INNOVATIONS IN EDUCATION FOR THE SEVENTIES: SELECTED READINGS

ACCOUNTABILITY
BEHAVIORAL OBJECTIVES
DIFFERENTIATED STAFFING
EDUCATION VOUCHERS
INDIVIDUALIZED INSTRUCTION
OPEN EDUCATION

Edited by

JULIA E. DE CARLO, Ph.D.
Associate Professor and Coordinator
of Elementary and Special Education
Graduate School of Education
Long Island University
C. W. Post Center

CONSTANT A. MADON, Ph.D.
Associate Professor, Graduate School of Education,
Long Island University
C. W. Post Center

Behavioral Publications   **New York**
1973

Library of Congress Catalog Number   **73-3084**
Standard Book Number 87705-114-3—Paperbound
                                 87705-115-1—Clothbound
Copyright © 1973 by Behavioral Publications

BEHAVIORAL PUBLICATIONS, 2852 Broadway—Morningside Heights,
New York, New York 10025

Printed in the United States of America
This printing   10 9 8 7 6 5 4 3 2 1

Library of Congress Cataloging in Publication Data

De Carlo, Julia E   comp.
    Innovations in education for the seventies.

    1. Educational innovations--Addresses, essays,
lectures. 2. Educational accountability--Addresses,
essays, lectures. 3. Differentiated teaching staffs--
Addresses, essays, lectures. 4. Open plan schools--
Addresses, essays, lectures. I. Madon, Constant A.,
joint comp. II. Title.
LB1027.D352   371.3   73-3084
ISBN 0-87705-115-1
ISBN 0-87705-114-3 (pbk)

TO
OUR PARENTS

Table of Contents

INTRODUCTION

As the decade of the seventies unfolds significant innovations are being tried in public schools across the country. These changes are very broad in scope encompassing such concepts as education vouchers, accountability, behavioral objectives, differentiated staffing, individualized instruction and open education. Each innovation has a unique feature which can have an important impact upon the instructional process and the entire structure of our public school system.

The educational voucher system which allows parents to choose the school which their child will attend may change the entire decision making process with regard to school selection, curricular offerings and staffing of our schools. In the area of program development three innovations are having noted impact. The first, individualized instruction, represents perhaps our most concerted effort at meeting individual needs, a textbook concept which has been discussed for many years but which only recently has been attempted on a large scale. Coupled with this idea is the concept of open education. If on the one hand teachers are able to deal with individual differences in a meaningful way, then it also becomes possible for them to open up their classrooms to accommodate to individual learning styles and to give youngsters a freer choice of learning alternatives. Another major innovation deals with the use of behavioral objectives for curriculum development. By specifying identifiable behavior and using this criterion as the evidence of learning, it becomes possible to monitor the child's progress more effectively.

Staffing patterns are also undergoing major revision. We have been accustomed to one teacher per class of 25 or 30 youngsters, but now a movement is

under way to hire a wide range of instructional personnel, with each person performing a specialized
function. The differentiation of staff is one way to
provide for the extensive variety of talents which
teachers and paraprofessionals possess while concomitantly providing more effective learning environments for students.

Finally, there is the overall movement toward
accountability wherein schools are being held responsible for their total program.

The diversity of these innovations when taken
together points to a stimulating decade of change.
Recognizing the significance and impact of these
innovations upon education, Dr. De Carlo and
Dr. Madon have developed an outstanding text, one
that will serve as a focal point for future trends in
American education.

Thomas F. Bowman, Dean
Graduate School of Education
Long Island University
C. W. Post Center

PREFACE

A variety of innovations are being introduced in schools throughout the country for the purposes of improving instruction and enriching the learning experiences of students. These experiments are being done on a selected basis, some through special funding and others as a result of the initiative of public school and university personnel. Descriptions, results, and reactions to these activities are being reported in professional journals of education. Changes are occurring in many different areas, making it increasingly difficult for the teacher or student to keep abreast of what is happeingin on the educational scene. As the decade of the seventies unfolds, it is likely that educators will be acquiring and using that information to improve the quality of education. The authors' purpose in developing this text was to bring together in a single volume a cross section of significant trends in order to facilitate the flow of knowledge from those actively engaged in specific aspects of these innovations to the larger assemply of professional educators.

The text covers six major innovations in education. They are: accountability, behavioral objectives, differentiated staffing, education vouchers, individualized instruction, and open education. Articles were selected which give the theory, description, analysis, and reaction to each innovation. Whenever applicable, material was selected which reflected actual classroom experiences so that a reader could formulate relationships between what has occurred in a particular situation and his own teaching activities. The text enables the reader to evaluate the merits of what has taken place in light of his own school and community's involvement in each innovation.

There are four major areas for which this

material could be used. These include:

1. Foundations of education courses

2. Curriculum courses

3. General methods courses

4. Student teaching seminars

The student in the foundations area can study the relationships between these innovations and their origins in the social, philosophical, and psychological foundations. In curriculum, it is important for the student, teacher, or curriculum specialist not only to be knowledgeable about these innovations, but also to be able to use the information in the formulation of new curricula. Since many of the articles are related to methodology, the student taking a general methods course should be able to incorporate these new ideas into his teaching strategies. Finally, the student teacher who may be faced with having to deal with these innovations, either in student teaching or later as a teacher, needs to be cognizant of their existence.

In addition, much of the material contained in this text is appropriate for in-service training as well as for general information purposes for each educator.

Long Island University   J. D. C.
C. W. Post Center   C. A. M.

CONTRIBUTORS

Allen, Dwight W.	Dean of the School of Education, University of Massachusetts
Barro, Stephen M.	Economist, The Rand Corporation
Bishop, Lloyd K.	Professor of Education, New York University
Carlton, Patrick W.	Professor of Education, New York University
Clayton, A. Stafford	Professor of History and Philosophy of Education, Indiana University
Cooper, James M.	Associate Dean, College of Education, University of Houston
Ellison, Martha	Director, The Brown School, Louisville, Kentucky
Esler, William K.	Associate Professor, Florida Technological University in Orlando
Gagné, Robert M.	Professor of Educational Research and Testing, Florida State University, Tallahassee
Glennan, Thomas K.	Director, Office of Research and Evaluation, Office of Economic Opportunity

Hawk, Richard L.   Assistant Professor of Education, University of Washington

Heller, Robert W.   Associate Professor, Department of Educational Administration, State University of New York, Buffalo

Heyman, Mark   Faculty Member, Sangamon State University, Springfield, Illinois

Hunter, Madeline   Principal, University Elementary School at UCLA

Janssen, Peter A.   White House Correspondent for Station WETA-TV, Washington, D.C.

Kimball, Roland B.   Chairman, Department of Education, University of New Hampshire, Durham

Kneller, George F.   Professor of Education, Graduate School of Education, University of California, Los Angeles

Miles, David T.   Assistant Professor, Southern Illinois University, Carbondale

Morris, John E.   Assistant Professor, Georgia Southern College in Statesboro

Nation's Schools   L. C. Hickman, Editor

Popham, W. James   Professor of Education, University of California, Los Angeles

Robinson, Roger E.   Director of the Educational Research Bureau, Southern Illinois University, Carbondale

Spodek, Bernard   Professor of Education, University of Illinois

PART ONE

ACCOUNTABILITY

In the United States taxpayers have been concerned not only with the rising cost of education,
but also with the quality of educational programs in
public schools. Accountability is an attempt to correlate academic achievement to expenditures for education. It allows the public as well as educators to
determine for themselves whether or not schools are
producing desired results.

Those who advocate accountability say that equal
educational opportunity is not enough, rather that
"every child will learn." Those opposed feel that
teachers should not be held accountable for achievement of every youngster because of the diversity and
range of variables in the teaching-learning process.
Notwithstanding these differing positions, the issue
of accountability remains one of the key forces in
education today as evidenced by the selection of
articles in this part.

An overview of accountability is presented in an
article by Morris. He describes the reasons for the
accountability movement; the requirements involved in
accountability; some vital questions that need to be
weighed; and the prospect for the future of accountability in the seventies.

In the second article Barro describes how accountability measures are employed in public schools
and in teacher education programs. He discusses ways
in which schools can become accountable and the need
for such measures. A framework for accountability,
the methodology and importance of experimental research are presented and developed. He concludes the
article with a description of some of the main uses
of accountability measures.

Popham offers a practical way of applying the concept of accountability to classroom teaching. The technique referred to is the instructional mini lesson. It is a four step process of: (1) setting an explicit instructional objective; (2) planning the lesson; (3) teaching the lesson; and, (4) measuring learning outcomes with a posttest evaluation. He cites evidence for improved teaching with the use of instructional mini lessons and feels that teacher competence would be improved with the use of such a technique.

In the last article, Esler discusses three important concerns which teachers have regarding the accountability movement. The first is related to setting goals and objectives. The selection of specific behavioral objectives may tend to restrict a given discipline and could exclude other equally important objectives. Secondly, the accountability model adopted by the school must provide the time, space and materials for instruction. Teachers cannot be expected to meet certain performance standards without the proper materials. Thirdly, there is a concern that accountability is equated with testing which may lead to less emphasis upon problem solving and creativity.

ACCOUNTABILITY: WATCHWORD
FOR THE 70'S

John E. Morris

To think about education in terms of decades
seems to be the "in" thing. Great emphases have been
placed on Schools for the Sixties and Schools for the
Seventies and in each decade much ado is made about
educational problems and reforms. Most of the sixties were devoted to curriculum reforms resulting in
a proliferation of NEWS--new math, new social studies,
new English, new science--which were to contribute to
the solution of many problems relating to student
achievement. If the sentiment of certain educators,
government, business, and lay leaders is an indication of what this decade holds, it is certainly the
dawning of the age of accountability wrapped in the
self-governance package of the educational profession
and bound by performance contracts.

As yet, there seems to be no definition which
can be considered an accurate index into the scope
and meaning of accountability. Yet, the focus is
certainly upon the achievement or lack of achievement
of students who enter our public schools in relation
to constantly increasing school budgets. The crux of
the issue, in greatly simplified form, seems to be
that if teachers cannot teach pupils to read; solve
mathematical problems; speak and write correctly;
memorize principles, laws, and formulas in science;
and regurgitate names of people, places, things, and
dates found in social studies texts; then some business concern will guarantee to do so at a predetermined level of performance and cost.

Accountability is not new to teachers and
*

Reprinted by permission from the February, 1971
issue of THE CLEARING HOUSE.

schools (although the use of the term in connection
with teacher performance did not appear in Education
Index until June, 1970), for we have always been
accountable to some one or some constituted authority.
One of the most revered teachers, Socrates, was
accountable unto death for his teaching. The sophists
were accountable to their students, for herein lay
their means of livelihood. The first universities
were, to a great extent, accountable to the student
body and the local community. Today, the classroom
teacher is legally accountable to the local school
board and morally accountable to self, profession,
community, and nation.

The form of accountability has varied from time-
to-time, but the end product--performance--has remained relatively constant. Since the family was the
first educational institution, parents were accountable for the instruction of their children in the
form of skills necessary for survival. With the
development of clans, tribes, and states, the functions of education became more formalized and the
fortunes of the clans, tribes, and states were more
or less determined by the performance of the educational system. In western education accountability
has often taken the form of examinations administered
at prescribed levels of the educational ladder. It
was not uncommon for teachers to be retained, dis-
missed, or promoted on the basis of pupil performance
on these examinations. A school whose students did
not consistently score high on examinations might
cease to attract sufficient students to make possible
its continued existence. Merit pay, compensation of
students for scholastic achievement as in the Martin
Luther King Junior High School in Portland, Oregon,[1]
and other "third factors" are means proposed or
applied in an effort to insure accountability. The
current emphasis for accountability has grown out of
the movement for national assessment of education and
President Nixon's "Message on Higher Education" which
stressed the wrongs in education and the necessity
for accountability.

In any country at any given time there exist
critics, both in and outside the profession, who complain about declining standards, failure of students
to learn basic fundamentals, teacher incompetencies,
parental unconcern, over permissiveness of administrators, decline of student morals, excessive expenditure of public funds, and a host of other real or

imagined shortcomings. This was particularly characteristic of the immediate post-sputnik period when
Russian education was considered by some, especially
Rickover, to be superior to ours. It would indeed be
interesting to know what public reaction would have
been had the United States launched the first satel-
lite. One can only assume that the opposite reaction
would have been the rule. Now that our astronauts
have walked on the moon on more than one occasion, it
seems as though our schools are producing students
who are capable of not only maintaining but advancing
the technological and scientific progress so necessary to our well-being. If one reads "The Schools
Behind Masters of the Moon,"[2] Polley's "What's Right
with American Education,"[3] and Rickover's "A Comparison: European Vs. American Secondary Schools,"[4] one
is confronted with the contradictions which are so
characteristic of American society. It may be that
the current emphasis on accountability is another
such contradiction.

REASONS FOR ACCOUNTABILITY MOVEMENT

There are several interesting generalizations
which can be made about the reasons for the current
emphasis on accountability. First, criticism and
reform movements seem to wax and wane in relation to
the current social milieu. The "roaring twenties"
resulted in rapid changes in economic, societal, and
personal values. Then came the depression and the
frantic search for explanations as to the causes for
such upheavals. The criticisms of this era are reflected by Professor Thomas H. Briggs when he stated
that education should be a

> ". . . long-term investment by the state
> to make itself a better place in which to
> live and in which to make a living, to per-
> petuate itself, and promote its own inter-
> ests. . . . authorities have made no serious
> efforts to formulate for secondary schools a
> curriculum which promises maximum good to
> the supporting state. . . . there has been
> no respectable achievement, even in the sub-
> jects offered in secondary school curricula.
> . . . no effort has been made sufficient to
> establish in students appreciation of the
> values of the subjects in the curricula

such as to insure continued study either in higher schools or independently after compulsory classes. . . . a state's attorney might conceivably present against an educational authority an indictment for malfeasance in office and misappropriation of public funds.[5]

The thirties witnessed rapid expansion of the progressive education movement aimed at eliminating many of these deficiencies.

Second, criticism and reform movements follow a shocking event in which we tend to come out second best. This is illustrated in the writings of Rickover, Bestor, and Conant in the post-sputnik era.

Third, since the schools are considered to be second only to the family in terms of safeguarding and extending traditional values, they are especially susceptible to attacks during times when these values are disappearing and new values to fill the vacuum have not been born. Such periods are characterized by mounting uncertainties, confusion, contradictions, and search, especially by youth, for identity. Jan Smithers, one of 775 youth included in a nationwide opinion poll, seems to express these conditions when she said: "Sometimes when I'm sitting in my room I just feel like screaming and pounding my pillow. I'm so confused about this whole world and everything that's happening."[6]

Fourth, schools are supposed to prepare leaders who are able to solve many of the pressing social, political, and economic problems which confront a nation. Today the magnitude and hopelessness of the military entanglements in Indo-China and the Middle East, poverty, race relations, the drug problem, and violence on our campuses and in our streets is, to a very great extent, directed toward the educational institutions and accountability is the battle cry.

Fifth, the general state of the economy, coupled with the social factors already mentioned, is a major cause of the current emphasis on accountability. There is widespread and increasing militance on the part of voters toward inflation and tax increases. A record defeat rate of school bond issues and millage increases does not necessarily mean that voters are anti-education. Instead, there is resistance to all tax increases and it so happens that those involving school finance are about the only increases voters directly control. This resentment has certainly increased as a result of action taken by various militant groups, violence on the campuses of junior highs, high schools and colleges, and by creation of unitary school districts in the South and massive busing of students in some areas outside the South.

Sixth, there is widespread agreement that some-thing is basically wrong with public education. Too many students cannot read, are deficient in basic communication skills, quit before completing the twelfth grade, and seem to be unpatriotic.

Seventh, today more parents are better educated because they have attended high school and college. They judge the progress of their children on the basis of their experiences and the widely publicized advancements in educational technology. They see the realities of the educational dilemma and are becoming more critical of and less willing to believe educa-tional authorities. They are demanding that adminis-trators and teachers be more accountable for the progress of students.

WHAT WILL ACCOUNTABILITY REQUIRE?

It is too early to envision all that will be required in terms of knowledge, skills, attitudes, personnel, money, and technology to put public edu-cation on an accountability basis as envisioned, for example, by Lessinger.[7] However, a number of require-ments are already evident.

First, Davies states that accountability will require ". . . changing people . . . and changing the institutions that control education."[8] Lessinger believes that ". . . educational accountability can be implemented successfully only if educational objectives are clearly stated before the instruction starts."[9] Since accountability implies predetermined levels of performance by students, an educational performance contract[10] would have to be initiated prior to the beginning of a prescribed program of instruction.

Second, accountability will most certainly

require application of principles involved in differentiated staffing similar to those advocated by Olivero[11] and Barbee.[12]   Perhaps a more fundamental requirement, and one which may be more difficult to secure, is self-determination of the teaching profession. Bain states that self-governance will have to become a reality before accountability is possible.[13]

Third, there must be more involvement of the community and teachers in determining policies, programs, performance levels, and incentive criteria.

Fourth, teacher education programs which are highly individualized, predicated on the basis of performance criteria, and providing more contact with the "real world" of teaching throughout the entire program instead of the limited experiences of present programs, will have to be inaugurated.

Fifth, there must be far more extensive and sophisticated use of educational technology than teacher education programs and public schools have been willing and/or able to use.

Sixth, a financial base to replace our present outdated and inequitable system of financing public education will have to be initiated.

Seventh, education must become, not only in theory but in fact, child centered. We will be forced to write programs for each child based on extensive results of highly sophisticated diagnostic instruments.

Eighth, the efficiency and effectiveness of the organization and administration of schools must be improved. The self-contained classrooms and principals who spend much of their time collecting lunch money and filling vending machines will have to go.

Ninth, instruments which are more reliable, individualized, and valid for measuring ability and performance in the cognitive and affective domains must be developed. Lessinger conceives of ". . . a process designed to ensure that any individual can determine for himself if the schools are producing the results promised. The most public aspect of accountability would be independent accomplishment audits that report educational results in factual, understandable, and meaningful terms."[14]

Tenth, new teacher-student roles and responsibilities will have to be defined and implemented. It is not certain what these would be, but the present ones of dispenser and container would either disappear or become more widespread.

SOME VITAL QUESTIONS

Accountability has already raised vital questions which must be considered before and if this concept advances beyond the experimental stages. The most serious questions center around accountability and the affective domain. We have long been aware of the vital role of such factors as attitudes, values, creativity, and self-contempt, but have never come to grips with them. We, as teachers and parents, have long observed that it is not always the "most intelligent" student who is "successful." Who is to determine what values, attitudes, creative abilities, etc., are to be taught? Who will write the performance contract? Who will perform the "independent accomplishments audits?" Who will determine what influences education is to have on the shaping of American democracy and the quality of life of the American people and how will these influences be measured? In short, how can we ". . . gauge behavior modifications that schooling is supposed to effect."[15] Similar, although not as controversial, questions are in order for the knowledge and skills for which we are to be accountable.

Accountability also raises the issue of further dehumanization of education. There is already much discontent with the dehumanizing effects of teaching machines; computer assisted instruction; the "do not fold, staple, or mutilate" system of identification, scheduling, and reporting; the lack of a humanizing curriculum; and the bureaucratic, impersonal school organization.

Would accountability virtually force teachers to "teach the test?" There is evidence that this has already happened in the Texarkana project.[16] The same practice has occurred in the United States and other countries when educational performance, teacher retention, and school finances were, to a greater or lesser degree, determined by examination scores.

Further questions are asked by Davies:

How do we move from a mass approach to
teaching and learning to a highly individual approach?

How do we go about the "simple" task
óf treating each child as an individual
human being?

How do we substitute a vigorous,
enjoyable classroom atmosphere for one that
has too often been marked by competition,
pain, fear, and failure?

. . . how do we build into ourselves
the capacity for continuing self-renewal,
for meeting increasing demands for adapting
to new roles?[17]

FUTURE PROSPECTS

It would be presumptuous to try to assess the
possible impact of accountability on public education
at this time. There are few certainties in those
areas involving human beings. But one thing is cer-
tain--Pandora's Box has been opened and education
will never be the same.

Approximately 200 school districts in various
parts of the nation are trying accountability in some
form. In Gary, Indiana, an elementary school has
been completely turned over to Behavioral Research
Laboratories for a three-year period. Dr. Alfonso
Holliday II, president of the Gary school board, is
quoted as saying: "With education costs rising 15 to
20 per cent a year, we didn't feel we could keep asking for more money when our children were learning
below their grade levels. . . . We are at rock bottom and must try new approaches. . . . We must be
willing to be pioneers, and no longer say our children lack ability to learn."[18] John Gardner is
quoted as saying that Accountability offers ". . . a
well-tested way out of the dizzying atmosphere of
talk and emotion . . ."[19] and Martin Filogamo of the
Texarkana project believes that: "If it succeeds, it
could well lead the way to the direct involvement of
private industry in the education of the nation's

school children."[20]   The 70's promise to be interesting and challenging years in education, and accountability may be the most interesting, challenging,
disruptive, and, in the end, productive issue of all.

FOOTNOTES

1.   Phi Delta Kappan, June, 1970, p. 510.

2.   "The Schools Behind Masters of the Moon,"
Phi Delta Kappan, September, 1969, pp. 2-7.

3.   Ira Polley, "What's Right with American Education," Phi Delta Kappan, September, 1969, pp. 13-15.

4.   H. G. Rickover, "A Comparison: European Vs.
American Secondary Schools," Phi Delta Kappan, November, 1958, pp. 60-64.

5.   Ellwood P. Cubberley, Readings in Public
Education in the United States (Boston: The River-
side Press, 1934), p. 468.

6.   "The Teenager," Newsweek, March 21, 1966,
p. 66.

7.   Leon Lessinger, "Accountability in Public
Education," Today's Education, May, 1970, pp. 52-53.

8.   Don Davies, "The Relevance of Accountability," Journal of Teacher Education, Spring, 1970,
p. 128.

9.   Lessinger, op. cit., p. 52.

10.   Ibid.

11.   James L. Olivero, "The Meaning and Application of Differentiated Staffing in Teaching," Phi
Delta Kappan, September, 1970, pp. 36-40.

12.   Don Barbee, "Differentiated Staffing:
Expectations and Pitfalls," TEPS Write-in Paper No. 1
on Flexible Staffing Patterns, Washington, D.C.:
National Commission on Teacher Education and Professional Standards, March, 1969.

13.   Helen Bain, "Self-Governance Must Come

First, Then Accountability," Phi Delta Kappan, April, 1970, p. 413.

14.   Lessinger, op. cit., p. 52.

15.   C. Grieder, "Educators Should Welcome Pressure for Accountability," Nations Schools, May, 1970, p. 14.

16.   Stan Elam, "The Chameleon's Dish," Phi Delta Kappan, September, 1970, pp. 71-72.

17.   Davies, op. cit., p. 129.

18.   "Where Private Firm Runs Public School," U.S. News and World Report, October 12, 1970, p. 41.

19.   Lessinger, op. cit., p. 52.

20.   Martin J. Filogamo, "New Angle on Accountability," Today's Education, May, 1970, p. 53.

AN APPROACH TO DEVELOPING ACCOUNTABILITY MEASURES FOR THE PUBLIC SCHOOLS

Stephen M. Barro

THE CONCEPT OF ACCOUNTABILITY

Although the term "accountability" is too new in the educational vocabulary to have acquired a standard usage, there is little doubt about its general meaning and import for the schools. The basic idea it conveys is that school systems and schools, or, more precisely, the professional educators who operate them, should be held responsible for educational outcomes--for what children learn. If this can be done, it is maintained, favorable changes in professional performance will occur, and these will be reflected in higher academic achievement, improvement in pupil attitudes, and generally better educational results. This proposition--that higher quality education can be obtained by making the professionals responsible for their product--is what makes accountability an attractive idea and provides the starting point for all discussion of specific accountability systems and their uses in the schools.

The unusual rapidity with which the accountability concept has been assimilated in educational circles and by critics of the schools seems less attributable to its novelty than to its serviceability as a unifying theme. Among its antecedents, one can identify at least four major strands of current thought and action in education: 1) the new, federally stimulated emphasis on evaluation of school systems and their programs; 2) the growing tendency

Reprinted from Phi Delta Kappan. 52:196-205, December, 1970 by permission of publisher and the Rand Corporation.

to look at educational enterprises in terms of cost effectiveness; 3) increasing concentration on education for the disadvantaged as a priority area of responsibility for the schools; and 4) the movement to make school systems more directly responsive to their clientele and communities, either by establishing decentralized community control or by introducing consumer choice through a voucher scheme. Under the accountability banner, these diverse programs for educational reform coalesce and reinforce one another, each gaining strength and all, in turn, strengthening already powerful pressures for educational change.

HOW THE SCHOOLS CAN BE MADE ACCOUNTABLE

Accountability in the abstract is a concept to which few would take exception. The doctrine that those employed by the public to provide a service--especially those vested with decision-making power--should be answerable for their product is one that is accepted readily in other spheres and that many would be willing to extend, in principle, to public education. The problems arise in making the concept operational. Then it becomes necessary to deal with a number of sticky questions:

To what extent should each participant in the educational process--teacher, principal, and administrator--be held responsible for results?

To whom should they be responsible?

How are "results" to be defined and measured?

How will each participant's contribution be determined?

What will be the consequences for professional educators of being held responsible?

These are the substantive issues that need to be treated in a discussion of approaches to implementing the accountability concept.

Various proposals for making the schools accountable differ greatly in the degree to which they would require existing structures and practices to be modified. In fact, it is fair to say they range from

moderate reform to revolution of the educational system. The following paragraphs summarize the major
current ideas that, singly or in combination, have
been put forth as approaches to higher quality education through accountability:

Use of improved, output-oriented management
methods. What is rapidly becoming a new "establishment" position--though it would have been considered
quite revolutionary only a few years ago--is that
school district management needs to be transformed if
the schools are to become accountable and produce a
better product. The focus here is on accountability
for effective use of resources. Specific proposals
include articulation of goals, introduction of output-
oriented management methods (planning-programming-
budgeting, systems analysis, etc.), and--most impor-
tant--regular, comprehensive evaluation of new and
on-going programs. Mainly internal workings of the
school system rather than relations between school
and community would be affected, except that better
information on resource use and educational outcomes
would presumably be produced and disseminated.

Institutionalization of external evaluations or
educational audits. Proposals along this line aim at
assuring that assessments of educational quality will
be objective and comparable among schools and school
districts and that appropriate information will be
compiled and disseminated to concerned parties. They
embody the element of comparative evaluation of
school performance and the "carrot" or "stick" associated with public disclosure of relative effectiveness. A prototype for this function may be found in
the "external educational audit" now to be required
for certain federal programs. However, the need for
consistency in examining and comparing school districts suggests that a state or even a federal agency
would have to be the evaluator. This would constitute a significant change in the structure of American public education in that it would impose a
centralized quality-control or "inspectorate" function upon the existing structure of autonomous local
school systems.

Performance incentives for school personnel.

Perhaps the most direct way to use an accountability
system to stimulate improved performance is to relate
rewards for educators to measure of effectiveness in
advancing learning. One way to do this is to develop
pay schedules based on measured performance to replace the customary schedules based on teaching
experience and academic training. An alternative
approach would be to use differentiated staffing as
the framework for determining both pay and promotion.
The latter is a more fundamental reform in that it
involves changes in school district management and
organization as well as changes in the method of
rewarding teachers. Professional organizations have
tended to oppose such schemes, partly out of fear
that performance criteria might be applied subjec-
tively, arbitrarily, or inequitably. Although this
may not be the only objection, if a measurement system could be developed that would be widely recognized as "objective" and "fair," the obstacles to
acceptance of a system of performance incentives
might be substantially reduced.

   Performance or incentive contracting. Performance contracting rests on the same philosophy as the
proposals for incentives, but applies to organizations outside the school system rather than individual professionals within it. A school district contracts with an outside agency--a private firm or,
conceivably, a nonprofit organization--to conduct
specified instructional activities leading to specified, measurable educational results. The amount paid
to the contractor varies according to how well the
agreed-upon objectives are accomplished, thereby
providing a very direct incentive for effective
instruction. At present, there is too little experience with performance contracting to support conclusions about its potential. However, a large number
of experiments and several evaluation efforts are
under way.* Should they prove successful, and should

---

*An experiment involving 18 districts and test-
ing several different forms of performance contracting is being carried out in 1970-71 under sponsorship
of the Office of Economic Opportunity. Also, the
Department of Health, Education, and Welfare has
contracted with the Rand Corporation to carry out an
evaluation of other efforts to plan and implement
performance contracts.

this very direct method of making the purveyor of
educational services responsible for his product
become widely used, there would undoubtedly be
substantial and lasting effects on both the technology and organization of American public
education.

Decentralization and community control. These
are two conceptually distinct approaches to accountability that we lump together under one heading only
because they have been so closely linked in recent
events. Administrative decentralization, in which
decision-making authority is shifted from central
administrators to local area administrators or individual school principals, can itself contribute to
accountability. The shift of authority should, for
example, favor greater professional responsiveness to
local conditions and facilitate the exercise of local
initiative. Also, it allows responsibility for results to be decentralized and, in so doing, provides
the framework within which various performance incentives can be introduced.

The movement for community control of the highly
bureaucratized, big-city school systems aims at
accountability in the sense of making the system more
representative of and responsive to its clientele and
community. In the context of community control,
accountability can be defined very broadly to include
not only responsibility for performance in achieving
goals, but also for selecting appropriate or "relevant" goals in the first place. Most important, community control provides the means of enforcing
accountability by placing decision-making and sanc-
tioning powers over the schools in the hands of those
whose lives they affect.

Alternative educational systems. Probably the
most radical proposal for achieving better education
through improved accountability is this one, which
would allow competing publicly financed school systems to coexist and would permit parents to choose
schools for their children. Usually this is coupled
with a proposal for financing by means of "educational
vouchers,"[1] although this is not the only possible
mechanism. The rationale for this "consumer-choice"
solution is that there would be direct accountability

by the school to the parent. Furthermore, there would be an automatic enforcement mechanism: A dissatisfied parent would move his child--and funds--to another school. Of course, the burden of becoming informed and evaluating the school would be on the individual parent. At present, there is very little experience with a system of this kind and little basis for judging how well it would operate or what effect it would have on the quality of education.

THE NEED FOR ACCOUNTABILITY MEASURES

These proposals, though not mutually exclusive, are quite diverse both with respect to the kinds of restructuring they would imply and the prospective educational consequences. However, they are alike in one important respect: Each can be carried out only with adequate information on the individual and the collective effectiveness of participants in the educational process. At present, such information does not exist in school systems. Therefore, a major consideration in moving toward accountability must be development of information systems, including the data-gathering and analytical activities needed to support them. This aspect of accountability--the nature of the required effectiveness indicators and the means of obtaining them--will be the principal subject of the remainder of this paper.

Progress in establishing accountability for results within school systems is likely to depend directly on success in developing two specific kinds of effectiveness information: 1) improved, more comprehensive pupil performance measurements; and 2) estimates of contributions to measured pupil performance by individual teachers, administrators, schools, and districts. As will be seen, the two have very different implications. The first calls primarily for expansion and refinement of what is now done in the measurement area. The second requires a kind of analysis that is both highly technical and new to school systems and poses a much greater challenge.

The need for more extensive pupil performance measurement is evident. If teachers, for example, are to be held responsible for what is learned by their pupils, then pupil performance must be

measured at least yearly so that gains associated
with each teacher can be identified. Also, if the
overall effectiveness of educators and schools is to
be assessed, measurement will have to be extended to
many more dimensions of pupil performance than are
covered by instruments in common use. This implies
more comprehensive, more frequent testing than is
standard practice in most school systems. In the
longer run, it will probably require substantial
efforts to develop and validate more powerful measurement instruments.

But no program of performance measurement alone,
no matter how comprehensive or sophisticated, is sufficient to establish accountability. To do that, we
must also be able to attribute results (performance
gains) to sources. Only by knowing the contributions
of individual professionals or schools would it be
possible, for example, for a district to operate an
incentive pay or promotion system; for community
boards in a decentralized system to evaluate local
schools and their staffs; or for parents, under a
voucher system, to make informed decisions about
schools for their children. To emphasize this point,
from now on the term "accountability measures" will
be used specifically to refer to estimates of contributions to pupil performance by individual agents in
the educational process. These are described as
"estimates" advisedly, because, unlike performance,
which can be measured directly, contributions to performance cannot be measured directly but must be
inferred from comparative analysis of different classrooms, schools, and districts. The analytical
methods for determining individual contributions to
pupil performance are the heart of the proposed
accountability measurement system.

A PROPOSED APPROACH

In the following pages we describe a specific
approach that could be followed by a school system
interested in deriving accountability measures, as
they have just been defined. First, a general rationale for the proposed approach is presented. Then the
analytical methodology to be used is discussed in
more detail.

For what results should educators be held responsible? Ideally, a school system and its constituent parts, as appropriate, should be held responsible for performance in three areas: 1) selecting "correct" objectives and assigning them appropriate priorities, 2) achieving all the stated (or implicit) objectives, and 3) avoiding unintentional adverse effects on pupils. Realistically, much less can even be attempted. The first of the three areas falls entirely outside the realm of objective measurement and analysis, assessment of objectives being an intrinsically subjective, value-laden, and often highly political process. The other two areas can be dealt with in part, subject to the sometimes severe limitations to the current state of the art of educational measurement. The answer to the question posed above must inevitably be a compromise, and not necessarily a favorable one, between what is desirable and what can actually be done.

Any school system aims at affecting many dimensions of pupil performance. In principle, we would like to consider all of them--appropriately weighed--when we assess teacher, school, or district effectiveness. In practice, it is feasible to work with only a subset of educational outcomes, namely, those for which (a) objectives are well defined and (b) we have some ability to measure output. The dimensions of performance that meet these qualifications tend to fall into two groups: first, certain categories of cognitive skills, including reading and mathematics, for which standardized, validated tests are available; second, certain affective dimensions--socialization, attitudes toward the community, self-concept, and the like--for which we have such indicators or proxies as rates of absenteeism, dropout rates, and incidence of vandalism and delinquency. For practical purposes, these are the kinds of educational outcome measures that would be immediately available to a school system setting out today to develop an accountability system.

Because of the limited development of educational measurement, it seems more feasible to pursue this approach to accountability in the elementary grades than at higher levels, at least in the short run. Adequate instruments are available for the basic skill areas--especially reading--which are the targets of most efforts to improve educational quality at the

elementary level. They are not generally available--
and certainly not as widely used or accepted--for the
subject areas taught in the secondary schools. Presumably, this is partly because measurement in those
areas is inherently more difficult; it is partly,
also, because there is much less agreement about the
objectives of secondary education. Whatever the reason, establishing accountability for results at the
secondary level is likely to be more difficult.
Pending further progress in specifying objectives and
measuring output, experiments with accountability
measurement systems would probably be more fruitfully
carried on in the elementary schools.

Fortunately, existing shortcomings in the measurement area can be overcome in time. Serious
efforts to make accountability a reality should,
themselves, spur progress in the measurement field.
However, for the benefits of progress to be realized,
the system must be "open"--not restricted to certain
dimensions of performance. For this reason, the
methodology described here has been designed to be in
no way limiting with respect to the kinds of outcome
measures that can be handled or the number of dimensions that can ultimately be included.

Who should be accountable for what? Once we
have determined what kinds of pupil progress to measure, we can turn to the more difficult problem of
determining how much teachers, principals, administrators, and others have contributed to the measured
results. This is the key element in a methodology
for accountability measurement.

The method proposed here rests on the following
general principle: Each participant in the educational process should be held responsible only for
those educational outcomes that he can affect by his
actions or decisions and only to the extent that he
can affect them. Teachers, for example, should not
be deemed "ineffective" because of shortcomings in
the curriculum or the way in which instruction is
organized, assuming that those matters are determined
at the school and district level and not by the individual teacher. The appropriate question is, "How
well does the teacher perform, given the environment
(possibly adverse) in which she must work and the
constraints (possibly overly restrictive) imposed
upon her?" Similarly, school principals and other

administrators at the school level should be evaluated according to how well they perform within the constraints established by the central administration.

The question then arises of how we know the extent to which teachers or administrators can affect outcomes by actions within their own spheres of responsibility. The answer is that we do not know a priori; we must find out from the performance data. This leads to a second principle: The range over which a teacher, a school principal, or an administrator may be expected to affect outcomes is to be determined empirically from analysis of results obtained by all personnel working in comparable circumstances. Several implications follow from this statement. First, it clearly establishes that the accountability measures will be relative, involving comparisons among educators at each level of the system. Second, it restricts the applicability of the methodology to systems large enough to have a wide range of professional competence at each level and enough observations to permit reliable estimation of the range of potential teacher and school effects.* Third, it foreshadows several characteristics of the statistical models needed to infer contributions to results. To bring out the meaning of these principles in more detail, we will explore them from the points of view of teachers, school administrators, and district administrators, respectively.

Classroom teachers. We know that the educational results obtained in a particular classroom (e.g., pupils' scores on a standard reading test) are determined by many other things besides the skill and effort of the teacher. The analyses in the Coleman report,[2] other analyses of the Coleman survey data,[3] and other statistical studies of the determinants of pupil achievement[4] show that a large fraction of variation in performance levels is accounted for by out-of-school variables, such as the pupils' socioeconomic status and home environment. Another large fraction is attributable to a so-called "peer group" effect; that is, it depends on characteristics of a

---

*This does not mean that accountability cannot be established in small school districts. It does mean that the analysis must take place in a broader context, such as a regional or statewide evaluation of performance, which may encompass many districts.

pupil's classmates rather than on what takes place in the school. Of the fraction of the variation that is explained by school variables, only part can be attributed to teachers. Some portion must also be assigned to differences in resource availability at the classroom and school level and differences among schools in the quality of their management and support. Thus, the problem is to separate out the teacher effect from all the others.

To illustrate the implications for the design of an accountability system, consider the problem of comparing teachers who teach very different groups of children. For simplicity, suppose that there are two groups of pupils in a school system, each internally homogeneous, which we may call "middle-class white" and "poor minority." Assume that all nonteacher inputs associated with the schools are identical for the two groups. Then, based on general experience, we would probably expect the whole distribution of results to be higher for the former group than for the latter. In measuring gain in reading performance, we might well find, for example, that even the poorest teacher of middle-class white children obtains higher average gains in her class than the majority of teachers of poor minority children. Moreover, the ranges over which results vary in the two groups might be unequal.

If we have reason to believe that the teachers associated with the poor minority children are about as good, on the average, as those associated with the middle-class white children--that is, if they are drawn from the same manpower pool and assigned to schools and classrooms without bias--then it is apparent that both the difference in average performance of the two groups of pupils and the difference in the range of performance must be taken into account in assessing each teacher's contribution. A teacher whose class registers gains, say, in the upper 10% of all poor minority classes should be considered as effective as one whose middle-class white group scores in the upper 10% for that category, even though the absolute performance gain in the latter case will probably be much greater.

This illustrates that accountability measures are relative in two senses. First, they are relative in that each teacher's contribution is evaluated by comparing it with the contributions made by other

teachers in similar circumstances. In a large city
or state school system, it can safely be assumed that
the range of teacher capabilities covers the spectrum
from poor to excellent. Therefore, the range of
observed outcomes, after differences in circumstances
have been allowed for, is likely to be representative
of the range over which teacher quality can be expected to influence results, given the existing
institutional framework. It may be objected that the
range of outcomes presently observed understates the
potential range of accomplishment because present
classroom methods, curricula, teacher training programs, etc., are not optimal. This may be true and
important, but it is not relevant in establishing
teacher accountability because the authority to
change those aspects of the system does not rest with
the teacher.

Second, accountability measures are relative in
that pupil characteristics and other nonteacher influences on pupil performance must be taken fully
into account in measuring each teacher's contribution.
Operationally, this means that statistical analyses
will have to be conducted of the effects of such
variables as ethnicity, socioeconomic status, and
prior educational experience on a pupil's progress in
a given classroom. Also, the effects of classroom or
school variables other than teacher capabilities will
have to be taken into account. Performance levels of
the pupils assigned to different teachers can be compared only after measured performance has been adjusted for all of these variables. The statistical
model for computing these adjustments is, therefore,
the most important element in the accountability
measurement system.

School administrators. Parallel reasoning suggests that school administrators can be held accountable for relative levels of pupil performance in
their schools to the extent that the outcomes are not
attributable to pupil, teacher, or classroom characteristics or to school variables that they cannot
control. The question is, having adjusted for differences in pupil and teacher inputs and having taken
account of other characteristics of the schools, are
there unexplained differences among schools that can
be attributed to differences in the quality of school
leadership and administration? Just as for teachers,
accountability measures for school administrators are

measures of relative pupil performance in a school
after adjusting the data for differences in variables
outside the administrators' control.

Consideration of the accountability problem at
the school level draws attention to one difficulty
with the concept of accountability measurement that
may also, in some cases, be present at the classroom
level. The difficulty is that although we would like
to establish accountability for individual professionals, when two or more persons work together to
perform an educational task there is no statistical
way of separating their effects. This is easy to see
at the school level. If a principal and two assistant principals administer a school, we may be able
to evaluate their relative proficiency as a team, but
since it is not likely that their respective administrative tasks would relate to different pupil performance measures there is no way of judging their
individual contributions by analyzing educational
outcomes. Similarly, if a classroom teacher works
with a teaching assistant, there is no way, strictly
speaking, to separate the contributions of the two.
It is conventional in these situations to say that
the senior person, who has supervisory authority,
bears the responsibility for results. However, while
this is administratively and perhaps even legally
valid, it provides no solution to the problem of
assessing the effort and skills of individuals.
Therefore, there are definite limits, which must be
kept in mind, to the capacity of a statistically
based accountability system to aid in assessing individual proficiency.

District administrators. Although the same
approach applies, in principle, to comparisons among
districts (or decentralized components of larger districts), there are problems that may limit its usefulness in establishing accountability at the district
level. One, of course, is the problem that has just
been alluded to. Even if it were possible to establish the existence of overall district effects, it
would be impossible to isolate the contributions of
the local district board, the district superintendent,
and other members of the district staff. A second
problem is that comparisons among districts can
easily fail to take account of intangible community
characteristics that may affect school performance.
For example, such factors as community cohesion,

political attitudes, and the existence of racial or
other intergroup tensions could strongly influence
the whole tone of education. It would be very difficult to separate effects of these factors from
effects of direct, district-related variables in trying to assess overall district performance. Third,
the concept of responsibility at the district level
needs clarifying. In comparing schools, for example,
it seems reasonable to adjust for differences in
teacher characteristics on the grounds that school
administrators should be evaluated according to how
well they do, given the personnel assigned to them.
However, at the district level, personnel selection
itself is one of the functions for which administrators must be held accountable, as are resource allocation, program design, choice of curriculum, and
other factors that appear as "givens" to the schools.
In other words, in assessing comparative district
performance, very little about districts can properly
be considered as externally determined except, perhaps, the total level of available resources.* The
appropriate policy, then, seems to be to include district identity as a variable in comparing schools and
teachers so that net district effects, if any, will
be taken into account. Districts themselves should
be compared on a different basis, allowing only for
differences in pupil characteristics, community variables, and overall constraints that are truly outside
district control.

A PROPOSED METHODOLOGY

The basic analytical problem in accountability
measurement is to develop a technique for estimating
the contributions to pupil performance of individual
agents in the educational process. A statistical
method that may be suitable for that purpose is
described here. The basic technique is multiple
regression analysis of the relationship between pupil
performance and an array of pupil, teacher, and school
characteristics. However, the proposed method calls
for two or three separate stages of analysis. The
strategy is first to estimate the amount of performance variation that exists among classrooms after

---

*In addition, of course, there are constraints
imposed by state or federal authorities. But these
are likely to be the same across districts.

pupil characteristics have been taken into account,
then, in subsequent stages, to attempt to attribute
the interclassroom differences to teachers, other
classroom variables, and school characteristics.[5]
This methodology applies both to large school districts, within which it is suitable for estimating
the relative effectiveness of individual teachers
and schools in advancing pupil performance, and to
state school systems, where it can be used, in addition, to obtain estimates of the relative effectiveness of districts. However, as noted above, there
are problems that may limit its utility at the inter-
district level.

Pupil performance data. Since we are interested
in estimating the contributions of individual teachers and schools, it is appropriate to use a "value-
added" concept of output. That is, the appropriate
pupil performance magnitudes to associate with a
particular teacher are the gains in performance made
by pupils while in her class. Ideally, the output
data would be generated by a program of annual (or
more frequent) performance measurement, which would
automatically provide before and after measures for
pupils at each grade level.

It is assumed that a number of dimensions of
pupil performance will be measured, some by standardized tests and some by other indicators or proxy
variables. Specific measurement instruments to be
used and dimensions of performance to be measured
would have to be determined by individual school
systems in accordance with their educational objectives. No attempt will be made here to specify what
items should be included.* The methodology is
intended to apply to any dimension of performance
that can be quantified at least on an ordinal scale.

---

*Realistically, however, almost every school
system will be likely to include reading achievement
scores and other scores on standardized tests of cognitive skills among its output variables. Also, it
will generally be desirable to include attendance or
absenteeism as a variable, both because it may be a
proxy for various attitudinal output variables and
because it may be an important variable to use in
explaining performance. Otherwise, there are innu-
merable possibilities for dealing with additional
dimensions of cognitive and affective performance.

Therefore, within a very broad range, it is not affected by the choice of output measures by a potential user.

Data on pupils, teachers, classrooms, and schools. To conform with the model to be described below, the variables entering into the analysis are classified according to the following taxonomy:

1.   Individual pupil characteristics (ethnicity, socioeconomic status, home, family, and neighborhood characteristics, age, prior performance, etc.).

2.   Teacher and classroom characteristics.

a)   Group characteristics of the pupils (ethnic and socioeconomic composition, distribution of prior performance levels, etc., within the classroom).

b)   Teacher characteristics (age, training, experience, ability and personality measures if available, ethnic and socioeconomic background, etc.).

c)   Other classroom characteristics (measures of resource availability: class size, amount of instructional support, amount of materials, condition of physical facilities, etc.).

3.   School characteristics.

a)   Group characteristics of the pupils (same as 2a, but based on the pupil population of the whole school).

b)   Staff characteristics (averages of characteristics in 2b for the school as a whole, turnover and transfer rates; characteristics of administrators--same as 2b).

c)   Other school characteristics (measures of resource availability: age and condition of building, availability of facilities, amount of administrative and support staff, etc.).

No attempt will be made to specify precisely what items should be collected under each of the

above headings. Determination of the actual set of
variables to be used in a school system would have to
follow preliminary experimentation, examination of
existing data, and an investigation of the feasibility, difficulty, and cost of obtaining various
kinds of information.

Steps in the analysis. The first step is to
determine how different pupil performance in each
classroom at a given grade level is from mean performance in all classrooms, after differences in individual pupil characteristics have been allowed for.
The procedure consists of performing a multiple
regression analysis with gain in pupil performance as
the dependent variable. The independent variables
would include (a) the individual pupil characteristics (category 1 of the taxonomy), and (b) a set of
"dummy" variables, or identifiers, one for each
classroom in the sample. The latter would permit
direct estimation of the degree to which pupil performance in each classroom differs from pupil performance in the average classroom. Thus, the product of
the first stage of the analysis would be a set of
estimates of individual classroom effects, each of
which represents the combined effect on pupil performance in a classroom of all the classroom and
school variables included in categories 2 and 3 of
the taxonomy. At the same time, the procedure would
automatically provide measures of the accuracy with
which each classroom effect has been estimated.
Therefore, it would be possible to say whether average performance gains in a particular classroom are
significantly higher or lower than would be expected
in a "typical" classroom or not significantly different from the mean.

Heuristically, this procedure compares performance gains by pupils in a classroom with gains that
comparable pupils would be likely to achieve in a
hypothetical "average" classroom of the system. This
can be thought of as comparison of class performance
gains against a norm, except that there is, in effect,
a particular norm for each classroom based on its
unique set of pupil characteristics. It may also be
feasible to carry out the same analysis for specific
subgroups of pupils in each class so as to determine,
for example, whether there are different classroom
effects for children from different ethnic or socioeconomic groups.

Estimation of teacher contributions. The second stage of the analysis has two purposes: 1) to separate the effects of the teacher from effects of non-teacher factors that vary among classrooms; and 2) to determine the extent to which pupil performance can be related to specific, measurable teacher attributes. Again, the method to be used is regression analysis, but in this case with a sample of classroom observations rather than individual pupil observations. The dependent variable is now the classroom effect estimated in stage one. The independent variables are the teacher-classroom characteristics and "dummy" variables distinguishing the individual schools.

Two kinds of information can be obtained from the resulting equations. First, it is possible to find out what fraction of the variation in performance gains among classrooms is accounted for by nonteacher characteristics, including group characteristics of the pupils and measures of resource availability in the classroom. The remaining inter-classroom differences provide upper-bound estimates of the effects that can be attributed to teachers. If there is sufficient confidence that the important nonteacher variables have been taken into account, then these estimates provide the best teacher accountability measures. They encompass the effects of both measured and unmeasured teacher characteristics on teacher performance. However, there is some danger that such measures also include effects of group and classroom characteristics that were inadvertently neglected in the analysis and that are not properly attributable to teachers. This problem is referred to again below.

Second, we can find out the extent to which differences among classrooms are explained by measured teacher characteristics. Ideally, of course, we would like to be able to attribute the whole "teacher portion" of performance variation to specific teacher attributes and, having done so, we would be much more confident about our overall estimates of teacher effectiveness. But experience to date with achievement determinant studies has shown that the more readily available teacher characteristics--age, training, experience, and the like--account for only a small fraction of the observed variance. It has been shown that more of the variation can be accounted for when a measure of teacher verbal ability is included.[6] Still more, presumably, could

be accounted for if a greater variety of teacher
ability and personality measurements were available.
At present, however, knowledge of what teacher characteristics influence pupil performance is incomplete
and satisfactory instruments exist for measuring only
a limited range of teacher-related variables. This
means that with an accountability information system
based on current knowledge, the excluded teacher
characteristics could be at least as important as
those included in determining teacher effectiveness.
For the time being, then, the interclassroom variation in results that remains after nonteacher effects
have been allowed for probably provides the most useful accountability measures, though the danger of
bias due to failure to include all relevant nonteacher
characteristics must be recognized.

The principal use of these estimates would be in
assessing the relative effectiveness of individual
teachers in contributing to gains in pupil performance. More precisely, it would be possible to
determine whether each teacher's estimated contribution is significantly greater or significantly
smaller than that of the average teacher. At least
initially, until there is strong confirmation of the
validity of the procedure, a rather stringent significance criterion should be used in making these
judgments and no attempt should be made to use the
results to develop finer gradations of teacher
proficiency.

The analysis will also make it possible to
determine the extent to which measured teacher
characteristics are significantly correlated with
teacher effectiveness. Potentially, such information
could have important policy implications and impacts
on school management, resource allocation, and personnel practices. A number of these potential applications are noted at the end of the paper.

Estimation of contributions by school administrators. The same analytical techniques can be used
in estimating the relative effectiveness of different
schools in promoting pupil performance. Conceptually,
a school accountability index should measure the difference between pupil performance in an individual
school and average pupil performance in all schools
after all pupil, teacher, and classroom variables
have been accounted for.

Such measures can be obtained directly if school dummy variables are included in the regression equation, as described earlier. Of course, the results measure <u>total</u> school effects, without distinguishing among effects due to school administration, effects of physical attributes of the school, and effects of characteristics of the pupil population. It may be feasible to perform a third-stage analysis in which the results are systematically adjusted for differences in the latter two categories of variables, leaving residual effects that can be attributed to the school administrators. These would constitute the accountability measures to be used in assessing the effectiveness of the principal and his staff. The results may have policy implications with respect to differential allocation of funds or resources among the different schools and, of course, implications with respect to personnel. Also, as would be done for teachers, an attempt could be made to relate measured characteristics of the school administrators to the estimated school effects. By so doing, it might be possible to learn whether administrator training and experience and other attributes are reflected in measured school output. Even negative results could provide important guidance to research on administrator selection and assignment.

   <u>Comparisons among districts</u>. For reasons that have already been stated, it would probably be desirable to treat comparisons among districts separately from comparisons among classrooms and schools. This could be done by means of yet another regression analysis, with individual pupil performance gain as the dependent variable and with independent variables consisting of pupil and community characteristics, measures of resource availability, and a dummy variable or identifier for each district being compared. The purpose would be to determine whether there are significant differences in results among districts once the other factors have been allowed for. If there are, the findings could be interpreted as reflections of differences in the quality of district policy making and management. But as pointed out earlier, there would be uncertainty as to the causes of either shortcomings or superior performance. Nevertheless, the results could have some important, policy-related uses, as will be noted shortly.

THE NEED FOR EXPERIMENTAL VERIFICATION
OF THE APPROACH

The methodology described here carries no guarantee. Its success in relating outcomes to sources may depend both on features of the school system to which it is applied and on the adequacy of the statistical models in mirroring the underlying (and unknown) input-output relationships in education. The validity and usefulness of the results must be determined empirically from field testing in actual school systems. Experimental verification, possibly requiring several cycles of refinement and testing, must precede implementation of a "working" accountability system.

Potential problems. Three kinds of technical problems can threaten the validity of the system: intercorrelation, omission of variables, and structural limitations of the models. None of these can be discussed in detail without mathematics. However, a brief explanation of each is offered so that the outlook for the proposed approach can be realistically assessed.

Intercorrelation. This is a problem that may arise where there are processes in a school system that create associations (correlations) between supposedly independent variables in the model. An important example is the process--said to exist in many systems--whereby more experienced, better trained, or simply "better" teachers tend to be assigned or transferred to schools with higher socioeconomic status (SES) pupils. Where this occurs, pupil SES will be positively correlated with those teacher characteristics. On the average, high SES children would be taught by one kind of teacher, low SES children by another. This would make it difficult to say whether the higher performance gains likely to be observed for high SES pupils are due to their more advantaged backgrounds or to the superior characteristics of their instructors. There would be ambiguity as to the magnitude of the teacher contribution and a corresponding reduction in the reliability of estimates of individual teacher effectiveness. Thus, the quality of accountability information would be impaired.

This problem can take many forms. There may be strong correlations between characteristics of pupils and characteristics of school staffs, between teacher characteristics and nonteacher attributes of the schools, between classroom-level and district-level variables, and so on. The general effect is the same in each instance: ambiguity resulting in diminished ability to attribute results to sources.[7]

There are several things that can be done to mitigate the effects of intercorrelation. One is to stratify the data. For example, if teacher characteristics were linked to pupil SES, it would be possible to stratify the classrooms by pupil SES and to perform separate analyses for each stratum. This would eliminate some of the ambiguity within strata. On the other hand, comparisons of teachers across strata would be precluded. Another possible solution would be to take account of interdependence explicitly in the statistical models. Some attempts along this line have been made in studies of determinants of school performance. However, this solution is likely to raise a whole new array of technical problems as well as questions about the feasibility of routine use of the methodology within school systems.

The problem of omitted variables. The validity and fairness of the proposed approach would depend very strongly on inclusion of all major relevant variables that could plausibly be cited by teachers or administrators to "explain" lower-than-average estimated contributions. This means that all variables would have to be included that (a) have significant, independent effects on performance and (b) are likely to be nonuniformly distributed among classrooms and schools.

It will never be possible to demonstrate in a positive sense that all relevant variables have been included. Many intangible, difficult-to-measure variables, such as pupil attitudes, morale, "classroom climate," etc., can always be suggested. What can be done is to determine as well as possible that none of the additional suggested variables is systematically related to the estimated teacher and school contributions. In an experimental setting, administrators could be interviewed for the purpose of identifying alleged special circumstances, and tests could be carried out to see whether they are systematically related to performance differences.

Structural limitations of the models. The
models described here may be too simple to take
account of some of the important relationships among
school inputs and outputs. One such shortcoming has
already been noted. The models do not allow for possible interdependencies among the various pupil and
school characteristics. Another, which may prove to
be more troubling, is that interactions among the
various output or performance variables have also not
been taken into account.

Researchers have pointed to two distinct kinds
of relationships. First, there may be trade-offs between performance areas.[8] A teacher or school may do
well in one area partly at the expense of another by
allocating resources or time disproportionately between the two. Second, there may be complementary
relationships. Increased performance in one area
(reading, for example) may contribute directly to
increased performance in others (social studies or
mathematics). Therefore, treatment of one dimension
of output at a time, without taking the interactions
into account, could produce misleading results.

Econometricians have developed "simultaneous"
models, consisting of whole sets of equations, speci-
ficially to take account of complex, multiple relationships among variables. Some attempts have been
made to apply these models to studies of determinants
of educational outcomes.[9] It may prove necessary or
desirable to use them in an accountability measurement system, despite the complexity they would add,
to eliminate biases inherent in simpler models.

Validity. Another important reason for thoroughly testing the accountability measurement system
is that its validity needs to be assessed. Some of
the procedures mentioned above contribute to this
end, but more general demonstration would also be
desirable. Two procedures that may be feasible in
an experimental situation are as follows:

Replication. A strong test of whether the
method really gets at differences in effectiveness
instead of differences in circumstances would be to

apply it to the same teachers and schools during two
or more years. Consistency in results from year to
year would strongly support the methodology. Lack of
consistency would show that major influences on performance remained unmeasured or neglected. Certainly,
if the results were to be used in any way in connection with personnel assignment, reward, or promotion,
the use of several years' estimates would be an
important guarantee of both consistency and fairness.

An external test of validity. The most direct
way to test the validity of the statistical approach
is to compare the results with alternative measures
of teacher and school effectiveness. The only measures that are likely to be obtainable are subjective
assessments by informed and interested parties.
Though such evaluations have many shortcomings, it
could be valuable in an experimental situation to see
how well they agreed with the statistical results.
Two important questions that would have to be answered
in making such a comparison are: 1) Who are the
appropriate raters--peers, administrators, parents,
or even pupils? and 2) What evaluation instruments
could be used to assure that subjective assessments
apply to the same dimensions of performance as were
taken into account in the statistical analysis? It
may not be possible to provide satisfactory answers.
Nevertheless, the feasibility of a comparison with
direct assessments should be considered in connection
with any effort to test the proposed accountability
measurement system.

POTENTIAL USES OF ACCOUNTABILITY MEASURES

Space does not permit a full review of the
potential uses of an accountability measurement system. However, an idea of the range of applications
and their utility can be conveyed by listing some of
the main possibilities.

Identification of effective schools. The most
rudimentary use of the proposed accountability measures is as an identification device. Once relative
school effectiveness is known, a variety of actions
can follow, even if there is ambiguity about causes.
As examples, less formal evaluation efforts can be

more precisely targeted once school effectiveness
with different kinds of children is known and cam-
paigns can be initiated to discover, disseminate, and
emulate good practices of high-performance schools.

Personnel assignment and selection.   Accountability measures may help to improve both staff
utilization and selection of new personnel. Personnel utilization could be improved by using information on teacher effectivemess in different spheres
and with different types of students for guidance in
staff assignment. Selection and recruitment could be
aided by using information from the models as a guide
to performance-related characteristics of applicants
and as a basis for revising selection procedures and
criteria.

Personnel incentives and compensation. An
accountability measurement system can be used to
establish a connection between personnel compensation
and performance. One use would be in providing evidence to support inclusion of more relevant variables
in pay scales than the universally used and widely
criticized training and experience factors. Another
possibility would be to use accountability measures
as inputs in operating incentive pay or promotion
systems. The latter, of course, is a controversial
proposal, long resisted by professional organizations.
Nevertheless, putting aside other arguments pro and
con, the availability of objective measures of individual contributions would eliminate a major objection to economic incentives and help to make the idea
more acceptable to all concerned.

Improved resource allocation. An accountability
measurement system could also contribute to other
aspects of resource allocation in school systems.
Analytical results from the models could be of value,
for example, in setting policies on class size, supporting services, and similar resource variables.
More directly, school accountability measures could
provide guidance to district administrators in allocating resources differentially among schools according to educational need. Similarly, state-level
results could be used in determining appropriate
allocations of state aid funds to districts.

Program evaluation and research. Models developed for accountability could prove to be valuable tools for program evaluation and research. They could be readily adapted for comparing alternative ongoing programs simply by including "program" as one of the classroom variables. Also, "norms" provided by the models for specific types of pupils could be used as reference standards in evaluating experimental programs. This would be preferable, in some cases, to using experimental control groups. Viewed as research tools, the models could help to shed light on one of the most basic, policy-related problems in education, the relationship between school inputs and educational output. The process of developing the models could itself be very instructive. The results could add substantially to our knowledge of how teachers and schools make a difference to their pupils.

In sum, there are many potential uses of the proposed measures and models, some going well beyond what is generally understood by "accountability." If the development of a system is undertaken and carried through to completion, the by-products alone may well prove to be worth the effort.

---

[1]See Education Vouchers: A Preliminary Report on Financing Education by Payments to Parents. Center for the Study of Public Policy, Cambridge, Mass., March, 1970.

[2]James S. Coleman et al., Equality of Educational Opportunity. Washington, D.C.: Office of Education, 1966.

[3]George W. Mayeske et al., "A Study of Our Nation's Schools" (a working paper), Office of Education, 1970.

[4]E.g., Eric A Hanushek, "The Education of Negroes and Whites," unpublished Ph.D. dissertation, M.I.T., 1968; and Herbert J. Kiesling, "The Relationship of School Inputs to Public School Performance in New York State," The Rand Corporation, P-4211, October, 1969.

[5]The statistical method described here is essentially the same as that used by Eric A. Hanushek in a study, The Value of Teachers in Teaching, to be

published in late 1970 by the Rand Corporation.

[6]Hanushek, The Value of Teachers in Teaching, op. cit.

[7]The existence of this type of ambiguity in analyses of the Coleman survey data is one of the principal findings reported in Mayeske, op. cit.

[8]See Henry M. Levin, "A New Model of School Effectiveness," in Do Teachers Make a Difference? Washington, D.C.: Office of Education, 1970, pp. 56-57.

[9]Ibid., pp. 61 ff.

THE NEW WORLD OF ACCOUNTABILITY:
IN THE CLASSROOM

W. James Popham

The educational battle lines for the impending
accountability showdown are drawn as clearly as in a
classic western movie. On one side we have the
underdog public school teachers, their portable
classrooms drawn into a circle. On the other side is
the marauding Accountability Gang who, although they
are viewed by teachers as mortal enemies, could
hardly be considered no account bandits. The Accountability Gang is beginning to fire some pretty potent
pistols at the embattled teachers. For instead of
Colt six-shooters and Winchester rifles, their guns
bear different markings. One is labeled "Teacher
Tenure." Another is called "Teacher Evaluation." A
third simply says "Taxpayer's Revolt." It is small
wonder that bullets from these guns may pick off a
teacher or two. And the terrifying part of this
script, at least to classroom teachers, is that there
may be no cavalry over the next hill coming to the
rescue.

AN ERA OF ACCOUNTABILITY

While perhaps a mite less melodramatic, the
present real world plight of classroom teachers who
are seriously trying to cope with the educational
accountability movement is equally serious. Teachers
are being quite literally bombarded with requests
and/or directives to become more accountable for
their instructional activities. Just what does this

Reprinted from the Bulletin of the National
Association of Secondary School Principals, 56:25-31,
May, 1970, by permission of the publisher.

mean and how can a willing teacher react sensibly to
the current quest for accountability?

Well, in general the concept of educational
accountability involves the teacher's producing evidence regarding the quality of his or her teaching,
usually in terms of what happens to pupils, then
standing ready to be judged on the basis of that evidence. An accountable teacher, therefore, takes
responsibility for the results his or her instruction
produces in learners. Characteristically, other
individuals, e.g., supervisors, administrators, or
school boards, will then take appropriate action
based on those results. The "appropriate action"
might range from decisions regarding which courses
the teacher should teach next year all the way to
termination of services or salary increases and
decreases. Clearly, the stakes are high.

FROM RHETORIC TO REALITY

Further, the situation has moved well beyond the
empty rhetoric stage. California legislators last
year enacted a teacher evaluation law requiring each
K-12 teacher in the state to be evaluated (probationary teachers annually, all others biennially) by
locally devised teacher appraisal systems. These
local evaluation systems must include certain state
stipulated elements. Prominent among these legis-
latively required elements is the teacher's role in
promoting learner progress in each area of study
toward locally defined standards. Thus, a learner-
results criterion has been mandated by California
lawmakers for teacher evaluation. A state-wide system of imposed accountability therefore exists in
California. Other states will surely be observing
the implementation of the California teacher evaluation law with keen interest.[1]

Beyond their individual involvement in the
accountability milieu as it affects job security and

---

[1]For a further treatment of the California
teacher evaluation law see the following document:
W. James Popham, Designing Teacher Evaluation Systems,
Instructional Objectives Exchange, Box 24095, Los
Angeles, California 90024, December, 1971, @ $1.25
per copy.

advancement, teachers are also being asked to play an
integral role in the appraisal of larger educational
units, e.g., the school or school district. The public is clearly subjecting educational institutions to
increased scrutiny. Citizens are not elated with
their perceptions of the quality of education. They
want dramatic improvements in the schools and, unless
they get them, there is real doubt as to whether we
can expect much increased financial support for our
educational endeavors. And the public is in no mood
to be assuaged by promises. "Deliver the results,"
we are being told. No longer will lofty language
suffice, and yesteryear's assurances that "only we
professionals know what we're doing" must seem laugh-
able to today's informed layman.

The distressing fact is that we haven't produced
very impressive results for the nation's children.
There are too many future voters who can't read satisfactorily, can't reason respectably, don't care for
learning in general, and are pretty well alienated
from the larger adult society.

AN APPROPRIATE RESPONSE

Well, what do educators do about this demand
that they produce results? How should they respond
to the mounting pressure that they become more
accountable? My recommendation is that we do just
that--we produce results and we become accountable!
For that stance, in my estimate, is the only professionally defensible posture available to us, and we
should be chagrined that it took external forces to
spur us to action.

Putting historical antecedents aside, let's
seize the initiative in this drive to make educators
responsible for their actions. The vast majority of
American teachers are well intentioned men and women
who want only the best for the children under their
tutelage. Impeded only by their human limitations
(There are only 24 hours available in most days, and
most human folk can't psychologically work 18 of
those), most teachers would like to do a better job
for their pupils if they only knew how. And here's
where the school principal comes in--his role should
be to increase the teacher's skill in achieving
demonstrable results with learners, while at the same

time making sure those results are the most defensible ones that can be attained.

In brief, I am suggesting that we accept the accountability challenge by increasing classroom teachers' skills in producing evidence that their instruction yields worthwhile results for learners. Not only is this the key ingredient in current accountability strategies, it represents a way of helping teachers do the best job they can for their students.

Space limitations preclude an exhaustive analysis of the numerous ways we can offer succor to the classroom teacher in promoting their increased results-producing competence. Thus, I would like to outline only two such strategies, but two strategies which seem to me to be high payoff schemes for implementing the principal's leadership role in this endeavor.

PROVIDE CRITERION-REFERENCED MEASURES

Since the emphasis is on getting demonstrable results, we should get into the teacher's hands suitable measures of such results. The teacher can then more readily monitor the quality of instruction in relationship to student progress on such measures and, insofar as resources permit, make individual diagnoses and prescriptions for different learners on the basis of their performance on such measures. This is a stance totally compatible with the continuing emphasis on measurable instructional objectives seen so frequently in today's educational circles. But rather than forcing the already too busy teacher to conjure up a host of specific objectives and measures related to them, we have to provide these measures.

I believe that criterion-referenced measures related to objectives will prove serviceable merely because experience suggests that explicit objectives will be a more parsimonious way of describing a class of learner behaviors than by using the measuring device itself. And please note that by measuring device I do not mean only paper and pencil tests. Surely the bulk of these measures will, for practicality's sake, be in a paper format. But we can use paper formatted measures for more diverse assessment schemes than the classic multiple choice test. Attitudinal inventories, interest questionnaires, indeed, affective measures of all sorts, can be handled by low cost paper measuring devices.

But why use such criterion-referenced measures rather than the time honored standardized tests? A simple question, with a simple answer. Because <u>for purposes of measuring results reflecting high quality instruction, standardized tests are usually inappropriate</u>. They were designed, developed, and refined with a totally different purpose in mind, namely, to permit us to distinguish between different learners. For the purpose for which they were intended, standardized tests are fine. When selections among learners are in order, for instance, in predicting which students will succeed in college, standardized tests are super. Well, at least, until some of their ethnic biases are better eliminated, they're the best available. But for purposes of assessing the quality of instruction and for making specific judgments about what certain pupils have learned, standardized tests will typically yield misleading information.

We need more short duration tests which have better <u>local curricular validity</u>. There are several ways school principals can attempt to promote the availability of more of these measures. First, they can bring concentrated pressure on America's major test publishers to encourage them to move more rapidly into the development of criterion-referenced measures. Second, they can inspect the suitability of those criterion-referenced measuring devices currently available. Third, if local resources permit, they can develop at least a few measures to deal with particularly high priority goals (perhaps in concert with neighboring schools or school districts).

Once the measures are available, teachers should be encouraged to use them frequently and to make instructional modifications as dictated by the results. And for purposes of instructional evaluation, not every pupil needs to complete every measure in its entirety. The use of <u>item sampling</u>, whereby different pupils complete only a small segment of the measuring device, can yield accurate estimates of group performance while conserving valuable instructional time.

The whole thrust of this particular strategy is to provide measures of pupil outcomes so that teachers will not have to judge intuitively whether their instructional tactics are effective, for such intuitions are often as likely to be wrong as they are to be right. Decisions regarding whether to modify or to retain a given instructional sequence can be better made by the classroom teacher on the basis of data yielded from criterion-referenced measures.

INSTRUCTIONAL MINI-LESSONS

One vehicle which appears to offer considerable promise in helping classroom teachers increase their ability to produce desirable results with learners is the instructional mini-lesson, or sometimes called the teaching performance test. By employing these mini-lessons in a systematic inservice or pre-service program there is evidence that instructors can increase their teaching proficiency. For example, teachers who have attempted to improve their instructional effectiveness through the use of mini-lessons have been able to significantly outperform comparable teachers not participating in a mini-lesson improvement program.[2] Further, teachers well versed in instructional principles and experienced with mini-lessons have been able to dramatically exceed the performance of novice teachers. There is evidence beginning to build up which, although only suggestive at the moment, offers considerable support for the role of mini-lessons in pre-service and inservice teacher education programs.

In general, instructional mini-lessons are designed to improve a teacher's skill in accomplishing a prespecified instructional objective while at the same time promoting learner interest in the lesson. Here's how they work:

> First, a teacher is given an explicit
> instructional objective along with a
> sample measurement item showing how the
> objective's achievement will be measured.

[2]Martin Levine, "The Effect on Pupil Achievement of a Criterion-Referenced Instructional Model Used by Student Teachers," unpublished doctoral dissertation, University of California, Los Angeles, 1971.

Second, the teacher is given time to
plan a lesson designed to achieve the
objective.

Third, the teacher instructs a group of
learners for a specified period of time,
perhaps as few as a half dozen students
or as many as a whole class. Certain
mini-lessons are designed to be used
with adult learners, others with younger
learners.

Fourth, the learners are measured with a
post-test based on the objective but
unseen previously by the teacher.
Learner interest in the instruction is
also measured.

On the basis of these two indicators, that is, learners' interest rating and post-test scores, a judgment
of the teacher's instructional skill can be derived.
Such a judgment does not reflect all dimensions on
which a teacher should be judged, only the teacher's
ability to accomplish a pre-specified instructional
objective with positive learner affect during a short
lesson. Nevertheless, this is an important aspect of
a teacher's instructional proficiency.

The use of mini-lessons to bring about increases
in a teacher's instructional skill is consistent with
a basic assumption regarding teaching, namely, that
the chief reason for a teacher's existence in the
classroom is to bring about desirable changes in
learners. Accordingly, one important competency
which a teacher should possess is the ability to promote the learner's attainment of specific instructional objectives. Mini-lessons are designed to
assess this ability, that is, the teacher's skill in
accomplishing pre-specified instructional objectives.
Mini-lessons, therefore, can be used as the central
focus of pre-service and inservice programs which set
out to improve this key instructional skill.[3] Unlike

[3]At least one firm is currently distributing
mini-lessons such as those described here. For information contact Instructional Appraisal Services,
105 Christopher Circle, Ithaca, N.Y. 14850. Film-
strip-tape programs describing how to construct and
use teaching performance tests are also available
from Vimcet Associates, P.O. Box 24714, Los Angeles,

the increasingly popular micro-teacher procedures, the focus of instructional mini-lessons is on learner outcomes, not the procedures employed by the teacher, that is, mini-lessons are product-focused rather than process-focused.

OTHER ALTERNATIVES

X

While the two specific procedures described here clearly do not exhaust the range of potential approaches we might employ to aid classroom teachers in improving their ability to produce better results, they are certainly consistent with the general theme of increasing the degree to which a teacher should become accountable. If educators can only capitalize on the correct state of educational affairs, rather than being cast in the role of progress-resistors, we may mark the age of accountability as the beginning of a new era indeed.

Calif. 90024.

ACCOUNTABILITY
THE TEACHER'S PERSPECTIVE

William K. Esler

From the coverage of the issue in newspapers,
magazines, and journals of professional educators, it
is obvious that the age of accountability is upon us.
The pressure from the business community for education to show some concrete results for the vast number of dollars it spends is being transmitted through
federal and state agencies to local school systems
with an ever-increasing force. Already the wave of
accountability has resulted in some fundamental
shifts in the ways that administrators and teachers
view their jobs. There is an increased emphasis upon
behavioral objectives and the need to define the
desired results of instruction.

There is an ever-increasing feeling among educators that what goes on in the classroom has become
public. We can no longer hide within the ivory walls
and behind closed doors. The threat of extensive
accounting systems for evaluating classroom instruction may well have the effect of awakening or rea-
wakening the energies of some teachers and principals
who have been satisfied to drift along, resting upon
the image of the kindly, well-intentioned, but largely unchallenged caretaker of public education. The
unsettling effects of accountability upon the public
schools are likely to be with us for some time.

Though the vitalizing effects of the accountability paradigm may be obviously a force for good
in many schools of the nation, it may be well to ask
a few questions concerning the effects of this movement upon the people at the firing line level before

Reprinted by permission from the May, 1972
issue of the CLEARING HOUSE.

proceeding with the evaluation throttle running wide
open. What will be the nature and extent of the
pressures created by systems of accountability upon
the individual teacher? How are the forces of
accountability likely to affect the curriculum--that
which is actually taught in the classroom? How much
of the teachers' energy must be devoted to satisfying
the testing and record-keeping requirements of
accountability? The answers to these questions, and
others like them, should be carefully considered by
persons who are contemplating the institution of performance contracts and other schemes of accountability.

Any model for dealing with the evaluation of a
curriculum must contain three essential parts:

(1) a statement of a small number of general goals of
    the curriculum and a much lengthier list of
    subordinate, specific behavioral objectives;

(2) an allotment of time, space, and materials for
    achieving the objectives;

(3) procedures for evaluating the extent to which the
    objectives have been achieved.

It is worth considering the effects of each phase of
the accountability model upon the teaching operation
as we know it today.

SELECTING GOALS AND OBJECTIVES

The broad goals of various disciplines may
remain fairly well intact with the institution of
accounting procedures. "The child will be able to
read with comprehension" is a worthy goal for a reading program, accountability or no. It is when one
attempts to answer the question "What is reading comprehension?" or more specifically "What tasks may a
child perform that indicates he has the ability to
comprehend what he reads?" that the real effect of
the evaluation process upon teaching objectives is
felt. There are several basic approaches to teaching reading which are popular today--sight reading,
phonics, linguistics, and combinations of these
instructional schemes. It has never been shown with
any degree of certainty that any one approach to

reading instruction is superior to all others for all types of children.

In the science and social studies areas one is faced with choosing process or content or some combination of the two approaches as the primary vehicle for building a curriculum. Evaluation instruments which measure content achievement are quite different from those that measure process.

Though educational research leaves open the question of the "best" instructional approach in all areas of the curriculum, a model of accountability must define quite specifically, and perhaps often arbitrarily, the behaviors which are to be achieved by the students in a school or system. The necessity for defining any discipline in terms of a list of specific behavioral objectives may result in a rather narrow version of that discipline, and additionally may exclude other quite legitimate goals and objectives that reflect other philosophies.

Choosing a single program in any discipline for an entire school system or for any one school may not be in the best interest of all other pupils of that school. If it is true that children learn in different ways, then it follows that a teacher may desire to structure several programs which utilize a number of procedures within a single classroom. It is even possible that a single set of objectives is not legitimate for all children in all classrooms within a school. A model for accountability, that is not unnecessarily restrictive to the teacher, must provide for a selection of goals and objectives from a larger pool of such objectives. And the evaluation of a teacher or school must consider the right and the obligation of teachers and principals to select the proper objectives that fulfill the needs of their own communities.

ALLOCATING TIME, SPACE, AND MATERIALS FOR INSTRUCTION

Any model of accountability worth its salt must spell out the conditions under which the students and teachers labor to achieve the desired objectives. If, for instance, a reading or science program along with its performance objectives are accepted by a school system, then the total package of teaching materials that comprise the program should be furnished to the teacher. If they are to achieve the desired behaviors the members of a teaching unit must not be deprived of all manipulative aids, workbooks, teaching aids, and the like, that are thought by the curriculum designers to be necessary for achieving the objectives.

This may work a hardship on the many school districts who have followed the practice of issuing textbooks and expecting the teacher to produce all other materials for doing the job at hand. Any teacher forced to operate with less than a full program of teaching materials has genuine cause to question the requirement for accountability. The same may be said for teachers forced to teach in cloakrooms, hallways, and under other such substandard conditions. Accountability implies at least minimally acceptable working conditions and a full set of tools for the job.

PROCEDURES FOR EVALUATION

Most teachers who think at all about the issues of accountability see it primarily as an increased emphasis upon standardized testing practices. And they are probably correct. The chief reason that the word accountability results in visions of increased standardized testing is that written, objective tests are the cheapest, most efficient form of mass evaluation of student performance known. Since instruments that measure changes in the attitudes, self-concepts, and even the problem-solving skills of students are much less reliable than the achievement test, does this mean that affective and higher level cognitive goals will not be measured?

What is lost when a student knows his history, but hates it? Or when he knows most of the names and dates of history, but is unable to generalize from a set of facts? What will the teacher teach when faced with a discipline that is defined in terms of 100 or 150 items on a test--items which emphasize primarily the lower classes of cognitive skills? Will that teacher lay aside possibilities of personal discomfort that may arise from the poor test scores of his students and provide ample opportunity for the development of positive attitudes and higher level problem-solving and creative skills? History and practice indicate that generally this will not happen.

Teachers in many school systems of the 1920's, 1930's, and 1940's were slaves to achievement testing programs. Some of the more mature among the readers may remember their teacher cramming a semester's work into a few weeks in order to prepare for the spring testing. Who does not remember teachers who maintained files of past scholarship tests, and who released the more able students from routine tasks that they might review and memorize the information the tests contained? It is often rumored that certain principals and teachers previewed actual test items with students prior to testing time. It is even said that some answer sheets and test grades were falsified to indicate a higher level of achievement for the students. It is not difficult to see the effects of such questionable evaluation procedures upon the validity of the whole assessment process.

Though the preceding examples of dishonesty are disheartening, the most serious effect was that the test dictated the curriculum. Whatever the purpose of a test item, whatever the cognitive level at which it might be aimed, the information that it contains could be memorized and the item, or like items, might be practiced.

Even if one assumes that all teachers and principals are basically honest, the observer may see how these professionals might come to view the objectives of the curriculum in terms of the narrow sample of evaluation tasks contained on a test. The effect of extensive emphasis upon testing has in the past, and will likely in the future, result in a narrowing of the goals and objectives of all school curricula.

The 1950's and 1960's have seen in public education an increased emphasis upon process, problem solving, and creativity. This movement has just begun to gain some small measure of success in the nation's classrooms. True, the use of the new methodology is far from universal. However, some inroads are being made by teacher preparation programs and in-service programs of public school systems upon the traditional read and memorize mode of classroom

operation. The advent of widespread accountability
procedures in the schools of the nation may well
spell the finish to this movement.

If one considers the concern by teachers for the
affective and higher level cognitive behaviors to be
a step in the right direction for public education,
then surely because of its deleterious effect upon
such concerns the widespread use of accountability
procedures must be considered a step backward, or at
least sideways. Just as many teachers are just
beginning to lose their unhealthy and restrictive
concern for traditional content-oriented teaching
objectives, the initiation of widespread testing programs will surely cause some measure of regression
and a reaffirmation of faith in the old values.

CONCLUSION

It should not be inferred from this writing that
teachers need necessarily fear accountability measures. Indeed, just the opposite is true. Since
curricula are to be well defined, and rather narrowly
defined, any teacher worthy of the title should be
able to meet his obligations. Free of many concerns
for student values and skills, the teacher will be
able to concentrate upon a curriculum of lesser
scope. In fact entering into performance contracts--
receiving pay commensurate with the performance of
his students--may do more to reduce the work-load of
the classroom teachers than any device yet conceived.
The greatest burden in a performance contracting
situation is placed upon the administrator who
chooses the curriculum and objectives that are suited
to the needs of the young people in his charge. The
cross of accountability may well be more than most
concerned public school administrators care to
shoulder.

Educators must pause before they, like the lem-
mings, run helter-skelter into the sea of accountability and destroy much which they have accomplished
in the past twenty years. Models for accountability
must provide flexibility for intrasystem and intra-
school curriculum options. And perhaps most importantly classroom teachers must be made to view
accountability not as something restrictive and to be
feared, but as an opportunity to objectively assess

their performance and ultimately to improve the level
of their instruction. Only if the obvious pitfalls
of the accountability paradigm can be avoided can
there be hope that it will work to the ultimate good
of public education.

PART TWO

BEHAVIORAL OBJECTIVES

In psychology, behaviorists hold that learning
is essentially a "change in behavior." Recently,
educators have utilized this concept in specifying
objectives for the learner in behavioral terms. Behavioral objectives focus upon the stimulus or input,
the conditions under which the subject is to perform
and the output or extent to which the subject has
mastered the content. In many instances, the pre-
test, post-test procedure is utilized.

Advocates of this process believe that it places
greater emphasis upon learning rather than teaching.
It helps the student to be more independent and makes
learning more efficient. Opponents of behavioral objectives feel that learning is too complex a process
to be reduced to an input-output system. The issue
is being widely debated as evidenced by the selection
of articles in this part.

The first article by Kimball is concerned with
the philosophy underlying behavioral objectives. He
not only discusses the rationale and limitations of
this approach, but also cites the need for a carefully delineated educational philosophy. This philosophy would provide the framework for the then ensuing
behavioral objectives.

Miles and Robinson in the second article offer
basic considerations dealing with behavioral objectives and attempt to answer criticisms leveled
against them. The authors give a detailed definition
and list specific attributes of such objectives.
Practical examples of behavioral objectives are
mentioned.

Arguments for and against behavioral objectives

are presented in separate articles by Gagné and Kneller respectively. Gagné holds that schools need a
clear set of instructional objectives in order to
communicate effectively. Objectives should identify
the capability learned and the performance required
to carry out the learned knowledge. Clearly stated
objectives can be used to communicate between curriculum specialist and course planner, between planner and teacher, between teacher and pupil, and
between teacher and parent.

In the last article Kneller argues that behavior
is highly complex and includes such areas as creativity and imagination. He further states that knowing and behaving are separate and distinct and that
it is impossible to coordinate the two processes.
Instead of behavioral objectives, the author would
rather have "specified" objectives which would be
identified for certain basic subject matter.   In
other areas, objectives should be consistent with a
defensible philosophy and psychology of learning.

EDUCATIONAL PHILOSOPHY AND
BEHAVIORAL OBJECTIVES

Roland B. Kimball

THE NEED FOR A BEHAVIORAL OBJECTIVES APPROACH

The educational world is currently caught up in an intensive examination of a behavioral objectives approach to curriculum planning and instructional method. This approach assumes the need and the possibility of stipulating learning outcomes in terms of discrete performance objectives. Whenever a teacher attempts to do this, he is forced to make a more considered analysis of just what it is that he seeks to teach, and to identify precisely just what performance by a student will serve as evidence that the concept or skill has in fact been learned.

Such an effort is laudable. For too long educators have formulated their educational purposes in vague generalizations, and have accepted as evidence of learning, actions which usually are judged by intuitive and subjective methods. Quite understandably, this practice has made many educational decisions highly idiosyncratic at best, capricious at worst. Analytical techniques which impose form, structure, and order on educational planning are indeed desirable. The behavioral objectives approach is one of the best techniques for assuring this sort of rigor in instructional planning.

Reprinted by permission from the April 1971 issue of THE CLEARING HOUSE.

THE LIMITATIONS OF THIS APPROACH

Yet there are important problems inherent in this approach. Most significant appears to be the inclincation to utilize this technique in a somewhat atomistic manner. This occurs in three ways:

(1) Overemphasis on Low-Level Cognitive Outcomes. There is a tendency to apply this approach only to the relatively low order cognitive or manipulative skills in particular areas of study. Thus, many groups have made good progress in creating behavioral objectives applications in elementary mathematics or science. And equally good results can be obtained in establishing performance outcomes for cognitive and skill learnings in spelling, vocabulary, typing, sewing, and the like. Higher order cognitive outcomes in areas such as creative writing or critical thinking apparently have not yet been subjected to the same type of analysis. Affective outcomes, directing attention to values, tastes, and attitudes, likewise have received only limited attention. Partly this is a function of the complexity of the task; but it may also be an indication that some of these outcomes do not yield to the behavioral objectives approach, given the present state of the art.

It will be interesting to follow the progress of those groups that apparently are seeking to apply the behavioral objectives techniques in curriculum areas which are most distinctly affective in nature. For instance, the ES '70 Arts Curriculum Project has this orientation,[1] and music educators also are moving to develop behavioral objectives for this area of study.[2]

(2) Overemphasis on a Single Discipline. In general the behavioral objectives technique has been applied on a subject-by-subject basis.[3] To the extent that this is so, decisions usually are made in terms of the internal requirements of the discipline, its logical structure, its central concepts, and its methodology. Cross disciplinary possibilities may not receive sufficient attention; instructional arrangements to help students synthesize learnings from different fields of study may not be created; and concerns for the formulation of attitudes, values, tastes, and interpersonal skills may not achieve the

central position they require.

(3) <u>Overemphasis on Selected Disciplines</u>. The evidence presently available indicates that certain disciplines have been the subject of fairly intensive applications of a behavioral objectives analysis. Two examples of this are mathematics in the Individually Prescribed Instruction Project[4] and science in the AAAS program known as "Science--A Process Approach."[5] There is less curriculum development in the area of language arts and the area of social studies. Fields such as music and art seem to have been almost totally neglected to the present time. Even though it is clear why this may be true, given the less definite intellectual structure and logical sequence in these disciplines, this does not eliminate the possibility that the disciplines receiving less attention by the behavioral objectivists may then receive less than their due in our educational priorities. Balance in the curriculum is important, and current developments to some degree threaten it.

THE NEED FOR A BROADER FRAME OF REFERENCE

If these limitations do occur on a very extensive scale, and there is some reason to believe that they do, the explanation seems simple. It lies in the failure to develop a complete and consistent philosophical frame of reference as a guide to the work of various groups preparing behavioral objectives in a specific field or for a specific grade level.[6] Without a carefully stated educational philosophy which sets forth a comprehensive and unified position regarding the total educational experience we seek for our learners, it is unlikely that we can expect separately undertaken efforts by various subject matter groups to create this for us. In short, some of the systems analysis techniques which the behavioral objectives proponents have been applying to selected disciplines must first be applied to the total educational effort of any given school system. Unless this is done the limitations of an atomistic approach will circumscribe our efforts.

Figure 1 depicts a generalized model for a curriculum development system which incorporates these features.

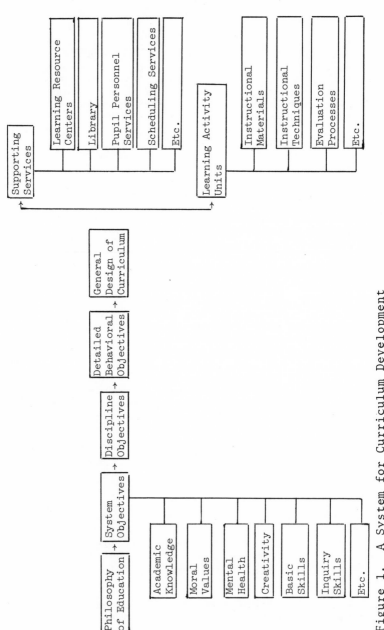

Figure 1. A System for Curriculum Development

Obvious problems appear. A general statement of educational philosophy may merely perpetuate the ills that the behavioral objectives approach has been designed to correct. Admittedly, any attempts to state a philosophy in terms of certain superordinate goals can become just one more exercise in glittering generalities. To avoid this, the educational philosophy should incorporate the spirit and sometimes the language of the behavioral objectives technique.

CRITERIA FOR A SYSTEM-WIDE STATEMENT
OF EDUCATIONAL OBJECTIVES

The preceding critique of the behavioral objectives approach suggests that a statement of educational purposes for a school system must be the starting point. Otherwise we risk putting old wine (the conventional academic subject matter) into new bottles (a behavioral objectives format).

Even though this change very well might be a forward step, it accomplishes only a part of what needs to be done. It is not enough to create a situation where teachers will take a hard and clear look at their claims regarding the intent of education, reformulating these intentions so that their accomplishment is indicated by the successful performance of particular tasks and the display of particular patterns of behavior by learners. Specific action of this nature will be fully effective only when it occurs in a larger context--in a context established by a comprehensive statement of educational purposes which seeks to identify the superordinate goals, the relative balance that is to characterize the educational enterprise, and the more subtle "humanizing" outcomes intended.

What are the criteria that should be met by such a statement?

(1) Mankind through the ages has developed patterns of personal and social survival, concepts of the good life, an understanding of his physical universe and his natural environment, and modes of expressing himself. These may be thought of as cultural universals. Because education has been a significant instrument for assuring man's cultural continuity, our statement of educational objectives

should recognize this conservator function.

(2)   Educational purposes are, to some degree, hierarchical in nature.   There is concern for enough factual knowledge to assure a cognitive awareness of the human condition and how it came to be what it is; there is concern for procedural competency in using the fundamental skills of language, number, science, and technology; there is concern for economic self-sufficiency and social responsibility; there is concern for creativity, productive thinking, and versatile intellectual and artistic endeavor; there is concern for aesthetic taste, moral standards, and sustaining interpersonal behavior.   Any statement of educational purpose should encompass the entire range of concerns, and should guide us in setting educational priorities so that appropriate emphasis is given to all levels and all domains of the hierarchy of concerns.

(3)   Given a cultural and environmental milieu which exerts both indirect and direct controls on human behavior, there exists a cause for the concern that individuality be protected and nurtured.   Hence, although a part of our statement of educational purpose should be derived from the characteristics of our culture, the complexity of our technology, and the needs of our society, it is equally true that a part of our statement should derive its authority from a concern that individuals be autonomous, that they play a part in defining the character of their educational experiences and in determining the sort of person they are to become.   This is to say that not all educational objectives, behavioral or otherwise, are to be set for the learner without his participation and consent.   Put a little differently, there is a need to identify educational objectives which make the learner a participant in shaping his life style.

(4)   Although the long-range, wholistic goals of education normally are not in conflict with the short-range, specific goals, the relationships between the two frequently are inadequately recognized. There is a tendency to stop short of the former, settling for competent performance by the student in the routine daily activities, the lessons and the responses related to specific purposes.   Emphasis on behavioral objectives increases the risk that our educational attention will be directed to the trees

at the expense of overlooking the forest, because behavioral objectives are discrete, analytic, hierarchical, whereas our long-range objectives are amorphous, synthetic, and interactive. A comprehensive educational philosophy, while recognizing the practical significance of the "here and now" as an educational concern, will also postulate a network of relationships which relate the specific events of day-by-day teaching to the longterm objectives which must be stated in comprehensive and, quite possibly, nonbehavioral terms.

FOOTNOTES

1. ES '70 News, Vol. 2, No. 14, April 1970, pp. 5,8.

2. Miriam B. Klapfer, "The Evolution of Musical Objectives," Music Educators Journal, February 1970, pp. 61-63.

3. A notable exception is an early effort published more than ten years ago: W. French and associates. Behavioral Goals of General Education in High School, Russell Sage Foundation, New York, 1957.

4. Mathematics Continuum: Individually Prescribed Instruction, Learning Research and Development Center, University of Pittsburgh, Pittsburgh, Pennsylvania. September 1968.

5. "Science--A Process Approach." AAAS Miscellaneous Publication 67-12, American Association for the Advancement of Science, Washington, D.C., 1967.

6. Ralph W. Tyler, "Some Persistent Questions on the Defining of Objectives" in Defining Educational Objectives (C. M. Lindvall, Editor), University of Pittsburgh Press, Pittsburgh, Pennsylvania, 1964, pp. 77-83.

BEHAVIORAL OBJECTIVES: AN EVEN CLOSER LOOK

David T. Miles and Roger E. Robinson

To many people associated with education, the term "behavioral objectives" evokes a classroom image of a free, open and humane environment with confident, self-directed and anxiety-free students joyfully acquiring complex intellectual and social capabilities. To others this very same term conjures up images of a factory-like room full of cubicles with dehumanized automatons repetitively memorizing useless facts. What is it about this concept that spawns such divergent impressions in people? Many of the reasons why people favor the use of behavioral objectives have been suggested by Tyler,[1] Mager[2] and Popham.[3] In a recent article entitled, "Behavioral Objectives: A Close Look," Robert Ebel[4] appears to have identified some of the fundamental reasons why many people oppose behavioral objectives. The present article examines some of these common criticisms and attempts to offer possible clarification regarding the nature and value of such objectives.

Before exploring these issues, we should first review the definition of the object of concern. A behavioral objective is a statement which describes what a student should be able to do after completing some unit of instruction. The three components which make up a behavioral objective are:

> 1.   Conditions: a description of the class
>   of stimuli to which the student is to
>   respond (e.g., the type of questions,
>   tasks or problems, and the form in which
>   they will be presented; the relevant

Reprinted from Educational Technology, 11:39-44, June, 1971 by permission of publisher.

conditions under which the student will
be expected to perform--materials or
equipment which will be available,
environmental conditions which may
affect the performance, special physical
or psychological demands which may exist).

2. <u>Behavior</u>: a statement containing an
action or behavioral verb which connotes
or denotes the behavior the student is
to perform (e.g., identify, write,
describe, solve, classify) and a general
reference to a product of the student's
behavior (e.g., an essay, a diagram, a
three-dimensional model).

3. <u>Criteria</u>: a description of the success
criteria by which the student's behavior
is to be judged acceptable or unacceptable (e.g., correctly applies three principles; identifies eight out of ten;
solves the problem; the idea must be
different from any in the textbook, discussed in class or produced by other
students).

COGNITIVE PROCESSES VS. BEHAVIOR?

One of Ebel's criticisms, which has helped
clarify a major source of potential conflict and confusion with behavioral objectives, deals with the
question of whether behavior <u>or</u> cognitive processes
should be the target of educational efforts. He
suggests that the real objectives of instruction are
knowledge, understanding, attitudes and values, as
opposed to actual behavior. What is proposed is that
cognitive processes and affective states are independent of behavior--that a person can think or feel
in a certain way without doing anything observable
that exposes his thoughts or feelings. Although some
people might deny this proposition, most people--
including behavioral objectivists--would probably
agree. Further, most people concerned with education
would probably agree what mental processes and emotional feelings are the "real" goals of education.
But this presents a problem for such people who want
to effect some change in other people's thoughts and
feelings. How can one find out what someone is

thinking or feeling unless the person <u>does</u> something?
Thinking and feeling are events which <u>go on</u> inside of
people and are not directly observable with the
unaided senses (such activity may, however, be observed by mechanical devices which measure electro-
chemical activities in the brain and other organs,
but this means of observation is presently of limited
use for most educators). We do not see a person
analyze a poem; we see or hear a report of his
analysis. We do not see the mental activity of problem solving; we see solutions to the problem. We do
not see the emotional feeling a person experiences
when listening to a favorite piece of music; we see
the results of his emotional experience in his verbal
response or facial expression, or in his future
selection of that music for listening. Thus, the
only way one can say anything with any certainty
about what another person is thinking or feeling is
through inference from observing his behavior. This
does not preclude the use of introspection to imagine
what one would think or feel if he were in the other
person's position. This method is one which is frequently used, but its validity is often questionable.

By suggesting that the goal of education is cognitive processes <u>instead</u> of behavior, we may be err-
ing in a direction opposite to that of many behaviorists, who claim that it is behavior--<u>instead</u> of
cognitive processes--that is the only concern of
education. For those concerned with education,
focusing upon cognitive processes without behavior is
essentially impossible; while on the other hand,
claiming that behavior is unrelated to cognitive
processes appears to be an equally naive position.

The question of whether the goal of education is
the inferred mental operations of students or the
observable indicants of the students' mental operations is essentially a misleading question since, for
the purpose of the educator, they cannot be separated.
The apparently little-appreciated virtue of behavioral
objectives is that they permit <u>inferences</u> to be made
regarding the cognitive processes required of the
student. To illustrate this point, consider the
following two objectives:

1. Given the ten recorded music excerpts
    which were played in class to illustrate
    acid rock, folk rock, soft rock and
    bubblegum, the student will classify

them in the named categories. Eight
out of ten correct will indicate
mastery of this objective.

2. Given ten unfamiliar recorded excerpts
from the following types of music: acid
rock, folk rock, soft rock and bubble-
gum, the student will classify them in
the named categories. Eight out of ten
correct will indicate mastery of this
objective.

In both objectives the performance and the success
criteria are identical, but due to the differences in
the stimulus conditions described, what is required
is quite different for each objective. In the first
objective, the student is required to identify previously heard musical excerpts and recall their
associated class names. In the second objective, the
student must discriminate among four classes of music
and generalize within each class on the basis of
characteristics associated with the different classes
of music--and also recall the names associated with
each class. The first objective requires what might
be called association learning, while the second
involves concept learning. Or, according to Bloom's
Taxonomy, the first is a knowledge objective and the
second belongs in the intellectual skills and abilities category.

Perhaps this incredibly important quality of
behavioral objectives can be shown with the diagram
below of the objective:

Given a common disposable object (e.g., paper
sack, bottle, cardboard box, plastic container) and the designation of a consumer
group (e.g., six- to ten-year-olds, college
students, housewives), the student will
describe in writing ideas for at least three
original marketable products. Each of the
three products must be previously unknown to
the instructor and class, and be something
the target group would be likely to buy, as
judged by class vote.

INSTRUCTIONAL OBJECTIVE

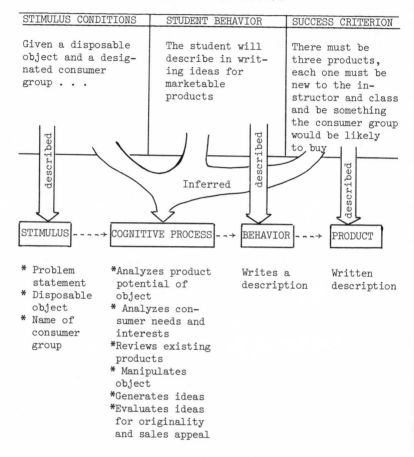

STIMULUS CONDITIONS	STUDENT BEHAVIOR	SUCCESS CRITERION
Given a disposable object and a designated consumer group . . .	The student will describe in writing ideas for marketable products	There must be three products, each one must be new to the instructor and class and be something the consumer group would be likely to buy

STIMULUS ----→ COGNITIVE PROCESS --→ BEHAVIOR ---→ PRODUCT

* Problem statement * Disposable object * Name of consumer group	*Analyzes product potential of object * Analyzes consumer needs and interests *Reviews existing products * Manipulates object *Generates ideas *Evaluates ideas for originality and sales appeal	Writes a description	Written description

This diagram attempts to illustrate the function of each component of the objective. The description of the stimulus conditions with which the student will be confronted and the performance expected of the student permit inferences to be made regarding the cognitive processes required of the student. Although it is seldom, if ever, possible to determine the precise nature of the cognitive process which occurs within people, it is possible to infer some of the general characteristics of such activities. The student behavior component defines the behavior to be employed in order to expose his solution. The

criterion component serves primarily as a guide to
the student and the instructor regarding the important characteristics of his behavior--or in this
case, the product of his behavior--which must be
present for the performance to be considered successful. This component also provides some inferential
information regarding the requisite cognitive
processes.

Several other functional features of behavioral
objectives could be pointed out here, but the major
intent is to show the relationship between behavioral
objectives and cognitive processes.

IS BEHAVIOR THE OBJECTIVE?

A second possible area of confusion with behavioral objectives deals with the term "behavior" itself. Since most people use the word "behavior" to
refer only to overt, observable actions--such as
speaking, writing, smiling, pointing, running, etc.
--many of the instructional objectives typically
referred to as behavioral objectives appear to be
mislabeled. These objectives in fact do not identify
specific, observable physical acts. Action verbs
such as describe, identify, construct, solve or classify, which are typically found in so-called behavioral
objectives, are not behavioral verbs if we accept the
common meaning of the word "behavior."[5] To further
clarify this point, consider the following objective:

> Given a copy of the state criminal code, a
> statement of his own moral code which he has
> previously defined, and descriptions of
> various acts performed by individuals with
> all relevant circumstances, the student will
> identify each act as one of the following:
> illegal and immoral; illegal but moral;
> legal but immoral; legal and moral; or not
> covered by either the state code or his
> personal code.[5]

The action verb "identify" used in this objective
could refer to many different behaviors:

<pre>
                                  Points to
                                  Writes a number by
                                  Orally names
              Identify   Marks an X by
                                  Draws a circle around
                                  Presses a button
                                  Wiggles nose at
</pre>

Two things seem to be important here. First, the
term "identify" does not refer to a specific behavior; second, the specific behavior employed in this
case to provide evidence that the student correctly
identified something is of little importance. Any of
the behaviors would probably be acceptable. It
should be pointed out here that some objectives do
contain behavioral verbs such as write, draw, speak,
or jump, and are thus truly behavioral objectives;
but frequently the choice of behavior specified
appears arbitrary.

There seems to be two situations in which it is
crucial that the particular form of behavior should
be specified in an objective. The first is when the
form of behavior expected of the student after completing instruction is important to the successful
performance of the learned capability. For example,
if after completing some instruction a person will
be expected to orally discuss his views on civic
matters in group situations, then an instructional
objective dealing with this capability should specify
the actual behavior--"orally discuss"--rather than
the more general "discuss," since the form of the
behavior is critical. Although a written discussion
of civic views might be a reasonable "enroute" or
preparatory performance leading to this capability,
it would probably not be an acceptable form of performance at the end of instruction. The second
situation in which the specific form of behavior
should be identified in an objective is where the
actual behavior is the focus of the objective, which
is the case with subjects in the psychomotor domain
--i.e., penmanship, a drawing class, a speech course,
athletics, playing musical instruments, shop courses,
etc. However, for much instruction in the public
schools and colleges, the behavior employed by students to communicate attainment of some capability
appears to be of secondary importance.

If the so-called behavioral verbs used in many
objectives do not refer to behavior--and in many

cases it is not important that they do--of what value
are they? Possibly their primary function is to suggest that the student will engage in some kind of
cognitive   activity and that he will do something to
expose this activity. Although this may seem to be a
trivial function, the difference between objectives
which contain such action terms and objectives which
use such static terms as "to understand" and "to
know" is not trivial at all. Since understanding and
knowing can only be understood or known by someone
else when a person does something, these action verbs
essentially supply the direction and purpose to
otherwise ambiguous states of knowledge or cognitive
ability. In addition, these terms appear to suggest
a range of relevant behaviors which might be used to
express and thereby observe cognitive activity. The
following diagram may illustrate the relationships
among verbs which describe internal states, action
verbs and behavioral verbs.

Internal State Verb	Action Verbs	Behavioral Verbs
	identify	
	define	
	describe	writes
understand	solve	points to
	classify	orally states
	evaluate	draws
	predict	

When we say we want a student to "understand," we
typically mean that he should be able to perform one
or more types of action such as listed under the
action verbs. These action verbs are more concrete
expressions of what is meant by understanding. The
behavioral verbs go one step further by specifying
the form in which the student will demonstrate the
process implied by the action verb. Often the same
behavior would be appropriate for expressing different actions; i.e., "writing" might be used to express
solving, identifying, describing, classifying, etc.

Perhaps a general rule regarding the degree of
specificity desired for defining the behavior in an
objective should be the same as that for any attempt
at communicating a message. One should use terms for
which the intended audience has a similar meaning.
If the expected reader of an objective has a similar

interpretation to that of the writer regarding what behavior would be associated with such terms as identify, describe or solve, then these terms would be appropriate. But when the form of the desired behavior is important and one cannot be sure how readers of these non-behavioral action terms will interpret them, then the actual behavior should be specified. It should also be recalled that the action verb is but one part of the three components in behavioral objectives, and by itself is of limited value. However, when action verbs such as these are combined with a description of the stimulus conditions to which the student will respond, plus a specification of the criteria which the student's performance must meet, we have what may be education's most valuable tool.

THE "REAL" OBJECTIVES OF INSTRUCTION

Another difficulty with behavioral objectives which Ebel mentioned is that the behavior specified in such definitions is "seldom the real objective of the instruction." In this instance his "real" objective appears to be what people are to do after completing their formal education. As Popham[6] has pointed out, the fact that a teacher uses a true-false test to measure music appreciation or good citizenship can hardly be blamed on the use of behavioral objectives. As a matter of fact, revealing discrepancies between intentions of instruction and the outcomes measured appears to be one of the greatest virtues of behavioral objectives. By stating objectives in this way, it is possible to assess the actual discrepancy between what students do to exhibit what was learned in a course, and what they are expected to do in the future. By talking in vague generalities about knowledge, understanding and attitudes students are to acquire from instruction and use afterward, any discrepancies between intentions of instruction and student performance required by traditional tests are not apparent.

The fact that many people are apparently unaware of the contribution which the use of behavioral objectives offers to facilitating transfer from the classroom to life activities is particularly discouraging. As Thorndike found, and countless other studies have conformed, the more similar the conditions and performances required from one situation to another, the greater the likelihood of transfer. In other words, the closer the match between what a student does to demonstrate successful completion of a course and what he will be expected to do in the future, the more likely that he will be able to perform successfully in the future. Although the use of behavioral objectives alone does not insure that a rigorous analysis and description of the post-instruction behavior will be performed to insure maximum congruence between objectives and post-instruction performance, the probability of such efforts appears much more likely with such an approach.

Certainly it is no simple job to identify the kinds of specific activities to be expected of students after completing a course for all subject areas. But if greater efforts are not expended in this direction, the current cry for "relevance" in education may grow louder and louder. This should not be taken to suggest that the arts and humanities should be de-emphasized in favor of a more occupationally oriented curriculum. On the contrary, it appears that what our society may need more than anything else is the kinds of attitudes and skills associated with tolerance, reason and a comprehensive perspective of human nature--which are often considered legitimate subject matter for the arts and humanities. But talking in vague and nebulous terms about citizenship, creative awareness, tolerance and critical thinking will do very little to solve any problem. It is only when such grand and virtuous qualities are operationally defined that progress will be made. It is only when objectives such as:

"The student will learn to critically examine the current political scene."

are translated into a set of objectives which may include the following:

"Confronted with two transcripts of political campaign speeches from opposing parties, the student will identify statements which contain the following: errors in reasoning, irrelevant arguments, unwarranted generalizations and invalid conclusions. As a minimum, the student must identify 80 percent of such statements identified by the course instructor."

that we can even find out what is being learned in
school, let alone its relevance to anything else.

SPECIFYING THE CRITERION LEVEL

There is general agreement among advocates of
"behavioral objectives" that the level of acceptable
performance or criterion level must be stated. Without this information, an objective may be of limited
use even if the other two components--the performance
and the conditions under which the performance is to
occur--are carefully stated. Consider the following
example:

> "Upon completion of a novel, the student will
> relate the novel to his experience."

The responses to this request by students could differ
considerably. Depending upon the teacher who reads
them, the judgments about the responses could also
vary widely. Obviously, there is no right answer to
this objective. Each teacher will probably be quite
subjective when evaluating these papers, and many
people would see this as good and noble. They would
see ultimate freedom for the student in relating a
novel to his experience in any way he sees fit, with
no predetermined criteria. As long as teachers
accept any response offered by the student and do
not place grades on the responses based upon some
hidden criterion, then there is no need for the
statement of an acceptable performance level.

However, most teachers do expect some minimum
level of performance from students. It may only
involve an indication that the student has attended
to the stimulus in question. As an example, the
objective above could be expanded to read as follows:

> "Upon completion of a novel, the student will
> relate the novel to his experience in any one
> of the following ways: (1) by discussing why
> he could or could not identify with any of
> the characters; (2) by stating what new ideas
> the author has presented, or what old ideas
> have been presented in a new persepctive for
> him; (3) by discussing any particular passage

or incident which evoked strong feeling in
him."[7]

Criteria for evaluating the first option may include:

1. Did the student state whether he did or
    did not identify with a character?

2. Did he provide reasons for his identifi-
    cation or lack of it?

3. Did he include specific examples from
    the book to support his answer?

In the case of these criteria, some restriction
is placed on the student regarding what the student
can discuss. He is asked to provide evidence that he
has attended to some aspect of a novel; and as long
as these criteria are met, the response is adequate.
This allows for unique responses by students, while
providing some cues about the expectations of the
teacher.

Stating a criterion level for an objective is a
difficult task. As Garvin[8] states, in some tasks
there are many levels of competence permissible, even
though a criterion level could be specified. In most
cases it is difficult, if not impossible, to determine an absolute criterion which should be met based
upon some external demand. Therefore, in most cases
criteria are established somewhat arbitrarily by
teachers. These criteria may be based upon knowledge
of future requirements in subsequent instruction or
in an occupation; upon expectations based on previous
experience with many students; or even upon value
judgments regarding important cognitive processes the
student should be able to use when faced with problem
situations. It would seem that criteria established
on these bases are better than none at all. Without
any criterion performance, our only apparent alternative is a norm-referenced evaluation scheme--a procedure which possibly has done more harm to education
than any other single phenomenon.[9]

Although knowledge of the comparative ability or
achievement of students is valuable information for
many functions--e.g., prescribing different instruction, selecting students for college or graduate
school, making occupational choices, selecting prospective employees, etc.--it is most unfortunate that

the philosophy and procedures of achievement testing
which are associated with these functions were ever
applied to evaluation in education. Some of the
direct and indirect effects of the norm-referenced
evaluation system commonly cited include:

1.   fixed amount of time allotted to courses
     of instruction;

2.   group pacing of instruction;

3.   a type of competitiveness among students
     in which the game strategy requires that
     some students be losers;

4.   emphasis on grades vs. learning;

5.   lack of accountability for instructional
     effectiveness;

6.   damage to self-concepts of average and
     slow learners;

7.   build-up of cumulative deficiencies in
     such skills as reading, due to social
     promotion.

Fortunately, criterion-referenced evaluation--
which is at the heart of the current move toward
instruction which is individualized, non-graded,
self-paced, continuous progress and competency-based
--promises to reduce and eliminate many of these
effects.

The function of evaluation in education should
very likely be restricted to finding out whether
students have learned what is intended and to provide
data for the improvement of instruction. To accomplish this function, it is more informative to be
able to say that a student achieved some known criterion level of performance, even though the level
was arbitrarily set, than to say that a student
achieved some unknown level, such as the 75th percen-
tile level, compared to some given group. The purpose of instruction is for students to acquire
certain capabilities and attitudes--not to continually prove that students learn at different rates
and, when given similar instruction and an equal
amount of time, that they will reach different levels
of achievement. The more clearly we can define what

students are to learn, the more likely we will be
able to improve the quality of our educational
efforts.

OBJECTIVES: TO HAVE OR NOT TO HAVE?

The preceding part of this article deals primarily with some specific attributes of instructional
objectives. The remainder of the article deals with
some more philosophic issues on the topic of behavioral objectives. Perhaps the pace to begin is at
the most basic level by "defining our terms."

We casually use the word "objective" in our
conversation and our writings without examining the
consistency of its use and the common meaning. It
appears that an objective is a future goal or aim
which one has in mind or states before it is achieved.
This implies that an objective, then, is a predetermined outcome which some person or group wishes to
achieve. Many teachers suggest that they do not know
the objectives for their course, but will determine
the learning outcomes at the end of instruction.
Certainly this is a practice which is not uncommon,
and many people feel they do not know ahead of time
what certain outcomes will be. However, to measure
outcome at the end of some instructional sequence and
then to call these "objectives" seems to be an illogi-
cal or inconsistent use of the term. On the other
hand, if one tries to determine objectives for future
courses based upon outcomes of past courses to get
some idea of the potential of the students, the
reasonableness of the material, etc., then this seems
to be a legitimate practice. What is suggested is
that when we use the term "objective," we imply predetermined knowledge of some outcome which is desirable to achieve. A consistent use of the word would
suggest that objectives are stated before instruction.

A second decision which must be made deals with
the issue of whether objectives should be made measurable or not. This raises a serious question which
may be stated as follows: "Is there such a thing as
a non-measurable objective?" If one considers the
use of the language carefully, it would be a linguis-
tic inconsistency to speak of a non-measurable
objective. If something is non-measurable, then to
say that it is a goal one wishes to achieve does not

appear to be a meaningful statement. To desire to achieve a goal implies that one must have knowledge of achievement; and this, of course, implies that one can detect the outcome. It does not matter if the objective is to be realized following the time when the instructor has the student in class. Many objectives deal with knowledge and skills to be used in real-life situations or in vocational situations. However, if a person never attempts to measure these future outcomes, his verbalization of them as objectives would be empty. On what basis can he continue to provide certain learning experiences without any knowledge about their effectiveness in achieving long-range goals? Most typically, data on post-course behavior are difficult or impossible to get; therefore, we should attend to end-of-course performance to assess instruction.

Since objectives imply measurability, the issue of measurable or behavioral objectives vs. non-behavioral objectives may be a false issue. Rather, the question appears to be whether the teacher should or should not have objectives for his instruction. It certainly may be the case that in some situations there are no outcomes which one hopes to achieve which can be stated previous to instruction. In these situations it may appear that whatever happens during some set of experiences or instructional procedures is acceptable to the instructor, and no predetermination of goals is considered necessary. Upon closer examination, it may be that there is implicitly an objective in these situations, such as students will learn some general processes in handling information, social-interaction skills, producing products, answering questions, making decisions, etc. An instructor who claims to have no predetermined goals should examine carefully whether,in fact, this is true; and certainly in all such situations where it is true, there will be no need for traditional evaluation of the students. Evaluation of the students would mean that there were standards or criteria to which they are held by the instructor. Even the use of a norm-referenced evaluation system in this situation would seem inappropriate, since it would be difficult to compare one student with another without any particular outcomes in mind.

Teaching is a goal-directed activity, as perceived in most people. As with any goal-directed activity, we need a clear statement of our objectives before proceeding with learning activities. If it is not a goal-directed activity, then it may best be labeled free association, and not teaching or instruction. Stated below is a general definition of teaching that the authors have used on occasion:

> "Teaching is the process of arranging learn-
> ing experiences to facilitate students'
> attainment of cognitive, affective and/or
> psychomotor objectives."

If you tend to agree with this definition, then it seems important to look very carefully at the problem of objectives. The use of behavioral objectives forces us to examine very carefully the evidence we will accept to infer sophisticated cognitive processes. Their use also tests our willingness to deal with data regarding our success as teachers.

At this point the use of an example may help to illustrate the importance of behavioral objectives in guiding the outcomes of instruction. Examine the following objective:

> "By the second semester of a course in
> social problems, the student will, after a
> classroom discussion in which he has parti-
> cipated and in which note-taking was not
> permitted, summarize in his own words at
> least five points made by other students in
> the discussion. The students who made the
> five points must agree on the accuracy of
> the summaries."

A teacher who would state an objective such as the one above exposes rather clearly one of the skills he wishes students to acquire as a result of his instruction and class discussions. Since listening to other discussants is a critical skill of a good participant, it has been singled out as <u>one</u> of the outcomes he hopes to achieve. Many other discussion skills could be developed or stated, but the point is made by this one example. Without some measurable evidence, as stated in a behavioral objective, a teacher may assume that everyone present during a discussion learned this listening skill. This may or may not be true, but without some measurable outcome to use as a criterion, we seem to be in the same position as contemplating "the number of angels on the head of a pin."

THE EVIDENCE

Many critics have made reference to the con-
spicuous "non-use" of behavioral objectives to
question their usefulness and the difficulty in writing them. The logic employed here seems highly
questionable under careful examination. To suggest
that a method or technique intended to improve
instruction lacks value because it has not been
properly or extensively used is to depart from any
resemblance of an empirical approach. We must agree
that there is not an extensive application of the use
of behavioral objectives. The same could be said for
many methods and techniques in education and other
fields, but this tells us nothing about their effectiveness to produce desired results. One may ask
another question which seems more appropriate: Given
a situation where behavioral objectives have been
developed and used to guide instruction as advocated
by people such as Popham, Mager, Harmes, Kibler[10] or
Gronlund,[11] were the results achieved--by any standard one wishes to apply--satisfactory? It may be
wise to await that verdict before pronouncing any
death sentences.

What empirical evidence is available to suggest
that pupils of teachers who use behavioral objectives
do better than those who do not? Many teachers ask
this question when confronted with a behavioral
objectives evangelist. It would be nice if there
were an answer, but there is none; and it does not
appear that there can be.

Raths[12] pointed out that any study which hopes to
compare the two treatments--one with pre-specified
objectives and one with no pre-specified objectives--
is biased in favor of the treatment using pre-specified objectives, because the criterion test usually
reflects the specific objectives. This is true when
there is a common criterion test to assess both
treatments, and when the test is based upon the specific objectives in the one treatment. The use of
dual criteria, one for each treatment, leaves no
basis for comparison. An analogy may make this point
more vivid.

Consider two men in St. Louis who are going on a
trip in their respective cars. They are analogous to
two teachers about to begin a class. We have decided

to compare their effectiveness as drivers on the basis on some criteria. Driver number one states rather clearly that he intends to drive straight to Cincinnati, and does so. Driver number two says he doesn't know where he is going; he will just start driving and stop somewhere. He ends up in San Francisco.

Now the dilemma begins in comparing these drivers in some way. If we choose to use as our criterion of effectiveness, arrival in Cincinnati, obviously Driver No. 1 is more effective; but it is just as obvious that driver No. 2 probably had no intention of going to Cincinnati, so this comparison makes no sense. We could select other criteria, such as who had the fewest accidents, who drove the most miles, who got the best gas mileage, etc. Clearly, without pre-specification, it is just as meaningless to compare the drivers on the basis of these criteria without their prior knowledge of them. The driver with the intent to meet any one of the criteria mentioned above will more likely achieve it than the one with no such intention. Similarly, the criteria we choose to compare teaching strategies will be biased in favor of the strategies designed to achieve the criteria. The argument for or against behavioral objectives based on a comparison between instruction with objectives vs. instruction without objectives is essentially meaningless.

There are, however, two important questions concerning behavioral objectives which can be posed and answered:

1. Does revealing objectives to students facilitate achievement of the objectives?

2. Does the degree of explicitness with which objectives are specified by teachers prior to instruction influence the quality of cognitive skills or attitudes achieved by their students?

These are questions to which some people are addressing themselves. The answers should ultimately guide our strategies in using objectives.

CONCLUSION

The history of education is characterized by continuous changes which have been influenced more by social and philosophical fads and fashions than empirical evidence. Behaviorally stated educational goals have also been "in" and "out of style" at various times. Behavioral objectives and the educational philosophy commonly associated with their use are similar to the computer and atomic energy. They have no inherent morality, and can be used for noble or destructive, human or inhuman ends. The use of behavioral objectives can improve the efficiency with which students learn either trivial skills and detrimental attitudes, or capabilities and inclinations which will prove valuable and productive to individuals and society. But since one of the basic purposes of such objectives is to clarify and expose what students learn in school, they appear to offer a unique potential for discovering what human characteristics are most valuable, and to facilitate their acquisition.

NOTES

1. Ralph W. Tyler. Constructing Achievement Tests. Columbus, Ohio: The Ohio State Univ., 1943.

2. Robert F. Mager. Preparing Instructional Objectives. Palo Alto, Calif.: Fearon, 1962.

3. W. James Popham & Eva L. Baker. Systematic Instruction. Englewood Cliffs, N.J.: Prentice-Hall, 1970.

4. Robert L. Ebel. Behavioral Objectives: A Close Look. Phi Delta Kappan, Nov. 1970, 52 (3).

5. Although common behavioral referents for such action terms as describe, identify and solve do not presently exist, the following writer has suggested that such a taxonomy of behavioral verbs be developed: H. M. Harmes. Behavioral Analysis of Learning Objectives. West Palm Beach, Fla.: Harmes & Assoc., 1969.

6. W. James Popham. Probing the Validity of

Arguments Against Behavioral Goals, a paper presented at the American Educational Research Association, 1968 Annual Meeting, Chicago. Printed in Miriam B. Kapfer (Ed.) Behavioral Objectives in Curriculum Development. Englewood Cliffs, N.J.: Educational Technology Publications, 1971.

   7. Instructional Objectives Exchange, Language Arts 7-9, The Center for the Study of Evaluation, UCLA, Los Angeles, Calif.

   8. Alfred D. Garvin. The Applicability of Criterion-Referenced Measurement by Content Area and Level. In W. James Popham (Ed.) Criterion-Referenced Measurement. Englewood Cliffs, N.J.: Educational Technology Publications, 1971.

   9. Benjamin S. Bloom. Mastery Learning for All, a paper presented at the American Educational Research Association, 1968 Annual Meeting, Chicago.

   10. Robert Kibler et al. Behavioral Objectives and Instruction. Boston: Allyn Bacon, 1970.

   11. Norman E. Gronlund. Stating Behavioral Objectives for Classroom Instruction. Toronto: The Macmillan Co., 1970.

   12. James Raths. Another Look at Behavioral Objectives. CAREL Report, University of Maryland, July 1967.

   The authors wish to acknowledge the contribution of the following people to the preparation of this paper: Reed Williams, Isadore Newman, Jack Byrne, Jack Kelly and particularly Judy Lyon.

BEHAVIORAL OBJECTIVES?   YES!

Robert M. Gagné

Few people who are professionally concerned with education in the United States are unaquainted with "behavioral objectives." Knowledge of this term and its meaning has become widespread. It is therefore timely to pose a question which inquires about the need for behavioral objectives, the possible uses they may have, and the educational functions that may be conceived for them.

NATURE OF INSTRUCTIONAL OBJECTIVES

The statement of a behavioral objective is intended to communicate (to a specified recipient or group of recipients) the outcome of some unit of instruction. One assumes that the general purpose of instruction is learning on the part of the student. It is natural enough, therefore, that one should attempt to identify the outcome of learning as something the student is able to do following instruction which he was unable to do before instruction. When one is able to express the effects of instruction in this way, by describing observable performances of the learner, the clarity of objective statements is at a maximum. As a consequence, the reliability of communication of instructional objectives also reaches its highest level.

To some teachers and educational scholars, it appears at least equally natural to try to identify the outcomes of learning in terms of what capability

Reprinted from Educational Leadership.   29:394-96, February, 1972 by permission of author and publisher.

the learner has gained as a result of instruction,
rather than in terms of the performance he is able to
do.   We therefore frequently encounter such terms as
"knowledge," "understanding," "appreciation," and
others of this sort which seem to have the purpose of
identifying learned capabilities or dispositions.
Mager (1962) and a number of other writers have
pointed out the ambiguity of these terms, and the
unreliability of communications in which they are
used.

Actually, I am inclined to argue that a complete
statement of an instructional objective, designed to
serve all of its communicative purposes, needs to
contain an identification of <u>both</u> the type of capability acquired as a result of learning, and also the
specific performance by means of which this capability can be confirmed (cf. Gagné, 1971a).   Examples
can readily be given to show that perfectly good
"behavioral" verbs (such as "types," as in "types a
letter") are also subject to more than one interpretation.   For example, has the individual learned to
"copy" a letter, or to "compose" a letter?   The fact
that no one would disagree that these two activities
are somehow different, even though both are describ-
able by the behavior of "typing," clearly indicates
the need for descriptions of what has been learned
which include more than observable human actions.
Complete instructional objectives need to identify
the capability learned, as well as the performance
which such a capability makes possible.

The implications of this view are not trivial.
If in fact such terms as "knowledge" and "understanding" are ambiguous, then we must either redefine
them, or propose some new terms to describe learned
capabilities which can be more precisely defined.   My
suggestion has been to take the latter course, and I
have proposed that the five major categories representing "what is learned" are motor skills, verbal
information, intellectual skills, cognitive strategies, and attitudes (Gagné, 1971b).   Completing the
example used previously, the statement of the objective would be "Given a set of handwritten notes,
<u>generates</u> (implies the intellectual skill which is to
be learned) a letter <u>by typing</u> (identifies the specific action used)."

The alternatives to such "behavioral" statements
have many defects, as Mager (1962) and other writers

have emphasized. However they may be expanded or
embellished, statements describing the content of
instructional presentations invariably fail to provide the needed communications. The fact that a
textbook, or a film, or a talk by a teacher, presents
"the concept of the family" is an inadequate communication of the intended learning outcome, and cannot
be made more adequate simply by adding more detail.
The critical missing elements in any such descriptions
of instruction are the related ideas of (a) what the
student will have learned from instruction, and
(b) what class of performances he will then be able
to exhibit.

USES OF BEHAVIORAL OBJECTIVES BY SCHOOLS

Statements describing instructional objectives
have the primary purpose of communicating. Assuming
that education has the form of an organized system,
communication of its intended and actual outcomes is
necessary, among and between the designers of instructional materials, the planners of courses and
programs, the teachers, the students, and the parents.
In order for the process of education to serve the
purpose of learning, communications of these various
sorts must take place. When any of them is omitted,
education becomes to a diminished degree a systematic
enterprise having the purpose of accomplishing certain societal goals pertaining to "the educated
adult." There may be those who would argue that
education should not serve such goals. Obviously, I
disagree, but cannot here devote space to my reasons.

Some of the most important ways in which the
various communications about objectives may be used
by schools are indicated by the following brief out-
lines:

1.   The instructional designer to the course
planner. This set of communications enables the person who is planning a course with predetermined goals
to select materials which can accomplish the desired
outcomes. For example, if a course in junior high
science has the goal of "teaching students to think
scientifically," the planner will be seeking a set
of materials which emphasize the learning of intellectual skills and cognitive strategies, having
objectives such as "generates and tests hypotheses

relating plant growth to environmental variables."

In contrast, if the goals of such a course are "to convey a scientific view of the earth's ecology," the curriculum planner will likely seek materials devoted to the learning of organized information, exhibited by such objectives as "describes how the content of carbon dioxide in the air affects the supply of underground water."

2.   The designer or planner to the teacher. Communications of objectives to the teacher enable the latter to choose appropriate ways of delivering instruction, and also ways of assessing its effectiveness. As an example, a teacher of foreign language who adopts the objective, "pronounces French words containing the uvular 'r,'" is able (or should be able) to select a form of instruction providing practice in pronunciation of French words containing "r," and to reject as inappropriate for this objective a lecture on "the use of the uvular 'r' in French words."

Additionally, this communication of an objective makes apparent to the teacher how the outcome of instruction must be assessed. In this case, the choice would need to be the observation of oral pronunciation of French words by the student, and could not be, for instance, a multiple-choice test containing questions such as "which of the following French words has a uvular 'r'?"

3.   The teacher to the student. There are many instructional situations in which the learning outcome expected is quite apparent to the student, because of his experience with similar instruction. For example, if the course is mathematics, and the topic changes from the addition of fractions to the multiplication of fractions, it is highly likely that the naming of the topic will itself be sufficient to imply the objective.

However, there are also many situations in which the objective may not be at all apparent. A topic on "Ohm's Law," for example, may not make apparent by its title whether the student is expected to recognize Ohm's Law, to state it, to substitute values in it, or to apply it to some electric circuits. It is reasonable to suppose that a student who knows what the objective is will be able to approach the task of learning with an advantage over one who does not.

4. The teacher or principal to the parent. It is indeed somewhat surprising that parents have stood still for "grades" for such a long period of time, considering the deplorably small amount of information they convey. If the trend toward "accountability" continues, grades will have to go. Teachers cannot be held accountable for A's, B's, and C's--in fact, grades are inimical to any system of accountability. It seems likely, therefore, that the basis for accountability will be the instructional objective. Since this must express a learning outcome, it must presumably be expressed in behavioral terms. Several different forms of accountability systems appear to be feasible: objectives would seem to be necessary for any or all of them.

These appear to be the major communication functions which schools need to carry out if they are engaged in systematically promoting learning. Each of these instances of communication requires accurate and reliable statements of the outcomes of learning, if it is to be effective. Such outcomes may be described, accurately and reliably, by means of statements which identify (a) the capability to be learned, and (b) the class of performances by means of which the capability is exhibited. There appears to me to be no alternative to the use of "behavioral objectives," defined as in the previous sentence, to perform these essential functions of communication.

REFERENCES

R. M. Gagné. "Defining Objectives for Six Varieties of Learning." Washington, D.C.: American Educational Research Association, 1971a. (Cassette tape.)

R. M. Gagné. "Instruction Based on Research in Learning." Engineering Education 61: 519-23; 1971b.

R. F. Mager. Preparing Instructional Objectives. Belmont, California: Fearon Publishers, Inc., 1962.

BEHAVIORAL OBJECTIVES?   NO!

George F. Kneller

The use of behavioral objectives in instruction
is characteristic of a culture which sets a high
value on efficiency and productivity.   Such a culture
seeks to measure accomplishment in standard units.
Theoretical justification for behavioral objectives
comes from behavioral psychology (Kendler, 1959,
p. 179).   This type of psychology defines learning as
behavior that is changed in conformity with predicted,
measurable outcomes and with little or no measurable
"waste."

Teacher education institutions that advocate the
use of behavioral objectives transmit methods of
instruction that are standardized, empirically tested,
and aim at measurable results.   Such methods work
best in school systems that are highly sensitive to
the economic and behavioral determinants of educational practice.

ANALYSIS

This approach to instruction rests on assumptions about human behavior that are reductionist,
deterministic, and physicalist.   It is opposed to the
view that learning is self-directed, unstructured,
and in large part unpredictable.

Advocates of the behavioral approach deny these
two points (Popham, 1968; Block, 1971).   Behavior,
they say, covers a wide range of experience,

Reprinted from Educational Leadership, 29:397-
400, February, 1972 by permission of author and
publisher.

including creativity, imagination, even serendipity. Nor need objectives be fixed; they can be modified, adjusted to individuals, even abandoned in favor of others (Baker, 1968; Block, 1971, p. 291). But if so, if the terms "behavior" and "objectives" can be made to mean many different things, what things could they not mean? If a term is to have a clear-cut meaning, we must at least be able to define its contradictory.[1]

Many advocates now speak of "instructional" rather than "behavioral" objectives (Mager, 1962). Nevertheless, one's notion of instruction depends on assumptions about the nature of the mind and of the persons involved in the instructional process (Noddings, 1971, p. 40). The new term may imply a more modest approach to instruction and force us to concentrate on matters more central to education. Yet learning still is conceived as a series of measurable responses to carefully prearranged stimuli (Steg, 1971). The sameness of individuals is judged to matter more than their differences; schooling is systems-oriented; adjustment to the curriculum is presupposed; replication is prized; and computer-assisted instruction is cordially welcomed (Broudy, 1970, p. 49; Dreyfus, 1967, pp. 13-33).

It is claimed that, using behavioral objectives, a teacher can teach an entire class and cater to individual differences as well (Block, 1971). He can do so, it is said, either by adapting predetermined objectives to individuals or by composing a special set of objectives for each member of the class. However, this proud claim entails that the teacher must

---

[1]The meaning of "behavior" becomes more complicated still when, in relation to learning, it is stratified according to dispositions. Learning defined as changed behavior then includes changes in dispositions to behave. See: James E. McClellan. "B. F. Skinner's Philosophy of Human Nature." Studies in Philosophy and Education 4: 307-32; 1966; and L. B. Daniels. "Behavior Strata and Learning." Educational Theory 20 (4): 377-86; Fall 1970. A satisfactory theory of human behavior has yet to be proposed.

(a) handle a staggering number of objectives,[2]
(b) accept a scientific theory of human behavior
which tends to exclude individualized (idiosyncratic)
learning, and (c) act on the false assumption that
learning, knowing, and behaving are the same process.

As regards (c), not only are there many kinds of
learning, pacing being only one of them, there are
also many kinds of knowing and behaving. These processes, psychologically speaking, are separate and
distinct. The subject is too complex to be argued
here, but this much may be said: Learning leads to
no particular behavior. It is impossible to coordinate learning or knowing with behaving, because there
is no theory which interrelates these phenomena, and
consequently there is no way of understanding how
their putative instances might be brought into relation in actual practice (Deese, 1969, 516-17). To
use behavioral objectives in individualized instruction is to overlook the essential differences between
individual learning, knowing, and behaving.

Behavioral objectivists are apt to be scornful
of teachers who refuse to adopt clearly specified
goals. This refusal, we are told, is partly responsible for the "present failure" of American education
(Popham, 1968). I do not see how this could be shown
to be the case. I am still less impressed by the
claim that if we adopted behavioral objectives, we
would solve most of our instructional problems.

All dependes on what one considers good teaching
and learning to be. Teachers might be held more
"strictly" accountable, learning might be evaluated

---

[2]Behavioral objectivists maintain that the
number of objectives for a single course could run as
high as two thousand, if the teacher sought to cover
everything. If there were 30 students in a class,
the number of individual objectives would amount to
as many as sixty thousand. The high school teacher
of 150 students would be handling millions of objec-
tives--conceivably. Given the behaviorists' claim
that behavior includes everything that can occur in a
learning situation, these figures are plausible
enough. Block (1971, p. 292) correctly observes that
the computer has a tremendous capacity to tailor-make
programs. Item banks could be constructed and
stored. Yet this of course would require that the
teacher specify goals in appropriate computer terms.

more "reliably," and parents might perceive their children's achievements more "accurately"--but only if teaching and learning are drastically circumscribed. Here is the heart of the matter. Undoubtedly, the process of education can be more tightly controlled, most simply by giving everyone less freedom of choice. This suits the behavioral objectivist, because his philosophy is one of control, but it does not suit educators of other persuasions.

SPECULATION

Under what circumstances may schools be said to "need" behavioral objectives? For one thing, such objectives can be used to define and measure accomplishment in those basic intellectual abilities that all students need if they are to pass successfully from one learning experience to another. Failure by a student to acquire a basic skill may, if uncorrected, hinder all his future learning and so his whole attitude toward education. The young man who desires to be a master mechanic must first acquire the skills of an apprentice, and then of a journeyman. He cannot acquire them unless he can read, write, and compute. A long history of painful, unsuccessful learning experiences can severely damage a student's self-concept, his personality development, and his entire life style (Block, 1971, pp. 297-98).

That many of our youth are damaged in this way, especially in the elementary school, is distressingly obvious. The school has a clear responsibility to ensure that all students succeed in learning basic skills. In order to meet this responsibility, the school must possess a schedule of clearly specified objectives for all students to achieve, together with adequate instruments for measuring what is achieved. Every student must know concretely and specifically what he is accomplishing relative to (a) what may reasonably be expected of him, and (b) what his peers are achieving.

"SPECIFIED" OBJECTIVES

The objectives I suggest are "specified" rather than "behavioral." They are chosen, or specified, by the school according to its own philosophy of education, and they are specified only for certain subject matter which the school considers basic.[3] Certain specific content (or skills) could be required of all students at certain levels, and the students could be tested on how well they had acquired it. It would be the sort of content on which it is fairly easy to test in accordance with minimum standards of achievement.

Yet at another level, a level at which standardization is difficult, impossible, or undesirable, the individual teacher should specify objectives, to be achieved by either the individual student or groups of students, in accordance with (a) a theory of knowledge and value adopted by the teacher himself, and (b) the talents and choices of the student. Take two subjects where rigorous evaluation is quite impossible, art and music. The teacher might perhaps stipulate that a certain number and kind of songs be learned, that at least one song be composed, and that a symphony be analyzed. He might also stipulate that a number of drawings be made, and that one essay be written on a painting and another on an art movement such as dadaism or impressionism. In teaching these and other subjects, the teacher should be guided by a defensible philosophy and psychology of learning and instruction.[4]

---

[3]I agree with Maccia (1962) and Steg (1971) that although some learning goals can be specified, we should give wide play to the discovery impulse in learning. Much knowledge may be set out for the student to acquire. Yet the teacher must also open the gate for students both to acquire knowledge that interests them personally and to inquire beyond the knowledge we now have.

[4]On learning goals and knowledge considerations, see Maccia (1962) and Steg (1971). Maccia shows that knowledge is an open system and Steg warns against using objectives as anything more than a means for focusing purposes: "They must never become the overriding concern of education." Although both writers deal primarily with teaching machines, they are concerned with means by which students can create knowledge (and values, for that matter) instead of simply absorbing it. Learning, says Steg, is "the possibility of going outside a frame of activity" (p. 49). "We must consider logical goodness," says

Ultimately, however, it is not the schools but the teachers who must decide what objectives should be specified, and they must do so as individuals taking their students into consideration. They must therefore acquire the knowledge and skills that are needed to specify educational objectives and evaluate the results obtained. Behavioral objectivists can help by providing models to spur investigation. Yet if these models are adopted uncritically by the rank and file of teachers, education will decline into an inauthentic and spiritless conditioning.

For, properly conceived, education is a dialogue between persons in the community of the school, a dialogue in which the teacher encourages the student to enter into acts of learning that fulfill him per- sonally. This is education at its finest, and the program of the behavioral objectivist has very little place in it.

REFERENCES

Eva Baker, Defining Content for Objectives. Los Angeles: Vincet Associates, 1968.

James H. Block. "Criterion-Referenced Measure- ments: Potential." School Review 79 (2): 289-98; February 1971.

Harry S. Broudy. "Can Research Escape the Dogma of Behavioral Objectives?" School Review 79 (1): 43-56; November 1970.

L. B. Daniels. "Behavior Strata and Learning." Educational Theory 20 (4): 377-85; Fall 1970.

James Deese. "Behavior and Fact." American Psychologist 24 (5): 515-22; May 1969.

H. I. Dreyfus. "Why Computers Must Have Bodies To Be Intelligent." Review of Metaphysics 21 (1): 13-33; September 1967.

Robert L. Ebel. "Behavioral Objectives: A Close Look." Phi Delta Kappan 52 (3): 171-73; November 1970.

Maccia, "in relation to [new] knowing as well as in relation to knowledge" (p. 238).

E. W. Eisner. "Educational Objectives: Help or Hindrance?" School Review 75 (3): 250-66; Autumn 1967.

E. W. Eisner. Instructional and Expressive Objectives: Their Formulation and Use in Curriculum. AERA Monograph Series. Chicago: Rand McNally & Company, 1969.

Howard H. Kendler. "Teaching Machines and Psychological Theory." In: Eugene Gallanter, editor. Automated Teaching. New York: John Wiley & Sons, Inc., 1959.

Elizabeth S. Maccia. "Epistemological Considerations in Relation to the Use of Teaching Machines." Educational Theory 12 (4): 234ff.; October 1962.

Robert F. Mager. Preparing Instructional Objectives. Belmont, California: Fearon Publishers, Inc., 1962.

Nellie L. Noddings. "Beyond Behavioral Objectives: Seeing the Whole Picture." Focus on Learning 1 (1): 35-41; Spring 1971.

David Nyberg. Tough and Tender Learning. Palo Alto, California: National Press Books, 1971. p. 68.

W. James Popham. "Probing the Validity of Arguments Against Behavioral Goals." Symposium presentation, AERA meeting, Chicago, February 1968.

D. R. Steg. "The Limitations of Learning Machines and Some Aspects of Learning." Focus on Learning 1 (1): 43-51; Spring 1971.

PART THREE

DIFFERENTIATED STAFFING

For many years educators have been trying to
discover ways of reducing the teacher-pupil ratio,
but economic considerations have not permitted them
to do so. Lately, interest in differentiated staffing has developed. Under this plan, staff members
are assigned within a hierarchical structure according to their level of specialization. A typical pattern might include the Master Teacher, Associate
Teacher, Assistant Teacher, Apprentice Teacher, and
Teacher Aide. Salary differentials are provided for
at each level in the team. By utilizing staff in
this fashion, it has become possible to reduce the
adult-pupil ratio thus enabling the staff to better
focus upon the individual needs of each child.

Proponents of differentiated staffing believe
that this schema enables teachers to spend more time
with each child. Opponents fear a career ladder because some positions are non-tenured. The articles
in this part center upon differentiated staffing and
offer the reader an opportunity to examine the ramifications of this timely issue.

Two articles, one by Allen and the other by
Bishop and Carlton provide an overview of differentiated staffing. Allen discusses the need to re-
examine the traditional model of teacher utilization
and offers a proposal for differentiated staffing.
He includes the following four categories of personnel: Associate Teacher, Staff Teacher, Senior Teacher, and Professor. Allen also lists the compensation
and responsibilities for each position. The advantages and problems of differentiated staffing are
summarized at the end of the article.

The model offered by Bishop and Carlton,

although similar to that of Allen, incorporates some varying aspects. Their staffing categories include: Intern Teacher, Probationary Teacher, Staff Teacher, Master Teacher, and Teacher Specialist. A supportive staff consisting of instructional or clerical aides and instructional associates is also mentioned.

The next article found in <u>Nation's Schools</u> describes practical applications of differentiated staffing in operation in Florida and Temple City, California. The Florida model includes a hierarchy of eight levels of personnel. These range from Teacher Aide to a Teaching Research Specialist. The Temple City model offers only four classifications ranging from Associate Teacher to Master Teacher.

Lastly, Cooper in answering a series of questions provides a summation of the current status of differentiated staffing. He deals with a definition of the term, locations where pilot projects are in operation, varying models of differentiated staffing, compensation of personnel, and reactions from the AFT and NEA to this concept.

A DIFFERENTIATED TEACHING STAFF

Dwight W. Allen

Central to the study of the organization of educational programs is the consideration of the role of the teacher in a professional staff. The current model of teacher-use is a model that was originated in the nineteenth century, and needs considerable re-examination, as we consider the problems faced by education today.

The present concept of help for the teacher dates back to a nineteenth century Normal School model where the teacher typically had completed a ninth grade education and one year of normal school. There was a valid assumption that the teacher was probably not able to cope with educational problems confronting him--or her, so we had to build help for the teacher, a hierarchy of professional staff who were available to teachers as consultants to backstop their inadequacies.

The training of teachers today is not even re-motely similar to that of a century ago. Teachers have four or five years of college education and are better able to deal with both their teaching subjects and their students. No longer is even the beginning teacher in danger of being run out of the classroom by his or her students. Yet help for the teacher remains the same: supervisors and consultants and curriculum coordinators and administrators.

We need a new concept of help for the teacher: clerks and proctors and technical assistants and teaching assistants and research assistants. The objective is not to eliminate curriculum coordinators

Reprinted from New York State Education, 57: 16-19, December, 1969, by permission of publisher.

and consultants and other kinds of specialized help, but the emphasis should be on the teacher as a professional, with various kinds of technical assistants to help the teacher with his professional responsibilities. Presently we fail to differentiate between instructional responsibilities which need five years of college experience, and the competence needed to run a ditto machine. The teacher today is cranking his own ditto machine and typing his own stencils, and proctoring and acting in the capacity of technical assistant as well as instructional leader. We have an undifferentiated staff, reminiscent of the medical profession at the turn of the century when the family doctor was responsible for the full range of medical services without nurses, laboratory technicians, or other assistants.

The current role of teacher is typified by no differentiation in staff responsibilities. A teacher is a teacher is a teacher. Teachers are interchangeable. Promotions are away from students. If a teacher becomes a department head, he teaches fewer students. If he becomes a counselor or administrator, it is likely that he does not teach students at all. It is a rather strange kind of profession where all promotions are away from the clients that we are attempting to serve.

The only way to get promoted as a teacher is either to grow older on the job, or go back to school and take more courses. These criteria do not emphasize the professional aspects of teaching, or the professional responsibilities of teachers. Consider the example of a fairly large high school where three teachers teach identical classes, say ninth grade English. The first teacher has been recognized as the outstanding teacher of the county so we assign thirty students to each of her classes. The next teacher has been on tenure for years but is mediocre almost to the point of being incompetent, so we assign thirty students to her. The third teacher is a first year teacher, untried, possibly outstanding, possibly incompetent, we just do not know, so we assign thirty students to her. We place students into these classes and pretend to them, to their parents, and to ourselves, that they are all getting something called ninth grade English, which is manifest nonsense. Parents would rather have their children in a large class with an outstanding teacher than in a small class with a marginally competent

teacher. Class size is not the prime issue. No
matter how few students are in a class, if the
teacher is not competent, the instructional situation
cannot be good. We need to find some way to differentiate the responsibility of the outstanding teachers and use other teachers in supporting roles. The
outstanding teacher should be responsible for the
education of more students.

This is not a merit pay proposal. Under merit
pay, teachers have the same responsibility but get
different compensation. A board of experts monitors
teaching competence and differentiates merit categories with special status and compensation. This
does not help the students who are not in these
favored classrooms. We need instead a differentiated
teaching staff where not only do teachers have different compensation, but also have differentiated
responsibilities.

For purposes of examining the idea we can identify four categories of teachers, four differential
teaching staff responsibilities (see Figure 1).
Based on a mean salary of $7,800, not atypical in
California school districts today, a proposed salary
range of $5,000-18,000 would be compatible with pres-
ent staff expenditures. Additional funds would not
necessarily be needed to differentiate staff in accordance with the present example.

The first category would be Associate Teacher,
with a range in compensation of $5,000-7,000, per-
haps in ten steps (the detail is not important).
This teacher would typically have at least an A.B.
degree. The staff category should not be tied specifically to preparation or course units, although we
can think of median levels of preparation associated
with the differential staff ranks.

The second level would be Staff Teacher, with a
salary range of $7,000-9,000. Advancement might be
more accelerated within this staff category perhaps
five annual increments. Typical preparation would be
a fifth year of college.

The third category would be Senior Teacher, with
a salary of $9,000-12,000, with probably an M.A.
degree.

The highest level might be designated a

A DIFFERENTIATED TEACHING STAFF

Compensation and Responsibility

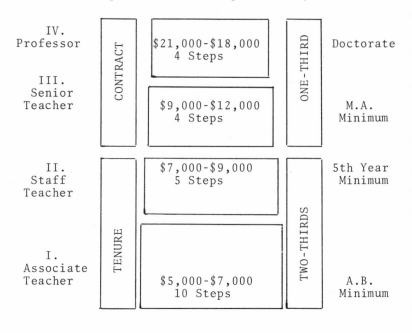

Professor. The title is not so important, but there should be a way to identify instructional responsibilities in the elementary and secondary schools that have commensurate professional responsibility and recognition with instructional positions in higher education. Compensation for the fourth staff category would range from $12,000-18,000 and similar to category three, would have perhaps four steps. This staff level would typically be associated with the doctorate and would enable a person who was interested in classroom teaching to have a full professional career in the classroom.

In the Secondary Teacher Education program at Stanford University approximately 140 candidates are trained each year. These students would compete favorably in any group of professionals. It is a very select group. One of our interns, four years ago at the end of his internship year, was noted the outstanding teacher at the high school in which he was interning, a fine school on the San Francisco Peninsula. The quality of the entire staff is consistently very high, but this intern was voted by the senior class as the outstanding teacher of the year at this high school. Where is this man four years later? He is completing his doctorate in Political Science and is a finalist in one of the outstanding post-doctoral fellowship programs nationally. He is an outstanding person. Could we recommend, in good conscience, that this person stay in the high school classroom? In the high school classroom, he would have to wait ten or twelve years before he could rise to the top level of teaching compensation and recognition, with little opportunity to exercise either his initiative or his enthusiasm in the process.

One of the inequities of teacher salary scales at present is the fact that if one examines the range of teacher competence and the range of teacher compensation, there is probably more concentrated competence in the middle range of the salary schedule than at the top ranges of the salary schedule. Teachers who have outstanding ability and initiative eventually promote themselves away from the classroom and monolithic salary schedules into counseling, administrative and higher education positions. Those who have less initiative and drive, although there are notable exceptions, remain in the high school and the elementary classrooms and eventually rise to the top of the salary schedule. There is no way under present staffing policies, to recognize unusual talent, or to extend its influence to benefit more students.

Consider the first and second staff levels as tenured positions and the third and fourth levels as contract positions. This would not require any modification in tenure laws; a person could be hired as an Associate Teacher and reach tenure as an Associate Teacher. He could be hired as an Associate Teacher or Staff Teacher, and receive tenure as a Staff Teacher. Teachers teaching in contract positions, at levels three and four, could still be tenured at level two, in much the same way that administrators now are not tenured as administrators, although they may hold tenure as teachers in the district in which they are serving as administrators. Typically levels three and four on the staff would be on twelve-month

contracts, rather than nine-month contracts, moving
in a desirable direction of professionalism. This
proposal initially provides for two-thirds of the
staff at levels one and two, and about one-third of
the staff at levels three and four.

A district would have to think through specific
differentiated staff responsibilities and promote
teachers to fulfill a particular responsibility.
When teachers are promoted by longevity, districts
have no control over the proportion of staff dollars
in relation to staff positions. Some districts in
California anticipate that their median salary level
will raise by some $500 over the next five years, on
the present salary schedule, simply because of longevity and tenure of staff.

Advantages of a Differentiated Staff

What are the advantages of a differentiated
teaching staff? Automatic promotion regardless of
competence is eliminated, a real key to improving
professionalism in education. There may be five
people in a particular school that have the capability to operate at the highest level with only one
position available, in the same way that there may be
five people that could competently serve as administrators with only one position open. However, once a
person is promoted, he undertakes a responsibility
which is different than the responsibility he had
previously discharged. We may not be able to promote
and recognize all of the talent that resides in the
teaching staff, but at least there is the potential
for the use of talent in differential service.
Secondly, if we develop a differential staff we will
identify specific responsibilities at each level.
The serious identification and development of these
responsibilities will take considerable time and
effort. A first approximation might be to think of
the Associate Teacher as the Doer who carries out
curriculum developed by more senior members of the
staff. The Staff Teacher may be the Illustrator who
works with the curriculum as it has been developed in
general, but illuminates it with different illustrations and enriches it in many ways. The Senior
Teacher will probably have some say in the shaping of
the concepts of the curriculum, and the person who is
operating at the top staff level should have a primary

role in anticipating directions of curriculum development. This person could be looking ahead ten and twenty years, rather than placing the educational enterprise in the position of having to respond to developments in the total society after the fact. We need to organize schools and staff to anticipate the changes that will be needed in the educational enterprise.

A third advantage is that the higher salary levels would be reserved for persons performing at levels commensurate with the salary level. This would encourage younger, talented staff members. There is a way to recognize talent early and reserve it for the high school or elementary classroom rather than lose it either to other professions or to other leadership positions in education.

A differentiated staff can make effective use of persons who do not wish to accept full professional responsibility. Under the present system, once a teacher is employed, his compensation and responsibility proceed independently of his professional interest or competence. There are a large number of teachers, primarily housewives, who do not wish to accept full professional responsibility and would be delighted to accept a more modest responsibility and compensation. There are many talented people who are unwilling to accept employment in the schools at all, at present, because employment implies this undifferentiated responsibility. We have to think much more imaginatively about the use of the total personnel resources available to the schools, full or part time, and at all levels of competence and responsibility.

The elimination of labor-management connotations in staff negotiations is another important consideration. We are in a decade of decision in terms of how teachers are going to negotiate for professional status. There is a real danger that we will sharpen the dichotomy between the teacher-professional and the administrator-professional, which is most undesirable in the development of more effective education. It is not appropriate to adopt a model in education that is relevant to other circumstances, but not to the development of a profession. By making it possible for classroom teachers to be compensated better and have more substantive responsibility than some administrators, we will recognize the fact that teaching performance and teaching competence is the heart of the education enterprise.

A differentiated staff will facilitate innovation. If a staff is prepared to undertake differentiated responsibilities, then we will not continue to find ourselves in a position where innovation is painful, traumatic, and difficult. We have to realize that we live in a world of change. We must learn to respond so that we do not have to make a disproportionate effort to institute minor changes.

There is a substantial organizational benefit from a differentiated staff. At present, organizational alternatives are severely limited by constant staffing formulas and monolithic requirements of staff use. The educational organization can become much more flexible--more alternatives can be considered. By identifying staff responsibilities more precisely, we can train staff to accept specific responsibilities. No longer will be tied to the limitations of retraining the entire staff whenever change is desired.

Finally, there are advantages in the identification and use of differential staff talents. Unsuccessful teachers might be used effectively if they did not have to perform the full range of teaching competencies. Some teachers who are excellent in terms of their creative ability have the fatal flaw of lack of classroom control. If we could differentiate staff responsibilities, to minimize the necessity for such teachers to exercise class control, they could be constructive members of a teaching staff.

Problems of a Differentiated Staff

A discussion of a differentiated teaching staff would not be complete without identifying problems associated with its implementation. First of all, it is difficult to identify differentiated staff responsibilities. We have not thought about the use of staff in such a manner and it would be a major undertaking to differentiate teaching staff responsibilities. Secondly, it would be difficult to establish working relationships among a differentiated staff. Thirdly, a differentiated staff implies

modification of the total school program. This may
mean that we have to consider different ways of
instructing pupils other than thirty at a time with a
single teacher, daily, for an hour. The notion of a
differentiated teaching staff goes hand in hand with
other organizational and program modifications, some
of which become possible and others of which become
necessary if a differential staff is to be developed.
Fourth, there is a lack of precedence of educational
decisions in systems in employing differential staff,
and we would have to examine the way in which decisions would appropriately be made. Fifth, we need to
develop new concepts of staff training. Teacher education programs would have to be modified substantially, recognizing which of the tasks of teacher
education would be pre-service and what portion of
teacher education would be in-service training. Some
formal training elements might be mid-career elements.
A sixth problem is the rejection of differential
teaching ranks by current staff threatened by performance criteria. There are now teachers who are
enjoying the benefits of an undifferentiated staff
without commensurate responsibilities, who are likely
to complain. A "grandfather clause" would take some
of the pressure off the present incumbents. And
finally, there is the need for over-compensation in
lower staff ranks during transition periods. We now
have teachers on salaries of $10,000-12,000 who would
be assigned at the lowest level of differentiated
staff. There will have to be provisions for the
extra finances necessary initially, to implement a
program of differential staffing.

As we look forward to the next decades, unless
we face the notion of a differentiated professionalism in the teaching staff, we will limit the quality
of American education. Approximately three out of
every ten college graduates presently go into teaching. It is likely that we can attract some more top
candidates and it is likely that we can eliminate
some at the lowest level. But, by and large, we will
have a 'body politic' teaching staff much on the
order of competence that we now have. We must use
them more effectively.

STAFF DIFFERENTIATION: A MODEL FOR
DEVELOPING PROFESSIONAL BEHAVIOR

Lloyd K. Bishop and Patrick W. Carlton

Most educators would recognize the need for, and
encourage, greater professional development among
teaching staffs in the nation's public schools.
Several public school programs have manifested this
concern in creating an organizational climate which
provides for greater staff professional recognition,
individual teacher autonomy, and organizational devices which allow the instructional staff a significant role in the decision making process of the
school. Although considerable progress in this regard has been made in a few isolated schools, public
school teachers generally continue to be relegated to
roles little different from those held by most sub-
ordinate bureaucratic employees. To date designs for
educational systems have provided only limited opportunity for the expression of staff individuality,
professional development, or teacher-initiated decision making activities.

CONVENTIONAL DIMENSIONS OF
TEACHER PROFESSIONALISM

Attempts to focus upon and to solve staff development problems have, in general, employed one of two
methods: 1) reduction of classload, or 2) increased
teacher salaries. While it is not intended to depre-
cate the importance of these activities in providing
a necessary occupational image for teachers, both

Reprinted from <u>High School Journal</u>, 54:   422-31,
April, 1971 by permission of publisher.

avenues have failed to establish a significant basis for professional advancement. No opposition to increased salaries for teachers is intended, for it is recognized that in some areas salary schedules are deplorable. However, salary increases per se are not a valid professionalizing influence.

We have created many educational myths concerning the importance of group size and class load to the instructional process. Although we may vary group size considerably within the conventional self-contained classroom, this technique alone has little significant impact upon instructional improvement or teacher professional development. The authors seriously disagree with those professional organizations which have perpetrated the conception that there is something magical about a teaching ratio of 25 students per class with no more than four classes assigned to each teacher. In terms of recognizable changes in professional behavior or instructional improvement, there is little evidence to date that this formula has had an appreciable effect upon the individualization of instruction in those school systems that have faithfully employed it. Issues concerning time and its relationship to instruction, individual student learning rates, and interaction processes within groups are not given appropriate consideration with the adoption of such an overly simplistic solution to otherwise complex educational relationships.

We now require an instructional system which recognizes the interrelationship between the size of the group and the specific instructional task or activity to be conducted. The system must also be flexible in order to accommodate the individuality of student and teacher, and the day-to-day professional judgments of the instructional staff. Some experimentation has been conducted in a few elementary and secondary schools. The deployment of students between large-group and small-group activities with the implementation of more flexible school schedules has provided an initial thrust in this important direction of wedding instructional task with group size and composition. Many teachers are finding that some learning activities can take place in relatively large groups (150 or more students) while other experiences need to be conducted in smaller groups where interaction between teacher and student, and more particularly between the student and his peer group is more informal.

It is concluded, then, that the conventional self-contained classroom, regardless of the number of students assigned, is definitely an educational anachronism. Moreover, it is detrimental to the professional development and needed interaction of teachers. Perhaps the greatest disadvantage is found in the utilization and development of professional strengths. Inasmuch as the conventional classroom forces the teacher into isolation, the teacher is deprived, to a great extent, of discourse with his colleagues out of which can arise common purposes, instructional improvement, and curricular innovation.

NEW DIMENSIONS OF TEACHER PROFESSIONALISM

What we require now are new directions in designing ways of approaching the issues of developing teacher professional status. The prototypes provided by the classical professions--theology, law, and medicine--although used on occasion, are not generally appropriate for providing theoretical or operational frameworks for education. Certainly, the unionism movement espoused by many large metropolitan teaching organizations has not yet encouraged the development of significant professional status among these teaching groups.

While it is not the intent of this paper to offer a completed design for teacher professional development, two criteria or elements of this design held to be extremely significant by some educators will be discussed. These include the dimensions of time control and differentiation of teacher responsibility. It is proposed that these criteria are central in any viable model which attempts to develop professional status in the coming years for public education. They are also prime requisites for any attempt to establish open and stimulating climates within a school program which wishes to allow for more interaction, open, healthy dialogue, and creative, professional expression.

TIME AS A FACTOR FOR DEVELOPING
PROFESSIONAL CLIMATE

In our enthusiasm to reduce class loads for
teachers, we have completely neglected considering
other equally significant alternatives. If we desire
to develop a climate for professional staff activities, and if we desire to provide opportunities for
greater individual teacher expression, autonomy of
action, and for a central role in structional decision making, no other facet of the teacher's school
activities is more critical than time. Few teachers
in conventional school situations, who are attempting
to develop exceptional instructional programs, have
sufficient time for these activities. Also, within
the limitations of most traditional school structures,
few teachers have the opportunity to control time in
respect to instruction, student groups, or the specific learning task. One of the critical elements of
most recognized professional bodies is the ability of
the professional to schedule or manage time in relation to his responsibilities and professional judgments. The best we have provided teachers in secondary education is the non-productive, preparation-
counseling period. Elementary teachers receive
little, if any, unscheduled time during school hours.

For any occupational group attempting to develop
recognizable professional status, control of time is
a critical dimension. One cannot expect teachers to
display professional behavior in public schools when
the complete organizational structure of these institutions is antithetical to the basic requirements of
a professional climate. The teacher, as a professional, requires more unscheduled time during the
school day for management and control than is normally provided. Teachers cannot assume professional
roles within the confines of most school programs as
presently constituted. The teacher, during the conventional school day, has little opportunity to re-
structure activities within groups, or to be a
manager of the instructional process in determining
the interrelationship between learning and specific
time requirements.

It is proposed that teachers be provided with
far more unscheduled, out-of-class time during the
school day, or school week, than is normally provided.
We would propose, at least as a point of departure,

that a 50/50 ratio be established between the teacher's scheduled, in-class time and his unscheduled out-of-class time. Fifty percent of the teachers' school week would be scheduled into regular assigned classroom activities; the other fifty percent would be unstructured, and the use of this time would be used at the professional discretion and control of the individual teacher. Because of the restrictions of traditional school scheduling practices, serious limitations are imposed by this proposition. However, with the development and implementation of various techniques for scheduling schools flexibly, this proposed time ratio for professional staffs does become feasible. A number of schools in the implementation stage of a modular or flexible schedule have taken advantage of this aspect of programming by providing a more significant professional climate for teachers through control of school time.

DIFFERENTIATION AS A FACTOR FOR DEVELOPING PROFESSIONAL CLIMATE

The present role of the teacher is characterized by non-differentiated responsibilities, assignments, or status positions. A teacher is a "teacher"; he is an interchangeable part. Paradoxically, education is one of the few social enterprises that rewards excellent performance by promoting the individual away from the client he is trained to serve. The only way to get promoted as a teacher is through longevity on the job, or a return to graduate school for more courses. No allowance has been made for rewarding the excellent, competent instructor short of promotion to some administrative position. Unfortunately, these promotion methods do not emphasize the professional aspects of teaching, or the professional responsibilities that should be attributed to teaching as a career. Methods must be found to differentiate roles, status, and responsibilities of outstanding teachers from those of less competent teachers.

Furthermore, the development of the conventional, monolithic salary schedule as found in most school systems has not provided the financial framework necessary for professional teaching and career development. This salary schedule assumes that all teachers are equally competent, and that all teaching activities and responsibilities are of similar importance

and magnitude. Such salary structures do not allow
for the differences in the psychological, physical,
and intellectual attributes present in any group of
teachers. Some teachers possess more potential, have
greater intellectual power, and are willing and capable of accepting more responsibility than others.
Concomitantly, it is assumed they should have a more
substantial impact upon the instructional decision
making process of the school.

It should be clarified that the present proposal
for differentiated teaching responsibilities and assignments is not a form of merit pay. Under most
merit pay systems teachers have the same responsibilities but receive different compensation. The
more experienced or meritorious teacher is deployed
in exactly the same way as the less experienced or
less competent teacher. Unfortunately, the merit pay
system allows those teachers to have little impact on
the decision making process of the school. Under the
concept of differentiated staffing as a career model,
teachers receive additional compensation for the assumption of additional responsibilities or differentiated duties which demand advanced levels of experience, training, skills, or professional competence.

For heuristic purposes in developing a differentiated professional salary structure, one can identify
several different categories or levels of teachers, or
differentiated teaching positions, with increasing
responsibilities as one moves upward through the
teaching hierarchy. In addition, it is possible to
develop a "career ladder" of paraprofessional or
auxiliary support roles leading upward into the
teaching ranks. Such a progression, composed of 7-9
levels, provides an excellent opportunity for satisfying instructional careers totally-related to the
classroom. Such a system, by recruiting early and
holding talented persons throughout their working
careers, can help to staunch the classroom "brain
drain" with which education is presently afflicted.

There are, of course, numerous ways in which
differentiated staffing structures can be established.
One type appears in Figure One. An explanation of
the staffing categories follows:

    1. Intern Teacher--This position is designed to
provide for smooth transition from student to

Figure 1

Differentiated Staffing Model
(Career Salary Schedule)

	10% of Teaching Staff	65% of Teaching Staff		20% of Teaching Staff	5% of Teaching Staff
	INTERN TEACHER	PROBATIONARY TEACHER	STAFF TEACHER	MASTER TEACHER	TEACHER SPECIALIST
Training Level	Non-Credentialed	Non-Tenure / Certified BA	Tenured / BA Degree	Special Contract / MA Degree	Special Contract / Doctorate or Equiv.
& Experience Teaching	No experience	1-2 yrs. exp.	3 yrs. exp.	3 yrs. exp.	5 yrs. exp.
Responsibility	Part or Full Time	100%	100%	60%-75%	50%-60%
Contract Per'd	10 mo. Full Time	10 months	10 months	10-11 months	12 months
Compensation	$7,500	$8,500-$9,950	$10,000-$15,500	$15,000-$17,500	$17,000-$25,000

Professional Service

1/3-1/2 ratio to teaching staff

para-professional support service

INSTRUCTIONAL ASSOCIATE $6,000-$7,500 (2 years college)

INSTRUCTIONAL ASSISTANT $5,500-$6,500 (high school diploma)

INSTRUCTIONAL AIDE $5,000-$6,000 (less than high school diploma)

professional status. It is the entering professional
category requiring only the A.B. degree and no previous teaching experience. The intern serves in an
apprentice relationship, receiving substantial inservice training from the teacher specialist and working
closely with the master teacher to whom he is assigned for on-the-job training and general supervision. The intern teacher's duties require a minimum
of teaching responsibility and average competence in
his subject field or teaching area. Teaching duties
are part-time in nature, and generally involve service on a teaching team. Other duties involve the
selection of instructional materials, development of
lesson plans, and attendance at professional meetings.

2. Probationary Teacher--These teachers have
completed a year of intern service or have served one
or two years in another school system. They are cre-
dentialed, non-tenured professionals who perform
full-time classroom teaching service. Probationers
receive some inservice training and are assigned to a
teaching team headed by a master teacher and composed
of one or more intern and staff teachers. Probationary teachers are responsible for the development of
instructional materials and lesson plans, and are
involved in evaluation of instruction. They are also
in regular attendance at professional conferences and
other activities of a professional nature.

3. Staff Teacher--The third level of differentiated responsibility is that of staff teacher (tenure). Typical preparation may include a fifth year
of college, but may not necessarily include the M.A.
degree. Teachers normally would be automatically
eligible for this level after having completed their
nontenure service. Some duties assigned to this
category include: (1) general classroom teaching or
team teaching; (2) specialized teaching duties;
(3) serving on curriculum committees; and (4) participating in curriculum research or study projects.

4. Master Teacher--The fourth category is
designated master teacher. The M.A. degree is required. The master teacher is one who has demonstrated his qualifications to assume responsibility
and leadership in teaching. This teacher is assigned
such duties as: (1) assisting in the training of

probationary or intern teachers; (2) assuming leadership positions on curriculum committees; (3) assisting in research projects; (4) serving as a team teaching leader; (5) serving in leadership positions in school faculty organizations; (6) evaluating other categories of teachers.

5. Teacher Specialist--The highest level is designated teacher specialist. While the title is unimportant, the philosophy underlying the creation of status positions with appropriate rewards which allow the teacher to remain in the classroom is important. This staff level may require the doctorate or comparable post master's degree work, and enables a person who is interested in teaching to have a full professional career in the classroom. The teacher specialist is a teacher who, through the quality of his experience, training, and demonstrated ability, is capable of assuming responsibility for teaching and curriculum development on a professional level beyond that expected to the regular classroom teacher. Typical duties include: (1) demonstration and consultation in areas of his particular competence; (2) research in areas of his specialized knowledge; (3) planning for programs that require system-wide coordination; (4) performance in experimental teaching situations; (5) inservice training programs for intern and probationary teachers; (6) evaluation of other categories of teachers; and (7) service on the special decision making committees of the school or school system.

Teachers serving in a differentiated situation are afforded an opportunity to engage in instructional decision making, a function too often denied them in the past. The vehicle for such service may be in the form of an instructional committee on which the principal, teacher specialists and master teachers serve, along with representatives of other ranks. In this way the professional expertise of teachers can be brought to bear upon educational problems in a positive manner. The democratic structure involved serves to assure that decisions will be based on the best possible professional judgment and not upon whimsy.

Supporting the professional staff is a three-level paraprofessional ladder composed of three categories. The ladder is designed to provide less

highly trained personnel an opportunity to enter
instructional work prior to the completion of a four
year college degree program. Such an "early-entry"
progression can serve to direct many potentially effective instructional personnel who might otherwise
drift into other occupations and be permanently lost
to public education.

The system combines service to the schools with
on-the-job and inservice training, plus advanced academic studies. Thus, an individual entering the
ranks of instructional aides receives on-the-job
training from the professionals with whom he works,
participates in a school district inservice program
conducted by district teacher specialists and instructional associates and attends adult education
courses leading to the completion of a high school
diploma. Upon completion of the diploma and inservice programs, plus a minimum period of satisfactory
on-the-job performance, he is eligible to apply for
advancement to the position of instructional assistant. The period for completion of these requirements is normally no more than two years.

Advancement from instructional assistant to
instructional associate is predicated upon the completion of an additional period of inservice training, a
period of satisfactory classroom service, and the
completion of two years of college work leading to
the bachelors degree. The time necessary for such
work normally does not exceed three years.

Following completion of the B.A. degree and a
third period of inservice training and satisfactory
service, the associate is eligible to apply for a
position as intern teacher. He may, of course,
choose to remain at any paraprofessional level but is
not encouraged to do so generally. During the intern
year, the individual completes certification requirements and rounds out his pedagogical and academic
training. From this point on individual progress
through the career ladder depends increasingly upon
personal aspiration and talent.

A description of duties for the paraprofessional
progression follows:

Instructional or Clerical Aide--The instructional or clerical aide provides services which

enable the teacher to give more time and energy to
the primary task of instruction by undertaking routine supervisory, clerical, and materials handling
tasks.   These tasks include: (1) record keeping;
(2) preparation of instructional materials; (3) monitoring of students; (4) scoring of simple, objective
tests; (5) duplication of materials for the teacher;
and (6) collection of funds; all under teacher
supervision.

Instructional Assistant--This individual carries
out many of the same duties performed by the aide but,
because of his greater experience and training, can
handle increasing instruction-related responsibilities under teacher supervision.   He may, for instance:
(1) work with small groups of students in an instructional situation; (2) assist in classroom management
and supervision of library and lunchroom periods, as
well as assisting on playgrounds and with bus duty;
(3) maintain all teacher-student records; (4) proctor
and monitor testing periods; (5) prepare more sophisticated instructional materials such as transparen-
cies, overlays, and slide presentations; and (6) take
charge for brief periods in the teacher's absence.

Instructional Associate--An associate is an
experienced assistant who acts in a role more directly supportive of the instructional program than those
filling the previously described positions.   That is,
he: (1) engages in direct instructional activities
on a regular basis with minimal supervision; (2) develops instructional materials and basic lesson
plans; (3) counsels students in disciplinary and personal matters; (4) assumes substantial responsibility
for class discipline; (5) supervises aides and assistants on grounds, bus, and cafeteria duty; (6) participates as an instructor in inservice programs for
aides and assistants; and (7) may serve on the instructional committee of the school, thus participating in the decision making processes.

The foregoing discussion has focused upon two
criterial influences in the drive for teacher professionalism: (1) control of time; and (2) differentiation of job responsibilities.   Each of these factors
has played an important role in the professional
lives of medical, dental, and legal personnel for a
substantial period of time.   While it would be

indefensible to contend that the institutionalization of these criteria on a broad scale would usher in the professional millenium in education, it is fair to assume that such action could only serve to move educators a step closer to that long coveted and highly elusive goal.

DIFFERENTIATED STAFFING

For educational trend watchers, the blue-ribbon candidate of the 70s has arrived. Its name is Differentiated Staffing and it is being carefully fed, watched and nurtured in an almost clinical environment.

What is differentiated staffing? There is no precise definition, but it implies a restructuring and redeployment of teaching personnel in a way that makes optimum use of their talents, interests and commitments, and affords them greater autonomy in determining their own professional development. A fully differentiated staff includes classroom teachers at various responsibility levels and pay--assigned on the basis of training, competence, educational goals, and difficulty of task--subject specialists, special service personnel, administrative and/or curriculum development personnel (who may also teach a percentage of the time), and a greater number of subprofessionals and nonprofessionals, such as teaching interns and teacher aides.

Differentiated staffing theorists assume three crucial benefits: (1) teachers will have opportunities to pull themselves up a career ladder; (2) good teachers can remain in the classroom instead of being "kicked upstairs" into administration when a promotion is in order; (3) all students will benefit from the new organization because there will be more individualization of instruction.

Hard-line opponents see it as a grandiose subterfuge for implementing merit pay, encouraging faculty separation and divisiveness.

_____
Reprinted from Nation's Schools, 85:43-49, June, 1970 by permission of publisher.

The answer to the merit pay objection, according to proponents, is that, under differentiated staffing, teachers are paid differently for different responsibilities, as opposed to traditional merit pay setups, where people are paid differently because they are judged to be performing similar tasks at different quality levels.

Where it started: One of the earliest differentiated staffing models was developed by Dr. Dwight Allen, dean of the University of Massachusetts' School of Education. It was presented to the California Board of Education in 1966, and first introduced in Temple City, California.

The Temple City program represents a stairstep, or hierarchical, model. Starting at the top and going down are master teachers, senior teachers, staff teachers, associate teachers, and three types of paraprofessionals--teacher aides, resource center assistants, and lab assistants. Responsibilities and salaries for these positions are varied, though the staff teacher and associate teacher are tenured.

Here is how the four basic positions at Temple City break down:

Associate Teacher--typically, a beginning teacher who spends most of his time in the classroom while simultaneously evaluating his performance in conferences with a supervisor.

Staff Teacher--has more experience and is assigned more difficult responsibilities, including tutorial sessions and small group instruction. Additionally he works on new curriculums and supervises their field testing.

Senior Teacher--in addition to teaching, consults with associate teachers, develops new teaching strategies, sets up inservice training programs, and develops resource banks for new instructional units, including the use of media.

Master Teacher--has district-wide responsibilities in the application of research to curriculum design. Teaches at least a part of the time.

Two other early models are noteworthy. One, a

TEMPLE CITY MODEL

A four-level teacher hierarchy is the basis for the differentiated staffing model being used at Temple City, California. The associate teacher, a novice, has a "learning schedule" and less demanding responsibilities; the staff teacher has a full teaching load and is aided by para-professionals; the senior teacher is a "learning engineer," or methodological expert in a subject; the master teacher is a scholar-research specialist who translates research theory into classroom possibilities.

Level	Tenure	Teaching Responsibilities	Salary Range
Master Teacher — Doctorate or Equivalent	NON-TENURE	2/5's Staff Teaching Responsibilities	$15,500-25,000
Senior Teacher — M.S. or Equivalent	NON-TENURE	3/5's Staff Teaching Responsibilities	$14,500-17,500
Staff Teacher — B.A. Degree and Calif. Credential	TENURE	100% Teaching Responsibilities	$7,500-11,000
Associate Teacher — A.B. or intern	TENURE	100% Teaching	$6,500-9,000

ACADEMIC ASSISTANTS AA DEGREE OR EQUIVALENT

EDUCATIONAL TECHNICIANS

CLERKS

hierarchical arrangement developed by Lloyd J. Trump, provided for teaching specialists, staff specialists, a number of general aides, and community consultants where needed. The other, the Head Start model (which evolved from the federal program of the same name), was a "flatter" model that had only two basic levels --a "lead" teacher without real authority and assistant teachers who composed the bulk of the team. The "lead" teacher received extra remuneration.

A major impetus for differentiated staffing appeared with passage of the Education Professions Development Act of 1967, which set aside federal funds for such experimentation.

One of the first districts to apply for EPDA money was Beaverton, Oregon, now completing its first year of differentiated staffing at a 975-student high school. For next year, the district has applied for funds to implement the program at the high school, a junior high, and an elementary school. One new position developed in the Beaverton program is the "domain chairman," who supervises development of interdisciplinary curriculum and provides leadership in teaching processes.

The Florida project: Unquestionably, the most extensive proposal for differentiated staffing is found in Florida, where, in 1968, the state legislature provided a mandate requesting the state department of education to "develop and operate model projects of flexible staff organization in selected elementary and secondary schools, based on differentiated levels of responsibility and compensation for services performed." As a result, a comprehensive feasibility study was completed, along with a plan that included role clarifications and cost analyses. Pilot projects are now set to begin this fall in three Counties--Dade (which includes Miami), Leon and Sarasota.

The Florida model has more levels than the one at Temple City. Starting from the top, there are: a teaching research specialist (equivalent to the principal), teaching curriculum specialists, senior teachers, staff teachers, associate teachers, assistant teachers, education technicians, and teacher aides. Each position has a different salary range and certain educational requirements.

FLORIDA MODEL

This is the differentiated staffing model and salary schedule developed in Florida. The first break into research responsibility comes at the senior teacher level, though the senior teacher will still spend four-fifths of his time in the classroom. Personnel at the two highest level positions will teach about three-fifths of the time. Within the salary schedules, each position from associate teacher on up has a range of $1,500, divided into three yearly increments of $500 each. The lower positions have a range of $1,000, for division into four yearly increments of $250 each.

Position	Tenure Status	SALARY RANGE
Teaching Research Specialist Doctorate degree	NON-TENURE	$17,500–19,000
Teaching Curriculum Specialist Master's degree	NON-TENURE	$15,000–16,500
Senior Teacher MS, MA, or M.Ed.	NON-TENURE	$12,500–14,000
Staff Teacher BA, BS or B.Ed.	TENURE	$10,000–11,500
Associate Teacher BA, BS, or B.Ed.	TENURE	$7,500–9,000
Assistant Teacher Associate degree (2 years)	NON-TENURE	$5,500–6,500
Educational Technician	NON-TENURE	$4,500–5,500
Teach. Aide	NON-TENURE	$3,500–4,500

Though many local districts have certain aspects of differentiated staffing (team teaching, flexible scheduling, etc.) already built into their programs, it is reported that a substantial number are now considering full-blown programs. And the states of Wisconsin and Massachusetts appear to be boosting the concept through changes in state certification regulations.

Teacher reaction: How do teachers feel about such proposals? The Association of Classroom Teachers, which has endorsed research on differentiated staffing, conducted a conference of representative teachers from all parts of the country to compile opinions. Conference participants cited these advantages:

The concept appears to provide a more meaningful educational experience and climate favorable to the development of each child.

It fosters good teaching technics, such as flexible assignments, modular scheduling, matching of instructional resources with learner needs, individualized learning experiences, and a clinical approach to meet student needs.

It provides for more effective use of human resources.

The opportunity is there for interaction among teachers, administrators, teacher aides, parents, and the community.

On the other hand, they also foresaw some obstacles:

A tendency on the part of some persons to move too quickly. The roles of administrators must change at the same pace as the roles of the classroom teachers.

Insufficient funds for an adequate program.

Personnel not prepared to operate within the new framework.

The tendency to bill differentiated staffing as a cure-all for educational ills.

A fear that assignments will be used as a means to cut school budgets by paying higher salaries to a few teachers who reach top· brackets and lower salaries to the vast majority.

Inadequate public relations and biased information programs.

It was admitted, however, that all these "obstacles" can be overcome by judicious planning.

One essential element cited, ironically, as an advantage by proponents and a disadvantage by critics is that teachers are generally evaluated for higher positions by committees composed of their own colleagues. This is fairer, say those in favor. It encourages conflict among the faculty, say those opposed. The proof of the pudding, whatever it is, has to be in the eating.

Additional points advocated for differentiated staffing are that it allows retention of good teachers while offering incentive for advancement; it offers the prospect of salaries equal to or greater than administrators at the higher stratification levels; it reduces the administrator-teacher gap considerably; it adds prestige to teaching; and it involves teachers more heavily in decision-making and planning.

Some have likened differentiated staffing in schools to the application of systems management technics used in industry. Others point out that it is only a natural evolvement in improving the quality of education. But its first champion, Dr. Allen, sees a simple goal: to compensate professional teachers at the same levels as other professional persons in a community. He says: "That goal is possible with differentiated staffing."

SOME QUESTIONS AND ANSWERS

James M. Cooper

Differential Staffing:

In the last three years, there have appeared
almost 100 articles, books, position papers, and
other writings examining the topic of differentiated
staffing for the public schools. Some of these
papers extol the virtues of differentiated staffing
while others are sharply critical of the concept.
Still others agree that it has merit, but at the same
time, see difficulties with its implementation. In a
paper as brief as this, it is impossible to give a
comprehensive treatment of the topic. An annotated
bibliography is therefore included, which will direct
the reader to a variety of positions on the topic. I
will attempt only to highlight some of the more pressing issues and questions that should concern anyone
interested in differentiated staffing.

What exactly is "differentiated staffing"?

Like "team teaching," most people believe they
know what the term means, but each person has a different conception, based on his own experiences.
While there are many possible variations, the term
"differentiated staffing" implies subdividing the
global role of the teacher into different professional and paraprofessional subroles according to
specific functions and duties that need to be performed in the schools and according to particular
talents and strengths that are evident within the
human resources of any given school community. Some

differentiated staffing models also include the creation of a hierarchy, with job responsibilities that are commensurate with the range of pay.

What's new about this? Haven't schools been differentiating for years?

Yes and no.   Yes, schools have been differentiating for years, ever since distinctions were made between the principal and the teacher and between social studies teachers and English teachers. However, the concept of differentiated staffing includes other factors that go beyond such distinctions.

What are some of these other ideas?

They include the notion of a career ladder for teachers, a vertical differentiation as well as a horizontal one along subject matter lines, increased decision-making responsibilities for teachers, pay scales for teachers that go upward of $20,000, and a wider variety of career patterns.

What problems do differentiated staffing and these other related ideas purport to solve?

Historically, promotion of teachers lead them away from the classroom, usually into administration. There is very little career incentive for the bright young teacher who traditionally must accumulate a number of years' experience and y credits in order to reach the top of the single salary schedule. Lacking the necessary patience, many talented teachers are forced out of teaching into other occupations or into administration. Creating a career ladder, with increased salaries commensurate with increased responsibilities, would serve to attract and keep talented teachers. By recognizing individual differences in teachers, as well as in students, differentiated staffing attempts to better utilize the talents and energies of the staff by allowing them to do the things that they do well, while not forcing them to perform functions ill-suited to their talents. Thus, by creating more and different kinds of teacher roles, such as evaluation specialist, curriculum developer, and diagnostician of learning difficulties, differentiated staffing tries to match functions to be performed with teacher interest, skills, and abilities more than do traditional staffing patterns. By recognizing the professional competence of teachers,

differentiated staffing incorporates more teacher
responsibility in decision making regarding curriculum and instruction. In several of the models, many
decision-making responsibilities that were previously
the domain of the administrator are now taken by
teachers.

What implications does differentiated staffing
have for curriculum, instruction, school structure,
and scheduling?

Staff differentiation in its full meaning recognizes the necessity for concurrent changes in scheduling, curriculum, decision-making power, and individualization of instruction. Merely adding or
subtracting personnel and calling it "staff differentiation" is tokenism. Without concurrent changes in
scheduling, curriculum, and instruction, staff differentiation is nothing new. In order to best use
differentiated staffs, the schedule should be flexible enough to allow teachers to meet with students
for varying lengths of time for varying instructional
purposes. Also, as teacher talent is released, new
curriculum offerings can be made to take advantage of
teacher interest and ability.

Is differentiated staffing just an idea, or has
it been tried out with all of its ramifications?

There are a number of school districts currently
implementing differentiated staffing plans of different types, including districts in California, Florida,
Arizona, and Missouri. The oldest and perhaps most
well-known differentiated staffing plan in operation
is the Temple City, California, plan. Its teaching
staff is divided into four professional levels: associate teacher, staff teacher, senior teacher, and
master teacher. A schema of their staffing hierarchy is represented in Figure 1. The specific functions to be performed at each of these levels are
carefully defined, and teachers are selected to perform these functions on the basis of their competencies. The associate teacher is conceived of as a
novice to the profession, and his teaching responsibilities are less demanding than those of the staff
teacher. The staff teacher carries a full teaching
load but is relieved of most nonprofessional tasks
such as yard duty, grading papers, hall supervision,
and so forth. The staff teacher is an experienced,
probably tenured, teacher. The senior teacher, the

| Tenure | Tenure | Nontenure | Nontenure |
ASSOCIATE TEACHER B.A. or Intern	STAFF TEACHER B.A. and Calif. Credential	SENIOR TEACHER M.A. or equivalent	MASTER TEACHER Doctorate or equivalent
100% teaching responsibilities	100% teaching responsibilities	60% staff teaching responsibilities	40% staff teaching responsibilities
10 months $6,500-$9,000	10 months $7,500-$11,000	10-11 months $14,500-$17,500	12 months $15,646-$25,000

INSTRUCTIONAL AIDE II $6,000-$7,500
INSTRUCTIONAL AIDE I $4,000-$7,500
CLERKS $5,000-$7,500

Fig. 1.   Temple City Differentiated Staffing Plan, 1969-71.

first level above the staff teacher, is an expert in
a subject, discipline, or skill area. The master
teacher is a scholar research specialist, someone
with the technical expertise to apply relevant research to classroom practice. All teachers function
as classroom teachers, though not for the entire day.

Some people have charged that differentiated
staffing is merit pay in disguise. Is there a difference between the two, and if so, what is it?

The basic distinction between differentiated
staffing and merit pay is that merit pay attempts to
distinguish who the good teachers are, usually based
on someone's judgment, and to pay them more for doing
a better job. In this instance, both the teacher who
receives merit pay and the teacher who does not perform essentially the same duties and have the same
responsibilities, but the merit pay teacher is deemed
to perform those duties in a better fashion. The
merit pay case usually leaves untouched any change in
instructional responsibilities and does not alter the
decision-making structure of the organization. Although teachers on a differentiated staff receive
different salaries, their functions and levels of
responsibility are also different. They are not paid
differently for performing the same duties but for
performing very different functions.

What are the reactions of the NEA and the AFT to
the concepts involved in differentiated staffing?

The main issue for both organizations concerns
the concept of a teacher hierarchy, illustrated by
the Temple City model, with its associate, staff,
senior, and master teacher levels. This type of vertical hierarchy is seen by the AFT and some organizations of the NEA as a wedge that will separate the
solidarity of teacher groups. As Robert Bhaerman,
Director of Research for the AFT, has said, ". . . for
the time being, we are left with a choice: to pay
teachers according to the role they fulfill (who can
judge priorities here?) or to pay teachers according
to their academic and experience background. . . .
Teaching is not competitive; it is a cooperative and
communal effort and so it should remain. Nothing
must be injected to create divisiveness."[1] Although
he accepts the notion of teacher differentiation
according to functions to be performed, Bhaerman does
not believe that these functions can be ordered in

terms of importance and a hierarchy of teacher roles created based on these functions. In March 1971 the Executive Council of the AFT supported Bhaerman's position and passed a resolution "opposing any vertical staffing patterns which reduce the total number of fully certificated staff responsible for the education of pupils, which results in an arbitrary reduction of financing for education, and which is a movement away from the concept of the single salary schedule. . . ."[2]

The NEA, composed of many different instructional divisions, does not present a unified position on the issue of differentiated staffing. The National Commission on Teacher Education and Professional Standards (NCTEPS) has enthusiastically endorsed the concept, and a number of position papers on the topic have been published through NCTEPS. The Association of Classroom Teachers, on the other hand, in its position paper echoed the AFT's concern about the establishment of a teaching hierarchy, asking ". . . can differentiated staffing be accomplished only by establishing a new hierarchy within the school system? Might there not be horizontal movement for the teacher rather than vertical movement or a plan of rotating assignments that could be equally effective?[3]

Although national officials of the two teacher organizations have publicly expressed their opposition to the notion of a teaching hierarchy, there appear to be pockets of support for the idea among teachers at the local levels. In Temple City, for example, the differentiated staffing plan was the result of administrators and teachers developing a plan that was agreeable to both groups. The teachers in Temple City have supported the plan enthusiastically. Because opposition to the vertical hierarchy has become widespread, models have been developed that differentiate only on the horizontal (subject and skill areas) dimension and do not attempt to differentiate teachers with respect to responsibilities and pay scales.

Why should some teachers receive more pay for performing different functions when it is impossible to say with certainty that some teacher functions are more important than others? Why can't teachers perform different functions but be equally compensated?

As a matter of fact, some staffing plans do differentiate according to functions but do not reward differently. Advocates of differentiated staffing argue, however, that those roles that require greater training or skill should receive greater compensation. Since the skillful in other occupations are rewarded more because of their talents and because of their increased responsibility, the teaching profession should be no different. Rather than forcing the talented and ambitious out of teaching because the opportunities for career advancement are practically nil, differentiated staffing advocates argue that opportunities for advancement and increased pay should be made available for the talented.

Another way of viewing the issue is that people who possess certain skills are in less supply than people who possess certain other skills. Since both kinds of skills are necessary for the operation of an instructional program, the people whose skills are in less supply--for example, an evaluation expert--command greater compensation than do those people whose skills are not so unique. When viewed in this manner, higher pay is given according to the law of supply and demand, rather than because certain skills are considered intrinsically more worthwhile and more valuable. Viewed either way, differentiated staffing plans seek to reward teachers for increased responsibility and for particular kinds of competencies.

Is differentiated staffing related to the accountablility movement in education and to the ideas of competency-based teacher education and competency-based certification?

Differentiated staffing embodies some of the same concepts as the accountability movement and competency-based teacher education. Before a differentiated staffing model can be constructed, an analysis of the teaching functions to be performed must be made. These functions can then be allotted to specific roles. After functions necessary for the achievement of instructional objectives have been identified, further analysis identifies units of performance, which are called tasks. Tasks are elements of a function that, when performed by instructional personnel in logical sequence, will fulfill the related function. Task analysis provides the teaching performance criteria that must be met in order that the function from which they are derived may be achieved successfully. Thus, in a differentiated staffing model, the stating of tasks in specific job descriptions for employment purposes will provide the formal identification of the teaching performance criteria that will establish a valid base for teacher performance evaluation. For each teacher role identified, there will be specific performance criteria that the teacher occupying that role must meet. In this respect, the teacher will be accountable for achieving the performance criteria associated with his job.

In the Temple City model, for example, teaching colleagues designed the job to be performed by the senior teacher, who was then held accountable to the teachers who received his services for effectively performing his job. Tenure is not granted to persons who occupy senior teacher positions; if they do not perform, they are not reemployed as senior teachers. Fenwick English, former Project Director at Temple City, describes the situation: "By tying the Senior Teacher's role directly to the recipients of the effects of that role and by systematically building into the system procedures whereby roles and role incumbents may be changed, debureaucratization occurs and the dominant one-way communication mode, and with it the traditional superior-subordinate concept, is radically altered . . . services become teacher-centered and teacher-designed."

Does differentiated staffing work on both the elementary and secondary school levels?

There was initial resistance to the Temple City model at the elementary school level. While the vertical differentiation was in terms of a hierarchy, or a teaching ladder, the horizontal differentiation at the secondary level was along subject matter lines-- senior teachers in mathematics, science, social studies, and so forth. In essence, this meant that almost no elementary school teacher would be chosen as a senior teacher, because the secondary teachers generally had more expertise in subject matter areas. The problem was solved by creating positions for senior teachers in instruction and in technology who would serve all elementary school teachers on a K-6 basis. When this was done, John Rand, Superintendent of Temple City Schools, reported that the primary grade teachers soon found ways in which a senior teacher could be valuable to them. Thus, the

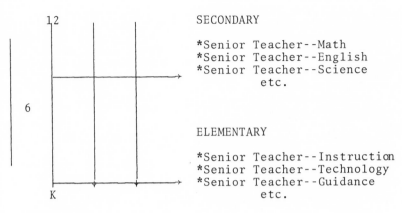

Responsibilities of Elementary School Senior Teachers

1. Pupil Diagnosis
   A. Pupil placement
   B. Pupil behavior analysis
      1) Preventive
      2) Remedial
   C. Parent conferencing

2. Instructional Analysis
   A. Program diagnosis/testing
   B. Prescription for learning: individual pupils/
      groups (to include mode of instruction/appro-
      priate software)
   C. Analysis and utilization of staff

3. Curriculum Development
   A. Coordination of curriculum development with
      master teachers
   B. Development of some curriculum in primary
      areas

4. Classroom Teaching
   A. Regular classroom teaching at least 40% of
      the time

Fig. 2. Refinement of Elementary/Secondary Differentiated Staffing Model.

elementary level is differentiating on the horizontal
axis along areas other than subject matter. The
Temple City school system is currently considering

another senior teacher position in human relations.
Figure 2 gives a schema that illustrates how the
senior teacher would operate for both elementary and
secondary schools, as well as a description of the
broad responsibilities of the elementary senior
teacher.

How can more information about differentiated staffing be obtained?

Readers are referred to the following bibliography and to a more comprehensive one--including
films, videotapes, and other media presentations on
differentiated staffing--which can be obtained from
Mr. Jerry Melton, School Personnel Utilization Resource Center, 908 W. Main, Mesa, Arizona 85201.

FOOTNOTES

1.   American Federation of Teachers. Several
Educators' Cure for the Common Cold, Among Other
Things. Quest Paper No. 7. Washington, D.C.: De-
partment of Research, the Federation, n.d. p. 6.

2.   American Federation of Teachers. "American
Federation of Teachers' Statement on Vertical Staff-
ing." Memo from the Federation to the Bureau of
Educational Personnel Development. U.S. Office of
Education. Washington, D.C.: the Federation, March
1971. (Mimeographed)

3.   National Association of Classroom Teachers.
Classroom Teachers Speak on Differentiated Teaching
Assignments. Report of the Classroom Teachers Na-
tional Study Conference on Differentiated Teaching
Assignments for Classroom Teachers. Washington, D.C.:
the Association, National Education Association, 1969.

A BASIC DIFFERENTIATED STAFFING LIBRARY

Allen, Dwight A. A Differentiated Staff: Putting Teacher Talent To Work. Occasional Papers No. 1.
Washington, D.C.: National Education Association,
National Commission on Teacher Education and Professional Standards hereafter NEA, NCTEPS), 1967.
7 pp. (Out of print)

Views teachers as interchangeable parts and current staffing patterns as inefficient. Proposes a four-level model and lists advantages of this kind of differentiated staff.

Barbee, Don. Differentiated Staffing: Expectations and Pitfalls. Write-In Papers on Flexible Staffing Patterns No. 1. Washington, D.C.: NEA, NCTEPS, March 1969. 7 pp.
Highlights various dangers of differentiated staffing--economy as a goal, using assistants as teachers, creating status and personality conflicts, overspecializing and increased bureaucracy.

Bhaerman, Robert D. A Study Outline on Differentiated Staffing. Quest Report No. 2. Washington, D.C.: Department of Research. American Federation of Teachers, n.d. 22 pp.
Weighs advantages and disadvantages of differentiated staffing. Gives AFT position on differentiated staffing and merit pay. Comments on current differentiated staffing literature. Comprehensive bibliography.

Cooper, James M., editor. Differentiated Staffing. Philadelphia: W. B. Saunders Publishing Co., 1972.
A book of readings on differentiated staffing with chapters giving case studies and exploring differentiated staffing's implications for administration, paraprofessionals, teacher education, and in-service education.

Davies, Don. "Education Professions Development: Investment in the Future." American Education 5:9-10; February 1969.
Former Associate Commissioner of Education, Bureau of Educational Personnel Development, describes the Education Professions Development Act and its objectives to individualize instruction and "open up" the teaching profession.

Edelfelt, Roy A. Redesigning the Education Profession. Washington, D.C.: NEA, NCTEPS, January 1969. 17 pp.
Executive Secretary of NCTEPS analyzes the teacher's role, teaching as a career, teacher supply and demand, the promise of a new differentiated staff organization and the governance of the education profession.

English, Fenwick W. "A Handbook of the Temple City Differentiated Staffing Project, 1965-1970." Temple City, Calif.: Temple City School District, June 1970. (Mimeographed)
    An up-to-date revision of the Temple City project, procedures, and policies. Excellent source of information.

English, Fenwick W. "Teacher May I? Take Three Giant Steps! The Differentiated Staff." Phi Delta Kappan 51: 211-14; December 1969.
    Warns that changing roles are not necessarily synonymous with changing attitudes about learning and analyzes some of the real dangers of differentiated staffing without adequate preparation.

Frinks, Marshall L. A Readiness for Differentiated Staffing: Questions Relevant to Development and Training Activities. Information Report No. 2. Tallahassee: Florida Department of Education, October 1969. 8 pp.
    Presents questions any educator must ask before contemplating a change in staffing pattern.

Hedges, William D. "Differentiated Teaching Responsibilities in the Elementary School." National Elementary Principal 47: 48-54; September 1967.
    Constructs a model for a differentiated elementary school staff. Also a position paper by the Department of Elementary School Principals, NEA.

Joyce, Bruce R. Man, Media, and Machines. Washington, D.C.: NEA, NCTEPS, 1967. 26 pp.
    Pictures a direct instruction team and its support centers. Predicts the school of tomorrow and how students and teachers will function in it--a program designed to complement the nature of learning.

McKenna, Bernard. School Staffing Patterns and Pupil Interpersonal Behavior: Implications for Teacher Education. Washington, D.C.: NEA, NCTEPS, 1967. 23 pp.
    Builds a staff organization on the basis of human relations and learning tasks. Differentiates teaching roles accordingly.

NEA, NCTEPS. A Position Statement on the Concept of Differentiated Staffing. Washington, D.C.: the Commission, May 11, 1969. 8 pp.
    NCTEPS endorses differentiated staffing as

worthy of trial. Developmental steps are suggested.
Definitions consistent with NEA goals are stated.

NEA, NCTEPS. Remaking the World of the Career
Teacher. Report of the 1965-1966 Regional NEA-TEPS
Conferences. Washington, D.C.: the Commission,
1966. 228 pp.
    Composite of speeches and papers focusing on the
title subject. An attempt to define excellence in
teaching and to redefine the teaching role.

NEA, NCTEPS. The Teacher and His Staff: Differentiated Teaching Roles. Report of the 1968
Regional NEA-TEPS Conferences. Washington, D.C.:
the Commission, 1969. 143 pp.
    Ten papers deal with the need for teacher spe-
cialization, relevant curriculum, principalship, team
teaching, teacher education, planned-change strategy,
and critiques of current education assumptions.

Rand, John M., and English, Fenwick W. "Towards
a Differentiated Teaching Staff." Phi Delta Kappan
49:264-68; January 1968.
    Fundamental and global rationale for differen-
tiated staffing. Role description; resistance to
change.

Ross, Marlene. Preparing School Personnel for
Differentiated Staffing Patterns: A Guide to Selected Documents in the ERIC Collection, 1966-1968.
Washington, D.C.: Educational Resources Information
Center, 1969. 74 pp.
    An ERIC publication listing 114 documents on
differentiated staffing. Teacher-administrator relationships, media, roles, team teaching, curriculum
organization, and innovation are included.

Ryan, Kevin A. A Plan for a New Type of Professional Training for a New Type of Teaching Staff.
Occasional Papers No 2. Washington, D.C.: NEA,
NCTEPS, 1968. 12 pp.
    Education courses and student teaching are
viewed skeptically. Sequence performance criteria
and simulated teaching experiences are suggested
training for candidates for a differentiated staff.

Stiles, Lindley I. "Certification and Preparation of Education Personnel in Massachusetts." Phi
Delta Kappan 50: 477-80; April 1969.
    Summary of an advisory report on certification

for Massachusetts; advocates distinctive performance levels and teacher self-regulation.

PART FOUR

EDUCATION VOUCHERS

Perhaps one of the most controversial, recent innovations in education is the education voucher. A voucher is a credit memo given to parents in the amount of their child's education which they can use to enroll their child in any school participating in the program. Such a plan enables parents to choose which school they feel offers the best education for their child.

Advocates of the voucher system hold that it enables parents of low income families to enroll their children in schools which offer high quality educational programs. Those opposing this plan fear that an imbalance in enrollments may result from the voucher system and that the traditional separation of public and private schools may be altered.

Heller describes how an education voucher system could be implemented in the schools. A voucher would be issued at a predetermined monetary value by either the public school district or an Educational Voucher Agency (EVA). The parent could then choose which school his child would attend. To ensure equal opportunity to low income parents, certain safeguards would have to be built into the system. Participating schools would need to agree that all vouchers would have the same value. Where there would be more applicants than places, a lottery system could be utilized. Furthermore, the EVA would pay all transportation costs.

The author also enumerates several areas of concern with the voucher system. Included are: (1) educators' concern for tenure; (2) what provisions should be made for parents who do not choose to participate in a voucher system; (3) how to help parents

to make intelligent choices for their children;
(4) the increasing cost of transportation for the
EVA; (5) the complexity of administrative details;
and (6) the method of school accreditation.

Glennan, who is director of the Office of Research and Evaluation for the Office of Economic
Opportunity, is involved with experiments that are
being conducted relative to the voucher system. He
cites the benefits of vouchers and gives specific
guidelines under which such a system would function.
Glennan then describes a proposal for a voucher experiment which covers three school systems for a period of five years.

The next two articles, one by Janssen and the
other by Clayton, give the reader reactions of educational groups and note areas of concern regarding the
voucher system. Janssen cites the positions of the
NACCP and the NEA who are opposed to the concept of
educational vouchers. Notwithstanding these objections, however, he feels that an experiment with an
educational voucher system would be a worthwhile
endeavor. Clayton tries to answer some fundamental
questions that need to be resolved concerning vouchers. Among them are: the way in which the EVA would
be funded; how controls would be exerted over local
EVA's; whether all parents would be able to make intelligent choices for their children; and, what would
be the policy of subsidizing private as well as public education.

PROBLEMS AND ISSUES

Robert W. Heller

An interesting phenomenon is now occuring in
American education. The introduction of the concept
of the Education Voucher, or Voucher Plan, has generated as much support and enthusiasm as it has
criticism without the plan's ever having become
operational. This plan is a proposed system for
financing schools through payment, directly to parents, of vouchers which are redeemable at schools of
their choice. The concept of the educational voucher
is not new. As perceived today, however, the educational voucher is quite complex, in that it concerns
itself with many of the crucial social, political,
and economic issues facing society.

Basically, the plan necessitates the issuance of
a voucher, at a predetermined monetary value, to
parents with school-age children. The voucher would
be issued by either the public school district or
other agency of government. Extra funds would also
be available for compensatory vouchers for disadvantaged or poor children. Parents could purchase
educational services at any participating voucher
school of their choice.

The philosophy behind this approach is that only
those schools offering a high quality of education
will attract clients and receive the necessary financial support to remain open. Proponents of the plan
perceive it as a mechanism providing for greater
parental choice and encouraging competition within
the educational system. Thus, the voucher plan is
seen as having the effect of making schools directly
accountable to their clients, since parents could

Reprinted from Educational Leadership. 29:424-
29, February, 1972 by permission of author and publisher.

take individual action for or against a school
through the use of their voucher.

Several forms of the voucher plan have been
developed in recent years.[1]   The model receiving
greatest attention was recommended in the study,
Education Vouchers,[2] which was prepared by Harvard
professor Christopher Jencks and his associates at
the Center for the Study of Public Policy. This
study was supported by funds from the Office of
Economic Opportunity.

All models of the voucher plan presently being
advanced closely resemble one another in their basic
design. Each provides a process for allocating funds
through a governmental agency, to be spent at the
discretion of parents for the education of their
children. The participating voucher schools in the
various plans call for an expenditure level comparable with per pupil costs within the existing school
districts where the plan would become operational.
Each plan also has its own approach for addressing
such questions and issues as desirable level of pupil
racial balance, church school eligibility, promotion
of unorthodox social or political views, level of
parental involvement in the decision-making process,
and relationship to already existing educational
agencies.

WHY THE EDUCATION VOUCHER?

The quality of American public schools is presently being seriously questioned. Educators frequently suffer serious embarrassment when pressed for
clearly stated written goals and objectives of American education. Far too few educational objectives
have been translated into behavioral terms with

----

[1]For a detailed description of the currently
advocated forms of education vouchers, see: Ray A.
Carr and Gerald C. Hayward. "Education by Chit: An
Examination of Voucher Proposals." Education and
Urban Society 2: 179-91; February 1970.

[2]Center for the Study of Public Policy. Educational Vouchers: A Preliminary Report on Financing
Education by Payment to Parents. Cambridge, Massachusetts: the Center, March 1970.

criteria for measurement which produce data to answer queries relative to the quality of the educational system's end product, the student.

Increasing numbers of people perceive schools as being unresponsive to minorities, the poor, and the disadvantaged. Schools also are not viewed as adjusting to the rapid social and cultural changes taking place in our society. Some argue that while some schools are performing better than ever, few educational systems have served the disadvantaged in a fashion which allows them to compete on an equal basis with the majority of Americans.

The concerns viewed here, coupled with recognition of the need for all children to receive a high quality of education, have led some people to look toward alternative forms of schooling. One such alternative, hailed as having potential for providing a high quality of schooling, is the educational school voucher.

OEO DEMONSTRATION PROJECT

The OEO, if February 1971, granted funds to the Gary, Indiana, public school district, and later to Seattle, Washington, and Alum Rock, California, for feasibility studies of the voucher plan. All three school districts sought the assistance of external agencies for conducting the preplanning studies.

OEO was interested in having several feasibility studies under way in municipalities which have heterogeneous populations of approximately 12,000 to 15,000 elementary students in public and private schools. The preplanning took about eight weeks and is being followed by a longer period of planning prior to the actual operation of a five- to eight-year experiment. Costs are estimated at 6 to 8 million dollars in each of the communities selected to participate in the demonstration project.

In the demonstration project, the vouchers will be administered by an Educational Voucher Authority (EVA). Several proposals as to membership on the EVA and its relationship to the existing board of education have been suggested and are still being discussed. The EVA will be responsible for establishing

the necessary policy and administering the voucher
demonstration project. The EVA will also operate an
extensive parent and teacher education program and
will provide parents and students with counseling
services. Proponents of the voucher plan are hopeful
that the resultant educational system will provide
educational freedom and flexibility of benefit to
both children and teachers and that it will revital-
ize the role of the family as an important agent in
the process of education. Of particular concern to
advocates of the voucher plan is whether it will provide a means of equalizing educational opportunity
for the disadvantaged.

Specifically, the education voucher is seen as
leading to improvement in the quality of education,
such as:

1. It would give individuals greater freedom to
move about within the public education system because
they would not be required to accept the standardized
program offered in the assigned public school. A
choice of schools would not necessarily be the privi-
lege of the wealthy.

2. It would give parents a more significant
role in shaping their child's education, and this
should renew the importance of the family's role in
education, which could improve the attitudes of both
parent and child. Also, it would allow teachers to
enter into a more direct relationship with parents
and children.

3. It would facilitate educational experimentation and diversification. A range of choices in
schools should become available. Small new schools
of all types would come into operation--Montessori,
Summerhill, open classroom, and traditional style
schools, among others.

4. It would give teachers and principals
greater freedom to vary their teaching methods. They
could arrange their curriculum to appeal to a particular group, or to reflect a particular school of
thought on educational methods. Schools could emphasize music, arts, science, or basic skills. Parents
not pleased with the emphasis of one school could
choose another. Thus, public school administrators
and teachers would be freed from the necessity of
trying to please everyone in an attendance area, a

practice that often really pleases no one.

    5. Special resources for the disadvantaged could be more accurately channeled directly to that group, since they would follow the child holding the voucher.[3]

    The OEO's voucher plan includes guidelines requiring the participating school districts to establish safeguards which would prevent discrimination against pupils or teachers by reason of race or economic position. Thought is still being given to the development of appropriate criteria and processes for handling student applications to avoid possible discrimination. Some form of lottery will likely be used for the selection of at least half a school's student body with the remaining half selected on the basis of criteria established by a particular school. Without regulation, some schools might attempt to exclude racial minorities.

    It is also possible that if no controls were set, some schools might require parents to add money to a voucher. This could result in economic segregation in the schools. Controls are also needed to prevent schools from making false or misleading claims as to their worth, particularly since the voucher plan is a system designed to function in the competitive market.

    The three school districts participating in the preplanning stage have now completed the feasibility studies and are moving slowly into the next phase of the study. How quickly the three districts will move now toward the field testing of the voucher plan is questionable. Some believe that the initial enthusiasm in evidence during the preplanning stages may have cooled off. It has recently been reported that the Gary school district has withdrawn from the OEO demonstration project.

    OEO's intention had been to have at least one demonstration project under way by the fall of 1971; but once the feasibility studes were under way, it was realized that this date was quite unrealistic. Any hopes for the operation of a demonstration project have had to be postponed for at least a year.

----

[3]The Feasibility of Implementing a "Voucher Plan" in Seattle. Seattle: University of Washington, May 1971. Appendix A-2, pp. 2-3.

POLITICAL CONCERNS

The education voucher is viewed as a vehicle for increasing the educational alternatives available to students, through greater involvement of parents in the decision-making process. Before any voucher plan becomes a reality in any state, enabling legislation must be passed to overcome many of the existing regulations related to the allocation of funds, curriculum standards of schools, certification of teachers, and allocation of power. This will not be an easy process, nor will it be a speedy one. While efforts have been made to introduce enabling legislation, no state legislature at present is on the verge of passing such legislation. The Center for the Study of Public Policy at Cambridge has been studying this issue for some time and has made available, to the school districts participating in the OEO's feasibility studies, legal assistance for drawing up draft legislation and for development of initial efforts to lobby support for the plan. All of this activity, however, is still in the early stages of development.

Of crucial concern is the question of the role of the local board of education and its relationship to the EVA. The EVA must be recognized as a legitimate authority, which means it needs to have "grassroots" support. If the EVA becomes too concerned with regulations, it will be immersed in a bureaucratic tangle and be subject to charges of conforming to existing educational systems. Without regulations and safeguards, however, the voucher plan could lead to a system of greater segregation and exclusiveness, with a smaller relative share of the available educational resources going to the poor.

In the course of implementing the Seattle feasibility study, in which this author was associated, we identified six political concerns which, while not perceived as insurmountable, certainly will necessitate careful study. They included:

1. One of the initial resistance forces to the education voucher nationally has been the professional education associations. Without the support of the professional educators, the voucher plan is in serious jeopardy. Concerns of educators include the issue of tenure, the quality of education that students will receive in voucher schools, and teacher's

involvement in the decision-making process. Teachers
perceive themselves as the professionals who rightly
have a role in the decision-making process.   Serious
questions are being raised as to what the teacher's
decision-making base would be in a voucher plan.
Voucher proponents stress greater involvement in
decisions by parent and community, not by the professional educator. Professional educators are a strong
lobbyist group and cannot be discounted.

2. A second major resistance force comes from
those opposed to the public support of parochial education. This resistance will appear if the voucher
plan includes parochial schools as one of the alternatives available to students. At present, parochial
schools are the single largest group of alternative
schools in existence. If the decision is made to
include parochial schools in a voucher plan, then all
of the traditional arguments regarding the use of
public monies to support religious education will be
used. The church-state issue involves a constitu-
tional or legal consideration which will have to be
settled in the courts prior to implementation of a
voucher plan.

3. Strong resistance forces will appear from
that segment of the population which feels that the
voucher plan is yet another attempt by those in our
society who wish to divide us further. This group
will advance the argument that our public schools
have been successful in the past and that any plan to
provide alternatives for education stressing diverse
goals will lead to further splitting of society. It
can be expected that this group will undoubtedly become more vocal as the alternatives for education
become more diverse.

4. With the implementation of a voucher plan,
there would have to be a decentralization of the
present educational system. This movement to decen-
tralize would be consistent with the trend in many
large cities, but the degree of decentralization
needed would be much greater than what is perceived
at the present time. Predicting the value and outcomes of greater parent involvement in decision making in the existing structure of control in public
education is largely a matter of speculation.

5. While the voucher plan need not work at
cross-purposes with racial integration, it does pose

questions as to its effect upon any school board's
present plans for integrating schools. Student
applications to voucher schools would have to be
carefully reviewed to ensure that a cross section of
the population was applying to all schools and that
no schools were predominately black or white or
excluding either group. It is also possible that if
application patterns indicated that integration was
not being achieved, then a quota system would have
to be included. Paramount is the issue of devising a
plan of action which ensures that the voucher demonstration plan can operate in conjunction with other
efforts being made to implement racial integration.
If such a plan cannot be developed, there would be no
real justification for continuing the planning of the
voucher model as a viable educational alternative.

6. In implementing a voucher plan, all participating schools would be open to all applicants, with
a selection process that suggests a random selection
or lottery process for determining admissions. This
process does not give any priority to parents living
in that attendance area. This raises a serious question for parents to consider. Do parents have
greater control in the decision-making process when
they cannot have their children placed in the school
of their choice? This situation can, and most likely
will, occur under the voucher plan. There may be
some animosity from parents who support the neighborhood school concept and find the voucher plan removes
their power of school selection. Supporters of the
voucher plan operate on the assumption that many parents will select schools because of geographical
location and that some parents will choose alternatives outside of the public schools--which means that
the probability is high that children will be admitted
to their neighborhood public school. It does not,
however, assure this choice.

It is hoped that the voucher plan would result
in imporvement in the educational program; however,
this is not an inherent outcome of an open market.
Competition and greater parental control can provide
some incentive for schools to imporve their programs.
This will require that those responsible for voucher
schools have a commitment to positive change and a
high quality of educational program. Conceivably, a
voucher system could foster the delusion in parents
that their child was receiving a better education
simply because he was attending a different school.

The OEO is now in the process of evaluating proposals from external agencies for performance of the
evaluation system of the voucher demonstration project. Those bidding had to submit proposals based
upon rigorous criteria established by OEO, which
include the gathering of a great deal of relevant
demographic data in addition to data relative to the
specific project and program involved. OEO is interested in obtaining an educational and political history of the project. An account of the political
climate and resultant pressures for and against the
voucher demonstration project needs to be analyzed.
Close examination of the effectiveness of the admissions process must be maintained to provide for suggested changes in the governing policies. Data will
also be needed as to the effects, if any, compensatory vouchers and the means of their distribution
have, particularly in light of conflicting reports on
past compensatory education programs.

The evaluation data must also provide a record
of the political consequences that the voucher demonstration brings about, both within the educational
system (teacher attitudes, parental involvement,
establishment of new schools, student progress, etc.)
and in the community (possible changes in voting
behavior, political pressure groups, population
shifts, etc.). Evaluation of the specific objectives
of the voucher plan must be continuous in order to
provide the necessary feedback for monitoring the
project and for taking appropriate corrective measures.

FURTHER EXPLORATION NEEDED

While the education voucher concept has gained
support in some quarters, several questions have not
yet been adequately answered. The very success of
any voucher plan may well rest upon these issues:

1. Greater parental involvement is a crucial
variable with the voucher model. For discussion purposes, let us say the parents' first choice, School A,
is not available due to not being selected via the
lottery system. The child then moves to the list for
second choice, school B. The question now becomes,
"Where does this child's name enter the list for this
school?" Many parents may have selected school B as
their first choice. This process could continue

until the child is far removed from the parents'
first, second, third, etc., choice schools, and may
enter the list of a school which the parent did not
want at all. There also will be the parents who do
not care to participate in the voucher plan, yet
whose child is enrolled in a school selected as one
of the voucher demonstration schools. By reason of a
random selection, this child is transferred from that
school to some other building despite the objections
of the parents. Is this considered greater parental
involvement? Policy still must be developed for
transferring and possible expelling of students within the voucher plan.

2. Success of the voucher plan depends upon the
availability of alternatives. What we are doing,
then, is putting great faith in an unknown quantity
and quality of schools to be established after the
voucher plan becomes operational.

3. Also to be considered is what happens to
those alternative schools which will emerge based
upon some specific educational need or focus. Is it
possible to maintain their focus when they cannot
control up to 50 percent of their clientele? A
school designed for students who are interested in a
nonstructured curriculum may find that many of the
students admitted because of the lottery system do
not have the intellectual capacity or psychological
orientation that meets the alternative school's needs
and expectations.

4. During the OEO demonstration project, any
financial loss incurred by the public school district's participation will be absorbed by OEO. Transportation costs are also to be covered. Is this a
realistic pattern for a demonstration project? If
the trial is declared successful and results in mass
implementation of the voucher plan, will anyone be
around to absorb the possible financial deficits the
school districts may suffer?

5. There seems to be some tendency on the part
of those advocating the education voucher to brush
over the administrative details needed to implement
the plan successfully.

6. A process for accreditation of schools in
the voucher plan must be developed, particularly in
view of past court decisions dealing with religious

and political considerations.

7.   The working relationship between the Office of Economic Opportunity and the U.S. Office of Education plus the education profession must be clarified.

In summary, a dangerous pattern is developing in American society, in which pessimism is being so reinforced that our negativism may turn out to be a self-fulfilling prophecy. Failure of some teachers and some schools becomes generalized to "the Educational Establishment has failed." Public education is written off as ineffectual and as bureaucratically mired down. Granted, many improvements are needed and large numbers of youths are being shortchanged, but necessary changes are occurring within the system. Paramount, of course, is faith by the American people that the so-called "Educational Establishment" has the capacity to change and seek alternative forms of education to better meet the needs of students.

The concept of the education voucher has met with some enthusiasm. Receiving strong financial backing from the Office of Economic Opportunity, the voucher model conceived by Jencks has a moderate chance of being implemented on a trial basis in one or more of three communities selected by OEO for their demonstration project. Many problems still remain unresolved, such as the legality of the plan; action on the part of state legislators in enacting enabling legislation for allocation of funds, both local and state, to parents; support of the plan by professional educators, students, and parents; and what effect the voucher plan will have upon the possible demise of our public school system.

The voucher plan warrants consideration as a potentially exciting innovation for making alternative forms of education available to children. The success or failure of the plan is largely dependent upon the soundness of the voucher models being planned for the OEO demonstration project presently under way. Some doubt still remains as to whether the demonstration projects will become fully operational. The hope is that they will, in order that the necessary data can be collected, analyzed, and then utilized to guide future action. The education voucher must be further developed conceptually, field tested, redesigned, mass tested, and evaluated prior to passing judgment on its merits as a viable alternative for <u>some</u> students, <u>some</u> teachers, and <u>some</u> parents in <u>some</u> communities.

OEO EXPERIMENTS IN EDUCATION

Thomas K. Glennan

Let me address the reasons why the Office of Economic Opportunity is involved in education and suggest why these activities are being carried out by the Office of Economic Opportunity rather than by the Office of Education. President Nixon, in his August 11, 1969 message on the reorganization of the OEO stated: "It is in the Office of Economic Opportunity that social pioneering should be a specialty. It is the OEO that should act as the 'R&D' arm for the government's social programs." He went on to say: "It should be free to take creative risks. It should set up a variety of demonstration projects, carefully test their effectiveness and systematically assess their results."

This is a broad charter indeed from the President; one which is extraordinarily difficult to carry out. But, why has the Office of Economic Opportunity emphasized education? I suppose that no one would deny the need for reforms and change in education. Even so, most of us would agree that taken as a whole the educational system performs better today than it has at any time in its past. More people have more skills and more knowledge than at any time in our history. At the same time, however, there is more public dissatisfaction with the educational system today than there has been at any time in its history in this country.

The nation's school system, public, private and parochial faces rising expectations on the part of many segments of the population concerning the performance of the schools. And, for no part of the

Reprinted from Compact, 5:3-5, February, 1971 by permission of publisher.

population is this more true than for the poor and
the disadvantaged who see the nation's school system
as an essential contributor--perhaps the main con-
tributor--to success of their children and an essential means of equalizing opportunity. But, in many
instances, it appears that the school system is failing to meet these expectations. In school system after school system we have found enormous numbers of
poor children who are far behind the skill levels
that we would judge to be appropriate and indicative
of future competence in our society.

OEO Experiments with Contracts

What is the Office of Economic Opportunity
doing? We are fielding a major experiment with performance contracting. The intent is to make information available to the nation's school system both on
the performance of the contractors and on the administrative problems associated with performance contracting. It is not our intent to support a national
program of performance contracting. Nor do we at
this time advocate large scale adoption of performance contracting.

And with Vouchers

We are also exploring the possibility of mounting a demonstration or experiment with education
vouchers. The basic idea of a voucher system is
relatively simple. A local public agency issues a
voucher to parents. The parents take the voucher to
the school of their choice. The school returns the
vouchers to the agency. The agency then sends the
school a check equal to the value of the voucher. As
a result, public subsidies for education go only to
schools in which parents choose to enroll their children. Schools which cannot attract applicants presumably do not remain in business.

Advocates of a voucher program claim a number of
potentially significant benefits. They suggest:

(1) Individuals would have a greater freedom
within the public education system because they would
not be required to accept standardized programs

offered in assigned public schools. Middle income
and poor parents will have the same freedom to choose
schools that wealthy parents can exercise. (2) Parents would be able to assume a more significant role
in shaping their child's education, thus renewing the
family's role in education. (3) A range of choices
in schools would become available. Small new schools
of all types will come into operation--Montessori,
Summerhill, open classroom and traditional style
schools. (4) School administrators and teachers
could arrange their curriculum to appeal to a particular group or to reflect a particular school of
thought on educational methods. Schools could emphasize music, arts, science, discipline or basic skills.
Parents not pleased with the emphasis of one school
could choose another. (5) Resources could be more
accurately channeled directly to a target group--the
poor--since funds would follow the child holding the
voucher. (6) A form of accountability to parents
would be introduced since parents would be free to
withdraw their children if the school did not perform
in accordance with their desires.

On the other hand, there are numerous problems
that a voucher system is alleged to have. It is said
that a voucher system will promote and encourage economic segregation within the school systems because
well-to-do parents will add money to the vouchers
and thus be able to choose schools that charge additional fees. A second alleged shortcoming is that
vouchers could lead to and be a vehicle for racial
segregation within the schools. Indeed, where vouchers have been tried in the South, courts have found
that they were unconstitutional because of this. A
third major issue is the concern that the system
would lead to the support of religiously sponsored
education and therefore violate the prohibitions of
the Constitution. A fourth concern is that the use
of a more nearly free market in education would lead
to false claims by providers of educational services
that would mislead and misinform an unsophisticated
public. In short, hucksterism would enter the educational market.

A fifth concern is that parents, particularly
low income parents, may not be competent to choose
sources of education for their children or, if competent, may not make the effort necessary to do so.
On the part of the administrators within the public
education system there is grave concern as to the

feasibility of adminstering an education vouchers program.   Critics have questioned whether alternative sources of education would be forthcoming, how they would be financed and whether their cost would be reasonable.   Finally, there is considerable concern that a voucher system would jeopardize the existence of the entire public education system in the country and that the public schools would become schools of last resort.

These are very legitimate concerns.   On the other hand, the suggested benefits are very attractive.   A year ago OEO made the assessment that the attractions were significant enough to merit giving the proposal further examination.   As a consequence, we commissioned a planning study that was intended to look at the desirability and feasibility of an educational voucher system and to consider possible designs for an experiment with such a system.   To do this we gave a grant to the Center for the Study of Public Policy in Cambridge, which has been studying the program for nearly a year.

Perhaps the most significant conclusion we have reached is that a simple unregulated voucher system of the sort most frequently envisioned would be a disaster for the nation's school system.   It would be likely to have most of the problems that critics of the voucher system have claimed.

On the other hand, the Center indicated that there was no need to view the educational marketplace as free of regulation.   As a consequence, the major part of the report they submitted to us last spring delineated the features of regulation that would be required in this market to meet many of the problems. These regulations focus on three areas: The admissions policy of the voucher schools; the type and quality of data that must be provided by the schools; and the services for which public monies can be used.

Specifically these basic rules have been recommended by the Center:

(1) No school may discriminate against pupils or teachers on account of race or economic status, and all schools must demonstrate that the proportion of minority pupils enrolled is at least as large as the proportion of minority applicants.

(2) Schools must be open to all applicants.
Where a school is over-applied, some portion of the
students may be selected by any criteria the school
wishes except race. Some schools may want to give
preference to siblings of children already enrolled,
to children of a particular neighborhood, to children
with particular capabilities and interests, or to
children of particular religious faith, etc. For the
remaining positions the choice from among applicants
should be on a fair and impartial basis. The Center
suggested the choice might be made by lottery among
the remaining applicants.

(3) The school must accept the voucher as payment in full for all educational services at the
school. In other words, no school may require parents to make additional payments out of pocket.
Schools may seek additional sources of funds from the
government, from foundations, or from interested citizens and parents; but in no case can the admission of
a child to a school be conditioned upon such contributions in the child's behalf.

(4) No school may use money to support religious
instruction. Parochial schools may participate, however, providing they raise money for religious activity from other sources and keep separate accounting
systems, and providing this support is consistent
with the state constitution. Of course, they must
also comply with all other rules including the requirement of open enrollment.

(5) All schools must make information available
to parents concerning the school's basic philosophy
of education, the number of teachers, teacher qualifications, facilities, financial status and pupil
progress. In short, schools must provide sufficient
information to enable parents to make wise decisions
when they select the schools.

These elements of regulation can be viewed as
leading to a very significant change in one's point
of view about the nature of the voucher system. In
most people's minds the voucher system is considered
to be, in part, a means of supporting private education. It might better be viewed as making education
in private schools more public. In order to participate, private schools (as well as current public
schools) would have to submit to regulation of their
admissions policy, publication of their curricular

objectives and capacities and regular audits of their books. In a real sense, they become "public" schools. The voucher system can be said to lead to a system of public schools that are open to the public and re- sponsive to the public but not necessarily managed by the public.

The Center also strongly recommended that in a voucher system focused on the disadvantaged, compen- satory payments must be given to schools enrolling disadvantaged youngsters. There are two reasons for this. One is to ensure that additional resources be focused on the disadvantaged child. The other is to provide an incentive to schools to enroll some pro- portion of disadvantaged youngsters. The Center also concluded that there is a need for excess capacity within community's school systems in order to ensure that free choice in fact exists for all students. If the capacity of the total school system, public and private, is just equal to the number of students, there will be a substantial proportion of students who get into only the schools of their last choice.

Many questions remain to be answered, questions that can only be answered by actual operations. Cur- rently, we are working with a number of communities to examine the implications of initiating such an experiment.

The most obvious questions are: Will the educa- tion of the children be improved? Will the community consider that the type of education provided by such a system meets the public needs of public education? Is a regulated voucher system administratively feasible?

The final questions concern such things as: Can an admissions policy such as that outlined by the Center work? What is to be done about late comers, transferrers, dropouts, etc.? How can the job secur- ity of tenured teachers be protected? What kinds of changes and administrative procedures within the cur- rent public schools will be required to allow princi- pals to respond to the interest of the community? What sorts of counseling should be provided to par- ents on educational alternatives and who should pro- vide it? How will capital for the startup cost of new schools be provided?

The Voucher Experiment

To investigate these questions we are proposing an experiment at the elementary school level. We have chosen the elementary level for several reasons. This level covers a period that is crucial in the development of children's basic skills and learning motivation. It is a time which the parents are particularly concerned with their children's education. In addition, since it is hoped that additional sources of education will be developed within a community, the elementary school level is desirable because it reduces the required capital necessary to start new schools.

The voucher plan would be administered by a locally selected Educational Voucher Authority (EVA). This would be a public body, which might be the current board of education augmented by members of the community and representatives of alternative sources of education. Alternatively, it might be a new board empowered to receive funds from the local school system and disburse them to the parents.

All students of appropriate age within the experiment area would be eligible to receive vouchers which could be used at schools meeting requirements established by the community. The Education Voucher Authority would pay particular attention to facilitating parents' choices of schools by providing information and counseling and technical assistance.

The experiment would continue for about five years to allow development of new schools. The educational results of such an activity would not be clearly apparent for three to five years. While the Office of Economic Opportunity is unable to commit funds for this length of time, it would do everything possible to insure continuity in the program.

A lengthy planning period, in addition to the planning already done, would precede the experiment to enable the establishment of political machinery responsive to parents, development of administrative procedures, and modification of the existing public school system's operations to fit into the voucher plan.

It is expected that the experiment would be

mounted in a large urban area with a fairly heterogeneous population. A variety of economic, social,
and racial groups is necessary so that the effect of
the voucher system upon integration of race and class
can be tested.

The value of the voucher would be approximately
equal to the total per-capita expenditures currently
being made in the local public school system. It is
not the intent of this agency to reduce the tax burden of the local taxpayer or to substitute federal
funds for local and state funds. As a consequence,
the Office of Economic Opportunity intends to provide
for expenses of administration and evaluation of the
project, expenses for additional transportation necessary to allow students a real choice of schools and
expenses associated with the transition of the public
school system to a voucher school system. The latter
might include the maintenance of unused facilities or
the fulfillment of obligations to teachers who would
not be required if the system lost some portion of
its students. OEO also would provide support for
those students in nonpublic schools who are not currently being supported by state and local funds. In
addition, the Agency would help support special compensatory programs if the community wishes to include
them in their program.

We would like to initiate such an experiment in
September, 1971. We will not do so unless both the
school system and we are convinced that a successful
experiment can be mounted. Because of the fact that
state and local funds are required in this experiment, the approval of a large number of people is
required before any program can move forward. Special enabling legislation would be required in virtually any state to permit such an experiment to take
place. We will require the active and enthusiastic
support of both the local superintendents of education and boards of education. The Economic Opportunity Act requires us to seek the approval of the
governor and of the local community action agency.

The Office of Economic Opportunity is not advocating the voucher system. We are not advocating the
widespread use of performance contracting. We find
both of the ideas attractive but unproven. We think
both of them merit examination and careful study. We
have tried to subject both to wide public debate and

scrutiny. The final test in both instances will be
the experiment.

EDUCATION VOUCHERS

Peter A. Janssen

In most U.S. public school systems, the school a
student attends is determined by where he lives. If
the local school does not respond to his needs, or if
his needs differ from his neighbor's, he can only
move to another district or enrol in a private school.
For years, middle-income parents have exercised
exactly those options. Lower-income parents, of
course, can do neither. They are forced to accept
the local public school as it is, and then hope--if
conditions are right and their patience holds--to
work for reform from within. More often, they and
their children give up.

Soon, however, the range of alternatives may be
broadened. This would happen under a voucher system,
a revolutionary concept that would allow parents to
use public money to buy an education for their children at any school they choose, public, private, or
parochial. Parents of all school-age children would
be given a voucher roughly representing their child's
share of the public school budget. The voucher would
be turned in at the school chosen, and the school
would turn it in to a government agency to collect
its money.

One study of the voucher concept has been developed at the Center for the Study of Public Policy in
Cambridge, Massachusetts, under grants from the
Office of Economic Opportunity. Christopher Jencks,
director of the Center, says the main argument in

Reprinted from Education Digest, 36:5-8, March,
1971, by permission of publisher and American
Education.

favor of the voucher system is that public schools
are unresponsive today because they have no competition. Vouchers would give students a choice, and the
schools then would have to be good enough to attract
students; the bad schools would be driven out of
business. The proposal also has some major side
effects. It would give parents a major responsibility in their children's education, and it would
overcome the limitations of the neighborhood school.

The voucher system is supported by liberals and
conservatives alike, ranging from psychologist Ken-
neth Clark and critic Paul Goodman to conservative
economist Milton Friedman. Friedman, a professor of
economics at the University of Chicago, has advocated
vouchers since 1953, because "I think parents should
be free to send their children to any kind of school
they want." The schools of the poor, he adds, have
to improve or lose their customers the same way other
schools have been losing the children of the middle
class.

Actually, proposals for some type of voucher
system far predate Friedman. In the 18th century,
Thomas Paine proposed that the state governments pay
poor families a small amount to provide for the education of each child. And the G.I. Bill provided a
type of voucher, permitting veterans to select their
higher education from the college and university
marketplace.

Despite this heritage, the voucher system has
potential problems and powerful opponents. Civil
rights organizations clearly remember that some
Southern states have used vouchers to avoid integration and to channel public funds to private schools
--until the Supreme Court ruled this unconstitutional.
The NAACP believes the voucher plan would result in
"the perpetuation of segregation in schools." Also
opposed is the NEA, which has passed a resolution
saying that vouchers "could lead to racial, economic,
and social isolation of children and weaken or
destroy the public school system." The NEA warned
that competition would widen the gap between rich and
poor schools, and leave the poor schools a dumping
ground for students whose parents didn't have the
sophistication or knowledge to use the system. Private schools might also try "hucksterism" to induce
parents to patronize them, an NEA official warned a
Senate subcommittee.

Responding to such attacks, OEO Director Donald Rumsfeld pointed out that existing schools are not doing a satisfactory job of educating the poor. In many cities disadvantaged students score three years below grade level by the ninth grade. Rumsfeld promised that the OEO "certainly will prohibit racial segregation or racial discrimination."

Jencks, too, says that the voucher system can be designed to insure integration and avoid church-state problems. Thomas K. Glennan, Jr., OEO director of research and evaluation, adds that OEO "is not wedded" to including parochial schools in all the pilot projects, particularly in a state with strong requirements for church-state separation. Glennan is more worried that the system would not help the most disadvantaged students. He fears that those who need the help most are those whose parents are least likely to hustle out with a voucher to enrol their children in a better school. Jencks responds that policymakers have assumed that middle-class parents are capable of making these decisions and should assume that, with enough information, poor parents can make them, too.

Many who favor vouchers say that giving parents more of a sense of control over their environment-- and their children's education--is a valid end in itself. The more control parents have over what happens to their children, the more responsible they will feel for the results; they also will tend to hold officials more accountable for the quality of education their children get.

The question of whether low-income parents actually will join in selecting a school for their children is crucial. "The success of the program," Jencks says, "depends on the effectiveness of the effort to give parents some idea of what constitutes a good school and what constitutes a bad school. They all want good schools, but most of them aren't sure how to get them. Nobody really knows how to do that; the experts are only right 49 percent of the time."

Jencks also is unsure about how much participation is necessary for the system to work. "If only 15 percent of the parents participate, does that justify the system? What makes it a success or failure? We don't know yet."

The OEO isn't sure what will make the system succeed either, but it is committed to trying to find out. "I believe that there's enough potential so that the vouchers are worth trying," says Glennan. "But we're not sure under what conditions they will work. I think the system's main advantage is that people can get some accountability. Teachers and principals will have to develop a style of education to attract and keep people in school. The schools will have to react to what people want. If a few people in a school are unhappy, if they don't like sex education or whatever, they can withdraw and go someplace else. If a large group withdraws, however, then the principal will have to react. He'll have to change something."

Glennan also hopes the plan will promote integration. "The great benefit of the voucher system," he says, "is that blacks who are now segregated by the restrictions of housing or school boundaries could choose not to be segregated any more." The proposed OEO experiment would require that each participating school have the same proportion of minority acceptances as it has minority applicants.

HOW IT WOULD WORK

The first step would be creation of a locally-controlled Education Voucher Agency (EVA) to which local and state education funds, plus an increment from the federal government to support "compensatory" vouchers for poor children, would go for distribution in the form of vouchers. Federal funds would also be available to provide additional transporation required.

In the spring, each participating school--public, private, parochial--would tell the EVA how many students it could take in the fall. It then would have to take everyone who applied. If it was over-subscribed, half its enrolment would be filled by a lottery. No one would be excluded from the school because his family was not rich enought--or white enough.

The EVA would publicize information about each school and give each parent a voucher equivalent to the average per pupil expenditure in the public schools. Under the plan proposed by Jencks, vouchers would be written on a sliding scale, so the voucher for the poorest child would be perhaps twice as much as the basic voucher. The parents would give the voucher to the school of their choice, which would cash it in through the EVA. The EVA would police the system to prevent discrimination in admissions.

In its preliminary report to OEO, the Center for the Study of Public Policy said the most important priority in American education is to reallocate resources so that disadvantaged children are exposed to their share of talented, sensitive teachers and classmates. "A student's classmates are probably his most important single 'resource,'" the report said. His classmates often determine how much instruction he will get from his teachers. "If, for example, a disadvantaged child attends a school in which most children never learn algebra," the report said, "his teachers will not expect him to learn algebra, even if he is perfectly capable of doing so."

To be eligible for the voucher system, a school would have to agree to accept a voucher as full tuition payment, to accept any applicant so long as there was room, to abide by uniform standards set by the EVA about the suspension and expulsion of students, and to make public a wide range of information about its facilities, teachers, programs, and students.

A voucher system, its advocates acknowledge, must contain many built-in safeguards. Jencks believes that the courts, Congress, and state legislatures will come to view schools in a voucher system as instrumentalities of the state and require them to meet the same responsibilities they make public schools face today. Only if the system is properly regulated, the Center adds, can it inaugurate a new era of innovation and reform in American schools.

The OEO is talking to several communities about the voucher system for next fall. OEO officials hope to develop a five-year pilot project in a large city with enough of a mix of public and private schools-- and disadvantaged and middle-class students--to create a valid experiment. They are determined to have the pilot program approved by the teachers' organizations, the school board, the mayor, and anyone else who might be involved.

School systems are not given to making difficult changes overnight, and it may be many years
before any of them embark on a voucher program on a
large enough scale to reverse the despair that now
grips schools in poverty areas. That despair, however, certainly is not going to be lessened by maintaining the status quo. Vouchers may possibly offer
a way out.

VITAL QUESTIONS, MINIMAL RESPONSES:
EDUCATION VOUCHERS

A. Stafford Clayton

The experiment which the OEO hopes to fund would
presumably provide some evidence that granting
vouchers in support of the school of parental choice
would lead to certain educational innovations. Professor Jencks tells us that these innovations are
presently restricted by the bureaucratic and political constraints of a monopolistic public school system. An experiment in this instance means trial of a
voucher system in some community as yet unidentified.
We are not told how the experiment will be designed,
what controls will be exercised, and what criteria
will be used in assessing its results. Without these,
there is little hope of determining whether the prescription helps to treat the disease without creating
more complications than the patient can withstand.

What Jencks offers is more an argument than a
description of an adequately planned experiment. The
source and character of the Education Voucher Agency
to be established in each community is not described
beyond saying that it is locally controlled. It is
not clear how the EVA will be funded so that the
redemption value of vouchers will "approximate what
the local schools are currently spending on upper-
income children" and be worth something more for
children of low-income families. More important,
what criteria are to be used in appraising results as
indicators of desirable national policy is not only
unclear but the argument itself is disturbing and
unsatisfactory.

The Educational Voucher Agency "will not operate

Reprinted from Phi Delta Kappan, 52:53-54, September, 1970 by permission of author and publisher.

schools of its own," will not restrain schools'
staffing practices, programs, and curricular policies.
It will inform parents about what each school is
doing. It will decide which of all schools, both
public and private, can cash the vouchers issued by
the EVA. It will lay down the basic requirements
that schools will have to meet in order to insure that
they are "really equally open to everyone within com-
muting distance." It will pay transportation costs,
establish the monetary value of vouchers so that the
poor will benefit from them more than the affluent,
and enforce the rule that participating schools "accept every child's voucher as full payment for his
education."

How these various responsibilities are feasible
of execution under a locally controlled EVA surpasses
understanding. But perhaps we are not to take local
control too seriously. Each EVA will receive federal,
state, and local funds, presumably in the amount of
those currently used in support of public schools.
It will distribute these according to stringent basic
rules. Nothing is said about the establishment of a
super-EVA, a kind of Education Voucher Authority, to
ride herd on locally controlled Educational Voucher
Agencies. However, what is said about the stringent
controls to be placed on participating schools'
admissions and tuition charges suggests a policing as
well as a policy function to be performed by somebody,
presumably the OEO. Without such an arm of federal
control it is difficult to see how local EVAs are
going to regulate the education marketplace. In the
light of the current politics of education, including
the policies of the White Citizens Councils, the
pressures from organizations on the radical right,
and the increasing effectiveness of teacher organizations, Professor Jencks has good reason to be concerned with the vigor with which local EVAs will
regulate the marketplace.

However, other fundamental questions "to be
resolved on policy grounds" plague the voucher system. These questions pertain to the four areas of
common objection to which Jencks offers rather minimal and superficial responses.

His consideration that "parents may be too ig-
norant to make intelligent choices" misses the heart
of the matter. Many of us, I should think, would
like to see parents make intelligent choices among

schools for their children,based on ingredients of
the schools' programs. But we must remember that
participation of the total range of parents in these
matters, especially under the conditions of modern
life, is a slender reed to lean upon. Jencks would
have parents apply to schools each spring to elect
the school in which their vouchers would be cashed.
Considering what we know about family living conditions in urban areas, in the South, and in many towns
and villages, is the proposed voucher policy not
highly preferential to white middle-class suburban
Americans?

Jencks' consideration of the question of "de-
stroying the public schools" and supporting denominational schools does not come off any better. The
case is made that a voucher system could be limited
to nonsectarian schools but that until the Supreme
Court rules on this kind of equal support for private
as well as public schools there is no "compelling
reason" to deny support to all schools.

The policy of providing subsidies from public
funds to pay for all schooling, public and denominational, is not without a history in other countries
as well as in our own. In France general subsidies
to pay for schooling have been in effect since 1951.
The question of aid to private schools has been one
of the most controversial questions in French politics, and some have found that the continuing conflict and divisiveness over the question contributes
to the parplysis of French educational reform. In the
Netherlands complete equal support of public and
denominational schools since 1920 has led to a reversal of the ratio of enrollments in public and private
schools. The denominational school is now the rule,
the "neutral" school the exception. Not only this,
but the pervasive columnization of Dutch society into
Roman Catholic, Protestant Christian, and "neutral"
ways of life--it has been said that the Dutch live
separately as three peoples--is traceable in large
part to decisions by parents to send their children
to schools of their choice. In England subsidy of
the parents' choice has led to Anglican and Free
Church efforts to reestablish in their schools their
own forms of denominational Christianity, largely in
response to the effectiveness of the Catholic hierarchy in obtaining support for its schools.

This is not to suggest that we should make

overly simplistic intercultural comparisons in attempting to assess the consequences of a voucher system. However, in the absence of an inclusive consideration of criteria by which a proposal is to be evaluated, are we justified in dismissing the dangers with the offhand suggestion that there may be "some shrinkage in the public sector"? Will denominational as well as racist interests see a voucher system, even under the benign scrutiny of the OEO and the federal courts, as an opportunity to extend equal access to schooling, including innovative educational programs? Or will a voucher system encourage those attitudes of exclusiveness which reduce community among us?

It may be that the OEO has in mind an experiment in education vouchers which will protect the interests of freedom and equality in the sense in which I have tried to point to them. It may be that criteria for the appraisal of the experiment will reveal that these values are operative as we search for a new educational policy. We cannot tell from what Professor Jencks has written here.

PART FIVE

INDIVIDUALIZED INSTRUCTION

The ways and means of dealing with individual differences has long been an area of concern in education. Recently, a new and concerted effort has been initiated to individualize the learning experience for each child. Attempts are currently under way to individualize both the cognitive and affective development of the learner through the use of custom tailored learning packages and through the accommodation of various learning styles within the teaching-learning process.

School districts are utilizing varying approaches to individualized instruction. Some are commercially prepared programs designed and distributed through outside corporations, while others are being developed by local school personnel. Supporters of the individualized approach to education feel that it offers the greatest opportunity for the unique growth of each child. Opponents note that, while the goal of individualized instruction is a worthy one, little conclusive evidence exists at the present time to support this approach over all others. They further point out that it is difficult to measure growth in the affective domain and would like to see further research to substantiate the concept of individualized learning styles.

Hunter in her article defines individualized instruction as "the process of custom-tailoring instruction to the needs of a particular learner." Her theory of individualization is based upon two premises. The first is that students learn at different rates and the second is that learning is incremental. She discusses how to individualize intellectual skills, attitudes and interests, and psychomotor skills. Her summary describes how each teacher can individualize her own behavior whether in a self-contained classroom or as a member of an instructional team.

Hawk points out that instructional technology is facilitating individualization in the schools. In his article, he discusses the changing role of the teacher under an individualized approach from a "giver of knowledge" to an advisor and counselor in teaching-learning process. Hawk also cites the problem of classroom management and some of the difficulties involved in the implementation of individualized instruction.

Fifteen suggestions on how the teacher can individualize instruction in the classroom are offered by Allen in the last article. Chief among these are the use of time waivers, cooperative student efforts, variable credits, multiple teacher assignments, student selection of teachers and the tutor course option.

INDIVIDUALIZED INSTRUCTION

Madeline Hunter

Individualized instruction is one of the most popular and most misunderstood concepts in education. Some teachers view it as the act of trying to juggle twenty-five to thirty-five child-shaped balls of different activities at the same time. Others view it as an electronic arsenal with each learner plugged into his appropriate socket. Still others perceive it as turning all responsibility for learning over to the students. None of these views is accurate.

Individualized instruction is no one way of conducting education, nor any one special program. It is the process of custom-tailoring instruction so it fits a particular learner. An individualized program is not necessarily different for each learner, but must be appropriate for each. It is based on the premise that there is no one best way for all learners, but that there are best ways for each learner, which may be different from those for another learner.

How do we achieve this "perfect fit"? An educational program has three major dimensions that can be adjusted to fit any learner: the educational task, or what is to be learned; the learner's behavior, or what the learner will do to accomplish the learning; and the teacher's behavior, or what the teacher will do to make the student's learning more efficient and more predictably successful. Each of these factors will be discussed on the following pages.

It is important to note that the word "individualized" modifies "instruction," implying that the teacher's role is still a vital one.

Reprinted from INSTRUCTOR (C) March 1970, The Instructor Publications, Inc., used by permission.

Individualized instruction is not an end in itself, but rather a means to achieve learning sucessfully, economically, and predictably. It is an effective and efficient means for achieving learning goals as well as increasing student learning.

ADAPTING LEARNING TASKS

Individualization of learning tasks is based on two major premises, both of which have been validated by research. These premises are:

1. Students learn at different rates. Age and grade level are in no way guides to the appropriateness of a learning task. A task which is right for one learner will be wrong for another who has already achieved that learning, or for one who is not ready for it. We wouldn't expect children of one age or grade level all to wear all the same size clothing. Neither should we give them identical tasks.

2. Learning is incremental. In most instances, the child builds his learning block by block, like a wall. Some learnings act as a foundation for other learnings. It is impossible to achieve a complex learning without first having mastered the simpler component learnings, even though some children may take bigger or faster learning steps than others. For example, in order to do long division, the student must have learned to add, subtract, multiply, and divide, as well as to understand place value.

INTELLECTUAL SKILLS

Having accepted these two premises we find we can no longer deal out to an entire class, on an assembly-line basis, the books and assignments of one grade level. In individualizing instruction, each objective will be custom-tailored to a particular learner, not homogenized for the whole class and in reality fitting only a few.

Individualizing instruction does not mean that we let certain students "get by" with doing less work. It means we begin where a student is able to perform and move systematically toward better and better academic performance.

Nor does individualized instruction mean that each student must work individually. What it means is that the teacher must thoughtfully and on the basis of the child's learning needs make the decision as to whether for this task he should be learning alone or in a group.

To begin the individualization of intellectual skills, we must first determine what each learner has already achieved in his learning sequence so he may move on to the next appropriate task. To iden- tify a pupil's instructional level in reading, for example, we may listen to him read. If he misses more than two or three words on a page, the book is too hard for him. If he misses no words, the book is too easy--too easy, that is, for us to discover the level of difficulty at which he needs reading instruction. In math, we check to see if he really understands the concepts in addition and subtraction before proceeding to multiplication and division. Thus, by checking what he already knows, we don't waste his time or ours by having him work on some- thing too simple or too advanced for him.

This determination of what each student is ready to learn has two dimensions. One dimension is that which ranges from easy learnings through learnings of increasing difficulty. An example taken from reading would be the learning progression in preprimer, primer, first-grade reader, second-grade, third-grade, and so on. For math this dimension would start with counting, addition, subtraction, multiplication, division, fractions and beyond.

The second dimension is one of increasing com- plexity in the student's thinking. The simplest level is where the student merely shows that he remembers what he has learned. In further steps, he demonstrates his understanding of that information; applies the information to new situations; uses that information to solve problems or generate ideas by analyzing, then synthesizing, and finally, evaluating.

To individualize instruction, a teacher can work with both of these dimensions, taking a tuck here and letting out a seam there to make the learning task fit the individual child. The task can be made eas- ier--having the child learn addition or use a first-grade reader. It can be made harder--teaching the child multiplication, or having him read a sixth-grade reader. The chart below shows an example of how a teacher may use the second dimension to adjust the learning task with a group for whom an assignment in fractions is appropriate.

Another example of this same type of individualizing takes place when a teacher reaches the subject of Daniel Boone in a class in American history. The subject remains the same but the teacher demands

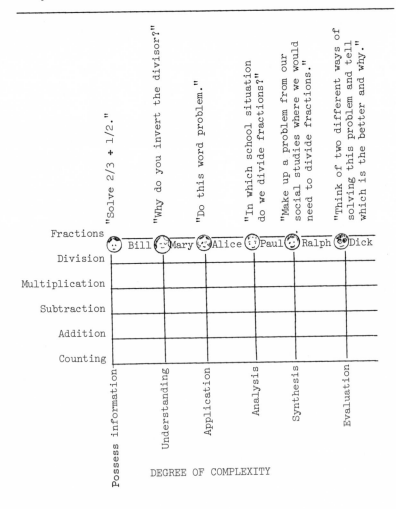

different levels of thinking from each student.
Billy, for example, is required only to be able to
answer the question, "Who was Daniel Boone?" He is
on the level of simply remembering information. Mary
is expected to have some understanding--to answer a
query like, "Why did Boone choose that area to explore?" Other students may be given assignments
which require them to apply their knowledge (From
this group of statements, select those which could
have happened to Daniel Boone), to analyze (What factors made Boone's trip dangerous?), to synthesize (As
if you had been a member of Boone's party, write a
story about your feelings and experiences), and
evaluate (Who do you think had the most difficult
trip--Daniel Boone or the moon explorers? Support
your position with evidence).

As you see, individualizing of instruction does
not mean that each student will be on a different
subject; nor does it mean that individualized instruction is instruction in isolation. Learners can be
grouped. It would be a waste of time for a skilled
learner to recite the "facts" about Daniel Boone; but
he needs that information for analyzing, synthesizing,
and/or evaluating. On the other hand, although the
less able learner cannot yet perform this more complex thinking, he will benefit from hearing others
deal with the information in advanced ways.

TEACHER PRACTICE

To individualize the difficulty of the task--
Have each child read aloud a page from his reader.
Which children miss more than two or three words on a
page? The book is too hard for them; use an easier
book for reading instruction. Which children know
all the words? For these children, the book is too
easy. Find a harder book; or let each select a book
of appropriate difficulty--although you must, of
course, check the selections.

To individualize the complexity of the thinking
--Make up questions at different levels of difficulty
for a story interesting to your class. If you chose
Goldilocks and the Three Bears, for example, your
questions might run like this:

1. Remembering information--What are some of the things Goldilocks did in the Bears' house?

2. Understanding--Why did Goldilocks like the Little Bear's things best?

3. Application--If Goldilocks had come into your house, what are some of the things she might have tried to use?

4. Analysis--What parts of this story could not have really happened?

5. Synthesis--How might the story be different if Goldilocks had visited the Three Fishes?

6. Evaluation--Do you think Goldilocks was "good" or "bad"? Why do you think so?

For which of your learners would each of your questions be appropriate? Try the story and questions on your class to check your judgment.

Readings for professional growth--

Taxonomy of Educational Objectives, Handbook 1:
Cognitive Domain, Benjamin S. Bloom, Editor (Longmans, 1956).

Classroom Questions, What Kind? M. Sanders (Harper, 1966).

ATTITUDES AND INTERESTS

Individualization of instruction is not limited to the intellectual domain. Individualization can also be accomplished in the development of interests, attitudes, and appreciations.

You must of course first realize that these feelings can be taught. A myth exists that we can't teach interests and attitudes, at least not directly and systematically. But much is known about their predictable development.

The first stage of such learning is for the child to receive or become aware of the thing beyond

himself--to recognize that there is something in
which to become interested or about which to form an
attitude or appreciation--whether it is an art work,
a poem, or another person with rights and feelings.
To teach consideration for others is a vain struggle
if the student is not aware of anything beyond himself. You will be equally unsuccessful in presenting
an "appreciation" lesson if a student has not experienced that which he is supposed to appreciate. Or
perhaps a child has been exposed to the experience,
but has paid little or no attention. He has not "received," so he cannot appreciate it.

The second step in developing an interest, attitudes, or appreciation is for the child to respond.
He must do something. He may listen, look, think,
feel, enjoy, comment, or in some other way react to
that which he has received.

Only after he has received and responded can the
student begin to value what he is learning; and, having begun, go on to make it characteristic of himself
so he becomes the kind of person who "is interested
in," who "feels that way about," or who "appreciates"
something.

Now let's translate these ideas into the individualization of instruction. Just as with intellectual skills, children's learning interests and attitudes will differ in their stage of learning, as well
as in their degree of possible development.

For example, your objective may be to develop an
appreciation of poetry, and you intend to start by
reading a selection aloud. To be successful, you
must remember that appreciation depends first on
"receiving," and select a poem that you judge your
group will listen to. No matter how excellent a poem
is or how valuable the experience would be, students
will not develop an appreciation of a poem that
"turns them off."

If you individualize, you will accept a wider
range of student responses--from simple attending
behavior to nonverbal evidence of enjoyment (such as
smiles, nods, or body movements), to verbal responses,
indicating enjoyment or understanding. Individualization can be accomplished by requiring a particular
learner only to listen; asking another which he likes
better of two poems; giving a third learner a choice

and hoping he will request poetry; and giving support
and encouragement to a fourth when he begins to write
his own poem. Future expectations for each learner
will also be individualized. Your aim for the passive listener will be to get him to respond; for the
learner who requests poetry, to increase his poetic
literacy by teaching him to appreciate different
poets and different poetic styles. In such individualized instruction, each of them will thus be given
an appropriate learning task.

Similarly, we can individualize the teaching of
attitudes such as "respect for the rights of others."
We can expect some learners merely to become aware
that there are others who are waiting to take a turn.
Learners already aware of the need for taking turns
can be required to do so. Some children will take
turns without our intervention, even if it is only
because they know we require it. Still others will
take turns because the game goes better. The objective for children is for them to take turns because
the other fellow has a right to one. This ideal may
not be obtainable for some at this time, but we can
take them a step along the way.

TEACHER PRACTICE

To individualize interests--Survey your group to
find out what interest each child would like to follow. After considering these interests in the light
of accessibility of materials, space, and need for
adult guidance, plan a program. You'll find some
students will flit from one activity to another, and
are unable to be independently productive; others
have the maturity to pursue an interest in depth. To
individualize instruction, work carefully with those
who need it, and give only occasional guidance to the
more independent. The dividends of such a program
will be growth in productive independence, expanded
fields of interest, and (most important) a growing
attitude that learning is zestful and rewarding.

To individualize attitudes--Together with your
class, identify some school situations that cause
problems. These might include having been a victim
of an unfair ruling in a ball game; being teased or
hit; finding the assignment too difficult; or any

problem related to the attitude you are trying to
build.   Then ask learners to suggest as many different ways to deal with the problems as they can think
of.   Don't be surprised if at first students can't
think of more than one way; or even if they merely
parrot previously heard preaching.   One reason   such
school problems exist is that students have not received and responded to acceptable alternative patterns of behavior.   Proceed by focusing their attention on more than one possible response.   When an
actual problem occurs, help them identify which
response they wish to use, then practice using the
response.

Readings--

Taxonomy of Educational Objectives: Handbook II:
Affective Domain, Krathwohl and Bloom (McKay, 1964).

Developing Attitudes toward Learning, Robert F. Mager
(Fearon, 1968).

PSYCHOMOTOR SKILLS

Instruction can also be individualized for the
psychomotor skills.   These are movement skills
through which a child expresses his feelings or
demonstrates his knowledge and ability, whether by
speaking, writing, jumping, dancing, playing ball, or
performing on a musical instrument.   Even though student aptitudes vary, each of these skills is learned
by building increasingly complex and automatic movement patterns.   To individualize instruction in movement skills, the teacher again must determine what
the student has already accomplished, and what he is
now ready to learn.

To determine the appropriate task, ask these
questions:

Has the learner perceived what he is to do--make
his letters touch the line, make his voice go up or
down, cup his hands to catch the ball?   You can waste
much time trying to teach a skill when the student
has not focused on the critical elements of the task.

Has he a "set" to perform the skill?   That is,

does he understand what part of his body is involved and does he know what to do with it--put the opposite foot forward, balance with his arms, place his lips correctly? Is he really trying, or simply going through the motions?

Has the student's performance been guided physically (placing his arms for him) or verbally ("Hold your arms this way") so he will get the feel of what is expected of him?

Has he "mechanized" his response--can he perform the sequence of movement without stopping to think what comes next?

Has the skill become an automatic, complex response to the appropriate stimulus--does he automatically track the ball with his eyes, run to where he expects it to land, and position his hands to catch it? In language does he have the movement skills to automatically communicate?

As has been previously pointed out, a teacher who individualizes instruction will have learners working at different stages. This is as true for instruction in psychomotor skills as any other type of skill. In handwriting, for instance, some learners will be working on the correct formation of difficult letters or letter combinations. Others will be writing sentences or paragraphs, automatically using their writing skill to communicate their ideas as they proceed in their learning.

In physical education, a teacher who individualizes will be teaching some students how to use their bodies properly in throwing, catching, running, or balancing. (It is just as unrealistic to put a learner who has not accomplished these basic skills into a complex ball game as it is to expect a first-grade reader to use the encyclopedia.) Students who have mastered the basics will be given the more advanced task of practicing throwing and catching to automate their responses. Still others will be automatically using their skills in a fast ball game, in a complex type of race, or in advanced gymnastics.

Each learner in an individualized program for psychomotor instruction will be using the skills he already possesses to learn more complex patterns. No learner will be trying to work on complex skills

without first having learned the simpler component
skills; he will never hear, "Just get in the game and
you'll learn to play."

TEACHER PRACTICE

Make a list of students for whom you think each
of the following learning tasks is appropriate:
Stopping and holding a ball rolled at his feet.
Catching a ball thrown to him between shoulder height
and waist height. Catching a ball thrown high, low,
or to one side. Tracking a ball through the air,
running to place his body in the right spot, catching
the "fly."

Readings--

"The Classifications of Educational Objectives:
Psychomotor Domain," Elizabeth Jane Simpson, in
Teacher of Home Economics, Winter 1966-67.

Developmental Sequence of Perceptual Motor Tasks:
Movement Activities for Neurologically Handicapped
and Retarded Children and Youth, Bryant J. Cratty
(Educational Activities, Inc.).

PROVIDING MANY WAYS OF LEARNING

Each individual finds that some learning behaviors are more productive for him than others. Some
children learn more quickly if they read, some need
to listen, others find it easiest to learn if they
talk about the material.

In planning an individualized program, a teacher
should provide different types of activities so a
student can participate in the ones that are best for
him. History, for example, can be learned by seeing
it re-enacted in a movie or a filmstrip, reading
about it in a book, writing a story about it, acting
it in a dramatization, painting a picture of it, dis-
cussing it with another individual or with a group,
visiting one of its scenes, viewing it in another
dimension through maps or on a time line, or constructing models or dioramas of it.

There are other dimensions of learning behavior which vary with individual students. Some can work productively with a friend; others are distracted. Certain children prefer to work alone and figure it out; others are more comfortable in a group. Boys tend to be active in learning styles, girls more passive. Some students are overwhelmed by a long and complex task--they need shorter assignments which give them frequent feelings of accomplishment. Others prefer a longer learning contract so they can make their own plans and proceed at their own pace.

When instruction is individualized for a certain student, the task to be accomplished is identified first. Next, both teacher and student proceed to seek the behaviors that will help him achieve understanding and accomplish the task.

Note that this does not mean that the student will always find the same type of learning behavior productive. The choice of learning style may vary with the pupil's previous experiences, with his ability, with the task, with the current interest of the student, and even with the style of presentation. A combination of learning behaviors is reinforcing; and, when a choice of learning styles is offered, the student can and should continuously expand his repertoire of learning behaviors that work well for him.

Thus by providing for many ways of learning, the teacher is accomplishing a major objective of the individualizing of instruction, that of helping the student to learn how to learn.

TEACHER PRACTICE

Make a list of learning behaviors which you think would be productive for your students. Be specific. You'll probably find you will have to do some careful thinking to be able to write down precise definitions of the learning behaviors. If you list "concentrate," for example, describe just what the student would have to do to convince you that he is concentrating. If you list "practice," describe what and how the student should practice. Making this list should stimulate you to increase your possibilities for individualizing learning behaviors.

Ask students to tell you what they would do if they really wanted to learn something in a hurry. Give them specific problems such as figuring out how many bottles of soft drink would be needed for a class party, memorizing the lyrics to a new Beatle song, learning enough about Joe Namath to interview him for the school paper, perfecting a trick on the parallel bars for a gymnastic show. Try to get them to reveal some real knowledge about how they themselves work, rather than repeating platitudinous adult admonitions.

Compare your list with the students'. You may find that you'll need to suggest some learning techniques that you know to be productive but that evidently the class does not know. A good example is making sure that pupils after learning something recall it at least once before moving on to new learning.

You may also find that your students have listed behaviors which you have not thought of. If they are productive, incorporate them in your plans.

Start a card file on how your pupils learn. Make a card for each pupil, listing the learning methods that seem to be best for him. Just doing the cards will help you organize your thinking about how each pupil learns best. It may also point out that some use only one or two ways of learning. Plan to have these pupils experiment with other types of learning activities. If a child, for example, seems to learn only by reading and then reporting what he has read, suggest that he broaden his base by reading an article on pottery, then show what he has learned by actually making a small piece rather than by reporting verbally on what was read. As each student moves into new learning methods, add those to the cards.

Set up a tentative plan for individualizing instruction when presenting a unit. Include activities which incorporate many ways of learning. For example, suppose your topic is the settlement of California during the 1850's. Your possibilities for learning might include: making a map showing early Spanish missions and trails; reenacting the discovery of gold at Sutter's Mill; developing a time line of California's historical events; making a report of life in a mining camp from a miner's point of view;

preparing an in-depth research paper on those who
came to prospect and stayed to farm and ranch.

Include some opportunities for a long-term
activity for the one or two persons in your room who
learn well when they can concentrate on one topic for
a long period. Often day-to-day work is frustrating
to the more able student who is anxious to really
attack a problem.

ADJUSTING YOUR TEACHING PATTERNS

The third dimension in the individualizing of
instruction is for the teacher to individualize his
teaching behavior--to decide what he must do to make
each student's learning more efficient and more successful. To accomplish this, you must gear your
teaching to the needs of the individual student
rather than to the demands of the large group.

Some teachers feel that teacher fairness and
consistency imply identical treatment of every
learner. On the contrary, it's these very qualities
that require a teacher to insure that each student
receives the assistance and support that are necessary to further his learning. For one student, this
may mean a great deal of assistance; for another, it
might mean encouraging or even insisting on independent performance.

Many teachers make these modifications in their
teaching behavior unconsciously. They joke with one
student, are solicitous with another; check every
problem with one, spot-check another; praise one,
scold another; insist that one work by himself, give
continuing help to another. Although the experienced
teacher automates these responses, it is important to
monitor them constantly to make sure they do not
become a rigid teaching pattern rather than genuinely
reflecting the needs of particular students. An
important factor in this aspect of individualization
is the sensitivity of the teacher to varying personality patterns and needs.

This does not mean that teacher behavior can
make up for errors in the individualization of the
learning task or in the student's learning behavior.
If the task is unattainable or the learning behavior

inappropriate for a particular learner, failure is
likely to occur in spite of any behavior on the part
of the teacher. For example, if a student's assignment is to learn to spell words he can't read, writing them fifty times even with teacher encouragement
will be a waste of time.

But when the tasks and the learning behaviors
have been individualized, the next step is to ask
yourself questions such as these for every student:

What can I do to increase his motivation to learn?

Should I praise him or prod him?

Should I give him many short assignments or a few
    long ones?

Is it better for him to experience continuing suc-
    cess, or does an occasional failure challenge
    him to greater effort?

How can I increase his speed of learning?

What kind and how much practice helps him most?

What are the reinforcers that strengthen his produc-
    tive behavior?

How can I make the material meaningful and interesting
    to him?

How can I encourage him to take more responsibility
    for his own learning?

What skills or knowledge does he already possess that
    will help him with this new learning?

How can I make his learning experiences more vivid?

What can I do so that he will remember more surely
    what he's learned?

How can I add "feeling tone" that will assist his
    memory?

How can I help him transfer what he has learned into
    other situations where it is appropriate--trans-
    fer his knowledge in spelling into his written
    work, transfer his good behavior in the class-

room to the assembly, transfer his hypothesizing in science into speculation in social studies?

How can I guide him into generalizations rather than isolated bits of knowledge?

You may be asking angrily or despairingly, "How can I possibly know all that about any <u>one</u> child, let alone all of them? Where can I find time to ponder each child's specific learning problem in such detail?" You are absolutely right; you can't possibly know all these things. But you will be amazed to find how thinking about these questions in relation to a particular child even at odd moments gives you valuable and productive insights into possible ways to individualize your teaching behavior.

Remember, however, that your purpose is to find out what behavior of yours best helps the child to learn in his own style. Don't fall into the trap of thinking that if you can just find the right technique--the right button or combination of buttons to push--all children will then move in whatever direction you have chosen, like obedient robots. Children know when a teacher is trying to manipulate them and rightfully resent it.

Another idea to watch is the notion that a child will always respond to the same teacher behavior in the same way. His needs and his responses will vary with the task, with the state of his health, with the progress of his maturity, with his mood, with your mood, and even the weather. But this flexibility is just an added dimension to your professional task of adjusting what you do to make it easier for each student to learn.

TEACHER PRACTICE

Make a list of questions for your students which begin, "Which helps you more . . ." "When do you learn more . . ." or "When do you try harder . . ." and complete them with some of your teaching behaviors. For example,

. . . When I give you one long assignments, or several short ones?

. . . When we practice together or you practice by
      yourself?

. . . When I am firm or when I joke?

. . . When I tell you what to do or let you figure it
      out yourself?

. . . When I decide which project you should do first
      or let you make the choice?

Collect the answers from each child. (You may be surprised at some of the replies.) Now proceed to individualize by trying each child's suggestions, after-
wards helping him to see the results. "You wanted a
long assignment, and you do very well when you have
one," or "You said you wanted me to joke with you but
now you're not settling down to business."

    If possible observe several teachers already in
an individualized situation, for the specific purpose
of noting the ways they adjust their teaching behaviors to the varying needs of the children. Some of
these may be deliberate, some unconscious. Make a
careful note of the different behaviors and how the
child responds. This is even more valuable in a
team-teaching situation or when a special teacher
takes over your class. Then you can observe someone
else with children you know, watching how specific
children react to various teaching patterns.

    Try different behaviors with your group and note
the children with whom they are effective. For example, tell them to be their own teacher for the next
twenty minutes and see who sets to work and who takes
undue advantage of the freedom. At another time let
them know you will not collect their papers, and
observe which children stop working or become care-
less. Offer a reward such as early dismissal for
completed learning and see which children try harder
or learn faster.

    If your school has videotape equipment, request
that it be used in your room as you work with children on a particular lesson. Pick one in which you
are especially confident and for which you have done
some good planning. When you view the videotape
later, make a list of the times when you individualized your approach to pupils, another list of times
when you tried to reach the entire group. Look for

these points:

Observe every person in the class. Was each being reached in some way?

What could you have done to reach the one or two who were not with you? (Perhaps only a nod, or a question worded especially for him?)

View the tape a second time. If you were teaching the same lesson again, what individualized activities would you introduce?

Read these programmed books on learning theory and try the ideas therein with your class: Motivation Theory for Teachers, Reinforcement Theory for Teachers, Retention Theory for Teachers, and Teach More--Faster, all by Madeline Hunter, published by TIP Publications, Box 514, El Segundo, California 90245. This series of books was written to make available to teachers important psychological knowledge that will result in significantly increased student learning.

YOU CAN INDIVIDUALIZE

Self-Contained Classroom

To individualize instruction for a self-contained class, begin by throwing out the notion that a student's age or grade determines what he should learn. You will no longer deal out the books of the grade level to everyone. You will overcome your compulsion to "cover the material." Instead, you will accept the responsibility of checking to see what each student already knows so you can plan what new material he is ready to learn. Informal tests and your own observation will show you where to start.

Begin to individualize instruction by checking each child's reading level. Have him read to you so you can see at what level he misses one to three words on a page. Then instruction can begin with groups that are able to use the same book. Slower readers will need daily instruction. More independent readers may not need to meet with you daily, but they will need instruction in certain skills and more practice in independent reading. You'll modify the complexity of the thinking task to suit each of the children reading in the same book. For some, it will be enough to know "what happened"; others in the same group should be able to use their knowledge of "what happened" to do the more complex tasks of comparing, applying, analyzing, synthesizing, evaluating.

The same procedure should be followed in math. Working usually with groups, you will teach new skills, always modifying your expectations for different students. For example, when a group is on multiplication, one learner may be doing the numerical problem, another can be solving word problems, and a third will be creating new word problems to go with the number problems.

Students will increasingly take charge of their own learning, at a rate appropriate for each. Some may work on "learning contracts," pacing themselves and designing their own ways for achieving the prescribed learning. Learning contracts may begin with a diagnostic test that will help teacher and students identify their areas of strength and weakness. Then, assuming differing degrees of responsibility, together they will design instructional procedures, making it possible for those who need to work on certain skills to work alone or in instructional groups.

At other times of day, it may be possible for students to pursue their own interests in other subject areas. However, simply scheduling "free periods" without learning expectations or without accountability is not individualized instruction. Other than time allowed for exploration, children should be required to make a commitment for what they intend to do and to present evidence they have done it or a reason why not.

There isn't any special way that individualized instruction should "look." But it must meet certain requirements. Each student must be working on an appropriate task, in the way most productive for him, and with the kind of teacher assistance which meets his needs.

As a Team Teacher

The staffing design of team teaching makes possible more alternatives in teaching style and competence, more dimensions in grouping, and more professional know-how in diagnosis and prescription.

In team teaching, learners are usually grouped
differently for instruction in each subject. When
instruction is individualized in a team-teaching
setup, the grouping continues. Occasionally the
total group will work together, but usually there
will be many smaller, flexible groupings. Children
may be grouped according to academic ability, but
this is only one of the many possibilities. Other
bases for grouping are the style of teaching that
students need, the interests or the friends they have,
the skills they are ready to learn, and the amount of
teacher help they require.

Most successful team teachers find that this
type of organization provides a richer environment
for student learning, and for teacher learning as
well.

The nongraded school was created on the basic
principal of individualized instruction, whether the
staffing pattern is team-teaching or self-contained.

Some schools that call themselves nongraded are
really levels systems; that is, all students reading
on a fourth-grade level go to this room, all on a
fifth-grade level go to that room, and so on. It is
an attempt to organize away achievement differences,
making it possible for one book and one assignment to
be used for the entire group. True nongraded instruction is designed to deal with differences; in
fact, this is the essence of individualized
instruction.

In a nongraded school, the learner is diagnosed
in terms of the style of teaching behavior that
should best propel his learning. He is assigned to
that kind of teacher or team. He is also diagnosed
as to the kind of group in which he will learn best
and assigned to that group. Only then, in an optimum
environment of teaching style and peer group, is he
diagnosed academically for the purpose of custom-

tailoring a program to his needs.

Sometimes the teacher will work with the total class; often he will work with subgroups, and occasionally with only one or two students. If the organizational pattern in the nongraded school is self-contained, a teacher must by necessity leave some students working by themselves when he works with a group. With team teaching, another teacher is available.

When a school is nongraded and instruction is individualized, a student is always working at the academic level appropriate to his present degree of learning. He is using ways of learning and receiving teacher assistance designed to promote his success.

QUESTIONS YOU MIGHT ASK

Should students always be "on their own" when instruction is individualized?

Some teachers think that individualizing instruction means turning over to students all responsibility for their own learning. This would be an abdication of professional responsibility. While it is highly desirable for a student to assume an increasing amount of responsibility for his learning, the rate of take-over must be individualized. The learning decisions a student is allowed to make should be commensurate with his ability and experience. The teacher should provide for the growth of each student toward maturity in learning decisions. He will not just hope the student will take over, nor will he expect the same degree of initiative and independence of all students.

Is individualized instruction an all-or-nothing proposition?

Completely individualized instruction and assembly-line instruction are at opposite poles, with most instruction falling somewhere between. Many learning activities are individualized in one of the dimensions of task, learning behavior, and teaching

behavior, but not in the other two. Sometimes a
teacher will individualize his expectations for student performance and his teaching behavior. But if
he has the same performance expectations for too
heterogeneous a group, he will have to adjust the
difficulty of the task in order to individualize it.
The behavior of the teacher who wants to individualize must at all times reflect the varying needs of
each of his students. The teacher who is an instructional artist will individualize all dimensions: the
task, what the learner does to achieve it, and what
the teacher does to assist him.

Doesn't individualizing take more time?

    If you have been arriving in school at the same
time as your students and leaving when they do,
you'll never be able to maintain that schedule when
you individualize your instruction. In the more
likely case that you have spent long hours planning
and suffering with frustration when students don't
learn, then individualizing instruction will save you
considerable time.

    All good teaching takes planning. When instruc-
tion is individualized, however, students work at a
level where they can be more independent. They don't
have long periods when they can't proceed because
they don't understand. Nor do they have free time to
get into trouble because the assignment was easy and
they finished ahead of the others; so control problems take up less of your teaching time.

    Many capable learners can proceed on their own
with only occasional stimulation or guidance. This
frees you to monitor more closely the learners who
would otherwise grind to a halt. Also, as you learn
to develop assignments with built-in flexibility the
same assignment can be appropriate and stimulating
for a greater number of students.

    Yes, individualized instruction takes much plan-
ning time. But never was your time better spent.

Will my students be ready for the next grade?

Since the purpose of individualizing instruction is to increase the amount of student learning, a good program will result in students' being better prepared for their next educational experience than they would have been with the typical instructional routine. Remember that good individualized instruction increases the amount of learning and decreases the time it takes to learn it. The more sturdy a child's educational foundation, the easier it is to build on it.

Doesn't it challenge a child to expose him to more advanced material?

If a student does not have the readiness and foundation for his "exposure" to any material, he will not only be unable to learn it, but precious time will be lost that could have been used to give him the learning he needs. Exposing students to fifth-grade reading when they can't read a third-grade book, or exposing them to multiplication when they don't understand addition, is actually detrimental. Imagine the rubble resulting from a bricklayer's putting in the sixth row of bricks when the first five were not securely in place. Just as real is the academic rubble which results from teaching "sixth-grade material" when previous learnings have not been thoroughly achieved.

Don't students feel that different assignments are unfair?

Do students feel it's unfair for a teacher to help a student who is having trouble with a problem and not give help to one who has solved it correctly? Of course not! Nor do they feel that assignments are unfair if each has work to do that is right for him.

Occasionally a student will ask, "Why do I have to do this when he only has to do that?" or "How come he gets to do that?" Your response might be, "It's either because I'm unfair, or I like one of you better, or I have a good reason. What do you think that reason might be?" The answer is usually a perceptive one, "Because he has finished his other work," or "Because it's harder for him." If there is a need to explain further, maintain the dignity of both students.

Students usually feel that individualized instruction is infinitely fairer, because everyone has a learning task he can accomplish with appropriate effort. Goldbricking no longer exists; neither are there insurmountable learning tasks.

How do I keep track of student progress?

The question of how to keep track of what students are learning is not a new one. It has always plagued conscientious teachers. Individualizing instruction merely brings into focus the fact that the question has seldom been satisfactorily answered.

The answer is not to load yourself down with bookkeeping chores, but to find ways to establish frequent learning checkpoints. Daily correction of work can be done by students who need both the responsibility and immediate feedback. For those who do not have the maturity or integrity to assume this responsibility, you may need to devise a daily monitoring system.

Your records should be simple and easily maintained. They should include this information: What has the student accomplished? Is he floundering, or is the task so easy he does not need to exert learning effort? Is he protected by a check-back system from forgetting something he once knew?

Devices can vary from checklists and anecdotal file cards to teacher-made tests and observations. It is important to have all the information you need, but on the other hand not to waste time collecting useless or obsolete data. Examine your records critically, and keep only those data that are indispensable.

Eventually, the computer will take over this chore. The machine is ready. It is waiting for humans to identify which data are most useful in making educational decisions.

Won't there be some children I just can't reach?

Regardless of your teaching procedures, there
will be some children who will be very difficult to
reach, especially those hard-core cases at low
ability or low motivation levels. But with individualized instruction you should have less trouble.
Having once accepted the idea that no materials or
procedures are inappropriate for any child, you can
select those which work best. And a pupil who real-
izes what you are trying to do is much more likely to
be motivated to try harder.

Won't I need lots of materials to individualize?

A teacher who follows the ideas outlined in this
feature can individualize instruction using whatever
materials are available. The more good materials he
has, the more alternatives he can make available to
learners. No amount of materials, however, can create a good individualized program when the teacher
does not have the incentive.

In short, use your materials and supplies to
give direction to your individualizing, not as ex-
cuses for not doing so. This is not to say good
materials are not needed. But demonstrations of good
individualized education have a way of stimulating
the financial support for material that will make a
program even better.

How do I explain individualized instruction to
parents?

Parents have been individualizing "instruction"
ever since their children were born. They know what
is right for Susie can be all wrong for Marty. Although not usually at a conscious level, parents set
different learning tasks for each child. Knowing
Marty's clumsiness, they don't demand he make his bed
as well as Susie, and so on.

Parents also know their children learn in different ways. Susie feels deserted if she does not
have the support of a more knowledgeable person in

new learning. Marty needs to figure out for himself;
he resents assistance, and looks on it as interference.

Parents are reassured by the knowledge that at
school their children are not anonymous "desk-
fillers"--that the individuality and learning style
of each child are being taken into account so he will
learn more in less time. When you explain your program to parents, don't be surprised if they respond,
"Why haven't schools been doing this all along?"

INDIVIDUALIZED INSTRUCTION IN
THE SCHOOL SETTING

Richard L. Hawk

INTRODUCTION

Focusing instruction upon the individual rather
than the group is not really a very new idea. Even
current techniques of grouping have been developed
to respond to needs of individuals caught in the
expediency of grouping. If "instruction" is viewed
in its broadest perspective, namely assisting a human
being in becoming mature and in learning how to cope
with life, then we see that all experiences both in
and out of school may be characterized in part as
individualized education. Outside of school, most
instruction is individualized. Education in the home
is done largely on a one-to-one basis. When stopped
by a policeman, we learn about traffic rules individually. In fact, most of life's experiences outside of the classroom are individual contacts with
the environment rather than group contacts, so individualization is nothing new.

Group approaches to instruction which are used
today were developed as an economic expedient. The
Lancasterian schools of England, with their large
groups and their monitors, provided a way of dealing
with large numbers of children with a minimum number
of teachers. In such systems where economy was
viewed as a curricular goal, instruction took a back
seat to the group-management design used. Such systems of dealing with education are so well established in our society that one seldom thinks twice
about how we have compromised the quality of

Reprinted from Educational Horizons, 49:73-80,
Spring 1971 by permission of the publisher.

educational experiences we know how to provide.

America's first schools--the one room type--pro-
vided many individualized learning opportunities. If
there was only one child at a given grade level, his
instruction of necessity was individualized to a considerable degree. As schools grew in size, financial
support trailed. Today a philosophy of economy as a
desirable ingredient in education has resulted in a
heavy dependence upon group or "herd" instructional
techniques. In fact, we have developed such techniques to a highly refined art. In contrast, recent
accents on individual rights are causing us not only
to respect and emphasize the student as a person but
also to provide him with individualized instruction.
We are moving back toward the individualization characteristic of the small school. This move is being
facilitated through the application of instructional
technology, as defined in the first article of this
publication. Such a move is typically stalled for
lack of funding--as usual.

I.   THE NATURE OF TECHNOLOGY'S IMPACT

As education has gradually expanded its use of
the technology of instruction, changes have occurred
in the classroom in a number of ways:

A.   Technology has demonstrated that the presentation of information can be mediated; the teacher
doesn't need to do it all. Traditionally, information has been presented most often by the teacher or
by text materials. While both may be considered as
media, they are being supplemented and replaced by
newer forms. As more media have become available,
the teacher's role as presenter is being decreased.

B.   Technology is not only decreasing the role
of the teacher as presenter but also helping to point
out other roles for the teacher to assume. The more
varied the mediating agent for teachers and students
to use, the more management problems are involved in
bringing students and appropriate media together. The
less time the teacher spends in "presenting," the
more time is available to manage the learning environment and to assist learners on an individual basis.

C.   Technology has helped and is helping to

sharpen a focus on a new economic philosophy for education. The level of utilization of technological devices in the home vastly exceeds that which a general public condones in the schools at the present time. For generations educators have lived with the philosophy that "keeping school" with the minimum possible investment in supplies, materials, and equipment is the most important objective. Today's world does not support such a philosophy. We are in the age of disposable technological devices. It is now cheaper to replace a small transistorized radio or an inexpensive watch or camera than to have them repaired. These things become almost as expendable in the minds of the young--who have never known a world without them--as were paper and pencil a generation ago. All these changes support a new technological standard of living for education and raise expectations among learners that these devices should be a natural part of the school environment.

D.   Instructional technology is helping to reveal new concepts about the role of education in society and to bridge the continuity of instruction outside and inside the classroom. Thanks to the mass media, information levels available outside the classroom compete with that inside the classroom, particularly where technological advances have not been achieved. To deny the potentials in the schools of utilizing many avenues for learning is an anachronism in today's society. Mass media are making us into mass man, while at the same time increasing the worth of the individual where instructional technology is applied to the individualization of instruction. Likewise, communication techniques facilitated by technology provide more time for individuals to interact with one another--if they will reorganize their management procedures to take advantage of such opportunities. H. S. Hayakawa, in his syndicated column, recently stated that he felt one reason for the alienation of youth today is the lack of experience in human interaction skills stifled by long hours of being passive interactors with the mass media. Schools must reverse this trend through increased opportunities for individual expression and interaction.

II.   THE NATURE OF INDIVIDUALIZATION IN THE PAST

Even though education in recent years has been based predominantly upon the group, individualized instruction occurs every time a teacher singles out a given learner for a conference regarding some learning problem.   Instruction is being individualized. When a student proceeds on his own with instructional materials he has selected, or someone has helped him select, or he completes a learning task assigned to him, he is functioning in the "individualized mode." Arrangements for such individualization have been largely informal in the past and generally in the category of lip service because true individualization, in part, has been limited by circumstances. Individualization--when it happened--was achieved in spite of the group system of instruction.   The learners who tended to receive individual guidance were either extremely bright children or children with severe learning handicaps.   Seldom did the youngster who learned to submerge himself in the group receive individual attention.   Individualization, therefore, was limited to the exceptional situation which demanded attention is spite of requirements upon the teacher to spend most of the time with a group.

Educators love to beseech one another to apply the best teaching techniques, but they seldom attack the fundamental reasons for failure to follow superior teaching methodology.   Elements within the situation, in addition to the desire of teachers to improve learning activities, must be changed before very much "real" action can occur.   As one example, effective materials must be readily accessible and in ample supply.

III.   THE DESIGN OF INSTRUCTION
FOR INDIVIDUALIZATION

In converting from the group instruction approach to individualization, several basic changes must be made.   As teachers place more dependence upon media for presenting information, they acquire greater responsibilities as learning managers.   Also, without constant supervision by his teacher, each student must accept new responsibilities for self-direction.   These changes demand adjustments in

organizational and administrative procedures, both
for manipulating the schedules for human activities
and for scheduling the use of facilities, materials,
and equipment. Let us look at each of these areas of
change.

A.   Role of the Teacher

Frequently teachers tend to think about their
jobs from the perspective of method. Traditionally,
the role of the teacher has been one of helping the
learner to "fix" content. The focus has been primarily upon the process of organizing information,
presenting content, and involving the learner for
this purpose. In strategies for individualized instruction, the emphasis must be switched from teacher
process to learner process, a switch from too much
concern about organizing teacher dominated lessons to
learner manipulation of learning experiences. One
must think in learner terms and de-emphasize achieving teacher goals. Emphasis should be upon how the
learner is to achieve <u>his</u> goals.

One of the best vehicles for such a change in
emphasis is the use of performance or behavioral
objectives. These are expressed in terms of processes and outcomes. Particularized for the learner,
objectives specify what he will need to do to complete a task, the nature of the task in specific
terms, and the level of performance expected for completion. Such objectives may take many forms.
Development of performance objectives is an art in
itself and much too complex to be fully covered in
this paper. The reader interested in this area
should refer to Robert F. Mager,[1,2] Norman E. Gronlund,[3] H. H. McAshan,[4] the performance objectives
catalog from Hughson High School,[5] or the new four-
volume "encyclopedia" of behavioral objectives published by the Westinghouse Learning Corporation
containing over 4,000 objectives.[6]

Even though more and more performance objectives
are becoming available in published form, in this
writer's experience, individualized instruction programs are most successful where the teachers employing the techniques have participated in their development and know how to write a performance objective.
This will not always be true. A number of the

packages for individualization, with their sets of
performance objectives, have been developed to such a
degree that teachers largely unacquainted with the
process can function quite successfully with them
after only a brief orientation. However, we are now,
and will be for some time, in a "selling phase" where
many teachers will need to participate in developmental work before they will be willing to accept and
promote the basic principles.

Literature abounds on the subject of individualization. Representative of articles which include
discussions of the preparation of objectives, Robert
Denby[7] and Lucius Butler[8] wrote of the necessity of
clear statements which are understandable by the
learners who are to use them. The importance of this
notion cannot be over-emphasized. Denby, in his
review of nine different independent study programs,
observed that understandability of objectives is
absolutely necessary if such programs are to succeed.
Butler pointed out that clear objectives not only help
the learner to know what he is to do and under what
conditions, they tend to make directions for learners
more precise because the student is able to go to
work directly with much less confusion or need for
assistance than from ordinary assignments. Regarding
the teacher's role in such programs, Ronald Edwards[9]
found in a community college typing course that individualization allowed the teachers to be free at all
times for consultation on specific learning problems.
Such freedom is not only a feature of thorough individualization, it is a necessity. As Madeline Hunter[10] pointed out, the teacher must be free to help
adapt any individualized system to the needs of specific learners. David Husband[11] observed the same
thing regarding teachers functioning in a learning
resources center. Raymond Oliver,[12] in individualizing a math program, emphasized the teacher's role
in helping students, as did Glenys G. Unruh[13] and
Bernice J. Wolfson.[14] Wolfson indicated that the
teacher might be compared to a travel agent who helps
the student plan his trip through the learning objectives. Donald Overly and Jon Kinghorn[15] feel that
this change in role of the teacher may be the biggest
roadblock in the change toward individualization. He
points out that many teachers cannot think of their
role in education as that of a guide and diagnostician. They view their role as a determiner of educational goals and a dispenser of information.

Success in individualized instructional programs is related to adequate staffing. This help does not consist exclusively of "conventional" teacher-types. When a visitor walked down the halls of a school just a few years ago (indeed, in many schools today) and encountered a staff member, he could feel fairly certain that this staff member was a teacher, the principal, the janitor, or the school secretary. Today such certainty does not exist; the person may be an aide, a clerk, a technician, a learning specialist or consultant of some sort, or even a doctor or psychiatrist. The "general teacher" may become as strange a bird in tomorrow's world as the "general practitioner" of medicine is becoming today. A recognition of the diversity of skills called for in a mediated technological learning environment leads to the involvement of persons with a variety of backgrounds, training, and job assignments.

B. Role of the Learner

If the teacher is not to stand at the learner's elbow "cracking the whip," the learner must take increased responsibility for his own learning activities. He must develop a new sense of responsibility for mastering material without someone always telling him when he has done the work correctly and when he has completed the lesson. He must develop new patterns of self-motivation if no one is to be constantly at hand to tell him to "get busy." These changes often can be facilitated through arrangements for the learner to participate in decision-making about what he learns, methods for learning, and with what materials. The performance-objective approach contributes toward this end. Given precise objectives and alternate learning packages, the learner can be given the responsibility to select tasks appropriate to his needs. The teacher's role in this regard is mainly as an adviser. Authoritarian "handing down of judgment upon the learner" is quite inappropriate for an individualized instructional system where the learner is taking major responsibility for his own activities. Gene Cisco and Dick Lake[16] point out that students must learn to take responsibility for their own decisions in order to live in a democratic society. As the student broadens his ability to assume responsibility, he is able to move out in an individualized program in many

exciting ways. Dorothy Wright[17] described such a program at the high school level where students selected
their own topics, defined their objectives, planned
all study activities and other relevant factors.
However, as Arthur Costa[18] points out, the teacher
must be ready and available to assist in such decision-making. Most students are never completely free
of a need for guidance. At the primary level, this
need is especially true. Primary teachers working
within individualized performance-based settings have
often commented to this writer that their biggest
task is getting students to pay close attention to
mastering the lesson content, not just going through
the motions of filling in blanks, answering questions
in a rote way, or "role playing" the part of a student doing a lesson rather than mastering the content.
Criterion testing upon completion of performance
objectives by a student often catches learning problems too late. At that point, he may have too much
material to repeat in the process of picking up the
loose ends (or major learnings) he may have missed
the first time. The task becomes psychologically
overwhelming. He feels defeated, and does not want
to return to the task. When this happens, both he
and his teacher share a motivational problem. The
careful monitoring of student progress that individualized instruction provides helps to solve this
problem.

Traditional grading and other authority-based
evaluation systems appear to be inappropriate and
inadequate in a system where each learner is functioning on his own. Rather, the learner must be
accountable in a simple, logical and easily managed
manner for the successes and failures he experiences
day after day. Writers who deal with the question of
evaluation in individualized instruction all make the
same point: the authoritarian "passing down of judgment" upon learners is "out," and carefully documented profiles of achievement are "in." Writers
such as C. Watson,[19] William Gordon,[20] Edwin A. Read,[21]
and Cisco and Lake[22] all point out that letter grading is dropped completely in individualized programs.
In its place is a careful logging of progress based
upon frequent and constant contact between learner
and teacher. In other words, inherent in individualized instruction is the way we always wanted to teach
when we were concerned about assessing the progress
of the individual learner.

Writers such as Dean S. Mentzer,[23] Roger Tunks,[24] and Lucius Butler[25] all recount examples of students achieving reduced time and increased learning in their experiences with individualized instruction.   Butler told of increasing manyfold the number of students that could be served through the use of a self-instructional laboratory.   Mentzer cited a significant reduction in the time invested by learners, as did Tunks.   Many writers refer to the enthusiasm which learners exhibit who are progressing satisfactorily through an individualized program, due in large measure to the fact that the learners are not held back by the restrictions of synchronizing their learning with a large group.   They are able to change working rates at will.   There seems to be something intrinsically reinforcing about one being able to "charge ahead" in a manner appropriate to his motivation of the moment.

IV.   A NEW SYSTEM OF MANAGEMENT

If each learner is to progress through a pattern of learning experiences which are exclusively his, then the problem of management of those experiences becomes acute.   The best answer to the question of management seems to be one of providing for a systematic approach, a method of instruction where all variables are planned and accounted for.   Ideally, each student should have a plan similar to what most of us are accustomed to making for the entire group.

Such a systematic design does not imply that each learner's activities will be prescribed for him in detail.   Quite to the contrary, alternatives will be spelled out from among which he will be able to choose.   The responsibility for routing through a given content area becomes the student's, with teacher advice.   He also assists in recording his own progress.

One helpful device which is being brought to bear on the problem of management is the computer.   Of all the technological innovations which support individualization, no single tool has had more impact.   It is useful in a number of ways, but generally in one of two categories: (1) either as a tool for direct instruction, or (2) as a management tool wherein record keeping, testing, and scoring are done

on an automated basis. A great deal of writing
exists on the role of the computer in individualized
programs. An example of the kind of impact the computer can have on direct instruction is described by
Patrick Suppes and Max Jerman.[26] They tell of the
many uses for instruction that the computer may be
put to simply through the process of having students
learn to program it. In the management area, Gail
Baker and Isadore Goldberg,[27] William J. Moore,[28] Wesley W. Walton,[29] Arthur M. Suchesk[30] and Robert
Steffenson and Edwin Read[31] all describe methods and
techniques where the computer helps in the enormous
bookkeeping job that individualized instruction
creates.

    If the teacher is not to be the major informa-
tion-presenter, the level and variety of learning
materials must increase drastically. Information
must be organized and packaged in a way where learners can interact with it directly without teacher
participation. The materials and media employed must
be chosen upon the basis of instructional efficiency,
not upon sentimental or traditional favoritism.
Teachers too frequently have favorite, familiar, and
comfortable books and films which they use consistently in a course or unit. In converting to an
individualized structure, new criteria for selection
are called for. Media and materials may be classified according to several different kinds of characteristics such as visual, auditory, expendable versus
enduring, machine-dependent versus machine-indepen-
dent, available or not available to the student, and
a number of other factors. An excellent discussion
of these variables was written by Donald T. Tosti and
John R. Ball.[32]   These characteristics must be
matched with the communicative requirements of the
lesson content so that the student has a variety of
media to choose from according to his preferences and
learning style.

    In an individualized program, media management
procedures are needed which are learner oriented, not
structured for administrative convenience. Too frequently library books, textbooks, workbooks, film-
strips, periodicals, audiotapes, films, and other
media are organized for use in incompatible ways.
They may be located in different places, may be bor-
rowed according to different rules, and may be retained for different lengths of time. It is simply
not logical for a learner to go to several different

places in the school to obtain materials he needs for
a given lesson or project. Incredibly, in the typical school, he must conform to as many as four or
five utilization procedures applying to the materials
he needs simply because those procedures were set up
in isolation from one another at some prior time, and
by different administrative personnel in the school,
with no attention given to the question of learner
efficiency or convenience.

Baker and Goldberg[33] emphasized that one of the
most important requirements for implementing individualized instruction is the availability of a wide
variety of instructional materials from which the
learner may select. John Bolvin and Robert Glaser,[34]
in an assessment of the developmental aspects of
Individually Prescribed Instruction (IPI), emphasized
the same notion. Gerald C. Ubben[35] expressed concern
for high quality materials. There are many, many
materials available, but they must be screened to be
sure they are appropriate for students to use individually. And John I. Thomas[36] adds that the materials must not only be good but also appropriate for
the learning styles of the students. In this writer's experience, the most successful materials and
media management programs call for the materials to
be in the classroom as well as in the library. Students work in both places, going to the library when
special materials and equipment are needed.

Probably the greatest impact upon management
techniques for individualized programs has come from
the area of performance contracting and commercially
developed systematic programs. Some of these efforts
make no attempt to create or publish materials. They
only organize those that exist. Others make little
attempt to systematize but concentrate upon the creation of learning packages which deal with all of the
necessary factors for the individualization of a
single activity. Teachers are participating in this
latter thrust, as may be exemplified by the Hughson
High School (California) listing of Learning Activity
Packages.[37]   John E. Arena[38] discusses the development
of the Learning Activity Package, its structure and
use. He gives ten steps to consider in implementing
a program of individualized instruction. Unruh,[39]
Franklin P. Morley,[40] Hulda Grobman,[41] and D. L. Davis
and Paul W. Kirby[42] all discuss the broader topic of
Learning Packages, pointing out to various degrees
their basic components and how they are utilized

(including most of the factors for the design of
individualized programs which had been discussed in
this article). The creation of materials such as
Learning Packages provides a substance and focus to
the processes of individualization which seem to have
far-reaching implications for the success of such
ventures. One commercial endeavor which merits special consideration is Project PLAN, developed by the
American Institute of Research and the Westinghouse
Learning Corporation, as described by Donald Deep[43]
and Robert A. Weisgerber.[44] PLAN organizes content
into units called "modules." Each "module" is broken
down into Teaching-Learning Units (TLU's). PLAN's
greatest contribution, in the opinion of this writer,
is in the enormous job of organization which has been
done. With the exception of the TLU's, PLAN produces
few of the things needed in the program. But they
provide everything needed for students to do the
TLU's. When a school, or school district, contracts
for PLAN, they are buying, more than anything else, a
management system which includes all of the necessary
materials and management procedures needed to make
the system operate successfully. Record keeping is
done by computer. Although teachers working within
the PLAN system are freed almost entirely from the
job of presentation, they are very, very busy in their
roles as learning managers, dealing with the many
problems each of the learners encounters along the
way, and providing the necessary feedback to the
learners needed to keep them on the right track.

V. PROBLEMS IN IMPLEMENTATION

Although many examples of individualized instruction are available for examination around the
country, there is no universal understanding nor
acceptance of such procedures. While basic purposes
for individualization are common to most programs,
many variations for implementing such purposes are
possible. Because this aspect of the educational
enterprise is innovative, change will come slowly.
Acceptance will come as everyone involved gains familiarity with the principles and techniques, and as
the problems encountered along the way are solved.
Among the problems that are the most clearly identified at the present time are these:

A. Shortage of Materials. If the teacher is
not the major source of information, and if information is to be packaged so that the learner may have
access to it when it is needed, the materials of
instruction must not only be readily available but
also carefully arranged and accounted for. Teachers
who individualize instructional opportunities on
their own invariably have collected and arranged
large inventories of materials. Maybe they are extensive vertical files of clippings and other printed
matter filed by topic, or they may be shelves of
audio tapes each containing a lesson of some value to
the objectives of the class. The one independent
study collection many schools have had for some time
is the school library, but the typical library book,
without supplementary curricular material, too frequently fails to fulfill all of the basic requirements of an individualized study lesson.

Materials collections of conventional schools
fall short of providing the necessary foundation for
much individualization. Major steps must be taken to
acquire appropriate materials, to provide functional
storage and accessibility for them, and to develop a
suitable management system that facilitates learner
acquisition and utilization. Such steps require
money, new service programs, and the changing of tra-
ditions and procedures within the school. These are
large problems which are solved only with time, patience, and hard work.

B. Organization. Not only does individualization call for reorganization of materials programs
within a school but such a curricular innovation requires that the entire staff management plan and student scheduling procedure be modified.   Teachers,
students, and administrators all must relinquish
unnecessary group procedures and develop new ones
which meet the requirements of learners working by
themselves much of the time. No proven and universally applicable plans are available for direct
adoption. Experts who can be brought in to expedite
such reorganization are few and expensive. Communities must be included in plans for change. All these
problems add to the complexity of the problem and to
the length of time needed to find solutions.

C. Staffing Levels and Assignments. With the

exception of the unusually motivated and dedicated
teacher who arranges individualized learning opportunities at personal sacrifice, few if any such programs operate successfully with conventional staffing
ratios and assignments. More help is needed, as well
as persons with different skills, to deal with the
many new management tasks. Such staffing changes are
hard to arrange in school systems where staffing configurations and pupil-teacher ratios are used as the
basis for budgeting. Parents become uneasy when the
conventional role of "teacher" for their children
becomes diffused. Most importantly, it is especially
hard for teachers to adjust to the new configurations
because of the major reshapings of professional role
concepts and because of old patterns for teacher
preparation and certification.

    D. Dehumanization. There is a very real con-
cern for the loss of individual identity and creative
freedom in programs that would so organize education
that the participants (both teachers and learners)
would simply follow prescribed patterns. It would be
just as possible to design individualized instructional situations to tightly control and rigidly
organize the learner's every move to the same degree
found in more tyranically managed conventional classrooms of today. Even in an environment based upon a
predominance of reward rather than punishment, detailed prescription of learning activities could lead
to the development of learners who are automatons
rather than thinking and feeling human beings. In
this writer's opinion, such a tendency springs not so
much from curricular design--like large group or
individualized learning environments--but from management design: how the teachers and administrators
actuate the curriculum. It is not inevitable that
individualization must lead to automation. Quite to
the contrary, through the increased opportunities for
interaction of a learner with the teacher and other
learners, and through the necessity for increased
assumption of responsibility by the learner, the opposite is encouraged. Safeguards can be built into
individualized curricular designs through a de-emphasis upon precise sequencing of experiences, with
an increase among alternative courses of action, one
of which is to ignore all of the other alternatives!
In actuality, carefully devised and managed individualization, in combination with other methods of
instruction, can be much more humane than traditional

teacher-dominated methods.

E.   Social Isolation versus Interaction.   As part of the question of dehumanization, there is great concern over the lack of social contact which working with materials rather than people implies. It is logical that students who would interact exclusively via mediated contacts with his teacher would not only be deprived of the many human values accruing from interaction with one's teachers but also of the similar values related to peer involvement through classroom discussions and other activities.   The need for the social experience is a vital part of our educational system.   As cited above, it has already decreased due to the impact of the mass media.

Social isolation need not be a component of an individualized instruction design.   The contrary may indeed be the case.   In a technological, methodical approach to the problems of instruction, opportunities for social contact can be defined and built in just as surely as independent work sessions.   In fact, through thorough planning such opportunities may be better and more valuable to learners.   Rather than casual or unstructured interaction, groups of various sizes and makeups may be brought together with specific goals to fulfill.   Such activities would be scheduled at appropriate intervals to ensure adequate contact time.   Furthermore, the scheduling plan for both teachers and learners allows more opportunities (and greater necessity) for them to get together when problems arise or the learners desire a conference.   Sometimes teachers invoke "social distance" in their relationships with students if they are too pressed for time to get involved in personal problems or if they simply don't care to get involved. The new emphasis on the teacher as instructional manager rather than presenter makes such separation undesirable and inappropriate.   More communication between teacher and learner from time to time would not only keep teachers "tuned in" to the needs of their students but would also reduce learner frustration arising from failure in a task or an entire course.   For many students, school is the one place where opportunities to learn how to relate constructively to their fellow human beings exists.   Individualized instructional plans, which include group experiences of many kinds, can help in this need.

Summary and Implications

Moving ahead with the reorganization of educational experiences for young people which are tailored to their individual needs means a new role for both teachers and learners. The principal attraction of teaching will no longer be the opportunity to stand before groups of people and to expound within one's favorite field of scholarship. Rather, the teacher of tomorrow must be concerned first and foremost with the welfare and development of each individual student. While he still certainly must be expert in his field, or in the discipline in which he works, he will put his expertise to work in different ways, helping young people in their task of learning and "becoming," helping them to cope with the ideas and challenges with which he has worked and coped.

The learner will have a wholly new role to play, as an authority-based philosophy gives way to one placing greater emphasis upon the rights and responsibilities of the individual. He no longer will be free to rest contentedly within a system that makes most basic decisions for him and provides few alternatives in what, where, when, and how he learns. If the teacher must make drastic changes in his style, so must the learner. The change must occur in nearly equal measure on both sides. As the teacher gives up the reins of authoritarian control, the learner must be more prepared to accept responsibility for his own destiny. The learner, freed from the reins of conventional controls, may at the least know so little of what to do with himself that he wastes much time. To the more drastic degree he may become disruptive, destructive, or in other ways, a negative force both to himself and society. The change toward individualization must show an adaptation balanced between learner and teacher. If it is not so, the indivualized school fails.

The school of tomorrow with its individualized instructional programs will have a new level of humanistic emphasis, not the de-emphasis which so many who do not understand the impact of technology fear. No longer will the "average student" be the major focus for the teacher. No longer will the bright student need to endure endless repetition of materials he has already learned, or presentations that go ploddingly for his active mind. No longer

will the slow learner know years and years of frustration and disappointment from a learning system
that goes too fast for him, and knows only to put him
in "remedial groups" which continue to "help" him not
to learn again what he has already failed to learn.
The school of tomorrow must have redefined group
goals. The concept of continuous progress (fundamental to the notion of individualization) will replace the present lockstep grade level system which
operates so unlike the way students learn. The computer which may assign mass man a number, and in its
thorough way, certainly does not lose track of him,
is a neutral factor. Humans are responsible for creating its dehumanizing aspect.

The unavoidable weight of social and technological change cannot help but have a major impact upon
the school of tomorrow. Some of the premises behind
individualized instruction presented in this article
may seem a bit farfetched and futuristic at this
point in time, if for no other reason than for the
economic problems involved. However, with acceler-
ating changes in the world today, these premises in a
later analysis may prove to be rather moderate. Time
will tell.

---

[1]Robert F. Mager, Developing Attitudes Toward
Learning (Palo Alto, California: Fearon, 1968).

[2]Robert F. Mager, Preparing Instructional Objectives (Palo Alto, California: Fearon, 1962).

[3]Norman E. Gronlund, Stating Behavioral Objectives for Classroom Instruction (New York: The Macmillan Co., 1970).

[4]H. H. McAshan, Writing Behavioral Objectives:
A New Approach (New York: Harper & Row, 1970).

[5]Hughson Union High School, Learning Activity
Packages (Mimeographed list. Available through
Jerry W. Carpenter, Curriculum Coordinator, P.O. Box
98, Hughson, California 95326).

[6]John C. Flanagan, William M. Shanner, and
Robert F. Mager, Behavioral Objectives: A Guide for
Individualizing Learning (New York: Westinghouse

Learning Corp., 1970, four volumes).

[7]Robert Denby, "Independent Study Programs," English Journal (December, 1969): 1396-1400.

[8]Lucius Butler, "Self-Instructional Lab Teaches Communication Skills," Audiovisual Instruction (February, 1970): 55-60.

[9]Ronald Edwards, "At Lansing Community College: Audiovisual Tutorial Instruction in Business," Junior College Journal (May, 1969), 56, 58, 60, 62, 64.

[10] Madeline Hunter, "Tailoring Your Teaching to Individualized Instruction," Instructor (March, 1970): 53-63.

[11] David Husband, "The Auto-Tutorial System," Audiovisual Instruction (February, 1970): 34-5.

[12] Raymond Oliver, "Math--To Each His Own," Montana Education (April, 1969): 9-10.

[13] Glenys G. Unruh, "Can I Be Replaced by a Package?" Educational Leadership (May, 1970): 763-6.

[14] Bernice J. Wolfson, "Pupil and Teacher Roles in Individualized Instruction," Elementary School Journal (April, 1968): 357-66.

[15] Donald Overly and Jon Kinghorn, "Individualized Instruction," Ohio Schools (October, 1968): 35 and 43.

[16] Gene Cisco and Dick Lake, "The Learning Laboratory," School and Community (February, 1970): 17 and 28.

[17] Dorothy Wright, "Try a Quest," English Journal (January, 1970): 131-33.

[18] Arthur Costa, "Strategies for Developing Autonomous Learners," Audiovisual Instruction (October, 1968): 832-4.

[19] C. Watson, "Learning and Liking It," American Education (May, 1970): 19-22.

[20] William Gordon and others. "ImPALLA--A New Approach to Secondary School Language Arts," English

Journal (April, 1970): 534-39.

[21] Edwin A. Read, "Educational Practice and the Theory of Continuous Pupil Progress," Audiovisual Instruction (February, 1970): 38-40.

[22] Cisco and Lake, op. cit.

[23] Dean S. Mentzer, "The Audiotutorial Laboratory," Audiovisual Instruction (April, 1970): 29-31.

[24] Roger Tunks, "A. V. Media and the Performance Curriculum," School Shop (April, 1968): 81-3.

[25] Lucius Butler, "Performance Objectives for Individualized Instruction," Audiovisual Instruction (May, 1970): 45-6.

[26] Patrick Suppes and Max Jerman, "Computer-Assisted Instruction," National Association of Secondary School Principals (February, 1970): 27-40.

[27] Gail Baker and Isadore Goldberg. "The Individualized Learning System," Educational Leadership (May, 1970): 775-80.

[28] William J. Moore, "A Program for Systematic Instructional Improvement," Audiovisual Instruction (February, 1970): 28-30.

[29] Wesley W. Walton, "Computers in the Classroom: Master or Servant," National Association of Secondary School Principals (February, 1970): 9-17.

[30] Arthur M. Suchesk, "Remote-Access Instructional Systems Model for a Regional Occupational Center," Audiovisual Instruction (April, 1970): 47-50.

[31] Robert Steffensin and Edwin Read, "A Computer Program for Management of Student Performance Information," Audiovisual Instruction (February, 1970): 56-9.

[32] Donald T. Tosti and John R. Ball, "A Behavioral Approach to Instructional Design and Media Selection," Audio Visual Communication Review (Spring, 1969): 5-25.

[33] Baker and Goldberg, op. cit.

[34] John Bolvin and Robert Glaser, "Developmental Aspects of Individually Prescribed Instruction," Audiovisual Instruction (October, 1968): 828-31.

[35] Gerald C. Ubben, "A Look at Nongradedness and Self-Paced Learning," Audiovisual Instruction (February, 1970): 31-3.

[36] John I. Thomas, "Individualizing Instruction in the Social Studies," The Social Studies (February, 1970): 71-6.

[37] Hughson Union High School, op. cit.

[38] John E. Arena, "An Instrument for Individualized Instruction," Educational Leadership (May, 1970): 784-7.

[39] Unruh, op. cit.

[40] Franklin P. Morley, "The Commercial Package and the Local Supervisor," Educational Leadership (May, 1970): 792-3.

[41] Hulda Grobman, "Educational Packages--Panacea." Educational Leadership (May, 1970): 781-3.

[42] O. L. Davis and Paul W. Kirby, "The Package: A New Way of Life," Educational Leadership (May, 1970): 767-71.

[43] Donald Deep, "Plan--Educational Automat," Pennsylvania School Journal (December, 1969): 107-9.

[44] Robert A. Weisgerber and Harold Rahmkow, "Individually Managed Learning," Audiovisual Instruction (October, 1968): 835-9.

HOW YOU CAN INDIVIDUALIZE
INSTRUCTION--RIGHT NOW

Dwight W. Allen

1.   Time Waivers

These waivers merely permit flexible examination
or assignment deadlines. If we're going to individualize instruction, why does everything have to be
turned in on Friday at 2? It isn't really a big deal
to let some kids turn in their work the following
Monday or Tuesday--or a few days early. Isn't it
more important to find out what he knows rather than
what he knows on Friday?

School administrators are preoccupied with
organizational considerations. It's very convenient
for the organization to have everything turned in at
2 o'clock on Friday. I was guilty of that as a
teacher because I used to hate to have tag ends. It
wasn't that I minded so much the student turning in
the project late; it was the problem of putting the
project with the rest of the stack so I could eventually grade them together. It was just messy.
Let's solve the administrative problem as such and
not confuse it with teaching and learning. One of
many possible solutions is to have nonprofessional
personnel available to receive and sort them. To get
time waivers going suggest to your faculty members
that they systematically explore changing the pattern
of due dates to individualize instruction or let students select their own due dates within reasonable
limits for projects and for examinations. Eliminate
"surprise quizzes," which accomplish little more than
dramatizing the teacher as a formidable antagonist.

Reprinted from Nation's Schools, 81:43-47,
April, 1968 by permission of author and publisher.

2.   Cooperative Student Efforts

This approach divides student labor and leads to a cumulative effort on assignments or tests. Sometimes you can take incorrigible students who really produce virtually nothing on tests and convince them they're getting away with something if you let them work together. You're really not jeopardizing much if you pick five students who are likely to come up with an F on an examination and allow them to put their efforts together.

This won't work with everybody. Some students react well; some don't. But I think schools have to get over the notion that is firmly ingrained in them --that education is a unique and individual competitive effort. It is a little unreal to train students competitively to go out in society and perform cooperatively.

School faculties might want to say, in effect: O.K., let's each agree that at some time during the year we will try some sort of cooperative collaboration. And at the end of the year, we'll get together and share the results and see what worked and what didn't work and how we might want to push the experiment out a little further another time around. This is a simple way of injecting some substance into the faculty meetings.

3.   Exceptional Loads

Greater or smaller student loads can be determined by educational consequence as well as schedule feasibility. This is suggested, of course, by the flexible schedule itself, where the number of courses that a student takes is no longer determined by the number of periods in the day. Once you start planning schedules with 30 and 40 and 50 per cent unscheduled time for students, then you can do a lot of adding to schedules and make some of them exceptionally heavy. We find students doing this regularly and extensively already. Let's crank into our mental processes the possibility that a student can absorb seven periods of class in a six-period day. Once we admit this possibility, we can examine the merit of exceptional loads in a way we haven't before.

There's nothing immoral about giving a student double credit if he's bright enough to divide his time between two classes meeting at the same time. For the same reason there is nothing wrong with a student being allowed to take fewer subjects--or an unusual combination of courses that will make him more positive about school. Often "six classes in six periods" mentality comes from a fear of leaving a student on his own. Why shouldn't we?

4.   Variable Credit

Such credit could be predetermined. You might ask:

"Johnny, how would you like to take art for two units of credit instead of one? Or for a unit and a half credit?" Or perhaps you could say: "Johnny, go into the art class, and after you finish, we'll figure out how much credit you get." That shouldn't be so revolutionary, but it is. At one school using flexible scheduling with a very flexible and wonderful teacher, a student was sort of poking his nose in the art laboratory. She invited him in. In a minute he started looking longingly at a piece of clay, and she asked: "Want to make something?" And after he got it made, he wanted to know if he could fire it in the kiln. Then he glazed it and got it all done, and he said, "Can I get credit for this?"

Well, now, we can't give students credit for something that they've already done! Books that are read over the summer don't count for book reports. But this teacher said: "O.K. That's about six weeks' worth of work. If you add such-and-such and such-and-such you can have one credit in art."

What's wrong with variable credit? Why can't we say, instead of "You've failed," that "You only get six week's worth of credit," or "one semester of credit for a year"? This would be a primitive but tentative step toward the definition of badly needed performance criteria.

5.   Roadblock Removal

Here the object is to define total procedures to
minimize a student weakness. For example, we know
that Johnny doesn't write very well--maybe we could
allow him a report that is dictated rather than written.   Lots of students have their own tape recorders.
Why shouldn't a student dictate his report, if he'd
rather--particularly if he has already demonstrated
conclusively his lack of ability in writing.   Another
alternative would be to take a student who has a ter-
rible time with grammar--who always comes out badly
"in writing."   You know in advance how he's going to
do on an assigned written project, and you also know
you can't remedy his grammar and spelling.   Why clob-
ber this student over the head again and again with
failure?   Wouldn't it be nice--think of the morale
boost--to assign an English teacher to work with him
on his report and edit it before it was turned in.
Put the English teacher on his side.

6.   Partial Participation

This is based on an agreed reduction in objectives and credit.   You can say to a student: "O.K.,
instead of getting a full year's credit in junior
English, if you only want a semester's credit, we'll
work out which of these objectives you don't have to
meet."

The temptation, of course, would be to do it in a
standard way--to say: "Anyone who doesn't want to
get a full unit of credit may skip these seven assignments."   But then, you're right back to the same
spot again.   The point is to get individualization.
Negotiate with the student.   Ask him: "What would
you like to leave out if we reduce the credit a little bit?"   And let him tell you.

7.   Multiple Teacher Assignments

Let more than one teacher help the same class or
the same student.   The arrangement can vary from consultation to complete multiple class participation.
Everybody knows that different people can learn from

different teachers in different ways. It can be very
valuable to have a student sit in on the same presentation given by two different teachers. It's one way
of getting at individualized instruction to say to
Johnny: "All right. You'll listen to a discussion
of positive and negative ions as explained by Miss
Jones, and then listen to Mr. Smith make the presentation."

Or--you know from last year that Johnny barely
got through ninth grade English. Your prediction is
that he will fail tenth grade English this year.
That means he may have to take tenth grade English
over again. And because English is required every
year for graduation, we finally wind up with some
kids taking English 10, 11 and 12 as seniors. If
that's a reasonable assumption, it may be a good idea
to assign some students to two tenth grade classes
simultaneously.

Let's have this as an option. If there are students who are having difficulty with a course, let
them sign up twice for that course. And if you're
concerned about credit, double the credit. We have
credit to burn in schools--we are shorter on learning.

8. Student Selection of Teachers

This isn't profound or novel; in some schools
it's done. For some students, we gain a motivational
advantage if we say to them: "All right, pick your
poison--Miss Smith, Miss Brown, or Mr. Jones."

Let students switch around if they want to. If
I get tired of Mr. Jones, let me go in and be bored
by Mr. Smith for a while. Maybe even keep track of
how it goes--that's called research.

9. Exceptional Sequences

In some cases, we should be able to waive prerequisites. The results might surprise you. Professor McDonald and I did an experiment in programmed
learning at Stanford University some years ago that
was terribly embarrassing.

We had a 32 frame programed learning program--a
research game that was well written and a lot of fun
to play. We knew we could control learning just the
way we wanted to. Then we said, let's see how bad
learning can get; let's have some students study this
program--but not in a carefully coordinated, logical
order. Logically we started out by telling them all
the information they needed--the name of the game,
the size of the board, the shape of the playing
pieces, and the basic moves. But we shuffled these
up for the test case and put them in random order.
The first frame told the students when they had to do
a forced capture. They didn't know the name of the
game, the playing pieces, how to move, or anything
else.

What were the results? They learned even better
than with our logically developed program. I think
it was quite presumptuous of the students to louse
up our results that way. But there they were, defy-
ing the logical nature of the development of the curriculum. The elementary social studies curriculum is
pretty much in the same boat. They start with the
child, and no one can argue with that. Then they go
to the neighborhood and the community and the state
and the nation and our Western neighbors and the
grand finale in the sixth grade is "our neighbors
around the world."

The trouble is, my kindergartner has been to
Puerto Rico and he hasn't been to the firehouse. The
tight light logic of progression that we have is
often nonsense. What confidence do we have that our
prerequisites are the right ones? In some schools
they are so silly as to define Art I as being art
that is taken by a freshman or sophomore, and Art II
as art taken by a junior or senior. What a wonderful
performance criterion that is.

What do you suppose would happen if we allowed
a student to take geometry before he had algebra?
What might happen if a student took chemistry as a
sophomore or a freshman, before he had the mathematics to cope with it? Maybe we could combine
another technic of individualization and let one of
the juniors or seniors tutor him in the math when he
gets stuck. When he got through as a senior, I wonder if this student would know less or more chemistry
than if he had taken it the standard way as a junior.

We could even allow for the fact that this would make chemistry two years more remote from graduation --but that shouldn't bother us because after six to eight weeks the retention is·down to about the 20 per cent level anyway, and it can't fall off much more than that.

Do you really know what would happen if you allowed freshmen to take the senior course in government? This needn't be assigned on a wholesale basis, but as a technic for individualizing or even to provide us with information on the real consequences of a particular set of prerequisites and their violation. What do you think would happen if we allowed kids to take two courses in the same sequence simultaneously? For example, algebra and geometry. I submit that if you let students take algebra and geometry together, not much would happen--at least for some students-- except the teacher would be traumatized.

10. Late Entries or Drops

Why does everything have to start in September and end in June? Along about the 15th of November, why can't we collar a student or two, and say: "Let's throw away your program and plan a new one. You can change anything that you want. Now that you've seen things for half a semester, what would you like to do differently?" Most students would be so aghast at the suggestion they wouldn't know how to deal with it. Likewise, if a student is doing poorly in a course in May, let him drop it. I'm not convinced we gain anything by putting failures on a transcript. A nonentry is eloquent testimony enough that he hasn't learned a course yet. Maybe there's a motivational tool here we haven't been using.

11. Routine Incompletes

Why not start a policy that would require the elimination of all borderline grades? Any time that a grade was on the borderline, the teacher can't give it. Instead of flipping a coin between a B- and a C+, the teacher should be required to get additional evidence. Have a tie-breaker.

Or have some sort of a standard incomplete
option. Encourage students to depose the regimen
with some agreed consequences. If a student says,
"I don't think I'm done with this course," say,
"O.K., you're not done; we'll give you an incomplete.
You tell us what you're going to do to complete it
and then we'll tell you what we'll do about the
grade."

He'll say: "I need a B in this course, because
it's a college course, and so far my grade is a C+."
We say: "Fine, if you don't want a C+, we'll give
you an incomplete instead. Now let's work out something that we can mutually agree will be a demonstration of sufficient competence to warrant the B."

12.   Substitute Assignments

Give students set performance criteria and allow
them to select alternative instructional procedures
to accommodate individual preferences. One reason
educators didn't get to this notion earlier is because it is built squarely on performance criteria--
knowing what the end is, knowing when we're done.
One big problem of education right now is that we
don't know when we're done. We have no way of knowing when a student is finished. If we could identify
performance criteria, if we could pinpoint what an
assignment is trying to accomplish, we would be able
to substitute assignments routinely.

My experience as a teacher--and here I'm citing
intuitive evidence, not research evidence--has always
been that whenever I allow students to pick their own
assignments, they usually pick more than I could
assign them. That's part of this idea.

13.   The Open Transcript

Why not revise performance reports the way you
would the chapters in a book? Think of the transcript not as a document that is compiled in February
and June, but as a document that reflects the current
state of the student's knowledge or even just "high
water mark" rather than the arbitrary designation of
that knowledge. I study algebra for a while and I

learn C's worth. If I want to come back and demonstrate later that the C's worth has changed to a B's
worth, I can substitute B for C. Still later that B
can be erased and made A. Any entry on the transcript would be considered temporary until the student left school. Who cares whether this happens in
September or February or May? It would be interesting to see if we doctored the transcript whether that
would produce a more accurate prediction of college
success than does the arbitrary transcript we now
use.

14. Lesson Alternatives

Allow students to provide alternatives to the
standard fare. The student says: "I know I'm not
very good at literature--but could I write some extra
poetry?" Or, a student says: "I hate to write short
stories. Could I do an extra book report?"

15. The Tutor-Course Option

This will work when we have genuine performance
criteria. Right now, in most schools, if you get an
A in Language I, you can go on to Language II. If
you get a B, you go on to Language II. If you get a
C, or D, you go on to Language II. But with an F,
you return to Language I; no credit and you repeat
the same course.

And yet we know that kids who get C and D in
Language I are doomed to failure in Language. How do
we defend an attrition rate in a language program
that often reaches 90 per cent? Seems to me that we
need to invent a Language 1 1/2, where students who
get C and D have a chance to get their performance
level up to an A or B in Language I. Then send them
in to Language II, and we can predict they will succeed. Once we get the performance criteria better
established, the tutor-course option will become a
much more significant part of the instruction and
grading in the school.

PART SIX

OPEN EDUCATION

For many years the self-contained classroom has
been the main environmental setting for children in
education. The fundamental instructional unit has
consisted of one teacher with one class of twenty-
five to thirty pupils. Presently, new developments
are taking place in school construction with the creation of large open spaces which can house the equivalent of several classes with different age levels.
These large areas provide added flexibility for both
student and teacher. By assigning students from two
or three grade levels to an open area, the teacher
can better meet the needs of youngsters who have
similar problems. Teachers are free to work with
varying size groups ranging from large ones to individual tutorial sessions.

Another aspect of open education is the increased focus upon the learner in the teaching-learning process with the teacher acting as a guide and
counselor, rather than a "giver of knowledge."

Advocates of open education hold that the added
flexibility not only provides for variations in instructional patterns, but also increases the opportunities for teacher-teacher, teacher-pupil and
pupil-pupil interaction.

Those who express caution are concerned that
traditional patterns of teacher-pupil interaction
which are found in self-contained classrooms would
be lost. Open education is one of the most creative
and dynamic forces in education today and it will be
interesting to follow its effect upon teachers and
pupils during the decade of the seventies.

Spodek introduces this part with an overview of

open education. Because of the failure of the
schools to provide for individual differences among
pupils, American educators have been seeking alternatives to traditional education. The author reviews
the British Infant School and discusses American
models of open education. The underlying assumptions
and the role of the teacher in the open classroom
setting are analyzed.

Ellison begins her article with an analogy between the one-room school and open education. She
then identifies two broad movements: one is toward
education as science or technology, while the other
is toward humanistic or affective education. The
author points to the difficulty of establishing educational goals within a new structure such as open
education. Nevertheless, she does identify three key
objectives. The first is the development of a
healthy self-image. A second task is the sensitivity
to readiness which the teacher must develop to bring
the child together with the subject matter at the
right time. The third is to replace extrinsic motivation for learning with intrinsic motivation. She
concludes the article by stating that the development
of a program in open education requires much dedica-
tion, hard work and willingness to try new instructional strategies.

In the next article Heyman discusses the factors
which are unique to the British system of open education. He states that there is little need for a uniform curriculum because of the qualifying exams which
serve as a screening device for higher education.
The Headmaster in the British system has usually been
trained in the classics and is primarily a teacher,
not an administrator. Another variable is the relatively formal relationship between parent and child
in the early childhood years which tends to make open
education easier to develop. In the British system,
learning is emphasized over teaching, independence is
stressed, and there is respect for the individual and
his abilities rather than uniformity of standards and
achievement. Because of the above differences between British and American systems, the author tends
to be pessimistic regarding widespread adoption of
open education in this country, unless a massive
effort is initiated to change the entire structure of
our present system.

The feasibility of whether or not open education

can be applied to the American system is presented in
the last article.   The background of this plan is
discussed; what constitutes an open classroom; the
theoretical basis for such a program; and criticisms
leveled against open education.

ALTERNATIVES TO TRADITIONAL EDUCATION

Bernard Spodek

A number of signs on the social scene have suggested that public education in the United States is
in a crisis state. Indeed a recently published book,
critical of public education and written by Charles
Silberman, is titled Crisis in the Classroom.[1] The
author characterizes American schools as dull, life-
less institutions which oppress children. Others
have used similar characterizations during the past
decade to describe American education.

From the time we began to press for universal
education as a social goal, we in the United States
have had problems in the schools--many of them problems of fit. When schools were designed for a small
minority of the population, any child who couldn't
conform to the school's expectations was simply expelled. If he didn't fit the school the problem was
with him, not with the school--so we let him go somewhere other than to school--home, or to work.

When schools serve all children, however, the
problem of fit becomes a more crucial one. By law a
child cannot be easily expelled, and the failure of a
child in school carries with it dire consequences.
Given the seriousness of the crises in American
schools, a number of alternative approaches to schooling are being suggested.

Some suggest that the problems of the schools

Reprinted from Peabody Journal of Education, 48:
140-146, January, 1971 by permission of the publisher.

[1]New York, 1970.

stem primarily from their sponsorship; the schools created by members of the majority group in society can never be sensitive enough or responsive enough to the needs of members of minority groups. Those who take this position, many times blacks, American Indians, or Spanish speaking citizens, often advocate the establishment of community schools--schools run by and for small elements of the larger society.

Others suggest that while public education as constituted today is unresponsive to the needs of children, the way to increase responsiveness of schools is to look outside the educational establishment for school sponsors. We are seeing the involvement of private corporations in providing educational service, these corporations suggesting that they can do a better job of educating children than can public institutions.

The concern for the failure of schools has also led to the creation of solutions relating to the content of education. A number of educators are suggesting that the way to solve the problems of the schools is to more narrowly define goals and to teach more directly to these goals in a more controlled fashion. By controlling goals and educational encounters, it is suggested that the educational needs of children can be matched more closely with the educational opportunities provided. Examples of these kinds of educational thought can be found in the advocacy of programmed instruction or systems such as Individually Prescribed instruction.

Other educators concerned with the failure of the schools reject this approach to educational reform. They see this solution as offering more of the same in a more systematic way. They suggest that the structure and content of educational experience needs to be changed if schools are to succeed. While no one particular approach to education may be fitting for all children, possibly a range of educational models ought to be provided for children. There is no reason why a school system could not support a number of alternatives within its confines. One of these alternatives that seems to make sense to a number of us has been characterized as Open Education.[2]

---

[2]Anne M. Bussis and Edward A. Chittenden, Analysis of an Approach to Open Education (Princeton, 1970).

The British Infant School

Twice in recent years I have been to England, visiting some of the most vibrant, vital educational programs to be seen anywhere: British Infant Schools. These are schools for children ages 5, 6, and 7. The most exciting of these schools have moved to a program characterized by what we call Open Education.

When visiting an English school, one first becomes aware of its organization. Many of the classes are family grouped; children of two or three different ages are in the same classes. The time schedule is also different from that of American schools and, apart from special times like lunch time and time for the use of the hall or multipurpose room, there may be no periods. Instead there is an integrated day. Many different subjects are taught or activities held at the same time, with the children working individually or in small groups; the teacher seldom lectures to all of them, but weaves in and out of groups helping children learn in their own fashion.

The class may be organized into interest centers. In each center materials, supplies and equipment are provided for the children's independent use. There will be a reading center, a math center, a play center, and other centers as well. Each room will be different and each will represent the interests and styles of the teachers and children who live in those rooms.

The mode of learning is an active one. Academics are being taught, but children are inquiring rather than being told. Play is seen as a legitimate mode of learning and the purposes of the children are taken into account in planning for learning.

Each child is considered an individual. Children aren't expected to be involved in an activity because it is the thing for fives to do. If a five-year-old is ready to read, he may. If he is not, well, he has another year or two to learn. Learning takes place as a result of expression and children are always encouraged to write, paint, draw, act, or dance--modes of expression that are used to move the child's level of understanding forward.

Nor is the teacher to be considered to be the

only instructor in the class. With as many as forty children under her tutelage the teacher learns to use other resources. Assignment cards extend the teacher's instructional role. The other children in the class also find themselves in the role of teacher. For children easily learn from other children, and teaching an idea to others is an aid to understanding.

American Models to Open Education

To attempt to superimpose an English institution on an American community would be foolish. Rather American models of Open Classrooms need to be worked on. At the early childhood level it often means breaking down artificial barriers that get in the way of children's learning. Some of these barriers relate to time, and traditional classroom schedules may be eliminated. Some of these barriers relate to activities or subjects, and learning activities may be developed in an integrated fashion. Some of these barriers relate to expectation, and teachers must reject age-grade norms as determiners of programs and begin to look at specific children, making classroom decisions based on their judgment of what each child needs.

Some of these barriers relate to institutional structures. The walls between some classrooms may be taken down to facilitate openness, or ages may be mixed in self-contained classrooms. Some schools have moved towards nongraded primary units. Others have developed integrated kindergarten-primary classes. An elaboration of the idea can be found in a recent pamphlet, published by the National Association for the Education of Young Children and titled Open Education.[3]

Assumptions Underlying Open Education

Open education is difficult to define. It does not adhere strictly to any single dogma. There is no single organizational model that it characterizes.

---

[3]Bernard Spodek, developer, Open Education (New York, 1970).

It does not narrowly define either the behavior of teachers or the behavior of children. It can best be understood in terms of the assumptions underlying it and the mode of decision-making used within it.

In open education learning takes place as a result of an individual's encounter with his environment. This assumption suggests that conceptually oriented education requires an active mode, especially for young children. The child develops understanding by observing things and thinking about them. Verbalizations take place after the child encounters reality and are never substitutes for experience.

Another assumption is that learning is not linear. Programmed instruction is a caricature of school organization. We slice up learning into a number of bits, assigning each bit to a grade level to be mastered sequentially. We assume that if a child has not mastered an early bit of learning, he will fail in later learning.

In an open educational environment there is no single way to master a concept or learn a skill. A single educational goal can be achieved using many avenues and, as a matter of fact, a child may be moving towards the mastery of a single concept from a number of different paths at the same time. Individual learning style is as important in determining instructional methodology as the definition of goals.

A third assumption underlying open education is that expression is a source of learning. In most traditional classrooms children are viewed primarily as receivers of learning. The teacher is the prime sender, using audio-visual devices or demonstrations as ways of telling children (Vincent Rogers calls it sneaky telling).[4]

In an open classroom there is more than inquiry learning taking place. Children will use arts and craft activity, movement or dancing, creative dramatics, the writing of stories, or the retelling of experiences as sources of learning. Out of expression grows understanding and these activities are given prime importance in the classroom, not relegated to Friday afternoons.

---

[4]Teaching in the British Primary School (New York, 1970).

A corollary of this assumption is one that states that feelings have a legitimate place in the classroom. It is impossible to express ideas without expressing feelings. These expressions of feelings are accepted as natural in the classroom and, while the teacher doesn't attempt to sweep feelings under the table, she also does not attempt to explain away all expressions of emotions or serve as a child therapist.

A final set of assumptions relates to children being viewed as competent, desirous of learning, and trustworthy. Many of the older views of children suggest they will learn only when they are somehow prodded from the outside, as if the natural state of children is to be inactive. This just is not so. In natural settings, children are always learning without being prodded either by external rewards or by external punishments. Few infants need to be given M&M's to learn to walk or talk, for example. It is only when the purposes of the adult are antagonistic to the purposes of the child that controls in the form of rewards or punishment must be given. When children's purposes are given legitimacy the activities have their own rewards.

If children are considered incompetent, then their activities need to be carefully controlled. As incompetents, others who are more competent must make all decisions for them. Error must be avoided and there is no way to correct oneself except by recourse to an external referee.

Decision-Making in an Open Classroom

As a result of the assumptions upon which open education is based, a new form of classroom decision-making is created. One finds that the old dichotomy between child-centered and adult-centered classrooms does not hold for open classrooms. These are not classrooms where children are allowed to "do their own thing" while the teacher acts as referee. Rather teacher and children both have major contributions to make in the decision-making process.

Educational decisions in the open classroom are not handed down from above. The activities of the classroom are jointly determined by teacher and child

as a result of a continued series of transactions.
The content of the field determines the goals and
parameters of the classroom learning environment.
Children's interests and competencies determine the
starting point of activities. Standards are maintained and they are high enough to be achieved while
requiring a certain amount of stretching from each
child. Learning is valued and progress is assessed
continually. What the children do in school provides
evidence of what they know and what they have yet to
know.

Teaching this way requires a continually progressive reorganization of the classroom. Teachers
need to be aware of the goals of instruction while
maintaining a flexibility in achieving these goals.
Teachers need to be constantly concerned with providing the resources needed for children to learn. Instead of finding new ways of telling things to children, teachers need to provide the class with experiences, things and people that will help children
explore areas of knowledge and help them to abstract
concepts and understanding. Teachers also need to
look for new ways of organizing themselves and the
learning environment and of keeping track of what's
happening to children. All this requires new techniques of teaching.

Teaching in an open classroom is a difficult
assignment. But then most worthwhile activities require effort, especially at the beginning. Teachers
may feel very unsure of themselves when they attempt
to do without textbooks. They may be extremely concerned about the learning of skills. They may not
trust children. It is easier to control the behavior
of children than to worry if the child will do what
you want them to do when you let him be free.

While there are difficulties there are also great
rewards. Discipline problems seem to diminish in an
open classroom. It is as if we create the discipline
problems in children by the way we organize schools.
Teachers can relax more since they are not in front
of the class acting (indeed there is no <u>front of the
class</u> in these classes), and their relations with
children are more vital and meaningful. They are
getting to know children.

Requisites for Teaching in an Open Classroom

Teachers need to know themselves and their children better if they are to teach in an open manner. They must begin to explore their own values and beliefs and to see the degree of consistency or inconsistency between beliefs and behaviors. They must provide legitimate ways to express feelings in the classroom.

As we work towards the establishment of open educational opportunities for children, we find a number of unresolved questions. Open education is difficult to define; because it is not an absolute it is hard to grab hold of. One must really talk about classes that are more or less open rather than classes that are open or closed. The difficulty with the definition of open education results in difficulty of description. Because the differences seem to be in the ideas that underlie classroom pactice and the nature of decision making, it is hard to spell out how such a class would look. Multi-age classes and open area schools may be quite closed and self-contained classrooms relatively open.

Another concern relates to the transmission of ideas related to open education. The language is easier to transmit than the behavior. Teachers may talk about open opportunities for children while actually maintaining prescriptive classrooms. Talking about education is not enough. What is needed is a way of communicating educational behavior.

Finally we come to the problem of evaluation. How do we know what we are really doing, how well we are doing it, and what the consequences of our actions are for children? Traditional evaluation procedures cannot really test the effectiveness of open education, for we have no good objective measures of the quality of expression, divergent thinking, or problem solving. This is an area that must be attacked in the near future if open education is to be made available to school children in any large numbers.

The kind of educational program we provide children is basically a function of our beliefs about children and about mankind. One cannot believe that children should be respected and still provide programs that show disrespect to children. One cannot believe that children should be trusted and yet provide programs that do not allow children independence of action. One cannot believe in the freedom of mankind and still provide educational programs that allow no freedom.

The basic qualities of trust, dignity, and freedom are as important in the development of human beings as are the skills of reading, writing, and arithmetic. Nor do these sets of educational goals need to be antagonistic to one another. It seems to me that the most important role of the teacher is to create a classroom atmosphere where children can learn academic skills and learn to be human and humane as well.

OPEN EDUCATION . . .
NOT FOR THE TIRED OR THE TIMID

Martha Ellison

From the moment the child is born, his activity
is willingly, even eagerly, directed toward learning
--about himself, his world, the people in that world,
how to communicate with those people who make all
those noises and act in certain ways as a response to
certain noises, how to get satisfaction of basic
human needs. The only boundaries of his learning are
those necessary for his health and safety, those imposed by a severely limited environment or, unwit-
tingly, by overly-conscientious parents.

Only when he enters school does his learning
meet arbitrary boundaries. Suddenly, learning is
circumscribed within certain spaces--sometimes as
small a space as his own desk. Suddenly, learning is
timed by the clock, and he must "put away the live
turtle to get on with the textbook science lesson
about crabs."

Suddenly, learning is work, for which he is rewarded with playtime, even though at the intuitive
level he must know that he often learns many useful
kinds of things through those activities that are
labeled "play." He also learns early that play means
fun, joy, physical movement, intellectual exercise,
and, most often, sharing with others.

If work is the opposite of play, by what emotions and activities is it logically characterized?

Reprinted from Kentucky School Journal, L (February, 1972, 17-20, by permission of the publisher.

Could this dichotomy have any bearing upon the fact that so many people view their work as drudgery, to be suffered through, and fun as a reward they earn in proportion to their perception of their suffering?

The open classroom does not distinguish between work and play. It recognizes that "play is a child's work" and that, through play, he learns concretely many of the things he is not ready to learn abstractly.

At whatever level it exists, open education extends the learning environment beyond the classroom, the pod, or even the campus, to include more of the real world. It enriches that environment by offering more choices or avenues for learning.

It says to children: "Come and find pleasure in learning, each in your own time and in your own way. We will guide you when you need guidance, help you when you need help, and trust you to become increasingly competent in making decisions and choices for your own and the common good. You will make many mistakes, but from them too you will learn."

Many people say the open classroom is like a one-room school; there are many similarities. My grandmother--and perhaps many of yours--had her limited education in a one-room school. The environment was not rich in books or hardware; but, partly because of the paucity of resources, my grandmother was forced to travel many avenues to learning.

Sometimes, she received rigorous formal instruction from the teacher; at other times, she worked independently. Occasionally, she had to seek help from older children; frequently, she reinforced her own learning by helping younger children.

The teacher--with 40 children ages 5 to 14-- could not be all things to all children. He, somehow, knew better than to try to be. He could only get the youngsters started in the right direction; then he remained sensitive to their needs for special help-- which he arranged for if he himself could not provide it. By today's standards, this was an impoverished educational environment; I am not suggesting that a return to such an environment would solve the ills of education.

What I am suggesting is that it accomplished one important goal we may have lost sight of as we have gained sophistication in other realms. It placed a great deal of responsibility on the individual stu- dent--not only for his own learning, but for that of others. Thus, at sixteen, my grandmother was con- sidered by herself, by her parents, and by society as mature enough to marry, to run a household, and to rear children--and she proved that she was.

We--society--delay the end of adolescence until the mid-twenties for great numbers of our youth. Meanwhile, we make their decisions for them (or try to)--in the schools, and in the homes--and we bear the responsibility for the consequences.

Suddenly, we say, "Now go and be an adult." Then, we wonder why so many do not seem to want the responsibilities that go with the comparative freedom of adulthood.

What would happen if we deliberately refocused much of the school experience on the development of skill in decision-making? What kind of person would emerge at the end of schooling if, at each step, he had been forced to assume a larger portion of the responsibility for his own learning and for his own behavior?

Proponents of open education in its broadest sense would say that the person who would emerge would have a better feeling about himself, be more self-directed, and be better prepared to assume a meaningful adult social role.

In addition, because he would have had experi- ence in identifying and managing much of his own learning, he would be more likely to continue learn- ing--with pleasure--as this marvelously "kooky" world continues to shift and change like a kaleidoscope propelled by perpetual motion--going ever faster, and never again showing any promise of slowing down.

For those who are attracted to the assumptions, goals, and methods of open education, the cautions are many. They abound in the literature of our pro- fession. Certainly, all educators are not likely to become disciples of open education tomorrow; nor should they.

Two broad movements are underway simultaneously in American education; on the surface, they seem to be antithetical to each other. However, those who seek beneath the surface will find that both movements start with the same hypothesis, and meet again in common agreement at the goals level. Both hold that free public schooling will become more effective when and if we begin to pay more than lip service to the goal of individualizing instruction.

The conflict, then, is basically a semantic one: What do we mean by <u>more effective</u> education?

One of the identifiable movements is toward education as <u>science or technology</u>. Under this broad umbrella lie such comparatively recent phenomena as behavioral objectives, performance criteria, systems approaches, computer-assisted instruction, computer-managed instruction, programmed instruction, instructional designs, management by objectives, storage and retrieval systems, and on and on. Many and loud are the cries that such paraphernalia are antihumanistic --that they threaten to turn our schools into assembly lines, our teachers into robots, and our students into pre-molded products processed along a 12-year assembly line by the robots.

The question is not whether we <u>use</u> the advances in science and technology for the purposes of education, but <u>what use</u> we make of them. If they become --as a result of our own fuzzy grasp of what we are about--the ends rather than the means, then there is indeed justification for indignant outcries. But, let them be directed inwardly--at ourselves--for our failure to remind ourselves that human beings put up a perverse resistance to the kinds of processing that airplanes and other machines undergo quite willingly.

The counter movement--or at least the movement viewed by many as antagonistic to attempts to make education a <u>science</u>--is, of course, the upsurge of interest in and programs addressed to <u>humanistic</u> or <u>affective</u> education, or, in short, to <u>education as art</u>.

Art--by its very nature--resides primarily in the affective domain. It is true that the language of any art becomes--in time--precise and formalized, so that its intellectual message can be more readily and widely understood.

Thus, we have color, line, form, rhythm, movement, and tone as speaking components of all of the arts--dance, drama, painting, sculpture, literature, and music. These carry a message to the intellect of those who know the language; but the way in which these elements come together to speak to the emotions is the final criterion by which we determine what is truly artistic and what is merely artful.

We ask, "What does this work of art mean?" out of intellectual curiosity. We ask, "What does it mean to me?" out of the deep need to internalize it emotionally, to be involved personally--at the most human level--with the personal expression of another human being.

The most recent trend--toward education as art-- is in the direction of arranging all of the components or elements in the child's schooling in such a way that he is not only intellectually involved, but that, in addition, he has very personal, positive feelings about that involvement. If we view education as art, we use the intellectual language of the various disciplines or subject areas to serve a larger goal than cognition: To bring about a productive and harmonious interaction of human beings in the learning and living endeavor which we call school.

Many people call one significant aspect of this latter movement by another umbrella term--open education.

Because we tend to latch onto new terms quickly, before their meanings become denotive rather than connotive, the term open education brings to mind many kinds of concurrent and related developments on the educational front: Free schools, new schools, alternative schools, open-space schools, open-campus schools, integrated day, informal education, and the open classroom. Although each of these terms tells us that someone--somewhere--is substituting new methods for traditional ones in some school, none of them tells us much about the changing goals which have mandated the changes in method.

For example, open education is a description of strategies for goal attainment, rather than a description of the goals themselves.

What, then, are the goals that give impetus to this movement? Have the old, established goals of education been tossed out, or merely rearranged in accord with new priorities?

One time-honored educational goal which has been elevated to high priority status by open educators is that each child shall come to think of himself as a worthwhile individual who can contribute meaningfully to his fellows.

The self-image each of us holds of himself is, in large part, a reflection of the image others hold of us. If I am viewed by important others (teachers, parents, fellow students) as a failure, I begin to think of myself as a failure, and I become unwilling to try new tasks that demonstrate and reinforce my sense of failure.

Certainly, no one ever intended the traditional organization of the school to become an instrument to sort youngsters into the "I can do's" and the "I can't do's." Yet, who will deny that this has been the general effect of the graded curriculum, with promotion or retention dependent upon traditional norms, and with instruction centered upon what is needed at the next level, rather than upon the immediate needs of each child?

In most open schools, the child is neither graded--in the sense of A, B, C, D, E--nor graded as to level--first, second, third, etc. Instead, he moves at the pace comfortable for him at a rate commensurate with his level of maturity and his experiential background for the learning task at hand.

He is not held back as an "I can't do," nor shoved along to widen the gap between his ability to perform and the performance expected of him at a particular grade level. His peer group may be broadly defined in terms of age, but they share with him a stage of readiness for certain types of learning.

Another high priority goal of open education is to help each child become a self-directed, willing, and, ultimately, an independent learner. Certainly,

the most effective strategy for attainment of this
goal seems to be to involve the child, quite early,
in making many of his own educational choices and in
managing some of the learning situations that arise
because of those choices.

In the open school, children find themselves, as
they move along their own continuum, increasingly
responsible for choosing, from a rich environment,
those experiences that speak clearly to their individual needs.

The teacher's role--and it is a much more difficult one than that in the traditional classroom--is
to structure the learning environment in such a way
that the child not only wants to do that which he
needs to do, but also finds the resources and the
adult guidance he needs to pursue the activity. In
other words, in the best open classroom, the activities the child needs to engage in (as judged by adult
standards) are seen by the child as needed, and are
further seen by the child as appealing.

Another task that takes on added significance
for the open classroom teacher is to be alert to each
child's readiness for structured learning in the various subject areas, and to help him move--at his
moment of readiness--from the exploratory behavior he
has been allowed, into a willing encounter with
learning of the skills, concepts, and information
integral to the subject.

This sensitivity to readiness on the part of the
teacher does not burst into bloom automatically as a
result of his training or because of his intention to
be sensitive. It grows--slowly but surely--in the
fertile milieu of a classroom brought alive by children freely exploring, investigating, and inquiring
among many kinds of resources and among themselves.

It comes about as teachers gain experience in
thoughtfully observing children at work and play, in
groups and independently. It comes about from quiet
exchanges between a single teacher and a single child
about something both view as important. It comes
about from time-consuming development of the highly
professional skill of diagnosis.

It results in bringing the child in contact with

the subject at just the right moment. The sensitivity to readiness is part of the art of education; the
prescription of the right materials for the right
content at the right time is part of the science.

Another goal of the classroom is to replace extrinsic motivations for learning with intrinsic motivation. We move in this direction when we eliminate
competitive grading, and encourage cooperation among
students. Another strategy for reaching this goal,
again, is to multiply the chances for success within
the school setting.

Each child brings with him to the school situation something he can do which makes him feel good
about himself. Too often, we minimize this competence or talent, and concentrate on remedying weaknesses. Holt refers to this as failure to "support
the powers of children." The open classroom recognizes the value of strengthening special talents,
abilities, and interests in children, and provides
the time and resources to do so.

It is, perhaps, an act of faith to assume that,
if a young person feels really good about his success
in one area, he eventually will be more willing to
dig in and struggle with another area in which he
does not feel so confident. Yet, who among us has
not at some time said to himself, "I know I can do
this if I try hard enough, because I already have
proved that I can do that?" So saying, we grit our
teeth and force ourselves to learn how to do a new
and difficult thing.

Such a willingness to tackle arduous or seemingly impossible tasks is peculiar in adulthood to the
kind of person who is self-confident, self-directed,
and, to a high degree, self-actualized.

By supporting the powers of children--that is,
by providing constant reinforcement of positive feelings about themselves--we help them gain psychic
strength for the intellectual and physical tasks they
find most difficult.

Thus, if Johnny finds it necessary or wishes to
work all of a particular day on a science experiment
he can conduct with ease and assurance, he may be
allowed to do so in the open classroom, with the

faith (usually justified in experience) that tomorrow
he will not only be more willing, but also more ready
for his next reading or math or social studies task.
At that time, he may be helped by the teacher or
another student, or he may be allowed to work independently on what other children completed the day
before.

Within the traditional classroom, order is
achieved in several ways--by seating arrangements, by
time schedules, by rules regarding movement and noise
within the room and beyond. Such arrangements do
indeed make it easier for a teacher to deal with a
group of youngsters as a unit.

Amazingly, many students learn, fairly quickly,
to sublimate their needs as individuals to the operational mode for the unit, to be still and quiet when
the clock and place and teacher say "worktime," and
to be noisy and animated when the clock and place and
teacher say "playtime."

To the suggestion that such behavior is not natural for children, we perhaps can answer that it is a
part of the socialization process and therefore "good"
for the young. The charge we have difficulty answering is that maximal learning does not occur naturally
in a teacher-clock-space dominated environment.

Those teachers and administrators who are discontent with the status quo, and are seeking ways to
bring about positive change, may want to take a
closer look at some of the existing programs in open
education as one of their alternatives. Across the
state of Kentucky and across the nation, elements of
openness are appearing--in the use of time, in the
use of space, in greater curriculum choice, and in
less rigid patterns of grade or age grouping.

Whether a school should try to effect comprehensive change rather quickly, or make small changes
gradually, depends not only upon the courage of the
school leadership, but also upon the community's
faith in that leadership to know what is best for the
children and youth of the community. Some of the
most dramatic failures in efforts toward open education have come about because of a lack of staff and
community involvement in exploration and planning
stages.

If, at this particular moment in history, open education seems to be the educational model most likely to prepare children well for tomorrow's world, then we can begin to demonstrate to the public--through gradual changes where these are indicated--that openness need not be synonymous with anarchy or chaos; that the school is not abdicating its role in giving children more responsibility, but subtly redefining the role for an unfolding drama quite different from that of yesterday.

Once in a while, one can stumble upon a demonstration of open education--unnamed and unheralded--in the classroom of a single teacher in a traditional school setting. You know that the attitudinal set essential to open education is present when you go into a non-authoritarian classroom where children are happily caught up in many different types of work-play activities--all going on simultaneously with the teacher somehow knowing and obviously caring about each activity and its effect upon each child's needs.

You may even find the same teacher working with an individual child in setting behavioral goals for that child--or helping another recycle himself through a multi-media learning pack or an instructional program provided by computer.

The science and the art of education are not antagonists in a good open classroom. Each is called upon when needed for a specific learning situation. The teacher's role is to know what is needed at this moment, and for which child.

The first requirement for a good program in open education is a teacher who is a welcome and frequent guest, if not a resident, of Olympus. It is not for those who are nostalgic for yeasterday and fearful of tomorrow.

AND IT IS NOT FOR THE TIRED OR THE TIMID.

LEARNING FROM THE BRITISH PRIMARY SCHOOLS

Mark Heyman

The newer British primary schools have been much
praised by American observers, and there is now available a significant and growing literature on the subject (1). As the years pass, more educators and journalists are going overseas to see for themselves.
There is little doubt that the ideas now coming from
Britain will have an impact on education in the U.S.A.

Just what are we learning from the British experience? One cannot question the factual accuracy
of the reports, but many, if not most of the conclusions drawn from these reports may be misleading.
Are we in danger of losing the value of another educational experiment, of not learning from the twenty
or more years of significant achievement in the British elementary schools? This possibility should not
be surprising, for we often struggle with the significance of educational innovations within our own
borders. In the present case, the cultural gap and
the physical distance present formidable barriers to
full understanding.

Perhaps the lessons we have to learn from the
British primary schools are not the lessons usually
seen. Perhaps the significance of the primary
schools is even greater than the most glowing enthusiasts have suggested. If we have been misreading
the British primary school either by drawing the
wrong conclusions or by underestimating their significance, or both, we are obliged to pay even closer
attention to British education than we have been.

Before turning to the conclusions that are

Reprinted from The Elementary School Journal,
72:335-342, April, 1972 by permission of author and
publisher.

usually drawn by and for Americans, it is useful to review the standard picture of the new British primary schools as that portrait is being developed on this side of the ocean.

As the usual description has it, the classroom in the new British primary school has no desks for children, no furniture bolted to the floor. Instead, light tables and chairs are arranged as activities require. Often there are semi-permanent learning centers providing special areas dedicated to modes of inquiry or selected subjects, such as mathematics, science, books, and crafts. A child does not have a fixed workspace, though he has a place to store his personal materials. The teacher rarely talks to the entire class, which typically has more than thirty-five members and occasionally more than forty. Instead, the teacher directs the children in tasks or projects, on which they work in small groups or as individuals. The teacher is free to walk about helping one group, then another. Or he is available for student requests for assistance. In general, the room is bustling with activity. Silence is as rare as interaction between the teacher and the entire class.

Small schools

Some classrooms have only one age level, but often the new primary school mixes age groups, a practice called "family" or "vertical" grouping. Or the children share teachers; "team teaching" is an American term coming into wider use in England. Or both techniques may be followed. In "the integrated day," the pacing of activities is not regulated by fixed time periods, but is varied and flexible. With family grouping, team teaching, and the integrated day--not all schools use all or any one to the same extent--the management of a school would be exceedingly complex, but the schools are small (generally between 250 and 350 children) so that flexibility, joint efforts, and the sharing of facilities and equipment are possible.

The head

Another feature of the primary school that draws the attention of foreign observers is the function of the principal, the "Head." Because the staff is small--it may have only eight or nine--the Head is able to work closely with each teacher. It is also possible for him to know all the children, and he can teach without shirking administrative tasks. One reason why he has less administrative work than his American counterpart is that he has the sole authority to determine curriculum and methods of instruction, which he usually does with staff participation. Schools are visited regularly by professional representatives of the Local Education Authority and the national Department of Education and Science, but the Head is not accountable, except in general terms, to outside direction. The inspectors and advisors are experienced former teachers who are respected and listened to. Frequently, they conduct workshops in which teachers from several schools can share ideas.

The physical aspects of the school afford additional insights into the educational program. The schools have a wealth of educational materials, including purchased equipment, donated apparatus (perhaps wheeled toys, rugs, and upholstered furniture), and natural and cast-off materials brought in by teachers and children. The resulting richness of the environment rivals that of schools in our most affluent districts.

The buildings

The buildings, as in the USA, are of a variety of ages, but many have been built since World War II in designs appropriate for the current programs. In the new schools, one large room, the Hall, is multipurpose. It can serve as a lunchroom, as a gym, and as an activity room for large groups, for music, and for movement (a form of interpretive exercise). Most rooms open directly to the outdoors, and there are several outside activity areas, more than one with play equipment. Arts and crafts are pursued in several classrooms, but there is also a separate room for crafts, pottery, and other messy work. There is probably cooking equipment somewhere, and various

rooms have sand tables, water tables, and other apparatus. Occasionally there is an outdoor wading pool,
usually built by parents.

A school may have a separate library, but there
are also books in many classrooms; the variety is
great, and multiple copies of a title are rare.
There are few scheduled times for reading and writing,
because the British regard reading and writing as
skills that should be acquired largely through the
pursuit of other activities, not as subjects to be
studied by themselves. Recognizing the relationship
between spoken and written language, the schools encourage talking rather than silence. Reading problems are rare, and the quality and quantity of writing impresses most visitors. There appears to be
merit in an approach that assumes that "reading and
writing are better learned when they are not taught."
A similar philosophy influences the primary-school
attitude toward many aspects of mathematics, though
often "maths" is studied for itself.

In summary, then, the school seems, to the American observer, to be a place of activity and a place
of learning; children generally like primary school,
and few "turn off." In the infant schools (ages five
through seven), the contrast between kindergarten
"fun" and first-grade "schoolwork"--a contrast that
is common in the USA--does not occur. And there appears to be more satisfaction and less frustration
among British teachers than among American teachers.

So much for the facts. What are the conclusions
that observers usually draw from this picture?

Start with the classroom

The key is the frequent use of the words "open"
and "informal" in descriptions of the British primary
classroom and its educational philosophy. Despite
warnings by some of the reporters about oversimplifi-
cation, the idea has come from England that informality is the critical characteristic of the new British
primary-schools. In addition, the work of contemporary critics of American education--such as Paul
Goodman and John Holt, who perhaps are often read
superficially--has served to support the "open classroom" and "informal education" interpretation of the

British schools. Charles Silberman's encyclopedic
Crisis in the Classroom (2) almost makes "informal
education" the only possible solution to our problems
in education. Finally, such powerful reporting as
Herbert Kohl's 36 Children (3) and his concise manual,
The Open Classroom (4), encourages the teacher and
the prospective teacher in the USA to see his own
efforts in the classroom (particularly in abolishing
traditional formality) as critical in the current
reform movement. As Joseph Featherstone says, in
concluding his significant 1967 series in The New
Republic on the British primary schools: "In the end,
you always return to a teacher in a classroom full of
children. That is the proper locus of a revolution
in the primary schools" (5:45).

This analysis appears to have been adopted by
many critics and reformers, and by many teacher
training programs in their efforts to contribute to
the reform of American public education.

Start with the system

In my view, the British experience teaches otherwise: the revolution in (or the evolution of) American education must occur in a larger arena, in "the
system." The introduction of informal methods, classroom by classroom, is not going to spread reform
throughout the vast American education enterprise.
Reform will not come by this method because the conditions for change that exist in the British classroom do not exist in the American classroom.   To
justify this viewpoint, let us briefly re-examine
education in the new British primary schools.

There can be no dispute about the fact that the
British classroom is unlike the American classroom.
In England, classrooms are activity rooms where projects are pursued, usually in small groups. The
teacher directs the class by encouraging children to
pursue their interests within a wide range of opportunities that the environment supports. (The pupil-
teacher ratio is high, but there can be much individual and small-group instruction because there is
little or no instruction of the class as a whole.)
The room is organized for activities, not for "instruction." It looks like a workshop; everything in
it has been brought in to help the children do their

work. The immediate environment of the building--and
more distant places--are used to provide an even
broader range of opportunities.

To understand this educational approach, and why
it works, it is necessary to consider some aspects of
the historical and cultural background of British
primary education.

The British background

Although England has a much older culture than
we do, compulsory education came later there. Because of the national examination system (now undergoing major changes) which guarded the portals to
higher education and to the type of secondary education that leads to higher education, there has been
little interest in developing uniform curriculums or
a mandatory program at the elementary-school level.
Furthermore, the assumption is widespread that, in a
civilized society, one knows what children should
learn, particularly if one is a professional concerned with children's education. Under these circumstances, it was possible for compulsory elementary
education to develop in a manner in which the teachers in each school, directed by the head teacher,
make the decisions about curriculum and methodology.
In this decentralized system, the discovery and development of successful techniques flourish for the
reason that Featherstone (and others) have noted:
learning in school occurs at the point of contact
between individual teachers and individual children.
Furthermore, the British are pragmatic, and their
social science theory relevant to education, particularly psychology and sociology, has never been so
weighted with data as ours has been. Not only did
this stance allow them to learn and apply successfully more of John Dewey's philosophy than we have,
but it also permitted them to learn from Piaget
decades before we paid much attention to him. They
were influenced by the "giant in the nursery" when
his reports were based on data from only a child or
two. A sharp contrast between what is regarded as
theory in the two countries can be seen in educational textbooks. Those in the USA are frequently
formidable analyses, while British textbooks are
generally brief surveys of the contributions of a few
major theorists, such as Bruner, Froebel, Piaget, and

Skinner, and interpretations of their ideas for
classroom use.

Administration

Another significant difference between the elementary school in Britain and in the USA is the difference in attitudes toward administration in the two
countries. Many British administrators in government
are trained in classics or other seemingly irrelevant
areas, and many English students who want a good
business administration degree look to graduate
schools in the USA. With this approach to administration, it is not surprising that the principal of a
British elementary school is primarily a head teacher,
not an administrator, a nonteacher. He functions as
the educational leader of his staff; his major concern is the educational program in his school, not
administrative or clerical responsibilities, or reports to external authorities. He knows the children
in his school, and he knows his teachers.(The size of
the school makes this possible.) Promotion to Head,
usually preceded by service as Assistant Head, is a
recognition of talent for teaching and for leadership
among teachers; the assignment is not "a promotion
out of teaching."

The national culture

Significant, too, for education is the difference in cultural homogeneity between the two countries. The Anglicization of immigrants has never
been a task of more than a minority of the British
schools; many of our schools have been concerned with
the Americanization of waves of newcomers and their
children. With foreign immigration reduced sharply,
our schools are now grappling with cultural disloca-
tions resulting from large internal migrations, especially to and within metropolitan areas.

Because of these important characteristics of
the British educational system and of the national
culture, informal education has developed in the primary schools and has succeeded in promoting children's learning. The new British elementary schools
promote the ability to work independently and in

small groups, the ability to accomplish research, and the acquisition of specific skills needed in further education, particularly reading and writing. Because children pursue topics that interest them, they want to acquire the skills needed to answer their questions. The school is structured and endowed so that assistance is readily available and the child develops his potential to a high degree in a relaxed environment free of stress.

In summary, the British are creating an elementary education system with many of the characteristics we seek: the emphasis on learning over teaching, the development of independence, and the fostering of creativity. They are building a system of elementary schools based on respect for the individual student and his abilities and aptitudes, rather than on uniformity and standards of achievement.

To repeat, the British have been able to develop informal education because their system encouraged this development. This, in a nutshell, is the major lesson of the new British primary schools.

For the USA, this conclusion suggests that changes in the individual classroom, made room by room, while good for the few children involved, are not likely to spread (or even be maintained) unless changes are made in the structure of the school. In addition, a lone informal classroom may have unintentional effects that are not beneficial for the children in it. The sociologists who have examined education, from Willard Waller to Edgar Friedenberg, tell us that one of the best-learned lessons in school is the value system of the school. If a teacher "gets away" with his different methods (often working behind a closed door and under pressure to conform), what do children learn about schools and about education? Perhaps the children will learn that a lone fighter can sometimes win, even if it takes diligence and skill. More often, however, the children learn that it does not pay to buck the system--especially if the teacher is (or feels) harassed or, as is not unusual, if he is forced to compromise his principles or give up the good fight.

If we had wanted to adopt the significant characteristics of the newer British primary schools, instead of focusing on the informal class, we might have looked at other--equally significant--features.

(We obviously did not look at class size!)   Rather
than adopting the philosophy of "the open classroom,"
we might have tried to relieve principals of paper
work and allowed and encouraged them to be educational leaders and change agents, working closely
with teachers and children.   We might have tried Paul
Goodman's ideas on small schools, breaking our larger
ones into reasonably sized subunits.   We might have
given more curriculum decisions to teachers instead
of developing better "teacher-proof" uniform curriculums.   That we narrowed in on the "free" or "open"
classroom and informality was probably inevitable.
We saw, among all the characteristics of British elementary education, those that are most traditionally
American, even if not typical of American schools.

Schools have settings

The conclusion that may be drawn from this analysis of our attempts to understand and absorb the
implications of British experience is that we have to
examine systems of education and the social environment of schools, not simply classrooms.   The current
approach of applying some aspects of the British primary schools in not likely to be productive.   We need
to deepen our examination of the British experience
and pay more attention to cultural background and the
social environment.   Few reports of the British experience, for example, have been concerned with the
nature of the parent-child relationship in England.
Is it possible that the more formal British home
develops attitudes and behavior in the preschool
child that make the informal approach of the school
possible?

The need remains for American observers and
critics, teachers and journalists, and others concerned with education to take another look at the
British primary school--and the system and the culture within which it functions.

NOTES

1.   See especially:
     M. Brown and N. Precious.   The Integrated Day in
     the Primary School.   New York: Agathon Press,

1970.
J. Blackie. Inside the Primary School. London: Her Majesty's Stationery Office, 1967.
J. Featherstone. Schools Where Children Learn. New York: Liveright, 1971.
A. Hertzberg and E. Stone. Schools are for Children: An American Approach to the Open Classroom. New York: Schocken Books, 1971.
G. Howson (editor). Children at School: Primary Education in Britain Today. London: Heinemann Educational Books, 1969.
C. Murrow and L. Murrow. Children Come First: The Inspired Work of the English Primary Schools. New York: American Heritage Press, 1971.
V. Rogers. "English and American Primary Schools," Phi Delta Kappan, 51 (October, 1969), 71-75.
V. Rogers (editor). Teaching in the British Primary School. New York: Macmillan, 1970.
J. Taylor. Organising and Integrating the Infant Day. London: George Allen and Unwin Ltd., 1971.
L. Weber. The English Infant School and Informal Education. Englewood Cliffs, New Jersey: Prentice-Hall, Inc., 1971.

Also useful is the new series of twenty-three slim paperbacks, "Informal Schools in Britain Today," published in 1971 and 1972 by Citation Press of New York City for the Anglo-American Primary Education Project, a joint venture of the Schools Council in England and the Ford Foundation. Some of the titles in the series are Environmental Studies; Evaluation of Achievement; From Home to School; Informal Reading and Writing; Mathematics for Older Children; Mathematics for Younger Children; Music; Recording Children's Progress; Space, Time and Grouping; The Head-Teacher's Role; The Pupil's Day; and Towards Informality.

2. C. Silberman. Crisis in the Classroom. New York: Random House, 1970.

3. H. Kohl. 36 Children. New York: New American Library, 1967.

4. H. Kohl. The Open Classroom. New York: Random House, 1970.

5.   J. Featherstone. <u>Schools Where Children Learn</u>.
New York: Liveright, 1971.

OPEN EDUCATION: CAN BRITISH
SCHOOL REFORMS WORK HERE?

Recently, American educators have been crossing
the Atlantic to take a look at what's going on in the
British infant schools and returning with some glowing reports and appeals to imitate them in this country. The infant school, with its stress on developing initiative, creativity and critical thought
processes in children, meets modern educational demands far more effectively than the traditional
American school, they contend.

To a surprising extent, the British school advocates have won a highly receptive audience in this
country. Within a very short space of time, adaptations of the infant school approach to elementary
education have been cropping up in scores of U.S.
classrooms from isolated farm towns in North Dakota
to Harlem neighborhoods in New York City. In America,
the infant school approach is referred to as "open"
or "informal" education. And lately it has been the
focus of some widespread attention from administrators, teachers, parents and school reformers who see
it as a way to improve learning possibilities in the
elementary school.

The approach is based on a new body of research
and theory on how children learn--notably the findings of Swiss psychologist Jean Piaget and recent
child development research. It discards the usual
classroom set-up and the traditional teacher and student roles for a freer, more informal and highly
individualized learning experience.

Although there is a world of difference between
the British infant school model and American schools

Reprinted from Nation's Schools, 87:47-51, May,
1971 by permission of publisher.

working with "open education," characteristics common to both are:

Decentralized classrooms divided into separate "learning areas" for math, reading, etc.

Freedom for children to move throughout the classroom, work together, and choose their own activities. Children from different grades frequently grouped together.

Teachers who work mostly with individual children or groups of two or three, while the rest of the children work on their own or with an aide.

A very rich classroom environment designed by the teacher, which offers a broad mix of resources.

British infant school background: The design for restructuring classrooms along these lines was one developed by a group of reformist British educators working in that country's infant schools--schools for children aged five to seven. Long before Piaget and other experimental psychologists added their insights about children's cognitive development, these educators' own observations supported what child development research now confirms about children's learning patterns: Namely, that children learn in different ways, at different times, from things around them which interest them, and from each other. And that children learn best when sparked by their own interests. In response to these observations, over a 50 year period, many of the infant schools have reorganized their classrooms, loosened curriculum requirements, and eased schedules to allow for a freer response to individual patterns of learning.

Since World War II, the reforms initiated in a scattered group of infant schools spread widely throughout England and have since been embraced by approximately 70 per cent of that nation's public infant schools and nearly half the junior schools (enrolling children up to age 12). Now that they have turned up in a number of U.S. elementary schools as well, the big question is: Can the British reforms work here?

Judging from the interest and support that the approach is generating in many parts of the country,

a number of U.S. educators think they can, despite
some formidable obstacles.

Schoolmen in New York and Vermont are seriously
considering introducing open education for the early
elementary grades on a statewide basis. In North
Dakota, where more than 10 per cent of the elementary
school children are attending "informal" open classrooms, the concept has swept across the state like a
January blizzard.

Teacher training, advisory services, and model
classroom adaptations of the British style are being
funded by the U.S. Office of Education and the Ford
Foundation. Study teams from American school districts, colleges and universities have been beating a
steady path to British schools over the past two or
three years, and British educators with infant school
experience are in great demand as advisors to new
American programs.

The Plowden Report, a 1967 document of Great
Britain's Central Advisory Council, which offers per-
suasive evidence of the effectiveness of the infant
school reforms, has become required reading for innovative educators in this country.

The most widescale attempt to introduce the British practices into American classrooms is a project
of the Educational Development Center (EDC), a federally assisted research lab based in Newton, Mass.
EDC serves as advisor and resource center to nine
school systems from Burlington, Vt., to Rosebud,
Tex., which are experimenting with open education in
more than 80 "Follow Through" classrooms. Also,
helping considerably to promote a national interest
is Charles E. Silberman's best-seller, Crisis in the
Classroom, in which he points to open education programs around the country as the most promising alternatives to the "grim," "joyless" and "oppressive"
scene he found in many traditional elementary schools.

The open classroom: While there seems to be little
uniformity among the open classrooms in the U.S., a
visit to any one of them, as Silberman also points
out, is nearly always a "disorienting" experience for
those used to formal schools.

Open classrooms don't look like classrooms at

all, but more like workshops divided into "learning areas" or "interest areas" for various subjects--generally math, science, reading, language and art. Often these are inviting nooks and corners, partitioned by cardboard tri-wall or pegboard room dividers and furnished with well-worn sofas, mattresses, rugs and lounge chairs, as well as tables, desks and workbenches. Corridors or extra rooms are used along with classrooms for an inestimable variety of activities that often include carpentry, ceramics, pottery-making, weaving, typography, photography, sculpture, cooking and sewing. Doors are open and children move around freely, working together, on their own, or in small groups with a teacher.

The over-all learning process appears to be casual, random and spontaneous.

Curriculum is flexible and interdisciplinary--with an interpenetration of various subjects, skills, and activities. Youngsters might be involved in math activities, writing and learning about science in making booklets on plants and animals, for example, or in reading, writing, spelling and drawing when they design and build carpentry projects.

Family or vertical grouping, which offers opportunities for children of different ages to work together, is another common practice. This grouping aims at capitalizing on the fact that children learn from each other, thus increasing the number of "teachers" in each classroom. Open classroom advocates say that younger children are motivated by a learning environment that includes older youngsters already involved in reading, writing and math work.

The environment: Within the open classroom, a child is free much of the time to choose his own activities. But as education writers Ronald and Beatrice Gross point out, "whatever choice he makes, he will be confronted with a wealth of opportunities for exploration and discovery. In the math section is everything he can use to measure and figure, including Cuisenaire rods, balance scales, rulers, and a stop watch, workbooks and counting games . . . similar riches await him in the language arts section where he can read, make a tape recording or type, write, play word games . . ."

The key to much of the learning that goes on in an open classroom grows out of the projects and experiences in which the child engages in response to the environment. In open education, the Montessori dictum that "things make the best teachers" is applied in full force--although the "things" available to children in open classrooms are much more wide-ranging than the strictly didactic materials found in Montessori schools.

While some classroom programs operate with a profusion of commercial materials, many others, such as Lillian Weber's OPEN DOOR project in New York City schools and various "Follow Through" classrooms, put the emphasis on improvisation with natural and home-made materials.

The Educational Development Center has published a 76-page set of guidelines* for open classrooms offering teachers and administrators a wealth of ideas for general classroom equipment and materials which can be obtained free or very cheaply in most communities.

As the EDC guide points out, the hardest job is investing these kinds of materials with meaning. The open classroom asks the teacher to invent multiple meanings, interpretations and learning uses for materials she might never have imagined working with in a conventional classroom.

Teacher's role: The role of the teacher in an open classroom is to serve as a facilitator or guide to learning for each child in her class. She is responsible for providing stimulating environment, materials, motivation, guidance and assistance. She works with individuals and small groups, helping youngsters to set goals and achieve them, posing questions, and diagnosing each child's progress. The emphasis is on teaching children how to learn--on motivating them to work on their own, dig for information, test out ideas, and solve problems. The goal: helping children to become independent thinkers who are self-propelled and continuing learners.

_____

*Copies of the "Instructional Aids, Materials and Supplies Guidelines" for open classrooms can be obtained free from the Educational Development Center, 53 Chapel Street, Newton, Mass. 02160.

Obviously, the approach asks a good deal of a teacher. For one thing, it requires a very radical shift in what she thinks education should be. For another, it asks her to throw out a lot of conventional wisdom about teaching: that learning goals should be identical for each child, that a teacher preplans and schedules the time and work for her students, and that specific times must be blocked out for presenting specific subjects.

The shift to an open classroom, most experts agree, means more work for a teacher, not less. For one thing, it is far more difficult to guide subtly, than to teach overtly. For another, the personal involvement with each child is much greater--and more time-consuming.

Teachers are asked to keep detailed and accurate records of what each child is learning and to plan for each student daily or weekly.

Although the best and most sophisticated open classrooms may seem to the casual visitor to provide an overly permissive setting for youngsters, they are also the ones in which teachers are fully in charge. Teachers expect responsible behavior and ground rules are well-defined. Antisocial behavior which interferes with other children's work is not tolerated. Children are expected to work together and with their teacher on the housekeeping duties--cleaning up and storing materials in their proper places.

While there is no abdication of adult authority, there is a conscious attempt, as one open classroom teacher put it: "to create an atmosphere of mutual respect . . . The rules are still there, but how a teacher enforced them is different."

The key word is respect. Along with most open education advocates, New York State's Commissioner of Education, Ewald B. Nyquist, puts this attitude of teachers at the heart of the approach:

"Respect and trust for the child are perhaps the most basic principles underlying open education," Nyquist told schoolmen recently.

Teachers begin, he went on, with "the assumption that all children want to learn and will learn, if the emphasis is on learning and not on teaching, on each child's thinking processes and not on rote skill acquisition, on freedom and responsbility rather than conformity and following directions."

Theoretical basis: If trust and respect are the heart of the approach, the intellect that makes it all plausible is Jean Piaget's. Piaget is the Swiss child psychologist whose research on how young children learn has been widely interpreted in connection with open education and whose theories provide the strongest part of its pedagogical base.

In essence, Piaget says that children learn over varying periods of time, in repeated encounters with concrete experiences, and in exchanging points of view. His message is very clear--that it is a waste of time to tell a young child what he cannot experience through his senses. The majority of young children, according to Piaget, grasp abstract concepts much more slowly than adults realize and the pattern for abstract thought, used in mathematics, for example, must be built on layers of direct experience: seeing, hearing, touching, and smelling.

For example, in one of Piaget's classic experiments, he found that if a given amount of water is placed in a flat saucer and then poured into a tall glass, most children said the amount of liquid had changed. It took both time and experience to get them to understand this wasn't really so.

Piaget's observations, says one EDC staffer, point strongly to the conclusion that: "Good pedagogy must involve presenting the child with situations in which he himself experiments, in the broadest sense of that term--trying things out to see what happens, manipulating things and symbols, posing questions and seeking his own answers, reconciling what he finds at one time with what he finds at another, and comparing his findings with those of other children."

Only after a good deal of these kinds of experiences is the child ready to move to abstract conceptualization.

In the framework of Piaget, open classroom advocates argue, quite persuasively, that most traditional classrooms--in which children are confined to

their desks and continually told to be quiet, in which
teachers "talk" and books are the basic instructional
media, and in which large group instruction is the
rule--are largely ineffectual settings for learning,
and often severely restrict children's intellectual
development.

But although Piaget's work has provided some
invaluable new insights for educators, nothing that
his advocates in the open classroom have to say about
reforming the schools is very new at all--nor is it
alien to American educational tradition. Some of the
basic reforms--and certainly the philosophy--espoused
by open educators were central to the progressive
movement in the U.S. during the 1920s and 30s under
the influence of John Dewey. In fact, one of the
chief objections that Americans raise about open education has a historical perspective. They argue that
the same kinds of reforms were tried in U.S. schools
during the progressive era and found lacking.

But that view misses a very fundamental point.
Most experts agree that progressive education never
got off the ground in U.S. public schools.

As Dr. Nyquist explains: "There was a great deal
of rhetoric about growth, personality development,
creative self-expression, and the importance of the
individual in the progressive schools, but little
basic change in the methods of teaching or understanding of learning . . . the underlying principles
of the philosophy were distorted in the implementation by classroom teachers. The important role of
the teacher as organizer of the environment, manager
of time, space, materials and guide in the learning
experience was neglected or misinterpreted."

Criticism of open education: Up to now, opposition
to open education in this country has tended to focus
on two or three important questions, raised by educators and parents alike. One common objection comes
from those who view the freedom and stress on individuality and creativity in the open classroom as an
improbably romantic conception, out of touch with the
harsh educational demands of today. To put it blunt-
ly, the question asked most often is:"Will anybody
learn to read, or are the kids just happy painting
pictures?"

This, of course, is the crucial question. As Dr. Sol Gorden of the Center for Urban Education points out: "In the climate of our times (demands for accountability, militant community preoccupation with control of the public schools) no educational program will survive--no matter how exciting its ego-enhancing and humanizing aspects--unless it teaches children to read, write and do arithmetic at functional elementary school levels."

So far, the available evidence indicates that open classroom children progress normally in reading and arithmetic skills as measured by standardized tests. There are also some indications of an increased desire to read and write among these youngsters and of higher scores, on the average, in math comprehension.

These are actually striking results its advocates contend, since traditional classrooms concentrate almost exclusively on reading and arithmetic skills the first two years, while open classrooms accord them equal status with activities like painting and playing with blocks.

While there is little pressure in the British schools to measure academic gains, there is here. Like many other educators, open classroom theorists feel that standardized tests are obsolete and agree that the problem is to create some alternatives. Currently, the Educational Testing Service is at work developing tests to measure the kinds of gains the open classroom focuses on: original thinking, creativity, problem-solving, independence.

Another serious argument against open education comes from critics who feel that it doesn't realistically prepare children for life. Many parents worry that the open classroom might handicap a child if he goes on to a more rigid school where teachers are far less solicitous of his feelings and spontaneity may be regarded as a behavior problem.

Open classroom advocates argue, on the other hand, that the self-confidence and independence children in their classes are likely to develop will stand them in good stead anywhere, and that most youngsters are much more adaptable than most parents think.

Besides, says Dr. Nyquist, if educators and parents are thinking about preparation for life, "we have to realize that education must prepare children for work that may not even exist today and whose nature cannot even be imagined. . . . This can only be done by teaching a child <u>how</u> to learn and teaching him to initiate his own learning."

There is some criticism, however, which isn't so easy to counteract. Detractors of the approach look to England where the infant schools are currently the target of some severe opposition in their own country. A series of "Black Papers" by a group of British educators indicates that British teachers are having a tough time measuring up to the demands of the "new progressivism" and "slipping into an easy acceptance of permissiveness." Critics say the same thing could happen here and open education advocates say that they are absolutely right. In fact, experts on both sides agree that the implementation of the approach presents great difficulty and considerable danger.

The danger which open classroom supporters seem most concerned about, is that open education may boom into the next educational fad and be used widely by teachers and administrators without the proper training and commitment.

To avoid this, open educators are urging their admirers to "think small"--stressing the difficulties and demands of the training for both teachers and administrators. They go out of their way, in fact, to caution that to open up classrooms without developing the necessary skills and strengths is to invite mindlessness and frustration. Interested schoolmen are urged to move slowly in starting up open classrooms so that teachers, children and parents can all understand, share in, and grow with the changes.

While there seem to be an increasing number of educators who feel the British reforms can make some significant improvements in primary school education --and in the upper elementary grades as well--they reject the more grandiose rhetoric from those who view open education as an importable scheme for radical reform.

In the main, there seems to be widespread agreement with Joseph Featherstone's advice that "careful work on a small scale is the best way to start making changes"--changes which will be well worth the time and effort, says Nyquist, "if they can help each of our youngsters become more of what he is capable of being."

DATE DUE

FEB 21 1975		
MAR 28 1975		
MAY 27 1975		
OCT 31 '75		
JAN 31 1978		
GAYLORD		

stress testing

PRINCIPLES AND PRACTICE
EDITION 3

stress testing

PRINCIPLES AND PRACTICE
EDITION 3

MYRVIN H. ELLESTAD, M.D., F.A.C.C.

Director, Memorial Heart Institute
Memorial Medical Center of Long Beach
Long Beach, California

Clinical Professor of Medicine
University of California, Irvine
California College of Medicine
Irvine, California

F. A. DAVIS COMPANY   Philadelphia

NOTE: As new scientific information becomes available through basic and clinical research, recommended treatments and drug therapies undergo changes. The author and publisher have done everything possible to make this book accurate, up-to-date, and in accord with accepted standards at the time of publication. However, the reader is advised always to check product information (package inserts) for changes and new information regarding dose and contraindications before administering any drug. Caution is especially urged when using new or infrequently ordered drugs.

Library of Congress Cataloging in Publication Data

Ellestad, Myrvin H., 1921-
    Stress testing.

    Includes bibliographies and index.
    1. Heart function tests.   2. Stress (Physiology).
3. Exercise tests.   I. Title.   [DNLM: 1. Exercise Test.
2. Stress.   WG 141.5.F9 E45s]
RC683.5.H4E44   1986   616.1'2'0754   85-10413
ISBN 0-8036-3112-X

DEDICATED TO MY LOVELY AND LOVING WIFE, LERA

FOREWORD TO FIRST EDITION

When the late Dr. Paul Dudley White was photographed riding his bicycle to work and when Dr. Sam Levine urged patients with myocardial infarction to get out of bed on the second or third day and when Dr. Arthur Master had patients with angina walk over the two step staircase, the old admonition to the cardiac patient to "take it easy" began to erode. The last 20 years have given rise to a strong surge of interest in exercise as a therapeutic measure for restoring functional capacity to patients with heart disease and as a possible preventive measure against myocardial infarction or the recurrence of other coronary events.

A prerequisite to using exercise as a therapeutic measure for cardiac patients is a reproducible and reliable method of stress testing that will define a patient's functional capacity and disclose the physiologic and symptomatic mechanisms that limit it.

Stress testing is unexcelled as a method for diagnosing unsuspected asymptomatic heart disease. For the detection of undisclosed myocardial ischemia, and in the management of established heart disease, it is indispensable in assessing the severity of impairment due to ischemia and for measuring the effectiveness of therapy. It then defines the level at which it is safe to exercise in the name of heart disease prevention.

Dr. Ellestad meticulously explains his own approach, based on 12 years experience, against the background of basic physiologic principles that provide foundation and reviews of the various testing methods, including treadmill, bicycle, and bench stepping, along with less formalized methods such as stair dashing and hand squeezing.

The book is valuable for its "how to" approach to performing stress tests that will yield the desired results. The directions are so straightforward and clear that a physician who has never done a stress test will be able to initiate a program of his own by close adherence to the principles and details defined by Dr. Ellestad.

Of particular interest to physicians already engaged in stress testing is the prognostic significance of the results of treadmill testing both in terms of sufficient patient sample and time to be of strong statistical importance. The ischemic ECG response to stress testing has proven to be the strongest known predictor of future coronary events both fatal and nonfatal.

With this book multistage exercise stress testing comes of age as a clinical diagnostic method. It has wide range of usefulness and can be the key to the liberation of the cardiac patient from the "take it easy" mentality.

Albert A. Kattus, M.D.
Professor of Medicine
UCLA School of Medicine

FOREWORD TO THIRD EDITION

This edition represents an update of a text that already has had two editions and four printings within the past decade. Thus its importance in describing the principles and practice of stress testing has been well established. The present edition is assured of continuing this tradition. The contents are well organized, clearly presented, and reflect the cumulative experience of a knowledgeable clinical investigator who skillfully incorporates the highlights of many studies in the medical literature. It is both readable and well illustrated with selected figures, diagrams, and tables from a variety of sources, and the information is clearly referenced.

The text begins with an historical perspective, and although a variety of stress testing procedures is cited throughout the volume, the emphasis of the information provided relates to noninvasive, clinically useful, multistage, dynamic exercise testing of cardiac patients who are not actively ill or who do not present specific contraindications to testing. Cardiovascular, pulmonary, extra-cardiac, as well as electrocardiographic responses to exercise are presented in relation to normal variations. The chapter on pathophysiology of cardiac ischemia is particularly informative because it integrates many experimental and clinical observations. Indications, contraindications, risks, safety precautions, practical details about procedures, techniques, observations, and interpretations of responses to each testing are well covered.

Difference in contemporary methods, protocols, and criteria for diagnosis are considered. Major emphasis is placed upon functional performance of individuals tested. Although clinical application is directed primarily toward probabilities of coronary artery disease, limitations in anatomic diagnosis are recognized, prognostic risk is emphasized, and representative responses in several other types of heart disease in both adults and children are included.

A personal point of difference with the author is use of hyperventilation, which is known to cause coronary and cerebral vasoconstriction, before exercise testing. But as the author also points out, details of testing procedure are explained to patients before testing begins. Thus, one hopes the explanation and answering of individual questions takes long enough for physiologic effects of respiratory alkalosis to subside before testing begins. (In patients with atypical chest pain syndromes, hyperventilation a few minutes after completing exercise and demonstrating fairly normal responses without chest pain is often more revealing.)

Special applications of testing after myocardial infarction, coronary bypass surgery, angioplasty, as well as in combination with thallium perfusion or radionuclide angiocardiographic imaging, various types of drug treatment, and risk assessment of asymptomatic persons and differences in responses of women are included in separate chapters. Electrocardiographic details, arrhythmias, and computer analysis are presented. Dr. Ellestad quite properly emphasizes the importance of incorporating all the observed responses and the relevant clinical information in evaluating each patient tested.

In summary, this is an excellent readable and well illustrated text for those students and physicians who are beginning to use exercise testing as well as experienced physicians seeking details about specific problems of the patients they encounter in daily practice. When more information is needed, the references listed provide many of the useful sources. As in any text by a single author, items selected for presentation reflect the scope of interests and depth of understanding and experience of the author. In this context, the foreword by Dr. Kattus for the first edition is equally applicable to the third edition.

Robert A. Bruce, M.D.
Professor of Medicine
University of Washington
Seattle

PREFACE

The years since the second edition of this book was published have passed with incredible rapidity. The acceptance of the basic tenets of the second edition have been gratifying, although the continued emphasis in the literature on the S-T segment, often to the exclusion of other equally important elements of exercise testing, is somewhat disappointing. The plethora of papers on the use of Baysean analysis, however, indicates an improved understanding of the importance of the application of multiple variables. Within a few years, the use of this type of analysis implemented by simple computer programs should become commonplace.

As with the second edition, most of the text has been rewritten to provide a current account of the state-of-the-art in exercise testing. To reorganize the material in a more useful format, seven totally new chapters have been added; these are:

Exercise Stress Testing After Myocardial Infarction
Stress Testing After Surgical Intervention and Coronary Angioplasty
Rhythm and Conduction Disturbances in Stress Testing
Stress Testing in Women
Chest Pain and Normal Coronary Arteries
Blood Pressure Measurement During Exercise
Sports Medicine and Rehabilitation

All revised and new chapters provide a significant number of up-to-date references from 1979 and later where appropriate. The third edition includes an expanded table of contents at the beginning of the book as well as at the beginning of each chapter to make the contents more accessible and easy to use as a reference.

I am indebted to many of my colleagues who have helped work on the projects in our laboratory designed to validate or sometimes discredit some of my ideas that kept surfacing during our analysis of the material coming through. The fellows in our cardiology training program have been greatly appreciated, not only because of their analysis of patient material but, especially when their questions and observations highlight gaps in our knowledge. My friend and colleague, Paul Greenberg, has been a significant factor in our continuing analysis of the patient data. I will be forever indebted to LaVergne Thomas, our research secretary, who does most of the day-to-day hard work. She organizes, calculates, runs the computer, draws graphs and tables, and generally keeps track of most of the projects underway. Finally, my two secretaries, Carol Fraser and Mildred Schwartzkopf kept the typewriters hot with never a complaint when I kept changing the manuscript after they thought it was complete.

It has been great fun and I hope that the fruits of our labors are well received.

MHE

CONTENTS

1

HISTORY OF STRESS TESTING

The cornerstone of modern stress testing is based on the empirical discovery that exercise in patients with coronary disease produced S-T segment depression. This discovery might be credited to Bousfield,[1] who recorded S-T segment depression in the three standard electrocardiographic leads during a spontaneous attack of angina in 1918, or it might be credited to Feil and Siegel[2] who, in 1928, actually exercised patients with known angina to bring about pain, and concurrently the S-T and T-wave changes we now recognize as showing evidence of ischemia. They described the changes as being due to a decrease in blood flow to the heart, and published tracings showing a return to normal after the pain had subsided and also after administration of nitroglycerin. They performed their stress tests by having the patients do sit-ups and, in selected cases, they held their hands on the patient's chest to increase the resistance and, therefore, the energy required to perform this maneuver. There is some question of whether or not Einthoven[3] may have actually recognized the changes associated with ischemia. He published a tracing in 1908 showing S-T segment depression after exercise, but did not comment on this.

Master[4] published his first paper on an exercise text in 1929 but did not recognize at that time the value of the ECG in the demonstration of ischemia. He used only pulse and blood pressure to evaluate the patient's cardiac capacity. His contribution must be labeled as being related to an exercise protocol rather than to the use of the ECG for the evaluation of ischemia in these early years.

In 1931, Wood and Wolferth[5] also described S-T segment changes with exercise and indicated its usefulness in diagnosis, but claimed it was too dangerous to deliberately exercise patients with coronary disease. They claimed that the precordial lead (lead 4) was more useful in revealing ischemic changes than were the standard leads.

Goldhammer and Scherf[6] reported in 1932 that S-T segment depression was present in 75 percent of 40 patients with angina and proposed the use of exercise to confirm the diagnosis of coronary ischemia. It is interesting to note that their percentage of false negatives was similar to that of some of the data being published at this time.

Katz and Landt[7] confirmed Wood's findings in 1935 in terms of their precordial leads and found lead 5 to be better in terms of discrimination than lead 4. They also demonstrated that the number of negative responses in patients with classical angina history could be reduced by using precordial leads. They tried to standardize their exercise test by having the subjects lift dumbbells while lying on a table. They also discussed the mechanism of pain and ischemia and implicated some irritative substance related to catabolism in the myocardium. Katz and Landt also reported on the use of anoxia to bring about characteristic changes in the S-T segment. They went on to produce the same changes with intravenous epinephrine.

By 1938, Missal[8] studied normal patients by having them run up from three to six flights of stairs and he may have been the first to use a maximum stress test. For convenience, he later elected to use Master's 9-inch steps to exercise his patients. He had his patients exercise to the point of pain and emphasized the necessity of taking the recording as quickly as possible thereafter. He cited a case report in which the stress test contributed to the management of a woman with hypothyroidism and angina who had an earlier onset of angina and S-T segment depression after taking thyroid. He also described its use in evaluating increases in exercise tolerance after nitroglycerin.

Riseman and colleagues[9] published an excellent review of the use of anoxia in the evaluation of ischemia in 1940. They compared exercise and the anoxemia test and suggested that the latter was more specific because there were fewer negative test results in patients believed to have coronary disease. They also described for the first time the use of continuous monitoring and thus discovered that S-T segment depression usually appeared before the onset of pain and usually persisted for a time after the pain subsided. They demonstrated the protective effects of oxygen breathing and described the presence of mild S-T segment depression in normal subjects (1.0 mm or less) as contrasted with 2.0 to 7.0 mm depression in some of their patients. In spite of all this information, they concluded that the exercise was of little practical value because of its poor discrimination between the normal and the abnormal subjects.

It is of interest to note that in 1941, 12 years after his original paper on an exercise test, Master, in collaboration with Jaffe,[10] proposed for the first time that an ECG could be taken before and after his "exercise tolerance test" to detect coronary insufficiency. In the same year, Liebow and Feil[11] reported that digitalis caused S-T segment depression and would confuse the diagnosis of ischemia in the exercise ECG. They also suggested the possibility of the drug reducing coronary flow.

Johnson and associates[12] working at the Harvard Fatigue Laboratory, developed the Harvard Step Test, which was similar in many ways to the original Master's Step Test. It was used widely in athletic circles to measure fitness, and a form of it (the Pack Test) was used for military purposes. These tests used pulse counts during recovery and provided an index of physical fitness, a technique that was to be carried forward in the indexes of fitness and aerobic power for a number of years. Brouha and Heath[13] also used this methodology to evaluate the cardiovascular response to various occupations and emphasized the influence of environmental factors such as room temperature. In 1949, Hellerstein and Katz[14] performed their classical studies describing the direction of the vector associated with subendocardial injury in various areas of the right and left ventricle. They also used direct current electrograms and established that S-T depression is primarily a diastolic injury current manifested during the T-Q interval.

By 1949, Hecht[15] was reporting his experience with the anoxemia test and claiming 90 percent sensitivity in coronary disease. He emphasized the important fact that pain is an unreliable end-point and accompanies ischemia in only 50 percent of the cases. He also pointed out that S-T segment changes associated with anoxemia may not be present if previous myocardial necrosis has occurred. Since then, Castellanet and colleagues[16] have confirmed that infarction tends to mask the electrocardiographic expression of ischemia.

In 1950, Wood and associates[17] at the National Heart Hospital in London described their experience with an effort test. It is interesting to note that they had patients run up 84 steps adjacent to their laboratory and also claimed that it was necessary to push the patients to the maximum level of their capacity. They established several points that still have validity:

1. The amount of work performed should not be fixed, but adjusted to the patient's capacity.
2. The more strenuous work (resulting in a heart rate of above 90) would produce a higher percentage of positive tests in patients with known coronary disease than if the heart rate were not accelerated above this level.
3. The reliability of their test (in effect, a maximum stress test) was 88 percent overall as compared with 39 percent in the Master's Test.

Wood and his colleagues, as Hecht before them, definitely recommended the use of the stress test to uncover latent myocardial ischemia, to determine the severity of the disease, and to evaluate therapy.

In 1951, Hellerstein and colleagues[18] used stress testing as a method of evaluating the work capacity of cardiac patients and began to amplify the work pioneered by Brouha. They deserve credit for demonstrating to employers that their cardiac employees might safely return to work. Thus, this continuing interest in the oxygen cost of various activities and in analysis of ischemia at various workloads began to plant the seed that flowered into our present cardiac rehabilitation program.

Yu and Soffer[19] reported in 1952 on the use of the Master's stairs with continuous monitoring and cited the following changes in the ECG indicting ischemia:

1. S-T segment depression of 1.0 mm or more.
2. Alteration of the T wave from upright to inverted or from inverted to upright.
3. Increase in the amplitude of the T wave of 50 percent or more over the resting deflection.
4. Prolongation of the QT/TQ ratio during exercise to more than two.

The last finding may still be a useful element in the evaluation of ischemia but this possibility has not been fully explored. They again emphasized the value of continuous monitoring previously described by Riseman and associates[9] and pointed out that the QT interval should be carefully measured.

Yu and coworkers[20] had previously reported a test using a motor-driven treadmill elevated to a 10 percent or 20 percent grade with continuous monitoring. They suggested that the lead system be set up as a bipolar lead from the right scapula to the V_5 position, a lead configuration that Bruce used for many years.

In 1953, Feil and Brofman[21] reviewed the bundle branch block patterns. They referred to transient bundle branch block developing with exercise and pointed out that this was first described by Bousfield[1] in 1918. They reported that S-T segment depression, when coexisting with the block pattern, indicates ischemia in both right and left bundle branch block (LBBB). They also reported false-positive stress tests in two or three patients with Wolff-Parkinson-White (WPW) syndrome, an observation subsequently confirmed by Sandberg[22] and Gazes.[23]

By 1955, the Master's Step Test had become widely accepted as a standard because of its simplicity. Its failure to apply adequate stress and the fact that information was lost by not observing the pulse response and the ECG patterns during exercise were rarely appreciated, even though these limitations had been pointed out by many of the earlier investigators. Although the Master's Test was originally proposed to provide information about the patient's functional classification, it remained for others to begin to combine a fairly satisfactory test of cardiac function with one that would provide information on the presence or absence of ischemic heart disease. Bruce[24] and Hellerstein[14] were early workers in this area and continue to make contributions.

An important push in the evolution of treadmill stress testing came from the work classification units. In 1950, Hellerstein's unit in Cleveland,[25] patterned after the original one in Bellview Hospital in New York established by Goldwater in 1944, set the stage for a proliferation of these clinics in many areas sponsored by the American Heart Association. My introduction to the treadmill test came when I worked in the Los Angeles Work Classification Unit. Familiarity with testing postmyocardial infarction patients led to the realization that this approach offered a more comprehensive evaluation than the Master's Step Test.

Modern stress testing might be dated from 1956 when Bruce[26] reported a work test performed on a treadmill and established guidelines that would more or less group patients into the New York Heart Disease Classifications I through IV. Many of the protocols for stress testing now in vogue have been based on an extension of the principles he established at that time. Shortly before this, Astrand and Ryhming[27] had documented that maximum oxygen uptake or aerobic capacity could be predicted by the heart rate at submaximal exercise. Thus, the groundwork necessary to establish the progressive exercise test as a physiologic exercise tolerance test had been laid.

About this time, Taylor and colleagues,[28] based on the work of Hill and Lupton,[29] proposed an index for circulatory performance that emphasized that if the strongest muscle was used, the amount of exercise would usually be limited by the cardiac output rather than by muscle weakness. Therefore, in walking or running, increases in pulse could be correlated with increases in cardiac output and thus, the aerobic capacity of the individual. In the late 1950s, Balke and Ware,[30] working in the Department of Physiology and Biophysics at Randolph Air Force Base, established the importance of stress testing in evaluating military personnel and published a formula that is still useful in estimating the oxygen uptake associated with treadmill walking.

In the early 1960s, numerous articles were written attempting to refine the criteria for ischemia S-T segment changes and the appropriate leads for recording.[22] Blackburn's[31] work in 1969 and the work of Blackburn and his associates[32] in 1966 demonstrated the incidence of S-T segment depression in various leads. His findings that 90 percent of the ischemic changes could be demonstrated in the CM_5 or V_5 lead made it possible to do stress testing with a relatively simple electrocardiographic recording system. This had a considerable impact because it spread the use of progressive testing outside the research laboratory. The CM_5 and the transthoracic or right scapula to apex bipolar lead are still in use today.

As the Air Force and NASA prepared to launch a man into space, Lamb[33] and Fascenelli and colleagues[34] in a continuation of the work pioneered by Balke, refined the methods necessary for accurate monitoring of multiple variables during exercise.

Shortly after this, in 1967, Robb and Marks[35] published their follow-up data on 2224 male applicants for life insurance and for the first time gave us statistical verification of the predictive value of the S-T segment depression. They demonstrated that the presence of horizontal or down-sloping S-T segments after the double Master's Test were more reliable in predicting subsequent coronary abnormalities than was the patient's medical history. They also established that deep S-T segment depression carried with it a more serious prognosis than a moderate degree of depression. By 1969 Bruce and associates,[36] Winter,[37] and Sheffield and colleagues[38] had reported on the use of computers to analyze S-T segments, and the correlation of these changes with coronary angiographic data was published by Najmi and associates,[39] Martin and McConahay,[40] Lewis and Wilson,[41] and Balcon and associates.[42] Because S-T depression and anginal-type chest pain were believed for a long time to be almost synonymous with coronary disease, many subjects underwent angiography who turned out to have normal coronary arteries. This helped us to gain insight into the limitations as well as the benefits of stress testing. We now understand more about the pathophysiology of the coronary system and recognize that many parameters besides the S-T segment need to be scrutinized in order to make maximum use of the procedure.

The years of the late 1970s and early 1980s might be labeled "THE DECADE OF BAYSIAN ANALYSIS." Numerous papers[43-45] have demonstrated the importance of disease prevalence and information content in applying the data. Although these concepts apply to any type of testing, most of the emphasis has been on exercise testing. Several methods of analyzing data by computers using a likelihood ratio[43] or multivariant analysis[46] are also being developed. Conventional exercise testing today, usually done with a treadmill, is being supplemented by nuclear techniques such as thallium scintography and blood pool nuclear ventriculograms as well as estimates of wall motion by echocardiograms and the kymocardiogram, a magnetic method for myocardial wall motion analysis.

These new techniques when combined with conventional testing improve the diagnostic certainty and often help localize the diseased vessels. I believe within the next four or five years the noninvasive diagnosis of myocardial ischemia will reach a reliability of well over 95 percent. We are beginning to understand that there are different types of ischemia, several of which are unrelated to fixed coronary obstruction. We will also have to revise our ideas about the character of the coronary lesions that restrict flow, as we study patients with new methods using dynamic measurements of flow reserve as well as anatomic analysis of the vessel caliber.

If I were to select one man who has made the greatest contribution to the technique, it would unequivocally go to Robert Bruce of Seattle, whose protocol is the standard in most laboratories in the United States. His meticulous work has given us a body of knowledge that provides a foundation for most other investigators.

Many workers have made major contributions that have not been mentioned. Their work will be discussed in the appropriate areas in the chapters that follow. As with the brilliant description of angina by Heberden, the understanding of basic physiology displayed by some of the pioneers in stress testing is remarkable. They have given us a tool that has and will improve our understanding of cardiac physiology and at the same time is now playing a major role in the detection and evaluation of coronary heart disease.

REFERENCES

1. BLOUSFIELD, G: *Angina pectoris: Changes in electrocardiogram during paroxysm.* Lancet 2:457, 1918.

2. FEIL, H AND SIEGEL, M: *Electrocardiographic changes during attacks of angina pectoris.* Am J Med Sci 175:225, 1928.

3. EINTHOVEN, W: *Weiteres uber das Elektrokardiogramm.* Arch ges Physiol 172:517, 1908.

4. MASTER, AM AND OPPENHEIMER, EJ: *A simple exercise tolerance test for circulatory efficiency with standard tables for normal individuals.* Am J Med Sci 177:223, 1929.

5. WOOD, FC AND WOLFERTH, CC: *Angina pectoris: The clinical and electrocardiographic phenomena of the attack and their comparison with the effects of experimental temporary coronary occlusion.* Arch Int Med 47:339, 1931.

6. GOLDHAMMER, S AND SCHERF, D: *Electrokardiographische untersuchungen bei Kranken mit Angina Pectoris.* Z Klin Med 122:134, 1932.

7. KATZ, L AND LANDT, H: *Effect of standardized exercise on the four-lead electrocardiogram: Its value in the study of coronary disease.* Am J Med Sci 189:346, 1935.

8. MISSAL, ME: *Exercise tests and the electrocardiograph in the study of angina pectoris.* Ann Int Med 11:2018, 1938.

9. RISEMAN, JEF, WALLER, J, AND BROWN, M: *The electrocardiogram during attacks of angina pectoris: Its characteristics and diagnostic significance.* Am Heart J 19:683, 1940.

10. MASTER, AM AND JAFFE, HL: *The electrocardiographic changes after exercise in angina pectoris.* J Mt Sinai Hosp 7:629, 1941.

11. LIEBOW, IM AND FEIL, H: *Digitalis and the normal work electrocardiogram.* Am Heart J 22:683, 1941.

12. JOHNSON, RE, BROUHA, L, AND DARLING, RC: *A practical test of physical fitness for strenuous exertion.* Rev Can Biol 1:491, 1942.

13. BROUHA, L AND HEATH, CW: *Resting pulse and blood pressure values in relationship to physical fitness in young men.* N Engl J Med 228:473, 1943.

14. HELLERSTEIN, HK AND KATZ, L: *The electrical effects of injury at various myocardial locations.* Am Heart J 36:184, 1948.

15. HECHT, HH: *Concepts of myocardial ischemia.* Arch Int Med 84:711, 1949.

16. CASTELLANET, MJ, GREENBERG, PS, AND ELLESTAD, MH: *The predictive value of the treadmill test in determining post-infarction ischemia.* Am J Cardiol 42:29, 1978.

17. WOOD, P, ET AL: *The effort test in angina pectoris.* Br Heart J 12:363, 1950.

18. HELLERSTEIN, HK, ET AL: *Results of an integrative method of occupational evaluation of persons with heart disease.* J Lab Clin Med 38:821, 1951.

19. YU, PNG AND SOFFER, A: *Studies of electrocardiographic changes during exercise (modified double two-step test).* Circulation 6:183, 1952.

20. YU, PNG, ET AL: *Variations in electrocardiographic response during exercise (studies of normal subjects under unusual stresses and of patients with cardiopulmonary disease).* Circulation 3:368, 1951.

21. FEIL, H AND BROFMAN, BL: *The effect of exercise on the electrocardiogram of bundle branch block.* Am Heart J 45:665, 1953.

22. SANDBERG, L: *Studies on electrocardiographic changes during exercise tests.* Acta Med Scand 169(suppl 365):1, 1961.

23. GAZES, PC: *False-positive exercise test in the presence of Wolff-Parkinson-White syndrome.* Am Heart J 78:13, 1969.

24. BRUCE, RA, ET AL: *Observations of cardiorespiratory performance in normal subjects under unusual stress during exercise.* Arch Indust Hyg 6:105, 1952.

25. HELLERSTEIN, HK: *Cardiac rehabilitation: A retrospective view.* Heart Disease and Rehabilitation 509, 1979.

26. BRUCE, RA: *Evaluation of functional capacity and exercise tolerance of cardiac patients.* Mod Concepts Cardiovasc Dis 25:321, 1956.

27. ASTRAND, PO AND RHYMING, I: *Nomogram for calculation of aerobic capacity (physical fitness) from pulse rate during submaximal work.* J Appl Physiol 7:218, 1954.

28. TAYLOR, HL, BUSKIRK, E, AND HENSCHEL, A: *Maximal oxygen intake as objective measure of cardio-respiratory performance.* J Appl Physiol 8:73, 1955.

29. HILL, AV AND LUPTON, H: *Muscular exercise, lactic acid, and supply and utilization of oxygen.* Quart J Med 16:135, 1923.
30. BALKE, B AND WARE, RW: *An experimental study of physical fitness of Air Force personnel.* US Armed Forces Med J 10:675, 1959.
31. BLACKBURN, H: *The electrocardiogram in cardiovascular epidemiology: Problems in standardized application.* In BLACKBURN, H (ED): *Measurement in Exercise Electrocardiography.* Charles C Thomas, Springfield, IL, 1969.
32. BLACKBURN, H, ET AL: *The electrocardiogram during exercise (Findings in bipolar chest leads of 1449 middle-aged men, at moderate work levels).* Circulation 34:1034, 1966.
33. LAMB, LE: *The influence of manned space flight on cardiovascular functions.* Cardiologia 48:118, 1966.
34. FASCENELLI, FW, ET AL: *Biomedical monitoring during dynamic stress testing.* Aerospace Medicine 9:911, 1966.
35. ROBB, GP AND MARKS, H: *Postexercise electrocardiogram in arteriosclerotic heart disease.* JAMA 200:110, 1967.
36. BRUCE, RA, ET AL: *Electrocardiographic responses to maximal exercise in American and Chinese population samples.* in BLACKBURN, H (ED): *Measurement in Exercise Electrocardiography.* Charles C Thomas, Springfield, IL, 1969.
37. WINTER, DA: *Noise measurement and quality control techniques in recording and processing of exercise electrocardiograms.* In BLACKBURN, H (ED): *Measurement in Exercise Electrocardiography.* Charles C Thomas, Springfield, IL, 1969.
38. SHEFFIELD, LT, ET AL: *Electrocardiographic signal analysis without averaging of complexes.* In BLACKBURN, H (ED): *Measurement in Exercise Electrocardiography.* Charles C Thomas, Springfield, IL, 1969.
39. NAJMI, M, ET AL: *Selective cine coronary arteriography correlated with hemodynamic response to physical stress.* Dis Chest 54:33, 1968.
40. MARTIN, CM AND MCCONAHAY, D: *Maximal treadmill exercise electrocardiography: Correlation with coronary arteriography and cardiac hemodynamics.* Circulation 46:956, 1972.
41. LEWIS, WJ, III AND WILSON, WJ: *Correlation of coronary arteriograms with Master's test and treadmill test.* Rocky Mt Med J 68:30, 1971.
42. BALCON, R, MALOY, WC, AND SOWTON, E: *Clinical use of atrial pacing test in angina pectoris.* Br Med J 3:91, 1968.
43. DIAMOND, GA: *Bayes' Theorem: A practical aid to clinical judgment for diagnosis of coronary-artery disease.* Practical Cardiology 10(6):47–77, 1984.
44. DIAMOND, GA, ET AL. *Application of conditional probability analysis to the clinical diagnosis of coronary artery disease.* J Clin Invest 65:1210–1220, 1980.
45. RIFKIN, RD AND HOOD, WB: *Bayesian analysis and electrocardiographic exercise stress testing.* N Engl J Med 297:681–686, 1977.
46. ELLESTAD, MH, ET AL: *The false positive stress test multivariate analysis of 215 subjects with hemodynamic, angiographic and clinical data.* Am J Cardiol 40:681–685, 1977.

2

CARDIOVASCULAR AND PULMONARY RESPONSES TO EXERCISE

A review of the mechanisms leading to the changes in cardiac output and other circulatory adaptations associated with exercise will be helpful. Various factors including venous tone, body position, blood volume, and depth of respiration control the input to the heart. The heart responds by pumping into the arterial circulation the volume delivered from the venous side. The amount per beat in milliliters is called the stroke volume. The total cardiac output (measured in liters per minute) is the stroke volume (usually 50 to 80 ml of blood) multiplied by the heart rate. For example, if each beat pumped 80 ml out and there were 70 beats per minute, the cardiac output would be 80 × 70 or 5600 ml, or 5.6 liters of blood per minute. This is an average value for an adult at rest. The output increases with exercise, depending on the efficiency of the system, up to about 30 liters per minute in a well-conditioned athlete. An individual's ability to increase pumping volume is the most important factor limiting the ability to increase physical work capacity.

When exercise signals the heart to increase its output, a rather complex set of events takes place, which influences the heart to increase pumping. The most important is the heart rate. However, if the stroke volume were to remain constant at 80 ml and the heart rate were to increase to its maximum (approximately 195 beats per minute for a 25-year-old man) the limit of the cardiac output would be 80 × 195 or 15,600 ml, or 15.6 liters per minute. We know that the peak heart rate for a man at a given age falls within a predictable range. How then is it possible to increase cardiac output to approximately double the above value, or 30 liters per minute? The only solution is to increase the stroke volume, which occurs during the early phases of increased work.

PRELOAD AND STROKE VOLUME

When exercise begins, a rather complex set of events can be measured that sets the stage for the events to follow. Probably the first is the increase in venous tone, which is mediated by autonomic reflexes. This squeezes the blood from the large vein into the right side of the heart, increasing the effective filling pressure. In a normal heart, the right ventricle is very distensible and accepts the increased volume of blood during diastole with very little increase in pressure (the filling pressure of both the right and left sides of the heart is usually from 5 to 10 mm Hg). Cardiac output increases immediately as a result of the increased filling and tachycardia (Fig. 2-1).

Evidence that the baroreceptor reflexes are progressively inhibited as exercise increases is suggested by denervation experiments.[1]

It is obvious that the heart cannot pump more blood out than it takes in; thus, the increased return is central to the problem of increased output. Besides the constriction in the veins, mediated by the sympathetic nervous systems forcing more blood into the heart, the pumping action of the muscles, especially those in the legs, propels the blood toward the heart. The increased negative pressure of deep inspiration, termed the abdominal thoracic pump, also tends to encourage this process. The tendency for blood to be preferentially shunted from certain organ systems, such as the kidney and splanchnic bed, the liver, and the spleen, also increases the venous return.

When exercise is first initiated, the stroke volume tends to increase as the increased venous flow takes place, but levels off somewhat short of the maximal pumping capacity[2] (Fig. 2-2).

Body position has considerable influence on stroke volume at rest because the return to the heart is greater in the supine position. This is due to an increased tendency for the veins to empty into the right heart when the gravity effect is removed. Thus, exercise in this position, such as swimming, may be associated with a larger stroke output and a lower heart rate. Chapman and colleagues[3] have shown, however, that after strenuous physical exercise is underway, the difference in stroke volume related to posture is minimized. A marked decrease in peripheral resistance has been recently established as an

Deconditioned Heart

Diastolic Vol. 120 ml.•Systolic Vol. 50 ml.
Stroke Vol. 70 ml.
Ejection Frac. 58%

Conditioned Heart

Diastolic Vol. 160 ml.•Systolic Vol. 30 ml.
Stroke Vol. 130 ml.
Ejection Frac. 84%

FIGURE 2-1. As training progresses, the increase in diastolic volume is accompanied by a simultaneous decrease in systolic volume. This results in an increase in stroke volume and the percentage of the diastolic volume expelled with each systole (ejection fraction).

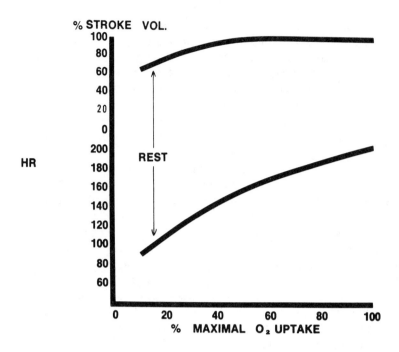

FIGURE 2-2. As the heart rate increases with exercise, there is a moderate increase in stroke volume, which reaches a maximum at approximately midway during the buildup of the exercise capacity.

aid to the increased stroke volume reported in trained athletes.[4] The cardiac dimensions are directly related to the diastolic volume and contractility. The heart gets slightly smaller near peak exercise but the systolic volume decreases even more than the diastolic, so that the stroke volume is maintained. As we will later see, this normal response is altered by some disease states and provides us with a mechanism for evaluating function during exercise.

STROKE VOLUME AND TRAINING

Numerous studies have demonstrated progressive increases in stroke volume after prolonged exercise programs. The stroke volume of endurance athletes has been reported to be 50 to 75 percent higher than that of sedentary individuals.[4] This enables those who are physically well conditioned to operate at a slower heart rate. It has been shown that an increased volume load is the most efficient method of increasing one's cardiac output in terms of myocardial oxygen consumption. Recent studies done with nuclear blood pool imaging[5] confirmed previous measurements in normals (normal subjects) and suggested that the increased stroke volume and maximal cardiac output seen in normals can also be achieved with coronary patients subjected to training.[6,7] The stroke

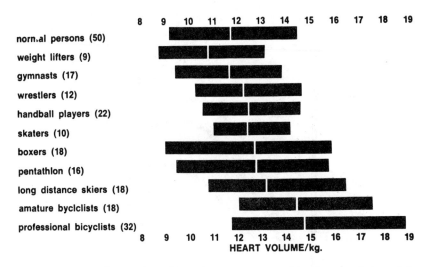

FIGURE 2-3. Heart volume estimated from the roentgenogram of the chest showing correlation with the type of physical activity. (From Roskamm,[8] with permission.)

volume can be correlated with heart volume estimated from a roentgenogram of the patient's chest. The volume averages for various athletes (Fig. 2-3) give some indication of the changes associated with various types of sports. It should be noted that the isometric type of exercise (weight lifting) produces no significant change in heart volume.

CONTRACTILITY

The mechanical response of the ventricle is based on Starling's law, which states that the force of contraction is a function of the degree of stretch during diastole (Fig. 2-4). Thus, as more blood enters the heart during each diastolic interval, the muscle is subjected to more stretch, which increases the force of contraction. During this process not only is more energy expended, but the increased fiber length results in a larger stroke volume if other factors, such as blood pressure, are not altered. The force of contraction is related to the inherent strength of the heart muscle as well as the amount of stretch taking place. At the same time, other mechanisms come into play that influence the final ability of the ventricle to pump.

Circulating catecholamines exert the most important influence because, by stimulating the production of adenyl cyclase and thereby, increasing the release of adenosine triphosphate, they increase the force of contractility, the amount of energy expended, and the heart rate. Another factor is the resistance in the vascular bed through which the heart must pump. The resistance in the lungs is so low in the healthy subject that it plays very little role as a limiting factor in exercise. The resistance in the systemic circuit as measured by the

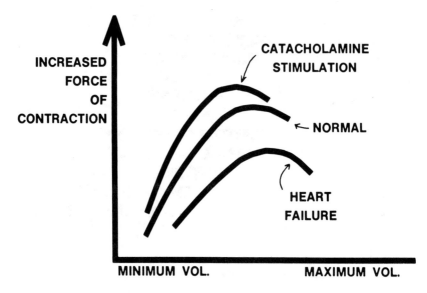

FIGURE 2-4. Starling's curves: the greater force generated by increasing the stretch on the myocardial fibers is influenced by many metabolic and mechanical factors. The effects of catecholamines and the still poorly understood state of heart failure are depicted.

brachial or aortic blood pressure is extremely important. We know it takes about twice as much energy to pump blood out against the resistance of 200 mm Hg as compared with 100 mm Hg. In the normal subject, the heart decreases its resistance to blood flow as exercise progresses. This may not be obvious to someone measuring blood pressure during exercise because it usually rises. Resistance is the product of blood flow multipled by blood pressure. When the heart pumps more blood, the cardiac output usually increases more than the resistance drops; therefore, there is a modest increase in systolic blood pressure during exercise in most patients.

Training has been shown to improve the inotropic properties of the myocardium,[9] probably due to an increase in velocity of enzyme activity.[10]

HEART RATE

The heart rate is the result of a number of physical and emotional influences that are mediated through the autonomic nervous system. These include excitement, fear, anticipation, temperature alterations, respiratory maneuvers, and physical work. Both the vagal and the sympathetic nerves are constantly stimulating the sinoauricular node so that if the influence of either is increased or decreased, a change in rate will be manifested. There are a number of complex inhibitory as well as stimulating reflexes in the vascular system that affect the heart rate, and during exercise the sympathetic is the most important, as vagal tone is gradually withdrawn as the workload increases.[11] At the onset of exercise, the heart rate has been shown to increase within 0.5 second,[12] probably secondary to an abrupt inhibition of a significant portion of the vagal tone. An interesting sawtooth effect in the heart rate has been described in the first few seconds of exercise,[13] suggesting that the autonomic nervous systems is "searching" for the proper balance.

Stimulating the sinus node with a pacemaker accelerates the heart rate, but the filling pressure does not increase; therefore, the stroke volume decreases. The result is a stable rather than an increased cardiac output. On the other hand, administering Adrenalin or other catecholamines causes both heart rate and venous return to increase, resulting in a net increase in cardiac output. Dog work suggests that about 50 percent of the cardiac acceleration is due to sympathetic drive, primarily beta stimulation.[13] A recent study by Swartz and Stone[14] indicates that the right stellate ganglion is an important pathway in this system.

A curious property of the heart is its apparent age-related ceiling on rate. It appears that the anatomy and physiology of cardiac function are so designed that when the body calls for the heart to increase its pumping, it can accelerate only to a predetermined peak and then does not further increase its rate of pumping or its output regardless of the demands of the body. As far as we can tell, pushing the heart to its maximum in a normal individual does no damage. If a person tries to push past this maximum pumping capacity, the peripheral tissues become anoxic because of inadequate oxygen delivery. The individual then rapidly builds up lactic acid and other metabolites, which terminates the ability to function in only a few minutes. Lactic acid depresses cardiac function and produces peripheral dilatation, which then decreases blood pressure (Fig. 2-5).

The knowledge of this peak heart rate in various age groups makes it possible for physicians to know when a subject has exercised to maximum pumping capacity. Although there is some disagreement about the range and variation around the mean, and the mean rates, the data adapted from Robinson[15] have been very useful in our experiences.

Bates[4] has studied cardiac output in relation to its limiting effect on exercise and has demonstrated that an oxygen uptake of up to 1500 ml per minute (Fig. 2-6), cardiac output, heart rate, and oxygen consumption increased in a linear relationship. However, near peak capacity (above 80 percent of maximum capacity) both heart rate and cardiac output tended to level off. It was possible at this point, however, to further increase the peripheral oxygen consumption another 300 to 500 ml, which was attributed to a widening of the arteriovenous oxygen difference. This ability of the peripheral tissues to extract more oxygen, especially when the subject is well conditioned, is a very important element of the circulatory adaptions to exercise. During the period when the oxygen consumption is increasing near peak workload, a very rapid increase in respiratory rate ensues.[16] It is postulated that the increase in oxygen consumption after the heart rate levels off is used to provide the extra work of breathing and is not available for useful external work.

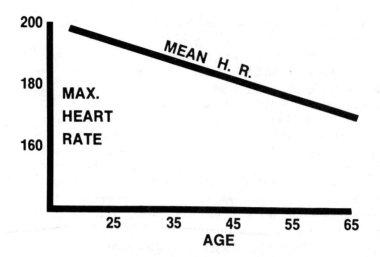

FIGURE 2-5. The maximum predicted heart rate is age-related. When the subject exercises to maximum capacity, the cardiac pumping reaches its maximum possible output at about the same time that the peak heart rate is attained.

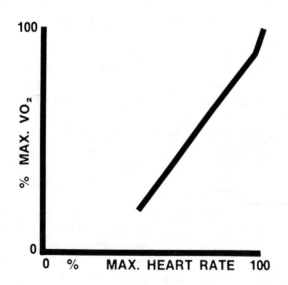

FIGURE 2-6. The relationship between maximum oxygen uptake by the body as a whole and the increase in heart rate tends to be almost linear until about 85 or 90 percent of maximum capacity is reached. At this point, there is a slight further increase in oxygen uptake without a significant increase in heart rate.

HEART RATE WITH TRAINING

The most dramatic and easiest alteration to measure in the physiology of physical conditioning is the heart rate response to a standard workload. Typical responses are depicted in Figure 2-7. It can be seen that at high workloads, the heart rate may be 40 beats per minute more in an unconditioned subject than in a conditioned one.

As was previously mentioned, the heart rate correlates well with the oxygen consumption of the heart, so that the heart of the well-conditioned subject is at least 25 percent more efficient. The decrease in resting heart rate is usually quite significant and is proportional to the duration of the period of increased activity. It is of interest to note that the total number of heart beats saved daily by a decrease in average heart rate of 10 beats per minute abouts to 14,400. Glagov and associates[17] actually measured the total number of heart beats in a 24-hour period by a cumulative counter and found that it varied from 93,615 to 113,988. The factors leading to the heart rate decrease are probably multiple. Not only the increase in stroke volume, but also a decrease in circulating catecholamines and an increased vagal tone are probably important. The optimum duration of exercise and repetition rate necessary to obtain the best pulse response from conditioning is still in doubt. However, a discussion by Pollack[18] suggests some guidelines of importance, as discussed below.

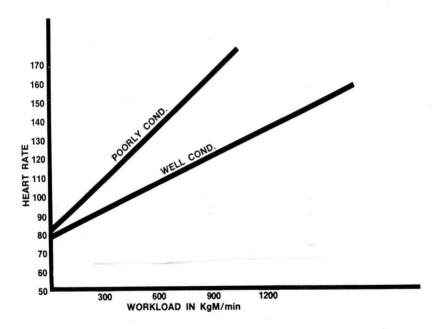

FIGURE 2-7. Heart rate response to exercise: as the workload is increased, the increment of pulse rise is more marked in the poorly conditioned subject.

TRAINING METHODS

Frequency

Although two days of fairly strenuous training will result in almost as much training effect as three days per week, the use of a minimum of three days allows the subject to get a good training effect with a less strenuous workout. It has been found that trying to fit in more than three days per week produces time demands that for many people are unrealistic. For the enthusiast to extend this to five days per week is acceptable, but allows for a much higher injury rate. Injuries that are common in middle-aged adults related to foot, ankle, and knee joints can be minimized by limiting the training somewhat. It would appear that the body needs rest between workouts.

Intensity

Most studies suggest that a minimal threshold for a satisfactory training response is 60 percent of the maximum capacity. In younger people, this would be training to heart rates of 130 to 150 beats per minutes; in older persons, this could be as low as 110 to 120. Studies in which very high levels of training are compared with those of a more moderate nature fail to show any significant increase in benefits as far as general health is concerned. It is obvious, of course, that a higher aerobic capacity can be obtained by pushing the intensity and the time of work. It has been shown in many studies that the drop-out rate in the very high intensity or interval training programs tends to be much higher than that in those using lower intensity work. The problem of intensity, however, is highly related to the subject's ego and the initial level of physical fitness.

Duration

Improvement in cardiovascular respiratory fitness is directly related to duration of training. While a moderate improvement in fitness can be obtained by 5 or 10 minutes, it has been shown that improvement in maximal oxygen uptake is probably optimum when the duration is from 30 to 45 minutes. On the other hand, a significant training effect can be shown in 15 minutes if the intensity is increased. It has been shown that the longer training program with a slightly slower pace is better tolerated, both in terms of drop-outs and in terms of ultimate injuries. I would; therefore, be inclined to urge people to strive for at least 30 minutes, and if vigorous, young, and not prone to injuries, possibly 45 minutes. However, individualization of the exercise prescription to account for age, fitness, and motivation is essential.

Mode

Although there are many enthusiasts who believe that jogging or running is the only approach to eternal life, this has yet to be proved. Any type of rhythmic training that burns calories and increases the heart rate, such as running, walking, bicycling, swimming, or jumping rope is equally effective. Exercise that fails to produce a significant increase in caloric demands, such as bowling, golfing, or moderate calisthenics, does not have much value. Weight lifting has been shown to be useful in a cardiovascular sense only if very light weights are used with multiple repetitions, and even in these types of programs very minor improvement in aerobic capacity has been shown. This, however, might be added to an exercise program in order to gain muscle strength, which is often very important to the individual. The amount of exercise necessary to maintain conditioning must be a great deal more strenuous if one is considering the type seen in long-distance runners.

CORONARY BLOOD FLOW

In the peripheral circulation of humans, about 25 to 30 percent of the oxygen is extracted from the blood as it runs through muscle or other tissues at rest. As

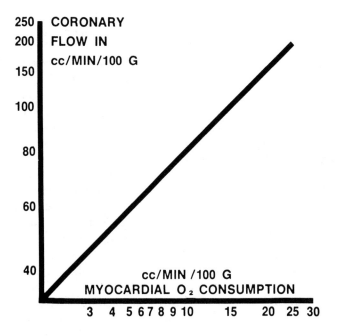

FIGURE 2-8. Because the heart extracts almost all the oxygen possible from the blood at rest, it is necessary for the coronary blood flow to increase linearly as myocardial oxygen demands increase.

the metabolic demands of the tissue rise or the blood flow decreases, a larger percentage of the oxygen is extracted. Thus, in a normal human at rest, the arterial saturation can be 95 percent and the venous 75 percent, resulting in an arteriovenous oxygen (AV-O$_2$) difference of 20 percent. This pattern is altered in cardiac patients with low outputs so that the AV-O$_2$ difference may be as high as 40 percent due to a drop in venous oxygen to 55 or 60 percent. The coronary circulatory system does not have the capacity to adapt to this degree because of the relatively high extraction rate of oxygen at normal work levels. Coronary sinus blood returning from the capillary bed of the myocardium is usually from 10 to 25 percent oxygen saturated, resulting in an AV-O$_2$ difference across the myocardium of 75 percent or more. This high degree of extraction is near the limits of the ability of hemoglobin to release oxygen, thereby, producing an absolute need for more blood whenever the heart requires more nourishment. Thus, in a normal man, there is almost a linear relationship between the increase in work done by the heart and the coronary blood flow (Fig. 2-8). Increases in coronary blood flow from 60 ml per 100 gms of ventricular myocardium per minute to 240 ml per minute during exercise are achieved by a marked reduction in coronary vascular resistance.

CORONARY RESISTANCE

The aortic pressure minus the resistance in the terminal arterioles and capillaries during diastole and the pressure of contraction during systole provides the driving pressure that nourishes the heart.

The resistance to flow has been subdivided into three types. *Viscous resistance* is defined as the resistance due to blood viscosity and the surface tension in the arterioles and capillary bed. *Autoregulatory resistance* is mediated through the smooth muscle in the arterioles and precapillary sphincters. This resistance is mostly under the control of metabolic processes in the heart muscle. *Compressive resistance* is due to the force of myocardial contraction. This compressive effect almost completely inhibits the flow during systole and depending on diastolic compliance, has considerable effect during relaxation.[19]

Studies involving the left anterior descending coronary artery actually demonstrate retrograde blood flow during the isometric phase of systole.[20] The diastolic blood flow is not only two or three times that of the systolic, but also, during this period, it preferentially goes to the subendocardium—an area relatively starved during systole (see Chapter 4).

Methods of blood flow regulation are still being studied, but certain factors have been established. Anoxia decreases the resistance in the coronary bed, possibly by the direct action of a low partial pressure of oxygen (PO$_2$) level, or indirectly due to the liberation of metabolites such as adenosine.[21]

These changes would be classified as autoregulatory. Flow is also subject to local pH changes, partial pressure of carbon dioxide (PCO$_2$), bradykinnins, and very likely to factors still to be discovered.[19] This type of regulatory function controls flow in a patient who becomes hypertensive, so that perfusion is restricted to the exact needs of the muscle in spite of the increase in diastolic driving pressure.

A great deal of interest has recently centered around the effect of adrenergic influences on coronary flow and resistance. The ability to block either alpha or beta receptors has made it possible to study this process in more detail. Intracoronary norepinephrine has been shown to reduce coronary flow in man,[22] as does dopamine.[23] Stellate ganglion stimulation and Isuprel in dogs reduce the inner/outer layer flow ratio,[24] but propranolol increases this ratio and favors subendocardial perfusion.[25] In spite of these findings, the direct role of adrenergic influences on the coronary circulation in normal and diseased individuals is still in doubt, but may have considerable importance.

MYOCARDIAL OXYGEN DEMAND

The myocardium uses 8 to 10 ml of oxygen per 100 gm of muscle per minute when the subject is at rest. Even when the heart is not beating, about 30 percent of this amount is still required.[25] The efficiency of the heart can be estimated by knowing its level of oxygen use both at rest and during work as illustrated by the following formula:[26]

$$\text{EFFICIENCY OF HEART} = \frac{\text{Work of heart in kg-m/min}}{\text{Oxygen consumption in ml/min} \times 2.059 \times 0.806}$$

Here, 2.059 is the energy equivalent (kg-m/ml) of oxygen at a respiratory quotient (RQ) of 0.82, and 0.806 is the fraction of oxygen used in the contractile work of the heart only.

According to these calculations, myocardial efficiency is approximately 37 percent in the dog and 39 percent in man.[27] With exercise, the oxygen consumption of the heart may increase 200 or 300 percent. Factors contributing to this would include the initial muscle fiber length or diastolic volume, the afterload or blood pressure, the velocity of contraction, and probably others not yet completely understood, such as the ability to use anerobic metabolism in some cases.

Figure 2-8 showed that the increase of coronary blood flow correlates well with myocardial oxygen consumption. It is apparent also that the heart rate increases with exercise and also correlates well with coronary blood flow (Fig. 2-9). Therefore, observation of the heart rate in an exercising individual allows us to predict how hard the heart is working or how well it is performing. If the peripheral resistance or afterload (blood pressure) increases excessively during work, the myocardial oxygen consumption will have to be increased considerably more per unit of pulse elevation than if it were to remain low. Therefore, it becomes evident that the work of the heart, the cardiac output, the coronary blood flow, and the heart rate all increase in a parallel

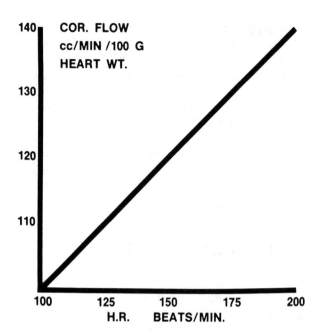

FIGURE 2-9. The coronary blood flow and pulse rate increase in a linear relationship as exercise progresses.

manner and attain a peak together. This means that when the cardiac output has reached its maximum, so have the coronary blood flow and the heart rate; hence, it is possible to make predictions about one based on another within certain limitations.

TENSION TIME INDEX

No discussion of coronary blood flow or myocardial oxygen requirements is complete without a discussion of the work on tension time index by Sarnoff and associates.[28] By controlling most of the variables with a heart lung preparation, it is possible to correlate coronary blood flow and myocardial oxygen needs with a number of parameters. Sarnoff and his associates found a positive correlation between heart rate, increase in blood pressure, diastolic volume, and myocardial oxygen consumption. The best correlation was with the so-called "tension time index," which was determined by multiplying the heart rate by the systolic blood pressure by the time of systolic contraction. Thus, the tension time index per heart beat is proportional to the area underneath the left ventricular pressure curve as shown in Figure 2-10. Because it is relatively easy to approximate this by noninvasive methods (see Chapter 1), it constitutes an important landmark in the physiology of exercise.[29] Subsequent stud-

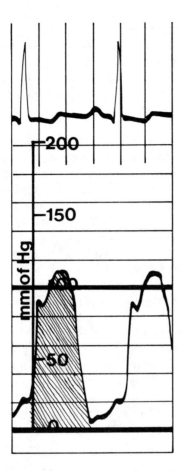

FIGURE 2-10. The area under the pressure curve (shaded area) tends to correlate with the myocardial oxygen uptake per beat. If the systolic pressure increases or the length of systole is prolonged, the oxygen requirements of the myocardium rise rapidly.

ies have demonstrated the importance of other determinants of myocardial needs. These are mentioned later.

Another important, but often overlooked, aspect in the research by Sarnoff and colleagues concerns the demonstration that the increase in stroke volume against a low systemic resistance has a relatively small extra cost in myocardial oxygen consumption. This may explain why the heart responds to exercise with this type of mechanism in a well-conditioned subject.

INTRAMYOCARDIAL TENSION

The tension or pressure developed by the ventricular wall has a very important influence in myocardial oxygen needs. It is not only related to the pressure of the blood in the ventricular cavity, but also to the thickness of the wall and the radius of the ventricle.[30]

Therefore, at a fixed pressure and wall thickness, an increase in ventricular volume will increase the tension and, thus, the oxygen consumption. The work performed by contractile elements in stretching the elastic components of the myocardium has been termed the internal contractile element work by Sonnenblick and colleagues.[30]

The discovery that wall tension is such an important determinant of myocardial oxygen consumption casts doubt on the validity of the tension time index as a reliable indicator of heart muscle demands. It now seems well established that the double product (systolic blood pressure times heart rate) is more reliable[31] than the triple product (systolic blood pressure times heart rate times systolic ejection time). This is because the systolic ejection time becomes shortened with increasing exercise and tends to decrease the total index with relationship to heart rate and blood pressure. When the time is excluded, the wall tension factor, which would increase oxygen uptake with increasing exercise and catecholamine load, approximately equals the negative influence left out of the equation when the ejection time is excluded.

No discussion of wall tension is complete without a comment on the relationship of ventricular diameter to the magnitude of tension. The Laplace relationship states that the wall tension is equal to the pressure within a cylinder times the radius of the curvature of the wall. Thus, the greater the ventricular volume, the less the curvature and the greater the radius, which will increase the tension. This is probably why dilatation is almost invariably associated with hypertrophy, so that the increased tension can be contained by the larger

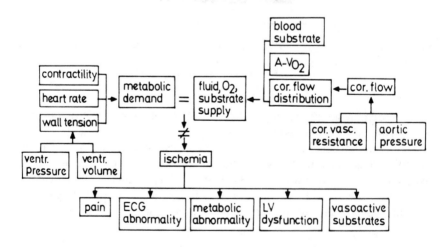

FIGURE 2-11. The oxygen supply-demand relationships are illustrated in subjects with ischemic heart disease. It can be seen that the supply and delivery are influenced by multiple factors. When contractility, wall tension, heart rate, or other parameters in the left side of the diagram are increased, there must be a corresponding increase in delivery. If not, ischemia may result.

muscle fibers. It must follow that the larger fibers also increase the oxygen demand as well as protecting the heart against the increased tension.

A schematic diagram summarizing the factors involved in the myocardial supply/demand equation are depicted in Figure 2-11.

SYSTOLIC AND DIASTOLIC TIME INTERVALS

During rest, the systolic interval time is about one third of the total cardiac cycle. As previously mentioned, most of the coronary blood flow takes place during diastole, which is alloted two thirds of the cycle when the heart rate is between 60 and 70. The time relationships become very significant in our understanding of the physiology of the coronary flow. As the heart rate accelerates, systole shortens, but not nearly as much as diastole. As a result, the heart is forced to do more and more work, but is given less and less time to obtain nourishment. This shortening of the diastolic interval may be the most important factor limiting heart rate. As the heart rate increases and diastole shortens, there just is not enough blood flow available in the time allowed to supply the demands of the heart.[25,32] Increasing diastolic stiffness as aging progresses might slow myocardial blood flow and be a factor in the progressive decrease in maximum heart rate with age. The tendency for patients with severe coronary disease and decreased compliance to have low peak heart rates and, thereby, a longer diastolic time, would tend to support this concept.

OXYGEN UPTAKE AND METABOLISM

Maximum Oxygen Uptake (VO$_2$max)

Although VO$_2$max has to do with the oxygen consumption of the total body during a maximal response to exercise, a brief discussion is warranted in this section.

Many years ago, the oxygen uptake at maximum exercise, termed VO$_2$max, was found to correlate well with degree of physical conditioning and has been accepted as an index of total body fitness by researchers in this field.[33] The capacity to take in oxygen is related not only to the effectiveness of the lungs, but also to the ability of the heart and circulatory system to transport the oxygen, and to the body tissue's ability to metabolize it. The VO$_2$max is a reproducible value, especially when corrected for body weight, and increases and decreases with the degree of physical conditioning.[34] In any given person, the intake of oxygen increases almost linearly with the heart rate or with the cardiac output (see Fig. 2-6).

Although maximal oxygen uptake values are reproducible in the same subject, considerable differences have been reported in various racial groups and in different geographic locations. Cummings[35] reported differences in data col-

TABLE 2-1. Children—Mean values for maximal oxygen uptake (ml/kg/min)

Age	Stockholm	Philadelphia	Indianapolis	Lapland	Winnipeg
6	48	—	—	—	52
8	55	—	—	—	49
10	52	29	—	51	40
12	50	30	28	48	42
14	46	34	—	44	38
16	47	23	—	42	39
18	47	19	—	42	44

Men—Mean values for maximal oxygen uptake (ml/kg/min)

Age	Boston	Stockholm	Dallas	Lapland	Norway Lumber	Norway Industry	Norway Office	Winnipeg Industry	Winnipeg Office
20–29	53	52	45	54	45	44	44	44	44
30–39	41	40	39	54	46	44	42	38	38
40–49	40	39	35	—	44	38	39	38	33
50–59	37	33	32	44	39	34	36	36	31
60	30	31	—	—	—	—	—	—	—

lected in various areas and suggested that some of the discrepancies seen between Europeans and Americans might be less pronounced if they were correct for lean body mass (Table 2-1). Even so, it would appear that in certain areas the fitness of children as well as adults is far superior to other cultures studied. The Norwegian Lapps seem to stand out among the adults as being more fit than any other population group.[21]

It is well established that VO_2max is influenced by the method used to elicit the exercise. For a time there was considerable controversy as to the limiting factor or factors affecting the capacity of the organism to take up oxygen. The data now suggest that the heart and cardiovascular capacity are the major determinants; however, the capacity of the muscle groups exercised is also critical. The oxygen demand of the working muscles is directly related to their mass and metabolic efficiency; therefore, exercise involving a larger mass of muscle is likely to be associated with a higher oxygen uptake. Indeed, running has been shown to result in a greater uptake than bicycling,[16] and both arm and leg work result in a greater VO_2max than running.[36]

Carbon Dioxide, pH, and Bicarbonate

THE EFFECTS OF CARBON DIOXIDE ON CORONARY RESISTANCE

The effects of alterations in carbon dioxide content on coronary resistance are discussed in Chapter 22. The remarkable increase in coronary resistance produced by hypocapnia with its resultant drop in myocardial oxygen extraction and coronary sinus oxygen content was demonstrated by Case[37] (Fig. 2-12). He

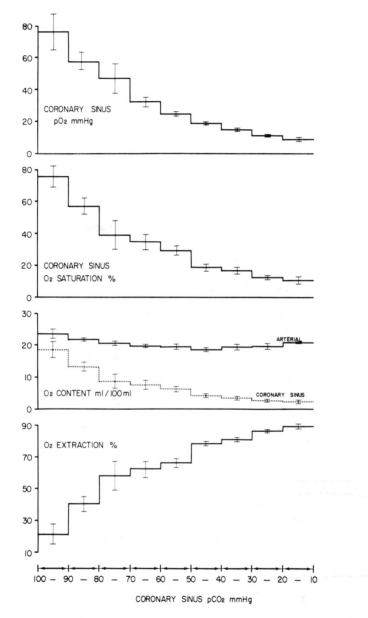

FIGURE 2-12. When the P_{CO_2} in the coronary arterial blood is varied, an inverse effect is registered on the coronary sinus oxygen content and P_{O_2}. As the coronary sinus P_{CO_2} is decreased, the extraction of oxygen from the arterial blood increases as flow decreases.

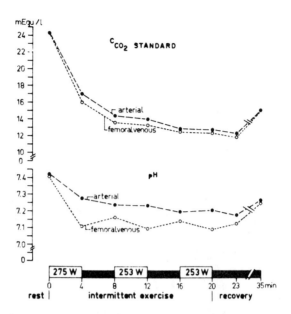

FIGURE 2-13. The pH and standard sodium bicarbonate buffer in arterial and venous blood both decrease during intermittent exercise.

showed that a reduction in arterial PCO_2 of less than 20 mm Hg will almost double the coronary vascular resistance, and that a severe reduction in coronary flow, possibly to the point of ischemia, can be produced by hypocapnia. This appears to be somewhat independent of the pH changes.[38] It has also been demonstrated that an increase in PO_2 in the coronary blood will decrease coronary flow,[39] and a decrease will cause a marked increase in perfusion. The fact that carbon dioxide has such a potent effect on flow questions the previously held view that the oxygen content of the myocardium is the primary regulator of coronary vascular resistance.

As exercise progresses, there is a consistent decrease in pH and sodium bicarbonate that correlates with a rise in blood lactate. The response to intermittent exercise as reported by Keul and Doll[40] is presented in Figure 2-13. It is of interest to note that the lactic acid in the working muscle is only partly liberated into the blood, thus decreasing the tendency toward acidosis, which would have a deleterious effect on the organism and its response to exercise if the pH falls much below 7.1.[41]

SUBSTRATE USE IN THE HEART

Carbohydrates

It is becoming increasingly clear that the cardiac metabolism varies considerably when comparing normal with hypoxic or ischemic conditions.[42] Hypoxia is used here to indicate adequate coronary flow with reduced oxygen content as distinct from a reduced or interrupted flow of blood with normal oxygen tension, constituting ischemia.

The metabolism of glucose, pyruvate, and lactate by the heart is determined by their levels of concentration in the arterial blood. Glucose and lactate are used at normal levels of concentration in about equal proportions in the blood, but the pyruvate level is so low that it plays a limited role.[43]

The total aerobic metabolism of carbohydrates accounts for about 35 percent of the total oxygen consumption. There is some evidence that the arterial insulin level is important in the regulation of glucose use by the heart according to Bing.[31] Under normal conditions, the human heart uses about 11 gm of glucose and 10 gm of lactate per day. Thus, the concentration levels in the coronary sinus of both lactate and glucose are lower than in the arterial blood. Acidosis has not only been demonstrated to increase coronary blood flow but also, in some degree, to increase glucose and lactate uptake. Alkalosis, on the other hand, decreases coronary blood flow and the uptake of both glucose and lactate.[44] It is of interest that the heart is unable to use fructose.

Noncarbohydrates

Bing[31] and Detry[34] have claimed that the human heart has a predilection for fatty acids as fuel. It has been shown that about 67 percent of the oxygen extracted by the heart goes toward the metabolic use of fatty acids. Ketones, triglycerides, cholesterol, lipoprotein, and the various free fatty acids make up this fraction depending on their level of concentration and on certain hormone and enzyme influences. For instance, diabetes decreases the relative use of oleic acid, at least in animals.[11]

It is often said that when the heart has access to carbohydrates and lipids together, it will preferentially use the lipid.[45] Although there have been some investigators who question this,[46] it has been clearly shown that an isolated perfused heart can maintain contractility for a long time by oxidizing endogenous lipids.[47] A buildup of long-chain acylcoenzyme A (acyl-CoA) ester will produce inhibition of adenine nucleotide translocase, which causes early loss of functional integrity of the mitochondrial membrane.[40] This can be inhibited by given carnitine, which might then restore the membrane's ability to mobilize calcium.[48] It has also been reported that a nicotinic acid analog that reduced plasma free fatty acids will minimize the S-T changes generated by ischemia in humans during exercise testing.[49]

Role of Nucleotides and Phosphorylase

The activity of nucleotides and phosphorylase is intimately related to coronary flow. Ischemia leads to a significant diminution of creatinine phosphate and an increase in inorganic phosphate. This results in a decrease in adenosine tri-phosphate (ATP) and an increase in adenosine diphosphate (ADP). The latter may be a major reason for coronary dilatation in myocardial anoxia.

AEROBIC METABOLISM

The accepted figure for oxygen consumption of the normally beating left ventricle is about 8 to 10 ml of oxygen per 100 gm per minute. When the output increases six- to eightfold in champion athletes, the oxygen consumption must increase to at least 35 to 40 ml per 100 gm per minute, and the ATP production must rise to 15 to 20 mmole of ATP per 100 gm per minute. This very high energy demand can be met because of the high concentration of mitochondria in the well-conditioned heart.[50] Under low metabolic rates, the oxidation rate will be determined by the availability of the free fatty acids and the rate of acyl-CoA oxidation of the citric acid cycle and, at high metabolic rates, by the rate of acyl translocation across the intermitochondrial membrane.

ANAEROBIC METABOLISM

Although the ATP concentration in the heart is about the same as that in the skeletal muscle, the glycogen content is about 5 gm per kg, a third of that in its skeletal muscle counterpart.[51] The heart begins to deteriorate about 8 to 12 beats after oxygen delivery ceases.[52] This is not due to depletion of high energy phosphates; therefore, must mean that the ATP available to the contractile protein compartment is limited or that the rapid buildup of metabolic end-products in some way inhibits contraction. In the experimental perfused heart, oxygen can be given without any other substrate and the myocardium will function for at least 40 minutes before glycogen is depleted,[53] indicating that there is normally an inhibitor that has been washed out in this experiment.

HYPOXIA AND ISCHEMIA

From the above discussion, it is evident that the metabolic effects of hypoxia (reduced oxygen content) and ischemia (reduced flow) are different. Biopsy material from ischemic hearts shows that contraction stops when ATP is only 20 percent depleted, but when the flow is maintained and ATP is reduced 40 percent, contraction continues to be almost normal.[45] Studies in the working rat heart clearly show the difference between hypoxia and ischemia. When coronary flow is maintained, but oxygen is replaced with nitrogen, there is a threefold increase in glucose use within five minutes, which is maintained for 30 minutes.[54] Glycogen stores drop by 70 percent in four minutes when these same animals are made ischemic by reduction in coronary flow of 50 percent or more. Glucose use drops immediately and is down to 50 percent of control within 12 minutes.[55] After 30 minutes of anoxia with normal coronary flow, intercellular lactate doubles, but after 30 minutes of ischemia with low coronary flow, the lactate increases tenfold.

It would appear that the accumulation of lactate is a significant factor in that the low pH reduces the rate of energy production by interfering with subcellular calcium transport. The importance of the above data is in the realization that even moderate reduction in blood flow (50 percent) will trigger biochemical changes and decrease myocardial function. There has been a tendency for cardiologists to assign some arbitrary number to the degree of coronary narrowing necessary to produce ischemia (usually 70 to 80 percent). It can be seen that a host of factors, especially those related to pH in the muscle will alter substrate use and, therefore, cardiac function. The factors leading to the ischemic changes reflected in the ECG and the associated decrease in contractility are further discussed in Chapter 4.

TEMPERATURE

External environment has a profound effect on the organism and its ability to adapt to exercise. This is due primarily to the need to dissipate the heat generated by the contraction of the muscles. Not only is there an increase in the heart rate with a higher body temperature, but there seems to be some decrease in the total efficiency of the heart[11] (Fig. 2-14). The data presented in Figure 2-14 are from a well-conditioned oarsman on the Harvard crew.[56]

Heat

Brouha[57] and Burch[56] have shown that the heart works less efficiently as the temperature rises and that a hot, humid environment results in a marked increase in cardiac work for any given level of external work. it has also been demonstrated that the recovery from work is much slower, apparently due to the body's failure to dissipate the heat generated. As temperature and humidity rise, the heart rate is increased for any given workload, as well as for the resting heart. If body temperature rises much over 107°F, heat stroke can result due to central nervous system (CNS) changes followed by a complete loss of vascular tone.

It is well known that the skin blood flow is reduced in subjects who have a cardiac output that is below the metabolic needs at whatever level of exercise. The gray skin color is easily recognized as clinical evidence of this condition. When this occurs, the body is not only signaling failure to provide adequate total blood flow, but is now unable to dissipate heat generated by muscle contraction. The resultant rising core temperature will then further inhibit cardiac output, thus initiating a vicious cycle.

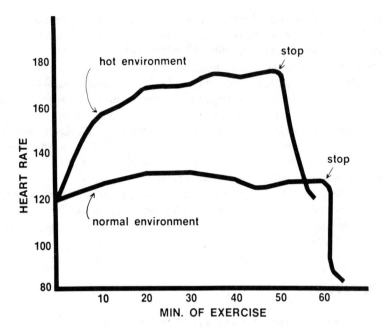

FIGURE 2-14. The increase in heart rate associated with a hot environment during exercise demonstrates the need for an increased cardiac output as the body temperature rises. This increased demand may be excessive if heart disease is present and the increased cardiac output cannot be generated.

In subjects with a normal cardiovascular system, repeated exposure to high temperatures will alter the ability to cope with this problem by the inhibition of sodium loss and, thus, reduce the expected decrease in central blood volume. With a larger blood volume and, therefore, a better stroke volume, there will be more cardiac output and more blood available to augment skin flow. This will improve heat loss and improve the cardiovascular function in general.

Robinson[15] reported that after conditioning has taken place, the effect of heat on performance is considerably reduced, confirming the adaptive mechanism described above.

Cold

The oxygen uptake at rest in a cool environment (50°F) has been demonstrated to be considerably higher than when a subject is exposed to moderate temperatures, that is, 60–70°F. Once exercise is underway, the oxygen consumption in a cool environment is about the same as in a warm one.[58]

Even though no measurable increase in oxygen uptake per unit of work has been documented, the general efficiency of the organism is less than optimum at a low temperature. It is well known that athletic endurance records are never established in extreme cold. Patients with coronary insufficiency have an earlier onset of angina in the cold due to an inordinant rise in blood pressure with exercise. This may be due to the vasoconstriction in the skin and other superficial vascular beds. Mice, in contradistinction to man,[59] do not adapt well to cold and have a consistently higher oxygen uptake when forced to exercise in a cold environment.

There is no doubt that physical fitness improves cold tolerance. This has been demonstrated by Hart,[59] of Ottawa, who also reports that training and the resultant changes in VO_2max are not altered by cold.

RESPIRATION

A detailed description of the pulmonary function in respiration will not be included at this point. On the other hand, a few remarks about the respiratory adaptation to exercise will be discussed. The heart has long been recognized as the limiting factor in the oxygen delivery system during exercise in the healthy individual. However, the respiratory apparatus is obviously involved and its basic function should be appreciated.

Exercise Hyperpnea

The ventilatory response to the onset of exercise is characterized by a rapid, almost instantaneous, increase in ventilation. It has been argued that because this starts within a few seconds and occurs before any metabolite from the exercising limbs could reach an appropriate sensor, that it must be due to a neurogenic stimulus. However, if this were totally true, one would expect to find a concomitant early drop in PCO_2, which is usually not present. Casaburi and colleagues[60] have shown that there is an abrupt increase in cardiac output at the onset of exercise that delivers an increased carbon dioxide load to the lungs, so that the ventilatory response is appropriately adequate to maintain the PCO_2 in the normal range. Later on, the respiration gradually increases in accordance with the metabolic needs and this process is believed to be controlled by a hormonal process. The exact pathways regulating volume of ventilation during exercise are still not completely established. There seems to be a large hypoxic component varying from 13–54 percent.[61] There is a smaller nonhypoxic component probably mostly carbon dioxide, so that the sensitivity of subjects to oxygen drive increases with exercise, but not to carbon dioxide. The endurance athlete seems to have less of a hypoxic drive than a sedentary counterpart; therefore, allowing the athlete to function at a slightly lower level of PO_2.

Rate Versus Depth

The rate and volume or depth of respiration are the obvious major mechanisms to be altered in increasing oxygen uptake. The respiratory muscles must overcome two types of resistance; the elastic resistance of the chest wall, the muscles, and the lungs themselves, and the airway resistance caused by the friction of air movement in the trachea, bronchi, and alveolae. The anatomical dead space between the alveolae and the mouth must be considered when the determination of optimal tidal volume and respiratory rate for any given increase in ventilation is considered.

In normal subjects, the increased ventilation at low levels of power is achieved by an increase in tidal volume up to a maximum that is about 60 percent of the subject's vital capacity.

Increasing the rate may merely move the air in the dead space in and out without increasing alveolar ventilation significantly. Therefore, as the demand for a greater total volume of air ensues, there must be an associated increase in tidal volume over and above that needed to fill the dead space. Increases in tidal volume are, however, more costly in terms of muscle work, especially if the airway or elastic resistance is above normal. The tidal volume at rest is usually about 500 ml (about 150 ml being dead space) with a respiratory rate of about 12–15 per minute. This produces a minute volume of about 6 liters per minute, but an effective alveolar ventilation of only about 4.2 liters per minute. Strenuous exercise may result in a minute volume of 140 liters per minute or more produced by respiratory rates of 60–70 and tidal volumes around 2 liters. When the respiratory rate and depth are increased, the extra oxygen expended on respiration reaches a point where it becomes a major metabolic burden.

The oxygen cost of breathing, therefore, assumes considerable importance. Factors such as emphysema or bronchospasm, which increase airway resistance; or pulmonary fibrosis or lung edema, which increase the elastic resistance; markedly increase the work of breathing and, thus, reduce the efficiency of the lungs. Bouhys[62] believes that the ability to function at higher tidal volumes decreases rapidly with age, making this one of the limiting factors in oxygen transport as well as in cardiac output.

Diffusion

The rate at which gas passes through the alveolar wall into the capillaries is often decreased in lung diseased states. There has been some question as to whether the rate of diffusion is a significant limiting factor in ventilation at high levels of performance. Measurements of diffusing capacity during exercise are markedly increased over the resting values, but it is not known if this is merely a function of increased pulmonary capillary blood flow or an actual physiologic alteration in the characteristics of the barriers to the passage of oxygen and carbon dioxide. The steady state diffusing capacity measured during exercise has been found to correlate with the vital capacity, which in turn correlates with the degree of physical conditioning and the VO_2max.[63]

SUMMARY

This chapter has reviewed the current concepts believed to best describe how the cardiovascular system responds to exercise. Although the changes are quite complex, our knowledge in this area has increased dramatically in the last few years. One must marvel at the capacity of the intricately interrelated systems to adjust to the wide range of stresses, such as an increase in cardiac pumping capacity of sevenfold, the elimination of heat in a variety of climatic extremes, and providing for the wide range of metabolic requirements of the various tissues of the body. When we consider that the mitochondria, the metabolic machines making it possible to increase our aerobic capacity to such extremes, may well be the product of what was once the symbiotic association between one-celled organisms, we can only marvel at how well the complex metabolic, chemical, mechanical, and neurogenic mechanisms fit together.

As we continue to learn about the intricate steps necessary to integrate the whole organism, our ability to deal with its tendency to dysfunction will certainly be enhanced. For a more detailed monogram on the coronary circulation, the reader should consult the work by Marcus.[64]

REFERENCES

1. McRitchie, RJ, et al: Role of arterial baroreceptors in mediating cardiovascular response to exercise. Am J Physiol 230:85, 1976.
2. Sheffield, LT, Holt, JH, and Reeves, TJ: Exercise graded by heart rate in electrocardiographic testing for angina pectoris. Circulation 32:622, 1965.
3. Chapman, CB, Fisher, NJ, and Sproule, BJ: Behavior of stroke volume at rest and during exercise in human beings. J Clin Invest 30:1208, 1960.
4. Bates, DV: Commentary on cardiorespiratory determinants of cardiovascular fitness. Can Med Assoc J 96:704, 1967.
5. Sheps, DS, et al: Effect of a physical conditioning program upon left ventricular ejection fractions determined serially by a noninvasive technique. Cardiology 64:256, 1979.
6. Hindman, MC and Wallace, AG: Radionuclide exercise studies. In Cohen, LS, Mock, MB, and Ringqvist, LG (eds): Physical Conditioning and Cardiovascular Rehabilitation. John Wiley & Sons, New York, 1981, p 33.
7. Wallace, AG, et al: Effects of exercise training on ventricular function in coronary disease (abstr). Circulation II–197.
8. Roskamm, H: Optimum patterns of exercise for healthy adults. Can Med Assoc J 96:895, 1967.
9. Penpargkul, S and Scherer, J: The effects of physiological training upon the mechanical and metabolic performance of the rat heart. J Clin Invest 49:1959, 1970.
10. Scherer, J: Physical training and intrinsic cardiac adaptations. Circulation 47:677, 1973.
11. Finkelstein, LJ, Spitzer, JJ, and Scott, JC: Society for the study of atherosclerosis: Myocardial uptake of free fatty acids in dogs. Circulation 22:679, 1960.

12. PETRO, JK, HOLLANDER, AP, AND BOUMAN, LM: *Instantaneous cardiac acceleration in man induced by a voluntary muscle contraction.* J Appl Physiol 29:794, 1970.

13. FAGRAEUS, L AND LINNARSSON, D: *Autonomic origin of heart rate fluctuations at the onset of muscular exercise.* J Appl Physiol 40:679, 1976.

14. SCHWARTZ, PJ AND STONE, HL: *Effects of unilateral stellectomy upon cardiac performance during exercise in dogs.* Circ Res 44:637, 1979.

15. ROBINSON, S: *Experimental studies of physical fitness.* Arbeits-physiologic. 10:251, 1930.

16. BORST, C, HOLLANDER, AP, AND BOUMAN, LM: *Cardiac acceleration elicited by voluntary muscle contractions of minimal duration.* J Appl Physiol 32:70, 1972.

17. GLAGOV, S, ET AL: *Heart rates during 24 hours of unusual activity.* J Appl Physiol 29:799, 1970.

18. POLLACK, ML: *How much exercise is enough?* Phys Sports Med 6:4, 1978.

19. KLOCKE, FJ: *Coronary blood flow in man.* Prog Cardiovasc Dis 19:117, 1976.

20. SCOTT, JC: *Physical activity and the coronary circulation.* Can Med Assoc J 96:853, 1967.

21. ANDERSEN, KL AND HERMANSEN, L: *Aerobic work capacity in middle aged Norwegian men.* J Appl Physiol 20:432, 1965.

22. GREENFIELD, JC, ET AL: *Studies of blood flow in aorta to coronary venous bypass grafts in man.* J Clin Invest 51:2724, 1972.

23. ROSS, G: *Adrenergic responses of the coronary vessels.* Circ Res 39:463, 1976.

24. UCHIDA, Y AND UEDA, H: *Nonuniform blood flow through the ischemic myocardium induced by stellate ganglion stimulation.* Jpn Circ J 36:673, 1972.

25. BECKER, LC, FORTUIN, NJ, AND PITT, B: *Effect of ischemia and antianginal drugs on the distribution of radioactive microspheres in the canine left ventricle.* Circ Res 28:263, 1971.

26. DOLE, VF: *The relations between non-esterified fatty acids in plasma and the metabolism of glucose.* J Clin Invest 35:150, 1956.

27. MIDIAL, G AND BING, RJL: *Myocardial efficiency.* Ann NY Acad Sci 72:555, 1959.

28. SARNOFF, SJ, ET AL: *Hemodynamic determinants of oxygen consumption of the heart with special reference to the tension-time index.* In ROSENBAUM, FF (ED): *Work and the Heart.* Paul B. Hoeber, Harper & Bros., New York, 1959.

29. GOBEL, FL, ET AL: *The rate-pressure product as an index of myocardial oxygen consumption during exercise in patients with angina pectoris.* Circulation 57:549, 1978.

30. SONNENBLICK, EH, ROSS, J, AND BRAUNWALD, E: *Oxygen consumption of the heart. Newer concepts of its multifactorial determination.* Am J Cardiol 22:328, 1968.

31. BING, RJ: *Cardiac metabolism.* Physiol Rev 45:2, 1965.

32. NAJMI, M, ET AL: *Selective cine coronary arteriography correlated with the hemodynamic response to physical stress.* Dis Chest 54:33, 1968.

33. TAYLOR, HL, BUSKIRK, E, AND HENSCHEL, A: *Maximal oxygen intake as objective measure of cardiorespiratory performance.* J Appl Physiol 8:73, 1955.

34. DETRY, JR: *Exercise Testing and Training in Coronary Heart Disease.* Williams & Wilkins, Baltimore, 1973.

35. CUMMINGS, GR: *Current levels of fitness.* Can Med Assoc J 96:868, 1967.

36. HERMANSEN, L: *Oxygen transport during exercise in human subjects.* Acta Physiol Scand (Suppl)39:91, 1973.

37. CASE, RB. *The response of canine coronary vascular resistance to local alterations in coronary arterial P_{CO_2}.* Circ Res 39:558, 1976.

38. KITTLE, CF, AOKI, H, AND BROWN, E: *The role of pH and CO_2 in the distribution of blood flow.* Surgery 57:139, 1965.

39. CASE, RB, BERGULUND, E, AND SARNOFF, SJ: *Changes in coronary resistance and ventricular function resulting from acutely induced anemia and the effect thereon of coronary stenosis.* Am J Med 18:397, 1955.

40. KEUL, J AND DOLL, E: *Intermittent exercise, metabolites, P_{O_2} and acid base equilibrium in the blood.* J Appl Physiol 34:220, 1973.

41. SIMSON, E: *Physiology of Work Capacity and Fatigue.* Charles C Thomas, Springfield, Illinois, 1971.

42. JENNINGS, RB: *Early phases of myocardial ischemia injury and infarctions.* Am J Cardiol 24:753, 1969.

43. BRAUN-MENENDEZ, E, CHOTE, AL, AND GREGORY, RA: *Usage of pyruvic acid by the dog's heart.* Q J Exp Physiol 29:91, 1939.

44. GOODYEAR, AVN, ET AL: *The effect of acidosis and alkalosis on coronary blood flow and myocardial metabolism in the intact dog.* Am J Physiol 200:628, 1961.

45. GUDBJARNASON, S, MATTHES, P, AND RAVENO, KG: *Functional compartmentalization of ATP and creatine phosphate in heart muscle.* J Mol Cell Cardiol 1:25, 1973.

46. OPIE, LH: *Metabolism of the heart in health and disease, II.* Am Heart J 77:100, 1969.

47. OLSON, RE AND HOESCHEN, RJ: *Utilization of endogenous lipids by the isolated perfused rat heart.* Biochem J 103:796, 1967.

48. SKROGO, E, ET AL: *Control of energy production in myocardial ischemia.* Circ Res (Suppl 1)38:75, 1976.

49. LUXTON, MR, MILLER, NE, AND OLIVER, MF: *Antilipolytic therapy in angina pectoris, reduction in exercise-induced ST depression.* Br Heart J 38:1200, 1976.

50. GIBBS, CL: *Cardiac energetics.* Physiol Rev 58:174, 1978.

51. FISHER, RB AND WILLIAMSON, JR: *The oxygen uptake of the perfused rat heart.* J Physiol (Lond) 158:86, 1961.

52. KUBLER, W AND SPIEKERMANN, PG: *Regulations of glycolysis in the ischemic and anoxic myocardium.* J Mol Cell Cardiol 1:351, 1970.

53. THORN, WG, GERCKEN, C, AND HURTER, P: *Function, substrate supply and metabolic content of rabbit heart perfused in situ.* Am J Physiol 214:139, 1968.

54. NEELY, JR, ROVETTO, MJ, AND WHITMER, JT: *Effects of ischemia on function and metabolism of the isolated working rat heart.* Am J Physiol 225:651, 1973.

55. OPIE, LH: *Effects of regional ischemia in metabolism of glucose and fatty acids.* Circ Res (Suppl 1)38:152, 1976.

56. BURCH, GE: *Influence of hot and humid environment upon the work of the heart.* In ROSENBAUM, FF (ED): *Work and the Heart.* Paul B. Hoeber, Harper & Bros., New York, 1959.

57. BROUHA, LA: *Effect of work on the heart.* In ROSENBAUM, FF (ED): *Work and the Heart.* Paul B. Hoeber, Harper & Bros., New York, 1959.

58. ANDERSEN, KL: *The effect of physical training with and without cold exposure upon physiological indices of fitness for work.* Can Med Assoc J 96:801, 1967.

59. HART, JS: *Commentaries on the effect of physical training with and without cold exposure upon physiological indices of fitness for work.* Can Med Assoc J 96:803, 1967.

60. CASABURI, R, ET AL: *Ventilating central characteristics of the exercise hyperpnea as discerned from dynamic forcing techniques.* Chest (Suppl 20th Aspen Lung Conference) 73:2280, 1978.

61. MARTIN, B, ET AL: *Chemical drives to breathe as determinants of exercise ventilation.* Chest (Suppl 20th Aspen Lung Conference) 73:2283, 1978.

62. BOUHYS, A: *Commentary to cardiorespiratory determinants of cardiovascular fitness.* Can Med Assoc J 96:704, 1967.

63. HOLMGREN, A: *Cardiorespiratory determinants of cardiovascular fitness.* Can Med Assoc J 96:697, 1967.

64. MARCUS, ML: *The Coronary Circulation in Health and Disease.* McGraw-Hill, New York, 1983.

3

EXTRA-CARDIAC EFFECTS OF EXERCISE

IMMEDIATE EFFECTS OF EXERCISE
  Autonomic Responses
  Blood and Plasma
  Lipids
  Blood Clotting
  Fibrinolysis
  Temperature
  Redistribution of Blood Flow
  Renal Function
  Gastrointestinal Function
  Muscles
  Metabolic Cost of Contraction
  Substrate Use in Exercising Muscles
      Energy Cost of Exercise: Walk Versus Run
      Steady State and Oxygen Debt
      Carbohydrates
      Proteins
      Fats
      Hormonal Influences
      Glucoregulatory Hormones
LONG-TERM EFFECTS OF EXERCISE
  Bed Rest
  Weightlessness
  Effects of Conditioning
  Maximum Oxygen Uptake (VO_2 max)
  AV-O_2 Difference

Blood Volume
Peripheral Resistance and Systemic Blood Pressure
Heat Dissipation
Heart Rate
Lipid Metabolism
Personality
Resistance to Sequelae of Coronary Atherosclerosis
Complications of Exercise
Influence on Aging
Summary

This chapter deals with the changes in the physiology and circulation not primarily associated with the pumping action of the heart, but closely interrelated to the pump and its function. Discussions of both the acute and the long-term effects of exercise are included.

IMMEDIATE EFFECTS OF EXERCISE

Autonomic Responses

The onset of exercise is associated with a number of cardiac and peripheral vascular responses mediated primarily through the autonomic nerve system. As exercise is initiated, there is an immediate withdrawal of vagal tone, creating sympathetic vasoconstriction in the capitence vessels, primarily the veins. This is associated with an increase in heart and respiratory rate and an increase in venous pressure and shortly after in respiratory minute volume. In the early stages of dynamic exercise, the cardiovascular system does not deliver enough blood to satisfy the increased metabolic needs of the muscles, resulting in an oxygen debt. If the level of exercise is submaximal, the cardiac output will "catch up" in a few minutes and deliver an appropriate volume of blood for the work being performed. Along with the increased blood flow a redistribution occurs, where the flow to the skin, viscera, and nonworking muscles is decreased and the flow to the active muscles is appropriately adjusted. An increase in the metabolic activity of the active tissue also increases oxygen extraction causing a greater difference between the concentration of oxygen in the arteries and veins in the vascular bed perfusing the working muscles. If the muscle group is large as with the legs, the AV-O_2 difference is significant enough to be detected in the venous return to the heart.

Blood and Plasma

As exercise-induced sweating produces loss of extracellular fluid, the circulating blood volume decreases. This is partially replenished at the expense of the intracellular water and electrolytes. The net decrease in plasma, however, tends to produce a relatively higher concentration of red blood cells, hemoglobin, and plasma proteins. Hemoconcentration produces increased viscosity and increased resistance to blood flow. The increased oxygen carrying capacity, as the unit volume of hemoglobin increases, is an important element in the increased capacity to perform work. However, if sweating and water loss from breathing and insensible loss reduces the central blood volume enough, a decreased cardiac output is unavoidable. A weight loss of 20 pounds in football players during a game has been measured, and a decrease of 7 percent of body weight in marathon runners is not unusual.[1] It is now known that the replenishment of this loss with fluid intake during prolonged exercise is essential to optimum function.

Lipids

Reports of a decrease in cholesterol levels at the time of exercise are conflicting, as researchers have reported both an increase and a decrease in its concentration. There may well be an increased mobilization of cholesterol during exercise, but little significant change can be expected.[2,3,4] On the other hand, plasma triglyceride levels drop at the time of exercise and do not return to control amounts for about 48 hours.[5] Thus, this lipid, which may be equally as important as cholesterol in the genesis of coronary atheroma, can be consistently reduced by a regular exercise program.[6,7] Evidence is now available that suggests that triglycerides are intimately related to high density lipoproteins (HDL) and as the triglycerides decrease, the HDL rises.[8] Exercise also initiates a progressive mobilization of free fatty acids and glycerols with an increase in plasma concentrations.[9]

Blood Clotting

One of the natural adaptive phenomena associated with an alarm reaction or with exercise is an increased tendency toward blood clotting.[10] Ikkala, Myllyla, and Sarajas have demonstrated that exercise shortens both coagulation and bleeding time.[11] The number of platelets also increases significantly. The most dramatic change occurs during contact activities such as football, which increases the platelet count over 150 percent. This reflects increases in Factors XI, XII, and VIII, all of which increase almost 100 percent with short-term strenuous exercise.* Egeberg[12] demonstrated that transfusions of plasma drawn

---

*These are substances found in the plasma and platelets that are important in the progression of the normal clotting process. Because some of the elements of clotting seem to play an important role in the development of atheroma and ultimately thrombi, which may form on these atheroma, more attention is being turned to this area in an attempt to determine its influence in the development of coronary heart disease.

immediately after exercise would correct the prolonged bleeding time of von Willebrand's disease. This is probably due to a rise in platelet adhesiveness, which is intimately associated with Factor VII.

Fibrinolysis

A detrimental connotation to the above changes might be implied because exercise is also associated with increased circulating fibrinolysis.[13] Thus, if one sustains a laceration, the blood will clot faster but the likelihood of intravascular coagulation is decreased. The increase in fibrinolysin normally associated with exercise has been found to be absent in patients with Type IV hyperlipoproteinemia.[14,15] Thus, the protective and probably beneficial effect of increased fibrinolysis, which might act to remove fibrin deposits from the vascular intima, is unavailable in some patients with coronary disease.

A number of studies have demonstrated that fibrinolysis is increased as much as sevenfold by 10 minutes of extremely severe exercise, and after 30 minutes of moderate exercise a similar result is achieved.[16,17] It would appear that mild exercise has almost no effect on fibrinolysis. The exact relationship of fibrinolysis to coronary atherosclerosis has not been established, but it seems that temporary decreases in this activity might alter the tendency to form atheromatous plaques in view of their demonstrated fibrin composition.

Temperature

During exposure to environmental heat stress, the body is acutely faced with thermal loads greater than 200 watts. Furthermore, steps to reduce this are usually initiated early on by seeking shade, protection from sun or some other means. Thermal loads associated with increased metabolic activity of the muscles can be in the excess of 800 watts for long periods and occasionally up to 1000 watts for a short time. Distribution of this much heat through the body in the absence of regulatory adjustments, would raise the core temperature (mean body temperature) one degree centigrade for every 5 to 8 minutes and result in a temperature high enough to cause brain damage within 15 minutes.[18] Without appropriate mechanisms to dissipate this heat, heavy exercise would be restricted to 15 or 20 minutes. An area in the hypothalamus responds to the temperature of the blood and mediates the various adjustments that protect us by balancing heat production and loss.[19] It is of interest that the "set point" or baseline temperature that controls the regulatory adjustments, such as an increase in skin blood flow, is believed to be the same in exercise as it is at rest. When a subject has a "fever" as might occur during an infection, the temperature "set point" is raised.[20] Thus, in this situation the increase in skin blood flow would not be activated until the new higher "set point" had been exceeded. The changes associated with the onset of exercise take place as depicted in Figure 3-1 from Mitchell's work,[20] where the muscle temperatures seem to increase rapidly followed by the core temperature and finally by the skin, acting as a radiator. The thermal energy depicted in the bottom panel is eventually dissipated with only about 20 percent of it being converted into mechanical energy by the muscles. The various heat loss mechanisms and their relative importance during exercise is depicted in Figure 3-2. It can be seen that the ambient air temperature is an important factor in the relationship between respiration (Eres), radiation (R), convection (C), and sweating (ESW). It can be seen that the skin temperature only changes 8°C over a 25°C change in ambient temperature. These changes in skin temperature are relatively independent of the level of exercise, while the changes in core temperature are relatively independent of the ambient air temperature. The sum of the energy

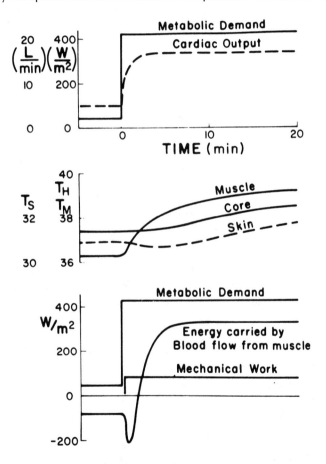

FIGURE 3-1. The three panels depict changes in cardiac output (*top*) with steady state exercise. Changes in temperature and time of change (*middle*), with muscle increasing early and core temperature following. The skin showing the least and latest rise. The thermal energy (*bottom*) carried from the muscle is dissipated in the skin with very little being used. (From Nadel,[18] with permission.)

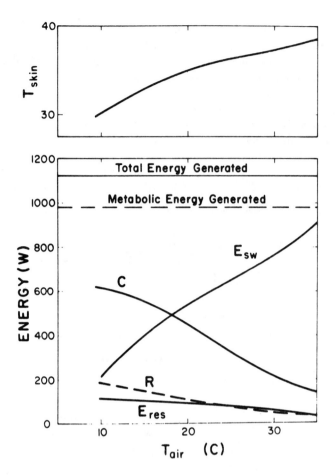

FIGURE 3-2. Heat loss mechanisms. As ambient air temperature rises during exercise, the heat loss by respiration (E res), radiation (R), and convection (C) play less of a role as sweating (Esw) increases rapidly. (From Mitchell,[20] with permission.)

transferred by the four methods mentioned above equal the energy metabolically produced and the absorption of solar energy. It can be seen that at high workloads, sweating is the most important aspect of this process and the ability to sweat, which varies from person to person, may be one limiting factor in endurance performance. In marathon running, for example, muscle temperatures have been recorded as high as 109°F, while at the same time the rectal temperature was 106°F. This "fever" of metabolic activity must be dissipated efficiently. The effects of the fluid and electrolyte loss, of course, are considerable as sweating continues. Failure of this system to function well in hot humid climates has a dramatic and deleterious effect on the heart and circulation. Likewise, a cold environment producing local vasoconstriction and, therefore, an increased peripheral resistance, will increase cardiac work; however, as the workload increases this effect is minimized.[21] Recent work[22] has demonstrated that exercise in patients with congestive heart failure produces a drop in core temperature. We have extended this to patients with coronary heart disease and find them to respond in the same way.[23] The exact reason for this is not yet clear.

Redistribution of Blood Flow

From the above discussion of temperature, it becomes obvious that the facility to selectively constrict certain vascular beds and preferentially shunt the blood to the areas of increased use is essential in adjusting to exercise.[1,24] With strenuous exertion, the splanchnic flow (hepatic, visceral, and renal) drops to about 20 percent of control within three or four minutes after exercise is initiated, as more blood is diverted to the skin and working muscles.[25] This delay explains why warmup is essential for optimum performance. When two major muscle groups are competing for flow (Fig. 3-3[20]), a balance is reached that is less than either might have when the opposing group is quiescent.[26,27,28] During upright exercise there is considerable competition between skin and muscles for the available cardiac output. It appears that in muscles even with very high blood flow there is minimal increase in the muscle blood volume, probably

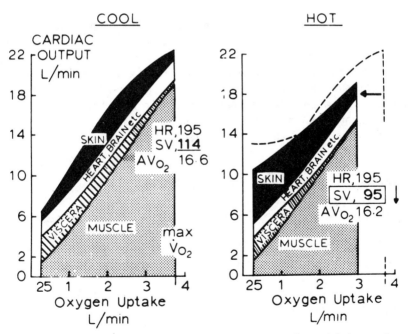

FIGURE 3-3. The relative flow in liters/min to various organs are depicted during maximum exercise in hot and cold environments. It can be seen that the skin gets more blood, at the expense of muscle in heat as compared with cold. (From Mitchell,[20] with permission.)

because the contracting muscle compresses veins as well as arteries, and because venoconstriction in this vascular bed is very active.[29] In the skin, however, no such containment occurs and when the forces of gravity are considered, the compensatory mechanisms are severely stressed. It must be remembered that 70 percent of the total blood volume is below the heart in an upright man and 80 percent of this volume resides in the veins and that cutaneous veins in contradistinction to arterioles have little ability to vasoconstrict.[30]

Renal Function

As mentioned above, renal blood flow is decreased during exercise in favor of flow to exercising muscles; therefore, the volume of urine is decreased as well as the ability to excrete nitrogenous waste products. This is undoubtedly one of the reasons why cardiac patients with marginal compensation diurese at night when the working muscles no longer need nourishment. At this time, a reestablishment of the renal blood flow takes place, thus increasing glomerular filtration.

Gastrointestinal Function

The gastrointestinal tract shares with the kidney, a relatively decreased blood flow during exercise. This results in a decrease in the secretion of digestive enzymes as well as a decrease in motility. These changes, however, are quite transient and rarely interfere with overall function. The absorption of fluid from the gastrointestinal tract is reduced however, especially if it is hypertonic. In low cardiac output states, a relative decrease in splanchnic blood flow may lead to gas and flatulence. This might be diagnosed as a primary disorder if the underlying cardiac insufficiency is not recognized.

Muscles

Changes in size and shape take place in working muscles because of the increased blood volume. These changes are temporary and the muscles return to normal soon after exercise is terminated. As has been previously discussed, a local increase in temperature occurs, depending on the activity of the muscle.

Metabolic Cost of Contraction

When the muscle is subjected to isometric contraction, the oxygen consumption rises linearly, but the oxygen debt rises more steeply and probably exponentially.[31] Thus, there is an increasing percentage of energy derived from anaerobic sources as the tension rises. This is probably related to the fact that muscle blood flow is decreased by sustained contraction. Rhythmic contraction is associated with better muscle perfusion and, therefore, can be continued longer than an isometric load. It appears that sustained isometric contraction actually shuts off blood flow to the working muscles and this is self-limiting to a significant degree.

Substrate Use in Exercising Muscles

ENERGY COST OF EXERCISE: WALK VERSUS RUN

As soon as a method for measuring oxygen uptake became practical in the early 1930s, intense interest in the measurement of the metabolic cost of various activities followed. An excellent review of this subject was published by Passmore and Durnin in 1955.[32]

Sleep is associated with a variable oxygen uptake, but usually averages approximately 10 percent below the conventional basal metabolic rate recorded while the patient is awake. The energy requirements associated with walking increase linearly until about 5.4 kg per hour, then rise curvilinearly at higher speeds and at progressively increased inclines.

Donnovan and Brooks[1] have reported that the efficiency of skeletal muscles decreases with increasing work, and that the caloric requirement increases exponentially when energy expenditure is plotted against speed. This may be due to the necessity of recruiting the less efficient white fast fibers to augment the work of the red fibers as speed of walking or running increases. Also, when running on the treadmill, the energy expended is greater than walking, even if the speed and grade are the same (Table 3-1).

TABLE 3-1. Estimated Substrate Depots in Normal Man

Fuel	Weight (kg)	Energy (kcal)
Tissues		
Fat (adipose triglycerides)	15	141,000
Protein (mostly muscle)	6	24,000
Glycogen (muscle)	0.350	1,000
Glycogen (liver)	0.085	340
		166,340
Circulating Fuels		
Glucose (extracellular water)	0.020	80
Free fatty acids (plasma)	0.0004	4
Triglycerides (plasma)	0.003	30
		114

STEADY STATE AND OXYGEN DEBT

When exercise is initiated, the demands of the body usually exceed the oxygen intake for a short time. If the work is relatively mild, this "debt" is paid back quite soon, because the body delivers just the right amount of oxygen to do the work. If work continues at a constant rate, oxygen intake and consumption come into balance. This balance has been called a steady state. This can be recognized during an exercise test by a stable heart rate. On the average, for a well-conditioned individual, it takes two or three minutes to reach this equilibrium after each increase in workload. As the subject reaches a workload near maximum capacity, however, the so-called steady state is rarely obtainable and the patient begins to accumulate metabolic waste products, such as lactic acid, indicating that more oxygen is being used than is being delivered. After exercise is terminated, the intake of oxygen continues at a higher level than it was during the resting state and actually requires some time to pay back the debt. This can be recognized by a higher than resting heart rate as well as a higher level of oxygen intake. The magnitude of the debt depends on the duration of the work and its relationship to the circulatory and metabolic capacity of the individual (Fig. 3-4).

CARBOHYDRATES

Hepatic glycogen is the major fuel for muscle work. Glycogen constitutes

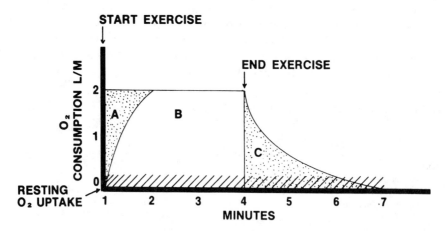

FIGURE 3-4. The concept of oxygen debt. At the onset of exercise, the immediate demand for oxygen by the tissues is not supplied by the oxygen transport system but is met by anaerobic metabolism (A). In moderate exercise, the transport system catches up with the oxygen demand within a few minutes, during which the subject is said to be in a steady state (B). At the end of exercise, the original deficit and any deficit accumulated during the exercise period is paid back by the oxygen transport system (C). The cardiac output exceeds the oxygen demand of the resting tissues during this period until the deficit accumulated during the initial anaerobic phase has been eliminated.

50 gm per kg of wet tissue in the liver. Therefore, in a liver weighing 1500 gm, 75 to 90 gm of glycogen are available. After a 10 to 12-hour fast in the resting subject, glycogen mobilization takes place at the rate of 50 gm per minute per kg of liver. This mobilization can continue about 24 to 36 hours. The muscle itself contains 9 to 16 gm of glycogen per kg, a value that varies little with age or sex, but is somewhat higher in the muscles of the lower extremities. When the muscles are at rest, very little of the muscle glycogen stores are used, even in prolonged fasting. Exercise, however, depletes the stores relatively rapidly, although glycogen cannot be transferred from one muscle to another. It has been shown that diets high in carbohydrates enhance muscle glycogen stores, especially if severe exercise precedes the carbohydrate intake. Exercise depletes the glycogen stores at a predictable rate as shown in Figure 3-5. This depletion is also affected by the supply of fuels carried by the blood, mainly hepatic glycogen and free fatty acids.

When the muscle glycogen supply becomes completely depleted, significant exercise capacity is suspended until replenishment takes place. Exercising muscle uses glucose from the blood 15 times faster than during rest after 10 minutes of exercise and 35 times faster after 60 minutes of exercise. The rest-

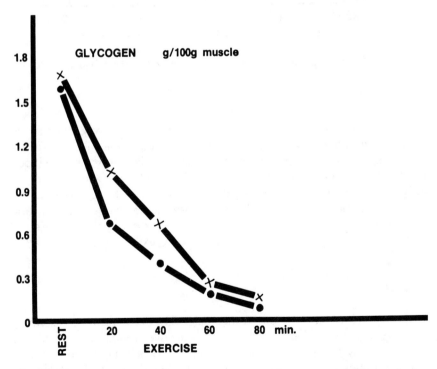

FIGURE 3-5. The glycogen content of the quadriceps muscle at rest and during exercise in groups of conditioned (X) and unconditioned (•) individuals. (Adapted from data suplied by Saltin and Astrand.[33])

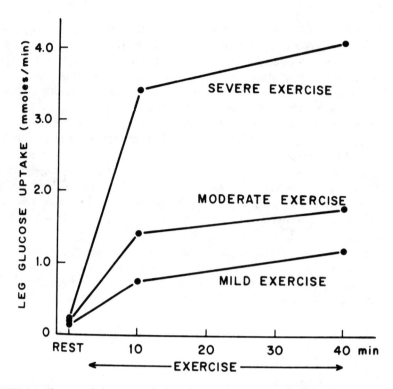

FIGURE 3-6. The rate of glucose uptake by exercising leg muscles. (From Felig and Wahren,[34] with permission.)

ing muscle uses free fatty acids for nutrients almost exclusively, but after 10 minutes of exercise, carbohydrates assume 90 percent of this role. As exercise progresses, the muscle component of glycogen steadily drops, and the blood component of glucose rapidly rises. After 40 minutes of exercise, approximately 75 to 90 percent of the oxidative metabolism of the carbohydrates in the muscle comes from the blood. There appears to be no selective reduction in glucose stores from other tissues besides the liver during this exercise.

The increased use of glycogen in muscle during exercise is shown in Figure 3-6.[34]

PROTEINS

Amino acids play very little role in the metabolism of resting muscles. During exercise, alanine is metabolized to a considerable degree, but is probably synthesized by the muscle itself. Its source is probably from free ammonia liberated during exercise or from pyruvate released during the breakdown of glucose. The increasing level of alanine in the blood during exercise is parallel to pyruvate and probably is an indirect measure of glucose metabolisms. Thus, the older idea that athletes should eat foods rich in proteins before competing seems to be in error, because it will be necessary to transform the protein to hepatic and muscle glycogen before it can play a significant role in metabolism.[35,36]

FATS

The average 70 kg man has approximately 15 gm of fat in the form of adipose tissue and triglycerides. This constitutes about 140,000 kcal, enough to permit survival for 2 to 3 months of total food deprivation. It has long been recognized that herein lies the principal source of stored energy. When exercise stimulates hydrolysis, it does so through the sympathetic nervous system with noradrenaline activating adenyl cyclase, forming an increased amount of cyclic adenosine $3',5'$-monophosphate (AMP). This in turn, activates the lipolytic system in the adipose tissue cell, catalyzing the hydrolysis of stored triglycerides. Albumin-bound free fatty acids (FFA) are transported to tissues through the body, mainly to the liver and muscle. Although the free fatty acid pool is usually small, its turnover is very rapid, varying from three minutes at rest to one tenth of this rate during exercise (Fig. 3-7[36]). The activity of fatty acids as seen in the figure demonstrates their role in exercise.

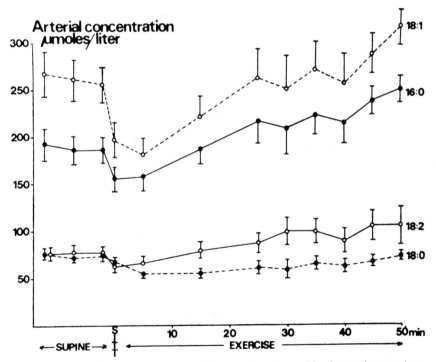

FIGURE 3-7. Arterial concentrations of palmitic, stearic, oleic, and linoleic acids at rest in supine and sitting positions and during upright exercise at 400 kgM per minute in healthy subjects. (From Wahren,[36] with permission.)

Maneuvers to increase plasma free fatty acids such as heparin[37] and caffeine[38] have been shown to increase use in the muscles and to decrease the uptake of carbohydrates as the blood sugar increases (Fig. 3-8[37]).

Felig and Wahren[34] have studied the comparative uptake of glucose and free fatty acids over 240 minutes of exercise in man. Their findings are illustrated in Figure 3-9.[34]

HORMONAL INFLUENCES

It has long been recognized that a number of endocrine systems are extremely important in the physiology of exercise.

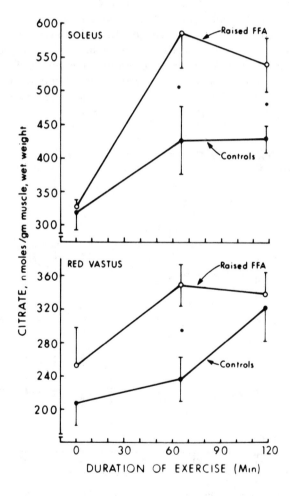

FIGURE 3-8. The increase in citrate, reflecting increased glucogen use, in exercising muscles in animals when the FFA are increased by heparin. (From Hickson et al.,[37] with permission.)

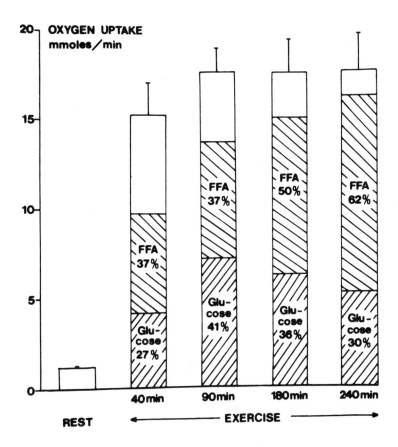

FIGURE 3-9. Uptake of oxygen and substrates in man during prolonged exercise. FFA take on a dominant role as exercise progresses. (From Felig and Wahren,[34] with permission.)

GLUCOREGULATORY HORMONES

A fall in plasma insulin and a rise in glucagon accompanying exercise is depicted in Figure 3-10.[34] The enhanced uptake of glucose with exercise is not totally regulated by insulin however, as it can take place in diabetic children with an inadequate production of insulin;[36] although in vitro it has been shown that insulin may have a permissive effect on glucose uptake. Catecholamines are believed to play an important role in the use of carbohydrates[7,34] as well as lipids and also mediate many of the changes in blood clotting seen with exercise. The changes in growth hormones seen with exercise are still poorly understood.[39]

The adrenal, which is probably the most important endocrine gland influencing exercise and other types of stress, deserves some consideration. It has been proposed by Selye[40] that the physiological response to stress, which he

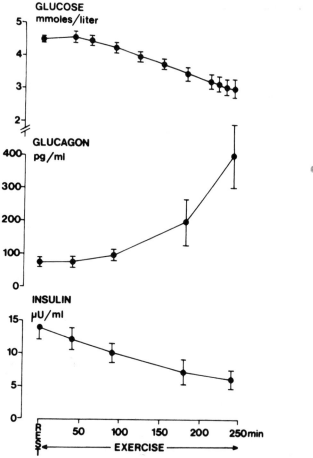

FIGURE 3-10. Plasma concentrations of glucose, glucagon, and insulin during prolonged exercise. (From Felig and Wahren,[34] with permission.)

has termed the General Adaptation Syndrome, consists of three phases: (1) the alarm reaction, (2) the stage of resistance, and (3) the stage of exhaustion. He proposes that the alarm reaction (in our case exercise) triggers an adaptation response associated with an increase in the secretion of adrenal cortical hormones, and hypertrophy of the adrenal cortex. Hypertrophy then allows the subject to establish the stage of resistance. Eventually, if the stress (or the alarm reaction) is continued too long or is too strenuous, the stage of exhaustion is reached; whereby, the organism develops adrenal cortical insufficiency with progressive deterioration. He believes that each organism has a certain amount of adaptive energy, the depletion of which will lead to the phase of exhaustion. If we subscribe to this theory, we might assume that heavy exercise (stress) will shorten life because it will exhaust the adaptive energy. Further research, however, seems to suggest that exercise produces a degree of protection against stress (not only exercise stress, but other types).[41] This might lead one to the conclusion that exercise would then help to conserve adaptive energy even though some would be depleted early in the development of resistance. Experimental heart attacks as well as natural ones seem to be prevented to some degree by regular exercise. Through observing a decrease in eosinophile counts and adrenal hormonal release, emotional stress has been demonstrated to have less impact on a regularly exercised organism.[42]

Experimental studies on hamsters have shown that exercise equivalent to about two thirds of the maximum capacity produces the greatest hypertrophy of the adrenal cortex.[43] It is of interest to note that trainers and coaches have arrived at a similar level of training as optimum for developing endurance.[44] It is also an opinion of coaches that overtraining or a decrease in performance after prolonged training in humans may be correlated with animal studies, indicating that adrenal exhaustion has occurred.

Hartley and coworkers[39] disclosed some interesting data on the hormone levels of seven subjects who were studied for seven weeks during an exercise program. They studied the levels of norepinephrine, epinephrine, growth hormone, insulin, and cortisol. The results are summarized in Figure 3-11. It can be seen that the hormonal response to exercise is generally decreased after training in the case of norepinephrine, epinephrine, and growth hormone. On the other hand, the insulin level increases in response to exercise, particularly in well-conditioned individuals. As the degree of conditioning progresses, the stress of exercise elicits less and less adrenal cortical response. Following conditioning, the lower levels of catecholamines are probably associated with the reduction of blood sugar use and an increase in the available free fatty acids. The reduction in the catecholamine response to exercise, therefore, results in higher insulin levels.

The changes in catecholamine concentration levels have been attributed to increased vagal tonus, but it would be more in keeping with the above reasoning to postulate that it would require less sympathetic drive to excite a stronger set of muscles than to stimulate an unconditioned subject. Therefore, as a stronger patient engages in an exercise program, which is easier for that subject, less stress is produced on the body as a whole.

The response of growth hormones is especially important because of the rise in concentration levels associated with moderate work and a drop with intensive work. There is evidence to suggest that this is not due to pituitary exhaustion, nor is it due to changes in blood lactate. The meaning of these changes are yet to be explained.

When young rats are exercised strenuously, their growth rate is retarded. Ekblom[45] has, on the other hand, reported that physical training in adolescent boys results in a more rapid growth than in untrained controls. The final effect on growth may be very complex and under the regulation of a number of agents, such as testosterone and the glucoregulatory hormones.

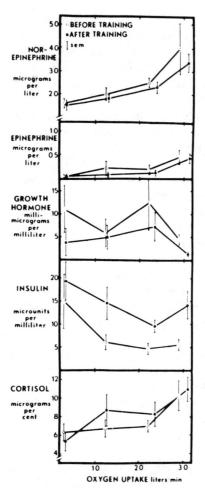

FIGURE 3-11. Mean concentration of hormones plotted at mean values of oxygen uptake before (o) and after (•) conditioning. (From Hartley, et al.,[39] with permission.)

LONG-TERM EFFECTS OF EXERCISE

Bed Rest

A preface to the discussion of the long-term effects of exercise should consist of a brief discussion of the effects of bed rest. A number of studies on bed rest have given us more insight into the contrasting effects of exercise.

Fortunately, the urge to use prolonged bed rest for the treatment of all kinds of diseases is on the wane. Symptoms produced by inactivity include stiffness, fatigue, weakness, incoordination, asthenia, ataxia, depression, and possibly many others.[46] Early writers who recognized the dangers of prolonged inactivity include Lusk,[7] Howard and associates,[47] and others.[33,48] The work by Saltin and associates[28] dramatically emphasized the decrease in VO_2max, stroke volume, heart volume, and the increase in resting and exercise heart rate.

Chapman and colleagues[49] found that 20 days of bed rest in healthy young men produced a decrease in lean body mass, total body water, red cell mass, plasma volume, and intracellular fluid volume. The average decrease in oxygen uptake was 28 percent. It took 55 days of intensive physical training to bring these values in the young men back to their pre-rest level. Morse[50] has found decreased rates of erythropoiesis by serial reticulocyte counts. Studies have shown elevated urinary calcium excretion of 30 percent above normal, and it has been demonstrated that 30 weeks of bed rest results in about 4 percent loss of the total body calcium. There is evidence that connective tissue is continually being removed and replaced, and if motion is limited, dense connective tissue is formed in replacement instead of loose areolar tissue. This will actually restrict the motion of a joint in less than a week. Kottke[51] reports an average increase in heart rate of $1/2$ beat per day for 21 days, and a negative nitrogen balance of 1 to 3.5 mg per day.

The effects attributed to zero gravity, which is a variety of inactivity studied in astronauts, confirm the above findings and emphasize the important loss of vasomotor control and psychologic effects of inactivity.[46] This is discussed in more detail below.

There is increasing evidence that physical rest has been overused in cardiac and pulmonary disorders and that an appropriate exercise program can have a beneficial effect on most patients with chronic diseases.

Weightlessness

The physiologic changes observed in space have been studied extensively—especially in the Skylab crews.[52] These include changes in body composition, including fluid and electrolyte balance, and neurophysiologic, musculoskeletal, cardiovascular, and pulmonary abnormalities. Weightlessness produces weight loss, measured as a decrease in body mass, and a redistribution of fluids headward so that the center of gravity moves in this direction. There is actually an increase in body height of at least 2 cm, thought to be due to expansion of the intervertebral discs. A reduction in total body water, potassium, extracellular fluid, plasma volume, and red cell mass was regularly seen, but could be minimized by regular exercise while in space.

Loss of calcium,[53] phosphate, and nitrogen were regularly identified as well as a loss of muscle mass, strength, and coordination. When these changes are compared with those reported by Saltin,[28] they are surprisingly similar in many areas; thus, the observations in space help us to understand better the need for a minimum amount of physical forces acting in the body and the dysfunction resulting from physical inactivity.

Effects of Conditioning

It has been demonstrated that a marked adaptive change is possible in muscle during a physical training period, and that an increased capacity for aerobic metabolism caused by alterations in the mitochondria takes place.[27] Not only do the size and number of mitochondria and mitochondrial protein increase, but also there is increased activity in the respiratory enzymes, especially those used in fatty acid oxidation. Training produces a much larger effect on oxidative enzymes than on oxygen uptake. There is also a rise in aerobic ATP generation. Because very little adaptive enhancement of carbohydrate metabolism occurs, it appears that physical conditioning shifts the emphasis toward use of fatty acids, thus bringing about a glycogen saving effect. This glycogen economy has been observed in well-conditioned individuals who underwent muscle biopsy during prolonged exercise periods. This tendency to mobilize fat deposits may also explain the trend toward less total body fat in conditioned individuals. Fatigue, then, is the result of depletion of glycogen stores, although the mechanism leading up to this event is profoundly dependent on fatty acid metabolism as well as carbohydrates.

Maximum Oxygen Uptake (VO$_2$max)

Although VO$_2$max was discussed in Chapter 2, some amplification seems to be warranted here. The total effect of physical training or conditioning seems to be best quantified by the individual's maximum capacity to extract oxygen. This is measured by collecting the expired air and measuring its volume per minute and the percentage of oxygen extracted during the individual's maximal effort. The difference in maximum uptake per kg of body weight has been studied by many investigators; Saltin and Astrand[28] have published ranges listed in Figure 3-12.

Improvement in VO$_2$max has been demonstrated not only in normal subjects who exercise regularly, but also in those who have coronary heart disease,[44] those with myocardial infarction,[54] and even in some with emphysema.[5] Siegel and colleagues[55] found that a 15-week conditioning program increased VO$_2$max from 24 to 28.5 mg per kg per minute, or 19 percent. Studies involving middle-aged men who led sedentary lives, but who had been endurance athletes in their youth, had a VO$_2$max 20 percent higher than age-matched men who had never engaged in strenuous athletics. These former athletes, however, were still 25 percent below an age-matched group who were still athletically active.

Hixon and colleagues[37] have shown that strenuous exercise for 40 minutes a day, 6 days a week, for 10 weeks produced a linear increase in VO$_2$max and endurance time for the total training period. The average increase in VO$_2$max for the 8 subjects was 0.12 liters per minute, or a total of 16.8 ml per kg per minute (44 percent). It was previously believed that several hours of training

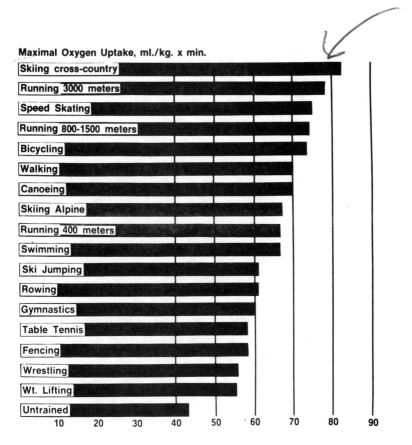

Maximal Oxygen Uptake, ml./kg. x min.

Skiing cross-country
Running 3000 meters
Speed Skating
Running 800-1500 meters
Bicycling
Walking
Canoeing
Skiing Alpine
Running 400 meters
Swimming
Ski Jumping
Rowing
Gymnastics
Table Tennis
Fencing
Wrestling
Wt. Lifting
Untrained

10   20   30   40   50   60   70   80   90

FIGURE 3-12. Maximal oxygen uptake per kg of body weight measured in members of the Swedish National teams. (From Saltin and Astrand,[33] with permission.)

would be necessary to produce this type of improvement, and that a much longer training period would also be required. Thus, while the attainment of very high maximum VO_2s usually takes a prolonged period of training, it may be achieved quite rapidly if a very strenuous exercise program is followed. When comparing equivalent training in sedentary students and Olympic athletes, the VO_2 increase in the students was about 18 percent, but as a group they still only averaged 73 percent of the athletes.[29] Whether this difference reflects an increased genetic endowment or previous prolonged training is still unsettled.

AV-O$_2$ Difference

The final step in the oxygen transport chain, the extraction by the tissues, is more efficient in well-trained subjects. This increase has been a consistent finding in trained young men and in men with ischemic heart disease, but not in women or older men.[29,56] This is thought to be due to an increase in capillary density and in mitochondrial content in skeletal muscles.[29] Of interest is the fact that improved extraction does not deteriorate with bed rest studies, although these are of short duration.

Blood Volume

It has been well established that although the immediate effect of exercise is to reduce blood volume,[50] long-term exercise and conditioning produce a significant increase in blood volume. This blood volume increase might be expected in view of the fact that bed rest produces a decrease.[28] The size and number of blood vessels are also increased significantly. It has been repeatedly observed in our laboratory that the number and size of arteries and veins in the arms and legs of vigorous athletic patients undergoing catheterization are greater than in those who are habitually sedentary. The increase in blood volume and red cell mass with endurance training does not increase hemoglobin concentration or the hematocrit. In fact, the hematocrit may drop a little with very strenuous training. This would cause a drop in viscosity and have a salutary effect on peripheral resistance. This increase in circulating volume results in a slightly increased venous pressure, which facilitates a higher cardiac preload.

Peripheral Resistance and Systemic Blood Pressure

One of the puzzling problems in exercise physiology is how the heart can increase its output so much in world class runners. It is now known that the marked drop in resistance to blood flow is a major factor. This effect is mainly due to a dramatic increase in blood flow to the skin and muscles. Ekblom and Hermansen[57] found that a group of athletes could reach their maximum cardiac output (36 liters per minute) at a mean blood pressure of only 116 mm Hg. This contrasts with a mean systolic pressure of 164 mm Hg in a group of sedentary women when only exercising to a cardiac output of 11.5 liters per minute. This reduction in afterload is probably mediated by marked change in the response of the peripheral arterioles rather than primarily by the increased capillary volume. Experiments involving one leg training have suggested that increased perfusion goes primarily to the trained limb and is probably mediated by local rather than systemic factors.[58,59]

A number of studies now suggest that the average systolic and diastolic blood pressure of exercising men decreases slightly. Hellerstein and Hornstein[60] studied 618 men in an exercise program for 7 years and noted a drop in mean systolic blood pressure from 129 to 121 and in diastolic pressure from 86 to 84. These changes were of questionable significance, but it is most important to recognize that in such a period in the age group studied, one would expect a gradual increase, not a decrease in blood pressure. Boyer and Kash[61] recorded a mean drop in systolic pressure of 13.5 mm and a 11.9 mm drop in mean diastolic pressure in hypertensive patients in their exercise program. They noted no significant change in normotensive patients who started the program. Johnson and Grover[62] reported on four severe hypertensive patients who exercised for half an hour, 3 times a week for 10 weeks. No improvement in their blood pressure resulted even though their physical strength, pulse response, and VO_2max improved. It would seem from a variety of studies that the most significant effect of exercise on blood pressure is observed in patients with mild, early hypertension. It may be that exercise might prevent their condition from evolving into a more serious, fixed elevation of pressure as they get older, or minimize an inherent tendency for this disorder.

Studies in rats by Buuk[63] indicate that hypertension, usually induced by feeding a high-salt diet, could be prevented by swimming one hour per day, five days per week. The exercise also prevented the coronary atherosclerosis seen in sedentary, sodium-fed rats who developed hypertension. Because blood pressure is a function of resistance, one would predict that as training reduced resistance it would have a similar effect on blood pressure.

Heat Dissipation

As mentioned in Chapter 2, heat dissipation is critical to prolonged exercise. Studies of skin blood flow suggest, however, that there is little increase in ability to dissipate heat associated with endurance training.[26] Senjay and Fortney[64] have reported that women have a reduced tolerance to exercise in a hot climate because they lose more fluid and proteins into interstitial spaces than men. The inherent ability to dissipate heat is highly variable among individuals and may be an important factor in adapting to endurance exercise.

A number of factors occuring with training would be expected to favor more efficient heat dissipation. A reduction in viscosity, an increase in capillary density in the skin, and the total increase in blood volume resulting in an adequate residual of blood volume necessary for sweating.

Heart Rate

As previously discussed in Chapter 2, the drop in heart rate with training is a sign of improved conditioning.[65] The ability to extract more oxygen from the blood may allow a decreased rate of blood flow to working muscles, and thus lower the heart rate. The improved metabolic efficiency of working muscles has been found even in cardiac patients after training, so that more work could be accomplished without increasing the cardiac output. Prolonged endurance training reduces maximum as well as resting heart rate, and a pulse of 40 to 45 is not an uncommon finding.

The low heart rate is probably vagally mediated and probably also reflects a decreased sympathetic drive for a given workload. It has been shown that the heart rate response is appropriate for the percentage of the maximum work for that individual. Thus, the heart rate response is a consistent measure of the percentage of maximal exercise, irrespective of conditioning[29] and provides us with an excellent measure of the effort during exercise testing.

Lipid Metabolism

In spite of the large number of studies, significant beneficial effects on serum cholesterol have been reported by some[66] and denied by others.[2,3,67] I think we must assume that the benefits of exercise will not effect important changes in serum cholesterol.

On the other hand, the level of high density lipoproteins (HDL) seems clearly to increase with regular activity.[68] This fraction of the cholesterol complexes may actually function to mobilize lipid deposits in the arterial wall.[69] Studies by Wood and colleagues[69] have shown consistently higher HDL fractions in runners compared with sedentary controls, while cholesterol was not significantly different (Figs. 3-13 and 3-14[69]). It remains to be demonstrated that HDL will rise in the absence of a drop in body fat, as the correlation between total body fat and HDL levels emerges as a consistent finding.[68] Triglyceride levels are consistently lower during and immediately after exercise, and although this may have a limited long-term effect, a good physical workout three times a week seems to be adequate to control their level in the average man.[2]

Personality

Nietzsche said, "What doesn't destroy me makes me strong." He was dealing primarily with our ability to tolerate the emotional stress of life. An interesting study by Barry[70] suggests that people fall into two groups in terms of their attitudes. Some are more orderly and self-controlled and respond to situations with judgment; others prefer mainly to perceive or observe events and are more flexible and open to new experiences. The latter tend to be more creative, while the former excel in business. Patients with coronary heart disease show a marked preference for judging. Those who judge have been found to be more conscious of work and physical discomfort, and to prefer less physical exercise. These individuals experienced a significantly higher incidence of coronary disease.

Hellerstein and associates[60,71] studied patients with coronary disease with a Minnesota Multiphasic Personality Inventory (MMPI) and found that a high score for depression was definitely improved after several months of physical conditioning.

There seems to be no doubt that trained subjects have a more positive attitude, are more confident, and have a better self-image. Because coronary

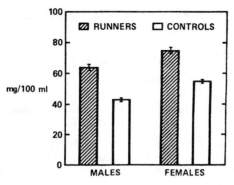

FIGURE 3-13. Plasma HDL in runners versus sedentary controls. (From Wood, et al.,[69] with permission.)

disease has such a profound impact on the male ego, one would expect to see, as we have, a profound psychologic improvement in male, coronary patients who undergo a conditioning program.

There has been a trend toward equating long-distance running with transcendental meditation. It seems in some subjects to be a satisfactory method of controlling anxiety[42] and promoting relaxation. Young[72] has demonstrated its ability to improve cognition. Ten weeks of running improved test scores on digit symbol and block design and associative learning as compared with sedentary controls.

Bowers and colleagues[73] tested memory-dependent reaction time before and after a 10-week walk/jog fitness program in a university faculty. They found a significant shortening in the exercisers as compared with the controls suggesting efficiency of recall is improved with fitness.

A study at the University of Wisconsin[74,75] indicates that nonpsychotic depression responds favorably to running 3 times a week in 6 of 8 patients, who

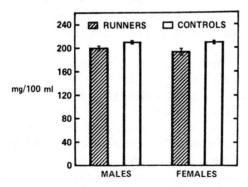

FIGURE 3-14. Plasma cholesterol in runners versus sedentary controls. (From Wood, et al.,[69] with permission.)

completely recovered from their depression. The patients began to feel better with the first week of running and steadily improved in most cases. As with any treatment, those who refused to take their medicine failed to respond. Although some preliminary data on exercise and psychotic patients look favorable, it remains to be demonstrated how often it can be applied in this area.

A group in Alberta[76] has studied alpha power, identified by electroencephalography in 20 subjects after 40 minutes of moderate exercise. They found an increase in alpha waves in the occipital and parietal cortical areas, which they claim identifies an altered consciousness and could explain the improvements in anxiety and depression that have been reported. Much work remains to be done in this fascinating area.

Resistance to Sequelae of Coronary Atherosclerosis

The literature is full of studies indicating that those who habitually exercise tolerate coronary atheroma better, or may develop less severe disease. A study by Frank and associates[54] of 55,000 men enrolled in the Health Insurance Plan of Greater New York is one of the most quoted. The mortality for the first myocardial infarction was 49 percent in those least active, 25 percent in those characterized as moderately active, and 17 percent in those most active. Kannel[8] reports from the Framingham study that the mortality from coronary disease is five times higher in sedentary than in the most active individuals.

Brunner's[56] elegant reports from the kubbutzim, when diet and environment seemed to be well controlled, indicate a twofold increase in coronary deaths and infarctions in those who are sedentary as compared with those who are physically active. A very interesting study by Paffenbarger and Hale,[77] who conducted a survey of 16,936 Harvard Alumni by questionnaire, indicates that the risk of heart attacks at all age levels related inversely to energy expenditure in their life routines. They also found that the correlation was independent of other risk factors. Paffenberger and Hale also come to a similar conclusion when analyzing the work records of the West Coast longshoremen. Similar data have been accumulated on a large number of patients who have exercised regularly after their myocardial infarctions as compared with sedentary controls.[54]

Barnard and associates[78] report that diet and exercise are a satisfactory approach to those with coronary disease; however, careful scrutiny of their results reveals that if the surgical case cross-overs are considered a coronary event, at least half of their 64 patients had death, an infarct, or required surgery in five years. This 10 percent per year event rate is discouraging and suggests that as a secondary prevention this approach has a number of short-comings. On the other hand, Shepherd and colleagues[79] from Toronto, reported a very low incidence of coronary events in their patients who continue the Rehabilitation Program as compared with the drop-outs. They have also trained a number of coronary patients to the point where they were able to finish a 26-mile marathon, a feat that is impressive for anyone in their age category, let alone someone who has had a previous myocardial infarction.

The one problem with correlating all this information with cardiac function is the possibility that those who exercise regularly are genetically less prone to coronary disease.

In an extensive review of the literature, Froelicher[67] concludes there is no definite evidence that exercise will prevent or improve existing coronary artery disease in man. For those interested in the subject, I recommend his analysis. On the other hand, the lifestyle of physically active subjects seems to favor a general reduction of known risk factors, and thus this "spin-off" may in itself be worth the effort.

In our own exercise program in Long Beach, California, we find that those patients who appear to need exercise the most are the most difficult to motivate. In light of this, we must consider the possibility that linked with genetic proneness to exercise comes a resistance to coronary atheroma. It is generally believed by adult distance runners that running will prevent coronary heart disease. Although it may aid in its prevention, we have seen a number of well-conditioned distance runners develop progressive coronary insufficiency during the course of their training schedules. Numerous authors report cardiac infarction and death in well-trained runners.[80-82]

Complications of Exercise

The frequent cases of severe exhaustion without a single incidence of myocardial infarction in the high altitudes of the Olympic Games in Mexico City suggests that exercise associated with proper warm-up rarely damages the heart of a normal person. On the other hand, most of the patients with coronary heart disease in the United States and Western Europe are yet to be identified. These people, if motivated to suddenly start a strenuous exercise program, may be in grave jeopardy. We have had two such cases resulting in cardiac arrest in our Coronary Rehabilitation Program (both successfully resuscitated), although we attempt to monitor the patients very carefully. There have been several reported[83-85] infarctions in such programs. Frequent reports of sudden death in the newspapers attest to the dangers of unsupervised physical conditioning programs. It seems incumbent to recommend that careful stress testing be used to evaluate sedentary men and women who might aspire to change their way of life in the direction of strenuous athletics.

The most frequent complications of exercise, especially in older patients, are muscular strains and other neuromuscular problems such as bursitis and arthritis.

The reduction in resistance to infection in those highly trained is now well established. This is thought to be due to a reduced level of immunoglobulins in the nasal and respiratory mucus membranes.[86] Other changes in the immune system may also be present, but need further study. It has also been claimed that some compulsive runners are really closet anorexics.[87] I believe that the running and dieting is a result, rather than the cause of the disorder in this case.

Influence on Aging

The methods of measuring the aging process are open to considerable discussion. There are no conclusive data to support the concept that exercise causes us to live longer. A report in the National Geographic Magazine describing areas in which an inordinate number of people live beyond 100 years suggests that hard physical work may be a factor.[88] It may be, however, that these subjects are not really as old as they claim to be, records being what they are in primitive areas. It may also be that the lack of medical care has allowed for natural selection to produce a hardier stock.

There is no doubt that exercise delays the normal decrease in stroke volume, VO₂max, vital capacity, and body strength.[89] A study by Robinson and associates[6] on former champion runners, some of whom still train, revealed a remarkable degree of fitness as compared with normal for age. It must be evident, however, that these men were favorably endowed and their unusual capacities may be more genetic than acquired.

In experimental animals, inactivity has been demonstrated to produce some of the metabolic and histologic changes seen in aging (see previous section Bed Rest). It is tempting to assume, therefore, that aging is retarded by habitual exercise. On the other hand, there is no evidence that the Gompertz plot[90] considered to be the index of the rate of aging, is different in populations engaging in life-long strenuous exercise.[91] At present, we must conclude that although exercise may improve the quality of life, it has not been demonstrated to extend its term very significantly. The studies done to determine the life expectancy of college athletes have been conflicting.[43] The original idea that athletes had more heart disease and died earlier has been largely disproven, but on the other hand, data to establish their increased longevity are in doubt.[2] It seems well established that mesomorphic individuals have a definitely increased susceptibility to cardiovascular disease.[61] Because a large number of athletes are of this body type, their increased tendency toward coronary disease may cancel the benefit of the exercise when analyzed statistically. Recent work in rats suggests that slower heart rates,[92] and low body weight caused by less food intake[93] prolong life. Fitness is usually associated with both these conditions and the old adage "a lean horse for a long race" cannot be completely discounted.

SUMMARY

Although there remain many unanswered questions regarding the effect of a physically active lifestyle, it seems well established that the beneficial effects outweigh the problems and risks.[28]

A careful analysis of our anthropologic heritage suggests the capacity to exercise had survival value for our ancestors for at least 3 million years. It seems unlikely that evolution has progressed fast enough to change our physiology significantly in the last five thousand years. I would agree with Paffenbarger and Kannel[94] that a sedentary lifestyle is a risk factor for coronary heart disease and probably for other degenerative conditions.

I would recommend some program of regular physical exertion and have found it to enhance the quality of life. On the other hand, the data fail to support the belief that excessive exercise, such as marathon running, provides an added benefit besides self-satisfaction and a good deal of camaraderie.

REFERENCES

1. DONOVAN, CB AND BROOKS, GA: *Muscular efficiency during steady rate exercise.* J Appl Physiol 43:431, 1977.
2. FOX, SM, NAUGHTON, JP, AND HASKELL, WL: *Physical activity and the prevention of coronary heart disease.* Ann Clin Res 3:404, 1971.
3. HOLLOSZY, JO, ET AL: *Effects of a six month program of endurance exercise on the serum lipids of middle-aged men.* Am J Cardiol 14:657, 1965.
4. SHANE, SR: *Relation between serum lipids and physical conditioning.* Am J Cardiol 18:540, 1966.
5. SKINNER, JS, ET AL: *Effects of a six month program of endurance exercise on work tolerance, serum lipids and balisto cardiograms of fifteen middle-aged men.* In KARVONEN, MJ (ED): *Physical Activity and the Heart.* Charles C Thomas, Springfield, IL, 1967.
6. ROBINSON, S, ET AL: *Physiological aging of champion runners.* J Appl Physiol 41(1):46, 1976.
7. LUSK, G: *The Science of Nutrition,* ed 4. WB Saunders, Philadelphia, 1928, p 400.
8. KANNEL, WB: *Recent findings of the Framingham study.* Res Staff Phys 16:68, 1978.
9. HOLLOSZY, JO, ET AL: *Effects of a six month program of endurance exercise on the serum lipids of middle aged men.* Am J Cardiol 14:657, 1965.
10. EGEBERG, O: *The effect of exercise on the blood clotting system.* Scand J Clin Lab Invest 15:8, 1963.
11. IKKALA, RR, MYLLYLA, SA, AND SARAJAS TE: *Proceedings of the Institute of Medicine of Chicao.* In KATTUS, AA: *Role of Exercise in the Management of Ischemic Heart Disease.* Chicago, 1970.
12. EGEBERG, O: *Changes in the activity of antihemophilic A factor (F VIII) and in the bleeding time associated with muscular exercise and adrenalyn infusion.* Scand J Haematol 1:300, 1964.
13. IATRIDIS, SG AND FERGUSON, JH: *Effect of physical exercise on blood clotting and fibrinolysis.* J Appl Physiol 18:337, 1963.
14. ASTRUP, I: *Effects of physical activity on blood coagulation and fibrinolysis.* In NAUGHTON, JP AND HELLERSTEIN, HN (EDS): *Exercise Testing and Exercise Training in Coronary Heart Disease.* Academic Press, New York, 1973.
15. EPSTEIN, S, ET AL: *Impaired fibrinolytic responses to exercise in patients with Type IV hyperlipoproteinemia.* Lancet 2:631, 1970.
16. ECKSTEIN, RA: *Effect of exercise and coronary artery narrowing in coronary collateral circulation.* Cir Res 5:230, 1967.
17. MENON, IS, BURKE, F, AND DEWAR, HA: *Effect of strenuous and graded exercise on fibrinolytic activity.* Lancet 1:700, 1967.

18. NADEL, ER: *Problems with Temperature Regulation During Exercise.* Academic Press, New York, 1977.
19. NAKAYAMA, T, ET AL: *Thermal stimulation and electrical activity of single units of the preoptic region.* Am J Physiol 204:1122–1126, 1963.
20. MITCHELL, JW: *Energy exchanges during exercise.* In NADEL, ER (ED): *Problems with Temperature Regulation During Exercise.* Academic Press, New York, 1977.
21. ANDERSEN, KL: *The effect of physical training with and without cold exposure upon physiological indices of fitness for work.* Can Med Assoc J 96:801, 1967.
22. SHELLOCK, FG, ET AL: *Unusual core temperature decrease in exercising heartfailure patients.* J Appl Physiol 54(2):544–550, 1983.
23. KOYAL, SN, ET AL: *Temperature response to upright exercise in patients with coronary disease* (abstr). Fed Proc 43:3, March 1, 1984.
24. BOCK, AV, ET AL: *Studies in muscular activity: Dynamical changes occurring in man at work.* J Physiol 66:136, 1928.
25. BERGMAN, HL, ET AL: *Enzymatic and circulatory adjustments to physical training in middle aged men.* Eur J Clin Invest 3:414, 1973.
26. CLAUSEN, JP, ET AL: *Central and peripheral circulatory changes after training of the arms or legs.* Am J Physiol 225:675, 1973.
27. JOSENHANS, WT: *Muscular factor.* Can Med Assoc J 96:842, 1967.
28. SALTIN, B, ET AL: *Response to exercise after bed rest and after training: A longitudinal study of adaptive changes in oxygen transport and body composition.* Circulation 37(7):VII–1, 1968.
29. BLOMQVIST, CG AND SALTIN, B: *Cardiovascular adaptations to physical training.* Ann Rev Physiol 45:169–189, 1983.
30. BJURSTEDT, H, ET AL: *Orthostatic reactions during recovery from exhaustive exercise of short duration.* Acta Physiol Scand 119:25–31, 1983.
31. ASTRAND, O AND RODAHL, K: *Textbook of Work Physiology.* McGraw-Hill, New York, 1970.
32. PASSMORE, R AND DURNIN, JVGA: *Human energy expenditure.* Physiol Rev 35:801, 1955.
33. SALTIN, B AND ASTRAND, O: *Maximal oxygen uptake in atheletes.* J Appl Physiol 23:353, 1967.
34. FELIG, P AND WAHREN, J: *Fuel hemostasis in exercise.* N Engl J Med 293:1078, 1975.
35. AHLBORG, G, ET AL: *Substrate turnover during prolonged exercise in man. Splanchnic and leg metabolism of glucose, free fatty acids and amino acids.* J Clin Invest 53:1080, 1974.
36. WAHREN, J: *Substrate utilization by exercising muscle in man.* Prog Cardiovasc Dis 2:255, 1973.
37. HIXON, RC, ET AL: *Effects of increased plasma fatty acids on glycogen utilization and endurance.* J Appl Physiol 43:829, 1977.
38. COSTILL, DL: ET AL: *Effects of elevated plasma FFA and insulin in muscle glycogen usage during exercise.* J Appl Physiol 43:695, 1977.
39. HARTLEY, LH, ET AL: *Multiple hormonal responses to graded exercise in relation to physical training.* J Appl Physiol 33:602, 1972.
40. SELYE, H: *The Stress of Life.* McGraw-Hill, New York, 1956.
41. PROKOP, L: *Adrenals and sport.* J Sport Med 3:115, 1963.
42. ANDRE, FF, METZ, KF, AND DRASH, AL: *Changes in anxiety and urine catecholamines produced during treadmill running* (abstr). Med Sci Sports 10:51, 1978.
43. PROUT, C: *Life expectancy of college oarsmen.* JAMA 220:1709, 1972.
44. DETRY, JM AND BRUCE, RA: *Effects of physical training on exertional ST segment depression in coronary heart disease.* Circulation 44:399, 1971.
45. EKBLOM, B: *Effects of training in adolescent boys.* J Appl Physiol 27:350, 1969.
46. JOHNSON, RS, DIETLEIN, LF, BERRY, CA (EDS). *Biomedical results of Apollo.* SP-368, NASA Scientific and Technical Information Office, Washington, DC, 1975.
47. HOWARD, JE, ET AL: *Studies in fracture convalescence. I. Nitrogen metabolism after fracture and skeletal operations in healthy males.* John Hopkins Hosp Bull 75:156, 1944.

48. LEVINE, SA AND LOWN, B: *The chair treatment of acute coronary thrombosis.* Trans Assoc Am Physicians 64:316–327, 1951.
49. CHAPMAN, HA, ET AL: *After 20 days in bed they ran.* JAMA 205:35, 1968.
50. MORSE, BS: *Red cell mass decrease seen in bed rest.* JAMA 200:23, 1967.
51. KOTTKE, FJ: *The effects of limitation of activity upon the human body.* JAMA 196:825, 1966.
52. JOHNSON, RJ AND DICTLEIN, LT (EDS): *The proceedings of the Skylab Life Science Symposium.* NASA, US Government Printing Office, Washington, DC, Aug 27, 1974.
53. DONALDSON, CL, ET AL: *Effect of prolonged bed rest on bone mineral.* Metabolism 19:1070, 1970.
54. FRANK, CW, ET AL: *Physical inactivity as a lethal factor in myocardial infarction among men.* Circulation 34:1022, 1966.
55. SIEGEL, W, BLOMQVIST, G, AND MITCHELL, JH: *Effects of a quantitated physical training program on middle-aged sedentary men.* Circulation 41:19, 1970.
56. BRUNNER, D: *Studies in preventive cardiology.* Monograph Pub C V Research Unit, Gov Hosp, Donolo, Tel Aviv Univ Press, Israel, 1973.
57. EKBLOM, B AND HERMANSEN, L: *Cardiac output in atheles.* J Appl Physiol 25:619, 1968.
58. CLAUSEN, JP: *Effect of physical training on cardiovascular adjustments to exercise in man.* Physiol Rev 57:779–815, 1977.
59. CLAUSEN, JP, ET AL: *Central and peripheral circulatory changes after training of the arms or legs.* Am J Physiol 225:675-682, 1973.
60. HELLERSTEIN, HK AND HORNSTEIN, TR: *Assessing and preparing a patient for return to a meaningful and productive life.* J Rehab 32:602, 1972.
61. BOYER, JL AND KASH, FW: *Exercise therapy in hypertensive men.* JAMA 211:1668, 1970.
62. JOHNSON, WP AND GROVER, JA: *Hemodynamic and metabolic effects of physical training in four patients with essential hypertension.* Can Med Assoc J 96:842, 1967.
63. BUUCK, RJ: *Effects of exercise on hypertension* (abstr). Med Sci Sports 10:37, 1978.
64. SENJAY, LC AND FORTNEY, S: *Untrained females: Effects of submaximal exercise and heat on body fluids.* J Appl Physiol 39:643, 1975.
65. GLAGOV, S, ET AL: *Heart rates during 24 hours of usual activity.* J Appl Physiol 29:799, 1970.
66. ALTEKRUSE, EB AND WILMORE, JH: *Changes in blood chemistries following a controlled exercise program.* J Occup Med 15:110, 1973.
67. FROELICHER, VF: *Does exercise conditioning delay progression of myocardial ischemia in coronary atherosclerotic heart disease?* In CORDAY, E (ED): *Controversies in Cardiology.* Cardiovascular Clinic Series, Vol 8, No. 1, FA Davis, Philadelphia, 1977, p11.
68. MILLER, GJ AND MILLER, NE: *Plasma high density lipoprotein concentration.* Lancet 1:16, 1975.
69. WOOD, PD, ET AL: *Plasma lipoprotein distribution in male and female runners.* Ann NY Acad Sci, 301:748, 1977.
70. BARRY, AJ: *Physical activity and psychic stress/strain.* Can Med Assoc J 96:848, 1967.
71. HELLERSTEIN, HK, ET AL: *The influence of active conditioning upon subjects with coronary disease.* Can Med Res J 96:901, 1967.
72. YOUNG, RJ: *Effect of regular exercise on cognition and personality* (abstr). Med Sci Sports 10:51, 1978.
73. BOWERS, RW, DEROSE, DV, AND MARTIN, J: *Memory dependent reaction time and improved C-V fitness in middle aged adults* (abstr). Med Sci Sports & Exercise 15(2):117, 1983.
74. GREIST, JH, ET AL: *Antidepressant running.* Behav Med 23:19, 1978.
75. MELLION, MB: *Effect of exercise on anxiety and depression: Cardiovascular manifestations of anxiety and stress.* Compr Psychiatry 1(3):4, 1983.
76. WEISE, J, SINGH, M, AND YEUDALL, L: *Occipital and parietal alpha power before, during and after exercise* (abstr). Med Sci Sports & Exercise 15(2):117, 1983.
77. PAFFENBERG, RS AND HALE, WE: *Work activity and coronary heart mortality.* N Engl J Med 292:545, 1975.

78. BARNARD, RJ, ET AL: *Effects of an intensive exercise and nutrition program on patients with coronary artery disease: Five-year follow-up.* J Cardiac Rehab 3:183–190, 1983.

79. SHEPHARD, RJ, ET AL: *Marathon jogging in post-myocardial infarction patients.* J Cardiac Rehab 3:321–329, 1983.

80. OPIE, LH: *Sudden death and sport.* Lancet 263–266, 1975, Feburary.

81. WALLER, BF AND ROBERTS, WC: *Sudden death while running in conditioned runners aged 40 years or older.* Am J Cardiol 45:1292–1300, 1980.

82. NOAKES, TD, ET AL: *Autopsy-proved coronary atherosclerosis in marathon runners.* N Engl J Med 301(2):86–89, 1979.

83. CANTWELL, J AND FLETCHER, GF: *Cardiac complications while jogging.* JAMA 210:130, 1969.

84. PYFER, HL AND DOANE, BL: *Cardiac arrest during exercise training. Report of successfully treated case attributed to preparedness.* JAMA 210:101, 1969.

85. BRUCE, RA, HORNSTEIN, TR, AND BLACKMON, JR: *Myocardial infarction after normal responses to maximal exercise.* Circulation 38:552, 1968.

86. TOMASI, TB, ET AL: *Immune parameters in athletes before and after strenuous exercise.* J Clin Immunol 2(3):173–178, 1982.

87. FLEISCHMAN, C AND SIEGEL, AJ: *Are compulsive runners really closet anorexics?* Ann Sports Med 1(3):98–99, 1983.

88. LEAF, A AND LAUNOS, J: *Every day is a gift when you are over 100.* National Geographic 143:1, 1973.

89. GRIMBY, G AND SALTIN, B: *Physiological analysis of physically well-trained middle-aged and old athletes.* Acta Med Scand 179:5, 1966.

90. SHOCK, NW: *Physical activity and the "rate of aging."* Can Med Assoc J 96:836, 1967.

91. MONTOYE, HJ: *Participatlion in athletics.* Can Med Assoc J 96:813, 1967.

92. COBURN, AF, GREY, RM, AND RIVERA, SM: *Observations on the relation of heart rate, life span, weight and mineralization in the digoxin treated A/J mouse.* Johns Hopkins Med J 128(4):169–193, 1971.

93. WEINDRUCH, R AND WALFORD, R: *Dietary restriction in mice beginning at 1 year of age: Effect on life-span and spontaneous cancer incidence.* Science 215:1415–1418, 1982.

94. PAFFENBARGER, RS AND KANNEL, WB: *Cardiovascular consequences of physical inactivity.* Primary Cardiology, April 1984.

4

PHYSIOLOGY OF CARDIAC ISCHEMIA

PAIN
  Endorphins
  Comment
BIOCHEMICAL CHANGES IN THE ISCHEMIC MYOCARDIUM
  Lactate
  Free Fatty Acids (FFA)
  Prostaglandins
MECHANISM OF S-T SEGMENT DEPRESSION
DIRECTION OF S-T VECTOR
S-T SEGMENT ELEVATION
SUMMARY

In this chapter, I review current concepts proposed to explain the pathophysiology of myocardial ischemia. Although our understanding of these mechanisms is constantly changing, a review seems important because it provides us with a framework on which to organize our clinical observations.

SUPPLY VERSUS DEMAND

Ischemia results from an imbalance between the oxygen supply and myocardial demand. In simple terms, supply is primarily a function of coronary artery luminal diameter times the driving pressure minus the non-coronary resistance to flow, modified by hemoglobin content and blood viscosity. Myocardial demand is primarily influenced by heart rate, wall tension, and contractile state. An imbalance in the supply/demand ratio may be either global or more often localized in certain areas of the heart muscle. This may be "silent" clinically or manifested by chest pain, arm or jaw pain, dyspnea, sudden weakness, or arrhythmias.

CORONARY ARTERIES

Vasomotion

For many years, we viewed the coronary epicardial arteries as passive conduits with the main regulatory process being located in the arterioles. Although this is usually the case, evidence presented by Masseri and colleagues[1-3] and others[4-5] has clearly demonstrated that spasm in the large epicardial coronary arteries often reduces flow enough to result in clinically important ischemia. While this occasionally occurs in a normal coronary, it is probably more common in a section of the arterial wall already altered by an atheromatous plaque. Thus, the dynamic aspect of the coronary tree becomes important in our understanding of the pathophysiology of this entity. A number of maneuvers can be used to precipitate the spasm. These include intravenous ergonovine, methacholine, histamine, cold pressure maneuvers, and hyperventilation. The reduction in flow can be reversed by nitroglycerin or by phentolamine. The latter is an alpha-adrenergic agent that may affect either epicardial coronary vessels or probably the coronary arterioles.

A coronary dilator that acts on the precapillary sphincter would only serve to send more blood through normal regions, so that nitroglycerin, if it acts in the heart, must mainly function to redistribute blood toward areas of reduced perfusion. A good deal has been written about the degree of coronary narrowing necessary to produce clinical signs of ischemia. It seems well established that function in a dog's heart begins to deteriorate when perfusion pressure drops to around 55 mm Hg, and as the reduction in flow increases, the loss of contractility progresses rapidly.[6] It has also been demonstrated that the drop in perfusion pressure is related to the velocity of the blood as well as the magnitude of the obstruction. The work of Young and associates[6] who demonstrated the relationship of velocity to magnitude of obstruction and its effect on pressure drop, is illustrated in Figure 4-1.[6] It can be seen that even restrictions of 50 to 60 percent can produce important pressure drops at high velocity. This

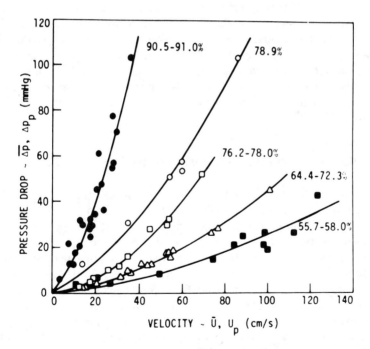

FIGURE 4-1. The pressure drop induced by various degrees of coronary narrowing as related to velocity of blood flow. The drop in pressure with high grade stenosis is manifested at low velocities, while a high velocity is necessary to cause a significant drop when the obstructions approach 50 percent. (From Young,[6] with permission.)

suggests that previous statements claiming 70 percent narrowing or more is required to compromise function[7] must be viewed with some skepticism. The resistance to flow secondary to muscle pressure during systole, left-ventricular end-diastolic pressure during diastole, and the lack of available time in a patient with tachycardia, are discussed on Pages 81 to 83.

Now that we realize that increased tone or spasm may further restrict flow in the region of a relatively small stenotic plaque, our blind faith in a coronary angiogram must be abandoned.

A patient who has typical angina or ischemic S-T changes, especially at rest, with an angiogram demonstrating only a 40 or 50 percent narrowing of a major coronary trunk, must be suspected of having temporary decreases in the stenotic orifice due to coronary spasm.

Collaterals

Intracoronary collaterals, connecting an ischemic arterial network to another coronary arterial bed, have definite functional benefit in providing improved perfusion to the starved myocardium. However, it appears that at best, these vessels replace up to about 40 percent of normal coronary flow. Thus, the flow is never enough,[8,9] that is, it may provide protection against myocardial infarction during low levels of metabolic activity; however, when metabolic demands on the heart muscle increase, ischemia almost invariably occurs. Thus, cardiac function is reduced to some degree, especially when significant increases in cardiac work are required, even in the face of well-developed collaterals. Also, we now know that collaterals that are visible during coronary angiography constitute a variable and often small portion of the actual intracoronary flow.

Stimulus to Coronary Collateral Formation

In animals, especially dogs, epicardial collateral vessels connecting to vascular beds seem to develop very rapidly, sometimes within a few minutes[8] after a myocardial infarction. If narrowing in the affected artery is slow enough, the rapidly developing collaterals will protect the heart from infarction altogether.[9] This is probably not always the case in humans, although a well-formed collateral system will certainly reduce the likelihood of myocardial necrosis. In humans, coronary narrowing of greater than 75 percent is probably necessary to stimulate collateral circulation;[10] however, there is a great difference among individuals as to the efficiency of this process, which may be inherited. It also seems established that the more rapidly the occlusion occurs, the less likely adequate collaterals will form and that complete obstruction of an artery is the best stimulus for collateralization.[11-13] When patients are compared, those with good collateralization to ischemic areas invariably have better function, especially when the muscle is stressed either by exercise or atrial pacing.

Exercise Stimulus to Collateral Formation

In 1967, Ekstein[14] performed a classical and often quoted study. He exercised dogs with partly occluded coronary arteries and found marked improvement in collateral flow compared with those dogs who were kept at rest. We now know that limitations in Ekstein's methodology adversely affected his conclusions. Coronary collaterals are very sensitive to extravascular compressive forces, thus his failure to account for this, the errors inherent in using retrograde flow as a measure of collateral flow, and the fact that he frequently used vascular beds where only an 80 or 90 percent antigrade obstruction was present probably led him to mistaken conclusions. More recent work by Schaper and colleagues[15] in a rigidly controlled dog model, found that exercise in dogs, at least, had no effect on collateral flow.

Heaton and colleagues[16] however, have studied myocardial blood flow to the epicardium as compared with that to the subendocardial areas in dogs. They found that in ischemic areas caused by previous coronary constriction, prolonged exercise improved the subendocardial flow when compared with control as estimated by radioactive microspheres. Scheel and colleagues,[17] Burt and Jackson,[18] and Kaplinsky and associates,[19] like Schaper, were unable to find that exercise was a stimulus to collateral growth in dogs. It has been stated that the epicardial collaterals in dogs and men are not exercise-induced, but intramyocardial collaterals as seen in pigs can be stimulated by exercise.[20] It is doubtful that the differences are significant. The question is yet to be answered satisfactorily in man, although many patients in Coronary Rehab Programs exercise religiously on the belief that it will stimulate collateral development. Evidence to establish this is difficult to come by, however.

Although MacAlpin and colleagues[21] have stated that 50 percent of patients who improved their exercise capacity during a Coronary Rehab Program also showed an improved collateral pattern on angiography, little confirmation of this has appeared. The one point that everyone seems to agree on is that the best stimulus to collateral formation is ischemia. We have seen collaterals associated with high-grade coronary disease disappear within a few minutes after the ischemia is relieved by percutaneous transluminal angioplasty. Thus, the collaterals visible on angiography at least, respond very quickly to changes in myocardial demand.

Coronary Size as Related to Workload

There seems no doubt that increased myocardial work increases the size of epicardial coronary arteries. Linzbach[22] has shown in autopsies and MacAlpin and colleagues[21] in coronary arteriograms that the coronary size increases appropriately for the increased myocardial work. We have tended to confuse the process of collateral proliferation associated with atheromatous disease with the increase blood flow to heart muscle that has been overworked either by exercise or by valvular abnormalities. These two processes probably have little to do with each other. MacAlpin[21] and associates have shown significant alterations in cross sections of coronary arteries of patients who have abnormalities that place excessive demands on their heart, such as aortic stenosis and mitral insufficiency. Studies in rats, ducks, and cats have been consistent in showing an increase in the absolute volume of coronary vasculature and an increase in the ratio of blood vessels to heart size with exercise.[23] Stevenson[23] found that forcing rats to exercise two days per week produced a greater increase in coronary size than exercising them five days per week. One hour per day of exercise produced the same increase in blood vessel volume as did five hours per day. One might conclude from this that moderate exercise is as good for the coronary circulation as strenuous exercise if collaterals act in the same way. The animal experiments cited and the angiographic studies by MacAlpin are in accord with the large coronary arteries reported in Clarence Demarr (Mr. Marathon) after his death from cancer. It is very tempting to correlate the increase in size found in his arteries with his long history of marathon running. It is also possible that he was an outstanding marathon runner because he was congenitally endowed with unusual coronary flow.

TRIGGER MECHANISMS FOR ISCHEMIA

Ischemia, either with or without anginal pain, comes on at unexpected times. Mechanisms that trigger this reduction in flow may be several. One theory is that when blood flows across a stenotic area, a passive collapse may occur; especially, if the velocity of flow is increased. Coronary spasm in patients with Raynaud's syndrome and migraine headaches suggest that altered autonomic tone may be a factor in some. A more common mechanism is thought to be platelet aggregation on the surface of the plaques. Prostacyclin mostly elaborated in the vascular endothelium is an important regulator of the interaction between platelets and the vessel wall. Activation of the prostaglandin mechanism in platelets results in an increased synthesis of thromboxane A2, which is both a vasoconstrictor and a promoter of platelet aggregation. The relative balance between this agent released from the platelets and prostacyclin, a vasodilator and an inhibitor of platelet adhesiveness manufactured in the endothelium, is probably crucial.[24] Factors known to shift this in the direction of thromboxane, thus favoring spasm and thrombosis formation are aspirin in large doses, coronary atherosclerosis, age, increased low-density lipoproteins, diabetes, mental stress, catecholamines, and vascular trauma.[24,25] There is some evidence that plaque rupture, exposing an ulcerated area, which then attracts platelets, is a trigger. Other complex chemical mechanisms in the coronary endothelium and arterial wall probably alter this dynamic process, but as yet are incompletely understood.

INTRAMYOCARDIAL PERFUSION

In recent years, a number of new techniques have been used to study the distribution of flow within the myocardium when there is narrowing of the epicardial vessels. These include radioactive microspheres to assess the distribution and volume of blood flow, and intramyocardial measurement of enzymes and substrate components in animals. In humans, coronary sinus catheterization and thermodilution flow probes and isotopes injected into the coronary circulation during catheterization help evaluate regional and total coronary flow. Radionucleotides, which are picked up by the myocardium when given intravenously or used to tag the circulation during first pass or gated blood pool imaging, have all greatly increased our understanding of this complex subject.

Even though considerable narrowing may occur in epicardial coronary arteries, the flow may not be significantly reduced because the resistance in the precapillary sphincters is greater than in the areas of the plaque in the proximal large artery. Figure 4-2 illustrates that the resistance to flow can come from any of a number of anatomic sites, or several in combination.

A patient whose heart is well perfused at rest may become ischemic when exposed to maximum metabolic demands shortly after the metabolic chemoreceptors in the myocardium dilate the precapillary sphincters and increase coronary flow to the point where the upstream narrowing becomes mani-

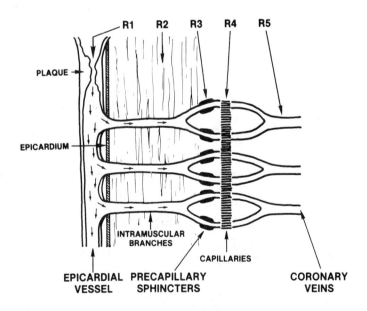

FIGURE 4-2. The diagram depicts the various resistances that influenced blood flow, from a plaque at R1 to the effect of coronary venous pressure at R5. When the heart is at basal state, the precapillary sphincters at R3 probably play the most important role.

fested. The function of shunt pathways to aid in these compensating adjustments is illustrated in Figure 4-3. Maximal dilatation of these pathways can often compensate for complete obstruction of a large coronary artery, especially if the patient rarely places increased metabolic demands on the system. When the heart is pushed past these compensating mechanisms, as in the bottom of the figure, the subendocardial areas become ischemic. When this occurs over time, it may result in a propagation of more ischemia as proposed by Guyton and colleagues,[26] who demonstrated an increased resistance after time in the artery distal to a critical narrowing. This could result in death of myocardial cells. It definitely has been shown to alter contractile properties for several hours, leading to the term "stunned myocardium."

Transmural Flow Distribution

Although there is no precise method of measuring transmural blood flow distribution in humans, data in mammals varying from very small to large body size are so consistent that there is no reason to predict that it will be different in man. Flow increases from the epicardium to the endocardium due to the increase in metabolic demands probably related to the increased wall stress on the inner layers. This increase of about 20 to 50 percent is maintained with increasing heart rates under normal conditions, but is profoundly altered in pathologic states as we see in Figure 4-3.[22,27] Flow is also altered by the fact that there is a definite reduction in driving pressure as the vessel penetrates the

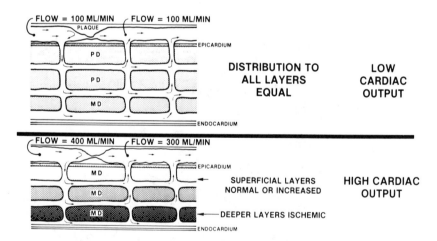

FIGURE 4-3. *Top:* The capacity of the collateral shunt pathways to compensate for severe epicardial coronary narrowing when the patient is at rest. *Bottom:* The same heart when the patient is exercising, requiring a greater cardiac output. The shunt pathways, maximally dilated with a low output, cannot increase flow to compensate for the greater metabolic demands, resulting in subendocardial ischemia. (MD = maximally dilated, PD = partially dilated.)

myocardium. The aortic pressure or epicardial coronary pressure is far higher than found in the inner one third of the myocardium (see Chapter 2). Also the tissue pressure is not just determined by the force of contraction, but by a combination of chemical and other neuroendocrine influences difficult to quantify. It has been shown that increased vagal tone will increase flow by a factor of 40 percent, while stimulation of the stelate ganglion will reduce flow initially and then later stimulate flow by coronary vasodilatation.[27] Epinephrine and dopamine reduce coronary resistance and increase flow while angiotensin causes a profound vasoconstriction. Of course, adenosine, glucagon, histamine, seratonin, the kinins, and other substances produced in the myocardium and vascular epithelium also play an important role.

Vasodilator Reserve

Recent studies by Wright and associates[28] in the operating room with doppler flow meters have documented that the ability of an area of the myocardium to increase flow is subject to a number of factors, some of which are still poorly understood. When they compressed the coronary artery for about 20 seconds,

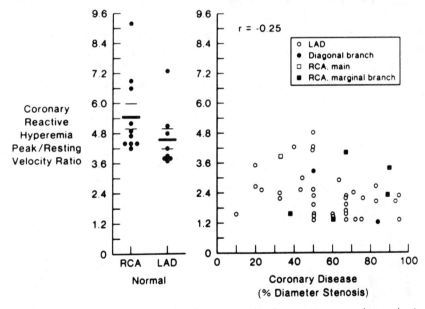

FIGURE 4-4. The response of the coronary flow measured in the operating room after mechanical occlusion for 20 seconds.[28] Note that normal coronary arteries (left panel) will increase flow approximately five times during reactive hyperemia but that this increase shows almost no correlation with the magnitude of coronary narrowing as determined by angiography. Some with LAD obstructions of 85 percent can increase flow almost threefold while some with only 20 percent are in the same range. (From White, CW et al.: Does visual interpretation of coronary angiogram predict the physiological importance of a coronary stenosis. N Engl J Med 310:819-824, 1984.

they found that reactive hyperemia would increase the flow about eightfold in normals. As stenosis in the coronary circulation progressed, this reserve capacity was reduced and became abolished when the stenosis was near 90 percent. On the other hand, they could not predict this response when coronary lesions, sized angiographically, were below 90 percent. Some subjects with apparent obstructions of as little as 30 percent would have a severely compromised flow reserve, while others with stenosis of 70 to 80 percent would have a near-normal reserve. Thus, angiographically measured coronary stenosis of less than 90 percent may have different dynamic implications for ischemia from patient to patient (Fig. 4-4). It is now easy to understand why the reliability of ischemic S-T depression in predicting coronary anatomy as estimated from angiography is so poor. Patients with left ventricular hypertrophy and so-called Syndrome X (ischemia with normal coronary arteries) have been found to have a reduced ability to increase flow even when the coronary vessels appear normal on angiography.[29] The exact reasons for this remain to be clarified.

PRESSURE RELATIONSHIPS OF LEFT VENTRICLE AND CORONARY ARTERIES

If we recall the concepts reviewed above and examine the myocardial circulation in relationship to the anatomic pathways and the pressure gradients in dogs (Figs. 4-5 and 4-6), it can be seen in Figure 4-6 that the flow gradient during diastole favors adequate perfusion in the normal heart. In the ischemic heart, however, the previously mentioned factors, which foster a decrease in

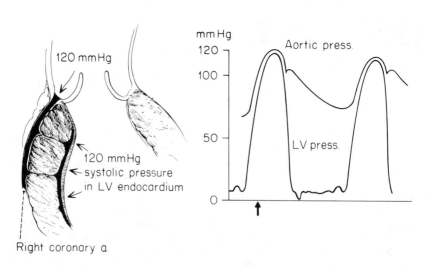

FIGURE 4-5. During systole in the normal heart, intraventricular pressure is the same as coronary artery pressure. Therefore, very little coronary flow occurs.

STRESS TESTING: PRINCIPLES AND PRACTICE

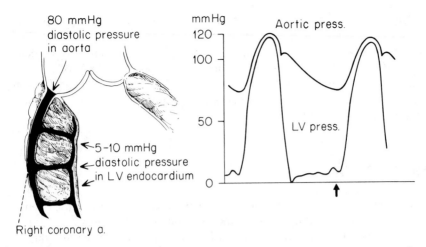

FIGURE 4-6. Normal diastole results in a fall in intraventricular pressure allowing for a flow gradient to develop, thus perfusing the myocardium.

ventricular compliance and promote the rise of end-diastolic pressure, result in a decrease in the driving pressure gradient across the myocardium, which then inhibits total myocardial perfusion.[30] This process is a vicious cycle because, as the stiffness of the ventricle increases, the decrease in total coronary flow is more profound. This would be even more marked if plaques in the proximal coronary arteries decrease the driving pressure gradient from epicardium to endocardium as illustrated in Figure 4-7. As progressive ischemia develops, the endocardium and subendocardial tissue are selectively starved.

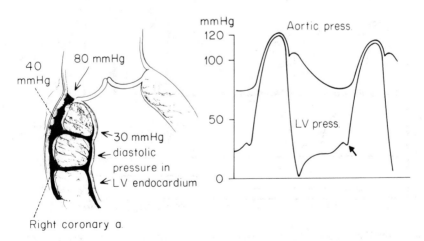

FIGURE 4-7. A large coronary plaque decreases the pressure in the coronary artery during diastole and at the same time the intraventricular pressure rises—resulting in very little flow gradient (40 − 30 = 10); therefore, very little myocardial perfusion.

This series of events explains why the end point of exercise and S-T segment depression is so reproducible in the patient with angina.[31,32] The work of Zaret and colleagues[33] suggests a marked decrease in relative myocardial perfusion with exercise-induced angina was measured by potassium-43 and thallium scanning, tending to confirm this concept. The chain of events finally results in a restriction of the necessary increased myocardial flow so that power failure eventually ensues.

TIME INTERVALS

Along with the variables related to pressure, we should understand the relative duration of systole and diastole. As the heart rate increases, relative diastolic time shortens. This may well be one of the major factors in limiting the increase in heart rate that is associated with exercise. Buckberg and coworkers[34] have produced dramatic decreases in subendocardial flow with a shortening of the diastolic time as well as with a diastolic pressure increase (Fig. 4-8). They proposed using a diastolic pressure time index to estimate the relative decrease in blood flow to the subendocardial layers of the myocardium and have shown with radioactive microspheres that this flow may decrease even as the total coronary flow increases. Barnard and associates[35] have shown S-T segment depression in apparently normal men who were exercising very vigorously without a warm-up. They demonstrated that these subjects had inordi-

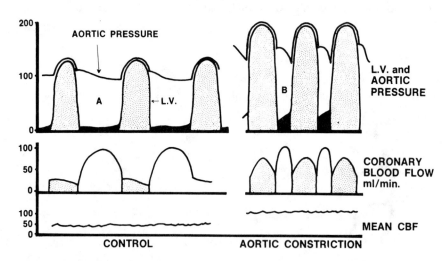

FIGURE 4-8. The area under the aortic diastolic pressure (A) becomes much smaller after aortic constriction and with an increase in heart rate (B) when related to the systolic area *(shaded)*. This results in a decrease in diastolic (endocardial) coronary blood flow as compared with the total flow, most of which must go to the more superficial layers of the myocardium.

nate shortening of a diastolic interval, thus, postulating a decrease in endocardial perfusion very similar to that which occurred in Buckberg's dogs.[34]

These concepts help us to conceptualize the mechanisms of flow in a working ventricle, but are inexact in their application. Efforts to predict thresholds by the ratio of the systolic to the diastolic pressure time interval (SPTI/DPTI) are based on some invalid assumptions. The influence of inertial factors, coronary capacitance, and blood velocity may be considerable. Also, the original assumption that the stop flow pressure (see Figs. 4-5 and 4-6) is the same as diastolic pressure has been demonstrated to be in error, and is non-uniform across the left ventricular wall. Thus, although the general understanding of these mechanisms help us to deal with clinical problems, it is too early to attempt to deal in exact values.[27]

RELATIONSHIP OF LEFT VENTRICLE TO PULMONARY ARTERY PRESSURES

Because left ventricular ischemia has been associated with a high filling pressure, we sometimes fail to remember that this is a function of not only myocardial compliance, but the volume and velocity of filling, which is dependent on the right side of the heart. An example is illustrated by a patient treated in our hospital for pulmonary edema (Fig. 4-9). Two days after obtaining relief from his symptoms through the use of a vasodilator, he was subjected to measurements of his pulmonary artery diastolic pressure at rest and after a rapid Levophed drip. The pulmonary artery diastolic pressure has been demonstrated to

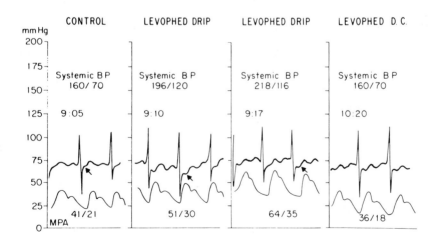

FIGURE 4-9. As the systemic pressure was increased by an alpha stimulator, the increasing left ventricular diastolic pressure, as reflected by the rising pulmonary diastolic pressure, resulted in transient S-T segment depression in the V_5 precordial lead.

be a fairly reliable indicator of the left ventricular diastolic pressure.[36] The increase in systemic resistance and arterial blood pressure that followed resulted in a return of chest pain and shortness of breath and an increase in pulmonary artery pressure reflecting the rise in left-ventricular diastolic pressure and a depression of the S-T segment. This rapidly abated when the peripheral resistance was allowed to return toward normal.

Myer and associates[37] reported the presence of S-T segment depression as a sign of a "ring-like" subendocardial infarction in 15 patients. Apparently this is the end stage of prolonged ischemia when the hemodynamic alterations became irreversible.

POSTURE AND FILLING PRESSURES

Occasionally S-T segment depression associated with treadmill exercise can be accentuated by placing the patient in a supine position.[38] When a person assumes the horizontal position, the central circulation is increased by 200 to 300 ml, increasing the filling pressure of the left ventricle.[39] If there is ischemia,

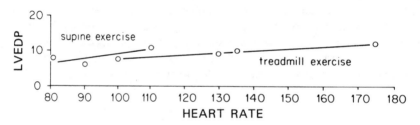

FIGURE 4-10. Pulmonary diastolic pressure response of normal subject to supine and treadmill exercise.

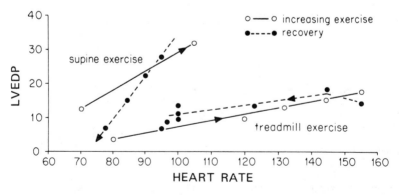

FIGURE 4-11. Pulmonary artery diastolic pressure (reflecting LVEDP) in patient with coronary disease in the supine position and on the treadmill.

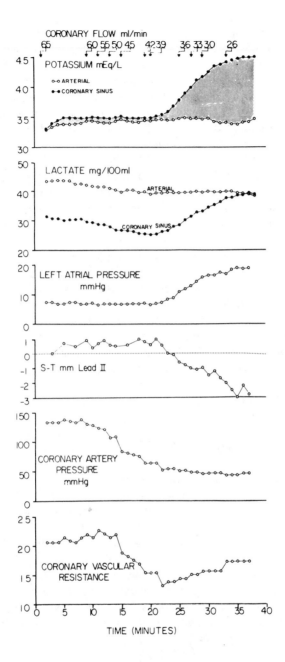

FIGURE 4-12. Data adapted from work of Case[40] demonstrated that the pressure, metabolic, and electrical changes occur at about the same degree of coronary ischemia.

and an increased stiffness of the ventricle, the end-diastolic pressure increases, accentuating the S-T segment depression. This process was further investigated by placing polyethylene catheters in the pulmonary arteries of 10 patients with known ischemic heart disease in an attempt to correlate the pulmonary diastolic and, thus indirectly, the left ventricular filling pressure with S-T segment depression. It was found, as might be expected, that when using the pulse as a guide to the amount of stress applied, the end-diastolic pressure increased much faster in the horizontal position, and with it an earlier onset of S-T segment depression (Figs. 4-10 and 4-11).

Case and coworkers[40] have eloquently demonstrated the relationship of S-T segment depression to the LVEDP elevation and also have correlated this with metabolic changes. These data have dramatized the importance of taking into consideration the metabolic and mechanical events associated with ischemia (Fig. 4-12).

A patient's heart may have normal compliance, as evidenced by a normal left-ventricular diastolic pressure, at one time and then a few minutes later, when subjected to exercise or anoxia, suddenly become quite stiff, only to return again to normal when the workload allows the muscle to equilibrate with its oxygen supply.[41] Echocardiographic studies of posterior wall motion by Fogelman and coworkers[42] reveal the rate of relaxation to be markedly reduced during or immediately after an angina attack. This change has also been demonstrated by Barry and associates[43] with left ventricular angiograms done at the time of atrial pacing, measuring pressure volume relationships, and by a number of other workers.[44-46]

SYSTEMIC BLOOD PRESSURE

Systemic blood pressure usually increases normally with exercise in coronary patients, but there is evidence to suggest that the peripheral resistance often increases inappropriately with the onset of myocardial ischemia. This has two effects: (1) the driving pressure in the coronary circulation is increased in diastole; thus, favoring better coronary perfusion and (2) the work necessary to eject blood is increased and the myocardial wall tension is increased, which requires an increase in myocardial oxygen use, the magnitude of which is often difficult to discern. I suspect that the extra work is more of a burden than can be compensated for by the increased coronary perfusion as a function of the increase in diastolic pressure. Blood pressure in relationship to stress testing is reviewed in Chapter 17.

CONTRACTILITY AND WALL MOTION

Although patients with decreased coronary flow and near-normal left ventricular function may have fair contractility as evidenced by observing an angio-

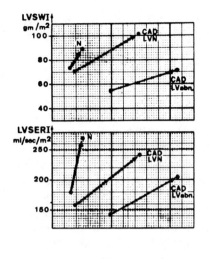
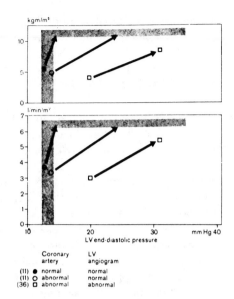

Coronary | LV
artery | angiogram

(11) ● normal | normal
(11) ○ abnormal | normal
(36) □ abnormal | abnormal

FIGURE 4-13. Left ventricular function curves correlated stroke work index and ejection rate index with LVEDP, where N = normal and CAD = coronary artery disease. (From Lichtlen,[47] with permission.)

gram, it is definitely less than that of normal subjects. This can be measured in a number of ways in the catheterization laboratory with the use of Vmax,* DP/DT,+ and circumferential fiber shortening. They all show a decrease when carefully measured, and as might be expected, the amount of decrease is related to the severity of the ischemia (Fig. 4-13).[47]

There is often a tendency for the contractility to be augmented by an excess of catecholamines, but the ability of the muscle to respond to these agents is somewhat depressed. It is noteworthy that the systolic ejection rate index (which equals the velocity of ejection over stroke input) is reduced so that under the stress of exercise, the time during systole, corrected for the heart rate, is actually longer. This can be measured from the aortic pressure with a catheter or from external recordings of the carotid artery or other peripheral arteries.

The contractility is often reduced in a localized segment so that a reduction in wall motion, or even a paradoxical bulge, becomes manifested during an ischemic episode.[6] This phenomenon occurs early in ischemia, even before the ATP in the involved muscle is depleted.[48] One can see how effective such a mechanism can be in preventing infarctions. As the ATP in muscle begins to deplete, some metabolic trigger mechanism suspends contraction, which then promotes increased blood flow to the ischemic segment by eliminating the

---

*Vmax = maximum velocity of pressure rise extrapolate to 0 pressure.
+Delta pressure over delta time characterizes the velocity of ventricular contractions.

resistance inherent in the systolic squeeze. Methods for detecting these bulges are now serving to identify ischemia when initiated by an exercise test.[49,50]

ABNORMAL RELAXATION

What is the metabolic process that alters compliance and slows relaxation? Evidence is accumulating that calcium ions that leave the sarcoplasmic reticulum and unlock the actin-myosin gate to initiate contractions must be returned by a calcium pump to bring about the muscle relaxation.[51] Langer[48] estimates that 15 percent or more of total myocardial energy costs may be expended to bring about this process. This involves moving about 50 milimoles of calcium ions per kg of heart muscle[48] back to the sarcotubular system. Hypoxia was thought to deplete the supply of ATP, which mediates this transfer, resulting in a cell with an excess of calcium ions and incomplete muscle relaxation. Support for this concept comes from the work of Bing and associates[52] who have shown that myocardial tension development extends into diastole. This is particularly true immediately after the hypoxia is relieved by adequate reoxygenation (Fig. 4-14).

More recent evidence, however, suggests that a trigger mechanism halts contraction before the ATP or other substrates are depleted.[53] This may be due to a drop in myocardial pH, as it has been shown that the reversal of acidosis in ischemic muscle improves the suppressed contraction.[54] As this sequence of events takes place, lactate release, probably the reason for the increase in hydrogen ion concentration, occurs prior to the recording of S-T segment shifts sampled at the epicardium.[55] At the same time, the increase in stiffness is asso-

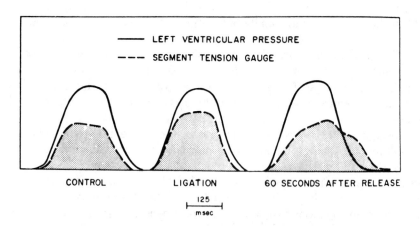

FIGURE 4-14. Isometric tension gauge tracings are superimposed on left ventricular pressure recordings of an open-chested dog during a control period, 3 minutes after coronary artery ligation, and 60 seconds after release. Note the prolongation of tension—thus incomplete relaxation is demonstrated. (From the work of Bing, et al.,[52] with permission.)

STRESS TESTING: PRINCIPLES AND PRACTICE

ciated with an increase in diastolic volume if the area of ischemic muscle is sufficient along with a marked decrease in systolic contraction.[56]

LEFT VENTRICULAR STROKE VOLUME

The normal tendency to increase stroke volume with exercise is not altered much in patients with coronary narrowing if their left ventricle is relatively normal and if the magnitude of coronary narrowing is not too severe. Lichtlen actually found it to be slightly, but not significantly, greater in a group of patients with angina when compared with normal subjects.[47]

When there is left main disease or severe three vessel disease, the normal stroke volume cannot be maintained with increasing myocardial demand in the face of inadequate delivery of oxygen. When this imbalance becomes manifested, the diastolic and the systolic volume both increase, resulting in a net drop in stroke volume and ejection fraction.[49] As this trend progresses, the cardiac output and systolic blood pressure begin to drop, resulting in the termination of exercise. It seems obvious, also, that as the left ventricle is replaced by increasing amounts of scar tissue, the stroke volume will decrease, especially during exercise. Occasionally, patients with large aneurysms have been studied who were able to compensate for the decreased ventricular function to the point that at rest the stroke volume and cardiac output were normal. This

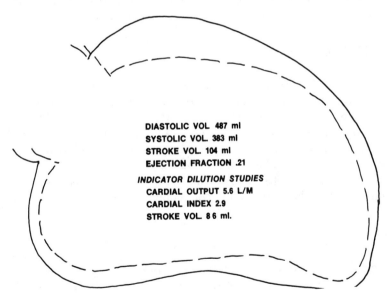

DIASTOLIC VOL 487 ml
SYSTOLIC VOL 383 ml
STROKE VOL 104 ml
EJECTION FRACTION .21

INDICATOR DILUTION STUDIES
CARDIAL OUTPUT 5.6 L/M
CARDIAL INDEX 2.9
STROKE VOL 8 6 ml.

FIGURE 4-15. Tracings of systole and diastole from the left ventriculogram of a 46-year-old man with severe two-vessel disease. Although the ejection fraction is low, the stroke volume and cardiac output are maintained by a very large diastolic volume. The stroke volume estimated from the angiogram is greater than that measured by indicator dilation studies due to error in adjusting for magnification.

can be seen even in the face of a very poor ejection fraction. The ability to compensate must be derived mainly through the Starling effect on the remaining muscle, but it may also be influenced by a chronic increase in the catecholamine concentration (Fig. 4-15).

The compensatory increase in contractility of the normally perfused muscle in this situation has been recognized by echocardiographers. The cardiac output required in patients with coronary disease after a training program may be less for a given workload than before, because of the increase oxygen extraction accomplished by the peripheral tissues.[57]

STROKE WORK

The inefficiency of the ischemic left ventricle is characterized by the stroke work index (left ventricle pressure minus LVEDP multiplied by stroke volume index). The response of the stroke work index to exercise is dramatized by the graphs from Lichtlen's work (see Fig. 4-13). The left ventricular function curves correlating left ventricular work and cardiac index and LVEDP clearly indicate that when a patient with coronary disease is performing normally, the patient is doing so at an increased metabolic cost. It is also rather obvious that the heart usually performs much better before a myocardial infarction takes place than after, even though the patient may be free from angina pain as a result of the infarction. It, therefore, behooves those involved in patient care to work toward preventing the infarction, or at least to attempt to reduce its size.

DOUBLE PRODUCT

As mentioned in Chapter 2, myocardial oxygen consumption correlates well with the tension time index. It has been shown that the time related to systole can be ignored and the so-called "double product" or systolic blood pressure times the heart rate can be used as a useful clinical index to estimate myocardial oxygen needs. Thus, when comparing a patient with himself, after an intervention, the peak double product or the double product at the onset of ischemia or at the onset of angina, provides a more precise end-point than the maximum exercise duration or other commonly used end-points.

PAIN

The anginal pain in coronary insufficiency considered to be the hallmark of myocardial ischemia is poorly understood. Although a classical anginal pattern is a fairly reliable marker for coronary disease, the exact metabolic and physiologic pathways responsible for its genesis are still an enigma. As early as 1935, Katz and Landt[58] postulated that the pain might be due to the release of metabolites by the anoxic myocardium. They also suggested that the pain and the ischemic ECG changes may be due to separate but coexisting processes.

Since that time a great deal of work has been done on myocardial ischemia but it has provided us with little improvement in our understanding. When a patient with coronary insufficiency is stressed as shown in Figure 4-16, the elevation in LVEDP consistently precedes the onset of pain, but in our experience, anginal pain rarely develops in the absence of the rise in diastolic pressure. The patient whose ECG is depicted in Figure 4-16 had pain at the time of the deep S-T segment depression and high LVEDP, but it was relieved shortly after the diastolic pressure began to fall and several minutes before the S-T segment depression had improved. This sequence of events is predictable. One would then surmise that the subendocardial ischemia is closely correlated with pain, as it is with the S-T segment changes.

One certainty is that the absence of pain is of no value in predicting the absence of coronary disease. A good deal has been written about the incidence of silent myocardial infarction, but the incidence of silent coronary disease is much harder to determine. We studied 1000 subjects referred for stress testing in 1968 and found that only 37 percent of those with ischemic changes had chest pain during the test. A group of executives believed to be normal were found to have ischemic changes at or near their peak exercise capacity and pain was uniformly absent.[59]

When 2703 subjects with a positive stress test were analyzed, only 26 percent had pain during the test. The distribution according to age is indicated in Figure 4-17. The similarity in the percentages of those with pain in each age group is somewhat surprising, once the very young are excluded. The higher incidence in young women ages 31 to 40 is surprising, but we also observed this in our 1968 study. It probably represents selective sampling.

It must be emphasized that many of those who do not have pain associated with ischemia during the test may have had some type of discomfort, possibly

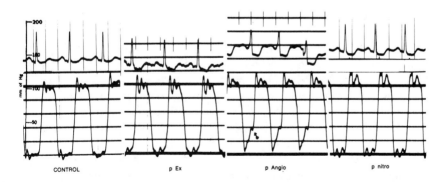

CONTROL p Ex p Angio p nitro

FIGURE 4-16. Left ventricular pressures and ECG recorded during exercise in a catheterization laboratory. Immediately after the angiogram, the patient developed angina that was associated with a very high left-ventricular end-diastolic pressure and deep S-T segment depression. Administration of nitroglycerine resulted in relief from the angina pain and a drop in LVEDP, but there was a delay in the resolution of the S-T segment depression.

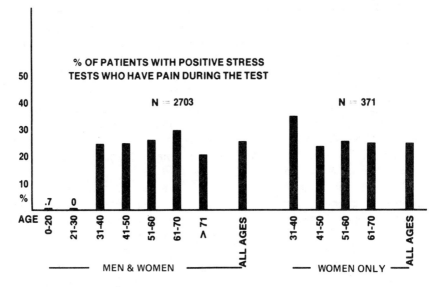

FIGURE 4-17. Analysis of the incidence of pain in subjects subjected to a maximum stress test. Only those with a positive test (S-T segments with depression of 1.5 mm or more) are depicted. Less than 30 percent of all positive responders had chest pain during the test with women having a slight increase in overall incidence.

recognizable as angina at other times. One of the mysteries of coronary disease is why angina may be manifested on one day and absent, even on maximum exertion, on another. Coronary spasm is suspect for some cases, but certainly does not explain all situations.

Endorphins

A great deal of interest in endorphins, the natural opium-like compounds manufactured by the body has recently occurred.[60,61] Because these substances when released by the brain are thought to reduce pain, we postulated that patients with ischemia who are not experiencing pain may have higher levels of endorphins.[62] To test this concept we exercised 10 subjects who had severe coronary narrowing to the point of S-T segment depression and injected naloxone expecting to neutralize their endorphins and initiate pain. Naloxone is known to neutralize endorphins as well as other opium-like drugs. None of our subjects had pain nor could we detect any other effect attributable to the agent. Thus, it appears that we are not much closer to understanding the absence of anginal pain in ischemic patients than before. Others have suggested that bradykinins and prostaglandin may be implicated in anginal pain.[63] Droste and Roskamm[64] studied the pain threshold in asymptomatic coronary patients and found it to be higher than in the usual patient with classical angina. Convincing evidence to implicate any mechanism in the final expression of coronary pain is still sketchy.

Some patients also discover that their angina pain will return if they stop the exercise regimens, but will again disappear if conditioning is resumed. For many years, therapeutic decisions have been made on the basis of pain patterns and yet it is now well-known how fallacious this can be. It has been our experience that moderate angina has an unpredictable pattern on the whole, but as the degree of disability increases, the threshold at which pain occurs becomes more constant.

It must be admitted that although there is a good deal of knowledge about the physiology of ischemic heart disease, at this time, this does not include the factors limiting or initiating anginal pain.

Comment

In some ways, the circulatory pattern and high metabolic requirements of the heart seem to be poorly designed, leaving it extremely susceptible to injury. On the other hand, we often see patients with 90 percent narrowing of all main coronary arteries who still have not only good left ventricular function at rest, but also surprisingly good exercise tolerance. The trigger mechanism, as yet poorly understood, that decreases or halts contraction in an ischemic segment prior to the depletion of ATP is an effective safeguard. It allows the most ischemic part of the myocardium to stop contraction prior to permanent injury, while the segments of the heart muscle with normal perfusion pick up the load to maintain pumping capacity.

The decrease in heart rate response for any given workload seen in some ischemic patients is also an effective way to improve myocardial circulation. The relatively longer diastole seen with a slow heart rate is very effective in providing more perfusion when the rate of flow through a coronary artery is reduced by a high-grade obstruction.

Finally, when we consider the remarkable performance required to make it possible for a patient with coronary narrowing to complete a marathon, the redistribution of flow from normal to ischemic areas, still incompletely understood, must be extremely effective.

BIOCHEMICAL CHANGES IN THE ISCHEMIC MYOCARDIUM

For a time, it was assumed that the loss of contraction in the ischemic area, which occurs within one minute of the onset of inadequate perfusion, was due to a loss of high energy phosphates (ATP). However, biopsies in experimental preparations demonstrated normal ATP for a time after contraction had ceased.[65] It seems likely that the increase in intracellular hydrogen ion following anaerobic metabolism interferes with the interaction of calcium in the contractile proteins and also restricts the release of calcium from the sarcoplasmic reticulum.[66] The increased lactate may also inhibit phosphorylase kinase, which suppresses use of glycogen. The mechanism that switches off contraction is really protective because when the flow of adequate oxygenated blood is re-established so that abnormal metabolites can be washed out, adequate ATP is still present to resume contraction; thus, preventing permanent damage during temporary supply/demand imbalance. The metabolic changes during ischemia and especially the early stages of recovery from ischemia, impairs ventricular relaxation; thus, increasing the left-ventricular filling pressure with its attendant reduction in subendocardial flow. The ability to metabolize free fatty acids also profoundly influences the effect of ischemia. It reduces the activity of carnitine palmityl coenzyme A, a key enzyme responsible for the oxidation of fatty acids, the usual substrate for myocardial metabolism when adequate oxygen is available.

Lactate

In normal subjects, increasing lactate levels in the blood are associated with increased lactate metabolism in the heart when adequate myocardial oxygenation is available. Cardiac muscle as well as skeletal muscle produces excess lactate when using anaerobic pathways, which liberates hydrogen ions and reduces pH. Not only does acidosis reduce the ability to metabolize lactate and fats and thus rapidly depletes myocardial glycogen, but the increasing level of free fatty acids causes further deterioration of myocardial contractility.[67] The mechanisms for this are incompletely understood, but they probably include inhibition of cellular enzyme systems and membrane transport functions. Studies in swine indicate a reduction in activity of adenine nucleotide transferase and a reduction in cytosolic free carnitine. The coronary sinus lactate rise has been shown to be more profound, the greater the ischemia, initiating a rapid deterioration in cardiac output, which further reduces myocardial perfusion.

Free Fatty Acids (FFA)

Because high FFA and low carnitine levels decrease myocardial contractility, carnitine has been used in both animals[68] and man[69] to improve cardiac function at times of ischemia. Whether this will become a practical clinical tool is yet to be determined. Oliver and associates[70] have used a nicotinic acid analog to reduce free fatty acids during myocardial infarction and have found that it suppresses arrhythmias. How the level of free fatty acid correlates with exercise-induced arrhythmias in ischemic patients is yet to be studied thoroughly, but is of considerable interest.

Prostaglandins

Berger and colleagues[24] have reported the release of prostaglandin F in the coronary sinus of ischemic patients after atrial pacing. The hemodynamic effects are yet unknown, but the material may have some type of protective effect, possibly by stabilization of lysosomes in the ischemic area. Many other vasoactive substances probably play some role in cardiac function during exercise. As previously mentioned, Staszewski-Barczak and colleagues[63] believe prostaglandin and bradykinin are the mediators of anginal pain, but evidence for this is still fragmentary.

MECHANISM OF S-T SEGMENT DEPRESSION

Extensive animal studies as well as data in man, have given information about the factors leading up to and responsible for the S-T segment changes that have long been empirically correlated with myocardial ischemia. Ischemia should be distinguished from hypoxia and anoxia. Ischemia is oxygen deprivation due to reduced perfusion; whereas, hypoxia is decreased oxygen supply despite adequate perfusion. Anoxia is the absence of oxygen in association with adequate perfusion. When the delivery of blood becomes inadequate, either due to temporary reduction in flow as might be caused by a coronary spasm, or a sudden drop in cardiac output as might occur with an intense vagal episode, or by an increase in myocardial demand in association with a significant coronary stenosis, the subendocardial area is the first to suffer.

The onset of ischemia is associated with a rapid loss of intracellular potassium resulting in a diastolic current of injury, outward toward the epicardium (Fig. 4-18). The figure depicts the outward diastolic current caused by the potassium leak with its resultant effect on the ECG baseline or the T-Q segment. The p and QRS are then inscribed on this elevated baseline. When ventricular depolarization occurs, inscribing the QRS, all the myocardial cells including those injured are depolarized. There is *no* current flow. At this point, which is the time of the onset of the S-T segment, the galvanometer deflection relates to the original 0 or null point, which is located below the previously elevated diastolic baseline. The result is S-T segment depression; which, when systole is completed, is followed by the elevated diastolic baseline due to the current of injury.

These changes have been associated with a shortening of the refractory period and a prolongation of the QT interval.[71] The transmembrane potential undergoes a reduction in amplitude and some prolongation as depicted in Figure 4-19.[72]

DIRECTION OF S-T VECTOR

With the picture of progressively more subendocardial ischemia before us, it is

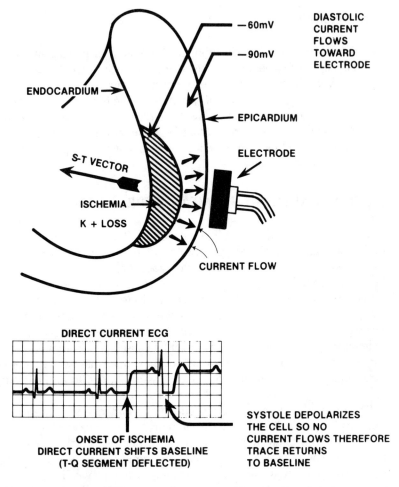

FIGURE 4-18. Mechanism of S-T segment depression. As the subendocardium becomes ischemic, potassium is lost from the cells resulting in a diastolic current flow toward the epicardium and the monitoring electrode. This would deflect the baseline inward, but is not recognized in our standard ECG because of the balancing current, until depolarization terminates the other potentials, resulting in the inscribed S-T segment depression.

now easy to see why the vector of a depressed S-T segment is fairly consistent in direction. The ischemic zone of endocardium, in many cases, may be relatively evenly distributed throughout the whole ventricular cavity, and due to the high left-ventricular filling pressure produces a diastolic injury potential characterized by a consistent vector force, which is opposite in direction to the major QRS vector (Fig. 4-20). The subendocardial ischemia demonstrated years ago[73] is characterized by S-T segment elevation within the cavity of the left ventricle[72] and by S-T segment depression on the precordium in the leads reflecting the appropriate area of injury. If the subendocardial ischemia is regional, then the vector will reflect this as depicted in Figures 4-21 and 4-22. It

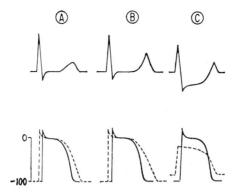

FIGURE 4-19. As ischemia is increased (A to C), the transmembrane potential alterations *(dotted line of lower row)* reveal a prolongation of electrical systole as the ECG in the top row reflects S-T segment depression (From Sodi-Pollares, et al.,[72] with permission.)

can be appreciated by inspection of these diagrams that the placement of the leads can easily determine the likelihood of detecting the abnormality.

On the other hand, Blackburn and associates[74] have shown that ischemic S-T segment depression is best demonstrated in 90 percent of all patients with a bipolar lead system with the negative electrode near V_5 position. Kaplan[82] and colleagues have shown that no matter what area of heart wall is ischemic as determined by coronary angiography, the incidence of S-T segment depression in the CM_5 configuration is very similar and the amount or number of collaterals detected by angiography does not alter this process. It would appear, then, that S-T segment depression and angina may not occur until the ischemia of the subendocardium has progressed enough to produce a general-

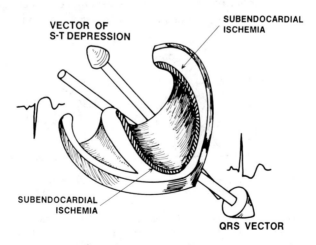

FIGURE 4-20. Schematic cross-section of the heart demonstrating generalized left-ventricular subendocardial ischemia and the vector of S-T segment depression most commonly recorded.

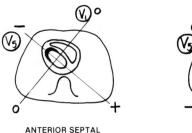
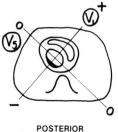

ANTERIOR SEPTAL   POSTERIOR

FIGURE 4-21. The schematic representation of the heart depicts an area of left-ventricular sub-endocardial ischemia where the cavity wall is thickened. The vectors of two leads, V_5 and V_1, are used to illustrate the presence or absence of S-T change. On the *left,* labeled anterior septal, the V_5 lead would show S-T segment depression and the V_1 lead would have an isoelectric S-T if the ischemia were localized to a small area. The reverse would be true *(right)* if the ischemia were isolated to a true posterior area of the left-ventricular subendocardium.

ized change in subendocardial blood flow. Operating from this frame of reference, it is possible to understand why considerable coronary artery disease may be present without producing S-T segment changes, even with maximum exercise, as long as the integrity of the total system is maintained,[74-77] and also why the CM$_5$ lead has proved to be so useful.

Many statements about the inadequacy of lead systems to demonstrate local ischemia imply that, if we used sufficient electrodes, even the most minute areas of ischemia would be revealed by S-T segment depression. Although there is no doubt that multiple leads identify more diseased patients than a single lead,[78] I have seen many examples of patients with severe ischemia who do not have S-T changes even with very complex lead systems. More data on multiple lead systems can be found in Chapter 7. In most cases, the decrease in total myocardial blood flow with its generalized subendocardial changes produces a consistent electrocardiographic pattern when the heart is disabled

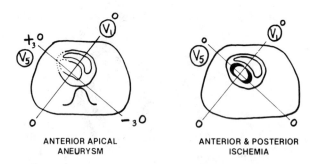

ANTERIOR APICAL   ANTERIOR & POSTERIOR
   ANEURYSM   ISCHEMIA

FIGURE 4-22. The schema used in Figure 4-21 is used here to depict an apical scar *(left),* which would result in S-T elevation at the V_5 position and depression over the right scapular area. On the *right,* two isolated areas of ischemia are at opposite sides of the cavity; therefore, they would cancel each other and the S-T segment at V_5 would be isoelectric. There is evidence to suggest this may happen clinically.

enough to cause a decrease in ventricular compliance and a rise in the diastolic pressure.

S-T SEGMENT ELEVATION

It may be that S-T elevation reflects transmural ischemia; whereas, S-T depression is mainly a marker for subendocardial ischemia. This is suggested by the transient S-T changes seen in the cath lab with coronary spasm or during angioplasty when the balloon causes complete closure of the artery being dilated. When no permanent cell death is present, and flow is re-introduced, the electrocardiographic changes resolve within a minute or two suggesting that transmural or subepicardial ischemia is the usual source of these changes. In certain patients with very high-grade proximal left-anterior descending stenosis, S-T elevation occurs with exercise, probably representing a very severe degree of ischemia[79] in association with transient bulging of the anterior wall during systole.

SUMMARY

In summary, the sequence of events leading to S-T segment depression may be as follows: as increased myocardial oxygen demands exceed that provided by

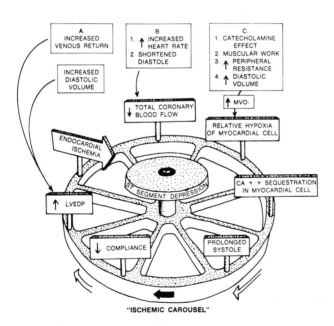

FIGURE 4-23. The ischemic carousel.

coronary perfusion, or when coronary flow is decreased by any means, the mechanism responsible for cardiac contraction is altered resulting in a failure to pump calcium out of the cell, and, thus, the prolongation of relaxation decreases the time remaining during diastole. This incompletely relaxed muscle is stiffer and the decreasing amount of compliance associated with an increasing rate of inflow into the ventricle applies a greater pressure to the subendocardial layers of the myocardium. This not only further inhibits coronary blood flow from the epicardium to the endocardium but accelerates the reduction in total myocardial perfusion and produces a subendocardial zone of injury[80] resulting in the characteristic S-T segment depressions recognized so many years ago by Bousfield.[81] This process causes the cardiac output to rapidly decrease in terms of the metabolic demand of the individual, thus bringing about a reproducible end-point in terms of work-related S-T segment depression, angina, and exercise tolerance.

This process might be depicted as in Figure 4-23. Factors setting the wheel in motion (boxes A, B, and C) are multiple and vary from patient to patient. They are not only initiated by increase in metabolic demand, but by reduction in blood flow. Spasm, changes in autonomic balance, and a drop in perfusion pressure are some of the causes. Once the mechanism is set in motion; however, it tends to compound the degree of dysfunction. Not only do a number of elements set the wheel in motion, but also, if they are blocked or reversed, the absence of the forces that keep the wheel turning will result in a return to more normal function. The presence of S-T segment depression on the ECG is then the electrical manifestation of a complex hemodynamic and metabolic chain reaction that we are only beginning to understand. It is important to consider as many of the above components as possible when dealing with coronary ischemia. Only in this way can we broaden our therapeutic and diagnostic horizons.

This chapter deals with myocardial ischemia as it pertains to exercise stress testing. For a complete work on the coronary circulation, I recommend the excellent text by Melvin Marcus.[27]

REFERENCES

1. MASERI, A, ET AL: Coronary artery spasm as a cause of acute myocardial ischemia in man. Chest 68:625, 1975.
2. MASERI, A, ET AL: "Variant" angina: One aspect of a continuous spectrum of vasospastic myocardial ischemia. Am J Cardiol 42:1019, 1978.
3. MASERI, A, ET AL: Pathogenic mechanisms of angina pectoris: Expanding view. Br Heart J 43:648, 1980.
4. SCHANG, SJ, JR AND PEPINE, CJ: Transient asymptomatic ST segment depression during daily activity. Am J Cardiol 39:396, 1977.
5. SEVERI, S, ET AL: Long-term prognosis of "variant" angina with medical treatment. Am J Cardiol 46:226, 1980.
6. YOUNG, DF, ET AL: Hemodynamics of arterial stenosis at elevated flow rates. Circulation Res 41:99, 1977.

STRESS TESTING: PRINCIPLES AND PRACTICE

7. HUMPHRIES, JO, ET AL: Natural history of ischemic heart disease in relationship to arteriographic findings. Circulation 49:489, 1974.

8. BERNE, RM AND RUBIO, R: Acute coronary occlusion: Early changes that induce coronary dilatation and the development of collateral circulation. Am J Cardiol 24:776, 1969.

9. SCHWARTZ, F, ET AL: Effect of coronary collaterals on left ventricular function at rest and during stress. Am Heart J 95(5):570–577, 1978.

10. WILSON, J, ET AL: Regional coronary anatomy in rest angina: Comparison of patients with rest and exertional angina using quantitative coronary angiography. Chest 82(4):416–421, 1982.

11. ELLIOT, E, ET AL: Day to day changes in coronary hemodynamics secondary to constriction of circumflex branch of left coronary artery in conscious dogs. Circ Res 22:237, 1968.

12. SCHAPER, W: The collateral circulation of the heart. American Elsevier Company, New York, Amsterdam, 1971.

13. ELLIOT, E, ET AL: Direct measurement of coronary collateral blood flow in conscious dogs by an electromagnetic flowmeter. Circ Res 34:374, 1974.

14. EKSTEIN, R: Effect of exercise and coronary artery narrowing in collateral circulation. Circ Res 5:230, 1967.

15. SCHAPER, W, ET AL: Der Einfluss korperlichen Training auf den kollateralkreislauf des herzens. Vereh Dtsch Ges Kreislaufforsch 37:112–121, 1971.

16. HEATON, W, ET AL: Beneficial effect of physical training on blood flow to myocardium perfused by chronic collaterals in the exercising dog. Circulation 57:575, 1978.

17. SCHEEL, K, INGRAM, L, AND WILSON, J: Effects of exercise on the coronary and collateral vasculature of Beagles with and without coronary occlusion. Circ Res 48(4):523–530, 1981.

18. BURT, J AND JACKSON, R: The effects of physical exercise on the coronary collateral circulation of dogs. J Sport Med 5:203–206, 1965.

19. KAPLINSKY, E, ET AL: Effects of physical training in dogs with coronary artery ligation. Circulation 37:556–565, 1968.

20. SCHAPER, W, ET AL: Quantification of collateral resistance in acute and chronic experimental coronary occlusion in the dog. Circ Res 39:371–377, 1976.

21. MACALPIN, R, ET AL: Human coronary artery size during life: A cinearteriographic study. Radiology 108:567, 1973.

22. LINZBACH, AJ: Heart failure from the point of view of quantitative anatomy. Am J Cardiol 5:370, 1960.

23. STEVENSON, JA: Exercise, food intake and health in experimental animals. Can Med Assoc J 96:862, 1967.

24. BERGER, H, ET AL: Cardiac prostaglandin release during myocardial ischemia induced by atrial pacing in patients with coronary artery disease. Am J Cardiol 39(4):481–486, 1977.

25. PITT, B, ET AL: Prostaglandins and prostaglandin inhibitors in ischemic heart disease. Ann Int Med 99:83–92, 1983.

26. GUYTON, R, MCCLENATHAN, J, AND MICHAELIS, L: Evolution of regional ischemia distal to a proximal coronary stenosis. Am J Cardiol 40:381, 1977.

27. MARCUS, ML: The Coronary Circulation in Health and Disease. McGraw-Hill, New York, 1983.

28. WRIGHT, C, ET AL: A method for assessing the physiologic significance of coronary obstructions in man at cardiac surgery. Circulation 62:111, 1980.

29. OPHERK, D, ET AL: Reduction of coronary reserve: A mechanism for angina pectoris in patients with arterial hypertension and normal coronary arteries. Circulation 69(1):1–7, 1984.

30. SONNENBLICK, E, ROSS, J, AND BRAUNWALD, E: Oxygen consumption of the heart. Newer concepts of its multifactoral determination. Am J Cardiol 22:328, 1968.

31. CASTELLANET, M, GREENBERG, P, AND ELLESTAD, M: The predictive value of the treadmill stress test in determining post-infarction ischemia. Am J Cardiol 42:24, 1978.

32. Grossman, W and McLaurin, L: *Diastolic properties of the left ventricle.* Ann Intern Med 84:316, 1976.

33. Zaret, B, et al: *Noninvasive assessment of regional myocardial perfusion with potassium 43 at rest, exercise, and during angina pectoris* (abstr). Circulation 46(Suppl 11):18, 1972.

34. Buckberg, GD, et al: *Some sources of error in measuring regional blood flow with radioactive microspheres.* J Appl Physiol 31:598, 1971.

35. Barnard, JR, et al: *Ischemic response to sudden strenuous exercise in healthy men.* Circulation 48:936, 1973.

36. Bouchard, R, Gault, J, and Ross, J: *Evaluation of pulmonary arterial end diastolic pressure as an estimate of left ventricular end diastolic pressure in patients with normal and abnormal left ventricular performance.* Circulation 44:1072, 1971.

37. Myers, G, Sears, C, and Hiratzka, T: *Correlation of electrocardiographic and pathologic findings in ringlike subendocardial infarction of the left ventricle.* Am J Med Sci 222:417, 1951.

38. Ellestad, MH, et al: *Maximal treadmill stress testing for cardiovascular evaluation.* Circulation 39:517, 1969.

39. Wang, TG, et al: *Central blood volume during upright exercise in normal subjects* (abstr). Fed Proc 21:124, 1962.

40. Case, R, Masser, M, and Crampton, R: *Biochemical aspects of early myocardial ischemia.* Am J Cardiol 24:766, 1969.

41. Epstein, SE, et al: *Angina pectoris: Pathophysiology, evaluation, and treatment.* Ann Intern Med 75:263, 1971.

42. Fogelman, AM, et al: *Echocardiographic study of the abnormal motion of the posterior left ventricular wall during angina pectoris.* Circulation 46:905, 1972.

43. Barry, WH, et al: *Analysis of ventricular compliance curves following pacing-induced angina.* Circulation 46(Suppl 11):483, 1972.

44. Cohn, PF: *Maximal rate of pressure fall (peak negative Dp/Dt) during ventricular relaxation.* Cardiovasc Res 6:263, 1972.

45. Grossman, W and McLaurin, LP: *Diastolic properties of the left ventricle.* Ann Intern Med 84:316, 1976.

46. Mathey, D, Bleified, W, and Franklin, F: *Left ventricular relaxation and diastolic stiffness in experimental myocardial infarction.* Cardiovasc 8:583, 1974.

47. Lichtlen, P: *The hemodynamics of clinical ischemic heart disease.* Ann Clin Res 3:333, 1971.

48. Langer, GA: *Ionic Movements and the Control of Contraction: The Mammalian Myocardium.* John Wiley & Sons, New York, 1974.

49. Rerych, SK, et al: *Cardiac function at rest and during exercise in normals and in patients with coronary artery disease.* Ann Surg 187:449, 1978.

50. Sharma, B and Taylor, SH: *Localization of left ventricular ischemia in angina pectoris by cineangiography during exercise.* Br Heart J 37:963, 1975.

51. Katz, AM and Tada, M: *The "stone heart": A challenge to the biochemist.* Am J Cardiol 29:578, 1972.

52. Bing, OH, et al: *Tension prolongation during recovery from myocardial hypoxia.* J Clin Invest 50:660, 1971.

53. Hillis, LD and Braunwald, E: *Myocardial ischemia.* N Engl J Med 296:971, 1977.

54. Regan, TJ, et al: *Myocardial ischemia and cell acidosis: Modification by alkali and the effects on ventricular function and cation composition.* Am J Cardiol 37:501, 1976.

55. Waters, DD, et al: *Early changes in regional and global left ventricular function induced by graded reductions in regional coronary perfusion.* Am J Cardiol 39:537, 1977.

56. Braunwald, E, Frye, RL, and Ross, J: *Studies on Starling's law of the heart.* Circ Res 8:1254, 1960.

57. Clausen, JP, Larsen, OA, and Trap-Jensen, J: *Physical training in the management of coronary artery disease.* Circulation 40:143, 1969.

58. KATZ, L AND LANDT, H: *The effect of standardized exercise on the four-lead electrocardiogram: Its value in study of coronary disease.* Am J Med Sci 189:346, 1935.

59. ELLESTAD, MH, ET AL: *Maximal treadmill stress testing for cardiovascular evaluation: One year follow-up of physically active and inactive men.* Circulation 39:517, 1969.

60. BUCHSBAUM, MS, ET AL: *Opiate pharmacology and individual differences. I. Psychophysical pain measurements.* Pain 10:357, 1981.

61. BUCHSBAUM, MS, ET AL: *Opiate pharmacology and individual differences. II. Somatosensory evoked potentials.* Pain 10:367, 1981.

62. ELLESTAD, MH AND KUAN, P: *Naloxone and asymptomatic ischemia: Failure to induce angina during exercise testing.* Am J Cardiol 54:982–984, 1984.

63. STASZEWSKI-BARCZAKS, J, FERREIRA, SH, AND VAN, JR: *An excitatory nociceptive cardiac reflex elicited by bradykinin and potentiated by prostaglandins and myocardial ischemia.* Cardiovasc Res 10:314, 1976.

64. DROSTE, C AND ROSKAMM, H: *Experimental pain measurement in patients with asymptomatic myocardial ischemia.* J Am Coll Cardiol 1:940, 1983.

65. COVELL, JW, POOL, PE, AND BRAUNWALD, E: *Effects of acutely induced ischemic heart failure on myocardial high energy phosphate stores.* Proc Soc Exp Biol Med 124:131, 1967.

66. HILLIS, LD AND BRAUNWALD, E: *Myocardial ischemia (first of three parts).* N Engl J Med 296:971–978, Apr 1977.

67. BOURASSA, MG, ET AL: *Myocardial lactate metabolism at rest and during exercise in ischemic heart disease.* Am J Cardiol 23:771–777, 1969.

68. LIEDTKE, AJ AND NELLIS, SH: *Effects of carnitine in ischemic and fatty acid supplemented swine hearts.* J Clin Invest 64:440–447, 1979.

69. THOMSEN, JH, ET AL: *Improved pacing tolerance of the ischemic human myocardium after administration of carnitine.* Am J Cardiol 43:300–306, 1979.

70. OLIVER, MF, ET AL: *Effect of reducing circulating free fatty acids on ventricular arrhythmias during myocardial infarction and on S-T segment depression during exercise-induced ischemia.* Circulation 53(3)(Suppl I):210–213, 1976.

71. HARUMI, K, ET AL: *Ventricular recovery time changes during and after temporary coronary occlusion* (abstr). Am J Cardiol 25:26, 1970.

72. SODI-PALLARES, E, ET AL: *Polyparametric electrocardiography concerning new information obtained from clinical electrocardiogram.* Prog Cardiovasc Dis 13:97, 1970.

73. HELLERSTEIN, HK AND KATZ, L: *The electrical effects of injury at various myocardial locations.* Am Heart J 36:184, 1948.

74. BLACKBURN, H, ET AL: *The exercise electrocardiogram during exercise: Findings in bipolar chest leads of 1449 middle-aged men, at moderate work levels.* Circulation 34:1034, 1966.

75. BLOMQVIST, CG: *Use of exercise testing for diagnostic and functional evaluation of patients with arteriosclerotic heart disease.* Circulation 44:1120, 1971.

76. MANVI, KN, ALLEN, WH, AND ELLESTAD, MH: *Elevated S-T segments with exercise in ventricular aneurysm.* J Electrocardiol 5:317, 1972.

77. SIMONSON, E: *Electrocardiographic stress tolerance tests.* Prog Cardiovasc Dis 13:269, 1970.

78. CHAITMAN, BR, ET AL: *Improved efficiency of treadmill exercise testing using a multiple lead system and basic hemodynamic response.* Circulation 57:71, 1978.

79. CAHAHINE, RA, RAEZNER, AE, AND ISCHIMORI, T: *The clinical significance of exercise induced S-T segment elevation.* Circulation 54:209, 1976.

80. BECKER, LC, FORTUIN, MJ, AND PITT, B: *Effects of ischemia and anti-anginal drugs on the distribution of radioactive microspheres in the canine left ventricle.* Circ Res 28:263, 1971.

81. BOUSFIELD, G: *Angina pectoris changes in the electrocardiogram during a paroxysm.* Lancet 2:457, 1918.

82. KAPLAN, MA, HARRIS, CN, AND PARKER, DP: *Inability of the submaximal stress test to predict the localization of coronary disease.* Circulation 47:250, 1973.

5

INDICATIONS

Only a few years ago, during the heyday of the Masters Test, stress testing was primarily used to identify or confirm the presence of ischemic heart process. Prior to World War II, it was mainly a research tool applied to problems related to exercise in athletes. More recently, as the method again evolved into a measure of functional capacity, as well as a means to diagnose coronary disease, the applications have been extended to a number of areas previously excluded, such as predicting prognosis in coronary artery disease and evaluating treatment in congestive failure.

In spite of the frequent editorials and papers criticizing its usefulness,[1,2] there has been an enormous increase in its use as cardiologists and other physicians have discovered how helpful stress testing can be in patient management. This chapter lists some of the indications and attempts to add some perspective to some of the present controversy.

Statistical data have established that coronary artery disease has reached epidemic proportions. Not only does the death rate average about 600,000 a year in the United States, but it exceeds all other causes of death. Death or a myocardial infarction is the first symptom in 55 percent of patients with coronary heart disease. An enormous amount of energy is being expended in search for the cause and a way to control this malignant process. Although it would be desirable to be able to map and quantitate the evolution of plaques in the coronary tree, an acceptable noninvasive means for doing this is not yet available. I know of no one who proposes routine coronary angiography for the asymptomatic population at large. Although the stress test is far from perfect, it is emerging as the most practical means of uncovering latent disease, and even though it may be that the coronary obstructive lesions must reach 50 percent or more in one vessel to reduce flow significantly, the majority of such lesions are probably still asymptomatic as far as the patient is concerned.[3] The study in dogs by Wegria and associates[4] suggests that blood flow must be reduced 75 percent before changes are routinely seen in the ECG.

Kaplan and associates[5] reported on the correlation of stress tests and coronary angiograms in 200 subjects. They found 19 (9.5%) had positive tests, yet had no more than 25 percent narrowing in a single artery. It must be concluded that some of these stenotic lesions were underestimated, but it points to the usefulness of the test in some patients with mild degrees of stenosis. Recent work by Marcus[6] illustrates the difficulty in predicting the metabolic significance from the coronary angiogram, suggesting the importance of a dynamic measure of function.

There are many forms of stress testing, such as the well known polygraph or "lie detector," the anoxia test, and the use of an isometric hand grip. Several of these will be reviewed; however, this chapter will concentrate on the indications for exercise testing, which are:

- Evaluating the patient with chest pain or with other findings suggestive, but not diagnostic of coronary disease.
- Determining prognosis and severity of disease.
- Evaluating the effects of medical and surgical therapy.
- Screening for latent coronary disease.
- Evaluation of congestive heart failure.
- Evaluation of arrhythmias.
- Evaluation of functional capacity and formulation of an exercise prescription.
- Evaluation of congenital heart disease.
- Stimulus to a change in lifestyle.
- Miscellaneous.

EVALUATION OF PATIENTS WITH CHEST PAIN

If the pain pattern is suspicious, but not classical for angina, the presence or absence of disease can often be established by a maximum stress test. Although there is a significant percentage of false-negatives when compared with coronary angiography depending on what is considered significant disease, the reliability is dependent on the magnitude and time of onset of the S-T changes, on the heart rate and blood pressure response and very importantly, on the prevalence of disease in the population under study. The influence of prevalence on the reliability of the S-T segment change is discussed in more detail in Chapter 14, under Bayesian Analysis. Suffice to say, in patients with chest discomfort selected because they are clinically apt to have coronary disease, exercise testing remains one of the more practical approaches to diagnosis, especially when using a number of parameters in combination with S-T changes.

PROGNOSIS AND SEVERITY OF DISEASE

In recent years, numerous studies[7,8] have confirmed that severity of disease, which is a major factor in prognosis, can be estimated with considerable accuracy with exercise testing. The details are presented in Chapter 14; however, it must again be emphasized that a clinical approach, considering multiple variables along with the presence of the S-T changes, will provide us with insight into the future course of the patient's disease process. In the last few years, the predischarge exercise test after myocardial infarction has become an accepted approach to stratification of risk for further events.[9]

EVALUATION OF THERAPY

The use of an objective method to evaluate therapy in coronary disease is essential. The "sham" operation for internal mammary ligation established dramatically how difficult it is to evaluate coronary disease by being dependent on the patient's reported symptoms. A good stress protocol should measure the patient's relative myocardial blood flow, onset of S-T depression in terms of the work applied, and aerobic capacity before and after treatment. Knowledge of this type can give us much more useful information than just asking patients how they feel. Because it is known that a myocardial infarction will terminate angina, it certainly follows that the presence or absence of pain is often a rather crude and misleading indicator of coronary disease. One of the logical applications is the evaluation of coronary patients before and after surgery. Stuart and Ellestad[10] and others[11,12] report that it has considerable value in predicting postoperative graft patency, but a certain amount of caution is indicated. The experience after angioplasty has also suggested its use in this area. When various medical regimens rather than invasive approaches, have been instituted, the test will be helpful. Cardiotoxic agents such as adriamycin, are being used more frequently and stress testing provides an evaluation of these effects.

SCREENING FOR LATENT CORONARY DISEASE

There is still widespread belief that significant coronary disease usually produces angina and that a good historian can usually elicit evidence of coronary disease during a complete medical workup by questioning the patient about chest pain.

As was noted in Chapter 4, our data indicate that only about 30 percent of those who have ischemia have chest pain concurrently.[13] When symptoms of typical angina are described by the patient, coronary disease can be predicted with considerable reliability, but when no history of pain is present, there is still a strong possibility of significant narrowing in the coronary tree in patients with appropriate risk factors.

The exact reliability of the positive stress test in predicting coronary disease is discussed in detail in Chapter 14, but using S-T segment changes alone, it is at least twice as useful as a high cholesterol level or any of the other risk factors

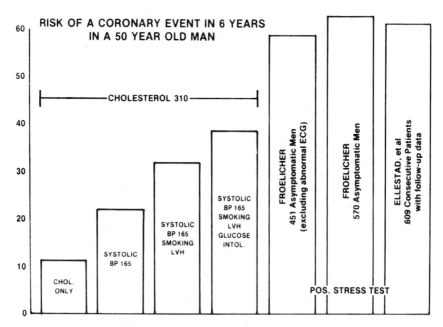

FIGURE 5-1. Graph of the relative capacity to predict coronary events among the various risk factors used in the Framingham Study as compared with the stress test.

usually mentioned. It could in some cases be one of the clues to the presence of unsuspected coronary narrowing, even though the false-positive rate in most asymptomatic groups is high.

Figure 5-1 illustrates the relative capacity to predict coronary events among the various risk factors used in the Framingham Study,[14] as compared with the stress test.[15,16] Chapter 14 discusses how the reliability of the test in asymptomatic persons is reduced because of the lower prevalence of the disease. In spite of the inherent limitations, it remains a useful cost-effective approach in evaluating asymptomatic individuals believed to be at risk.

EVALUATION OF PATIENTS WITH CONGESTIVE HEART FAILURE

Until recently, congestive heart failure was considered an absolute contraindication to exercise testing. Recently, a number of workers[17,18] have used this approach to try to understand functional changes, to establish mechanisms and to measure response to therapy. At this time, it does not seem to have much use in routine patient care outside the research protocol.

EVALUATION OF ARRHYTHMIAS

Many rhythm disturbances are initiated by exercise, and when this is so, it is very important to document. It is also important to establish that some abnormalities in rhythm are terminated by exercise. When we treat an arrhythmia that is influenced by exercise, we are deluding ourselves if we believe the efficiency of the therapy can be determined by observing the patient only at rest. The significance of exercise-induced arrhythmias on the ability to predict future events in coronary patients has been determined and is reviewed in Chapter 13. The presence of exercise-induced arrhythmias also becomes an important public health issue when the arrhythmias developed in subjects engaged in hazardous activities or in occupations in which coordination and alert performance affect the lives of others. Young and colleagues[19] have used the symptom-limited exercise test routinely to evaluate malignant arrhythmias referred to their group.

EVALUATION OF FUNCTIONAL CAPACITY

One of the most important decisions a physician must make in the case of a patient who has angina or has had a myocardial infarction is how much exercise the patient can tolerate. Testing two to three weeks after a myocardial infarction has established it as a safe and useful adjunct to patient management. If the patient has a strenuous job, this is especially critical. All too often,

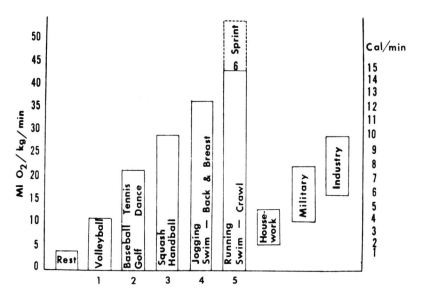

FIGURE 5-2. Various types of exercise presented in relation to oxygen uptake in ml per kg of body weight and calories expended per minute. (Adapted from classification schema of Wells, Balke, and Van Fossan by Falls, HB, in J. S. C. Med. Assoc. (Suppl.), December, 1969.)

the patient's physician is inclined to be conservative and insists on restrictions based on an unsubstantiated guess rather than on hard data. There is no substitute for watching the patient actually exercising. The next best thing is to have a detailed report from someone knowledgeable in exercise physiology who has watched the subject exercise. It is also important to be able to advise patients with coronary insufficiency, either latent or manifest, how much exercise they can do during their leisure time or if they plan to launch into some new endeavor requiring a higher input of stress. Good data are available as guides to the metabolic demands for various occupations and sports. From a properly designed stress test, the response can be translated into a proper exercise prescription (Fig. 5-2).

The ability to predict a patient's aerobic capacity is now well established and this knowledge can be useful in noncardiac conditions as well as in those with valvular and other forms of noncoronary disability.[20]

The whole concept of the cardiac rehabilitation unit was formulated on the concept that a safe exercise prescription can be predicated on the results of the stress test. This is being expanded to patients who have had coronary bypass surgery as well as angina and a previous myocardial infarction.

CONGENITAL HEART DISEASE AND VALVULAR DYSFUNCTION

The management of children with congenital heart disease is being made after function as well as anatomic data have been considered. It has been especially useful in congenital aortic stenosis,[21] and also in studying postoperative patients with tetralogy and other complex defects.[22]

One of the most difficult decisions in cardiology is deciding when to replace damaged valves. Exercise testing provides invaluable guidelines in this determination. This is especially true in aortic and mitral insufficiency when used in conjunction with nuclear blood pool imaging.

STIMULUS TO MOTIVATE CHANGE IN LIFESTYLE

One of the most serious problems in our sedentary population or in those with coronary disease is the need to motivate patients to stop smoking, follow a diet, exercise regularly, and to make other necessary changes in their lifestyles. Because the results associated with such change in their habit patterns are not readily apparent to them, a stimulus of some sort is often needed. The patient's performance on a stress test often serves just such a function. In our cardiac rehabilitation program, the stress test response is explained to the patient and its meaning in regard to the progress often serves to motivate cooperation not otherwise forthcoming. This has been the experience of cardiac rehabilitation units across the country.

SPORTS MEDICINE

In the last few years, there has been renewed interest in research in exercise physiology in sports medicine.[23-25] In a large number of these reports, exercise testing plays an indispensable role. A significant segment of the new information in exercise testing is now coming from this sector. As fitness becomes more and more of an obsession in our culture, the stress test emerges as a useful method for measuring this parameter. This is often desirable prior to sports training so that a baseline may be established in order to compare the efficiency of a certain program.

SUMMARY

As mentioned by Kattus in the Foreword to the first edition of this book, we have progressed beyond the "take it easy" mentality and realize the importance of evaluating cardiovascular function during exercise as well as rest. The indications discussed here will undoubtedly be expanded in future years. The recent trend to do stress tests prior to hospital discharge for an acute infarction is an example. The expansion in the field of pediatric cardiology is another. The recent work by Marcus[6] emphasizes that even the coronary angiogram needs to be correlated with functional testing to provide the information we need to make sound clinical decisions.

REFERENCES

1. BORER, JS, ET AL: *Limitations of the electrocardiographic response to exercise in predicting coronary artery disease.* N Engl J Med 293:367, 1975.
2. REDWORD, DR, BORER, JS, AND EPSTEIN, SE: *Whither the ST segment during exercise.* Circulation 54:703, 1976.
3. ASTRAND, I: *Exercise electrocardiograms recorded twice with an 8-year interval in a group of 204 women and men 48-63 years old.* Acta Med Scand 118:27, 1965.
4. WEGRIA, R, ET AL: *Relationship between reduction in coronary flow and appearance of electrocardiographic changes.* Am Heart J 38:90, 1949.
5. KAPLAN, MA, ET AL: *Inability of the submaximal treadmill stress test to predict the location of coronary disease.* Circulation 47:250, 1973.
6. MARCUS, ML: *The Coronary Circulation in Health and Disease.* McGraw-Hill, New York, 1983.
7. DAGENAIS, GR, ET AL: *Survival of patients with a strongly positive exercise electrocardiogram.* Circulation 65(3): 452–456, 1982.
8. GOLDSCHLAGER, N, SELZER, A, AND COHN, K: *Treadmill stress tests as indicators of presence and severity of coronary artery disease.* Ann Int Med 85:277, 1976.
9. BARON, DB, LICHT, JR, AND ELLESTAD, MH: *Status of exercise stress testing after myocardial infarction.* Arch Intern Med 144:595–601, 1984.
10. STUART, RJ AND ELLESTAD, MH: *Postoperative stress testing.* Angiology 30:416, 1979.
11. ASSAD-MORELL, JL, ET AL: *Aorta-coronary artery saphenous vein bypass surgery, clinical and angiographic results.* Mayo Clinic 50:379, 1975.
12. FRICK, MH, HARJOLA, PT, AND VALLE, M: *Persistent improvement after coronary bypass surgery: Ergometric and angiographic correlations at 5 years.* Circulation 67(3):491–496, 1983.
13. KEMP, GL AND ELLESTAD, MH: *The incidence of "silent" coronary heart disease.* Calif Med 109:363, 1968.
14. KANNEL, WB (ED): *Framingham study: An epidemiological investigation of cardiovascular disease.* Pub Nat Heart, Lung and Blood Institute. 1948 to present.
15. ELLESTAD, MH AND WAN, MCK: *Predictive implication of stress testing.* Circulation 51:363, 1975.
16. FROELICHER, VF, YANOWITZ, FG, AND THOMPSON, AJ: *The correlation of coronary angiography and the electrocardiographic response to maximal treadmill testing in asymptomatic persons.* Circulation 48:597, 1973.
17. FRANCIOSA, JA: *Exercise testing in chronic congestive heart failure.* Am J Cardiol 53:1447–1450, 1984.
18. KRAMER, BL, MASSIE, BM, AND TOPIC, N: *Controlled trial of captopril in chronic heart failure: A rest and exercise hemodynamic study.* Circulation 67:807–816, 1983.
19. YOUNG, DZ, ET AL: *Safety of maximal exercise testing in patients at high risk for ventricular arrhythmia.* Circulation 70:184–191, 1984.
20. BRUCE, RA, KUSUMI, F, AND HOSMER, D: *Maximal oxygen intake and nomographic assessment of functional aerobic impairment in cardiovascular disease.* Am Heart J 85:546, 1973.
21. JAMES, FW AND KOPLAN, S: *Exercise testing in children.* Primary Cardiol 3:34, 1977.
22. STRIEDER, DJ, ET AL: *Exercise tolerance after repair of tetralogy of Fallot.* Am Thorac Surg 19:397, 1975.
23. CORQUIGLINI, S (ED): *Biomechanics III.* Medicine and Sport Vol. 8 Karger, Basel, 1971.
24. KEUL, J, DOLL, E, AND KEPPLER, D (EDS): *Energy metabolism of human muscle.* Medicine and Sport Vol. 7, Karger, Basel, 1972.
25. WILSON, PK (ED): *Adult Fitness and Cardiac Rehabilitation.* University Park Press, Baltimore, 1976.

6

CONTRAINDICATIONS, RISKS, AND SAFETY PRECAUTIONS

A good deal of controversy over the safety of exercise in various population groups has occurred in recent years. Because Americans have gone on a "health binge" with millions jogging and entering in organized runs, some understanding of the risks involved warrant discussion. Some of these same issues pertain to the prescribing of exercise and/or exercise testing. Shephard[1] of the University of Toronto has taken the position that there is little risk involved in initiating an exercise program of a sedentary asymptomatic middle-aged man and advised against an exercise test. He does so because of the evidence that a high percentage of abnormal electrocardiographic stress tests are false-positives in this population, and he believes the information may lead to other unnecessary tests, such as angiography.

The American Heart Committee on Exercise,[2] however, recommends stress testing prior to the initiation of exercise programs in normals over 40 or in others with risk factors that increase the probability of coronary artery disease. Fletcher and colleagues[3] and others [4-7] concur in this decision. The data from the Seattle Heart Watch[8] clearly indicate that in asymptomatic subjects with two or more risk factors, stress testing identifies a cohort with a risk of a coronary event at least 15 times greater than the negative responders. It would seem prudent that such a group might be worthy of careful scrutiny to determine the presence of a life-threatening process. If exercise testing is used in these subjects, or in cardiac patients in general, safety is an important aspect of the procedure.

It should be emphasized that the most important safety factor in stress testing is a knowledgeable and experienced physician in charge of the test. Knowing when to stop or when not to start a stress test requires considerable familiarity with exercise physiology, cardiology, and electrocardiography. Experience combined with the above knowledge is essential in undertaking the risk of exercising cardiac patients. On the other hand, it has been demonstrated that even maximum testing is safe if one follows available guidelines after receiving some degree of training and experience.[9,10] Verbal but unpublished reports of high mortality occurring with enthusiastic untrained novices come to us quite frequently.

A reasonable knowledge of the patient's past medical history and present problems is essential. A fairly good idea of the patient's capacity to exercise can be obtained when this information is combined with auscultation of the heart and inspection of the resting ECG. Then, by carefully observing the patient's response to the early stages of the exercise protocol, the physician can be alerted to potential dangers and take steps to make certain that no harm is done.

WHEN NOT TO STRESS (ABSOLUTE CONTRAINDICATIONS)

It is generally agreed that stress testing should not be done on:
1. Patients with an acute myocardial infarction.
2. Patients suffering from acute myocarditis or pericarditis.

STRESS TESTING: PRINCIPLES AND PRACTICE

3. Patients exhibiting signs of unstable progressive angina. This includes the patient who has long periods of angina of fairly recent onset while at rest.
4. Patients with rapid ventricular or atrial arrhythmias.
5. Patients with second or third degree heart block and patients with known severe left main disease.
6. Acutely ill patients, such as those with infections, hyperthyroidism, or severe anemia.
7. Patients with locomotion problems.

Over the years, exercise was believed to be dangerous in certain conditions, which lead to there being included in a list of absolute contraindications to exercise testing. In some of these, such as unstable angina, experience has led us to this conclusion, while in others common sense seemed to justify such a statement. Every so often one of the absolutes is moved to the relative contraindications list. This has happened in both aortic stenosis and congestive heart failure in the last few years, and may also pertain to left main coronary disease and various types of heart block before too long. Thus, the above list comprises a current consensus but may be changed as new knowledge is accumulated.

RELATIVE CONTRAINDICATIONS

Aortic Stenosis

Early reports of cardiac arrest in patients with aortic stenosis resulted in a cautious approach with this valvular lesion. This should be applied. If the auscultatory findings, clinical symptoms, and laboratory data suggest very high-grade stenosis in adults, stress testing should be avoided. In adults with moderate valvular disease, however, it can be a very useful procedure with an acceptable risk when used cautiously. We have never had a serious problem with a patient with aortic stenosis. In children, it has been found to be useful and quite safe (see Chapter 20).

Suspected Left Main Equivalent

Because we frequently fail to identify this lesion before the stress test and discover later what we have done, considerable experience is available. Most patients tolerate the test safely, but usually have a limited exercise capacity. It has been our practice to withhold stress testing if we have prior knowledge that the left main lesion is over 70 percent or if there is a left main equivalent (very high-grade proximal obstruction in all branches of the left coronary artery). One of our deaths was in a patient with left main disease (see Case History 2 later in this chapter).

Severe Hypertension

If the patient has severe resting hypertension (240/130) requiring multiple medications, we believe the test should be withheld or used with extreme caution. The clinical status, such as history of strokes, carotid bruits, age, and heart size must be taken into consideration.

Idiopathic Subaortic Stenosis and Asymmetric Septal Hypertrophy

In these conditions in which outflow obstruction may be quite severe, caution is important. Sudden death after exercise occasionally occurs even in young patients irrespective of the degree of obstruction.[11]

Severe S-T Segment Depression at Rest

In a patient with a history of angina who is not on digitalis, S-T segment depression at rest should be viewed with caution. It may indicate severe subendocardial ischemia. Such a patient failed to tolerate a stress test in our laboratory (see Case History 3 later in in this chapter).

Congestive Heart Failure

Patients with basal rales and leg edema should as a rule not be tested; however, the evaluation of patients with compensated heart failure is often helpful in regulating their exercise schedule. Recent studies on patients with congestive failure have been accomplished without complications, however.[12]

WHEN TO TERMINATE THE EXERCISE TEST

In a patient with known or suspected heart disease, the physician or trained technician administering the test must continually observe the patient and the monitor, and have the ability to record the ECG on paper for further analysis. The electrocardiographic printout is often more informative than the image on the oscilloscope and must be available for immediate inspection. The proper application of electrodes and capacity electrically to filter the signal are also very important. Some filtering designed to minimize baseline wandering will also eliminate the S-T segment depression. Details on electrical filtering and standards for ECG equipment are discussed in Chapter 7.

It is generally agreed by most workers in the field that the test should be terminated when:

1. Premature ventricular contractions (PVCs) develop in pairs or with increasing frequency as exercise increases, or when ventricular tachycardia develops (runs of three or more PVCs).
2. Atrial tachycardia, atrial fibrillation, or atrial flutter supervenes.
3. There is onset of heart block, either second or third degree.
4. Anginal pain is progressive (grade three pain if grade four is the most severe in patient's experience).
5. S-T segment depression has become severe. Some would terminate with 3 mm or more, but if the patient looks good and feels good, it has been safe in our experience to proceed with changes of greater magnitude.
6. S-T elevation of 2 mm or more in precordial or inferior leads that do not have a resting Q-wave.
7. The heart rate or systolic blood pressure drops progressively in the face of continuing exercise.
8. The patient is unable to continue because of dyspnea, fatigue, or feeling of faintness.
9. Musculoskeletal pain becomes severe, such as might occur with arthritis or claudication.
10. The patient looks vasoconstricted, in other words, pale and clammy.
11. Extreme elevations occur in systolic and diastolic blood pressures associated with a headache or blurred vision.
12. When the patient has reached or exceeded the predicted maximum pulse rate, one can be satisfied that the patient has performed satisfactorily. However, if the subject is able and willing to continue, it is safe to proceed in the absence of other indications for termination.
13. Equipment problems, that is, loss of ECG on monitor.

Patients should understand that they can stop voluntarily, but are encouraged to try to reach or exceed maximum predicted heart rate.

CONTROVERSIAL INDICATIONS FOR TEST TERMINATION

Submaximal Target Heart Rates

Many investigators in this field discontinue the test at some arbitrary heart rate below maximum capacity.[13,14] Some use the heart rate of 150 for all patients.[15] Some use 75, 80, or 90 percent of maximum predicted heart rate.[16] Any arbitrary cutoff, when not adjusted for age, must be recognized as being unphysiologic just as is any predetermined load, such as 150 or 200 watts, on the bicycle. It has been stated that stopping short of maximum heart rate is safer, and the available support for this will be presented. In our laboratory, the predicted rate seems to be a safe target, but is often exceeded in fit patients. If a predetermined heart rate is used, the ability to estimate aerobic capacity is lost.

S-T Segment Elevation

After exercise is underway, some patients will develop S-T segment elevation. In the absence of a previous infarction, this pattern in the anterior precordial leads usually indicates ischemia involving the total thickness of the myocardium rather than just a subendocardial problem.[17] When seen, it is almost always associated with a high-grade obstruction in the proximal left anterior descending coronary. If exercise persists, infarction may be eminent and it would be wise to terminate the test. Sheffield and associates[14] have described a patient with a history suggesting variant angina who had resting S-T segment elevation reverting to normal on exercise. Shortly after the test the patient sustained an anterior wall infarction. They believe that S-T segment elevation should be treated with extreme caution.

S-T segment elevation in leads reflecting a previous infarction need not generate concern, but usually reflect dyskinesia and a full thickness scar.

S-T segment elevation on the anterior/posterior lead, either V_1 or V_2 or the orthogonal Z may be a reflection of subendocardial changes in the septum and should be considered to be equivalent to S-T segment depression in other leads.[3]

EQUIPMENT AND SUPPLIES NECESSARY TO TEST SAFELY

Although it is generally stated that the Master's Test is associated with no significant risk, two of the three patients who died in our laboratory exhibited problems at a workload commensurate with the double Master's Test. Therefore, it is strongly urged that all stress testing be done in a setting where emergencies can be treated efficiently and expeditiously. Monitoring should be continuous. If, for some reason, interference caused by muscle artifact or the battery effect of the electrode-skin interface produces an uninterpretable tracing, the test should be terminated. Blood pressure monitoring should be done before, during, and after the test. The standard cuff method is still to be preferred, although a number of automated devices are on the market. There is no method now in use, as far as I know, that will accurately record blood pressure in all patients during running, short of intra-arterial catheterization. Fortunately, only those subjects in quite good condition spend much of the test time jogging at over 4 miles per hour on most protocols. Those able to reach this level of activity are usually less likely to have sudden changes in blood pressure; therefore, the failure to record, accurately, the pressure at high workloads is not as serious as it would be for one in poorer physical condition. Fortunately, the pressure immediately after the test is similar to the one just before termination of the test and is much more accurately measured. An early rise may often occur about one minute after the termination of the test and is usually a sign the subject has exceeded anaerobic threshold and has performed near maximum capacity.

STRESS TESTING: PRINCIPLES AND PRACTICE

Drugs

An emergency kit of appropriate drugs should be adjacent to the testing area, along with syringes, intravenous equipment, and Ambu bag. The medicines to be included will vary with the experience of the physician and the methods and concepts of treatment in the area. Those kept in our unit are:

Adrenalin 1:1000, 30 ml vial
Aminophylline IV, 500 mg, 20 ml ampule
Amobarbital, 500 mg ampule
Metaraminol, 10 mg/ml, 10 ml vial
Atropine, 0.4 mg/ml, 20 ml vial
Diphenhydramine hydrochloride, 50 mg/ml, 1 ml ampule
Calcium gluconate, 1 gm, 10 ml ampule
Deslanoside, 0.4 mg/ml, 2 ml ampule
Dexamethasone sodium phosphate, 4 mg/ml, 5 ml vial
Digoxin, 0.5 mg/ml, 2 ml ampule
Diphenylhydantoin, 100 mg vial
Isoproterenol hydrochloride 1:500 5 ml ampule
Propranolol hydrochloride, 1 mg ampule

Heparin, 1000 U/ml ,10 ml vial
Furosemide, 20 mg/ml, 2 ml ampule
Lidocaine 2 percent, 5 ml syringe
Lidocaine 2 percent, 50 ml vial
Naloxone hydrochloride, 0.4 mg 1 ml ampule
Potassium chloride, 20 mEq, 10 ml vial
Sodium bicarbonate, 3.75 gm/ml, 50 ml vial
Hydrocortisone sodium succinate, 250 mg vial
Diazepam, 10 m, 2 ml ampule
Glucose 50 percent, 50 ml vial
Dopamine, 5 ml ampule
Bretylium tosylate, 500 mg, 10 ml ampule
Verapamil, 10 mg ampule

Defibrillator

It is generally agreed that a DC defibrillator should be on hand and frequently tested to assure that it is functioning properly. Although it will be used very rarely if the proper care is exercised in testing. The rapid conversion of ventricular tachycardia or ventricular fibrillation will be lifesaving. Those in attendance should be fully trained in its use, as in other matters of resuscitation.

It is of interest to note that we have used the defibrillator on three patients with ventricular fibrillation. One who was converted immediately did not have an infarction. Another, who also converted immediately, did prove to have an infarction, but recovered. The third patient sustained an infarction and failed to survive.

CASE HISTORIES OF PATIENTS WHO DIED

Although it has been over 10 years since we have had a death related to stress testing, it still seems appropriate to describe the patients who died in our early experience. Tragedy should always be analyzed carefully.

CASE 1: H.G. was a 53-year-old machine operator with a history of angina subsequent to a myocardial infarction sustained four years before. Progression of his angina had recently accelerated to the point that prolonged pain at rest had been common. Examination disclosed a sustained apical heave suggestive of a myocardial aneurysm and a loud fourth sound. The resting ECG revealed an old inferior and an anterior septal infarction. A coronary angiogram and catheterization disclosed a large calcified apical aneurysm and severe three-vessel coronary disease. The left-ventricular end-diastolic pressure was 24 mm Hg at rest and increased to 36 mm Hg with three minutes of straight leg-raising.

When the treadmill test was performed, he walked five minutes without pain, reaching a pulse of 164 and stopped because of dyspnea. The physician noted several PVCs just before the patient stopped the exercise; S-T segment elevation was also recorded during stress. Two minutes after termination of the test, he suddenly developed ventricular fibrillation and although he reverted to sinus rhythm several times with cardioversion, ventricular fibrillation repeatedly returned and he eventually expired. The autopsy revealed a fresh infarction (Fig. 6-1).

CASE 2: G.M., a 43-year-old meperidine addict, had undergone Vineberg surgery nine months before the stress test. He had almost continuous chest pain, but it seemed to be pleural in nature and was not relieved by nitroglycerin. Angiography had documented patency of the internal mammary implants and 90 percent stenosis of the left main coronary artery.

The stress test was done in an attempt to evaluate his pain pattern. The resting tracing revealed inverted T waves and 1.0 mm S-T segment depression. He walked for two minutes, achieving a heart rate of 112, and his S-T segment depression reached 2.0 mm by the second minute in the CM_5 lead. The test was terminated due to increasing S-T segment depression and the development of typical substernal pain superimposed on the patient's lateral chest pain. He was given sublingual nitroglycerin and an oxygen mask and was apparently getting some relief when a slow sinus bradycardia developed three minutes after termination of exercise. His blood pressure also dropped and although atropine was given intravenously, his heart rate did not show an increase. An isoproterenol drip was then instituted because he was becoming vasoconstricted and sweaty. Shortly after this had been started, ventricular fibrillation ensued and a prolonged resuscitative effort was unsuccessful. Autopsy disclosed no evidence of a new infarction, but confirmed the high-grade disease of the left main coronary artery and evidence of an old anterior septal infarction (Fig. 6-2).

CASE 3: A.S. was a 53-year-old man with a two-year history of progressive angina limiting his walking to half a block on level ground. Physical examination was negative except for a loud fourth sound and a double apical impulse. The resting ECG did not show an infarction, but did disclose S-T segment

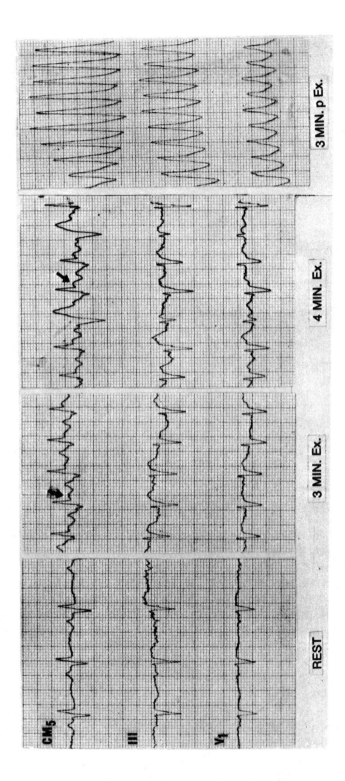

FIGURE 6-1. The ECG shows resting Q waves in CM_5 and S-T segment elevation with exercise as well as an increasing incidence of premature ventricular contractions. Two minutes after exercise, ventricular fibrillation supervened.

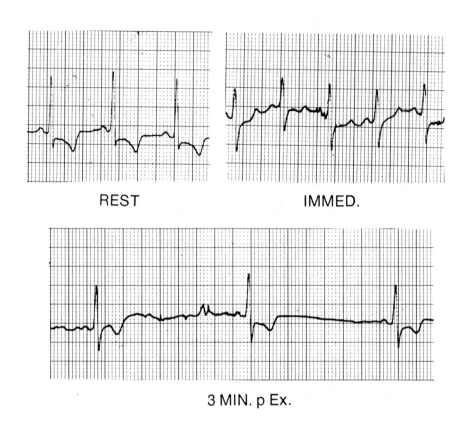

REST   IMMED.

3 MIN. p Ex.

FIGURE 6-2. Three minutes after exercise, a very slow sinus bradycardia developed, which failed to respond to atropine intravenously.

depression of 1.0 mm in V_4, V_5, and V_6.

He walked for two and a half minutes, reaching a heart rate of 138 and stopped because of fatigue, dyspnea, and a slight pressure sensation in his chest. S-T segment depression increased from 2.0 mm at rest on the CM_5 lead to 3.0 mm at peak exercise. Two minutes after the test was terminated, he developed severe dyspnea, a drop in his systolic blood pressure to 80, and cold, sweaty skin. No arrhythmia or evidence of infarction was manifested on three monitoring leads. Intermittent closed chest massage failed to improve his condition, and for two hours various attempts to improve his status failed, including massage, ionotropic agents, and oxygen. All during this time his ECG remained stable (Fig. 6-3). After two hours, he succumbed to fibrillation and expired. Autopsy disclosed an acute myocardial infarction of the inferior and lateral walls.

What can we learn from these cases? First, we no longer stress a subject with known left main coronary disease or its equivalent (Case 2). Second, we avoid stressing those patients who have experienced recent rapid acceleration of their angina. Third, if resting S-T segment depression of 2.0 mm or more is

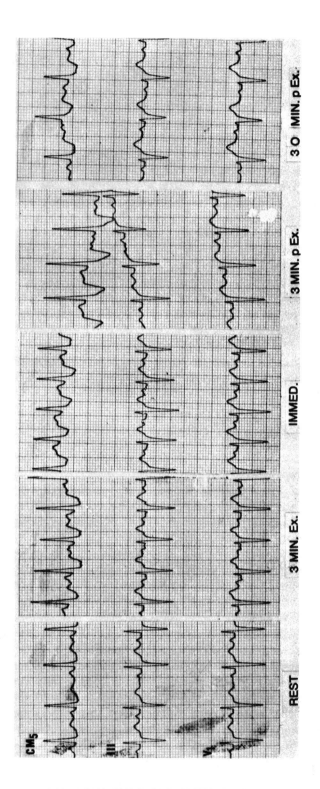

FIGURE 6-3. A 53-year-old man developed a low cardiac output after a stress test without a significant arrhythmia or electrocardiographic signs of an acute myocardial infarction. Note stable sinus rhythm after 30 minutes of closed chest massage, which was associated with almost no significant cardiac output.

present in the CM$_5$ lead, we do not subject the patient to a stress test unless we know the condition of the coronary anatomy and can be sure there is good left ventricular function as well as adequate myocardial perfusion.

By following these guidelines as well as those previously listed, we have not had a myocardial infarction or a death in the last 12,000 patients tested, many of whom have had advanced coronary insufficiency.

RISKS REPORTED IN THE LITERATURE

Rochimis and Blackburn[9] surveyed 73 medial centers in 1971 to evaluate their procedures with references to methods and complications present in stress testing. Their data summarized approximately 170,000 tests. Sixty percent of the centers used the treadmill, with the Master's Step Test the next most popular. In 66 percent of the centers questioned, subjects were stressed to 75 percent or more of their maximum heart rate. Twenty-five centers, or 34 percent, used the maximum work capacity of each patient as their end-point. Sixteen deaths were reported resulting in a mortality of about 1 per 10,000 (0.01 percent). Four per 10,000 required hospitalization within one day of the test for events such as arrhythmias and prolonged chest pain. Brock[16] surveyed 17,000 cases from work evaluation units and found 1.7 deaths per 10,000. No information on how many deaths or other complications occurred in the various types of test was available.

In 1977, we[10] surveyed 1,375 centers who reported on 444,396 treadmills, 44,460 bicycle stress tests, and 25,592 Master's Tests from the previous year's experience. Complications reported were 3.5 infarctions, 48 serious arrhythmias, and 0.5 deaths per 10,000. Scherer and Kaltenbach[18] report on 1,065,923 tests, mostly bicycle ergometry, done in German-speaking regions of Europe. Stress testing done in 353,638 "sports persons" had no mortality or morbidity, while in 712,285 coronary patients, there were 17 deaths and 96 life-threatening complications—mostly ventricular fibrillation. Thus, bicycle ergometry in a disease population results in about 2 deaths in 100,000 in their experience. They found that the recumbent ergometer test resulted in pulmonary edema seven times more commonly than with the upright test and the mortality increased from 0.6 to 1.2 per ten thousand.

Sheffield and associates[19] have recently analyzed the results of the Lipid Research Clinics prevalence study on 9,464 patients. They had no mortality with near-maximal testing in this group and attributed the safety to careful patient selection and termination of the test appropriately.

It would appear from these data that, even in the face of an enormous increase in volume, the mortality from stress testing has decreased at least 50 percent, and possibly more. It would seem that the risks of serious complications in stress testing are reasonable and, when using established techniques with continuous monitoring, they can be greatly minimized.

LEGAL IMPLICATIONS

Although lawsuits against physicians doing stress tests are fairly common; few, if any, have been appealed so that precedence is not yet established. Sagall[20] has written extensively, however, on the necessity of informed consent and exercising reasonable care. Testing according to published standards seems to be the best protection. When complications arise, the physician should document that he was familiar with and able to deal with problems in a manner commensurate with the standards in the community. Having a procedure manual available to show adequate preparation would be of benefit. Suits have also been filed for mis-diagnosis of the test in patients who later had an infarct. It would behoove all those engaged in this procedure to be up-to-date on the current literature and methodology and be able to demonstrate this when a hungry barrister attacks.

SUMMARY

As in the previous chapter on indications, the contraindications are also in a state of flux. Whereas, it used to be completely contraindicated to test people with aortic stenosis, it is now known to be safe if the degree of stenosis is not severe and the patient is watched meticulously. This is particularly true in younger patients, and has been practiced in pediatric cardiology now for some time. Also, a number of research protocols have been recently proposed in which patients in congestive failure have been tested on a treadmill or bicycle. This apparently is safe when done under carefully controlled conditions. The common use of stress testing in patients with subacute myocardial infarction has also been recently established as a practical adjunct to the management of this process. We have tested patients with both second- and third-degree heart block at times, but this also should be done with great caution. At present, I believe the most important contraindication is an unstable anginal pattern. These patients should be carefully evaluated by other methodologies, particularly coronary angiograms, and then if the coronary anatomy is found to be of minimal nature, it would be safe to proceed with a stress test.

REFERENCES

1. SHEPHARD, RJ: *Do risks of exercise justify costly caution?* The Physician and Sports-medicine February: 58–65, 1977.
2. ELLESTAD, MH (CHAIRMAN), BLOMQVIST, CG, AND NAUGHTON, JP: *Standards for adult exercise testing laboratories.* Am Heart Association Sub-committee on Rehabilitation, Circulation 59:421A–443A, 1979.
3. FLETCHER, GF, ET AL: *Exercise in the Practice of Medicine.* Futura Publishing, Mount Kisco, New York, 1982.
4. MCHENRY, PL: *Exercise in the practice of medicine.* J of Continuing Education in Cardiology, October 14, 1984.

5. HASKELL, WL: *Design of a cardiac conditioning program.* In WENGER, NK (ED): *Exercise and the Heart.* Cardiovascular Clinics Vol. 15(2), FA Davis, Philadelphia, 1979.

6. WILSON, PK: *Cardiac rehabilitation, adult fitness, and exercise testing.* Lea & Febiger, Philadelphia, 1981.

7. FROELICHER, VF AND MARION, D: *Exercise testing and ancillary techniques to screen for coronary heart disease.* Prog in Cardiovasc Dis 24:261, 1984.

8. BRUCE, RA, DEROUEN, TA, AND HOUSSACK, KF: *Value of maximal exercise tests in risk assessment of primary coronary heart disease events in healthy men: Five years experience of the Seattle Heart Watch Study.* Am J Cardiol 46:371–378, 1980.

9. ROCHIMIS, P AND BLACKBURN, H: *Exercise test: A survey of procedures, safety and litigation experience in approximately 170,000 tests.* JAMA 217:1061, 1971.

10. STUART, RJ AND ELLESTAD, MH: *National survey of exercise stress testing facilities.* Chest 77:94, 1980.

11. FRANK, S AND BRAUNWALD, E: *Idiopathic hypertrophic subaortic stenosis.* Circulation 37:159, 1968.

12. FRANCIOSA, JA: *Exercise testing in chronic congestive heart failure.* Am J Cardiol 53:1447–1450, 1984.

13. FOX, SM, NAUGHTON, JP, AND HASKELL, WL: *Physical activity and the prevention of coronary heart disease.* Ann Clin Res 3:404, 1971.

14. SHEFFIELD, LT, ET AL: *Electrocardiographic signal analysis without averaging of complexes.* In BLACKBURN, H (ED): *Measurement in Exercise Electrocardiography.* Charles C Thomas, Springfield, Ill, 1967.

15. BORER, JS, ET AL: *Limitations of electrocardiographic response to exercise in predicting coronary artery disease.* N Engl J Med 293:367, 1975.

16. BROCK, LL: *Stress testing incidents in work evaluation units in WEU subcommittee newsletter.* Am Heart Assoc, New York, 1967.

17. TAKAHASHI, N: *How to evaluate the S-T segment elevation during or after exercise.* Am Heart J 79:579, 1970.

18. SCHERER, D AND KALTENBACH, M: *Frequency of life-threatening complications associated with stress testing.* Dtsch Med Wshcr 104:1161, 1979.

19. SHEFFIELD, LT: ET AL: *Safety of exercise testing volunteer subjects: The lipid research clinics' prevalence study experience.* J Cardiac Rehab 2(5):395–400, 1982.

20. SAGALL, EL: *Malpractice aspects of medically prescribed exercise.* Legal Medicine Annual 30:275–289, 1975.

7

PARAMETERS
TO BE MEASURED

HEART SOUNDS AND OTHER AUSCULTATORY FINDINGS
First and Second Heart Sounds
Fourth Heart Sounds
Third Heart Sounds
Aortic Murmur
Mitral Murmur
PALPITATION
PULSUS ALTERNANS
SUMMARY

As we learn more about the physiology of exercise and the perturbations in the normal process brought on by disease-states, it would stand to reason that our ability to separate disease from normal function should improve and, indeed, it has. One of the most important revelations is the acceptance that ischemia is often due to a reduction in delivery of blood flow to the myocardium rather than just an increase in the demand. Maseri[1] must be credited for this turnaround in our thinking, which has also led to the concept of a reduced coronary vasodilator reserve.

This implies that the increased flow, required by increasing myocardial action demands remains unmet, probably because of some problem in vasomotion of the myocardial arterioles. For instance, Marcus[2] has shown that reactive hyperemia, caused by mechanical obstruction of a coronary for 20 seconds normally results in a five- to eight-fold increase in perfusion. Some patients, however, with normal epicardial coronary arteries can only increase flow to double the resting level for reasons not yet fully understood. He has also demonstrated that reductions in flow associated with coronary plaques varies a great deal when the obstruction is estimated by angiography; thus, the old idea that a 70 percent obstruction implied reduced perfusion and a 40 percent obstruction did not, is untenable. Some subjects with angiographic narrowing of 30 to 40 percent show a very poor increase in flow with increased metabolic demand, while others with from 60 to 80 percent obstruction will respond almost normally. The implications of these findings are far-reaching.

It seems likely that many so-called false-positives and false-negatives may be true positives and true negatives when considering myocardial perfusion rather than coronary anatomy. We should also recognize the need for analyzing as many different facets of the exercise response as possible rather than concentrating too heavily on the S-T segment.

It might be well to remember when searching for parameters that are useful in identifying disease that powerful predictors are *infrequent,* and *frequent* predictors are rarely powerful.[3]

ELECTROCARDIOGRAPHIC SPECIFICATIONS

The wide recognition of the importance of faithful recording at the lower end of the electrocardiographic frequency range has been a significant development in the instrumentation necessary for accurate stress testing.[4-5] The standards recommended by the Committee on Electrocardiography of the American Heart Association in 1967[6] require errors of less than 0.5 mm (0.05 mV) in the early part of the ST-T (0.05 Hertz cutoff with a 0 decible per octave rolloff) segment. Technical aspects of the electrocardiographic recording during muscular activity are clearly interdependent. Poor frequency response at the lower end of the spectrum in the older ECG units would "smooth" the record, giving apparently better records, but obscuring the most important information, the low frequency S-T segment changes. As impedence at the skin source is reduced by better electrodes and as the skin preparation techniques are improved, the fidelity of the recorder can be improved and still give "clean" readable records. Faris and colleagues[7] claim 10 percent of the ischemic S-T changes will only appear during exercise so that good quality is essential. Special systems for noise reduction are considered in the chapter on computers.

LEAD SYSTEMS

As early as 1931, it was noted by Wood and Wolferth that the precordial leads gave a greater sensitivity in detecting the S-T segment depression of ischemia than did Einthoven's standard leads. Various types of unipolar and bipolar precordial systems have been in use for a number of years and have produced satisfactory results.

Bipolar Leads

CM$_5$. This system locates the negative electrode on the upper sternum and the positive one in the V$_5$ position. This was probably the most popular single lead for exercise monitoring for many years, and has been demonstrated to have the highest incidence of positive changes in patients with known ischemia.[8]
CC$_5$. The negative electrode is in the right lateral part of the chest in the axilla, and the positive electrode is in the V$_5$ position.[9] This lead has been credited with showing less contamination by the Ta wave and is preferred by MacAlpin and Kattus.[59]
CA Lead. The negative electrode is on the medial scapular ridge on the right side and the positive electrode is in the V$_5$ position.
CB Lead. The negative electrode is on the inferior scapular angle on the right and the positive electrode is in the V$_5$ position (Fig. 7-1).

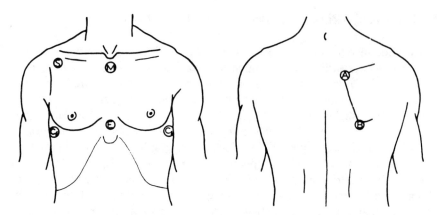

FIGURE 7-1. The diagram depicts a simple bipolar transthoracic lead with the positive electrode at the V_5 position. The negative reference electrodes include those over the right scapula, C-A and C-B, on the manubrium of the sternum (M), below the right scapula C-S, and low on the anterior axillary line on the right side (C-C). These leads all give good QRS and S-T segment display and a fairly minimum amount of muscle artifact during muscle activity. (From Blackburn,[10] with permission.)

CS$_5$. The negative electrode just below right clavicle and the positive electrode is in the V_5 position.

When testing patients with ischemic S-T segment depression, maximum S-T segment depression is usually 180 degrees opposite to the maximum R wave amplitude. Blackburn[10] studied this in 25 men and plotted the R wave as shown in Figure 7-2. It can be seen that using the various lead systems discussed above, the CM$_5$ and CS$_5$ fall near the regression line of 45 degrees. In the same study, the other parameters of the ECG complexes were tabulated as seen in Table 7-1. Examination of this table reveals that bipolar leads with the exploring electrode at V_5 generally resemble a true V_5 of the Wilson systems except that these have a higher QRS voltage and are more sensitive to S-T segment depression.[10] The bipolar systems that combine the highest R wave amplitude and the greatest display of S-T depression are CM$_5$ and CS$_5$. They have been reported to identify 89 percent of all S-T segment depression found by multiple lead systems. These leads might be termed "optimally" distorted.

Hakki and associates[11] have demonstrated that a lead with a low R wave amplitude is likely to exhibit no S-T depression even when ischemia is present.

McHenry and Morris[12] locate the bipolar system by examination of the resting precordial leads. They then place the positive monitoring lead at the position of the maximum R wave amplitude.

Conventional 12 Leads

The use of all 12 leads of the conventional systems has the advantage of wide familiarity, but also the disadvantage of redundancy and some decrease in

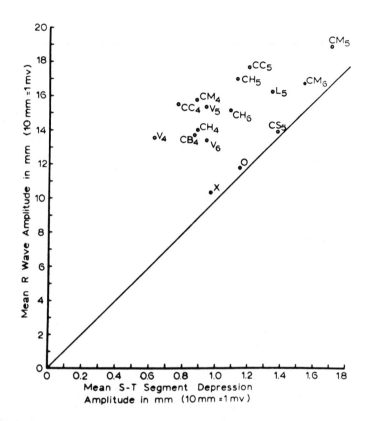

FIGURE 7-2. The S-T segment amplitudes are plotted against the R wave amplitude in men exhibiting positive ischemic responses. It can be seen that there tends to be a regression line correlating the R wave amplitude and the amount of S-T segment depression. However, it is not linear. (From Blackburn,[10] with permission.)

relative sensitivity to the display of S-T segment depression. Virtually all the S-T segment information in common usage at the present time is found in 2, AVF, V_3, V_4, V_5, and V_6. When patients were studied by Blackburn and associates[8] with a 3-minute step test, recording 12 standard leads, a fairly high incidence of 0.5 mm S-T segment depression in one lead or another was recorded. Isolated changes in lead 3 were 1 percent, in VF 3 percent, and in both 3 and VF another 3 percent. The use of multiple leads becomes much more practical with the newer recorders and probably will become the standard. The option of adding CC_5 and CM_5 probably provides the optimal approach. We use such a system and monitor exercise with the three leads AVF, V_1, and CM_5.

XYZ Orthogonal Leads

As the computer techniques are applied more and more to exercise testing,

TABLE 7-1. Four simultaneously recorded bipolar monitoring ECG leads immediately postexercise among a mixed group of normal subjects and patients*

		CB N=25	CA N=25	CS N=25	CM N=25
Q-wave amplitude	M	0.5	0.8	0.9	1.4
	SD	0.7	1.0	0.9	2.0
R-wave amplitude	M	16.0	19.0	17.9	19.9
	SD	7.3	9.1	9.2	9.8
S-wave amplitude	M	4.5	5.8	4.8	3.4
	SD	2.5	3.7	2.2	2.6
T-wave amplitude	M	2.3	2.7	2.7	2.5
	SD	2.1	1.9	2.0	2.2
S-T junction	M	-2.5	-2.6	-2.3	-2.4
Maximum amplitude	SD	1.6	1.8	1.9	1.9
S-T midpoint amplitude	M	1.8	1.8	1.8	1.9
	SD	0.4	0.3	0.3	0.4
S-T segment maximum amplitude when depressed	M	-3.8	-6.0	-5.0	-4.9
% Total Depressed		48	36	36	44

		Reference Electrode	Exploring Electrode
CB	inferior scapular angle, right		Common to all in
CA	medial scapular ridge, right		position C_5
CS	subclavicle, right lateral		
CM	manubrium sternum		

*Amplitude in mm (10 mm = 1 mV); M = mean; SD = standard deviation. The amplitude of the waves varies somewhat with the different lead systems plotted. The tallest R-wave amplitude is with the CM lead. The highest percentage of positive test results of the four leads was with the CB lead, although it is very similar to that of the CM. (From Blackburn,[10] with permission.)

there may be a trend toward the use of XYZ leads. Computer programs are available that can synthesize the standard 12 leads from the orthogonal leads, and some excellent studies have been done in normal subjects for standardization.[13]

However, with exercising patients, the noise level of muscle activity is considerable, making digital filtering and noise reduction essential when using this approach. Information as to the sensitivity and specificity of the XYZ leads has been published by Simoons[13] suggesting that with computer measurements the results are excellent. Blackburn[10] in a limited study has reported the XYZ leads to be less sensitive, but Hornsten and Bruce[62] found them to be equal in sensitivity to the bipolar system.

Camp and colleagues[14] compared the orthogonal lead with CM_5 in 93 patients who had stress testing and coronary angiography. They reported the true positive tests in the Y, CM_5, and X leads to be 57, 66, and 69 percent respectively. They found the total sensitivity of the X, Y, and Z leads to be 84 percent as compared with 71 percent for CM_5. In 1966, Isaacs and colleagues[15] claimed that the analysis of the vector loop in the Frank system produced better sensitivity than the scaler tracing. They found the loop positive in 80 percent, while the scaler S-T segments were positive in only 60 percent. This method has never become popular, however, and has not been confirmed by others using angiograms as a check.

Most of the work on vectorcardiographic analysis of exercise tracings has been done with the Frank system. There seems to be general agreement that the X lead, which is equivalent to a bipolar lead from right to left axilla, provides the most useful information on the S-T segment.[16] The other leads are of lesser value. Blomqvist[16] described in greater magnitude of S-T segment depression recorded simultaneously in the CH_4 and CH_6 bipolar leads than in the orthogonal leads. He has also provided excellent data on variations seen during exercise in normal subjects.[17] It would seem that unless one has a computer available, the orthogonal leads have less use.

Polarcardiographic Measurements

Dower and coworkers[18] have described the polarcardiograph as a graphic display of the sequential changes in spatial and planar magnitudes of the cardiac vectors expressed in spherical coordinates of longitude and latitude. Bruce[63] has studied normal subjects and demonstrated abnormalities with exercise thought to be due to compliance abnormalities as well as ischemia. He believes this method of study provides a more sensitive approach to the evaluation of ischemic heart disease. Adequate experience to determine the exact place of polarography in stress testing has not yet been accumulated. Simoons,[13] however, after evaluation of orthogonal systems, Chebyshere polynomials, S-T slopes, and integrals, as well as polar coordinates found that the approach of Dower and associates failed to offer any advantages.

Precordial Maps

Fox and colleagues[19,20] have reported a number of studies using a 16-lead precordial map or grid and report a sensitivity when comparing with coronary angiography of about 87 percent, similar to that obtained by Chaitman and coworkers[21] with their 14 leads. In a more recent report, Chaitman has reported a sensitivity of as high as 95 percent, with a specificity of approximately 78 percent. It is important to realize that these numbers come from a case load with a very high prevalence of coronary disease and might well be less reliable if the prevalence of disease is as low as 50 percent or less. He did find that S-T elevation had a sensitivity of 100 percent although only 4 percent had this finding. Fox and colleagues feel they have had enough experience to recommend that this method be used clinically on a day-to-day basis. They also believe it can be used to localize the coronary artery involved when single-vessel disease is present. They found a sensitivity of 74 percent with their map

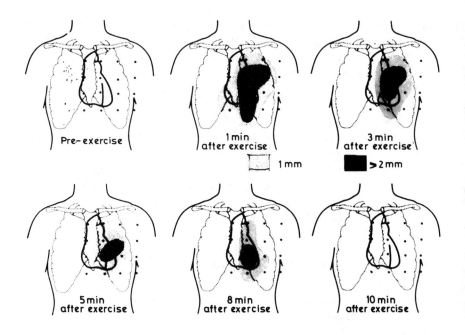

FIGURE 7-3. Example of sequence of contour maps showing areas of S-T segment depression after exercise. Striped = 1 mm, Black 2 mm. (From Fox, et al.,[19] with permission.)

as compared with 42 percent when a standard 12-lead system was used (Fig. 7-3).

A recent editorial by Spach and Barr[22] from Duke University, however, presents some theoretical insights into the practical application of this method. After reading this, it would seem there is a good deal of work to be done before we can accurately identify localized epicardial electrical events on the surface of the torso. Be that as it may, there is renewed interest in this approach and it would appear that we may soon find a broader clinical application.

Mixed Lead Systems

Studies will continue to be published claiming that various lead combinations are superior. Chaitman and associates[21] evaluated a number of systems and reported that a 14-lead system including CM_5, CC_5, CL, and the standard 12 leads with the exception of AVR was superior to the others with a sensitivity of 88 percent and a specificity of 82 percent. They reported the two most sensitive single leads in this system to be CM_5 and CC_5. Froelicher and coworkers[9] reported CC_5 and V_5 to be superior to CM_5. However, they excluded the upsloping patterns in their abnormal group (see Chapter 11). We evaluated CM_5 and CC_5 simultaneously in our laboratory for one year and found more false-positives in CM_5, but more false-negatives in CC_5.

Although the final chapter on the best lead system has not been written, there are important differences among many of the systems and by far the most sensitive exploring electrode position is at the V_5 chest location. The CH (forehead to chest), CC, or C5R to C_5 a transthoracic lead and the CC lead (right back to apex) all provide very good data. The right ear, the ensiform cartilage and the C_7 position seem to stand out in this regard also.

Data now seem to be accumulating to indicate that computer analysis of S-T segment changes is somewhat superior to the standard visual approach.[13] Simoons[13] suggests that correction for heart rate with analysis of very minor S-T changes by computer increases sensitivity. It may also be that accurate measurements of intervals such as the QT, S-T integral, and correction of the S-T for R wave amplitude by computer will be important.

For many years we used a 3-lead system and concentrated on the use of multiple variables to improve detection. I now believe a 12-lead system with additional leads such as CC_5 and CM_5 is justified. Although it only increases detection by about 7 or 8 percent, it appears that an increased number of leads does not decrease the specificity. The reduced cost of newer equipment providing these options is encouraging. It may eventually turn out that some type of maping will be the most desirable.

R WAVES

Although normals usually have a decrease in precordial R waves with exercise, an increase is present in a relatively small number of patients with ischemia. A recent study[23] in our laboratory indicated it is less sensitive than we originally believed, but the R wave still should be measured and considered along with other variables discussed below (See Chapter 12).

ST/HEART RATE SLOPE

Although preliminary calculations of the ST-heart rate (ST/HR) slope were equivocal, considerable interest has been generated by the reports from the group at Leeds,[24] England claiming their application of this concept resulted in a perfect identification of patients with coronary disease. They found the slope not only separated subjects without significant narrowing from those who did, but also could separate single from double, and double from three vessel disease.

They used 13 leads, the conventional 12 plus CM_5. Patients were exercised on a bicycle for 3 minute intervals at steps chosen to increase the heart rate with each workload of about 10 beats.

Using a magnifying glass the S-T depression was measured on each lead and the ST/HR slope was plotted and the steepest was taken as representative for that patient.

Although Elamin and associates[24] are convinced of the accuracy of their methods, others have been unable to reproduce their findings.[25] The variation in degrees of myocardial ischemia, related to the number of vessels done, negates the kind of results they have reported. Also a few patients with severe CAD and normal S-T segments (a fairly common finding) along with the usual type of false-positive we see all the time would make these results impossible.

Even so, the work has stimulated others to correct S-T segments for heart rate in various ways and it may be that some improvement in discrimination will result. At this time, the subject needs more work to warrant any final conclusions.

BLOOD PRESSURE

Observation of the blood pressure response is important both to insure the safety of the patient and to provide information on the strength of the cardiac contraction and the state of the peripheral resistance. It may also be of value in predicting hypertension in the future. It should be recorded before and with exercise at each work level as well as in recovery (see Chapter 17 for details).

PRESSURE PULSE PRODUCT

The systolic blood pressure is multipled by the heart rate to provide the double product or modified tension time index (MTTI). As was described in Chapter 2, this value gives an index of myocardial oxygen consumption and provides a parameter for comparison of tests before and after some type of intervention. Figure 7-4 illustrates the relative use of myocardial oxygen before and after treatment with propranolol as reflected in the pressure pulse product or double product. During the second test, the exercise end-point is about at the same pressure pulse value even though it took two minutes longer to reach it.

Figure 7-5 depicts the pressure pulse product at each minute of exercise before (5-23-72) and after (12-12-72) vein graft surgery. The second determination with the lower pressure pulse product was due to thrombosis of the graft. The third test (4-12-73) was after reoperation and the establishment of good flow to the left anterior descending coronary artery.

Because the double product is dependent on both blood pressure and heart rate, the finding that they appear to be related variables is of some interest. Thulein and Werner[26] studied the heart rate response in hypertensive persons during stress testing and holter monitoring, as compared with normal persons. Those with blood pressure above average on causal findings have consistently higher heart rates for a given workload as well as higher systolic and diastolic blood pressures. It would seem that they must be hyper-reactors; therefore, as a group, would have a much higher double product and, accordingly, a higher myocardial oxygen consumption than normal persons.

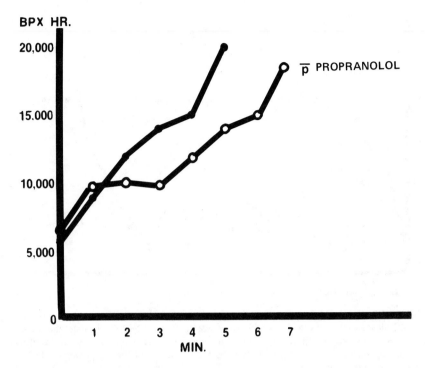

FIGURE 7-4. The double product (systolic blood pressure times pulse) plotted for each minute of exercise until maximum capacity was reached. The patient went longer after propranolol but his myocardial oxygen consumption as estimated by the double product was about the same during both tests.

DPTI/SPTI RATIO

In recent years, there has been a good deal of interest in predicting the adequacy in transmural myocardial perfusion by the ratio of the diastolic pressure time interval (DPTI) to the systolic pressure time interval (SPTI) (see Chapter 4). It is possible to arrive at reasonable estimates of these values noninvasively with systolic time intervals or even from heart sounds alone when combined with the blood pressure measurements. Regional work on animals[25,27] suggested that underperfusion of the subendocardium occurred when the ratio[28] fell below 0.7; however, now it appears that a critical ratio is about 0.4. Unfortunately, a number of difficult-to-estimate parameters confound the predictive value, such as myocardial thickness, edema, contractility, blood viscosity, as well as left-ventricular end-diastolic pressure. Significant data are yet to be presented to establish this ratio as a clinically useful parameter during stress testing; however, it should be studied further.

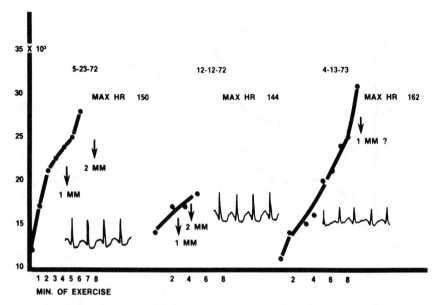

FIGURE 7-5. The double product plotted against time on the treadmill in a 44-year-old man. 5-23-72 illustrates the stress test when the patient was first seen. 12-12-72 illustrates the decreasing coronary blood flow approximately four months after a saphenous vein bypass graft had become obstructed by a clot. 4-13-73 illustrates the improvement after reoperation, which established patency of the graft. Severe anginal pain and a characteristic ischemic S-T segment change were present on 12-12-72, but not on 4-13-73.

HEART RATE RESPONSE TO EXERCISE

The heart rate response is the best indicator of the magnitude of exertion. A good estimate of the maximum heart rate obtainable is 220 to 230 minus age. It is essential that the person doing the test knows the approximate predicted maximum heart rate and is familiar with the average response to the protocol selected for each of the various age groups.

Although it has long been known that the heart rate gives a reasonably reliable measure of the cardiac output, the tendency to a lower heart rate under a standard exercise load has been frequently considered to be a matter of better conditioning. Indeed, the observable decrease in resting and exercise heart rate after physical fitness programs is regarded as a most desirable result and is carefully recorded.

The interesting work of Jose and Taylor,[29] however, suggests that as myocardial contractility decreases, the so-called intrinsic heart rate becomes slower. After constructing nomograms characterizing the heart rate response to our standard protocol, we began to see patients who had a peculiar lack of chronotropic response to exercise, even though they were severely deconditioned. One of these subjects who had previously complained of a vague chest pain at night suddenly died of a myocardial infarction, even though his S-T segments during the stress tests were considered by us to be perfectly normal. Subsequent study of this phenomenon has led us to believe that "chronotropic incompetence," as we call it, is a fairly reliable sign of poor myocardial function. Figure 7-6 illustrates the heart rate response to our protocol of a 53-year-old man who had progressive myocardial disease, including one myocardial infarction and progressive angina between the two tests. The change in the slope as compared with the predicted normal pulse for his age and sex is easily apparent because the slower heart rate for the same workload was associated with decreasing ventricular function.

Figure 7-7 depicts the heart rate response of another man, age 51, with severe three-vessel coronary disease before and after a successful saphenous vein graft operation. Not only did his chronotropic response to exercise become normal, but his deep S-T segment depression recorded on the preoperative test also disappeared.

Hinkle and associates[30] reported this type of response and documented its correlation with coronary disease and an increased incidence of coronary death. They called it "sustained relative bradycardia." They believe it was due to ischemia of the sinus node and described a 46 percent mortality over a

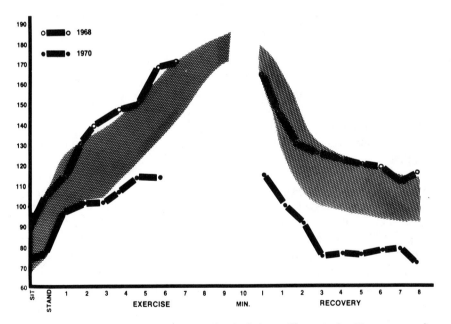

FIGURE 7-6. Chronotropic incompetence. The shaded area illustrates the 95 percent confidence limits for the average heart rate response to our protocol. The subject was tested twice; once in 1968, at which time his heart rate response fell along the upper margin of the normal range. Two years later, after a myocardial infarction and continuing angina, the patient's ability to accelerate his heart rate had diminished, and at this time his pulse was far below the normal range.

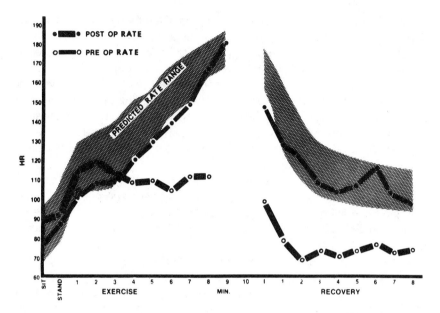

FIGURE 7-7. The pulse response of a 51-year-old man with a severe three-vessel coronary disease shows a very definite plateau with an inability to increase appropriately. Following successful bypass surgery, which completely relieved his pain, his pulse response to the same protocol returned to the normal range.

7-year period (N = 34) as against a 12 percent rate in subjects with normal heart rate response (N = 301). Grimby and Saltin[31] found that the peak heart rate capacity in athletes correlated well with the resting rate (r = 0.81). We have not found a similar correlation in our patients, most of whom are in poor physical condition.

When we analyzed the eight-year follow-up data on subjects with this abnormality, the high incidence of coronary heart disease can be seen not only in those with ischemic S-T segments, but in those with no electrocardiographic evidence of coronary disease (see Chapter 14). A subsequent study during catheterization revealed that they have more severe coronary disease than comparable patients with a normal heart rate response.[32]

In order to recognize this process, it is necessary to construct standard heart rate response graphs for whatever protocol one elects. The information used in our protocol is listed in Appendix 6. If this response is searched for, a significant number of subjects with normal S-T segments but who have poor ventricular function as evidenced by bradycardia, will be recognized.

AUTONOMIC STRESS TESTING

As was mentioned in the previous paragraph, the heart rate response to exercise is due to the balance between the sympathetic and parasympathetic neurogenic impulses acting on the sinus node. Although the exact mechanisms are yet to be worked out, it has now become apparent that the exquisite balance between these opposing systems is altered in many patients with heart disease. A chronic state of vasoconstriction has long been recognized in congestive heart failure, but it is only recently that we have recognized the changes present in subjects with coronary heart disease who are not in failure. Over the years, a number of simple methods for identifying abnormalities in autonomic response have been proposed, such as the Valsalva maneuver, tilting the patient from horizontal to vertical, face emersion, and carotid sinus massage.

We have studied the heart rate response to standing,[33] hyperventilation,[34] cough,[35] deep breathing, and isometric hand grip, and attempted to determine whether the changes could be used to discriminate patients with coronary disease from normals. It has been recognized that S-T changes initiated by hyperventilation are more common in subjects with normal hearts than in coronary artery disease.[36] The reduced heart rate response to exercise associated with poor ventricular function is undoubtedly mediated through auto-

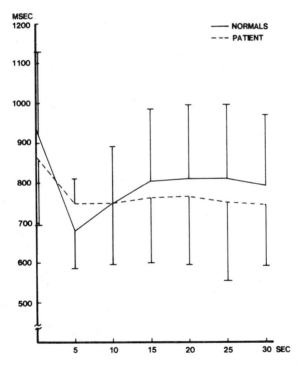

FIGURE 7-8. Mean RR intervals—control, lying and immediately after standing in normal subjects and patients with heart disease. Vertical lines = 2 SD. Note: Heart rate increases rapidly then rebounds in normals but has a lesser increase in patients with coronary artery disease. Wide SD, however, illustrates significant overlaps diminishing the discrimination between groups.

nomic pathways. Carotid stimulation has been shown to increase the incidence of sinus arrest in subjects with severe coronary artery disease.[37] The maneuvers mentioned above are usually associated with a blunted heart rate response in patients with coronary narrowing. The mean changes when comparing normals with patients with heart disease are significantly different. However, the variations are wide enough that the diagnostic accuracy is less than desirable. Age, degree of conditioning, and many unknown factors alter the autonomic response. Figure 7-8 illustrates the mean heart rate response to standing in a group of heart patients versus normals. Although the normals are quite different than those with coronary artery disease, subjects with chest pain syndromes who have been subjected to coronary angiograms respond quite similarly to those with coronary artery disease and different from normal volunteers and athletes. These changes appear to be useful as an aid to diagnosis, but are weak discriminators.

OXYGEN CONSUMPTION

Over the years, there has been a great deal of interest in measuring the oxygen consumption of subjects undergoing stress testing.[38] This measurement has been accomplished in various centers by collecting expired air in Douglas bags or balloons at measured intervals. This is usually done at rest, during exercise, and at peak stress. Because the amount of work expended by the individual depends a great deal on the type of stress applied, the metabolic cost of walking up stairs is different than the cost of walking on a treadmill, which is different than running on a treadmill, and different than riding a bicycle. Comparative studies have been published that allow us roughly to estimate one or the other (see Appendix 9).

The actual measurement of oxygen intake for each patient is expensive, time consuming, and probably not indicated in a routine stress test. Unless the patient is familiar with the proceedings, the patient does not accommodate to the mouthpiece and the nose clip necessary to obtain accurate data. This is especially difficult for cardiac patients who may be anxious and having chest pain as well as muscular fatigue. Ford and Hellerstein[39] have published data on the energy cost of the Master's test. Balke and Ware[40] published a formula that can be applied to a treadmill program that gives a rough estimate of the oxygen requirements of any speed and grade. It must be recognized, however, that the efficiency of walking and strength of the subject affect the capacity to walk or run uphill a good deal, so that the variation around a mean must be quite large.

$$VO_2 = v \times w \times (0.073 + \frac{ml}{100}) \times 1.8$$

where:

VO_2 = oxygen consumption in ml/min (STPD)
v = treadmill speed in m/min
w = body weight in kg
ml = treadmill angle in percent
1.8 = factor constituting the oxygen requirement in ml/min for 1 m/kg of work.

Mastropaolo and colleagues[41] checked this method of estimating VO_2 against measured uptake and found it to be very satisfactory.

Bruce and associates[42] describe uptake values measured in mg per kg per minute (Fig. 7-9). This is a simplified approach to the problem for practical application in day-to-day testing. Givoni and Goldman[43] have also published a formula that we have found very reliable at lower workloads. A number of online systems have been devised (Fig. 7-10) that can measure continuous oxygen uptake.

In day-to-day testing of CAD[42] patients, oxygen measurements probably add little to the understanding of their disease process and are unnecessary. The estimates from the various formulae are satisfactory for clinical purposes.

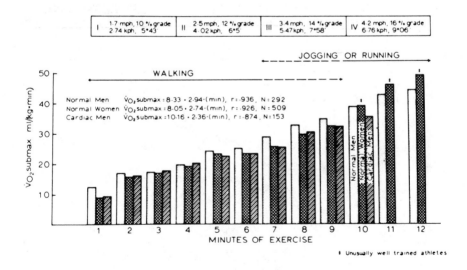

FIGURE 7-9. Aerobic requirements of healthy adult men and women and cardiac men walking without support on a multistage treadmill protocol. It can be seen that the ability to predict the oxygen consumption for each level of work is quite reliable. (From Bruce, et al.,[42] with permission.)

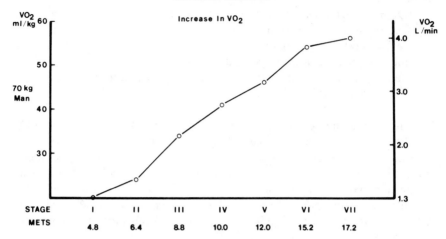

FIGURE 7-10. Oxygen consumption in a 70 kg man according to treadmill stage.

RESPIRATORY DATA DURING STRESS TESTING OTHER THAN OXYGEN UPTAKE

Up to this time, there has been little attention paid to respiratory rates or to volumes in conjunction with stress testing. In normal subjects, ventilation increases in a linear relationship to oxygen intake and carbon dioxide output up

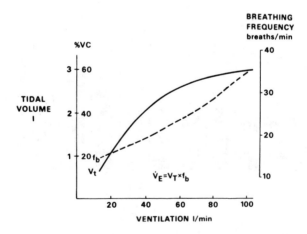

FIGURE 7-11. The *solid line* depicts the rapid change in tidal volume as ventilation increases until about 60 percent of total capacity then begins to level off. The frequency of breathing *(dotted line)* increases in a more linear manner, but increases excessively after about 80 percent of maximal capacity is reached.

to power outputs of 50 to 60 percent of maximal capacity. Above this, ventilation is more closely related to carbon dioxide output, which increases to a greater extent than oxygen intake. At about this same time, the tidal volume increases at a slower rate as the respiratory rate increases more rapidly to compensate[44] (Fig. 7-11). The final tidal volume is a primary function of airway resistance and compliance. The lower the compliance, the more efficient a small tidal volume with its resultant increase in respiratory rate.

A large number of our patients discontinue their exercise because of extreme dyspnea. There is some evidence that this type of dyspnea in patients with cardiac disease is due to a rising left atrial and pulmonary venous pressure. It might be that it would be important to know the tidal volume because as the lungs become less compliant, it is more efficient to ventilate with a smaller tidal volume.

RESPIRATORY GAS EXCHANGE
AND ANAEROBIC THRESHOLD

In 1964, Wasserman and McIroy[45] proposed a noninvasive method of detecting the onset of aerobic metabolism during exercise. This occurs earlier than the peak work capacity of the patient and will signal the point at which the patient is being deprived of adequate aerobic energy substrates. Although this point during exercise can be detected by an increase in lactic acid concentration in the blood or a decrease in arterial blood bicarbonate of pH, they proposed determination by an increase in the respiratory gas exchange ratio (R) on a breath-by-breath basis. They calculated "R" from the end-tidal gas concentrations monitored continuously during exercise using the formula:

$$R = \frac{F_A CO_2}{1.26\ F_A N_2 - 1 + F_A N_2}$$

where:

$F_A CO_2$ = end-tidal carbon dioxide concentration
$F_A N_2$ = end-tidal nitrogen concentration

R was then determined by a nomogram. They were able to show that the increase in R was related principally to a decrease in end-tidal nitrogen concentration. In a typical subject, they found that the anaerobic threshold was between 60 and 70 percent of the maximum oxygen capacity when R suddenly changed from 87 to 96 percent. Experience has shown it can usually be predicted from a change in the slope of the ventilatory equivalent, as well as the RQ.

Since the original work, Wasserman and Whipp[46] have studied the phenomenon intensely and the level of anaerobic threshold has been used to estimate $VO_2 max$ and has been shown to increase with training. It's usefulness in evaluating exercise physiology in patients with coronary artery disease has yet to be determined.

This method requires careful monitoring of expired gases and the attendant discomfort to the patient. Unfortunately, many cardiac patients do not tolerate this type of instrumentation well. However, as techniques improve, it would seem to be a worthwhile adjunct to the study of patients with CAD. Recent data suggest the possibility that the anaerobic threshold might be detected by integrating electromyographic potentials as exercise progresses.[47] When the slow twitch fibers become anoxic, the fast twitch fibers are recruited and increase the potential voltage of the electromyogram. If this method turns out to be validated, it might be a useful noninvasive parameter.

BODY AND SKIN TEMPERATURES

Skin temperature variations on the precordium associated with angina have been reported by Potanin and associates[48] using heat sensitive tapes. During angina, a cold area develops, apparently caused by cutaneous vasoconstriction. They reported that when pain was unilateral, skin coldness was invariable and was within the distribution area of the pain. When the pain was central, skin coldness was inconstant and did not correlate with the pain distribution area. They found also that the thermographic patterns did not show cooling in subjects without pain arising in the chest wall. The coldness appeared about one minute or less before the pain, but persisted five or six minutes after the pain had subsided.

A more recent study of core and skin temperature by thermisters has been surprising. The normal increase in core temperature with exercise, at least for the first 10 minutes,[49] is replaced by a decrease in coronary artery patients. This was first demonstrated by Shellock and colleagues[50] in heart failure and in our own laboratory in patients who did not have failure, but had coronary artery disease. Although preliminary studies suggest a high predictive accuracy, it is too early to know how helpful this finding will be when tested in a larger population (Fig. 7-12).

SYSTOLIC TIME INTERVALS

At this time, it is difficult to measure an external carotid pulse and to take a phonocardiogram during exercise on a treadmill. If a bicycle ergometer is used rather than a treadmill, data of this sort can be recorded. Because of the demonstrated value of these noninvasive parameters of ventricular function, they have been studied before and immediately after stress in a number of centers. It should be noted that the stroke volume in a sitting or standing position is lower than that in a horizontal position; thus, the normal data supplied by the nomogram by Weissler and associates can be applied only if the measure-

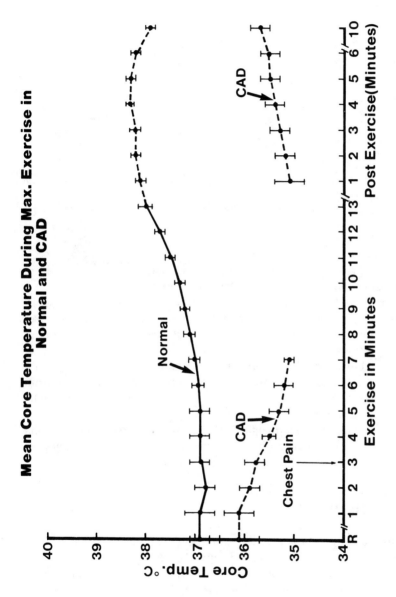

Mean Core Temperature During Max. Exercise in Normal and CAD

FIGURE 7-12. The mean core temperature response to treadmill exercise in 26 normals and 14 patients with coronary artery disease. Arrow indicates onset of angina in the patient with the most severe disease.

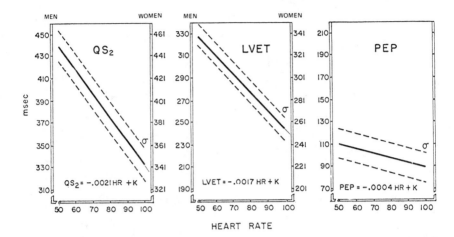

FIGURE 7-13. These nomograms illustrate the changes in systolic time intervals correlated with heart rate. Observing deviations from these normals is useful in the evaluation of left ventricular function in subjects with ischemic heart disease. (From Weissler, et al.,[51] with permission.)

ments are taken in a horizontal position (Fig. 7-13).

Pouget and associates[52] have recorded the carotid ejection time and pre-ejection period with exercise, and demonstrated that the ejection time is longer than would normally be predicted for the heart rate when a patient develops coronary insufficiency during exercise. Their group has proposed that this is due to the increased peripheral resistance known to be common with the onset of angina.

Gillian and associates[53] and Van der Hoeven and colleagues[54] have found ejection time prolongation with exercise in 85 and 86 percent of patients studied, respectively, and propose this as an adjunct to stress testing and identification of coronary disease.

Data on wall motion abnormalities[54] initiated by exercise might suggest that the ejection time prolongation is due to the decreasing force of ventricular contraction coincident with areas of hypokineses or akinesis.

WALL MOTION

Several methods of recording wall motion patterns during exercise are now available. When ischemia is associated with a loss of contractility, the changes can be recorded with isotope techniques[55] or by a magnetic precordial transducer called a cardiokymogram by Silverberg and colleagues.[56] We have used this method and have confirmed the reports that it often identifies anterior wall ischemia, occasionally in the absence of S-T segment depression. It would appear to be especially useful when the electrocardiogram cannot be interpreted, such as in patients with left bundle branch block or Wolff-Parkinson-

STRESS TESTING: PRINCIPLES AND PRACTICE

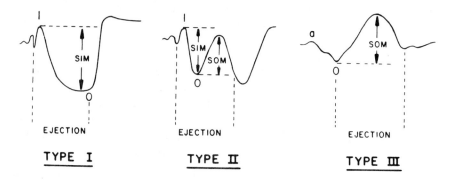

FIGURE 7-14. Kymocardiographic tracings of wall motion. Type I—Normal; Type II—Abnormal; Type III—Abnormal. SIM = systolic inward motion; SOM = systolic outward motion.

White syndrome. Crawford and coworkers,[57] however, studied this method and found a number of serious limitations. Since their study, improvements in design and engineering have made the device easier to use and we now include it as a routine measurement, recorded before and immediately after exercise. Reports that the sensitivity is near 73 percent and the specificity 95 percent in patients being evaluated for chest pain syndromes, indicate its usefulness.[58] The inability to position the transducers so that a normal tracing before exercise can be recorded in about 10 percent of those tested, limits its application somewhat (Fig. 7-14).

WALK THROUGH PHENOMENON

In 1966, MacAlpin and Kattus[59] reported that when subjects who were having pain while walking on the treadmill could be continued at a set rate, the angina would eventually disappear, even though there was no apparent decrease in their metabolic workload. At the same time, the ischemic S-T segments returned to normal. This adaptive capacity can also be demonstrated by repeating the test after the patient has recovered from the first one. The capacity to improve after a warmup probably reflects a similar process. They reported that the pain usually remains constant at a set workload for about five minutes, and then begins to decrease. It usually takes approximately 7 to 10 minutes to completely disappear and another 5 to 7 minutes for the S-T segments to become isoelectric. Many patients will report a similar type of response during their efforts to exercise in their work or recreation. We have not studied this process, but would guess that the adaptive process is less likely to be related to the heart than to peripheral effects. The lowering of peripheral resistance known to accompany exercise might well reduce the myocardial oxygen demands, and thus, allow the heart to function more efficiently in relationship to the total organism.

HEART SOUNDS AND OTHER AUSCULTATORY FINDINGS

First and Second Heart Sounds

Prior to every stress test, the physician should listen to the patient's heart to note the character of the heart sounds. It is a well established fact that the amplitude of the first sound correlates well with the DP/DT of the left ventricle. Thus, it is possible to predict to some degree how well the left ventricle will respond to stress. Paradoxical splitting of the second sound, usually associated with left bundle branch block, also indicates decreased function.

Fourth Heart Sounds

A fourth heart sound is a very common finding in ischemic heart disease. If this is fairly loud, the compliance of the left ventricle may be reduced, resulting in an elevation of the left ventricular end-diastolic pressure. If this appears after exercise, it is a useful diagnostic sign. If it gets louder with exercise, it is of added significance.[60] However, it can also occur with primary myocardial disease.

Third Heart Sounds

Third heart sounds are usually associated with very poor left ventricular function and should cause the physician to seriously reconsider a decision to proceed with the stress test. In most cases, it should be considered a major contraindication to testing. On the other hand, if it is heard after the test, it constitutes clear-cut evidence of serious ventricular dysfunction.

Aortic Murmur

An ejection murmur of aortic stenosis should alert one to the possibility that testing the patient carries an increased risk. Before the stress test is done, a good deal of information regarding the patient's status should be at hand. This is particularly true if the patient is over age 40. Aortic insufficiency murmurs, however, do not preclude testing, but should be noted and correlated with the patient's blood pressure.

Mitral Murmur

The most commonly heard mitral murmur will be associated with papillary muscle insufficiency or a prolapsed mitral leaflet. Short, late systolic murmurs

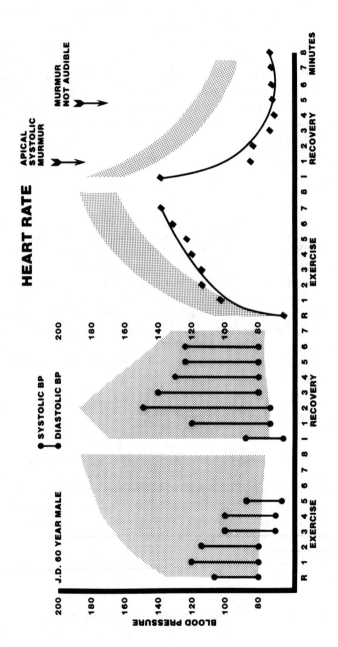

FIGURE 7-15. Blood pressure, heart rate, and time of auscultation of mitral insufficiency in a 60-year-old man without angina who had severe three-vessel disease.

associated with a click should alert one to the possibility that S-T segment depression recorded may not be due to coronary disease. Holosystolic murmurs, however, may indicate a more serious degree of mitral insufficiency. These usually do not constitute a significant contraindication to testing, however. The papillary muscle insufficiency murmur will usually get much louder near the peak of exercise. The diastolic murmur of mitral stenosis should tell the examiner that atrial fibrillation may be initiated by the stress. If tight mitral stenosis is present, a very modest increase in cardiac output is all that can be expected. Figure 7-15 depicts the blood pressure, heart rate, and time of auscultation of a murmur of mitral insufficiency in a man without angina who had severe three-vessel disease.

PALPITATION

A double impulse may be felt when a fourth heart sound is heard, confirming the presence of alterations in left ventricular compliance. Occasionally, a prominent left ventricular heave will be indicative of either a very dilated heart or a large apical ventricular aneurysm. Such a finding should be noted, as it may have a definite bearing on the presence or absence of the characteristic S-T segment changes seen with ischemia (see Chapter 14). An abnormal apical impulse is also common in patients with aortic or mitral valve disease. The typical thrill, or vibration palpable on the chest wall, associated with various valvular lesions is something to be particularly watchful for, because it indicates that the physiologic abnormality associated with the accompanying murmur is producing an increased workload on the heart.

PULSUS ALTERNANS

Banks and Shugoll[4] described pulsus alternans occurring in 4 out of 12 patients during attacks of spontaneous angina. We have not searched for this routinely, but it has been occasionally observed in those with severe angina and poor left ventricular function. One should be especially alert for pulsus alternans if alternating S-T segment depression or QRS amplitude is observed on the monitor during the stress test (see Chapter 6).

SUMMARY

It is hoped that this chapter has provided enough information to convince the reader that there is more to stress testing than S-T segment depression. As late as the latter part of 1979, an article in the New England Journal of Medicine[61] was widely quoted emphasizing that exercise-induced S-T depression added little to the diagnosis in patients with classical angina. The authors, however, ignored many of the important parameters demonstrated to be useful in patient evaluation. These will be reviewed again in Chapter 14. The term positive or negative stress tests, while still in use, is mostly to help understand some of the concepts relating to prevalence and the Bayesian theories of probability. It should be abandoned in the clinical setting when based on S-T segments only, as it denotes an all-or-none phenomenon that completely distorts our thinking about the use of stress testing. Because there are now so many hemodynamic and other clinical findings that are useful in evaluating the stress test, we may not need such complex approaches as precordial mapping. Although the S-T segment remains important, we should always combine it with as many variables possible.

REFERENCES

1. MASERI, A: Pathogenic mechanisms of angina pectoris: Expanding views. Br Heart J 43:648, 1980.
2. MARCUS, ML: The Coronary Circulation in Health and Disease. McGraw-Hill, New York, 1983.
3. STANELOFF, H, ET AL: The powerful predictor pitfall in prognostication. Circulation 68(III):136, 1983.
4. BANKS, T AND SHUGOLL, GI: Confirmatory physical findings in angina pectoris. JAMA 200:107, 1967.
5. BERSON, AS AND PIPBERGER, HV: The low frequency response of electrocardiographs, a frequent source of recording errors. Am Heart J 71:779, 1966.
6. REPORT OF COMMITTEE ON ELECTROCARDIOGRAPHY, AMERICAN HEART ASSOCIATION. Recommendations for standardizations of leads and of specifications for instruments in electrocardiography and vector cardiography. Circulation 35:583, 1967.
7. FARIS, JV, McHENRY, PL, AND MORRIS, SN: Concepts and applications of treadmill exercise testing and the exercise ECG. Am Heart J 95:102, 1978.
8. BLACKBURN, H, ET AL: The standardization of the exercise ECG. A systematic comparison of chest lead configurations employed for monitoring during exercise. In SIMONSON, E (ED): Physical Activity and the Heart. Charles C Thomas, Springfield, Ill, 1967.
9. FROELICHER, VF, ET AL: A comparison of two bipolar exercise ECG leads to lead V_5. Chest 70:611, 1976.
10. BLACKBURN, H: The Exercise electrocardiogram: Technological, procedural and conceptual developments. In SIMONSON, E (ED): Measurement in Exercise Electrocardiography. Charles C Thomas, Springfield, Ill, 1967.
11. HAKKI, AH, ET AL: R wave amplitude: A new determinant of failure of patients with coronary heart disease to manifest ST segment depression during exercise. JACC 3(5):1155–1160, 1984.
12. McHENRY, PL AND MORRIS, SN: Exercise electrocardiography-current state of the art. In SCHLANT, RC AND HURST, JW (EDS): Advances in Electrocardiography. Grune & Stratton, New York, 1976.
13. SIMOONS, M: Optimal measurements for detections of coronary artery disease by exercise ECG. Comput Biomed Res 10:483, 1977.
14. CAMP, J, ET AL: Diagnostic sensitivity of multiple leads in maximal exercise testing. Circulation 44:1120, 1971.
15. ISAACS, JH, ET AL: Vector electrocardiographic exercise test in ischemic heart disease. JAMA 198:139, 1966.

16. BLOMQVIST, CG: *The frank lead exercise electrocardiogram.* Acta Med Scand 440(suppl):9, 1965.

17. BLOMQVIST, CG: *Heart disease and dynamic exercise testing.* In WILLERSON, JT AND SANDERS, CA (EDS): *Clinical Cardiology.* Grune & Stratton, New York, 1977.

18. DOWER, GE, HORN, HE, AND ZIEGLER, WG: *The polarcardiograph: Terminology and normal findings.* Am Heart J 69:355, 1965.

19. FOX, KM, ET AL: *Projection of ST segment changes on to the front of the chest.* Br Heart J 48:555–559, 1982.

20. FOX, KM, SELWYN, AP, AND SHILLINGFORD, JP: *Precordial exercise mapping: Improved diagnosis of coronary artery disease.* Br Heart J II:1596–1598, 1978.

21. CHAITMAN, BR, ET AL: *Improved efficiency of treadmill exercise testing using a multiple lead system.* Circulation 57:71, 1978.

22. SPACH, MS AND BARR, MC: *Localizing cardiac electrical events from body surface maps.* Int J Cardiol 3(4):459–464, 1983.

23. ELLESTAD, MH: *Stress testing: A review.* In SOBEL, B, ET AL (EDS): *Perspectives in Cardiology.* Current Medical Literature, Ltd., London, 1984, p 29.

24. ELAMIN, MS, ET AL: *Accurate detection of coronary heart disease by new exercise test.* Br Heart J 48:311–320, 1982.

25. QUYYUMI, AA, ET AL: *Inability of the ST segment/heart rate slope to predict accurately the severity of coronary artery disease.* Br Heart J 51:395–398, 1984.

26. THULEIN, T AND WERNER, O: *Exercise test and 24-hour HR recording in men with high and low casual blood pressure levels.* Br Heart J 40:534, 1978.

27. BUCKBERG, GD, ET AL: *Subendocardial ischemia after cardiopulmonary bypass.* J Thorac Cardiovasc Surg 64:699, 1972.

28. BUCKBERG, GD, ET AL: *Experimental subendocardial ischemia in dogs with normal coronary arteries.* Circ Res 30:67, 1972.

29. JOSE, AD AND TAYLOR, RR: *Autonomic blockade by propranolol and atropine to study the intrinsic muscle function in man.* J Clin Invest 48:2019, 1969.

30. HINKLE, LE, CARVER, ST, AND PLAKUN, A: *Slow heart rates and increased risk of cardiac death in middle-aged men.* Arch Int Med 129:732, 1972.

31. GRIMBY, G AND SALTIN, B: *Physiological analysis of physically well-trained middle-aged and old athletes.* Acta Med Scand 179:513, 1966.

32. CHIN, CF, GREENBERG, PS, AND ELLESTAD, MH: *Chronotropic incompetence, an analysis of hemodynamic and anatomical findings.* Clin Cardiol 2:12, 1979.

33. GREENBERG, PS, COOKE, BM, AND ELLESTAD, MH: *Use of heart rate responses to standing and hyperventilation at rest to detect coronary artery disease: Correlation with the ST response to exercise.* J Electrocardio 13(4):373–378, 1980.

34. KEMP, GL AND ELLESTAD, MH: *The significance of hyperventilation and orthostatic T-wave changes on the electrocardiogram.* Arch Intern Med 121:518–532, 1968.

35. GREENBERG, PS, ET AL: *Value of autonomic maneuvers in detecting cardiac disease.* Practical Cardiology 9(10):92–100, 1983.

36. JACOBS, WF, BATTLE, WE, AND RONAN, JA, JR: *False-positive ST-T wave changes secondary to hyperventilation and exercise.* Ann Intern Med 81:479–482, 1974.

37. BROWN, KA, ET AL: *Carotid sinus reflex in patients undergoing angiograms.* Am J Cardiol 40:681, 1977.

38. FOX, SM, NAUGHTON, JP, AND HASKELL, WL: *Physical activity and the prevention of coronary heart disease.* Ann Clin Res 3:404, 1971.

39. FORD, AB AND HELLERSTEIN, HK: *Energy cost of the Master's two-step test.* JAMA 164:1868, 1957.

40. BALKE, B AND WARE, RW: *An experimental study of physical fitness of Air Force personnel.* US Armed Forces Med J 10:675, 1959.

41. MASTROPAOLO, JA, ET AL: *Physical activity of work, physical fitness and coronary heart disease in middle-aged Chicago men.* In KARVONEN, MD AND BARRY, AJ (EDS): *Physical Activity and the Heart.* Charles C Thomas, Springfield, Ill, 1967.

42. BRUCE, RA, KUSUMI, MS, AND HOSMER, D: *Maximal oxygen intake and nomographic assessment of functional aerobic impairment in cardiovascular disease.* Am Heart J 85:546, 1973.

43. GIVONI, B AND GOLDMAN, R: *Predicting metabolic energy costs.* J Appl Physiol 30(3):429–433, 1971.

44. JONES, HL: *Clinical exercising testing.* WB Saunders, Philadelphia, 1975.

45. WASSERMAN, K AND MCILROY, MB: *Detecting the threshold of anaerobic metabolism in cardiac patients during exercise.* Am J Cardiol 14:844, 1964.

46. WASSERMAN, K AND WHIPP, BJ: *Exercise physiology in health and disease.* Am Review of Respiratory Disease 112:219, 1979.

47. MORITANI, T AND DEVRIES, HA: *Reexamination of the relationship between the surface IEMG and force of isometric contraction.* Am J Phys Med 57:263, 1978.

48. POTANIN, C, HUNT, D, AND SHEFFIELD, LT: *Thermographic patterns of angina pectoris.* Circulation 42:199, 1970.

49. KOYAL, SN, ABATE, JA, AND ELLESTAD, MH: *Temperature response to upright exercise in patients with coronary artery disease.* Abstract presented at the FASEB meeting, April 1984.

50. SHELLOCK, FG, ET AL: *Unusual core temperature decrease in exercising heart-failure patients.* J Appl Physiol 54(2):544–550, 1983.

51. WEISSLER, AM, HARRIS, WS, AND SCHOENFELD, CD: *Systolic time intervals in heart failure in man.* Circulation 37:149, 1968.

52. POUGET, JM, ET AL: *Abnormal responses of systolic time intervals to exercise in patients with angina pectoris.* Circulation 43:289, 1971.

53. GILLIAN, RE, ET AL: *Systolic time intervals before and after maximal exercise treadmill testing for the evaluation of chest pain.* Chest 71:479, 1977.

54. VAN DER HOEVEN, GMA, ET AL: *A study of systolic time intervals during uninterrupted exercise.* Br Heart J 39:242, 1977.

55. JENGO, JA: *Evaluation of LV ventricular functions by single pass radioisotope angiography.* Circulation 57:326, 1978.

56. SILVERBERG, RH, ET AL: *Noninvasive diagnosis of regional ischemia: Superiority of this method over EKG treadmill in the detection of coronary disease* (abstr). Am J Cardiol 39:288, 1977.

57. CRAWFORD, MH, MOODY, JM, AND O'ROURKE, PA: *Limitations of the cardiokymograph for assessing left ventricular wall motion.* Am Heart J 97:719, 1979.

58. WEINER, DA, ET AL: *Cardiokymography during exercise testing: A new device for the detection of coronary artery disease and left ventricular wall motion abnormalities.* Am J Cardiol 51:1307–1311, 1983.

59. MACALPIN, RH AND KATTUS, AA: *Adaptation to exercise in angina pectoris: The electrocardiograms during treadmill walking and coronary angiographic findings.* Circulation 33:183, 1966.

60. GOOCH, AS AND EVANS, JM: *Extended applications of exercise stress testing.* Med Ann Dist Col 38:80, 1969.

61. WEINER, DA, ET AL: *Exercise stress testing: Correlations among history of angina, ST segment response and the prevalence of coronary artery disease in the coronary artery surgery study (CASS).* N Engl J Med 30:230, 1979.

62. HORNSTEN, RR AND BRUCE, RA: *Computed S-T forces of frank and bipolar exercise electrocardiograms.* Am Heart J 78:346, 1969.

63. BRUCE RA, ET AL: *Polarcardiographic responses to maximum exercise in healthy young adults.* Am Heart J 83:206, 1972.

8

STRESS TESTING PROTOCOL

REQUIREMENTS

The protocol for stress testing should be structured to include the following:
1. Continuous ECG monitoring.
2. ECG recording when desired; preferably several simultaneous leads before, during, and after exercise. A minimal recording of muscle potential is essential to an artifact-free recording.
3. A type of activity that can be performed by the sedentary, poorly developed, and underconditioned subject as well as by the trained athlete.
4. A workload that can be varied according to the capacity of the individual, but is standardized enough to deliver reproducible results and allow comparison with other patients tested.
5. Repeated frequent blood pressure measurements before, during, and after exercise.
6. A way of estimating the aerobic requirements of individuals tested.
7. Maximum safety and minimum discomfort for each individual tested.
8. The highest possible specificity and sensitivity in the discrimination between health and disease.
9. There should be a sufficient body of information available as to the response of normal and cardiac patients.
10. It should provide a first stage long enough for a warmup to occur.
11. The procedure should be short enough to be practical.

SINGLE LOAD TESTS

Master's Step Test

The protocol for the Master's Step Test, the best known of this type, was constructed originally as an exercise tolerance test rather than a screening test for coronary disease. The subject walked up and over a device two steps high with three steps, two of which were 9 inches above the floor and a top step 18 inches high.[1] Even though he used three steps in each ascent, two up and one down, it was called a two-step test. After going up and over, the patient then turned and walked over the steps again for a prescribed number of ascents. Blood pressure and pulse were then recorded; by knowing the patient's weight and the time required to complete the test, the work per minute could be derived. It was suggested that the prescribed number of ascents be completed in one and a half minutes. The tables for the number of ascents for men and women are reproduced in Appendix 7.

Many years later, Master added the electrocardiogram and suggested that it be recorded before and after the test and largely abandoned the original criteria that were proposed to evaluate exercise tolerance until about 1937. Until about 1973 or 1974, this test was accepted as the standard and for years was the most widely used in spite of its clinical limitations.

A survey completed in 1978[2] suggested it was decreasing in popularity and in 1985 one can rarely find a set of Master's Steps. As with other protocols listed below it has been included largely for historical reasons. Heart rate and blood pressure are not recorded during the test, thus, no measurements are available to evaluate the percentage of maximal work. Master recommended that 0.5 mm of S-T depression be accepted as abnormal, which in conjunction with the reduced workload resulted in approximately 60 percent false-negative results. Master reported in 1935, that 100 patients with coronary artery disease were tested, none developed anginal pain on the test. This gives ample evidence that the workload was too low to provide the maximum use.

Harvard Step Test

The Harvard Step Test was developed in the Harvard University Fatigue Laboratory around 1940. It is basically an exercise tolerance test somewhat similar to the original Master's Test before the ECG was applied.[3] The patient is asked to step up and down on a 20-inch platform 20 times a minute for five minutes. The pulse is counted from one to one and a half, two to two and a half, and three to three and a half minutes after stopping work. The score is obtained by dividing the duration of exercise in seconds, multiplied by 100, by twice the sum of pulse counts during the recovery period. The meaning of the figure is as follows: below 55 is indicative of poor conditioning, 55 to 64 is low average, 65 to 70 is high average, 80 to 89 is good, and above 90 is excellent.

The major advantages of single stage tests are their simplicity and the fact that little special equipment is needed. They almost all share the limitations detailed in the discussion of the Master's Test.

INTERMITTENT TESTS

The concept of an intermittent test is basically sound because progressive workloads can be interspersed with short rest periods, thus giving the subject time to recover somewhat before starting the next period of exercise. This time also allows one to take ECGs and make blood pressure determinations free of the motion artifact attendant on walking or running. Experience has shown that muscle strength can be restored when frequent rest periods are allowed; therefore, a greater total stress can be applied. Intermittent tests of this sort are often associated with continuous monitoring and an estimation of the aerobic capacity can be made.

Examples of this include Hellerstein's and Hornsten's[4] version of the work capacity test (PWC 150) and the widely used Swedish bicycle test[5] or a number of its modifications proposed by Mitchell and associates.[6] Hellerstein still believes the intermittent test is more physiologic and prefers it to a continuous protocol. While bicycle tests are commonly used for intermittent tests, a treadmill is equally applicable. The chief disadvantage inherent in interrupted tests is the time involved in waiting out the rest periods between exercise.

CONTINUOUS TESTS

Continuous tests are similar to intermittent tests in basic design, but vary in the use of either a treadmill, bicycle, or some type of stepping device. They also vary in the amount of work applied and the duration of effort required. By not allowing the patient to rest between work periods and progressively increasing the work, the patient's peak capacity or end-point is reached earlier. The ability to predict aerobic capacity, observe the chronotropic response to stress, measure blood pressure, and continuously record the ECG is similar to that of the intermittent tests.[7]

Heart Rate Targeted Testing

Increasing the exercise workload is usually accomplished by selecting some arbitrary increase in bicycle resistance or treadmill speed or grade. Another approach to increasing work is to set a target heart rate for each workload and then increase the work until it is reached. This can be done on either a bicycle or treadmill. Because heart rate is a major determinant of myocardial oxygen consumption, the work corresponding to a prescribed heart rate will then be a way of estimating the patient's aerobic capacity. Using this method, it might also be possible to evaluate subjects at predetermined percentages of their predicted maximum aerobic capacity. The patient's physiologic response theoretically adjusts the heart rate according to individual physical fitness.[8,9]

Bicycle Test

The use of the bicycle has several advantages. The patient's thorax and arms are relatively stable, allowing ECGs to be recorded with less muscle artifact and making it easier to record blood pressure accurately. The patient's body weight does not influence exercise capacity appreciably and sitting on a bicycle often produces less anxiety than walking on a mechanically driven treadmill. In addition, the bicycle requires less space in the laboratory and is usually less expensive than the treadmill.

It is my feeling, however, that the treadmill applies a more physiologic workload. This view seems to be shared by most stress testing laboratory personnel in the United States, and a number of studies have shown that subjects are much more likely to reach their aerobic capacity or their peak predicted heart rate on the treadmill, especially if they are not athletic in nature. The muscles necessary for bicycling are generally not well developed in the American population. We have also found that when patients are somewhat reluctant to push on because of fatigue, it is easier to obtain their cooperation on a treadmill because it is difficult to terminate voluntarily when the treadmill is still moving.

Bicycle test protocols may be intermittent or continuous but usually involve a progressively increasing workload. The bicycle may be mechanically or electrically braked, and the workload is easily calibrated in watts or Kg meters and it tends to be less dependent on the patient's weight and physical efficiency. A small person may be spending a much larger portion of maximal oxygen intake at a given workload than a large person, but the work applied takes a much less complex set of muscles and, therefore, is more predictable from one time to another. If one correlates the body weight and workload with the oxygen consumption per Kg of body weight, the latter can be estimated with an accuracy of approximately 10 percent. Nomograms have been constructed, and Table 8-1 lists the aerobic capacity of individuals exercised on a bicycle ergometer. It can be seen that as the subject's weight increases, the oxygen consumption per ml per minute per Kg of body weight decreases.

Koyal and colleagues[10] have reported that the small muscle mass used during bicycle tests causes more metabolic acidosis, which cannot be compensated by increased ventilation. Therefore, respiratory rate for equivalent workloads was higher. It has been shown[11] that supine bicycling is more likely to result in ischemia than upright pedalling. This may cause more ischemia when used in nuclear tests and thus explains their increased sensitivity.

Treadmill Test

The use of a treadmill presents a number of advantages because it is possible to adjust the speed and grade of walking to the agility of the subject. For example, Taylor and associates[12] found that groups of young men being stud-

TABLE 8-1. Oxygen requirements of bicycle ergometric workloads*

Workload										
Watts	25	50	75	100	125	150	175	200	250	300
Kg-m/min	150	300	450	600	750	900	1050	1200	1500	1800
Total oxygen used	600	900	1200	1500	1800	2100	2400	2700	3300	3900
K cal/min	3.0	4.5	6.0	7.5	9.0	10.5	12.0	13.5	16.5	19.5

Body weight		Oxygen used (ml/kg/min of body weight)									
(lbs)	(kg)										
88	40	15.0	22.5	30.0	37.5	45.0	52.5	60.0	67.5	82.5	97.5
110	50	12.0	18.0	24.0	30.0	36.0	42.0	48.0	54.0	66.0	78.0
132	60	10.0	15.0	20.0	25.0	30.0	35.0	40.0	45.0	55.0	65.0
154	70	8.5	13.0	17.0	21.5	25.5	30.0	34.5	38.5	47.0	55.5
176	80	7.5	11.0	15.0	19.0	22.5	26.0	30.0	34.0	41.0	49.0
198	90	6.7	10.0	13.3	16.7	20.0	23.3	26.7	30.0	36.7	43.3
220	100	6.0	9.0	12.0	15.0	18.0	21.0	24.0	27.0	33.0	39.0
242	110	5.5	8.0	11.0	13.5	16.5	19.0	22.0	24.5	30.0	35.5
264	120	5.0	7.5	10.0	12.5	15.0	17.5	20.0	22.5	27.5	32.5

*Based on data of Fox, et al.,[17] with permission.

STRESS TESTING: PRINCIPLES AND PRACTICE

Treadmill test; 5.5 km/h, 8° (3.4 mph, 14%)

Subject's bodyweight 75kg

Oxygen uptake (L/min)	2.9	2.2	3.2	2.9
Heart rate (beats/min)	155	138	168	158

FIGURE 8-1. Figures depict the increased oxygen cost of walking without holding on to the handrail, and of running over walking at the same speed and grade. (From Astrand,[19] with permission.)

ied always contained a few individuals who could not run more than 7 mph. Mitchell and coworkers[6] reported that most middle-aged men find 6 mph to be their peak capacity. Our experience with 5 mph at a 10 percent grade would suggest this to be about maximum for most middle-aged physically unfit individuals. The starting speed of 1.7 mph at a 10 percent grade recommended by Bruce and associates,[13] resulting in an oxygen consumption of about 4 METS, has been very satisfactory. There are, however, reports of success with higher or lower speeds and inclines.[14,15]

In some old or debilitated subjects, 1.7 mph is clearly faster than they can walk, and if stress testing is to be used in this group, a lower speed is useful. We also start with a lower speed when testing patients two or three weeks after myocardial infarction.

Balke and Ware,[16] Fox and associates,[17] and Naughton and coworkers[15] believe that the speed should be kept constant and the grade should be gradually increased. This is because running is quite difficult for many people, especially the old, sick, or obese. There has been a good deal of disagreement as to how steep the grade should be. We have kept the grade constant at 10 percent throughout most of our tests, as has Kattus,[18] mainly because walking or running up steep grades often causes pain in the calf muscles, especially in those who are poorly conditioned. Astrand[19] has emphasized that running at the same speed and grade (Fig. 8-1) requires more oxygen than walking.

Climbing Step Test

Kaltenbach[20] in Frankfurt, prefers a climbing test for cardiac screening (Fig. 8-2). He has had extensive experience with this approach for over 15 years and finds it has the advantages of allowing subjects to use their arms as well as

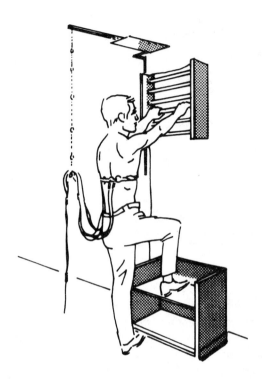

FIGURE 8-2. Climbing step test of Kaltenbach.[20] This approach is said to be more physiologic because the arms contribute to exercise; however, it precludes recording the blood pressure.

their legs and thus provides for the use of more muscles, resulting in a slightly higher VO_2max. He has worked out tables allowing for the prediction of workload and calculated oxygen uptake. The speed of climb is regulated with a metronome. The cost of equipment and space required are minimal. I have no first hand experience with this technique, but it has the major drawback that the blood pressure cannot be recorded during exercise and thus would seem to have reduced safety for patients with significant coronary disease.

Bruce Protocol

Bruce[21] who has probably done more maximum tests than anyone in the field, however, finds both an increase in speed and grade to be very satisfactory. He reports that his protocol produces nine times as many positive responders as the Master's test. His subjects start out at 1.7 mph on a 10 percent grade and progress to their maximum capacity at three-minute intervals (Fig. 8-3). (See Fig. 7-9 for O_2 consumption at each workload.)

STAGE	SPEED	GRADE	TIME	CUMULATIVE TIME
5	5.0	18%	3+	15+
4	4.2	16	3	12
3	3.4	14	3	9
2	2.5	12	3	6
1	1.7	10	3	3

FIGURE 8-3. The incline and speed are both increased every three minutes with the Bruce protocol.

COMPARISON OF VARIOUS PROTOCOLS

A number of excellent treadmill protocols have been used by various investigators and are highly satisfactory. One of the older and well established ones is that of Balke and Ware[16] who keep the speed constant and increase the grade gradually. One by Astrand[22] and Astrand and Rudahl[23] other pioneers in exercise physiology, starts at 3.5 mph at 2.5 percent grade with a 5-minute warmup, followed by continuous multistage run to exhaustion. This test is probably better suited to testing athletes than coronary patients. Other useful protocols (Fig. 8-4) have been published.[18,24-27] Pollock[28] published an excellent analysis of four popular protocols to determine the relative heart rate response and oxygen cost (Figs. 8-5 and 8-6). It becomes evident from examination of Figures 9-5 and 9-6 that although there is some variation in the rate at which the workload increases, most protocols accomplish about the same thing. Notice the leveling off near maximum workload of heart rate, but not oxygen consumption. This suggests that the heart rate plateaus, prior to reaching the VO$_2$max. Redwood[29] at the National Institutes of Health demonstrated the importance of warmup at a reasonably low workload when using the exercise test to quantitate ischemia or for comparison of various interventions such as medication or surgery. They found that if the initial exercise load was at or

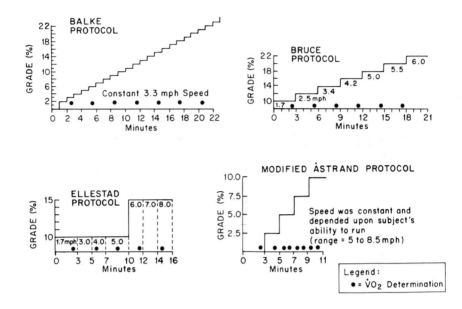

FIGURE 8-4. Diagrams of workloads used on a number of popular protocols. (From Pollock,[29] with permission.) The workload in the ninth minute of the Ellestad protocol has changed. See Figure 9-4 on page 192.

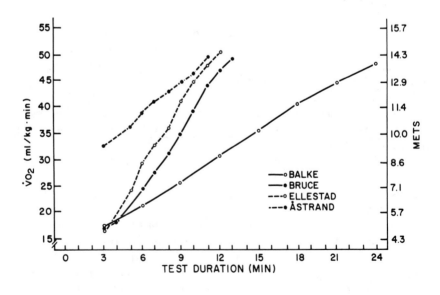

FIGURE 8-5. Mean VO$_2$ measured according to time of exercise on four different protocols. (From Pollock,[28] with permission.)

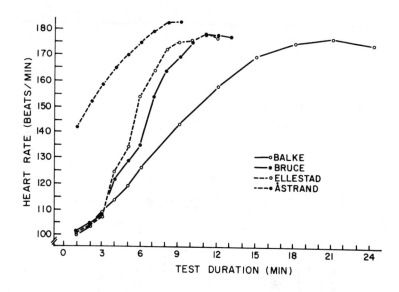

FIGURE 8-6. Mean heart rate response according to time on different protocols. Note in this and the previous figure that the start and stopping points are similar for most protocols. The major difference is how fast you get there. (From Pollock,[28] with permission.)

above the anginal threshold, a higher pulse pressure product or exercise work-load could be achieved than if a warmup workload was used. When the high initial workload was used, the end-points were also found to have low repro-ducibility.

ESTIMATION OF OXYGEN CONSUMPTION

Blackburn and associates[30] studied the oxygen consumption and heart rate of 10 men stressed by different protocols using steps, bicycle, and treadmill. As might be expected, the variability of oxygen consumption expressed as liters per minute on the bicycle tests was least because of the constant external load and very small variability of efficiency among subjects. However, since bicy-cle testing is independent of body weight, a marked variability in oxygen con-sumption expressed as per kg per minute was found. The treadmill, with its weight-dependent workload, shows a small variation in oxygen reported as ml per kg per minute and a larger variation when reported as liters per minute. In the Master's test, the variability of oxygen consumption for both liters per

TABLE 8-2. VO$_2$ STPD Estimate Compared With Direct Measurement

Stage	Treadmill Speed & Grade	ELLESTAD PROTOCOL Watts	Givoni & Goldman (L/M)	Ml/Kg For 70 Kg Man	METS	Direct Measurement By MMC (L/M)
I (3 min)	1.7 mph @ 10%	50	1.40	20	4.8	1.28
II (2 min)	3.0 mph @ 10%	100	1.68	24	6.4	1.67
III	4.0 mph @ 10%	150	2.4	34	8.8	2.07
IV	5.0 mph @ 10%	200	2.92	41.7	10.0	2.74
V	5.0 mph @ 15%	250	3.22	46	12.0	3.17
VI	6.0 mph @ 15%	300	4.15	59.3	15.2	3.8
VII	7.0 mph @ 15%	350	4.8	68.5	17.2	3.96

N = n(W+L) (2.3+0.32 [V−2.5] 1.65 + G[0.2+0.07(V−2.5)])

M = Metabolic Rate, Kcal/hr

n = Terrain Factor, Defined as 1 for Treadmill Walking

W = Body Weight (Kg); L = External Load (Kg); V = Walking Speed, KM/hr

G = Slope (grade) percent

minute and kg per ml per minute lies somewhere in between. There is no significant difference in the variability of the heart rate response. Bruce has published oxygen data describing the mg per kg per minute for subjects using his protocol, which is excellent. When he adjusts for the sex and physical activity of the subject, the VO_2max was estimated with what appears to be acceptable accuracy[31] (see Chapter 7, Fig. 7-9).

Froelicher and coworkers,[32] on the other hand, tested the time on the protocol proposed by Bruce as an estimate of oxygen consumption and found it to be unreliable.

We have used the formula published by Balke and Ware[16] and also by Givoni and Goldman[33] to estimate VO_2max. Table 8-2 illustrates data from the latter formula and has been fairly accurate at lower workloads (below about 12 METS).

EXERCISE INTENSITY

There has been a good deal of reluctance on the part of physicians to apply maximal stress to the general population because of fear of producing injury, either cardiac or musculoskeletal. Lester and associates[34] have reported that ventricular and supraventricular tachycardias are more apt to occur at between 90 and 100 percent of maximal heart rate, and suggest that 90 percent of maximal predicted pulse be the point of termination. The Scandinavian Committee on Electrocardiogram Classification[35] recommend target heart rates of approximately 85 percent of the maximal. Sheffield and associates[24] found the maximal predicted heart rate to be 198 (0.14 × age) for conditioned men and 205 (0.41 × age) for unconditioned men and compiled Table 8-3.

The problem with heart rate-related end-points that are still in common usage is due to the variability in the maximal heart rate, even when adjusted for age. If a test of 85 percent of maximal heart rate is used to terminate exercise, it may be much less or more than 85 percent of capacity depending on the patient's actual and unknown maximal heart rate. Also one has to forego the estimation of aerobic capacity; a useful calculation made from the patient's symptom-limited exercise duration. Although we have used a symptom-limited maximum test using an age-corrected maximum heart rate as a guide for years, advocates of the submaximal testing claim that the S-T changes occuring at heart rates above this level have less significance.

Gibbons and colleagues[36] reported a 20-month followup in 550 patients with abnormal exercise electrocardiograms. They found that in subjects with known coronary artery disease, S-T depression occuring at heart rates below 85 percent of maximal were six times more predictive of a new event than changes occuring at heart rates greater than 85 percent. In those with no known disease, S-T depression occuring above and below the 85 percent cutoff had about the same predictive power.

The controversy over what constitutes maximum heart rate deserves a few words. The disagreement regarding what constitutes a maximum heart rate

TABLE 8-3. Maximum heart rate predicted by age and conditioning

Age	20	25	30	35	40	45	50	55	60	65	70	75	80	85	90
Unconditioned	197	195	193	191	189	187	184	182	180	178	176	174	172	170	168
90%	177	175	173	172	170	168	166	164	162	160	158	157	155	153	151
75%	148	146	144	143	142	140	138	137	135	134	132	131	129	128	126
60%	118	117	115	114	113	112	110	109	108	107	106	104	103	102	101
Conditioned	190	188	186	184	182	180	177	175	173	171	169	167	165	163	161
90%	171	169	167	166	164	162	159	158	156	154	152	150	149	147	145
75%	143	141	140	138	137	135	133	131	130	128	127	125	124	122	121
60%	114	113	112	110	109	108	106	105	104	103	101	100	99	98	97

(From Sheffield, et al.,[24] with permission.)

STRESS TESTING: PRINCIPLES AND PRACTICE

response probably stems from the analysis of different population groups. Our studies are taken from a relatively sedentary population, while others have analyzed athletes and other selected groups. The variation above and below the mean is at least 10 beats, and although subjects with this variance are fairly rare, they are occasionally seen. Cooper and colleagues[37] have published data showing the variations associated with fitness (Fig. 8-7). Thus, we should recognize that our tables are only guidelines.

Lester and coworkers[34] studied normal men ranging in age from 40 to 75 with a near maximum graded test and also with the Master's Step Test. The submaximal test resulted in positive findings characterized by 1.0 mm horizontal or downsloping S-T segment depression in one subject. Five more abnormal tracings were recognized with the maximal test. In the analysis of 1000 tests in our laboratory, 19 percent of the men with abnormal findings manifested S-T segment changes in our fourth stage at 5 miles per hours at a 10 percent grade. Most subjects will be very near their peak heart rate at this level. Twenty-one percent of the women with abnormal tracings were also detected at this stage. This suggests that pushing the patient to maximal effort is feasible. However, a higher yield of abnormal tests in so-called normal patients with the maximal stress test[24,38] might cause an increased false-positive response. In our series of tests on healthy executives,[39] 14 percent had abnormal S-T segment depression of 1.5 mms or more and almost all developed near peak heart rate. We have no information on how many of these had coronary disease. Strandell[40] reports a relatively high prevalence of abnormal responders in apparently normal men that increases with age. Aronow[41] found

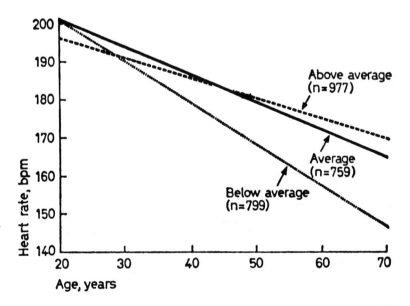

FIGURE 8-7. Maximum heart rates achieved according to fitness and age. (From Cooper,[37] with permission.)

TABLE 8-4. Ages and maximal heart rate (MHR)*

Age	MHR	Age	MHR	Age	MHR
20	200	37	185	54	171
21	199	38	184	55	171
22	198	39	183	56	170
23	197	40	182	57	170
24	196	41	181	58	169
25	195	42	180	59	168
26	194	43	180	60	168
27	193	44	180	61	167
28	192	45	179	62	167
29	191	46	177	63	166
30	190	47	177	64	165
31	190	48	177	65	164
32	189	49	176	66	163
33	188	50	175	67	162
34	187	51	174	68	161
35	186	52	173	69	161
36	186	53	172	70	160

*Mean maximum heart rates used as a guide for determining approximate end-point of stress in our laboratory.

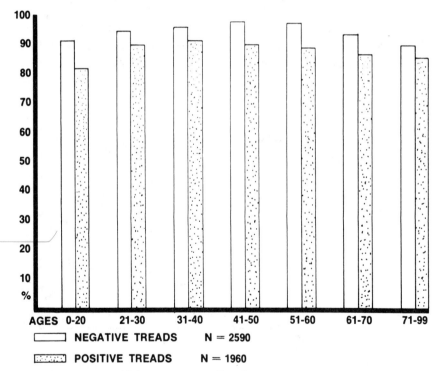

FIGURE 8-8. Average peak heart rate attained by all subjects exercised according to age and diagnosis. The poor averages in the younger age groups are due to our failure to push these subjects to maximum.

13 percent abnormal maximal tests in normal men with a mean age of 51. It is of some interest to note that none of the executives we tested with positive S-T segment depression had chest pain of any type when the changes were recorded near maximum capacity. It must be emphasized that the clinical significance of S-T segment depression discovered at maximal exercise levels is yet to be clarified.

Blomqvist[42] has published data on S-T depression in normal persons at high workloads (see Chapter 14). Kasser and Bruce[43] believe these changes represent some abnormality in myocardial function, but not always coronary ischemia. The relative absence of such changes in young persons and in a significant number of older people indicates that they are probably correct. During heart catheterization, we have found that many patients with left ventricular dysfunction have exercise-induced S-T segment depression in spite of normal coronary arteries.

Bruce has done over 10,000 maximum stress tests without a fatality. In our series of 10,000 tests, we have had three deaths, but two of the three developed trouble at far below their maximum heart rate.

Our recent survey of stress testing facilities[2] suggests the mortality has decreased in the face of increased use of maximum stress testing. It has been our practice to suggest to patients that they may stop the test once their maximum predicted heart rates have been reached (Table 8-4), unless they want to continue. This maximum is rarely exceeded by more than 5 to 10 beats per minute, even in those individuals who are pushed to exhaustion. On the other hand, those who voluntarily elect to continue and achieve heart rates 10 or 20 beats above the mean for their ages may be physiologically younger than their chronological age. Figure 8-8 depicts the ability by various age groups to approach the peak predicted heart rate response. A high percentage were surprisingly good.

In summary, when maximum stress is used, there will be an increase in the number of subjects identified as having abnormal hearts if the S-T segments alone are used as a marker for disease. As we develop data to validate other findings, the exact significance of S-T depression at high workloads will probably be clarified. Those who have abnormalities identified at the higher workloads will obviously have less serious disease than those identified early in the procedure or by submaximal tests.

PROTOCOL FOR EARLY STRESS TESTING (AFTER MI)

It is now common to use exercise tests to evaluate patients about ready to leave the hospital after acute myocardial infarction.[44] This has been shown to be useful in predicting the subsequent course of the disease and in the analysis of arrhythmias. A less demanding protocol is usually used. Figure 8-9 illustrates the protocol in use in our laboratory. Most investigators terminate exercise at heart rates near 120 to 130; however, some have used maximal testing as early as 3 weeks.[45]

STAGE	SPEED	GRADE	TIME	METS	TOTAL TIME	VO$_2$ ml/mm/Kg
1	1.5	0	3 min	2.8	3	6
2	1.5	4	3	3.2	6	9
3	1.5	8	3	3.7	9	12
4	1.7	10	3	4.0	12	15
5	2.0	12	3	5.0	15	20

FIGURE 8-9. Submaximal treadmill protocol used when patients are tested just before discharge after a myocardial infarction (2 to 3 weeks following infarction). A heart rate of 120 is now used as a target but this may finally be less than desirable.

ARM EXERCISE TESTING

In subjects who are unable to exercise with their legs because of orthopedic problems or vascular insufficiency, arm crank ergometry provides an excellent substitute.

Maximal Work

Maximal oxygen consumption achieved with the arm crank is between 65 to 80 percent[46] of that maximally achieved by the legs, depending on the strength of the arm and shoulder muscles. Studies of VO$_2$ capacity demonstrate that exercising with the arms is a poor predictor of leg capacity and vice versa.[47] Although maximum cardiac output is lower with arm work, the maximal heart rate, systolic blood pressure and double product are quite similar. Thus, myocardial oxygen consumption is greater per unit of total body work probably due to the relative increase in peripheral resistance when using the arms.

Although there is some disagreement, most investigators find the identification of ischemia to be quite similar when subjects are tested with both methods.[48,49] DeBusk and associates[50] found leg exercise to be better, but Shaw and colleagues[48] and Schwade and coworkers[49] could demonstrate no difference.

Equipment

Bicycle ergometers with either a mechanical or an electrical brake are satisfac-

STRESS TESTING: PRINCIPLES AND PRACTICE

tory. We use a Collins ergometer that functions for either arm or leg tests, depending on positioning. Other makes are available on the market.

Protocol

A number of progressive continuous protocols are in use starting at about 200 to 300 kilogram meters of work and increasing by about 100 kilogram meters at each workload, usually of 2 or 3 minutes each.[51] Blood pressure and electrocardiograms are recorded at each stage and the electrocardiogram is continually observed during the test as it is in conventional leg-exercise testing. During blood pressure measurements, the patient may continue to crank with the opposite arm, but will probably have to slow the rotation somewhat.

This type of testing is not only a practical alternative in subjects who cannot walk, but is also useful when arm exercise is necessary in certain occupations or avocations. Planning a training or rehabilitation program for someone who plans to use their arms preferentially may find the arm ergometer a most practical testing device.

ISOMETRIC TEST

The procedure consists of squeezing a dynomometer at from one fourth to three fourths of the maximum hand strength and sustaining this for as long as possible. The resultant increase in myocardial oxygen consumption is mainly due to the rise in systolic blood pressure, although there is also an increase in heart rate. If one measures the pulse pressure product at the end-point of angina or of S-T segment depression, such a heart rate is reasonably reproducible. The increase in heart rate is probably due to the withdrawal of vagal influence. The cardiac output increases but the stroke volume usually remains constant until the grip is increased above 50 percent of the individual's total capacity, and it may then decrease.[52] It has been shown that, in spite of the rise in blood pressure, the blood flow to noncontracting muscles does not increase, probably due to reflex vasoconstriction. LVEDP rises and abnormal heart sounds such as S_4 or S_3 may be accentuated. The murmurs of aortic and mitral regurgitation are also accentuated. Thus, it may be a useful test to do at the bedside for subjects who are unable to walk. It must be remembered, however, that isometric exercise can produce arrhythmias and the other hazards of exercise stress testing; therefore, continuous electrocardiographic and blood pressure monitoring should be routinely used. The test result cannot be correlated to aerobic capacity, thus, it is difficult to relate to other types of activity. The isometric test would seem to have a limited application, but is useful in certain situations.

Kerber and colleagues[53] have studied the relative relationship of isometric to dynamic exercise in coronary patients. They reported an isometric test to be an inefficient way of initiating ischemia. They also found that when isometric exercise was combined with treadmill exercise (carrying a briefcase), more coronary artery patients failed to have S-T depression than when walking without a briefcase. Systolic and diastolic pressures (and thus, the double product) were increased by the isometric load, but they postulated that the higher diastolic pressure improved perfusion enough to compensate for the increase in myocardial oxygen demands. Sheldahl and associates[54] found that post-myocardial infarction patients carrying weights up to 50 pounds had a high prevalence of diastolic hypertension (greater than 120 mms of mercury), but little ischemia.

HYPOXEMIA TEST

Although the reduction in T wave amplitude with hypoxemia was first demonstrated in 1921 and described by many researchers since then, the routine use of this type of stress testing has never been popular.[55,56] The credit for developing a standardized procedure should probably go to Leevy and coworkers[57] who, in 1939, proposed breathing a mixture of 10 percent oxygen and 90 percent nitrogen for 20 minutes.

Mechanisms

In normal persons, a decrease in oxygen saturation can be compensated for by increased coronary flow. This cannot be accomplished satisfactorily when critical blood vessel narrowing is present. There is little increase in ventilation when breathing low concentration levels of oxygen because the carbon dioxide liberated by muscles during exercise is the primary stimulus increasing respiratory volume. The decrease in carbon dioxide relative to exercise, results in alkalosis with hypoxemia and acidosis with exercise. The latter has a slightly more suppressive effect on arrhythmias. The ECG changes associated with the decreased myocardial oxygen supply are similar to those resulting from exercise. The hypoxemia may produce cerebral dysfunction, although the myocardial difficulties usually occur first. Thus, brain damage may occur, especially in patients who have cerebrovascular disease or pulmonary insufficiency.

Broch[58] reviewed the subject and proposed a calibrated hypoxemia test by monitoring the oxygen saturation as the concentration of oxygen in the inspired air was decreased. T-wave amplitude decreased in normal and coronary patients alike. No false-positive tests were demonstrated in five normal patients. Out of 13 patients with established angina, however, 5 did not show S-T segment depression. Many years ago, Katz and Landt[59] reported that the specificity and sensitivity of the hypoxemia tests were better than an exercise test

STRESS TESTING: PRINCIPLES AND PRACTICE

and this may still be valid. Roskamm[60] tested 10 subjects with angina who were known to have ischemic S-T segment depression using exercise and correlated this with the hypoxemia test. The correlation was extremely good ($p = 0.05$). A good study using subjects who have had coronary angiograms needs to be done to establish the validity of this test on a sound basis.

Procedures

A wide variation in arterial oxygen saturation may be observed in subjects breathing a 10 percent oxygen mixture. Simonson[61] reported a difference in subjects ranging from 5 to 25 percent measured by an earpiece oximeter. He felt this was due to variations in vital capacity, residual air, and the volume of pulmonary ventilation.

Therefore, there has been a trend toward standardizing the oxygen saturation rather than the oxygen concentration of the inspired air. Penneys[62] stabilized the arterial saturation at progressively lower levels, in other words, 80, 75, and 70 percent saturation, with ECGs recorded at each concentration level. This allows the progressive hypoxemia to be graded, much as the workload during exercise is graded.

Criteria

Most investigators[59,61,62] agree that a positive test based on S-T segment depression is extremely rare in healthy subjects. In this test, an inversion of the T waves in any lead except III, AVL, AVR, or VR has also been reported to indicate coronary disease.[61] In 126 cases studied by Simonson,[61] none developed anginal pain, although its occurrence is a possibility and is considered to be abnormal even in the absence of S-T segment depression. The usefulness of the Q-T interval is controversial[14] as well as the QX/QT ratio.

The absence of significant tachycardia with this test results in a smaller Ta* wave and, thus, the S-T segment depression is easier to measure.

Predictive Data

A number of followup studies are available that further document the validity of the hypoxemia test. Based on a study of 254 subjects over an 8-year period, Mathers and Levy[63] reported a cumulative mortality of 61 percent in those with positive tests. This is considerably higher than the mortality reported by Robb and Marks[64] and Mattingly[65] for patients studied for a 7-year period after a positive Master's Test (20 and 22.2 percent, respectively).

---

*Ta wave = wave of atrial repolarization

We have experienced a 22 percent mortality over an 8-year period for those who had a positive response to our maximum stress test. It would appear from the higher mortality and the lack of false-positive studies with the anoxemia test that it identifies only patients with two- to three-vessel disease.

I believe that this method of testing has never become popular because:

1. What we really want to know is how the heart responds to exercise.
2. Breathing gas mixtures with low oxygen content is uncomfortable and produces a great deal of anxiety.
3. An individual's aerobic capacity cannot be estimated by this method. On the other hand, almost immediate termination of the anoxic state can be accomplished by switching to 100 percent oxygen.

CATECHOLAMINE STRESS TEST

Catecholamine stimulation has been used by many investigators to produce an increase in cardiac work.[59] Gorlin and Raylor[66] gave isoproterenol intravenously in order to evaluate coronary sinus lactate excretion in subjects with known coronary disease. Chun and coworkers,[67] in our laboratory, used isoproterenol to increase cardiac work and simultaneously monitored the ECG and systolic time intervals. Gubner[68] gave patients 15 mg of isoproterenol sublingually just prior to the Master's Test. He reported that a significant number of negative or equivocal responders became positive as a result of this procedure. The exact significance of this has not been statistically presented. In our experience with intravenously administered isoproterenol, we were more interested in evaluating left ventricular contractility and chronotropic response than in producing ischemic S-T segments. We found that the failure to increase the pre-ejection period and the pulse pressure were usually reliable evidences of severe left ventricular dysfunction. It is also interesting to note that all our normal subjects developed an audible systolic ejection murmur while those with poor left ventricular contractility failed to do so. It would appear that a strong muscle is necessary to produce the flow murmur associated with an increased catecholamine stimulus.

DIPYRIDAMOLE TESTING

This agent has been recognized to be a potent coronary dilator for many years. Its usefulness in angina was limited, however, because it preferentially dilated the coronary arterioles and precapillary sphincters, so that the areas of the heart where perfusion was normal were over-perfused, thus resulting in reduced flow to the ischemic areas. This has resulted in a "coronary steal" actually shunting blood away from ischemic areas. Because of this, the agent has been used recently primarily because it inhibits platelet adhesiveness. The very property that makes it inappropriate for treating angina recommends it as a way to pharmacologically produce ischemia. In patients who are unsuitable for exercise testing, the agent has been used intravenously in doses of 0.6 mgs/kg infused over a 10-minute period. Ischemia can be detected by S-T response, thallium scintograms, or by the appearance of angina.

Reliability

Slany and colleagues[69] and Tauchert and associates[70] have reported a very high sensitivity, when testing patients with a high prevalence of critical coronary stenosis. When normal subjects and those with false-positive S-T depression are included, however, its reliability decreases considerably. DeAmbroggio and coworkers[71] found it was not only a poor predictor of high-grade stenosis, but frequently produced an abnormal response in subjects with normal coronary arteries, especially those with a "false-positive" S-T response to exercise. None of their patients with single-vessel disease had an abnormal response. They believed it produces chest pain and ECG changes in patients by mechanisms other than the "steal" syndrome that are yet to be identified.

Work by DaiHyon and Gluckman[72] and Hamilton[73] suggest that dipyridamole may increase myocardial sensitivity to catecholamines. This would explain its demonstrated propensity to produce ischemic changes in subjects with a hyperdynamic circulation. Thus, the use of this agent to identify coronary artery disease has little to recommend it at this time.

ERGONOVINE TESTING

Demonstration of coronary spasm, during angiography with ergonovine, has become fairly routine. When patients with a history of angina at rest, especially when it occurs early in the morning, undergo angiography, the demonstration of the vasospastic process by intravenous administration of ergonovine maleate in doses of 0.01, 0.1, and eventually 0.2 mgs intravenously is the common practice. A positive responder usually has anginal chest pain, S-T segment elevation and angiographically demonstrated localized spasm in a large epicardial coronary artery. A generalized reduction in epicardial coronary caliber is normal and not considered to be significant. In some centers, ergonovine has been given in the isotope laboratory and in the coronary care unit[74] and the effects recorded with thallium scintograms. Occasional patients who require intracoronary nitroglycerin to terminate spasm have however dampened enthusiasm for this approach outside the catheterization laboratory.

HISTAMINE TESTING

Ginsburg and colleagues[75] at Stanford have recently reported on the use of histamine in place of ergonovine to initiate spasm in Prinzmetal angina. The agent is infused at a dose of 0.5 ugs/kg/min for 3 minutes. The concentration is increased to 1 ug/kg/minute if no pain or S-T elevations occurred. Patients were given Cimetidine prior to testing to prevent GI problems and hypotension. They had a positive response in 4 of 12 patients suspected of having vasospastic angina and recommended it if ergonovine fails to demonstrate spasms when clinically suspected. The GI and other systemic effects, however, must be blocked with Cimetidine to make the side-effects tolerable. More work with this agent needs to be done before it can be recommended outside the research laboratory.

COLD PRESSOR TEST

The autonomic response to immersion of one hand in ice water has been demonstrated to produce ischemia in subjects with coronary artery disease as well as those with vasospastic angina.[76,77] Although it will increase heart rate and blood pressure modestly in most subjects, a few (the reactors) will have a major rise in blood pressure; thus, increase myocardial oxygen demand. It has been used in conjunction with simple electrocardiographing and blood pressure monitoring and in the nuclear laboratory using blood pool angiographic monitoring.[78] Jordan and colleagues[78] from Cornell have demonstrated a reduced magnitude of rise in both heart rate and blood pressure than with conventional stress testing, and suggest this test has limited usefulness. In occasional situations, it may initiate coronary spasm, and should be considered when other methods fail to document this type of physiology. On the whole, however, it has been disappointing in its ability to initiate ischemia and will probably only work in patients with very severe degrees of coronary obstruction.

LEFT VENTRICULAR WALL FUNCTION

The use of an epinephrine drip during the recording of the left ventricular angiogram to study changes in segmental and total muscle function is underway in our laboratory. A useful way to help identify muscle that is noncontractile or hypokinetic from underperfusion as contrasted to that replaced by scar tissue. The same data can now best be studied by isotope methods (see Chapter 13).

EMOTIONAL STRESS TEST

It is well known by every physician who treats coronary patients that emotional stress may initiate angina. Very little systematic work has been done to analyze this element of our environment to determine how it impacts on the clinical problem of coronary heart disease.

Mcneil[79] has studied coronary patients with a series of emotional challenges and monitored blood pressure and heart rate in much the same way as during an exercise test. Patients were then given a probing interview to explore areas of possible concern, such as the impact of heart attack on their families, occupations, sexual activities, longevity, and so forth. The patients then watched a videotape of a child suffocating, a man having a heart attack, and an erotic scene. After a period of relaxation, they were asked to solve a geometric puzzle and assured it was quite easy, although most found it difficult. The interview and the puzzle provided most physiologic stress as measured by the double product. It was of interest that patients who were judged to have anger or denial regarding their coronary disease had a lesser response in heart rate and blood pressure. This implies that the emotionally responsive subject is less physiologically responsive, a surprise finding. There are no data to correlate the findings with subsequent coronary events or severity of coronary disease. Spachia[80] has used mental arithmetic testing in a large group of patients with CAD and was able to induce S-T segment abnormalities in 18 percent, all of whom also had an abnormal exercise test.

ATRIAL PACING

Although this test requires that a pacing catheter be placed in the right atrium, it serves as a practical approach to the evaluation of ischemic heart disease and for quantitation of its severity during heart catheterization or if a catheter has been placed, for monitoring. The correlation of heart rate and increased myocardial oxygen consumption indicates that at some heart rate, most patients with ischemic heart disease will have either chest pain or ischemic S-T segments. It should be re-emphasized that when the rate is increased by pacing, the cardiac output does not increase; therefore, the stroke volume progressively decreases. This means that the cardiac work with atrial pacing is not comparable to the same heart rate associated with exercise in which the increased venous return not only keeps the stroke volume near resting, but may actually result in a slight increase.

In practice, the rate is increased by 10 or 30 beats each minute until 160 is reached or until S-T segment depression or pain occurs. Souton and associates[81] studied 22 patients with atrial pacing, 13 of whom developed angina during the study. The onset of pain was at a consistent time tension index (5 percent variation) confirming that in patients with coronary insufficiency, the heart's ability to perform is predicably limited by the amount of oxygen delivered. End-diastolic roentgenograms were made at various pacing rates and, in all but one case, the ventricular volume was smaller at the anginal threshold. This finding was consistent with the decrease in stroke volume demonstrated by indicator dilation curves. Tzivoni and coworkers[82] report an increased sensitivity for ischemia over treadmill stress testing in postmyocardial infarction patients. They also claim abnormalities induced by this method are better predictors of subsequent morbidity and mortality.

CIRCADIAN INFLUENCE

A word about the timing seems in order. Yasue[83] has found patients with vaso-spastic angina, even if they have fixed lesion, are more likely to have changes in the morning. Joy and associates,[84] on the other hand, report that patients with stable angina have more S-T depression in the afternoon. Autonomic changes that are responsible are still poorly understood.

SUMMARY

The preceding material describes the various protocols that have been or are being used to evaluate patients with suspected coronary disease. There are, no doubt, many that are not listed and many yet to be described. The reader is urged to examine the evidence available and select a method or methods best suited to the patient or to the reader's own understanding of exercise physiology. There are numerous advantages, however, to selecting one or two methods and using them enough to become familiar with the response of normal and abnormal subjects alike. Using a protocol for which there is ample clinical experience available, makes it possible to better categorize each individual's performance. Consistency will also make it easier to compare the patient's performance from one year to the next, and to compare one patient with another. The details of the protocol should also be clearly outlined when data are sent to other physicians.

REFERENCES

1. MASTER, MA: *Two step test of myocardial function.* Am Heart J 10:495, 1934.
2. STUART, RJ AND ELLESTAD, MH: *National survey of exercise stress testing facilities.* Chest 77:94–97, 1980.
3. HART, JS: *Commentaries on the effect of physical training with and without cold exposure upon physiological indices of fitness for work.* Can Med Assoc J 96:803, 1967.
4. HELLERSTEIN, HK AND HORNSTEN, TR: *The coronary spectrum: Assessing and preparing a patient for return to a meaningful and productive life.* J Rehab 32:48, 1966.
5. ARSTILA, M: *Pulse conducted triangular exercise ECG test: A feedback system regulating work during exercise.* Acta Med Scand 529(Suppl):9, 1972.
6. MITCHELL, JH, SPROULE, BJ, AND CHAPMAN, CB: *The physiological meaning of the maximal oxygen intake test.* J Clin Invest 37:538, 1958.
7. THE COMMITTEE ON EXERCISE. *Exercise testing and training of apparently healthy individuals.* American Heart Association, Dallas, 1972.

8. ASTRAND, I: *The physical work capacity of workers 50-64 years old.* Acta Physiol Scand 42:73, 1958.

9. LANCE, VO AND SPODICH, DH: *Constant load vs. heart rate targeted exercise: Responses of systolic time intervals.* J Appl Physiol 38:794, 1975.

10. KOYAL, SN, ET AL: *Ventilatory responses to the metabolic acidosis of treadmill and cycle ergometry.* J Appl Physiol 40(6):864–867, 1976.

11. CURRIE, PJ, KELLY, MJ, AND PITT, A: *Comparison of supine and erect bicycle exercise electrocardiography in coronary heart disease: Accentuation of exercise-induced ischemic S-T depression by supine posture.* Am J Cardiol 52:1167–1173, 1983.

12. TAYLOR, HL, BUSKIRK, E, AND HENSCHELL, A: *Maximum oxygen intake as an objective measure of cardiorespiratory performance.* J Appl Physiol 8:73, 1958.

13. BRUCE, RA, ET AL: *Exercise testing in adult normal subjects and cardiac patients.* Pediatrics 32(Suppl):742, 1963.

14. KASSEBAUM, DG, SUTHERLAND, KO, AND JUDKINS, MP: *A comparison of hypoexmia and exercise electrocardiography in coronary artery disease.* Am Heart J 7:371, 1932.

15. NAUGHTON, J, BALKE, B, AND NAGLE, F: *Refinements in methods of evaluation and physical conditioning before and after myocardial infarction.* Am J Cardiol 14:837, 1964.

16. BALKE, B AND WARE, RW: *An experimental study of physical fitness of Air Force personnel.* US Armed Forces Med J 10:675, 1959.

17. FOX, SM, NAUGHTON, JP, AND HASKELL, WL: *Physical activity and the prevention of coronary heart disease.* Ann Clin Res 3:404, 1971.

18. KATTUS, AA: *Physical training and beta adrenergic blocking drugs in modifying coronary insufficiency.* In MARCHETRTI, G AND TOCCARDI, B (EDS): *Coronary Circulation and Energetics of the Myocardium.* S Karger, New York, 1967.

19. ASTRAND, PO: *Principles in ergometry and their implications in sports practice.* Sport Med 1:1–5, 1984.

20. KALTENBACH, M: *Exercise Testing of Cardiac Patients.* Williams & Wilkins, Baltimore, 1976.

21. BRUCE, A: *Comparative prevalence of segment S-T depression after maximal exercise in healthy men in Seattle and Taipei.* In SIMONSON, E (ED): *Physical Activity and the Heart.* Charles C Thomas, Springfield, Ill, 1967.

22. ASTRAND, I: *The physical work capacity of workers 50-64 years old.* Acta Physiol Scand 42:73, 1958.

23. ASTRAND, PO AND RUDAHL, K: *Textbook of Work Physiology.* McGraw-Hill, New York, 1970.

24. SHEFFIELD, LT, HOLT, JH, AND REEVES, TJ: *Exercise graded by heart rate in electrocardiographic testing for angina pectoris.* Circulation 32:622, 1965.

25. HELLERSTEIN, HK: *Exercise therapy in coronary heart disease.* Bull NY Acad Med 44:1028, 1968.

26. FROELICHER, VF, ET AL: *A comparison of the reproducibility and physiological response to 3 maximal treadmill exercise protocols.* Chest 65:512, 1974.

27. TAYLOR, HL, ET AL: *The standardization and interpretation of submaximal and maximal tests of working capacity.* Pediatrics 32:703, 1963.

28. POLLOCK, ML: *A comparative analysis of 4 protocols for maximal exercise testing.* Am Heart J 93:39, 1976.

29. REDWOOD, DR: *Importance of the design of an exercise protocol in the evaluation of patients with angina pectoris.* Circulation 63:618, 1971.

30. BLACKBURN, H, ET AL: *The standardization of the exercise electrocardiogram: A systematic comparison of chest lead configurations employed for monitoring during exercise.* In SIMONSON, E (ED): *Physical Activity and the Heart.* Charles C Thomas, Springfield, Ill, 1967.

31. BRUCE, RA, KUSUMI, F, AND HOSMER, D: *Maximal oxygen intake and nomographic assessment of functional aerobic impairment in cardiovascular disease.* Am Heart J 85:546, 1973.

32. FROELICHER, VF, ET AL: *A comparison of the reproducibility and physiological response to 3 maximal treadmill exercise protocols.* Chest 65:512, 1974.

33. GIVONI, B AND GOLDMAN, RF: *Predicting metabolic energy cost.* J Appl Physiol 30(3):429, 1971.

34. LESTER, FM, ET AL: *The effect of age and athletic training on the maximal heart rate during muscular exercise.* Am Heart J 76:370, 1968.

35. SCANDINAVIAN COMMITTEE ON ELECTROCARDIOGRAM CLASSIFICATION. *The Minnesota code for ECG classification.* Acta Med Scand 183(Suppl 481):3, 1967.

36. GIBBONS, L, ET AL: *The value of maximal versus submaximal treadmill testing.* J Cardiac Rehab 1(5):362–368, 1981.

37. COPPER, KH, ET AL: *Age-fitness adjusted maximal heart rates.* Medicine and Sport 10:78, 1977.

38. BELLET, S AND MULLER, OF: *Electrocardiogram during exercise: Value in diagnosis of angina pectoris.* Circulation 32:477, 1965.

39. ELLESTAD, MH, ET AL: *Maximal treadmill stress testing for cardiovascular evaluation.* Circulation 39:517, 1969.

40. STRANDELL, T: *Circulatory studies on healthy old men, with special reference to the limitations of the maximal physical working capacity.* Acta Med Scand 175(Suppl 414):1, 1964.

41. ARONOW, WS: *Thirty month follow-up of maximal treadmill stress test and double Master's test in normal subjects.* Circulation 47:287, 1973.

42. BLOMQVIST, CG: *Heart disease and dynamic exercise testing.* In WILLERSON, JT AND SANDERS, CA (EDS): *Clinical Cardiology.* Grune & Stratton, New York, 1977, p 218.

43. KASSER, IS AND BRUCE, RA: *Comparative effects of aging and coronary heart disease on submaximal and maximal exercise.* Circulation 39:759, 1969.

44. ERICSSON, M, ET AL: *Arrhythmias and symptoms during treadmill 3 weeks after myocardial infarction in 100 patients.* Br Heart J 35:787, 1973.

45. STYPEREK, J, IBSEN, H, AND KJOLLER, E: *Exercise in ECG in patients with acute myocardial infarction before discharge from the CCU* (Abstr). Am J Cardiol 35:172, 1975.

46. STENBERG, J, ET AL: *Hemodynamic response to work with different muscle groups, sitting and supine.* J Appl Physiol 22:61, 1967.

47. ASMUSSEN, E AND HEMMINGSEN, I: *Determination of maximum working capacity at different ages in work with the legs or with the arms.* Scand J Clin Lab Invest 10(1):67, 1958.

48. SHAW, DJ, ET AL: *Arm-crank ergometry: A new method for the evaluation of coronary artery disease.* Am J Cardiol 33:801, 1974.

49. SCHWADE, J, ET AL: *A comparison of the response to arm and leg work in patients with ischemic heart disease.* Am Heart J 94:203, 1977.

50. DeBUSK, RF, ET AL: *Cardiovascular responses to dynamic and static effort soon after myocardial infarction.* Circulation 58:368, 1978.

51. FRANKLIN, BA, ET AL: *Arm-exercise testing and training.* Practical Cardiology 8(8):43, 1982.

52. NUTTER, DO, SCHLANT, RC, AND HURST, JW: *Isometric exercise and the cardiovascular system.* Mod Concepts Cardiovasc Dis 41:11, 1972.

53. KERBER, RE, MILLER, RA, AND NAJJAR, SM: *Myocardial ischemic effects of isometric dynamic and combined exercise in coronary artery disease.* Chest 67:388–394, 1975.

54. SHELDAHL, LM, ET AL: *Response of patients after myocardial infarction to carrying a graded series of weight loads.* Am J Cardiol 52:698–703, 1983.

55. HECHT, HH: *Concepts of myocardial ischemia.* Arch Intern Med 84:711, 1949.

56. WOOD, P, ET AL: *Effort test in angina pectoris.* Br Heart J 12:363, 1950.

57. LEEVY, RL, BRUEEN, HG, AND RUSSELL, HG: *The use of electrocardiogram changes caused by induced anoxemia as a test for coronary insufficiency.* Am J Med Sci 197:241, 1939.

58. BROCH, OJ: *Calibrated hypoxemia test in normal subjects and coronary patients: Hemodynamics and acid-base equilibrium in hypoxemia of short duration.* Acta Med Scand 191:181, 1972.

59. KATZ, L AND LANDT, H: *Effect of standardized exercise on the four lead electrocardiogram:*

Its value in study of coronary disease. Am J Med Sci 189:346, 1935.

60. ROSKAMM, H: *Comparison between ECG during exercise and ECG during hypoxia in patients with angina pectoris.* Mal Cardiovasc 10:73, 1969.

61. SIMONSON, E: *Electrocardiographic stress tolerance tests.* Prog Cardiovasc Dis 13:269, 1970.

62. PENNEYS, R: *The oximeter-controlled induced anoxemia test: Seventy tests on coronary suspects.* Arch Intern Med 101:747, 1958.

63. MATHERS, JAL AND LEVY, RL: *The prognostic significance of the anoxemia test in coronary heart disease: A follow-up study of 254 patients.* Am Heart J 43:546, 1952.

64. ROBB, GP AND MARKS, HH: *Postexercise electrocardiograms in arteriosclerotic heart disease: Its value in diagnosis and prognosis.* JAMA 200:918, 1967.

65. MATTINGLY, TW: *The postexercise electrocardiogram: Its value in the diagnosis and prognosis of coronary arterial disease.* Am J Cardiol 9:395, 1962.

66. GORLIN, R AND RAYLOR, WJ: *Selective revascularization of the myocardium by internal-mammary-artery implant.* N Engl J Med 275:283, 1966.

67. CHUN, G, ELLESTAD, MH, AND ALLEN, WH: *Isoproterenol infusion test: Effects on systolic time intervals in normal subjects and patients with coronary disease.* Abstracts of Asian Pacific Congress of Cardiology. Singapore, F–5, p 66, Oct 1972.

68. GUBNER, RS: *Newer developments in exercise electrocardiography and evaluation of chest pain.* Trans Assoc Life Ins Med Dir Am 52:125, 1969.

69. SLANY, J, ET AL: *Einfluss von Dipyridamole aug das ventrikulogramm bei koronarer Herzkrankheit.* Z Kardiol 66:389, 1977.

70. TAUCHERT, M, ET AL: *Ein neuer pharmakologischer Test zu diagnose Koronaroinsuffizienz.* Dtsch Med Waschr 101:35, 1976.

71. DEAMBROGGI, L, ET AL: *Assessment of diagnostic value of dipyridamole testing in angina pectoris.* Clin Cardiol 269–274, 1982.

72. DAI HYON, Y AND GLUCKMAN, MI: *The effect of dipyridamole on the metabolism of cardiac muscle.* J Pharmacol Exp Ther 170:37, 1969.

73. HAMILTON, TC: *The effects of some phosphodiesterase inhibitors on the conductance of the perfused vascular beds of the chloralosed cat.* Br J Pharmacol 46:386, 1972.

74. WATERS, DD, ET AL: *Ergonovine testing in a coronary care unit.* Am J Cardiol 46:922, 1980.

75. GINSBURG, R, ET AL: *Histamine provocation of clinical coronary artery spasm: Implications concerning pathogenesis of variant angina pectoris.* Am Heart J 105(5):819–822, 1981.

76. MUDGE, GH, ET AL: *Reflex increase in coronary vascular resistance in patients with ischemic heart disease.* N Engl J Med 295:1333–1337, 1976.

77. ENDO, M, ET AL: *Prinzmetal's variant form of angina pectors: Re-evaluation of mechanisms.* Circulation 52:33–37, 1975.

78. JORDAN, LJ, ET AL: *Exercise versus cold temperature stimulation during radionuclide cineangiography: Diagnostic accuracy in coronary artery disease.* Am J Cardiol 51:1091–1099, 1983.

79. MCNEIL, MS: *Continuous monitoring during stress interviews in coronary patients: Scope of ambulatory monitoring in ischemic heart disease.* Medical Communications and Services Administration, Seattle, Washington, 1977.

80. SPACHIA, H: *Direction of anger during laboratory stress.* Psychosom Med 16:404, 1954.

81. SOUTON, EE, ET AL: *Measurement of the anginal thresholds using atrial pacing: New technique for the study of angina pectoris.* Cardiovasc Res 1:300, 1967.

82. TZIVONI, D, ET AL: *Early right atrial pacing after myocardial infarction. II. Results in 77 patients with predischarge angina pectoris, congestive heart failure, or age older than 70 years.* Am J Cardiol 53:418–420, 1984.

83. YASUE, H: *Circadian variation in response to exercise: An important variable in interpretation of the exercise stress test.* Practical Cardiology 9(12):43–49, 1983.

84. JOY, M, POLLARD, CM, AND NUNAN, TO: *Diurnal variation in exercise responses in angina pectoris.* Br Heart J 48:156–160, 1982.

9

MEMORIAL HOSPITAL PROTOCOL

TIMING
QUESTIONNAIRE AND INFORMED CONSENT
CLOTHING
SKIN PREPARATION FOR ELECTRODES
ELECTRODE POSITIONS AND ATTACHMENTS
EXAMINATION AND EXPLANATION
EXERCISE
HANDRAIL SUPPORT
REASSURANCE
MONITORING
EXERCISE DURATION
TERMINATION OF TEST
RECOVERY PERIOD
RECORD PREPARATION
GENERAL DISCUSSION
SUMMARY

The description of the methodology used in our laboratory can be used as a lesson in "How to do it." For this reason, it will be described in considerable detail.

The protocol has been structured to obtain a maximum amount of information in as short a time as possible.[1] It is used for testing normal subjects who have a sedentary lifestyle, or for the evaluation of cardiac patients. By extending the time and the exercise load, one can evaluate trained athletes. By establishing a standard protocol for almost all patients, we have been able to compare the responses of individuals to their own previous tests and to the tests of other subjects. Although this has been a practical and useful routine, there is nothing absolute about its design. The majority of laboratory staff doing stress testing today, use some type of a graded continuous system, that of Bruce being the most popular. The advantages of using a protocol that has been established will be obvious as we review the procedure.

TIMING

Although it would be best to test each patient, the first thing in the morning before breakfast, the volume of tests makes this impractical. We do tests, therefore, at any time of the day and only suggest that patients eat lightly prior to the test.

QUESTIONNAIRE AND INFORMED CONSENT

When the patient arrives at the laboratory, the patient is asked to read a description of the procedure and then is asked to sign a consent form that includes the statement that the patient has read and understands the description. The subject then fills out a questionnaire that includes statements about previous myocardial infarction, anginal pain, smoking, and exercising (see Appendix 2). It is often necessary for the secretary to help the patient with some of the answers.

CLOTHING

It is important that the subject be lightly clothed. We often dress men and women alike in hospital surgical scrub pants. The men go without a top and a standard hospital gown is placed on the women backward so that it opens in the front. Patients should be advised to bring appropriate footwear, such as tennis or running shoes.

SKIN PREPARATION FOR ELECTRODES

The quality of the recording is highly dependent on good electrode contact. The discovery of this simple fact has had more to do with the good quality of exercise records than all the advances of electronic engineering up to this time. The elimination of the horny layer of the epidermis is the most important

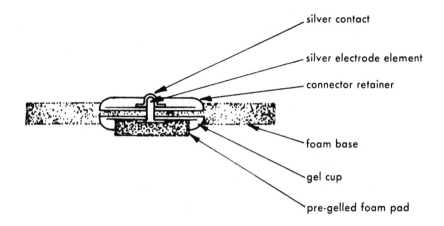

silver contact

silver electrode element

connector retainer

foam base

gel cup

pre-gelled foam pad

FIGURE 9-1. Diagram of disposable electrode used in our laboratory.

factor. This may be, but is not as a rule, accomplished by superficial cleansing and application of electrode paste. By removing the oil with a fat solvent such as acetone and than abrading the skin with a fine file, fine sandpaper, or a dental burr, one can obtain excellent electrode contact with the body fluids. A number of lightweight liquid-contact relatively nonpolarizing silver chloride electrodes are now available. They have a plastic housing and light flexible cable and have improved the quality of tracings immensely. Disposable electrodes are now available from: American Hospital Supply, Medical Measurements Corporation, Johnson & Johnson, NDM (New Dimensions in Medicine), IMI Corporation, Electrodyne, Travenol, Avionics, Beckman, and IBC. We have experimented with a number of these and are presently using the ones from NDM, which are very satisfactory and in the middle price range. They have a plastic ring with a sponge-like middle, prefilled with paste and have a good silver chloride core (Fig. 9-1).

ELECTRODE POSITIONS AND ATTACHMENTS

The 12-lead system with electrodes as demonstrated in Figure 9-2 is attached in the appropriate positions. The plastic adhesive electrodes have self-contained electrode jelly in the cap and need only to be stuck on and attached to the lead wires. A few minutes delay between application and exercise allows for better contact; therefore, less "battery effect" at the skin contact point. This will minimize the baseline wandering.

EXAMINATION AND EXPLANATION

During the time that the technician is applying the electrodes to the chest and

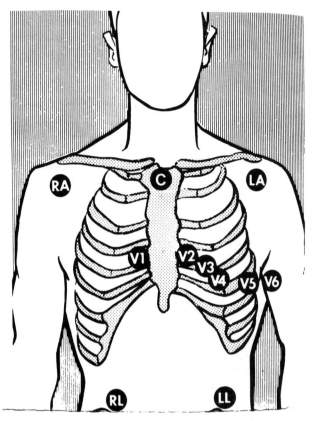

FIGURE 9-2. Lead positions adapted from Mason and Likar with "C" as location for negative electrode for CM_5.

the blood pressure cuff to the arm, the technician is explaining the test and reassuring the patient about the safeguards available. The technician will also demonstrate how to mount the treadmill and the most comfortable gait. The physician then reviews the patient's questionnaire and asks the patient about possible pain patterns, exercise capacity, cardiac history, and reviews the resting ECGs. Careful attention is given to determine what drugs might have been taken and when. The physician then listens to the patient's heart and lungs, especially noting third or fourth heart sounds and murmurs. The blood pressure is recorded when the patient is sitting and standing while simultaneous ECGs are recorded. The patient is asked to hyperventilate for 20 seconds while standing and the electrocardiographic response is noted. The physician explains the protocol, then explains and demonstrates the method for stepping on the treadmill. The physician also discusses the type of pain used for an endpoint for termination if the patient has been subject to angina in the past. The method for terminating the test is also explained and the subject is given the option to terminate if the patient feels unable to continue. The subject then lies on a couch and a baseline cardiokymogram is recorded during breath holding.

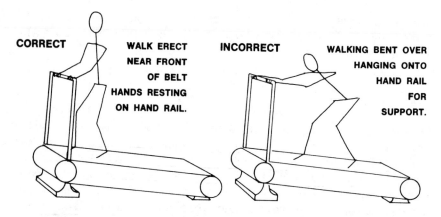

CORRECT WALK ERECT NEAR FRONT OF BELT HANDS RESTING ON HAND RAIL.   **INCORRECT** WALKING BENT OVER HANGING ONTO HAND RAIL FOR SUPPORT.

FIGURE 9-3. Correct and incorrect posture for treadmill walking. It is very important to instruct the patient in the proper technique. The erect posture is all-important.

EXERCISE

The treadmill is elevated to a 10 percent grade and then started at 1.7 mph and the patient is asked to step on. If necessary, the patient is supported by the physician and/or technician during the first few seconds of walking to be certain of the ability to keep up with the moving belt. It is often necessary to advise the patient as to the length of stride, the position of the belt, and postural adjustments to walking up a 10 percent grade (Fig. 9-3). At the end of each minute of exercise, an ECG and blood pressure are recorded. This can be done more accurately if the patient lets the arm hang rather than resting it on the bar or handrail.

HANDRAIL SUPPORT

Many patients who are weak, fearful, or short of breath find it essential to hold tightly to the handrail while walking. If accurate aerobic information is to to obtained, it is mandatory that support from the handrail be prohibited. On the other hand, we feel it is better to get some information than none at all, so we do not insist on the total absence of support. The heart rate and pulse pressure product are good estimates of the magnitude of coronary flow and aerobic capacity as well as the time on the protocol.

REASSURANCE

The physician constantly talks to the patients while they are being tested, reassuring them as to their progress and asking how they feel. When it is time to increase the speed of the treadmill, patients are notified and asked if they think they can go faster for a short time. We think this continuous discussion is particularly important for those who are fearful and especially for those who are being tested for the first time.

MONITORING

The oscilloscope is under constant observation by both the technician and the physician doing the test. At the end of each minute, the blood pressure and ECG are recorded and the heart rate is noted on the worksheet. Premature ventricular contractions (PVCs) or other arrhythmias are noted on the worksheet and reported by the technician to the physician. The technician reminds the physician of the heart rate at the end of each minute. At the end of the third minute, after the blood pressure and ECGs are recorded, the treadmill speed is increased to 3 mph and, thereafter, according to the protocol in Figure 9-4.

If S-T segment depression is noted on the monitor or on the recorder, the patient is frequently questioned as to the presence of pain or tightness in the chest. If must be remembered that the ability or propensity to report discomfort varies a great deal from patient to patient. Patients are asked to grade the intensity of the pain from one to four, with four being the most severe they can remember. Men are less likely to report pain than women.

After the subject is walking or jogging 4 mph or more, it is often very difficult or impossible to obtain the subject's blood pressure. Therefore, the general appearance in terms of skin color, facial expression suggesting anxiety, and the apparent strength and vigor of the patient's walk will give clues as to the adequacy of the circulatory system. The blood pressure tends to increase moderately with exercise until the maximum aerobic capacity is reached (see Chapter 17). After this, if the patient continues to exercise, the blood pressure begins to drop. If this drop is not detected by the technician, the patient may

STAGE	SPEED	GRADE	TIME	METS	TOTAL TIME	VO$_2$ ml/mm/Kg
1	1.7	10%	3	4	3	15
2	3	10%	2	6-7	5	25
3	4	10%	2	8-9	7	35
4	5	10%	2	10-12	9	45
5	5	15%	2	13-15	11	55
6	6	15%	2	16-20	13	65

FIGURE 9-4. The Memorial Hospital maximal treadmill protocol. Over 95 percent of our subjects are unable to progress past the fourth stage. (See Chapter 8, Fig. 8-9 for submaximal treadmill protocol.)

STRESS TESTING: PRINCIPLES AND PRACTICE

faint. Most patients, however, refuse to continue past their peak capacity and voluntarily decide to terminate exercising long before fainting occurs. If the peak heart rate has been reached, it can be predicted that the subject will elect to terminate the exercise within a minute or so unless they are very well conditioned. It has been our practice to suggest that they may stop when this occurs, although we encourage them to continue if they feel like it.

EXERCISE DURATION

A majority of our subjects reach their peak predicted heart rate response or have been terminated for other reasons within 8 to 10 minutes. For selected cases in which the subjects are well-conditioned athletes, we continue as long as necessary at an increased grade of 15 percent and by increasing the speed of the belt 1 mph every two minutes. This usually results in the subject reaching peak heart rate response and maximum capacity within a total exercise time of 12 to 15 minutes.

TERMINATION OF TEST

Although the indications for termination have been discussed in Chapter 6, it seems appropriate to review them here. It is generally agreed by most workers in the field that the test should be terminated when:

1. PVCs develop in pairs or with increasing frequency, or when ventricular tachycardia develops (runs of 3 or more PVCs).
2. Atrial tachycardia or atrial fibrillation supervenes.
3. There is onset of heart block, either second or third degree.
4. Anginal pain is progressive (grade three pain, if grade four is the most severe in patient's experience).
5. S-T segment depression has become severe, that is, 6 to 7 mm or more in vigorous asymptomatic subjects. If the patient is known to have severe coronary disease or angina at low workloads, or if the patient has S-T segment depression at rest, exercise should be terminated with only minor increases in S-T segment depression over the baseline tracing.
6. The heart rate or systolic blood pressure drops progressively with continuing exercise.
7. The patient is unable to continue because of dyspnea, fatigue, or feelings of faintness.
8. Musculoskeletal pain becomes severe, such as might occur with arthritis or claudication.
9. The patient looks vasoconstricted, that is, pale and clammy.
10. Extreme elevations in systolic and diastolic blood pressures associated with a headache or blurred vision occur.

11. The patient has reached or exceeded the predicted maximum pulse rate.

We have found that it takes experience to determine how far to push a sick patient. Our policy is to stop the test if in doubt. It can always be repeated another day. On the other hand, there are times when a few more seconds on the treadmill can result in a more certain diagnosis with no significant increase in risk.

RECOVERY PERIOD

At the instant exercise is discontinued, the electrocardiographic recorder is turned on and left running while the patient is helped to a seat on the couch next to the treadmill. Blood pressure is then recorded and the patient lies down to have the cardiokymogram recorded. The evaluation of the S-T segments and other ECG change sin the first few seconds is often very important. Occasionally, a more stable baseline can be obtained by asking the patient to hold the breath for a few seconds. Blood pressure will often be quite low at the period just after the exercise only to rise temporarily again about one minute later. This drop in blood pressure may be due to the temporary inadequacy in cardiac pumping capacity in relation to metabolic demand, or it may be due to the vasodilation associated with increasing lactic acid concentrations at peak stress. The blood pressure and ECG are then recorded at minute intervals for eight minutes while the patient is supine. Electrocardiographic changes during exercise and recovery are entered on the work sheet.

It is quite common for the electrocardiographic pattern to be equivocal immediately after exercise. If this is so, elevating the patient's legs will increase

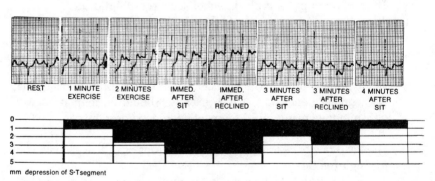

mm depression of S-T segment

FIGURE 9-5. The S-T segment depression recorded in a patient with classical ischemic heart disease subjected to a treadmill stress test. Note the tendency for the S-T segments to flatten when the patient is placed in the horizontal position. After sitting the patient up, the S-T segments began to improve, but become more pathologic when again placed in the horizontal position in the third minute. We believe that the increased venous return in the horizontal position produces a higher left-ventricular end-diastolic pressure and therefore promotes more S-T segment depression.

the venous return at a time when the ventricular compliance is most likely to be reduced. This results is an increased LVEDP and a resultant increase in S-T segment depression (Fig. 9-5).

Late S-T segment depression and T-wave inversion should also be noted as well as the absence or presence of arrhythmias. At the end of the eight-minute observation, if the patient is stable and comfortable, the patient is reassured by the physician doing the test and it is explained that the data will be forwarded to the patient's personal physician.

RECORD PREPARATION

Following termination of the test, the patient's heart rate is compared with the normal for age and the ECGs are marked for mounting. It has been our practice to mount and send out examples of the ECGs demonstrating the important positive or negative findings as well as representative samples at each workload and during selected recovery intervals. The total record is kept on file in the laboratory for review if necessary. The appropriate computer codes designating the phrases to be printed out and the diagnostic implications are entered on the work sheet along with the designations for the electrocardiographic patterns. The diagnostic computer code phrases are designed to represent the overall final diagnostic conclusion. The items listed under abnormalities constitute the events observed that influence the final diagnosis.

Comments are also added if indicated. The work sheet is given to the secretary who enters it on the computer keyboard and sends the print-out for filing with the mounted ECG strips.

GENERAL DISCUSSION

Various parts of the procedure described need special emphasis. It will be remembered that in the chapter on protocol a number of idealized standards were listed and discussed. It was stated that the protocol should provide:

1. Continuous electrocardiographic monitoring.
2. Electrocardiographic recording when desired and preferably several simultaneous leads before, during, and after exercise. A minimum of muscle artifact is essential to good recording.
3. A type of stress that can be performed by the sedentary, poorly developed, and underconditioned subject as well as the trained athlete.
4. A workload that can be varied according to the capacity of the individual but is sufficiently standardized to be reproducible and to allow comparison with other subjects tested.
5. Repeated frequent blood pressure measurements.
6. A way of estimating the aerobic requirements of the individual.
7. Maximum safety and minimum discomfort for each subject.

8. The highest possible specificity, sensitivity, and discrimination between health and disease.
9. A sufficient body of available information so that the response of both patients and normal subjects can be compared with those previously examined.
10. An initial stage of exercise long enough for a warmup to occur.
11. Practicality with respect to the amount of time involved.

Our protocol is designed as a practical approach to day-to-day stress testing. Our experience has led us to believe it has some unique advantages and fulfills most of the above requirements. On the other hand, any well-established protocol can give the same information if the above items are included.

The print-out (Fig. 9-6) contains some calculations that would be impractical if done manually.

1. Aerobic capacity in percent: The inverse of Bruce's aerobic impairment, so that if a subject exceeds the average, aerobic capacity will be greater than 100 percent.
2. Estimated VO_2MAX in milliliters per kilogram per minute, by the formula of Giovoni and Goldman[2] (see Chapter 8).
3. Efficiency index: This value relates to the estimated myocardial oxygen consumption (taken from the double product) to the estimate of VO_2MAX; for example: When a high-exercise level is reached with a low-double product, the patient has a more efficient circulatory system. This index was first proposed by Aptecacs and colleagues[3] in Buenos Aires (see Chapter 8).
4. Treadmill score. Numbers are assigned to each exercise minute and to each minute during recovery, and are multipled by the S-T segment

```
STRESS TEST SUMMARY:  The patient was exercised for a total of  4 minutes
                      achieving  70 percent of predicted maximal pulse rate.

        TREADMILL TEST PROTOCOL..........:  ELLESTAD MAXIMAL
        MAXIMUM VO2 CONSUMPTION..........:  25.06 ML/MIN/KG
        R-WAVE CHANGE....................:  + 0.0 MM
        TEST TERMINATED DUE TO...........:  Chest pain (anginal)


TREADMILL SCORE:     80  - Based on S-T depression values obtained during the
                          exercised and recovery stages of the test.

AEROBIC CAPACITY:    74% - Based on VO2 consumption during the time exercised.

EFFICIENCY INDEX:   121% - Based on VO2 consumption, heart rate, and systolic
                          BP compared with a value of 1.25 for the age group.

MULTIVARIANT ANALYSIS:    Analysis of this patient considering age, ECG at rest,
                          minutes exercised, S-T depression, achieved heart
                          rate, anginal pain, and R-wave changes suggest a
                          PROBABILITY OF SIGNIFICANT CORONARY DISEASE OF  89.1%


ABNORMALITES RECORED:
        History of angina
        Atypical chest pain, probably anginal equivalent
```

FIGURE 9-6. Part of front sheet of computer print-out showing calculations that are useful in patient evaluation. See text.

STRESS TESTING: PRINCIPLES AND PRACTICE

depression in millimeters. High scores will be registered if deep S-T segment depression occurs early or persists long during recovery (see Fig. 9-7).

5. Multivariate analysis. Using a group of variables previously assigned a number designating their ability to separate patients with coronary disease from normals, a probability of disease is calculated. This has been shown to be more reliable than using the S-T change alone (see Chapter 23).

6. Physician's diagnosis. After thoroughly considering all the findings, the cardiologist codes in the cardiologist's best impression. The cardiologist may qualify this with appropriate comments if desired.

7. Heart rate, blood pressures, measured S-T changes, and arrhythmias according to their time on the protocol.

We believe that the use of the above calculated indices gives more information by far than can be obtained from the same test without the computer.[4] The probability statement of disease is the most important. The state of the art no longer allows us to use the term "positive and negative" tests. For example,

PRE-TEST	Minutes	Pulse	BP	S-T Seg Depression	FACTOR	SCORE
Prone						
Sit						
Stand						
Hyp-Vent						

EXERCISE TIME						
1				0	10	
2				0	9	
3				1	8	8
4				1	7	7
5				2	6	12
6				2	5	10
7					4	
8					3	
9					2	
10						

RECOVERY						
Immediate				2	4	8
1				1	5	5
2				0	6	50
3					7	
4					8	
5					9	
6					10	
7						
8						
9						
10						

TOTAL SCORE

FIGURE 9-7. Treadmill Score-The number is derived by adding the magnitude of S-T segment depression at each minute of exercise and recovery after multiplying them by a factor adjusting for the workload and the persistence of S-T depression during the recovery period. The score has helped us to discriminate between patients with mild and severe ischemia.

when the probability of disease is high (95 percent) or low (20 percent), then the diagnosis has a high degree of certainty. If the probability is 47 percent or 54 percent, the certainty of the diagnosis is in doubt. Thus, the reliability of the diagnosis is apparent from the report in contradistinction to previous methodology.

SUMMARY

This protocol has shorter exercise times than most and because of this, allows completion in less than 10 minutes except for highly trained runners. We have found it satisfactory for clinical use as well as research. Our long experience provides data on large populations that allow comparisons that are useful in clinical practice.

REFERENCES

1. ELLESTAD, MH, ET AL: *Maximal treadmill stress testing for cardiovascular evaluation.* Circulation 39:517, 1969.
2. GIOVONI, B AND GOLDMAN, RF: *Predicting metabolic energy cost.* J Appl Physiol 30(3):429–433, 1971.
3. APTECACS, M, VASQUEZ, A, AND MINDLIN DE APTECAR, FR: *The assessment of myocardial efficiency by an exercise testing index.* J Cardiac Rehab 2:271–279, 1982.
4. ELLESTAD, MH AND GREENBERG, PS: *Multivariate approach to the treadmill stress test: Prospective study.* Cardiology 68(2):24–27, 1981.

10

EXERCISE STRESS TESTING AFTER MYOCARDIAL INFARCTION

ADVANTAGES AND BENEFITS
SAFETY AND PATIENT SELECTION
PROTOCOLS
ABNORMAL STRESS TEST RESPONSES
  S-T Segment Depression
  Angina
  Exercise-Induced Ventricular Arrhythmias
  Hemodynamic Responses
  S-T Segment Elevation
RELIABILITY OF ABNORMALITIES
ESTIMATING THE EXTENT OF CORONARY DISEASE
RADIONUCLIDE TECHNIQUES
  Thallium Scintigraphy
  Radionuclide Ventriculography
  Findings Predictive of Events
EXTENDED FOLLOW-UP
SUMMARY

As we improve our approach to the management of patients with an acute myocardial infarction, we must include a re-evaluation of our concepts about the period immediately after discharge from the hospital. If we are to advise our patients on the most appropriate long-term management, we need to find methods of risk stratification.

ADVANTAGES AND BENEFITS

The majority of postinfarction deaths are sudden and occur within the first six months.[1-4] Mortality at one year ranges from 6 to 20 percent and declines thereafter to about 3 to 4 percent a year.[2-5] The occurrence of nonfatal MI follows a similar pattern in which 11 percent of patients reinfarct in the first year and 16 percent in the first two years.[6] Indicies that determine patients at-risk have been identified by reviewing the complications that develop during convalescence. The presence of pulmonary edema or heart failure, renal failure, ventricular arrhythmias, and angina are but a few of the problems imparting a poor prognosis.[1,4,5,7] Most of the indicies identified as prognostically significant relate to residual ischemia, left ventricular dysfunction, and electrical instability.[1,4,8] However, a large number of patients with myocardial infarction have an uncomplicated convalescence.

An MI almost always indicates the presence of coronary artery disease, but does not imply its severity. Patients that are clinically stable, irrespective of the size of infarction, will commonly have severe coronary disease.[9]

However, up to one third of patients with a myocardial infarction may have single-vessel disease and if the tissue at-risk has undergone necrosis, they may remain stable for long periods.[8] At present, the ability of medical and surgical therapies to alter the natural history of asymptomatic postmyocardial patients is not yet clarified. Therefore, routine invasive diagnostic procedures cannot be universally recommended. Nonetheless, in selected patients with two- and three-vessel disease coronary artery bypass probably prolongs survival, especially in left main coronary artery and three-vessel disease.[10] Moreover, medical therapy such as anti-platelet and beta-blocker drugs also appear to reduce mortality.[11]

Attempts to identify high-risk groups noninvasively began to appear about two decades ago. Peel and associates[12] and Norris and colleagues[13] suggested demographic, historical, and clinical factors that might be used, and settled for indices of severe left-ventricular impairment as the most useful. Clinical signs of this impairment included sustained tachycardia, heart failure, a third heart sound, and an enlarged left ventricle on roentgenogram. By 1975, hemodynamic data collected in the coronary care unit were being added.

The use of exercise testing early after infarction was originally believed to be too dangerous and early ambulation and discharge had to be accepted before the idea that deliberate exercise testing within two or three weeks might be safely performed. In 1971, Atterhog and associates[14] reported on 12 patients tested 3 weeks and 18 months after infarction and reported that it was not only safe, but might have prognostic value. This was followed, again in Sweden, by Ericsson and coworkers[15] in 1973 who reported its use in initiating serious arrhythmias that were believed to be a factor in sudden death during the first six months after the event. Soon many reports of both the safety and predictive ability of testing patients from 10 days to 3 weeks after a myocardial infarction appeared.[16,17] Although the risks of doing this type of testing have probably been underreported, at this point, it seems reasonably safe. The post MI stress test then has emerged as providing us with a means of selecting patients at high-risk among those who are asymptomatic and have an uncomplicated convalescence, permitting the implementation of aggressive management that might reduce mortality and morbidity.

Stratification of patients soon after an MI with exercise stress testing offers several other benefits. Patients at low-risk may be spared needless invasive and costly studies. Exercise testing defines the patient's functional cardiac capacity by which activity level and rehabilitation can be rationally prescribed. It provides a safe basis to advise patients regarding return to normal activities and work. Psychologically, the test promotes self-confidence and reassures both patient and physician that routine daily tasks can be performed safely; thereby, avoiding unnecessary restrictions. Even if the convalescent cardiac patient is subject to ischemia or arrhythmias during exercise testing, the patient is best served by exposing these problems under supervision.

SAFETY AND PATIENT SELECTION

A sizable experience with post MI stress testing has been amassed and its safety has been demonstrated. Several thousand predischarge and post MI exercise tests have been reported with only a few serious complications.[11] The major determinate of risk is probably patient selection. Generally, post MI patients with clinical heart failure, recent angina, uncontrolled high-grade ventricular ectopy, unstable ECG, and severe hypertension are excluded from stress testing. These patients are in a high-risk subset of their own with defined morbidity and mortality that may already place them in a category for interventional therapy. The remaining patients that have an uncomplicated hospital course constitute approximately one third to two thirds of survivors.[11] In these patients, the protocol and time after infarction are other factors influencing the risk.

PROTOCOLS

Most early treadmill stress tests performed either at discharge or within two weeks of an MI are terminated with the attainment of a specific heart rate, usually 70 percent of the maximum predicted heart rate for age (normally 120 to 130 beats per minute) or when a workload of 3 to 5 METS (multiples of resting energy expenditure) has been achieved. These modified protocols begin with a low initial workload and are advanced in small increments. Figure 8-9 is an example of such a protocol. Modified heart rate or workload limited tests are referred to as submaximal treadmill stress tests and impose a stress equivalent to that encountered during routine daily activity.[18] Some studies, however, use symptom-limited or sign-limited tests using greater workloads.

These protocols have been generally recommended for patients in the later post MI period, beyond two weeks after infarction. Symptom-limited tests are terminated with the onset of angina, dyspnea, or fatigue regardless of the magnitude of S-T segment depression. Sign-limited protocols are concluded at the onset of significant S-T segment depression, ventricular arrhythmias, or hypotension.

DeBusk and Haskell[19] compared symptom-limited and heart-rate-limited modified treadmill protocols at three weeks after an MI and found both equally safe and effective in provoking ischemic abnormalities and identifying patients at-risk of subsequent coronary events. Higher peak heart rates and workloads were achieved with the symptom-limited protocol, yet the prevalence of ischemic test abnormalities were similar with both protocols with the abnormalities usually occurring at heart rates of 130 beats per minute or less. However, a similar study by Starling and colleagues[20] demonstrated a greater yield with a symptom-limited modified test. At 6 weeks, a standard maximum symptom-limited stress test protocol appears superior to a modified symptom-limited test but at 10 days to 2 weeks, I still believe a low-level modified protocol is more appropriate (See Fig. 8-9).

ABNORMAL STRESS TEST RESPONSES

There has been some confusion regarding the relative importance of the various stress test abnormalities in predicting morbidity and mortality. The low incidence of many cardiac events after an MI, especially death and recurrent infarction, necessitates a highly specific test to perform adequately as an accurate predictor. Most abnormalities with stress testing are of moderate specifity; therefore, only low-risk and high-risk groups can be identified. Despite these problems certain trends and conclusions are be inferred that are clinically useful.

S-T Segment Depression

The development of S-T segment depression with exercise is probably the most reliable sign of myocardial ischemia and appears to be the most useful parameter of prognostic importance. In post MI patients, the incidence reportedly varies from 15 to 40 percent.[16,17,21] Theroux and coworkers[16] found exercise-induced S-T segment depression of 1 mm or greater on a submaximal treadmill protocol was highly predictive of subsequent mortality during a one-year period. This ECG response carried a 27 percent mortality while patients with normal exercise responses had a 2.1 percent mortality, indicating a 13-fold increased risk. Only 30 percent of patients demonstrated significant S-T segment depression, but 91 percent of sudden deaths and 85 percent of all deaths occurred in this group. Neither the occurrence of angina or the magnitude of S-T segment depression influenced mortality. Of note, S-T segment depression was not associated with nonfatal recurrent infarction or the development of angina.

Sami and colleagues[21] similarly noted an eight-fold increased risk of cardiac arrest and recurrent infarction in patients with S-T segment depression of 2 mm or greater on a modified symptom-limited treadmill test. In this study, there was a tendency toward increased risk with greater S-T segment depression. Although the number of patients was small, the risk of a cardiac event doubled between S-T segment depression of 1 to 2 mm and S-T segment depression of 2 mm or greater.

Ischemic S-T segment changes alone or in conjunction with other stress test abnormalities predict a group of patients at risk of subsequent cardiac events such as stable and unstable angina,[22] serious ventricular arrhythmias,[23] heart failure,[24] and coronary artery bypass surgery.[21]

The accuracy of exercise-induced S-T segment depression in providing prognostic information can be influenced by several factors. Early termination of the stress test at a predetermined level of exercise may result in underestimating the incidence of ischemic S-T changes. Resting S-T segment abnormalities, digitalis effect, myocardial hypertrophy, and conduction abnormalities make interpretation of exercise-induced S-T segment changes difficult.

Recent myocardial infarctions may increase the number of false-negative responses with exercise testing. Castellanet and associates[26] found that ischemia after an anterior MI was less apparent than with the same process following an inferior MI. This is because an anterior wall aneurysm appears to mask or alter significant S-T depression in most leads.

Angina

Few studies have investigated exercise-induced angina as an isolated prognostic factor, although it occurs in 5 to 40 percent of patients undergoing post-myocardial infarction exercise testing.[15,21] Although Theroux and coworkers[16] could not demonstrate that angina predicts mortality or morbidity, they found it does correlate with the development of stable angina within one year.

Davidson and DeBusk[25] found angina in the absence of S-T segment depression was not predictive of future medical events except that it was predictive of eventual coronary bypass surgery. Angina reflects the subjective status of patients and provides an incentive to intervene therapeutically.

Exercise-Induced Ventricular Arrhythmias

The prognostic significance of ventricular ectopy provoked by stress testing after an MI is controversial, as it is with routine treadmill stress testing. Complex ventricular arrhythmias detected by ambulatory ECG monitoring during the late hospital phase of an infarction has been reported to adversely affect prognosis.[1,4,27,28] Reports of the incidence of ventricular ectopy with postinfarction exercise tests range from 20 to 60 percent.[16,17,21] Some investigators have found that ventricular ectopy during post MI exercise tests is predictive of mortality.[29,30] Other studies have found it of little prognostic significance for predicting subsequent coronary events, even if high-grade ventricular arrhythmias or a high frequency of premature beats are observed.[19,23,25] Rarely in this population is there a relationship between arrhythmias and S-T segment depression and no datum indicates whether antiarrhythmic medications influence the incidence of exercise-induced ventricular ectopy or alter mortality.

It seems well established, however, that ventricular ectopy associated with left-ventricular dysfunction is more onerous.[30,31] Schultz and coworkers,[30] using Holter monitoring, demonstrated that only patients with an ejection fraction of less than 40 percent and complex ventricular activity had sudden death within six months after an MI. Borer and colleagues[51] noted a relationship between impaired ejection fraction, determined by nuclear studies, and ventricular ectopy frequency and complexity. They found ventricular ectopy provided no more predictive information than ejection fraction alone.

Ambulatory electrocardiographic monitoring is superior to exercise testing in detecting ventricular arrhythmias,[20,32] although there is some evidence that the arrhythmias may have somewhat different mechanisms. Also, exercise testing may demonstrate advanced grades of ventricular ectopy not detected by ambulatory monitoring, and it would appear that both tests may be complimentary.[33] If arrhythmias are of concern, ambulatory ECG monitoring should be performed in addition to stress testing because the prognostic importance of ventricular arrhythmias detected by ambulatory ECGs are well established.

Hemodynamic Responses

Certain hemodynamic responses to predischarge treadmill stress testing are also important. Reduced exercise capacity roughly reflects impaired left ventricular function[34] and may attribute its prognostic value to this association. Performing modified workload-limited stress tests at two weeks post MI on all patients even if significant heart failure was present, Weld and associates[35] found exercise duration provided the most useful variable for predicting mortality. Completing a workload of at least 3 METS implied a favorable prognosis even if S-T segment depression or ventricular arrhythmias occurred. Excluding patients with clinical heart failure, Davidson and DeBusk[25] found a maximum workload of less than 4 METS at three weeks after infarction to be a risk factor for future cardiac events.

Inadequate blood pressure response (defined as an increase of 10 mm or less in systolic blood pressure with a peak systolic pressure of 140 mm or less, or a fall of greater than 20 mm in systolic pressure from peak systolic blood pressure) also appeared predictive of coronary events and seemed to correlate with exercise duration.[22] Additionally, high peak heart rates at low workloads have implied a poor prognosis, presumably indicating an impaired myocardial function and low-stroke volumes. Granath and colleagues[29] and Lundvall and Kaijser,[36] exercising patients on a bicycle ergometer, found heart rates of greater than 125 to 130 beats per minute at workloads of 33 to 50 watts (2.6 to 4 METS) was a significant prognostic factor. Naturally, heart rate and blood pressure responses will be blunted if the patients are on beta-blockers, nitrates, or antihypertensive medications.

S-T Segment Elevation

Exercise-induced S-T segment elevation is common in subjects with post-myocardial infarction stress tests in leads where Q-waves are present.[31,37] It has been correlated with abnormal wall motion in the area of infarction, however, approximately one half of the S-T segment elevations observed initially with predischarge stress tests will be absent on retesting at six weeks, which may reflect improvement of abnormal wall motion with fibrosis and scarring.[10] Most post MI patients with S-T segment elevation on exercise have ventricular aneurysms.[38] It rarely occurs with inferior infarction and the ejection fraction is significantly lower in patients demonstrating S-T segment elevation. Thus, when the S-T segment elevation is noted on post MI stress testing, it may signify segmental or global left-ventricular dysfunction. We have wondered if S-T segment elevation represented peri-infarction ischemia and would identify muscle still at-risk for further damage. Gewirtz and colleagues,[39] using thallium perfusion scans, found that these changes correlate with the size of the scar and with the increase in heart rate during the test. They found no evidence that ischemia was a consistent finding when S-T elevation was present, and furthermore, their patients with the most marked S-T elevation (4 mm) had no ischemia detected by thallium.

RELIABILITY OF ABNORMALITIES

Knowledge of the consistency of post MI exercise test abnormalities is important in assessing the validity of its prognostic value. Different timing in the performance of stress tests with relation to the infarction may alter the ability to provide prognostic information. DeBusk and associates[19,21,23] exercised patients with modified limited treadmill stress tests starting at 3 weeks after infarction and then every 2 weeks until 11 weeks. A stress test at 3 weeks identified most ischemic responses and ventricular arrhythmias compared with tests performed at 11 weeks. However, a single test at 3 weeks did not predict all patients that have cardiac events occurring within a 2-year period. Interestingly, the frequency of exercise-induced ventricular ectopy increased during the period of testing. Patients with normal treadmill tests at 11 weeks identified a group of patients with an excellent prognosis in 2 years. It would appear that most information concerning exercise capacity, ischemic S-T changes, and ventricular arrhythmias can be obtained by 2 tests performed at 3 to 5 weeks and 7 to 11 weeks following an MI.

Starling and coworkers[33] compared modified symptom-limited treadmill tests performed at predischarge (two weeks) and six weeks post MI. The frequency of S-T segment depression was similar on both stress tests results and exhibited a high reproducibility. The frequency of angina, inappropriate blood pressure response, and ventricular arrhythmias for the group were also similar; however, these abnormalities demonstrated limited reproducibility and substantial variation in individual patients. Furthermore, almost one fourth of abnormal predischarge tests were normal at six weeks, and nearly one third of abnormal tests became normal. Also, the patients that had an intervening cardiac event between three and six weeks had abnormal predischarge stress tests.

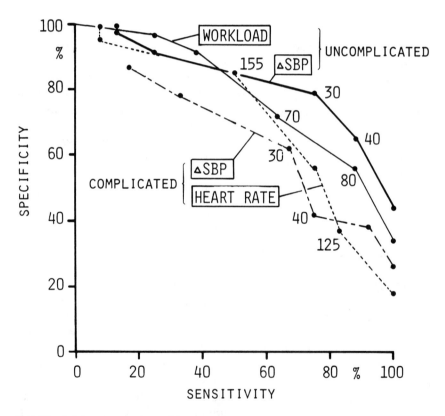

FIGURE 10-1. Sensitivity and specificity in predicting survival of patients according to the findings during exercise testing three weeks after myocardial infarction. (From Deckers, et al[55] with permission.)

STRESS TESTING: PRINCIPLES AND PRACTICE

The disagreement on predictive capacity of various stress test findings was further fueled by the report of Deckers and associates[55] from Rotterdam. They tested patients with a symptom-limited test at three weeks after discharge and found S-T depression to be a poor predictor of events. They followed 403 uncomplicated myocardial infarction patients for 1 year and only found a 4 percent mortality as compared with a 13 percent for those judged complicated or too sick to test. The best predictors of survival in their study were increased in systolic blood pressure of 30 mm over rest and the ability to reach 80 percent of their age predicted maximum workload. The sensitivity and specificity for survival of the above markers is depicted in Figure 10-1.

Therefore, early or predischarge stress tests identify a group of patients at early risk, as well as determine the exercise capacity, ischemic S-T response, and ventricular arrhythmias that aid in predicting long-term prognosis. A second test performed several weeks after an MI is important to further identify patients that had previously normal early stress tests and may still be at-risk for subsequent cardiac events.

ESTIMATING THE EXTENT OF CORONARY DISEASE

Because the severity of coronary artery disease has been demonstrated to be an important determinate of survival[40,41] and because multivessel disease has been demonstrated angiographically in as many as 50 to 75 percent of patients soon after an MI,[8,9,31,37] it would be helpful if testing would predict the severity of disease. In asymptomatic patients with an inferior MI, Miller and associates[8] found the prevalence of proximal left anterior descending disease was 63 percent and left main stenosis has been reported in up to 10 percent.[37,42] Although symptomatic patients appear to have a higher prevalence of multivessel involvement, symptoms or complications are relatively insensitive discriminating factors.[42,43]

It would be desirable if the absence of exercise-induced ischemic ECG responses signified no further coronary disease; therefore, single-vessel disease, and that stress test response reflected ischemia at sites adjacent to or remote from the infarction where viable myocardium is supplied by stenotic vessels; thereby, reflecting multivessel involvement.

Two studies, Fuller and colleagues[44] and Schwartz and associates,[9] found that S-T segment depression of greater or equal to 1 mm, angina or both, correctly identified most patients with multivessel disease. Hemodynamic parameters such as achieved workload or double-product, however, did not assist in predicting patients with multivessel involvement. Both studies found a positive ischemic response was of moderate sensitivity, approximately 55 to 67 percent in detecting multivessel disease and had a high specificity of about 90 percent with a predictive value also near 90 percent. Fuller found 73 percent of negative responses on exercise tests identified single-vessel disease. However, Schwartz found that a negative exercise test could not reliably indicate single-vessel disease because over one half of the patients with negative responses had multivessel disease. Therefore, an abnormal post MI stress test identifies most patients with multivessel disease, but a negative test does not necessarily preclude multivessel involvement.

RADIONUCLIDE TECHNIQUES

Thallium Scintigraphy

Besides predicting the presence of ischemia, it would be helpful to know the location of the stenosed arteries. Abnormal stress test responses cannot distinguish peri-infarction ischemia occurring with one-vessel disease from ischemia remote from infarction due to multivessel disease.[45] In contrast, stress thallium scintigraphy can at times provide noninvasive anatomic localization of abnormal myocardial perfusion created by infarction or induced ischemia and, therefore, provide further important prognostic information.

Gibson and colleagues[46] performed submaximal treadmill tests two weeks post MI and found multiple thallium defects as the best indicator of multivessel disease. Arteries supplying infarcted myocardium had a high rate of detection. However, despite a high specificity of 92 percent, the sensitivity of identifying individual stenosis remote from the infarction was 62 percent, a value similar to that in patients without prior MI.[43,47] The test is a better identifier of left anterior descending stenoses than right coronary or left circumflex artery stenoses. As with the ECG, there is evidence that an anterior MI may diminish the sensitivity of detecting stenosis in other vessels, although evidence is conflicting.

Turner and associates[48] also found reversible thallium defects, when combined with ischemic S-T responses, had a sensitivity of 81 percent at identifying multivessel disease with stenosis greater than 70 percent. This test helps to detect viable myocardium perfused by stenotic vessels, thus providing a physiologic assessment of residual jeopardized myocardium.

Stress thallium scintigraphy is a useful adjunct to exercise ECG testing following infarction. Its use is most evident, as in conventional stress testing, in circumstances when the ECG response cannot be interpreted adequately or is equivocal. Conventional predischarge exercise testing selects with reasonable sensitivity post MI patients having multivessel disease but, if indicated, thallium imaging may provide a noninvasive method of localizing coronary disease and evaluating the extent of jeopardized myocardium.

Radionuclide Ventriculography

A depressed left-ventricular ejection fraction in the post MI period has been shown to impart a poor prognosis.[31,37,49] Sanz and colleagues[49] stratified patients one month post MI by ejection fraction and the number of significantly diseased vessels. Patients with ejection fractions greater than 50 percent, despite three-vessel disease, had an excellent prognosis. As expected, patients with severely impaired ejection fractions, less than 20 percent had a poor prognosis. Those patients with intermediate ejection fractions, between 21 and 49 percent, had a prognosis worse than patients with normal ejection fractions only if associated with three-vessel disease.

One might reason that treating patients falling between these extremes might be the most fruitful. Radionuclide ventriculography provides an accurate noninvasive method of quantitating left-ventricular ejection fraction as commonly used in patients with a complicated convalescence in which an exercise test might prove overly demanding. Thus, this would provide valuable information as to the prognosis and possible suitability for coronary bypass surgery. When exercise ventriculography is used, a decrease in ejection fraction from rest signifies myocardial ischemia. This appears to be a highly sensitive means for detecting coronary disease prior to an MI and is now being investigated (the postinfarction setting). Wasserman and coworkers[50] demonstrated that a fall in the ejection fraction with exercise was the most sensitive in predicting multivessel disease following inferior infarction, but was unable to predict additional disease in those with an anterior wall infarction.

Borer and associates[51] could not demonstrate any prognostic advantage of an abnormal exercise ejection fraction response over an impaired resting ejection fraction. On the other hand, Corbett and colleagues[52] found exercise radionuclide angiography was a better predictor of events in the first six months than either a resting nuclear ventricular function study or an exercise electrocardiogram.

Findings Predictive of Events

1. S-T segment depression.
2. Short-exercise duration.
3. High-heart rate at low workload.
4. Failure to increase blood pressure or fall below control.
5. Complex PVCs with poor left-ventricular function.

EXTENDED FOLLOW-UP

Most of the follow-up data reported are for fairly short periods. Theroux and associates[53] report a five-year follow-up that is of special interest. They found that the usual markers—S-T segment depression, decreasing blood pressure, and short-exercise duration, were excellent predictors for events in the first year, but, thereafter, factors that were markers for decreased ventricular function such as the size of the infarct from the electrocardiogram, the history of

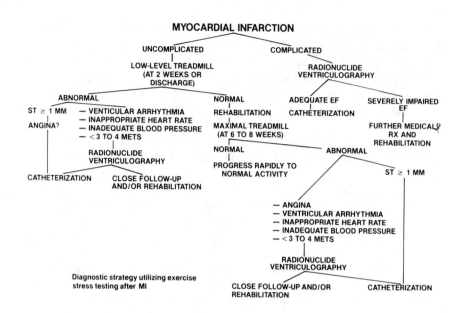

FIGURE 10-2. Strategy. The suggested strategy for management after myocardial infarction presents a plan for categorizing patients into subgroups that are expected to need early intervention or allow rapid return to full function with low risk of future problem.

previous infarctions, and ventricular arrhythmias, were more important. Thus, when making a short-term determination, the decision-making process is different than when the first year is behind us and we are going for the long-haul.

SUMMARY

In conclusion, the diagram in Figure 10-2[54] might provide a strategy for dealing with patients after a myocardial infarction providing Streptokinase, early PTCA, coronary bypass has not been performed. The data are yet to come in on this group so that recommendations made at this time will have no relevance. Although statistical data suggest the clinical approach recommended makes sense at this time, individual patients often present individual problems and our responsibility is to try to do what is best for each person. It is the mark of a good clinician that the clinician not only knows the statistics, but can apply their probabilities to each patient. Many exceptions will occur and our ability to deal effectively with each complex situation will be the true test of our medal.

REFERENCES

1. Moss, AJ, ET AL: *The early posthospital phase of myocardial infarction: Prognostic stratification.* Circulation 54:58–64, 1976.

2. WEINBLATT, E, ET AL: *Prognosis of men after first myocardial infarction: Mortality and first recurrence in relation to selected parameters.* Am J of Public Health 58:1329–1347, 1968.

3. Moss, AJ, DeCamilla, J, and Davis, H: *Cardiac death in the first 6 months after myocardial infarction: Potential for mortality reduction in the early posthospital period.* Am J Cardiol 39:616–620, 1977.

4. BIGGER, JT, ET AL: *Risk stratification after acute myocardial infarction.* Am J Cardiol 42:202–210, 1978.

5. KANNEL, WB, SORLIE, P, AND McNAMARA, PM: *Prognosis after initial myocardial infarction: The Framingham Study.* Am J Cardiol 44:53–59, 1979.

6. VERDIN, A, ET AL: *Death and non-fatal reinfarctions during two years followup after myocardial infarction: A follow-up study of 440 men and women discharged alive from hospital.* Acta Med Scand 198:353–364, 1975.

7. DAVIS, HT, ET AL: *Survivorship patterns in the posthospital phase of myocardial infarction.* Circulation 60:1252–1258, 1979.

8. MILLER, RR, ET AL: *Chronic stable inferior myocardial infarction: Unsuspected harbinger of high-risk proximal left coronary arterial obstruction amenable to surgical revascularization.* Am J Cardiol 39:954–960, 1976.

9. SCHWARTZ, KM, ET AL: *Limited exercise testing soon after myocardial infarction: Correlation with early coronary and left ventricular angiography.* Ann Intern Med 94:727–734, 1981.

10. RAHIMTOOLA, SH: *Coronary bypass surgery for chronic angina—1981: A perspective.* Circulation 65:225–241, 1982.

11. MILLER, DH AND BORER, JS: *Exercise testing early after myocardial infarction: Risks and benefits.* Am J Med 72:427–438, 1982.

12. PEEL, AAF, ET AL: *A coronary prognostic index for grading the severity of infarction.* Br Heart J 745:760, 1962.

13. NORRIS, RM, ET AL: *A new coronary prognostic index* ' ancet Feb: 274–278, 1969.

14. ATTERHOG, JH, EKELUND, LG, AND KAIJSER, L: *Electrocar* graphic abnormalities during exercise 3 weeks to 18 months after anterior myocardi; farction. Br Heart J 33:871–877, 1971.

15. ERICSSON, M, ET AL: *Arrhythmias and symptoms during treadmill testing three weeks after myocardial infarction in 100 patients.* Br Heart J 35:787–790, 1973.

16. THEROUX, P, ET AL: *Prognostic value of exercise testing soon after myocardial infarction.* N Engl J Med 301:341–345, 1979.

17. SMITH, JW, ET AL: *Exercise testing three weeks after myocardial infarction.* Chest 75:12–16, 1979.

18. ELLESTAD, MH, COOKE, BM, AND GREENBERG, PS: *Stress testing: Clinical application and predictive capacity.* Prog Cardiovasc Dis 21:431–460, 1979.

19. DeBusk, RF AND HASKELL, W: *Symptom-limited vs. heart rate limited exercise testing soon after myocardial infarction.* Circulation 61:738–743, 1980.

20. STARLING, MR, CRAWFORD, MH, AND O'ROURKE, RA: *Superiority of selected treadmill exercise protocols predischarge and six weeks post-infarction for detecting ischemic abnormalities.* Am Heart J 104:1054–1059, 1982.

21. SAMI, M, KRAEMER, H, AND DeBusk, RF: *The prognostic significance of serial exercise testing after myocardial infarction.* Circulation 60:1238–1246, 1979.

22. STARLING, MR, ET AL: *Exercise testing early after myocardial infarction: Predictive value for subsequent unstable angina and death.* Am J Cardiol 46:909–914, 1980.

23. MARKIEWIEZ, W, HOUSTON, N, AND DeBusk, RF: *Exercise testing soon after myocardial infarction.* Circulation 56:26–31, 1977.

24. KOPPES, GM, ET AL: *Response to exercise early after uncomplicated acute myocardial infarction in patients receiving no medication: Long term follow-up.* Am J Cardiol 46:764–769, 1980.

25. DAVIDSON, DM AND DEBUSK, RF: *Prognostic value of a single exercise test 3 weeks after uncomplicated myocardial infarction.* Circulation 61:236–242, 1980.

26. CASTELLANET, M, GREENBERG, PS, AND ELLESTAD, MH: *Comparison of ST segment changes on exercise testing of angiographic findings in patients with prior myocardial infarction.* Am J Cardiol 42:24–35, 1978.

27. MOSS, AJ, ET AL: *Ventricular ectopic beats and their relation to sudden and non-sudden cardiac death after myocardial infarction.* Circulation 60:998–1003, 1979.

28. BIGGER, T, WELD, FM, AND ROLNITZKY, LM: *Prevalence, characteristics and significance of ventricular tachycardia (three or more complexes) detected with ambulatory electrocardiographic recording in the late hospital phase of acute myocardial infarction.* Am J Cardiol 48:815–823, 1981.

29. GRANATH, A, ET AL: *Early workload tests for evaluation of long term prognosis of acute myocardial infarction.* Br Heart J 39:758–763, 1977.

30. SCHULTZ, RA, STRAUSS, HW, AND PITT, B: *Sudden death in the year following myocardial infarction: Relation to ventricular premature contractions in the late hospital phase and left ventricular ejection fraction.* Am J Med 62:192–199, 1977.

31. DEFEYTER, PJ, ET AL: *Prognostic value of exercise testing coronary angiography and left ventriculography 6-8 weeks after myocardial infarction.* Circulation 66:527–536, 1982.

32. WEINER, DA, ET AL: *S-T segment changes post-infarction: Predictive value for multivessel coronary disease and left ventricular aneurysm.* Circulation 58:887–891, 1978.

33. STARLING, MR, ET AL: *Treadmill exercise tests predischarge and six weeks post-myocardial infarction to detect abnormalities of known prognostic value.* Ann Intern Med 94:721–727, 1981.

34. PAINE, TD, ET AL: *Relation of graded exercise test findings after myocardial infarction to extent of coronary artery disease and left ventricular dysfunction.* Am J Cardiol 42:716–723, 1978.

35. WELD, FM, ET AL: *Risk stratification with low-level exercise testing 2 weeks after acute myocardial infarction.* Circulation 64:306–314, 1981.

36. LUNDVALL, K AND KAIJSER, L: *Early exercise tests after uncomplicated acute myocardial infarction before early discharge from hospital.* Acta Med Scand 210:257–261, 1981.

37. TAYLOR, GJ, ET AL: *Predictors of clinical course, coronary anatome and left ventricular function after recovery from acute myocardial infarction.* Circulation 62:960–970, 1980.

38. MANVI, KN AND ELLESTAD, MH: *Elevated ST segments with exercise in ventricular aneurysm.* J of Electrocardio 5:317, 1972.

39. GEWIRTZ, H, ET AL: *Role of myocardial ischemia in the genesis of stress-induced ST segment elevation in previous anterior myocardial infarction.* Am J Cardiol 51:1289–1293, 1983.

40. HUMPHRIES, JO, ET AL: *Natural history of ischemic heart disease in relation to arteriographic findings: A twelve year study of 224 patients.* Circulation 49:489–497, 1974.

41. REEVES, TJ, ET AL: *Natural history of angina pectoris.* Am J Cardiol 33:423–430, 1974.

42. TURNER, JD, ET AL: *Coronary angiography soon after myocardial infarction.* Chest 77:58–64, 1980.

43. RIGO, P, ET AL: *Value and limitations of segmental analysis of stress thallium myocardial imaging for location of coronary artery lesion.* Circulation 61:973–981, 1980.

44. FULLER, CM, ET AL: *Early post-myocardial infarction treadmill stress testing: An accurate predictor of multivessel coronary disease and subsequent cardiac events.* Ann Intern Med 94:734–739, 1981.

45. KAPLAN, MA, ET AL: *Inability of the submaximal treadmill test to predict the location of coronary disease.* Circulation 47:250–256, 1973.

46. GIBSON, RS, ET AL: *Predicting the extent and location of coronary artery disease during the early post infarction period by quantitative thallium-201 scintigraphy.* Am J Cardiol 50:1272–1278, 1982.

47. MASSIE, BM, BOTVINICK, EH, AND BRUNDAGE, BH: *Correlation of thallium 201 scintigrams with coronary anatomy: Factors affecting region by region sensitivity.* Am J Cardiol 44:616–622, 1979.

48. TURNER, JD, ET AL: *Detection of residual jeopardized myocardial 3 weeks after myocardial infarction by exercise testing with thallium-201 myocardial scintigraphy.* Circulation 61:729–737, 1980.

49. SANZ, G, ET AL: *Determinants of prognosis in survivors of myocardial infarction: A prospective clinical angiographic study.* N Engl J Med 306:1065–1070, 1982.

50. WASSERMAN, AG, ET AL: *Non-invasive detection of multivessel disease after myocardial infarction by exercise radionuclide ventriculography.* Am J Cardiol 50:1242–1247, 1982.

51. BORER, JS, ET AL: *Sensitivity, specificity, and predictive accuracy of radionuclide cineangiography during exercise in patients with coronary artery disease: Comparison with exercise electrocardiography.* Circulation 60:572–580, 1979.

52. CORBETT, JR, ET AL: *The prognostic value of submaximal exercise testing with radionuclide ventriculography before hospital discharge in patients with recent myocardial infarction.* Circulation 64:535–544, 1981.

53. THEROUX, P, ET AL: *Exercise testing in the early period after myocardial infarction in the evaluation of prognosis.* Cardiology Clinics 2(1):71–77, 1984.

54. BARON, DB, LICHT, JR, AND ELLESTAD, MH: *Status of exercise testing after myocardial infarction.* Arch Intern Med 144:595–601, 1984.

55. DECKERS, JW, ET AL: *Bayesian analysis of exercise test after myocardial infarction* (abstr). JACC 5(2):563, 1985.

11

STRESS TESTING
AFTER SURGICAL INTERVENTION
AND CORONARY ANGIOPLASTY

Most patients, prior to undergoing coronary bypass surgery, have a major decrease in function, especially during exercise, and the aim of surgery is to improve their performances. The expected improvement as measured by stress testing includes an increase in aerobic capacity, ability to exercise without undue dyspnea and without significant chest pain or discomfort. Because it is common for most cardiac patients to be asymptomatic at rest, a test of functional capacity before and after a treatment is important in evaluating the benefit derived from the intervention.

Stress testing has become established as one of the most useful ways to measure the response and to evaluate progress or the lack of it immediately after the procedure and in the ensuing years. It has been used in valvular surgery, coronary bypass surgery, and recently in angioplasty. It is often used to measure changes expected from medical therapy as well.

QUESTIONS

Questions we would like to answer in the evaluation of bypass patients are as follows:

1. Can we predict the postoperative result from the preoperative stress test?
2. Does postoperative S-T depression depict graft closure or residual or new myocardial ischemia? Is it as reliable as the preoperative stress test?
3. Does comparison of the preoperative and postoperative exercise tests have more value in assessing graft patency than the postoperative test alone?
4. Does angina or its lack during stress testing postoperatively predict the presence or absence of myocardial ischemia?
5. Does the postoperative exercise tolerance correlate with ischemia or graft patency?
6. Does serial postoperative testing aid in patient evaluation and follow-up?

CORONARY ARTERY BYPASS SURGERY

Prediction of Postoperative Results
From Preoperative Stress Testing

We conducted a study of 387 postoperative patients, 196 of whom had completed preoperative and postoperative exercise tests.[1] We compared age, sex, workload at onset of ischemia, and the presence of anginal pain during testing and found none of these helped to discriminate between those who would have a good or a poor result, thus it appeared that it failed as an adjunct in determining the need for surgery. We had believed angina manifested on the preoperative treadmill would be a predictor for both ultimate survival and relief of ischemia. This was because we knew generalized scarring of the myocardium, which is more common in coronary patients without angina, should carry a poor prognosis while exercise pain signaling a viable myocardium should predict a better result after bypass. We found no evidence to confirm this hypothesis in our data.

On the other hand, Weiner and colleagues[2] when analyzing the nonrandomized patients in the CASS Registry found those with a high-risk exercise test (S-T depression greater than 1 mm and a short exercise time—Bruce First Stage only) had better survival if operated than treated medically. Those reaching Bruce Stage IV, irrespective of the S-T changes, also did better with surgery than those with limited exercise capacity. The CASS group[3] also found that those who had angina during the preoperative exercise test did better when treated surgically than medically (5-year survival of 94 percent for surgery versus 87 percent for medical therapy). It is also well known that the high crossover from medical to surgical treatment (23 percent) in the CASS study favors good results in the medical cohort; so that if these patients were counted as poor results, the data would force surgery even more.

The so-called high-risk treadmill patients also had an improved quality of life, characterized by less angina and a longer exercise time if they had bypass surgery. This also fits with the findings of the European Coronary Surgery Randomized Trial.[4]

Thus, when comparing operated versus nonoperated patients, our original thesis was confirmed, that is, the exercise test is useful in deciding who should have surgery.

Prediction of Ischemia and Postoperative Testing

Does postoperative S-T depression predict graft closure or residual or new ischemia? Is it as reliable as the preoperative treadmill stress test?

Several studies[5-9] found complete disappearance of S-T depression was usually associated with complete revascularization. However, Siegel and associates[9] reported that 30 percent of their patients with complete revascularization continued to have S-T depression after surgery. When part of the bypass grafts are open and some are closed, there is also a high likelihood of a normal S-T response. Although the postoperative S-T response is helpful, a significant number of those with all grafts closed will have normal S-T segments.[10] Our experience has been similar to Siegel and coworkers[9] in that some patients with open grafts will continue to have S-T depression. Although it is somewhat difficult to document, postoperative S-T segment depression is probably not as reliable as preoperative in predicting the presence or absence of ischemia. Assad-Morrel[8] reported an excellent correlation between graft patency postoperatively and exercise-induced S-T depression. When all grafts were patent, only 9 percent had S-T depression and none of their patients with total failure to be revascularized had normal S-T segments. However, no other study has been reported where the exercise test provides quite as good discrimination (Table 11-1).

Preoperative and Postoperative S-T Segment Depression

When preoperative and postoperative S-T segments are compared, most investigators report that the conversion from abnormal to normal is associated with a high likelihood of total revascularization. Hartman and associates[10] reported this in 88 percent. They also found that in those with improved coronary flow, but less than total revascularization, S-T depression disappeared in 79 percent and even in those who were shown to be unimproved by angiography, 50 percent lost their S-T depression postoperatively.

From the data available, it appears that when an abnormal S-T pattern converts to normal, there is a high probability of total revascularization.[5,11] On the

TABLE 11-1. Postoperative treadmill exercise response by number of vessels left ungrafted (VLU)

	No VLU	One VLU	Two VLU	Three VLU
Total patients (no.)	23	33	24	5
Treadmill exercise response:				
Positive	2 (9%)	23 (70%)	23 (96%)	5 (100%)
Negative	21 (91%)	10 (30%)	1 (4%)	0 (0%)
Patients by vessels				
diseased (no.):	10	2	0	0
One vessel	11	18	7	0
Two vessels	2	13	17	5
Three vessels	38	56	46	9
Total grafts*				
Grafts patent:	38	42	23	0
No.	100	75	50	0
%				

*Total number of grafts in group.
(From Assad-Morell et al.,[8] with permission.)

other hand, a significant number of patients with total revascularization will continue to have S-T depression and there will also be some with failed grafts who have a normal S-T response.[12]

Diagnostic Value of Angina

The diagnostic value of angina during postoperative testing has been studied by a number of authors.[5,7,9] Almost all patients with complete revascularization are free of exercise-induced angina; in fact, over 90 percent of those who have had bypass surgery lose their angina. The loss of angina, however, is a weak predictor for graft patency. Seventy-nine percent of patients with at least one patent graft in the early postoperative period fail to have angina and Hartman and colleagues[10] found that 50 percent of those without any revascularization became free of angina. It is important to remember that 38 percent of patients either lost or had marked improvement in their angina after the now discarded Vineberg Procedure,[13] which may have improved collateral flow a little, but was, by no means, a complete revascularization.

Postoperative Exercise Performance

It is known that exercise performance can be very bad in patients with normal function and quite good in those with severely compromised cardiac output.[14] Therefore, it is not too surprising that total exercise time, maximum achieved heart rate, and maximum achieved double product have not been shown to have much validity in predicting the degree of revascularization.[15,16] Although most patients with good anatomic results improve their exercise capacity after surgery, as an individual predictor it fails to stand up. This may be because the loss of pain—so common in those even with failed revascularization, determines the exercise end-point in many cases. We know that in the absence of angina, patients will often exercise longer, often reaching an increased double product. Therefore, there is fairly good correlation between the loss of induced angina and increased function capacity. The paper by Block and coworkers[17] demonstrates this concept. They studied 23 patients following unsuccessful revascularization and reported a statistically significant improvement in maximum heart rate and lesser improvement in functional aerobic impairment, absolute duration of exercise and pressure-rate product (Fig. 11-1).

The reverse is important, however. When patients fail to have pain relief after coronary bypass surgery, they almost invariably have a significant amount of unbypassed myocardium,[9] unless they have vasospastic angina. Although there is still inadequate confirmation by other authors, we believe the double product at the onset of ischemic S-T depression is the most reliable stress testing measure of a change in the degree of ischemia over time, or due to an intervention. We found this index to be improved in 61 percent of our patients after coronary bypass surgery.[2]

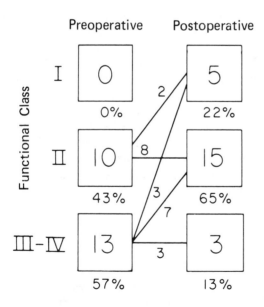

FIGURE 11-1. Changes in functional class in 23 patients after unsuccessful revascularization. Note the improvement in spite of the lack of functioning grafts. (From Block, et al.,[17] with permission.)

Serial Postoperative Exercise Testing

Although in clinical practice it is common to use the exercise test in following and re-evaluating postoperative coronary bypass patients, there is not much documentation of its usefulness. Guttin's group[18] in Houston found 20 percent of those who were negative after coronary bypass surgery converted to an abnormal test in 23 months. Many of these had progression of disease or graft failure. In our experience, the onset of S-T depression at a lower workload or lower double product has usually led us to the discovery of progressive ischemia.

ANGIOPLASTY

It would be suspected that the concepts presented in postoperative coronary bypass patients might hold for angioplasty. Insufficient time and experience make it difficult to determine if this is so. Because at this time, the majority of patients undergoing coronary angioplasty have single-vessel disease, one might suspect some variations in findings compared with CAB patients. Marco and colleagues[19] from Toulouse, followed 62 patients with successful angioplasty and found that exercise testing within 2 days of the procedure reliably predicted the 32 percent who developed restenosis. In our experience, anginal pain is a reliable predictor of re-stenosis or progression of disease in another vessel in angioplasty patients. Also, postangioplasty resolution of S-T depression has been a reliable indicator of a successful result. Meier and associates[20] at Atlanta used bicycle ergometry on those with successful angioplasty and found their work capacity increased from 72 watts to 122. Rosing and colleagues[21] reported on 66 patients from the National Heart, Lung, and Blood Institute Registry that had undergone successful angioplasty. They found only 33 percent had S-T depression prior to the procedure and 7 percent of these were abnormal afterward. If angina was used as an indicator of abnormality, 68 percent were abnormal before and 7 percent afterward. The low sensitivity of S-T depression in this group probably reflects the original restrictions of this procedure to single-vessel disease. It is of interest that those patients who had an abnormal thallium test after the procedure had a higher probability of re-stenosis.

DISCUSSION AND SUMMARY

The reason S-T depression may be absent in patients with failed bypass surgery remains obscure. Fibrosis or injury of the subendocardium, the origin of the S-T changes, may be a cause.

Until recently, we had no clear explanation why some patients with angiographic evidence of total revascularization continue to have S-T depression in the postoperative period. The recent measurement of coronary flow as generated by digital angiography by Bates and coworkers[22]may give us an explanation. They found that the reactive hyperemia associated with contrast media increased velocity in normal coronaries about 1.8 times normal. This reactive increase is reduced depending on the severity of the coronary lesion. When they studied normal appearing bypass grafts, the increased flow was about half that seen in normal vessels. It may be that even though the graft is patent, the rigid tube almost universally found after a year or so, cannot deliver the magnitude of flow increase necessary to supply myocardial needs during exercise.

The work of Riberio and colleagues[23] in Selwyn's laboratory in London is of special interest. They found some patients with bypass surgery who had open grafts, yet had ischemia documented by Holter Monitor, exercise testing, and positron tomography using rubidium-82. Their work supports that of Bates and associates[22] in that ischemia can be present in areas of the myocardium, which one would expect to be adequately perfused when viewing the angiogram. Mechanisms responsible for this still need further study.

Even though the exercise test has limitations in the postoperative patient, it can be very useful. The aerobic capacity, blood pressure, and heart rate response, initiation of arrhythmias, and other findings are probably as valuable as the detection of S-T segment depression when considered as a whole and with knowledge of the patient's previous performance.

ANSWERS

1. The preoperative exercise test can help predict those who will do better with surgery. The best predictor is a short exercise time.
2. Reversion of postoperative S-T segments to normal usually indicate complete revascularization, but there are many exceptions to this. It almost always indicates improved perfusion.
3. It would appear that postoperative testing can be interpreted with much more reliability when the preoperative test is available.
4. Anginal relief occurs with improvement of perfusion in almost every case, but may also occur in patients with little or no change in myocardial blood flow.
5. Exercise tolerance, postoperatively. There is poor correlation between postoperative exercise tolerance and graft patency. If strength and conditioning can be taken into account, it may be a weak predictor of changing patterns of perfusion. The double product at onset of S-T depression provides a more objective assessment of myocardial blood flow.
6. Serial postoperative testing. Changes in onset of S-T depression and the work level at onset of angina are useful markers for progression of disease. Postoperative testing is a useful and practical approach to patient evaluation and should be used as an aid in following coronary bypass patients.

REFERENCES

1. STUART. RJ AND ELLESTAD, MH: *The value of exercise stress testing in predictive benefits from aorto-coronary bypass surgery.* Angiology 30:416, 1979.

2. WEINER, DA, ET AL: *Value of exercise testing in identifying patients with improved survival after coronary bypass surgery* (abstr). Circulation II 70:771, 1984.

3. RYAN, TJ, ET AL: *The role of exercise testing in the randomized cohort of CASS* (abstr). Circulation II 70:78, 1984.

4. EUROPEAN CORONARY STUDY GROUP: *Long-term results of prospective randomized study of coronary artery bypass surgery in stable angina pectoris.* Lancet Oct-Dec:1173, 1982.

5. MCCONAHAY, DR, ET AL: *Accuracy of treadmill testing in assessment of direct myocardial revascularization.* Circulation 56(4):548–552, 1977.

6. KNOEBEL, SB, ET AL: *The effect of aortocoronary bypass grafts on myocardial blood flow reserve and treadmill exercise tolerance.* Circulation 50:685–693, 1974.

7. BODE, RF, JR AND ZAJTCHUK, R: *Evaluation of saphenous vein bypass surgery with multistage treadmill test and ventricular function studies.* J Thor Cardiovasc Surg 74(1):44–46, 1977.

8. ASSAD-MORELL, JL, ET AL: *Aorto-coronary artery saphenous vein bypass surgery, clinical and angiographic results.* Mayo Clinic Proc 50:379, 1975.

9. SIEGEL, W, ET AL: *The spectrum of exercise test and angiographic correlations in myocardial revascularization surgery.* Circulation (Suppl I):51–52, 156–162, 1975.

10. HARTMAN, CW, ET AL: *Aortocoronary bypass surgery: Correlation of angiographic, symptomatic and functional improvement at 1 year.* Am J Cardiol 37:352–357, 1976.

11. GLASSER, SP AND CLARK, PI: *The Clinical Approach to Exercise Testing.* Harper & Row, New York, 1980.

12. DODEK, A, KASSEBAUM, DG, AND GRISWOLD, HE: *Stress electrocardiography in the evaluation of aortocoronary bypass surgery.* Am Heart J 86(3):292–307, 1973.

13. KASSEBAUM, DG, JUDKINS, MP, AND GRISWOLD, HE: *Stress electrocardiography in the evaluation of surgical revascularization of the heart.* Circulation 40:297, 1969.

14. BLOCK, T, ENGLISH, M, AND MURRAY, JK: *Changes in exercise performance following unsuccessful coronary bypass grafting* (abstr). Am J Cardiol 37:122, 1976.

15. LAPIN, ES, ET AL: *Changes in maximal exercise performance in the evaluation of saphenous vein bypass surgery.* Circulation XLVII:1164–1173, 1973.

16. MERRILL, AJ, JR, ET AL: *Value of maximal exercise testing in assessment of results.* Circulation (Suppl I):51–52, 173–177, 1975.

17. BLOCK, TA, MURRAY, JA, AND ENGLISH, MT: *Improvement in exercise performance after unsuccessful myocardial revascularization.* Am J Cardiol 40:673, 1977.

18. GUTTIN, J, ET AL: *Longitudinal evaluation of patients after coronary artery bypass by serial treadmill testing* (abstr). Am J Cardiol 35:142, 1975.

19. MARCO, J, ET AL: *Two years and more follow-up after successful percutaneous transluminal coronary angioplasty* (abstr). Eur Heart J 5(Suppl 1):76, 1984.

20. MEIER, B, ET AL: *Long-term exercise performance after percutaneous transluminal coronary angioplasty and coronary artery bypass grafting.* Circulation 68(4):796–802, 1983.

21. ROSING, DR, ET AL: *Exercise, electrocardiographic and functional responses after percutaneous transluminal coronary angioplasty.* Am J Cardiol 53:36C–41C, 1984.

22. BATES, ER, ET AL: *The chronic coronary flow reserve provided by saphenous vein bypass grafts as determined by digital coronary radiography.* Am Heart J 106(3–1):462–468, 1984.

23. RIBEIRO, P, ET AL: *Different mechanisms for the relief of angina after coronary bypass surgery.* Br Heart J 52:502–509, 1984.

12

ECG PATTERNS
AND THEIR SIGNIFICANCE

ROUNDED S-T SEGMENT DEPRESSION

S-T SEGMENT ELEVATION WITH EXERCISE

S-T SEGMENT ELEVATION AT REST NORMALIZED BY EXERCISE
(EARLY REPOLARIZATION)

Q-T INTERVALS

Q PEAK T (QPT) WAVE INTERVALS

QT/QX RATIO

SEPTAL Q-WAVES

SEVERE HYPERTROPHY PATTERNS

TALL T-WAVES

FLATTENED OR INVERTED T-WAVES

NORMALIZATION OF T-WAVES WITH EXERCISE

THE U-WAVE

HYPERVENTILATION AND ORTHOSTATIC CHANGES

CONCLUSION

Although computers are now being used more and more to evaluate the electrocardiographic changes associated with exercise,[1,2] it is still essential to carefully scrutinize the electrocardiogram visually. Careful personal inspection of tracings from appropriate lead systems, using properly applied electrodes and recording systems with a good frequency response, can usually result in accurate evaluation of changes now known to be clinically significant.

THE NORMAL EXERCISE ELECTROCARDIOGRAM

As the heart rate increases with exercise, a number of predictable changes occur in a normal electrocardiographic tracing. The P-R interval is definitely shortened after one minute of exercise.[3] The P-wave becomes taller[4] and the Ta-wave (wave of repolarization) increases, resulting in a downward displacement of the P-Q junction. This is particularly important because the so-called baseline, for terms of evaluating S-T segment change, is below that usually considered to be isoelectric in the resting tracing (Fig. 12-1). With exercise, the Ta-wave tends to extend through the QRS and may influence the junction between the S-T segment and the T-wave. Lepeschkin[5] believed that this alteration in baseline extends also well into the S-T segment and may cause fictitious S-T segment depression (Fig. 12-2).

It has been our practice to use the line marked 2 on Figure 12-2 or the P-Q or P-R junction, indicated in Figure 12-1, as a marker for the baseline rather than line 3 (Fig. 12-2). A discussion of this point with Bruce and associates[6] confirmed our position. The excellent computer analysis of this problem, done in the laboratory of Bruce and colleagues,[7] has been followed by the study of Blomqvist[8] indicating the appearance of progressive depression of the junction, and when the S-T segment is measured at one fourth the distance be-

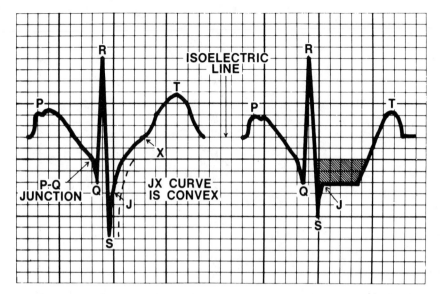

FIGURE 12-1. *Left,* the normal exercise electrocardiographic complex. It can be noted that the P-Q segment is deflected below the isoelectric line. This point is considered to be a baseline for determining S-T segment abnormalities. *Right,* a horizontal S-T segment depression of 2.0 mm as measured from the P-Q segment.

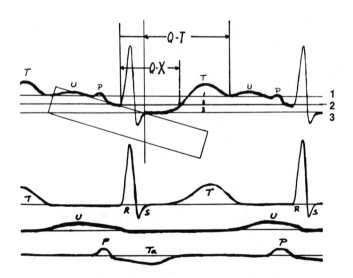

FIGURE 12-2. Deviation of S-T segments associated with exercise. It was Lepeschkin's premise that the repolarization wave of the U-wave and the repolarization wave of the P-wave combined to depress the S-T segment to the line marked 3 in the illustration. For practical purposes, most workers in the field use the line marked 2 as the point of measurement for the evaluation of S-T segment depression. (From Lepeschkin,[5] with permission.)

ECG PATTERNS AND THEIR SIGNIFICANCE 225

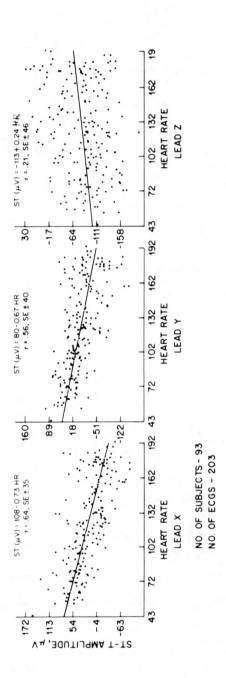

FIGURE 12-3. S-T segment depression or elevation in millivolts according to heart rate in a group of normal men tested by Blomqvist. Note the wide scatter in lead Z. (From Blomqvist,[8] with permission.)

STRESS TESTING: PRINCIPLES AND PRACTICE

tween the QRS and peak T in left to right leads, considerable depression is usually seen. The anterior posterior lead changes (V_1 to V_2) are less prominent than those in the lateral and vertical leads.

Figures 12-3 and 12-4 illustrate the findings in the orthogonal leads at the various heart rates. Depression in the Y or vertical lead gives us a clue as to why this lead has been shown to have a high incidence of so-called false-positive S-T changes.[9] It can be seen that the changes are less significant in the frontal or transverse lead, X.

The absence of significant S-T segment depression in young, vigorous boys and in athletic, middle-aged men exercised in our laboratory suggests that the effect of the Ta-wave can be easily recognized because of the short duration (usually 0.04 second) of the J-point depression (Fig. 12-5).

QRS CHANGES

The total amplitude of the QRS complex with exercise usually decreases near peak workload as does the T-wave amplitude, and there is a tendency toward right axis deviation. The QRS duration does not change significantly. If the stroke volume increases, the T-wave may actually increase, which occurs early in exercise with moderate workloads. A decrease in R-wave is more likely to be seen immediately after, however, rather than during the exercise period. When considering the QRS in the various leads during maximum exercise, there is a tendency toward a reduction in R-wave or S-wave amplitude; this is more marked in normal than abnormal subjects. The decreased amplitude following a peak exercise period is possibly due to a decrease in systolic and possibly diastolic volumes,[10] which often develops after peak cardiac output is attained. A study of this phenomenon was done by Brody[11] in 1956, and Pipberger and coworkers[12] in 1971. The latter investigators have termed this the "Brody Effect" and find that left ventricular forces decrease as stroke volume decreases, and right ventricular forces usually increase at the same time. In ischemia, the systolic volume increases and stroke volume decreases and the left-ventricular R-waves become taller. This would correlate with our experience in the observation of respiratory-related R-wave and S-T segment amplitude changes.

R-WAVE AMPLITUDE

The R-wave amplitude in the lateral precordial leads usually decreases more in the normal than in the abnormal subjects, and correlates with left-ventricular function. Bonoris and coworkers[13] in our laboratory demonstrated the usefulness of observing changes in R-wave amplitude during stress testing. They reported that ventricular function correlates with R-wave changes and that patients with severe coronary disease are likely to have an increase in R-wave

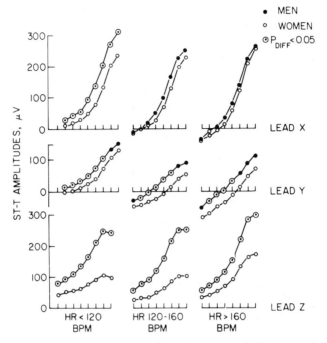

FIGURE 12-4. Variations in measurements of the S-T segment, divided into eight equidistant points between Q and peak T-wave, in normal men and women. Note that the deviations, even at high heart rates in lead X are less pronounced than in the other leads, as are the differences between men and women. (From Blomqvist,[8] with permission.)

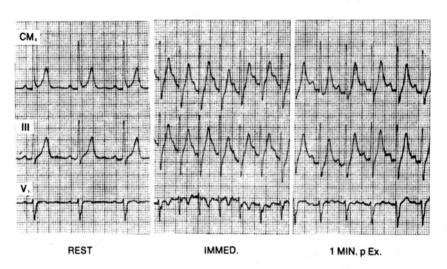

FIGURE 12-5. The tracing of a normal 19-year-old boy illustrating the electrocardiographic response to exercise usually seen in this age group. Note the steep slope of the S-T segment and the tall T-waves.

amplitude with exercise. As exercise progresses and the heart rate increases, there is a normal increase in R-wave amplitude until the heart rate is approximately 120 or 130, and then the amplitude begins to decrease. This suggests that for the R-wave to have significance an increase in amplitude should be at a heart rate above 120 (Fig. 12-6). When the exercise changes in R-wave amplitude of normals and patients with coronary disease are compared, the response was as depicted in Figure 12-7.

Three basic types of patterns were recognized (Fig. 12-8). Those in panel A are normal and have a marked reduction in R-wave amplitude. Those in B reduced their R-wave, but also have S-T depression. These usually have moderate coronary disease, but have good left-ventricular function. In C, the changes seen are more likely to illustrate patients with severe triple-vessel disease and global ischemia. Note the marked increase in R-wave and a moderate degree of S-T depression. Some of these types of patients have no S-T depression or they may have 3 or 4 mm of S-T depression.

An attempt to apply R-wave criteria to patients with left bundle branch block has been reported by Orzan and associates,[14] who report that it will not help in identifying those with coronary disease as compared with other cases with conduction abnormalities. On the other hand, Lee and colleagues[15] report that R-wave changes in 23 patients with LBBB had a 93 percent sensitivity, 88 percent specificity, and 93 percent predictability. Our experience tends to confirm that of Lee and coworkers[15] in that a reduction in amplitude is an aid in predicting normal coronary arteries and good left-ventricular function in left bundle branch block. Morris and coworkers[16] have determined that the trend in amplitude changes, in the first few minutes after exercise is a more reliable predictor of coronary disease than when the exercise tracing is compared with the control. Berman and associates[17] used the sum of the R-waves in AVL, AVF, and V_3 to V_4, plus S and V_1 and V_2 and were able to identify coronary disease in 93 percent of 230 patients subsequently studied with coronary angiography. Van Tellingen and colleagues[18] found that when the R-wave was combined with S-T depression, the sensitivity was only 51 percent, but

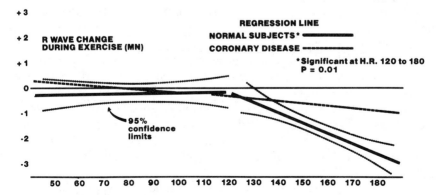

FIGURE 12-6. R-wave responses to exercise.

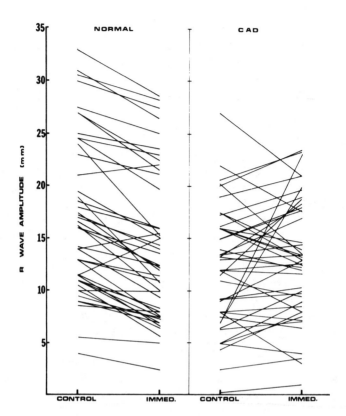

FIGURE 12-7. Direction and magnitude of R-wave changes after exercise in normal patients as compared with patients with angiographically demonstrated disease. Note that most of the normal patients had a decrease, while in those with disease both decreases and increases are seen.

the specificity increased to 93 percent. It has also been reported to be useful in patients on digitalis, as the R-wave amplitude fails to be altered by the drug in contradistinction to the S-T segment.[19]

Although we were quite enthusiastic about the R-wave measurements initially, reports from other centers found the exercise-induced changes in R-wave had very little, if any, discrimination for ischemia.[20,21] Studies on the mechanism of these changes also demonstrated that an enlarging ventricular volume as determined by nuclear blood pool angiograms, did not correlate very well with R-wave changes.[22] Excellent work by David and associates[23] has indicated that the R-wave increase seen with ischemia probably represents an alteration in intraventricular conduction. An R-wave increase has been reported with vasospastic angina,[24] and early in the course of a myocardial infarction, where it is predictive of severity and the likelihood of severe arrhythmias.[25]

The paper by DeCaprio and colleagues[26] and our subsequent studies[27] suggest that changes in R-wave amplitude are often correlated with heart rate, and

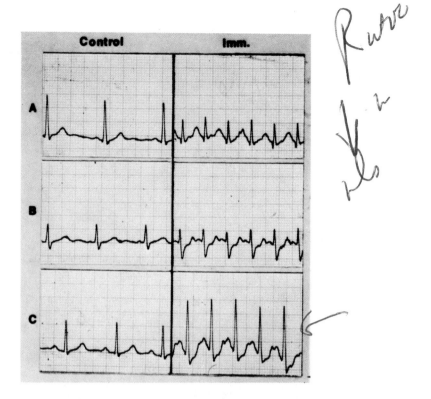

FIGURE 12-8. Three common patterns seen in lateral precordial electrocardiographic exercise tests comparing control at rest with that recorded immediately after exercise. A, Normal response equals a marked decrease in R-wave. B, Mild S-T depression but a reduction in R-wave, caused by mild ischemia with residual good left-ventricular function. C, Marked increase in R-wave and coexisting S-T depression. In these subjects, there is very poor ventricular function with an enlarging cavity and a reduction in ejection fraction as exercise progresses.

that their capacity to discriminate disease from normals is less than we originally believed. If the coronary patient terminates exercise at a low heart rate, there is very likely to be an increase in R-wave amplitude, but if the patient can achieve a high heart rate, the R-wave will usually decrease or stay the same. At this time, the evidence suggests that as a single discriminator, the R-wave change has limited value, although when combined with other variables, it may still be quite useful (Fig. 12-9).

S-T SEGMENT AND J-POINT DEPRESSIONS

A conclusive evaluation of S-T segments may still be some time away; however, the following data are representative of the current thinking. In our laboratory, we have considered the normal S-T segment with exercise to be steeply

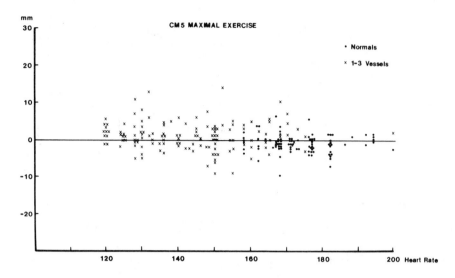

FIGURE 12-9. The changes in R-wave plotted according to the maximum heart rate achieved. CAD Patients = x, Normals = •. There is a trend toward a decrease in R-wave as the heart rate increases. The large number of abnormal CAD patients showing a reduced R-wave amplitude, especially at lower heart rates, reduces the diagnostic power.

upsloping and slightly convex in form, so that within 0.04 to 0.06 second after the J-point, it has returned to the baseline estimated from the P-Q junction (slope = −0.70 uV/sec) (see Figs. 12-1 and 12-2). Our followup data, revealing a low incidence of infarction in subjects with negative tests over a period of eight years, indicate that patients with this type of S-T segment response have the same life expectancy as those considered to be normal by the standard life table method. This would lead us to believe that our analysis of the normal S-T segment is reasonably reliable. The question as to whether every normal subject, if stressed enough, will have ischemic S-T segment depression has been discussed by Kahn and Simonson[28] and Simonson and Enzer.[29] It has been stated that the difference between the ECGs of normal and abnormal subjects is not only quantitative, but qualitative,[28] that is to say, the quantity of the S-T segment depression is not the only important determinant. The shape and slope of the S-T segments, time relationships of the S-T and T-waves have emerged as significant determinants of pathology. The fact that there are many tracings considered to be borderline indicates that our information is still limited. Stuart and Ellestad[30] have analyzed the various ECG patterns and determined their ability to predict subsequent events. These data will be presented as each pattern is discussed in detail.

Robb and Marks[31] reported that J-point (junction between S-wave and S-T segment) depression was not only normal after exercise, but that the survival rate for the insurance policyholders who had this finding after exercise was better than that of individuals with completely normal S-T segments. In our

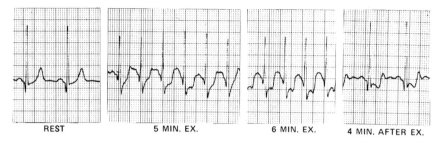

| REST | 5 MIN. EX. | 6 MIN. EX. | 4 MIN. AFTER EX. |

FIGURE 12-10. The ECG of a 50-year-old man with severe disease of the right and left anterior descending coronary arteries. Note J-point changes, which evolve into horizontal and finally downsloping S-T segment depression.

experience, J-point depression is a normal finding, but is often the first sign of a series of abnormalities developing in a patient with ischemic heart disease.[32] Figure 12-10 shows the tracings of a patient who first had J-point depression and, as exercise continued, developed a flat S-T segment and then finally a downsloping pattern during the recovery period. This sequence of events is so common that it would seem that J-point depression seen on a submaximal test such as the Master's might well be the first stage of progression to ischemic S-T segment change.

An effort to quantify J-point slope by Salzman and coworkers[32] led to the conclusion that a J-point slope of 30 degrees above horizontal was probably not indicative of ischemia, those less than this were borderline cases, and those horizontal or below were abnormal. They found that after an exercise program, some abnormal subjects increased their conditioning and at the same time the slope of their S-T segment. This increase in slope was interpreted as showing improvement.

UPSLOPING S-T SEGMENTS

From our material, the upsloping S-T segment is considered to be indicative of ischemia if at 0.06 second after the J-point, the segment is 1.5 mm below the baseline level of the P-Q junction (Fig. 12-11). Of 70 subjects with these changes who were catheterized in our laboratory, 57 percent had either two- or three-vessel disease. Bruce and Blackman[33] as well as a number of other experts[34] concede that "upsloping" S-T segments may be indicative of ischemia. Brody[35] found what he called junctional S-T segment depression of 1.5 mm or more in 756 business executives tested with a double Master's test. Twenty-one percent of these men later developed coronary disease. Brody also found that patients with junctional changes from 0.5 to 1.4 mm had a 2.5 percent occurrence of coronary disease. This incidence of coronary disease is very similar to that of subjects with completely normal exercise tracings. Kurita and coworkers[36] also found a high correlation between angiographically demonstrated stenosis and upsloping S-T changes when the depression was greater

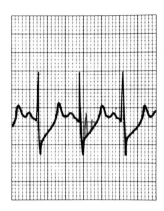

FIGURE 12-11. The upsloping S-T segment depicted here is at an angle of 50 degrees. Although some would label this J-point depression, we have called this "upsloping S-T segment" and it is usually associated with ischemia.

than 1.5 mm. Goldschlager and associates,[37] however, found the upsloping pattern to be somewhat less sensitive than horizontal or downsloping patterns. It would, therefore, appear that upsloping S-T segment changes should be considered abnormal when the degree of depression at 0.06 seconds from the

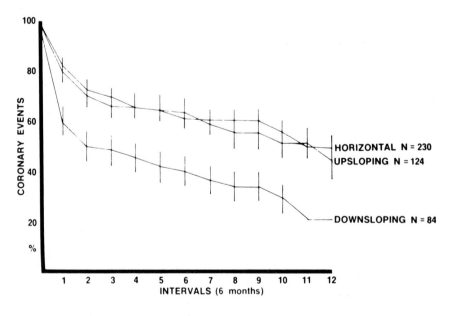

FIGURE 12-12. Life table analysis of new coronary events (progression of angina, myocardial infarctions, and death) in patients manifesting horizontal, upsloping, and downsloping S-T segment depression with exercise. The incidence of coronary events in patients with upsloping S-T segment depression is the same as in those with horizontal S-T segment depression. Those with downsloping S-T segment depression have a higher incidence of events.

STRESS TESTING: PRINCIPLES AND PRACTICE

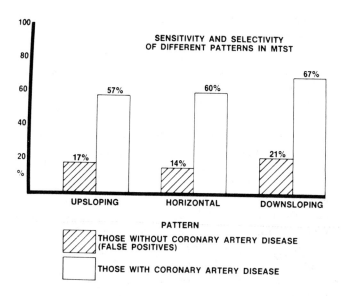

FIGURE 12-13. Subjects with various patterns of S-T segment depression are depicted according to the percentage having two-vessel coronary disease of more than 50 percent obstruction and those with no disease as determined by coronary angiogram. The incidence of patients with disease is similar in all groups.

J-point is down 1.5 mm or more. Figures 12-12 and 12-13 illustrate that the frequency of coronary disease diagnosed by angiography and new coronary abnormalities in patients with upsloping S-T segments is the same as those with flat S-T segments. On the other hand, junctional changes with very steep upsloping S-T segments are probably not pathologic.

Table 12-1, compiled from the data of Bruce and colleagues[7] describes the evaluation of J-point and S-T segment changes in normal subjects as a result of exercise. These changes are similar to those of Blomqvist[8] and will help us to separate the abnormal from the normal.

TABLE 12-1. S-T measurements 50 to 59 msec after nadir of S-wave

HR	Normal	Abnormal
75	+0.5	+0.5
100	0.0	−0.25
125	−0.5	−1.0
150	−0.7	−1.5
175	−1.0	−2.0
	N=48	N=22
	−0.4 ± 0.52	−1.36 ± 0.52

HORIZONTAL AND DOWNSLOPING S-T SEGMENTS

It seems ironic that 60 years after the significance of depressed S-T segments was first recognized, the criteria for identification of these changes are still not totally agreed upon. The physiologic basis for the observed electrocardiographic abnormalities is quite complex and may be multifactorial. One reason there has been so much confusion is that investigators have attempted to correlate S-T segment depression with the degree of coronary disease. It is obvious that the electrical changes in the muscle producing abnormalities in the ECGs are the results of many influences, including those caused by electrolytes, hormones, and hemodynamic and metabolic, as well as anatomic changes (see Chapter 4).

It is known, the magnitude of the stenosis in an artery, estimated by angiography may not accurately predict the amount of restruction in flow.[38]

There is general agreement, however, that an increased magnitude of S-T segment depression usually denotes an increased degree of ischemia. Robb and associates[39] reported this from their follow-up studies of subjects using the Master's protocol.

In the early days of our stress testing program, we were most anxious not to affix a diagnosis of coronary disease to someone who was normal, so we selected 2.0 mm of depression with a horizontal or downsloping S-T segment as the only definite criterion for an abnormal finding. Careful follow-up of our patients has convinced us that we were being too stringent. Our criteria were later modified to accept 1.5 mm of depression at 0.08 second from the J-point even if the S-T segment slopes upward. I believe 1.0 mm is probably the best

TABLE 12-2. Recommended criteria for significant S-T segment depression with maximal exercise

Resting ST-T configuration	Exercise or postexercise S-T configuration	S-T depression in mm and point of measurement
Normal	Horizontal	1.0 mm at 60 msec from J-point
	Upsloping	1.5 mm at 80 msec from J-point
	Downsloping	1.0 mm more depressed than at rest
Flat or sagging S-T and T	Horizontal	1.0 mm more depressed than at rest
	Upsloping	1.5 mm more depressed than at rest at 80 msec from J-point
	Downsloping	1.0 mm more depressed than at rest
Inverted T	Horizontal	1.5 mm at 60 msec from J-point
	Upsloping	1.5 mm at 80 msec from J-point
	Downsloping	1.5 mm at 20 msec from J-point

Note that these current criteria are slightly different depending on the configuration of the resting S-T segment and T-wave.

available minimum level to use in horizontal S-T segment changes (Table 12-2). The problem of marginal or equivocal findings can sometimes be resolved by urging the patient to exercise a little longer and, therefore, increase the metabolic load on the heart. This will often result in tracings that appeared to be equivocal with moderate stress evolving into a diagnostic pattern with an increased workload.

If one accepts S-T segment depression of 0.5 to 1.0 mm as abnormal, as recommended by Master and Jaffe,[41] the number of false-positive tests will increase even though the number of false-negative tests will decrease. When examining our follow-up data, the increased incidence of coronary abnormalities in our tests rated equivocal (S-T segment depression of 0.5 to 1.3 mm), indicated that a significant number of patients with coronary disease or decreased ventricular function were included in this group (Fig. 12-14). Mason and associates[42] in a study of correlation with coronary angiography, found that the sensitivity, when using 0.5 mm S-T segment depression, was 83 percent while the specificity was 60 percent. On the other hand, when 1.5 mm was used, the sensitivity dropped to 44 percent but the specificity rose to 90 percent (see Chapter 14 for discussion of sensitivity and specificity). Martin and McConahay[43] found that, when using 1.0 mm of depression in correlation with angiographically demonstrated 50 percent or more narrowing, the specificity was 89 percent and the sensitivity was 62 percent. Again, in the series by Mason and colleagues, when they reduced the depression of the S-T segment to 0.5, the sensitivity increased to 84 percent but the specificity decreased to 57 percent. They found the S-T segments alone at maximum exercise levels correlated best with an increased left-ventricular filling pressure in 90 percent of the patients.[42] In our laboratory, we have measured S-T segment depression as illustrated in Figure 12-15.

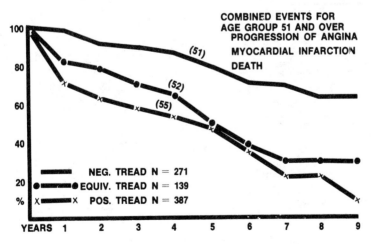

FIGURE 12-14. The incidence of coronary events in those with equivocal S-T segment depression (0.5 to 1.4 mm marked 52) is so close to that of the positives that it must be assumed that many of them have coronary disease.

ECG PATTERNS AND THEIR SIGNIFICANCE

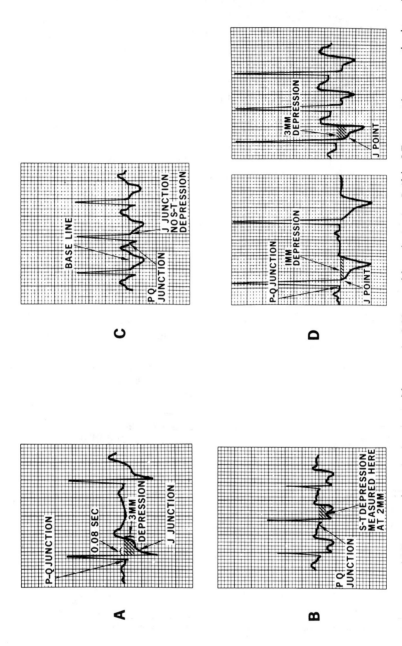

FIGURE 12-15. A, Horizontal S-T segment depression is measured from a point 0.08 second from the J-point. B, If the S-T segment is convex, the depression is measured from the top of the curve to the level of the P-Q junction. C and D, With downsloping S-T segments, the depression is measured at the point where the S-T segment changes slope, which is very close to the point usually called the J-junction.

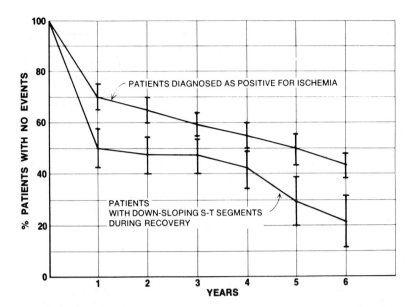

FIGURE 12-16. Incidence of coronary events in patients with S-T segment depression. Those patients who have horizontal or upsloping S-T segments immediately after exercise, but which evolve into a downsloping pattern, have a higher prevalence of coronary events in all positive responders as a group.

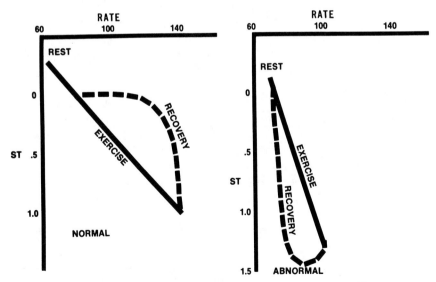

FIGURE 12-17. The heart rate is presented on the abscissa and the magnitude of the S-T segment depression on the ordinate. The normal subject tends to immediately correct the minor S-T segment depression associated with exercise when recovery begins. The abnormal subject may actually increase the S-T segment depression somewhat during the early periods of recovery, even though the heart rate is slowing down. (Adapted from Bruce and McDonough.[44])

ECG PATTERNS AND THEIR SIGNIFICANCE

When exercising patients with ischemic heart disease, the first abnormality seen is often a moderate degree of J-point depression, which then evolves into a progressively more depressed horizontal S-T segment pattern, which then remains horizontal as exercise continues (see Fig. 12-10). Pain may be experienced after the onset of S-T depression, but rarely before the pattern is recorded. At the termination of the test, the S-T segment may evolve into an upsloping configuration similar to the previously recorded J-point pattern, or it may progress to a downsloping pattern with a deeply inverted T-wave. The latter evolutionary change has been associated with a high incidence of ischemia. When we analyzed our life table data, we found the incidence of subsequent coronary events to be greater in those with this type of pattern (Fig. 12-16). Bruce and McDonough[44] have proposed that the so-called hysteresis of the S-T segment depression during recovery is a method of increasing diagnostic specificity. They believe the S-T segment depression that resolves rapidly during recovery is probably not due to ischemia, while the depression that increases during the recovery period is pathologic. They have displayed these patterns, using a counterclockwise loop when the magnitude of the S-T segment depression is depicted in normal patients, and a clockwise loop in abnormal patients (Fig. 12-17). A significant number of exceptions to this line of reasoning have been observed in our material, however.

INTRAOBSERVER AGREEMENT

The analysis of S-T segment depression by a group of 14 experts from seven medical centers was correlated by Blackburn.[45] They reported that the accuracy of positive responses with undefined criteria varied from 5 to 55 percent for each physician. Agreement of all 14 observers was obtained on only seven normal patients and one abnormal patient. The mean estimation of accuracy was only 10.8 percent.

Hornsten and Bruce[46] analyzed 100 tracings by computer that identified 0.10 mV (equivalent to 1.0 mm) depression at 40 to 70 msec after the nadir of the S-wave. This gave a specificity for true-negatives of 91 percent and a sensitivity for true-positives of 85 percent when averaging 20 complexes with the computer; however, transient ischemia was "averaged out." It was their conclusion that this degree of depression was the most reliable in predicting ischemia. They also found that there was some degree of S-T segment depression in the so-called normal patients as a result of tachycardia.

Although agreement was poor in Blackburn's intraobserver study, he believes that it can be improved by following strict criteria.

Although the criteria in Table 12-2 are generally useful, especially in men, there are more and more exceptions now recognized. Simoons[47] has suggested the S-T be corrected for heart rate, a concept that would fit with the observations of Blomqvist.[8] It is also essential to consider the patient as a whole, including age, sex, blood pressure, murmurs, and other findings. This dictum is repeated several times in this book.

Sandberg[48] analyzed S-T segment depression and T-wave amplitude in a series of patients with coronary disease or with vasoregulatory asthenia. The S-T segment depression was significant and predictable in the patients with coronary disease, but 13 of the 32 patients showed no significant change in T-wave amplitude. Those with vasoregulatory asthenia often had a decrease in T-wave amplitude, but none had S-T depression of more than 1.0 mm after reaching their maximum level of exercise.

DISTRIBUTION OF S-T SEGMENT DEPRESSION

Although the majority of S-T depression is manifested in the anterior lateral precordial leads, it will also be seen in others depending on severity and location. It appears that the more leads manifesting S-T depression, the more widespread and severe the ischemia. Although data to accurately localize areas of myocardium are limited, it appears that S-T depression in AVF and 3 often reflect inferior ischemia, while S-T depression in CM_5 and V_4, V_5, and V_6 reflect anterior and apical problems. S-T elevation in V_1 and AVL indicate ischemia in the septum, caused by left anterior descending stenosis, while S-T depression in V_1 indicates inferior wall ischemia.

S-T INTEGRAL AND SLOPE

The use of computers to record the voltage changes associated with the electrocardiographic complex lends itself to measurements that are otherwise laborious. Two that have been used in several centers are the slope of the S-T segment in the area subtended by the negative deviation and the integral (Fig. 12-18). In Figure 12-18, A depicts the slope of the S-T segment. It is usually measured in milivolts per second. A positive number if upsloping and a negative one if downsloping. In B of Figure 12-18, the shaded area under the isoelectric line subtended by the S-T segment defines the integral. Imperical correlations with coronary narrowing have been published.

Most of the measurements of the slope are combined with a measurement of the S-T depression in order to predict ischemia because the slope could be quite flat when the deflection below the baseline is minimal, resulting in a pattern that usually at least looks normal. In 1968, McHenry and colleagues[49] reported an analysis of the S-T interval by combining a computerized slope and S-T measurement and indicated its usefulness in analysis of exercise tracings. Shortly afterward, Sheffield and associates[50] reported on both the slope and the integral. Ascoop and coworkers[51] measured the slope during the first 50 msecs, (0.05 sec) after the J-point and used a slope of no greater than 180 microvolts per msec as the upper limit for an abnormal value. The integral selected as the best discriminator was 8 microvolt seconds for CC_5 and 10 microvolt seconds for CM_5. Using these numbers, sensitivies of 0.42 and specificities of 0.93 could be obtained. When the S-T depression of 50 msecs after the J was combined with the slope, better discrimination was possible

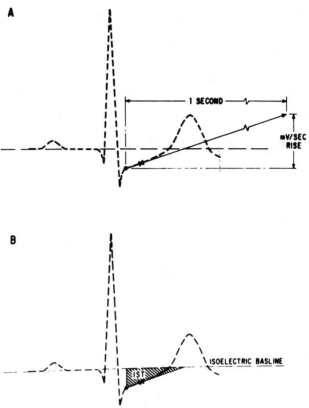

FIGURE 12-18. S-T slope and integral. A, Illustrates the slope of the S-T calibrated in millivolts per second. In B, The integral is the area below the isoelectric line subtended by the S-T segment. The area will increase as the depression increases and the slope decreases.

with the sensitivity increasing to 70 percent, without much loss in specificity. Forlini and colleagues[52] in San Francisco used the slope and integral, but isolated the integral by extending the slope through the T-wave and reported a sensitivity of 79 percent, somewhat better than the results previously cited by Ascoop and associates. The calculation of slope and integral are standard on a number of commercially available computerized stress testing systems and seem to add some improvement to the analysis of the S-T segment, especially when the S-T is marginal. One of the best evaluations of the integral was done by Sketch and coworkers[53] who were able to correlate the integral with severity of disease and found that it provided an improved predictive value (see Fig. 23-3 and Chapter 23 for more on slope and integral).

I believe the method shows promise even though enthusiasm is still limited more than 10 years after the measurements have become technically practical.

HYPOKALEMIA

Hypokalemia has long been known to flatten T-waves and prolong the Q-T

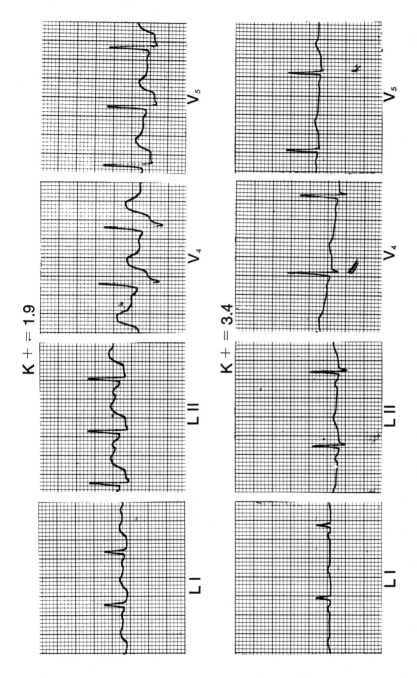

FIGURE 12-19. The tracings in the bottom panel were taken one day after those in the top panel in a 46-year-old woman admitted with long-standing excessive furosemide administration.

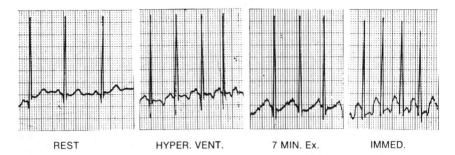

REST   HYPER. VENT.   7 MIN. Ex.   IMMED.

FIGURE 12-20. Note the shape of the early part of the S-T segment especially after hyperventilation in "Reynolds syndrome." We believe this pattern can be differentiated from classical ischemic S-T segment changes. Note deep septal Q-waves.

interval. There is no doubt that it will lower the S-T segments in an exercising patient. As a result of injudicious use of diuretics, many women in their 30s and 40s have a tendency toward hypokalemia with resultant S-T segment depression. Potassium depletion, as a diuretic side effect, is extremely common among American women (Fig. 12-19) (see Chapter 22). Hypertensive individuals taking thiazide diuretics are also likely to be a problem in this regard.

INCREASED SYMPATHETIC TONE (REYNOLDS SYNDROME) (VASOREGULATORY ASTHEMIA)

Yanowitz and associates[54] have demonstrated that many types of S-T and T-wave abnormalities can be induced in dogs by stellate ganglion stimulation. We have seen a number of patients with increased sympathetic drive who have exhibited T-wave inversion and S-T segment depression upon exercising. The first one of the patients that we were able to do coronary angiograms on who was found to have normal coronaries and relatively normal left-ventricular function was named Reynolds. We, therefore, named the syndrome associated with increased sympathetic drive and abnormal T-wave and S-T segment change the "Reynolds Syndrome" (Fig. 12-20). It is possible that this may be a variant of the vasoregulatory asthemia described by Holmgren and colleagues.[55] However, Reynolds and patients with similar changes did not exhibit symptoms typical of Holmgren's syndrome in that they did not give evidence of poor peripheral oxygen extraction.

S-T SEGMENT DEPRESSION AT REST EVOLVING TOWARD NORMAL WITH EXERCISE

Patients with abnormal autonomic drive have demonstrated S-T segment depression after hyperventilation as well as after exercise. In our experience, those patients with S-T segment depression at rest and those who have an increased S-T segment depression after hyperventilation, but tend to return to normal with exercise, do not usually have coronary disease. Jacobs and co-workers[56] also report that changes associated with hyperventilation are usually associated with normal coronary arteries. Propranolol and other beta blockers have been shown to block the S-T changes associated with hyperventilation, suggesting an autonomic etiology.[57,58] The common finding that body position may produce similar changes tends to support this concept. These types of changes are common in patients with mitral prolapse.[59]

It is a well-established fact that chronic hyperventilation and its resultant hypokalemic alkalosis is characterized by total body potassium depletion. This and the coronary vasoconstriction demonstration to be associated with alkalosis[56] could also explain the resting S-T segment depression (see Fig. 2-12). The tendency for an increase in serum potassium during exercise might explain why the patient's S-T segment returns to normal (Fig. 12-21). Unfortunately, the benignity of this phenomenon cannot be guaranteed. Figure 12-22 shows the tracing of a 62-year-old woman with severe three-vessel disease who also demonstrates this phenomenon. In our experience, it seems to be much more common in women.

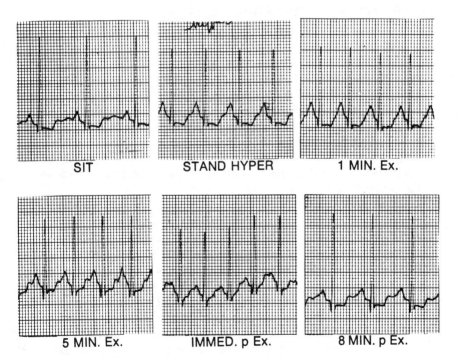

SIT   STAND HYPER   1 MIN. Ex.

5 MIN. Ex.   IMMED. p Ex.   8 MIN. p Ex.

FIGURE 12-21. Changes seen in a 29-year-old woman exercised to maximum capacity who had no stigma of coronary disease. The resting S-T segment depression accentuated by hyperventilation returns to a normal pattern as exercise progresses. Note changes at eight minutes.

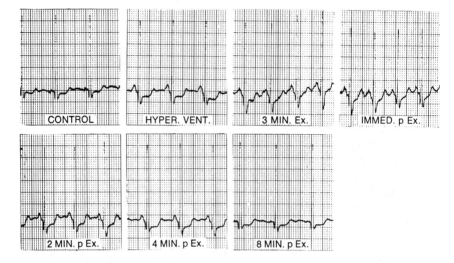

FIGURE 12-22. A 62-year-old woman with severe three-vessel disease demonstrated on coronary angiography. Note that the changes are quite similar to those illustrated in Figure 12-21 taken from a subject without coronary disease.

INTERMITTENT S-T SEGMENT DEPRESSION ASSOCIATED WITH RESPIRATION

Early in our experience with stress testing, we observed S-T segment depression that varied from beat to beat. It was obviously not due to baseline drift and was often apparently associated with respiration. We had reason to believe that some of these subjects were not suffering from coronary disease. For example, a 28-year-old pathology resident showed this change (Fig. 12-23). He led a sedentary life and had a stress test prior to entering into a physical conditioning program at our hospital. After three months of a moderately rigorous training schedule, his abnormality completely disappeared. We have observed a number of similar cases.

On the other hand, we have seen several patients who progressed from variable S-T segment depression, often associated with respiration, to the classical S-T segment changes typical of ischemia. We examined a 59-year-old man who had never experienced cardiac symptoms of any type, but who underwent a stress test as a routine screening procedure. Two years after a tracing similar to the one illustrated in Fig. 12-24, he had evolved from the variable S-T segment depression into a classical ischemic pattern, but still exhibited moderate variability. Subsequent coronary angiography studies disclosed advanced two-vessel disease. The mechanism of this condition seems to be related to the fact that inspiration and expiration are associated with different rates of left-ventricular filling. If the compliance of the left ventricle is slightly decreased, the increased rates of the filling may produce an elevation in the end-diastolic pressure and, therefore, S-T segment depression for only a

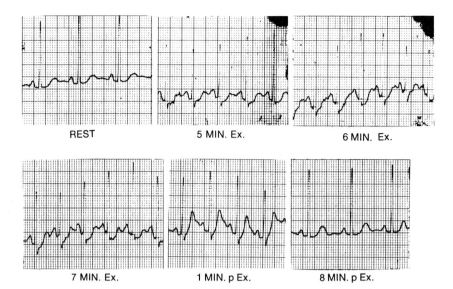

| REST | 5 MIN. Ex. | 6 MIN. Ex. |
| 7 MIN. Ex. | 1 MIN. p Ex. | 8 MIN. p Ex. |

FIGURE 12-23. Transient variable S-T segment depression occurred after seven minutes of exercise in a 28-year-old pathology resident. Two months later, a stress test was perfectly normal after a physical fitness program.

few beats. This is almost always seen near maximum stress levels when one would expect that the compliance of the ventricle would be decreased the most and when the thoracioabdominal pump would be returning the blood to the heart at the greatest velocity.

The reason this phenomenon is seen in patients with hearts believed to be relatively normal is difficult to explain. It might be that an unconditioned subject, such as the pathology resident, actually has loss of left ventricular compliance in the absence of overt disease. It is not unusual to do coronary angiograms and left ventricular dynamic studies on patients with odd types of pain syndromes who seem to exhibit this type of change. It may be that, as the subject becomes better conditioned, the heart improves its ability to increase the diastolic volume and makes a physiologic adaptation to filling at high rates without an associated rise in pressure. We have seen this phenomenon in both normals and CAD patients, but have found it most commonly in subjects believed to be free of disease.

In an effort to understand this phenomenon, left-ventricular pressures have been recorded during deep respiratory cycles in subjects with poor left-ventricular function. The LVEDP fluctuates and seems to increase near the end of inspiration and decrease late in expiration. The S-T segment depression follows this same pattern with a drop in S-T segments at the same time the LVEDP is rising. The changes described here have never been recorded in patients with completely normal ventricles and are usually seen only in those with some degree of dysfunction. Apparently, the inflow of blood to the chamber increases late in inspiration resulting in changes in pressure caused by the

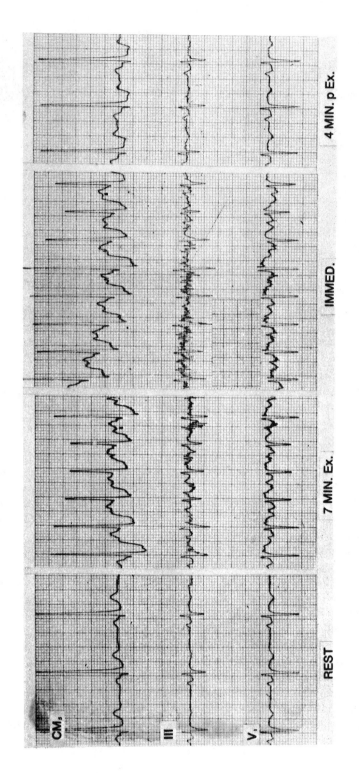

FIGURE 12-24. Exercise-induced variations in R-wave amplitude and S-T segments in a 59-year-old man. The R-wave amplitude and S-T segment depression were related to respiration. Coronary angiography revealed a complete obstruction of the right coronary artery, 90 percent obstruction of the left anterior descending, and 100 percent obstruction of the left marginal.

STRESS TESTING: PRINCIPLES AND PRACTICE

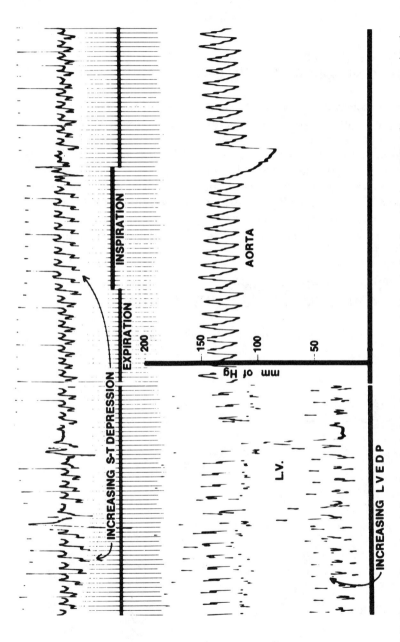

FIGURE 12-25. Recordings taken during a heart catheterization illustrating an increase in the left-ventricular end-diastolic pressure and in the amount of S-T segment depression associated with respiration. It can be seen that with inspiration, there is a tendency for the LVEDP to rise and the S-T segment depression to increase.

lack of normal compliance. The amplitude of the R-waves also increases at the same time that the S-T segment is depressed, so that the respiratory pattern is evident both in terms of the increased amplitude of the R-waves and in the depth of the S-T segment depression (Fig. 12-25).

S-T SEGMENT DEPRESSION ASSOCIATED WITH LONG DIASTOLIC FILLING

For the person with a slow heart rate and a long period of diastole after a premature ventricular contraction, the next beat is often associated with S-T segment depression. It is well established that the individual has "overfilling" of the ventricle and if the compliance is compromised, the increased diastolic pressure may be associated with S-T segment depression. This is seen repeatedly and correlates well with the diagnosis of clinical ischemia. It is most commonly recorded immediately after the exercise is terminated. This type of S-T segment depression has not been recognized in our laboratory in very young people with sinus arrhythmia or with congenital heart block (Fig. 12-26).

S-T SEGMENT DEPRESSION WITH NODAL PREMATURE CONTRACTIONS

S-T segment depression is often associated with the wide complex of a PVC or

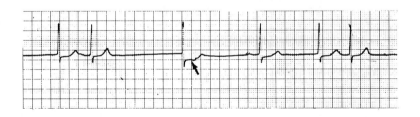

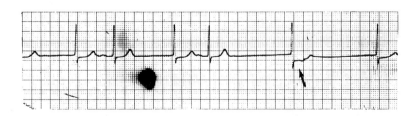

FIGURE 12-26. Tracings recorded shortly after exercise. The complexes marked by the arrow represent a nodal escape with a retrograde P-wave. Note the increased S-T segment depression in these complexes.

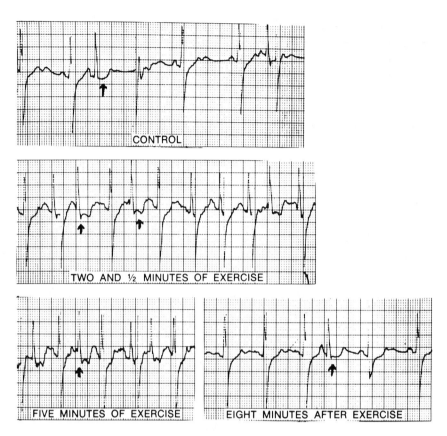

FIGURE 12-27. Exercise tracings on a 73-year-old woman with a pacemaker. Note the nodal extra beats, which have deep S-T segment depression with exercise only.

an LBBB pattern. These changes are thought to be secondary to the abnormal conduction pathway and may not be a sign of abnormal left-ventricular function. On the other hand, nodal or atrial premature contractions when seen in the so-called "normal heart" are not usually associated with S-T segment depression.

A number of patients with significant coronary disease, demonstrated by angiography, have exhibited S-T segment depression with nodal or atrial extrasystoles during or immediately after exercise. These same patients, when having nodal or atrial extrasystoles at rest, did not have S-T segment depression. As a result, we consider such a finding to be presumptive evidence of ischemic heart disease; however, the number of cases seen is too small to offer much conclusive evidence. Figure 12-27 represents the tracings of a 73-year-old woman with a previous myocardial infarction and a sick sinus syndrome with a demand ventricular pacer. Note that the nodal premature contractions at rest demonstrate only slight S-T segment depression but during exercise, it evolved to at least 3.0 mm. This same beat again presents almost no S-T segment de-

ECG PATTERNS AND THEIR SIGNIFICANCE

251

pression during the recovery period. No significant S-T segment depression is present in either the sinus or the paced beats. It may be that the degree of muscle relaxation is incomplete, resulting in a decreased compliance even with a shorter diastolic filling period, and thus decreased subendocardial perfusion.

ALTERNATING S-T SEGMENT DEPRESSION

The alternating S-T depression pattern is invariably associated with severe ischemia. It is quite unusual and has rarely been reported in the literature. Roselle and coworkers[60] were able to produce this in dogs by severely decreasing the coronary flow. They observed pulsus alternans in these animals, and it is of interest to note that the strongest pulse was associated with the complexes with the deepest S-T depression. Their observations tend to fit our physiologic concepts in that the beat with the greatest degree of filling and the higher

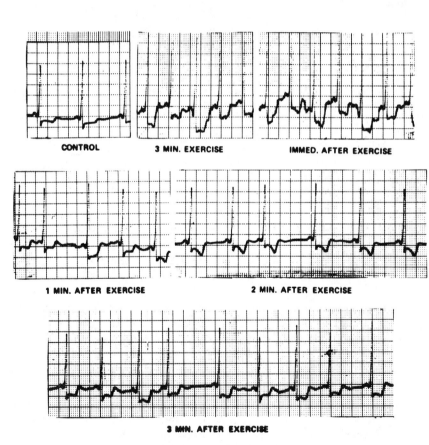

FIGURE 12-28. Alternating S-T segment depression with exercise in a 49-year-old, hypertensive man with a 90 percent occlusion of the proximal anterior descending coronary artery.

diastolic pressure would be the one to produce the strongest peripheral pulse. Figure 12-28 represents the tracing of a 49-year-old, hypertensive man with a left anterior descending coronary artery that is about 90 percent obstructed. Left-ventricular function was somewhat hypokinetic even though the patient never had a recognized myocardial infarction.

Wayne and associates[61] reported on a 61-year-old man with severe three-vessel disease who had alternating S-T segment elevation with exercise. They disputed the likelihood that a hemodynamic cause could be postulated because the alternation was not effected by PVCs. The S-T depression in our patient was not altered by atrial premature contractions.

S-T SEGMENT DEPRESSION LATE IN THE RECOVERY PERIOD

There is a significant number of subjects who do not have S-T segment depression with or immediately after exercise, but who develop changes from three to eight minutes after the stress test has been terminated. This was recognized many years ago by Master and Jaffe.[41] The hemodynamic, metabolic, and electrophysiologic reasons for this have never been clearly understood. It has been postulated that, as the cardiac output suddenly drops due to venous pooling, an inordinate decrease in coronary blood flow may occur and ischemia may be manifested even though it was not present during exercise.[40] Empirically, it has been observed that such a pattern may be seen in ischemic heart disease; however, these changes are usually of very moderate magnitude (1.0 mm depression or less) and are quite difficult to evaluate (Fig. 12-29). McHenry and colleagues[49] believe that if hyperventilation produces even moderate T or S-T changes prior to exercise, then S-T changes occuring late in recovery are almost always associated with normal coronaries. Also, if this occurs in subjects without either hyperventilation changes and also without even marginal exercise S-T change, then it probably can be ignored as insignificant. They think some changes are due to carbohydrate consumption prior to the test and can be abolished by repeating the test in the fasting state.

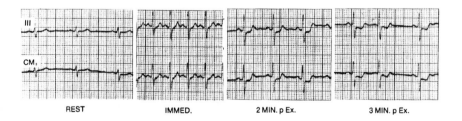

REST   IMMED.   2 MIN. p Ex.   3 MIN. p Ex.

FIGURE 12-29. Although the S-T segments immediately after exercise are normal, classical ischemic changes develop in the second and third minutes of recovery in a 51-year-old man with a proximal 95 percent obstruction of the right coronary artery.

In a follow-up study of 308 subjects with this pattern, we found it to be a definite but weak predictor of subsequent coronary events. These patients must be differentiated from those who have S-T segment depression at rest, return to normal with exercise, and again develop S-T segment depression late in the recovery period. The latter pattern is usually, but not always, associated with a normal heart.

CONVEX S-T SEGMENT DEPRESSION

Lepeschkin and associates[63] reported that the prominent Ta-wave (wave of atrial repolarization) and the superimposition of the U-wave on the baseline adjustments tend to accentuate the depression of the proximal part of the S-T

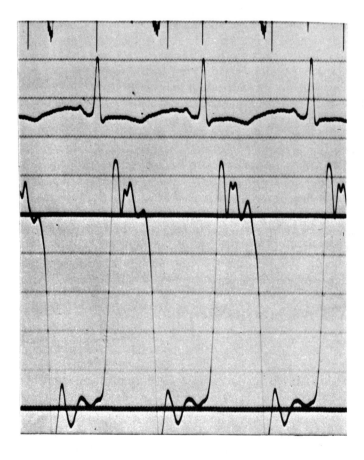

FIGURE 12-30. A 44-year-old woman with normal coronary arteries and normal left-ventricular function. The left-ventricular pressure curve is completely normal but the T-waves are inverted and there is upward curving of the S-T segments.

STRESS TESTING: PRINCIPLES AND PRACTICE

segment and may lead one erroneously to the diagnosis of ischemia (see Fig. 12-2). When the T-wave is biphasic during exercise, significant S-T segment depression will result in a pattern similar to Figure 12-30. This pattern is fairly common in classical ischemia, but the S-T segment is not as flat as it is in typical horizontal S-T segment depression. When significant depression of 1.5 mm is manifested, myocardial dysfunction can usually be predicted. When these changes are not associated with significant S-T segment depression as measured from the middle portion of the convex part of the S-T segment curve (see Fig. 12-15-B), it may be a variation of the normal, or at least associated with autonomic overdrive such as might be found in vasoregulatory asthenia or other neurasthenic disorders. The 44-year-old woman with atypical angina whose tracings are depicted in Figure 12-30 had normal coronary arteries and normal left-ventricular function.

ROUNDED S-T SEGMENT DEPRESSION

A rounded S-T segment depression pattern in the CM₅ lead, as well as in other leads, is quite common and is often associated with ischemia. Figure 12-31 depicts the ECG of a 48-year-old physician who was experiencing classical anginal pains. Substernal pressure developed during the test and one year later he sustained a myocardial infarction. This pattern is somewhat difficult to evaluate if the duration of the S-T segment sagging is very short, but usually reflects ventricular dysfunction. Stuart and Ellestad[30] found this pattern to be associated with a slightly increased incidence of subsequent coronary events in a follow-up study. Patients with a rounded pattern had a 5.8 percent per year incidence of coronary events as compared with 8.3 percent per year for those with a horizontal pattern.

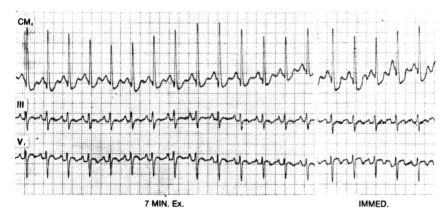

FIGURE 12-31. A tracing taken during and immediately after exercise in a 48-year-old physician who had typical angina and severe two-vessel disease on angiography. Note the rounded S-T segments and the variable R-wave amplitude.

S-T SEGMENT ELEVATION WITH EXERCISE

When S-T segment elevation occurs during exercise, it has been associated with a ventricular akinetic or dyskinetic segment in most of the cases studied by means of angiography in our laboratory.[64] On the other hand, it will occasionally be seen in a subject who has not had a previous infarction and in such a case is almost invariably associated with a very high-grade proximal LAD lesion. Cahahine and colleagues[65] proposed that it may reflect a dyskinetic anterior wall, a concept that tends to be confirmed by studies with exercise nuclear angiography.[10] One might suspect that when S-T segment depression is seen, ischemia is mostly subendocardial, but when S-T elevation is recorded in the anterior lateral precordial leads, the ischemia may be transmural. Although it had been our experience that most patients with variant angina (Prinzmetal's syndrome[66]) had either no change or S-T depression with exercise, Detry and colleagues[67] have reported S-T elevation in variant angina as have others.[24,65,68] These changes occur in leads from V_4 to V_6, and may also be associated with episodes of exertional angina. They also have angiographically demonstrated coronary narrowing in most cases. There is a high occurrence of arrhythmias with exercise and they are at risk from this mechanism, as well as the danger of infarction. It would appear that if the patients have angiographically normal coronary arteries and Prinzmetal's syndrome due to spasm as described by MacAlpin and colleagues,[69] they will usually have no change during exercise. If they have coronary disease, with or without spasm, one may see S-T elevation as well as depression. Exercise-induced S-T elevation in a subject with variant angina probably indicates hemodynamically significant coronary atheroma (Fig. 12-32). Belik and Gardin[70] report a case with alternating S-T elevation, S-T depression, ventricular conduction abnormalities, and U-wave inversion. Most of the classical signs of ischemia in one patient.

Occasionally, we have seen S-T depression occur during stress testing and then elevation develop if exercise is continued. A physiologic aneurysm may be provoked by the relative increase in myocardial perfusion deficit during exercise. The opposing vectors of S-T segment elevation and depression may often cancel each other out, and thereby explain the decreased incidence of S-T segment depression upon exercise in patients who have had a myocardial infarction.[71] The localization of a dyskinetic segment was correctly identified by S-T segment elevation in 86 percent of the patients in one study.[42] *S-T elevation during exercise is always associated with pathology* in my experience.

S-T SEGMENT ELEVATION AT REST NORMALIZED BY EXERCISE (EARLY REPOLARIZATION)

Although a stable left-ventricular aneurysm may often manifest S-T segment elevation in the precordial leads at rest, there are quite a few subjects who

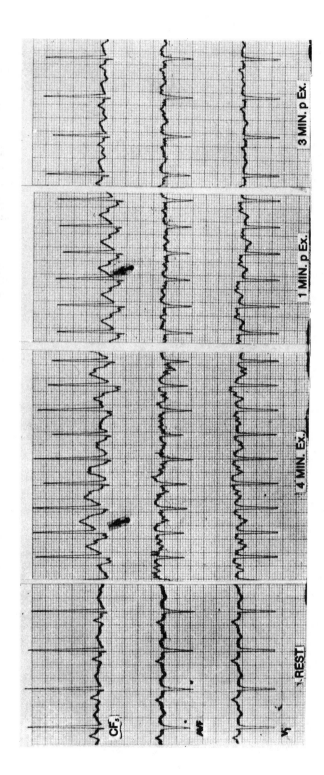

FIGURE 12-32. These tracings were recorded from a subject with a large apical left-ventricular aneurysm. Note that S-T segment deviation with exercise in the CM_5 lead and depression in V_1.

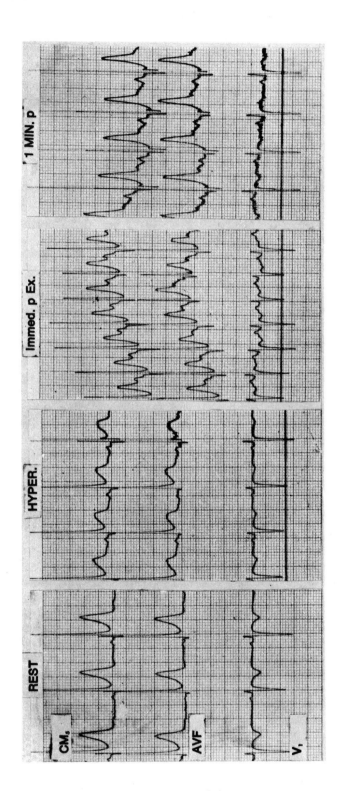

FIGURE 12-33. Resting S-T elevation in a 13-year-old boy who was studied because he had a functional murmur. Subsequent heart catheterization failed to reveal any pathologic findings. Note the increase in S-T segment elevation after hyperventilation.

have some degree of elevation in the CM_5 or other precordial leads and have normal hearts. This is most likely to be seen in young black men[72] but is by no means limited to this group. This has been termed early repolarization. Kambara and Phillips[73] have reviewed this syndrome and report that 26 percent of these patients have eventual disappearance of the characteristic findings as they get older. We have found it to be very common in well-conditioned athletes. If this type of S-T segment elevation returns to normal during exercise, it is usually associated with a normal heart. When measuring for significant S-T depression, we do not use the resting S-T level as baseline, as in those with normal S-T segments. Any exercise-induced S-T depression seen should be analyzed as if the resting S-T were isoelectric. Reports describing this syndrome have also been published by Chelton and Burchell[72] and Lloyd-Thomas[74] (Fig. 12-33).

Q-T INTERVALS

Yu and coworkers[75] in 1950 and Yu and Soffer[76] in 1952 studied Q-T intervals and their relationship to ischemia. They found a definite prolongation in cor-

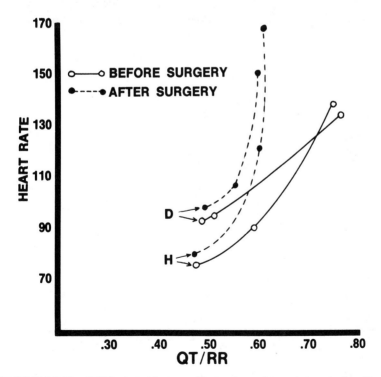

FIGURE 12-34. The QT/RR plotted in two subjects who underwent stress testing (D and H) before and after coronary vein bypass surgery. Note the tendency for the Q-T interval to become much shorter with exercise in subjects with a good surgical result.

rected Q-T intervals in patients with ischemic and hypertensive heart disease. They also correlated it with the severity of the disease as measured by the patient's endurance and the presence of S-T segment depression. The Q-T interval correlates well with the carotid ejection time, which is also prolonged when patients with ischemic disease exercise (see Chapter 8). The interest in the analysis of the Q-T interval and its association with ischemia has diminished partly because it is quite difficult to measure accurately. As the rate increases, the T-wave merges with the U-wave and then finally with the P-wave. Thus, the end of the T-wave can only be recognized as a notch between the T-wave and the P-wave. Nevertheless, changes in the Q-T interval are often very significant and more research needs to be done on the subject (Figs. 12-34 and 12-35). The data in Figure 12-35 were assembled from a small group of patients with severe S-T depression several years ago, and suggested there might be useful information in the Q-T interval. We studied the Q-T intervals, along with S-T segments, R-wave changes and QX/QT ratios in 74 patients who had both stress tests and coronary angiograms.[77] The QTc (corrected Q-T interval) was found to be most useful in patients who have an upsloping S-T pattern, but was a weak predictor when used alone (Table 12-3). It will be noted that it failed to outperform the S-T and R together, but has a better sensitivity although a lower specificity than the S-T segment alone. We are only able to make satisfactory measurements on 91 percent of the patients,

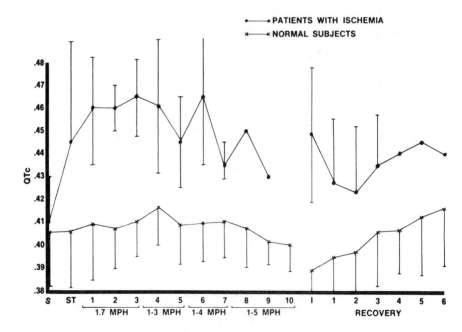

FIGURE 12-35. The corrected Q-T interval plotted for each minute of our exercise protocol in 10 normal and 6 abnormal subjects with classical ischemic changes. Note the tendency for the Q-T to become quickly prolonged early in exercise as compared with the normal subjects.

TABLE 12-3. Comparison of various measurements as predictors of ischemic disease

	ST	R	ST or R	QTc	QX/QT	QX/QT or QTc	ST or QTc
Sensitivity	50	58	76	76	81	89	89
Specificity	89	89	81	76	38	39	73
PV	83	85	81	80	54	60	79

however. I believe that, when combined with other findings, it may turn out to be a definite adjunct in the analysis of the exercise electrocardiogram.

Q PEAK T (QPT) WAVE INTERVALS

Because prolongation in the Q-T interval is an established sequelae of ischemia and is difficult to measure after exercise because of the overlap of the T and P, we decided to use the interval from the onset of the Q to the peak of the T as an estimate of ischemia prolongation. Vaselamanolokis and associates,[78] working in our laboratory, were able to show a correlation between ischemia, as judged by coronary angiography and a prolongation of this interval (QPT). When the QPT corrected by Bezett's[79] formula is greater than 40 milliseconds longer after exercise than before, it identifies ischemia with an accuracy similar to that of the S-T segment depression. Furthermore, it is often abnormal in patients who fail to manifest S-T depression. We were able to re-classify about 50 percent of the false-negative exercise tests as estimated by S-T changes correctly by applying the measurement. It is also useful in our multivariate program as a discriminator for ischemia.

QX/QT RATIO

The concept of measuring the QX/QT ratio was introduced by Lepeschkin and Surawicz[80] as a method of evaluating S-T segment depression in order to separate moderate J-point changes from true ischemic abnormalities (Fig. 12-36). The assumption was that the S-T segment depression due to ischemia would

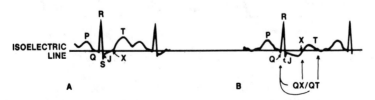

FIGURE 12-36. When the Q-X interval exceeds 50 percent of the Q-T interval it has been inferred that ischemia is present.

persist longer than that associated with tachycardia or changes in the ventricular gradient. It was proposed that a QX/QT ratio of 50 percent or more would be a relatively reliable point of differentiation. They reported, however, that the QX/QT was greater than 50 percent in 13 percent of their normal control subjects. This was later studied by other authors including Roman and Bellet,[81] who reported on 150 supposedly normal subjects. They found that 61 percent had a negative test by the QX/QT criterion, but that the remainder would have been classified as abnormal. Their conclusion was that this measurement was not valid in determining the presence or absence of ischemic heart disease. Master and Rosenfelt[82] and Robb and Marks[31] supported their position. Our study[77] of this measurement led us to believe it is a weak predictor of disease.

SEPTAL Q-WAVES 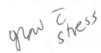 *grow c̄ stress*

For a number of years, we had noted an increase in septal Q-waves in normals and a lack of this response in subjects with significant ischemic S-T depression. Remembering the work of Burch and DePasquale[83] on the loss of septal Q-waves in resting electrocardiograms, we postulated that the disappearance was due to the loss of contractility secondary to ischemia. Morales-Ballejo and associates,[84] working in our laboratory, correlated this change with angiographic findings. Since then, we have shown a high correlation with LAD disease when the septal Q-waves decreases[85] and our work recently has been confirmed by O'Hara and colleagues.[86] Although Q-waves in the anterior precordial leads are often missing, when they are present, they may aid in the

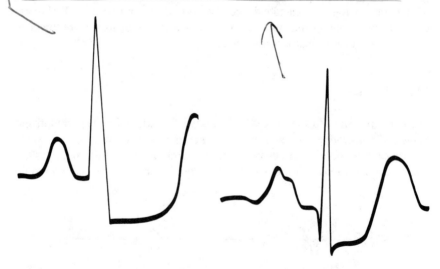

FIGURE 12-37. Septal Q-wave in two patients with S-T depression. Left, After exercise, the S-T depression and deep septal Q are seen in a man with normal coronary arteries. Right, The septal Q at rest has disappeared in a man with a 95 percent proximal left-anterior descending obstruction, who has significant S-T depression (From Morales-Ballego, et al., with permission.[84])

differentiation between true-positive and false-positive electrocardiograms. When S-T depression is associated with an enlarging septal Q, it is rarely due to ischemia; at least not due to left anterior descending narrowing (Fig. 12-37).

SEVERE HYPERTROPHY PATTERNS

One of the more difficult problems in the evaluation of stress testing is in weighing the significance of S-T segment depression changes when superimposed on those of left-ventricular hypertrophy. The prevalence of positive S-T segment depression in hypertensive patients is documented by Wong and associates.[87] They found that if the subjects had hypertension only and no patterns indicative of hypertrophy on the ECG, there was no impairment in exercise capacity and no increase in the incidence of S-T segment depression after exercise. When left-ventricular hypertrophy was present on the resting ECG, however, the incidence of significant S-T segment depression in 19 patients after exercise was 42 percent. They found that in patients who had a clinical history of angina and coexisting hypertension, the prevalence of a positive treadmill stress test was 63 percent.

Stuart and Ellestad[30] studied mortality and coronary events in 45 patients who had left-ventricular hypertrophy and exercise-induced S-T depression. We found the annual incidence of coronary events to be 13.3 percent, which is almost twice that found in subjects with classical horizontal S-T depression. Mortality was also increased in the same ratio.

Harris and associates[88] also reported an increased prevalence of positive stress tests in patients with hypertension and emphasized that S-T segment depression does not necessarily mean that they have coronary disease. It would be my feeling, however, that it does represent abnormal left-ventricular function, especially in view of the observation that many hypertensive patients who do not have coronary disease have a negative stress test. It has also been our experience that on catheterization, the left-ventricular function in hypertensive patients may be either normal or abnormal when the patient has normal coronary arteries. I believe it is safe to say that the absence of S-T segment depression in a hypertensive patient is strong evidence against coronary disease, but not the reverse (Fig. 12-38) (see Fig. 12-15D for method of measuring S-T segment depression).

TALL T-WAVES

Scherf[89] and Scherf and Schoffer[90] together have reported that tall T-waves, during or after exercise indicate inferior wall ischemia. From our experience, it appears that this is unusual. We have found that tall T-waves in the lateral precordial leads after exercise are a normal result of an increased stroke volume and are usually seen in subjects with a normal myocardium. Figure 12-39 illustrates the test of a 23-year-old man who has congenital heart block. Be-

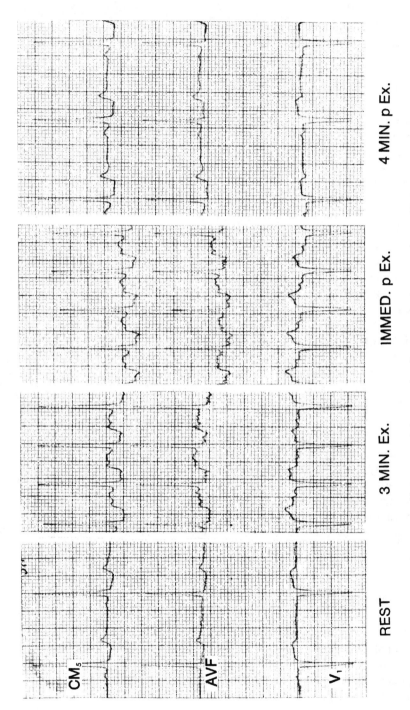

FIGURE 12-38. Exercise tracing of a 50-year-old woman with long-standing hypertension. Angiography revealed normal coronary arteries but an elevated LVEDP. Classical S-T segment depression develops with exercise.

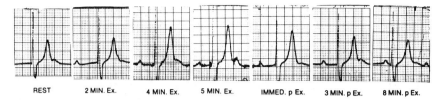

| REST | 2 MIN. Ex. | 4 MIN. Ex. | 5 MIN. Ex. | IMMED. p Ex. | 3 MIN. p Ex. | 8 MIN. p Ex. |

FIGURE 12-39. Tracings from a 23-year-old man with congenital heart block. The T-wave amplitude increases as exercise progresses.

cause he was unable to increase his heart rate as much as is normal, it has to be assumed that his stroke volume became larger to meet the increasing metabolic demands. The progressively increasing height of the T-waves would appear to correlate with the increasing stroke volume. This phenomenon is seen in many healthy teenage boys immediately after the exercise period. At this time, the pulse drops very rapidly and it would appear that the stroke volume must increase to make up for the lingering metabolic debt.

The incidence of tall T-waves (characterized by T-waves more than twice as tall as those at rest) is listed below:

Age	N	Percentage of Total in Age Group
10 to 20	22	15.0%
21 to 30	10	6.0%
31 to 40	14	5.5%
41 to 50	31	1.2%
61 to 70	1	0.2%
N	78	

The increased prevalence in tall T-waves in the younger age groups would weigh heavily against its being an abnormal finding.

Blomqvist[91] has postulated that tall T-waves are due to a higher serum potassium level after exercise. However, the transient nature of the phenomenon in our material suggests that potassium is of only secondary importance. Figure 12-40 demonstrates the tall T-waves in a 56-year-old man admitted with severe chest pain before and after the development of an inferior wall myocardial infarction. Note that the tall T-waves extend from V_1 to V_4 but in V_5, the lead most like our CM_5, the T-waves are flattened. In summary then, tall T-waves in lead CM_5 following exercise are not usually associated with ischemia, but may be in leads V_2 to V_4.

FLATTENED OR INVERTED T-WAVES

In the early days of stress testing, a change in the direction of the T-wave was considered to be an important indicator of ischemia.[74] Then after a time, it was believed that it was so nonspecific that the T-waves could be completely ig-

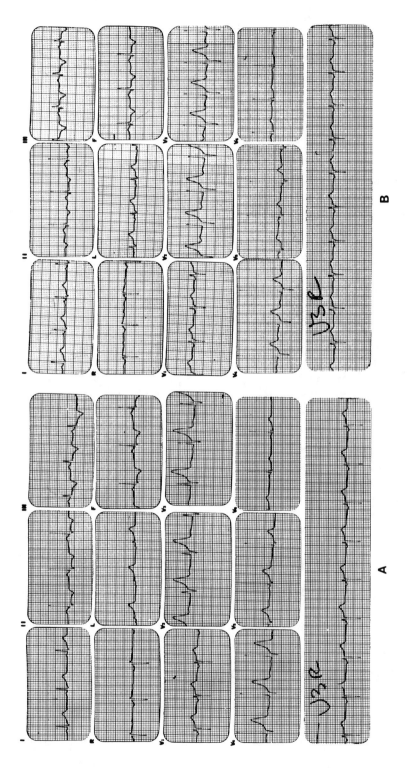

FIGURE 12-40. Twelve lead tracings before (A) and after (B) development of an inferior wall infarction. Note the S-T segment and Q-wave changes in lead III and the tall peaked T-waves in V_2, V_3, and V_4. The T-waves in V_5 and V_6 do not show abnormal T-wave configurations.

nored. Barker and coworkers[92] were able to produce T-wave depression by feeding sodium bicarbonate, and T-wave elevation by feeding ammonium chloride, to experimental subjects. Perfusion experiments on animals have demonstrated an increase in T-wave amplitude with a decrease in pH and an increase in PCO_2 and a decrease or inversion in the T-wave by increasing the pH and lowering PCO_2.[93]

The practice in most laboratories is to pay almost no attention to alternations in T-waves in the evaluation of ischemia. T-wave inversion during exercise almost never occurs in normal subjects and rarely in patients with abnormal function caused by ischemic heart disease.[74] The inversion of T-waves during exercise, however, is quite common in subjects with left-ventricular dysfunction due to hypertension or due to nonspecific types of myopathy. Subjects with normal coronary arteries and angina may show this. Lepeschkin[5] gave normal subjects epinephrine intravenously and found that as the heart rate slowed, the T-waves first got taller for a time, but after the blood pressure rose, the T-wave amplitude was reduced. As epinephrine increased the heart rate, there was a definite decrease in T-wave height in a near linear relationship. This would then suggest that increased catecholamines in the blood as well as a variety of noncardiac influences are often the reason for inverted or flattened T-waves.

On the other hand, the evolution of a downsloping T-wave after exercise is often associated with ischemia (see Fig. 12-10).

NORMALIZATION OF T-WAVES WITH EXERCISE

In patients with flat or inverted T-waves at rest, the evolution to an upright T-wave has been considered by some to be a sign of ischemia.[75,76] Bellet and colleagues[94] reported this as being present in patients with clearcut angina and considered it to indicate ischemia. As was mentioned in the section on tall T-waves, this may well be due to changes in the potassium balance in the body or to other factors that are, as yet, poorly elucidated. Noble and colleagues[95] studied 38 patients with angiographically demonstrated ischemia and inverted T-waves at rest. They found that angina that was exercise-induced or caused by intravenous isoproterenol would cause the T-wave to revert to upright in most cases. Aravindaksham and associates,[96] however, compared the T-wave response in both ischemic patients and asymptomatic subjects with primary R-wave abnormalities. They showed that 27 percent of those with ischemic heart disease had all T-waves revert to normal with exercise, while 57 percent of those without disease reverted to normal. They excluded subjects with R-wave inversion due to hypertrophy, left bundle branch block and drugs, but included in their ischemic group those with a previous infarction. They found that complete T-wave normalization was associated with significant S-T segment depression in 90 percent of ischemic patients, and with a negative test in all patients without ischemic heart disease.

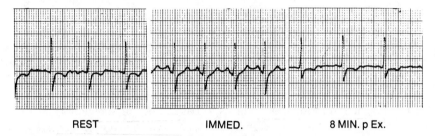

REST   IMMED.   8 MIN. p Ex.

FIGURE 12-41. A 32-year-old asymptomatic woman with normal exercise tolerance whose inverted T-waves became upright with exercise. History and physical examination failed to reveal any evidence of cardiac abnormality.

Many patients with inverted T-waves on the basis of metabolic abnormalities will manifest upright T-waves at the time of exercise. This is particularly true in women. Figure 12-41 illustrates the tracing of a 32-year-old woman who had no coronary symptoms and came in for a screening test. In our experience, this finding does not usually indicate ischemia. On the other hand, ischemia associated with coronary spasm has been shown to cause inverted T-waves to become upright. When the patient is not exercising, this type of change has considerable significance.

THE U-WAVE

Lepeschkin[97] has published an excellent review of the significance of the U-wave. The U-wave is usually upright if the T is also upright, and is highest at low heart rates. It usually follows the T-wave at the same time ventricular relaxation is occurring. When the heart rate increases to over 90, the U-wave is rarely visible because it becomes merged with the end of the T-wave and the ascending limb of the P-wave. Most workers believe that this represents afterpotentials of the T-wave. The U-wave is accentuated by a larger diastolic volume, hypokalemia, and increased digitalis or calcium. Occasionally, in patients with very low potassium, the U-wave can become so tall that it is mistaken for a tall T-wave. Patients with inverted U-waves may have an overload of their central volume, and the tall U-wave may represent a distended papillary muscle.[98] Lepeschkin[97] reports that in patients with coronary disease, the incidence of inverted or diphasic U-waves is about 30 percent at rest and 62 percent after exercise. If one makes an analysis of all patients with inverted U-waves, left-ventricular hypertrophy is the most common cause with angina being responsible for about 20 percent.

Farris and coworkers[99] report that an inverted U-wave, usually during recovery, can often be a clue to ischemia, even in the absence of S-T depression, and in 28 patients with exercise-induced U-wave inversion, 24 had a high-grade proximal left anterior descending stenosis and 3 had significant coronary disease in other vessels. Only 1 had normal coronary arteries. They concluded that this finding predicts coronary disease with considerable reliability (Fig. 12-42). This supports the dictum that powerful predictors are infrequent.

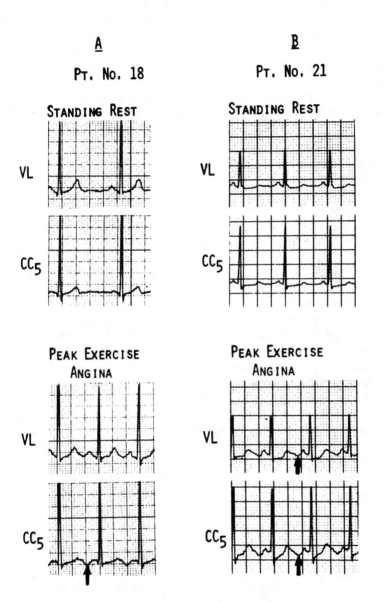

A

Pt. No. 18

STANDING REST

VL

CC₅

PEAK EXERCISE
ANGINA

VL

CC₅

B

Pt. No. 21

STANDING REST

VL

CC₅

PEAK EXERCISE
ANGINA

VL

CC₅

FIGURE 12-42. A, Demonstrates simultaneously recorded vertical (VL) and modified CC₅ lead ECGs during standing rest and at peak exercise for patient 18. Marked U-wave inversion appeared in lead CC₅ at the time of exercise-induced angina pectoris. The exercise S-T segment remained normal. B, Patient 21 was taking digoxin, making the S-T segment response to exercise difficult to interpret. However, during exercise-induced angina pectoris, this patient demonstrated marked U-wave inversion in both leads. The appearance of detectable U-wave inversion in the vertical lead was unusual in this study. (From Faris,[99] with permission.)

ECG PATTERNS AND THEIR SIGNIFICANCE

HYPERVENTILATION AND ORTHOSTATIC CHANGES

Changes in T-waves with hyperventilation or standing are relatively common and are thought to be mediated through the autonomic nervous system. When they are associated with S-T segment depression, the prevalence decreases and it has been reported to be less than 1 or 2 percent.[59] The mechanism is somewhat obscure and has been attributed to pH changes, electrolyte changes (especially potassium), changes in heart position, coronary arteriolar vasospasm, and excessive catecholamines. Because they can be reduced by beta blockers and accentuated by intravenous epinephrine,[100] they probably are due to asynchronous repolarization, probably mediated through the sympathetic pathway. Because the response of the autonomic system may be blunted in coronary disease, these changes are strong negative predictors for ischemia.[101]

Sandberg,[48] Holmgren and associates,[55] Sjostrand,[102] and others have studied such patients and labeled some as having vasoregulatory asthenia. This syndrome is usually seen in young and middle-aged women who often appear to be hyperreactive emotionally and who are usually quite sedentary in their lifestyles. When studied by heart catheterization, they usually exhibit a rapid heart rate, decreased blood volume, higher than normal cardiac output, and a very small arteriovenous difference in their oxygen saturation. This last finding appears to be caused by a decreased capacity to extract oxygen as the blood passes through the capillary bed. These patients often have moderate S-T segment depression with exercise, but the most characteristic change is its appearance when standing and its absence while sitting or lying down.

More recently, it has been shown that mitral prolapse is commonly associated with S-T segment depression secondary to hyperventilation.[59] It may be that some of Holmgren's patients have unrecognized mitral prolapse. It is now accepted that this syndrome is associated with major disturbances in autonomic balance and exercise-induced S-T depression with exercise is not uncommon.

Marcomichelakis and colleagues[103] believe that when exercise-induced S-T depression is found in patients who are likely to have non-coronary causes, it can be identified if the changes are abolished by a beta blocker. They found that the drug did not eliminate the S-T depression in any patients with significant coronary disease, but did correct the S-T in those with normal coronary angiograms.

Hyperventilation, then, should be part of the routine in every stress test, and when identified, used in evaluation of any S-T depression that may occur.

Figure 12-43 is the tracing of a 28-year-old woman who suffered from chronic hyperventilation and a neurotic personality. The marked S-T segment depression after hyperventilation improved with exercise, but returned during the recovery period.

CONCLUSION

This chapter has reviewed most of the electrocardiographic patterns believed

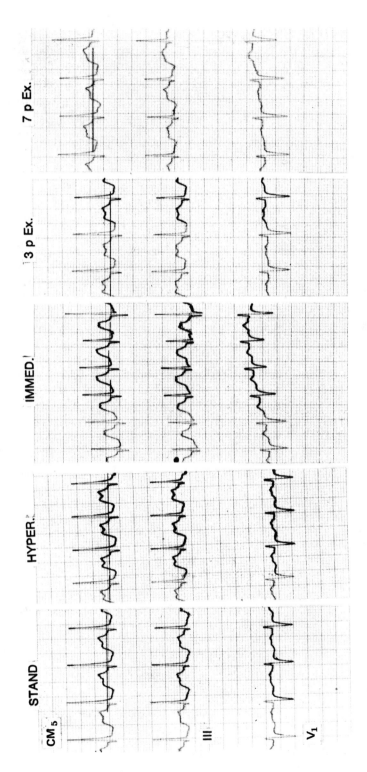

FIGURE 12-43. Exercise test of a 28-year-old woman with chronic hyperventilation and a neurotic personality. The resting S-T segment depression increased by hyperventilation tends to return to almost normal with exercise.

to have known significance in detecting coronary disease. There may well be others of importance that have escaped notice to this date.

By the time this book goes to press, there may well be new electrocardiographic criteria worth considering. All one needs is a little curiosity and a sharp eye to find new things in old places. The changes associated with conduction abnormalities and arrhythmias are covered in Chapter 13.

REFERENCES

1. ELLIOTT, SE, ET AL: *The use of the digital computer in the study of patients during exercise induced stress.* Am Heart J 79:215, 1970.
2. SHEFFIELD, LT, ET AL: *On-line analysis of the exercise electrocardiogram.* Circulation 40:935, 1969.
3. KAHN, KA AND SIMONSON, E: *Changes of mean spatial QRS and T vectors and of conventional electrocardiographic items in hard anaerobic work.* Cir Res 9:629, 1957.
4. BELLET, S, ET AL: *Radioelectrocardiographic changes during strenuous exercise in normal subjects.* Circulation 25:686, 1962.
5. LEPESCHKIN, E: *Physiological factors influencing the electrocardiographic response to exercise.* In BLACKBURN, H (ED): *Measurements in Exercise Electrocardiography.* Charles C Thomas, Springfield, Ill, 1969.
6. BRUCE, RA, ET AL: Personal communications, 1973.
7. BRUCE, RA, ET AL: *Electrocardiographic responses to maximal exercise in American and Chinese population samples.* In BLACKBURN, H (ED): *Measurements in Exercise Electrocardiography.* Charles C Thomas, Springfield, Ill, 1969.
8. BLOMQVIST, CG: *Heart disease and dynamic exercise testing.* In WILLERSON, JT AND SANDERS, CA (EDS): *Clinical Cardiology.* Grune & Stratton, New York, 1977.
9. FROELICHER, VF, ET AL: *A comparison of two bipolar exercise ECG leads to V_5.* Chest 70:611, 1976.
10. RERYCH, SK, ET AL: *Cardiac function at rest and during exercise in normals and in patients with coronary heart disease.* Ann Surg 186:449, 1978.
11. BRODY, DA: *A theoretical analysis of intracavitary blood mass influence on the heart lead relationship.* Circulation 4:731, 1956.
12. PIPBERGER, HV, ISHIKAWA, K, AND BERSON, AS: *QRS amplitude changes during heart filling and digitalization.* Am Heart J 83:292, 1972.
13. BONORIS, PE, ET AL: *Evaluation of R wave changes vs. ST segment depression in stress testing.* Circulation 57:904, 1978.
14. ORZAN, F, ET AL: *Is the treadmill test useful for evaluating coronary artery disease in patients with complete LBBB?* Am J Cardiol 42:36, 1978.
15. LEE, G, ET AL: *Accuracy of left precordial R wave analysis during exercise testing in reliably detecting coronary disease in LBBB patients.* Personal Communication, 1981.
16. MORRIS, SL, LOVELACE, E, AND MCHENRY, PL: *Comparison of R wave and QRS amplitude during treadmill testing in normals and patients with coronary disease* (abstr). Am J Cardiol 43:353, 1979.
17. BERMAN, JL, WGNNE, K, AND COHN, P: *Multiple lead treadmill exercise tests.* Circulation 61:53, 1980.
18. VAN TELLINGEN, C, ASCORP, CA, AND RIJNEKA, RD: *On the clinical value of conventional and new exercise ECG criteria.* Int J Cardiol 5:689, 1984.
19. DEGRE, S, ET AL: *Analysis of exercise-induced R wave amplitude changes in detection of coronary artery disease in patients with typical or atypical chest pain under digitalis treatment.* Cardiology 68(Suppl 2):178–185, 1981.
20. FOX, K, ET AL: *Inability of exercise-induced R wave changes to predict coronary artery disease.* Am J Cardiol 49:674–679, 1982.

21. Fox, K, Selwyn, A, and Shillingford, J: *Precordial electrocardiographic mapping after exercise in the diagnosis of coronary artery disease.* Am J Cardiol 43:541–546, 1979.

22. Greenberg, PS, et al: *Radionuclide angiographic correlation of the R wave, ejection fraction, and volume responses to upright bicycle exercise.* Chest 80:459–464, 1981.

23. David, D, et al: *Intramyocardial conduction: A major determinant of R wave amplitude during acute myocardial ischemia.* Circulation 65:161–166, 1982.

24. Ekmekci, A, et al: *Angina Pectoris.* Am J Cardiol, April: 521–532, 1961.

25. Madias, JE and Krikelis, EN: *Transient giant R waves in the early phase of acute myocardial infarction: Association with ventricular fibrillation.* Clin Cardiol 4:339–349, 1981.

26. DeCaprio, L, et al: *R wave amplitude changes during stress testing: Comparison with ST segment depression and angiographic correlation.* Am Heart J 99(4):413–418, 1980.

27. Ellestad, MH, Greenberg, PS, and Thomas, LK: *The R wave revisited.* In press.

28. Kahn, KA and Simonson, E: *Changes of mean spatial QRS and T vectors and of conventional electrocardiographic items in hard anaerobic work.* Circ Res 9:629, 1957.

29. Simonson, E and Enzer, N: *Physiology of muscular exercise and fatigue in disease.* Medicine 21:345, 1942.

30. Stuart, RJ and Ellestad, MH: *Upsloping ST segments in exercise testing.* Am J Cardiol 37:19, 1976.

31. Robb, GP and Marks, HH: *Postexercise electrocardiograms in arteriosclerotic heart disease: Its value in diagnosis and prognosis.* JAMA 200:918, 1967.

32. Salzman, SH, et al: *Quantitative effects of physical conditioning on the exercise electrocardiogram of middle-aged subjects with arteriosclerotic heart disease.* In Blackburn, H (ed): *Measurements in Exercise Electrocardiography.* Charles C Thomas, Springfield, Ill, 1969.

33. Bruce, RA and Blackmon, JR: *Exercise testing in adult normal subjects and cardiac patients.* Pediatrics 32(Suppl):742, 1963.

34. Blomqvist, CG: *The frank lead exercise electrocardiogram.* Acta Med Scand (Suppl)178:440, 1965.

35. Brody, AJ: *Master's two-step exercise test in clinically unselected patients.* JAMA 171:1195, 1959.

36. Kurita, A, Chartman, BR, and Bourassa, MG: *Significance of exercise-induced ST depression in evaluation of coronary artery disease.* Am J Cardiol 40:492, 1977.

37. Goldschlager, N, Selzer, A, and Cohn, K: *Treadmill stress tests as indicators of presence and severity of coronary artery disease.* Ann Intern Med 85:277, 1976.

38. Marcus, ML: *The coronary circulation in health and disease.* McGraw-Hill, New York, 1983.

39. Robb, GP, Marks, HH, and Mattingly, TW: *The value of the double standard two-step exercise test in the detection of coronary disease: A clinical and statistical follow-up study of military personnel and insurance applicants.* Trans Assoc Life Ins Med Dir Am 40:52, 1956.

40. Detry, JR: *Exercise Testing and Training in Coronary Heart Disease.* Williams & Wilkins, Baltimore, 1973.

41. Master, AM and Jaffe, HL: *The electrocardiographic changes after exercise in angina pectoris.* J Mt Sinai Hosp 7:629, 1941.

42. Mason, RE, et al: *Correlation of graded exercise electrocardiographic response with clinical and coronary cinearteriographic findings.* In Blackburn, H (ed): *Measurements in Exercise Electrocardiography.* Charles C Thomas, Springfield, Ill, 1969.

43. Martin, CM and McConahay, DR: *Maximum treadmill exercise electrocardiography: Correlations with coronary arteriography and cardiac hemodynamics.* Circulation 46:956, 1972.

44. Bruce, RA and McDonough, JR: *Stress testing in screening for cardiovascular disease.* Bull NY Acad Med 45:1288, 1969.

45. Blackburn, H: *The exercise electrocardiogram: Technological, procedural and conceptual development.* In Simonson, E (ed): *Physical Activity and the Heart.* Charles C Thomas, Springfield, Ill, 1967.

46. HORNSTEN, TR AND BRUCE, RA: *Computed ST forces of frank and bipolar exercise ECGs.* Am Heart J 78:346, 1969.

47. SIMOONS, ML: *Optimal measurements for detection of coronary artery disease by exercise ECG.* Comput Biomed Res 10:483, 1977.

48. SANDBERG, L: *Studies in electrocardiogram changes during exercise tests.* Acta Med Scand 169(Suppl):365, 1969.

49. McHENRY, PL, STOWE, DE, AND LANCASTER, MC: *Computer quantitation of the ST segment response during maximal treadmill exercise.* Circulation XXXVIII:691–701, 1968.

50. SHEFFIELD, LT, ET AL: *On-line analysis of the exercise electrocardiogram.* Circulation XL:935–944, 1969.

51. ASCOOP, CA, DISTELBRINK, CA, AND DELAND, PA: *Clinical value of quantitative analysis of ST slope during exercise.* Br Heart J 39:212–217, 1977.

52. FORLINI, FJ, COHN, K, AND LANGSTON, MF, JR: *ST segment isolation and quantification as a means of improving diagnostic accuracy in treadmill stress testing.* Am Heart J 90(4):431–438, 1975.

53. SKETCH, MH, ET AL: *Automated and nomographic analysis of exercise tests.* JAMA 243(10):1052–1055, 1980.

54. YANOWITZ, F, ET AL: *Functional distribution of right and left stellate innervation to the ventricles: Production of neurogenic electrocardiographic changes by unilateral alteration of sympathetic tone.* Circ Res 18:416, 1966.

55. HOLMGREN, A, ET AL: *Electrocardiographic changes in vasoregulatory asthenia and the effect of training.* Acta Med Scand 165:21, 1967.

56. JACOBS, WF, BATTEE, WE, AND RONAN, JA: *False positive ST-T wave changes secondary to hyperventilation and exercise.* Ann Intern Med 81:479, 1974.

57. LARY, D AND GOLDSCHLAGER, N: *ECG changes during hyperventilation resembling myocardial ischemia in patients with normal coronary arteriograms.* Am Heart J 87:383, 1974.

58. WASSERBURGER, RH, SIEBECKER, KL, AND LEWIS, WC: *The effect of hyperventilation on the normal adult ECG.* Circulation 13:850, 1956.

59. TOMMASO, CL AND GARDIN, JM: *Pseudoischemic ST segment changes induced by hyperventilation.* Primary Cardiology, April 111–119, 1983.

60. ROSELLE, HA, CRAMPTON, RS, AND CASE, RB: *Alternans of the depressed ST segment during coronary insufficiency: Its relation to mechanical events.* Am J Cardiol 18:200, 1966.

61. WAYNE, VS, BISHOP, RL, AND SPODICK, DH: *Exercise-induced ST segment alternans.* Chest 5:824–825, 1983.

62. FARIS, JV, McHENRY, PL, AND MORRIS, SN: *Fundamentals of clinical cardiology.* Am Heart J 95(1):102–114, 1978.

63. LEPESCHKIN, E, ET AL: *Effect of epinephrine and norepinephrine on the electrocardiograms of 100 normal subjects.* Am J Cardiol 5:594, 1960.

64. MANVI, KN AND ELLESTAD, MH: *Elevated ST segments with exercise in ventricular aneurysm.* J Electrocardiol 5:317, 1972.

65. CAHAHINE, RA, RAEZNER, AE, AND ISCHIMORI, T: *The clinical significance of exercise induced ST segment elevation.* Circulation 54:209, 1976.

66. PRINZMETAL, M, ET AL: *Variant from angina pectoris.* JAMA 174:1794, 1960.

67. DETRY, JMR, ET AL: *Maximal exercise testing in patients with spontaneous angina pectoris associated with transient ST segment elevation.* Br Heart J 37:897, 1975.

68. HEGGE, FN, TURA, N, AND BURCHELL, HB: *Coronary arteriography finding in patients with axis shifts and ST elevation in exercise testing.* Am Heart J 86:613, 1973.

69. MACALPIN, RN, KATTUS, AA, AND ALVARO, AB: *Angina pectoris at rest with preservation of exercise capacity: Prinzmetal's variant angina.* Circulation 47:946, 1973.

70. BELICK, N AND GARDIN, JM: *ECG manifestations of myocardial ischemia.* Arch Int Med 140:1162–1165, 1980.

71. KASSER, IS AND BRUCE, RA: *Comparative effects of aging and coronary heart disease on submaximal and maximal exercise.* Circulation 39:759, 1969.

72. CHELTON, LG AND BURCHELL, HB: *Unusual ST segment deviations in electrocardiograms of*

normal persons. Am J Med Sci 230:54, 1955.

73. KAMBARA, H AND PHILLIPS, J: Long-term evaluation of early repolarization syndrome. Am J Cardiol 38:157, 1976.

74. LLOYD-THOMAS, H: The effect of exercise on the electrocardiogram in healthy subjects. Br Heart J 23:260, 1961.

75. YU, PNG, ET AL: Observations on change of ventricular systole (QT interval) during exercise. J Clin Invest 29:279, 1950.

76. YU, PNG AND SOFFER, A: Studies of electrocardiographic changes during exercise (modified double two-step test). Circulation 6:183, 1952.

77. GREENBERG, PS, FRISCHA, DA, AND ELLESTAD, MH: Comparison of the predictive accuracy of ST depression, R wave amplitude, QX/QT and QTc during stress testing. Am J Cardiol 44:18, 1979.

78. VASILOMANOLAKIS, EC, ET AL: Identification of exercise induced ischemia by measurement of Q to peaked T interval (abstr). American Heart Association 56th Scientific Session, Anaheim, Calif, November 1983.

79. BEZETT, HC: An analysis of the time relations of electrocardiograms. Heart 7:353–370, 1920.

80. LEPESCHKIN, E AND SURAWICZ, B: Characteristics of true-positive and false-positive results of electrocardiographic exercise tests. N Engl J Med 258:511, 1958.

81. ROMAN, L AND BELLET, S: Significance of the QX/QT ratio and the QT ratio (QTr) in the exercise electrocardiogram. Circulation 32:435, 1965.

82. MASTER, AM AND ROSENFELT, I: Two-step exercise test: Current status after 25 years. Mod Concepts Cardiovasc Dis 36:19, 1967.

83. BURCH, GE AND DEPASQUALE, N: A study at autopsy of the relation of absence of the Q wave in leads 1, AVL, V_5, and V_6 to septal fibrosis. Am Heart J 60:336–340, 1960.

84. MORALES-BALLEGO, H, ET AL: The septal Q wave in exercise testing. Am J Cardiol 48:247–251, 1981.

85. FAMULARO, M, ET AL: Identification septal ischemia during exercise by Q wave analysis: Correlation with coronary angiography. Am J Cardiol 51(3):440–443, 1983.

86. O'HARA, MJ, ET AL: Changes of Q wave amplitude during exercise for the prediction of coronary artery disease. Int J Cardiol 6:35–45, 1984.

87. WONG, HO, KASSER, I, AND BRUCE, RA: Impaired maximal exercise performance with hypertensive cardiovascular disease. Circulation 39:633, 1969.

88. HARRIS, CN, ET AL: Treadmill stress test in left ventricular hypertrophy. Chest 63:353, 1973.

89. SCHERF, D: Fifteen years of electrocardiographic exercise test in coronary stenosis. NY State J Med 47:2420, 1947.

90. SCHERF, D AND SCHOFFER, AI: The electrocardiographic exercise test. Am Heart J 43:44, 1952.

91. BLOMQVIST, CG: Use of exercise testing for diagnostic and functional evaluation. Circulation 44:1120, 1971.

92. BARKER, PS, SHRADER, EL, AND RONZONIA, E: Effects of alkalosis and of acidosis upon human electrocardiogram. Am Heart J 17:169, 1939.

93. TRETHEWIE, ER AND HODGKINSON, MM: Influence of carbon dioxide and pH on electrocardiograms of isolated perfused heart. Quart J Exp Physiol 40:1, 1955.

94. BELLET, S, DELIYIANNIS, S, AND ELIAKIM, M: The electrocardiogram during exercise as recorded by radioelectrocardiography: Comparison with the post-exercise electrocardiogram (Master's two-step test). Am J Cardiol 18:385, 1961.

95. NOBLE, J, ET AL: Normalization of abnormal T-waves in ischemia. Arch Intern Med 136:391, 1976.

96. ARAVINDAKSHAM, V, SURAWICZ, B, AND ALLEN, RD: ECG exercise test in patients with abnormal T waves at rest. Am Heart J 93:706, 1977.

97. LEPESCHKIN, E: Physiological basis of the U wave. In SCHLANT, RC AND HURST, JW (EDS): Advances in Electrocardiography, Vol. 2. Grune & Stratton, New York, 1977.

98. FARBETTA, D, ET AL: *Abnormality of the U wave and of the T-A segment of the electrocardiogram.* Circulation 14:1129, 1956.
99. FARIS, SV, MCHENRY, PL, AND MORRIS, SN: *Concepts and applications of treadmill exercise testing and the exercise electrocardiogram.* Am Heart J 95:102, 1978.
100. KARJALAINEN, J: *Function and myocarditis-induced T-wave abnormalities.* Chest 83:6, 1983.
101. MCHENRY, PL: *Treadmill exercise testing in the diagnosis and evaluation of coronary heart disease.* J Continuing Ed in Cardiol, October, 11:14–25, 1978.
102. SJOSTRAND, R: *Experimental variations in T-wave of electrocardiogram.* Acta Med Scand 138:191, 1950.
103. MARCOMICHELAKIS, J, ET AL: *Exercise testing after beta-blockade: Improved specificity and predictive value in detecting coronary heart disease.* Br Heart J 43:252–261, 1980.

13

RHYTHM AND CONDUCTION DISTURBANCES IN STRESS TESTING

Alterations in cardiac rhythm occur frequently with exercise and have considerable importance in understanding a patient's function as well as providing predictive information as to the mortality and morbidity. Arrhythmias during exertion result from sympathetically enhanced Phase IV repolarization of ectopic foci, alterations in recovery time of cardiac tissues caused by ischemia, and probably battery effects associated with ischemic tissue adjacent to normally perfused myocardium. The prevalence increases steadily with age[1] and has reported to be 100 percent in one study of older subjects.[2]

The imbalance between oxygen supply and demand induced in exercising patients with coronary disease may be augmented during the recovery period. Peripheral dilatation induced by exercise, coupled with a reduced venous return caused by abrupt cessation of muscular activity, may cause cardiac output and coronary flow to fall at a time when myocardial oxygen demand is still quite high, owing to tachycardia. These changes, in combinations with elevated catecholamines, may explain the increase in arrhythmias commonly seen during recovery.

SICK SINUS SYNDROME (Chronotropic Incompetence)

There exists a heterogeneous group of subjects who often have inappropriately low resting heart rates. Some of these are symptomatic and others may be unaware of this abnormality. Many have been diagnosed as having sick sinus syndrome. It would appear that some have a high vagal tone, some have intrinsic disease of the nodal tissue—possibly due to ischemia or degenerative changes, and some are due to causes not yet elucidated. When a slow resting pulse fails to accelerate normally with exercise, we have labeled it "chronotropic incompetence;" however, it would appear that our understanding of these syndromes is somewhat incomplete. A slower than normal acceleration of the heart rate would be a protective mechanism in ischemia, preserving a longer diastolic time to perfuse the myocardium. It has been suggested that the Bezold-Jarrish reflex, initiated by mechanical receptors in the left-ventricular wall when dilatation occurs with ischemia, may be a mechanism.

We have found[3,4] that the reduced heart rate response to exercise identifies a cohort of patients with poor ventricular function and severe coronary narrowing who are subject to an increased prevalence of future coronary events. The predictive power of this response is presented in Chapter 14.

Abbott and colleagues[5] performed bicycle ergometry on 16 patients with electrophysiologically confirmed sinus node dysfunction who had a blunted heart rate response to exercise. Atropine increased their chronotropic response to normal at lower workloads, but with peak exercise their heart rates were still below predicted, suggesting vagotonia was not the only mechanism. These patients probably suffer from a number of autonomic aberrations and much remains to be done to improve our understanding of the complex factors controlling heart rate in patients with cardiac dysfunction.

STRESS TESTING: PRINCIPLES AND PRACTICE

SUPRAVENTRICULAR ARRHYTHMIAS

Although sinus arrhythmias tend to be reduced by the vagal withdrawal accompanying the onset of exercise, this and wandering pacemakers tend to recur early during the recovery period and have no special significance. The loss of the atrial transport mechanism, however, results in a loss in stroke volume of from 5 to 30 percent depending on the ventricular compliance and the heart rate. As early as 1912, Sir Thomas Lewis[6] demonstrated a drop in cardiac output and aortic pressure at the onset of atrial fibrillation and reports by Kaplan and colleagues[7] and Killip and Baer[8] both substantiate the belief that atrial contraction is important to function. Thus, the sinus node not only determines the chronotropic response to increased metabolic load, but the appropriately timed atrial boost of ventricular filling is critical for optimal function at high workloads.

Atrial Fibrillation and Flutter

Transient atrial fibrillation or flutter is seen frequently and can be associated with coronary heart disease, rheumatic heart disease, thyrotoxicosis, or myocarditis. It is also occasionally seen in people of all ages who have no other apparent abnormalities. Although no specific diagnosis can be made when this condition develops, it is an indication of malfunction and it should be noted that the cardiac output with rapid rates of atrial fibrillation or flutter is far below that of a subject with sinus rhythm who has a similar ventricular response. Upon testing a subject with atrial fibrillation or flutter, the ventricular response tends to accelerate very rapidly, probably due to inadequate left-ventricular filling resulting in a decreased stroke volume. The S-T segment changes associated with ischemia are similar to those observed with a sinus rhythm and may be seen in rheumatic heart disease and with other cardiac abnormalities. In these cases, the S-T segment depression may indicate left-ventricular dysfunction due to primary muscle change rather than to coexisting coronary disease. It may also be that the very short diastolic intervals produce subendocardial ischemia because of the inadequate perfusion time in the face of an otherwise normal ventricular function. When supraventricular rhythms are initiated by exercise, they do not necessarily implicate coronary disease as the underlying etiology, although this is usually the primary factor in older subjects.

Atrial Tachycardia (PAT)

Two- or three-beat bursts of atrial or junctional tachycardia are occasionally seen with exercise, but sustained PAT is relatively rare. Graboys and Wright[9] reported 29 patients with sustained paroxysmal atrial tachycardia in 3000

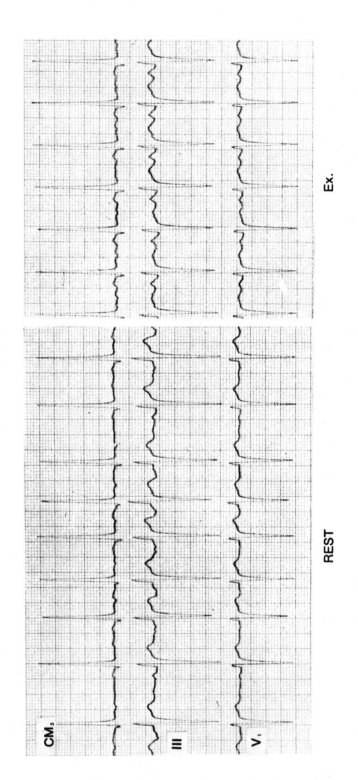

FIGURE 13-1. Tracings of a 33-year-old alcoholic whose unusual PAT could be terminated by intravenous atropine or by exercise.

stress tests. These were from a cohort of 207 patients referred for evaluation of atrial arrhythmias. Gough[10] reported on 880 stress tests, 315 of which were believed to be normal subjects. Eleven had atrial and nine had junctional tachycardia and two had atrial fibrillation in short bursts. All but one spontaneously terminated within 90 seconds. Even in subjects prone to paroxysmal atrial tachycardia, this rhythm is rarely initiated by exercise. In one of our cases, an intermittent supraventricular tachycardia was consistently terminated by exercise (Fig. 13-1). The exact cause for this is obscure, but it may have been that the re-entry pathway responsible for the tachycardia had become refractory during the exercise period. When PAT does appear during a stress test, S-T segment depression is commonly seen and is often, but not invariably, associated with ischemia.

VENTRICULAR ARRHYTHMIAS

Resting

There is considerable disagreement in the significance of resting ventricular ectopic beats. Fisher and Tyroler[11] studied 1212 white, male factory workers and concluded that although there was an increase in incidence of PVCs from 2 to 15 percent with age, they could not statistically predict the incidence of sudden death or myocardial infarction. When Goldschlager and associates[12] compared the coronary angiograms of patients exhibiting premature contractions with those who did not, they found a much more severe degree of disease associated with the arrhythmia. Rodstein and coworkers[13] studied 712 insured persons with extrasystoles for an average period of 18 years. No change in mortality was observed, even when those over and under age 40 were compared. However, when exercise produced an increase in the number of arrhythmias in either age group, the incidence of mortality did increase. There are a number of other studies that claim that the occurrence of sudden death in subjects with resting ventricular arrhythmias is increased by two- to threefold.[14] Alexander and colleagues[15] from the Lahey Clinic reported follow-up studies on 539 patients with PVCs at rest. They found that in patients with heart disease there was a small but statistically significant increase in mortality when PVCs were recorded.

Recently Buckingham and associates[16] have demonstrated that frequent PVCs detected in Holter recordings in normal subjects are usually benign. On the other hand, if they occur in subjects with significant ventricular dysfunction, they are often harbingers of subsequent trouble. As it turns out, the same thing can be said for PVCs recorded during exercise testing.[17]

Exercise-Induced Ventricular Arrhythmias

In clinically normal subjects, maximal stress testing will produce occasional ventricular arrhythmias in from 36 to 42 percent, usually at high workloads. In coronary patients, the prevalence is reported to be about 50 to 60 percent. In general, coronary patients manifest arrhythmias at a lower heart rate, and they are somewhat more reproducible than those seen in clinically normal subjects. Sheps and coworkers[18] have reported that when stress tests are done consecutively on the same day, the second test produced significantly fewer PVCs.

In actively employed normal policemen[19] and airmen,[20] exercise-induced PVCs have been studied and found to have no influence on the subsequent morbidity and mortality.

We have reported follow-up data on 1327 patients who had PVCs either before, during, or after exercise testing who were referred to our hospital mostly for chest pain syndromes.[17] In this population, we found that the PVCs were associated with a moderate increase in morbidity and mortality as compared with the normal, even when they failed to have ischemic S-T depression. However, when they developed S-T depression, the mortality and number of coronary events almost doubled. Also, ominous PVCs increased the risk even more to about twice that of the others. Ominous PVCs were defined as multifocal, multiform, repetitive, and also ventricular tachycardia. Follow-up data on PVCs after myocardial infarction have also shown that when associated with mild disease and good left-ventricular function they are of lesser

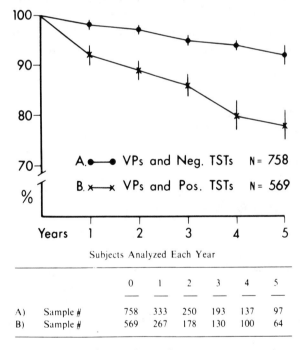

| A) | Sample # | 758 | 333 | 250 | 193 | 137 | 97 |
| B) | Sample # | 569 | 267 | 178 | 130 | 100 | 64 |

FIGURE 13-2. Life table depicting the prevalence of coronary events according to patients with ventricular premature beats and normal S-T segments, A, and the same rhythm in patients with S-T depressions. B. Patients in whom both abnormalities are present have more than a twofold prevalence of coronary events (angina, myocardial infarction, and death).

STRESS TESTING: PRINCIPLES AND PRACTICE

clinical significance, but when recorded in patients with a low ejection fraction, they indicate a more grave prognosis (Fig. 13-2).

The recent report from Durham, North Carolina by Califf and colleagues[21] on 1293 stress tests in patients undergoing coronary angiography is of interest. Their survival data are quite similar to ours. They also found that those with greater ischemia, that is, three-vessel disease, had a higher incidence of more serious ventricular arrhythmias. McHenry[22] reported a 27 percent incidence of exercise-induced ventricular arrhythmias in cardiac patients as compared with 7 percent in those with normal coronary arteries. It is of interest that Califf[21] found a much higher incidence of ventricular arrhythmias in those on digitalis, confirming previous report by Gouch[23] who report one half of the six patients taking digitalis in their series developed ventricular tachycardia.

Abolition of Arrhythmias by Exercise

The induction of arrhythmias by exercise is well recognized, but the abolition of ectopic activity is less commonly appreciated. The mechanisms responsible for this include rapid heart rate, which increases the relative time during the refractory period providing a measure of overdrive suppression and decreased automaticity of the Purkinje system, associated with rapid stimulation.

It is common to see young, apparently healthy subjects who have PVCs at rest that are abolished with exercise. These individuals have no evidence of cardiac abnormalities other than the PVCs at rest. It had been our policy to consider this type of arrhythmia benign as proposed by Bourne[24] in 1977. This seemed to be so logical that we were surprised when our own study indicated that patients referred for stress testing in our laboratory whose PVCs were suppressed by exercise had a similar prevalence of cardiac events as those whose PVCs were initiated by exercise. Helfant and colleagues[25] have also reported a significant incidence of coronary disease in a small group (N = 22) of subjects with PVCs that were decreased by exercise. McHenry and associates[19] report exercise suppression of ventricular arrhythmias in 42 percent of these coronary patients.

PVCs During Recovery

As the rate rapidly slows during recovery, PVCs commonly occur and usually have no clinical significance in our experience. As previously mentioned, this may be a time when metabolic adjustments in the heart are somewhat inappropriate and, therefore, occasionally serious disturbances in rhythm may be initiated. A recent report, however, suggests that the danger from arrhythmias during the cool-down may be considerable.[26] Dimsdale found epinephrine and norepinephrine can shoot up to 10 times normal. The hormonal fluctuations can be minimized by a gradual cool-down. The drop in blood pressure during recovery appears to trigger the response.

Ventricular Tachycardia

When this rhythm, defined as three consecutive VCs or more, comes on during exercise, it constitutes an indication for termination and has been found to be associated with a high incidence of coronary events. Sandberg[27] claims that ventricular tachycardia does not have any more serious implications than any other type of ventricular arrhythmia in terms of the incidence of underlying coronary disease. This seems at odds with the observation by Rodstein and associates[13] who reported a definite increase in mortality in their insurance subjects who had multifocal premature contractions. Castle and coworkers[28] reported on a patient with a negative maximal stress test who had ventricular fibrillation while playing tennis. Although this is very possible, the X lead in his illustration recorded immediately after the test looked to me as though it indicated myocardial ischemia. Perhaps if a more sensitive lead had been used, it might have been easier to recognize the abnormality.

I believe that *most adult men with ventricular tachycardia associated with exercise have significant coronary disease,* although occasionally they may have some other type of left-ventricular dysfunction. This rhythm is occasionally seen in children and young adults as a relatively benign process. Several subjects under our supervision with quite severe ventricular tachycardia have had either myocardiopathies or very minimal coronary atheroma. In our follow-up study, there was a 12 percent death rate over a 5-year period in this group, and when the occurrence of ventricular tachycardia was analyzed alone, the 5-year mortality was 37 percent. Therefore, we must conclude that *the more irritable the ventricle, the more severe the implications.*

Reproducibility

It has been experimentally shown that PVCs are consistently seen at the inception of acute ischemia. Thus, exercise-induced PVCs and/or V-tachycardia may be an "ischemic equivalent" and one would expect good reproducibility. Unfortunately, this is not the case. Faris and colleagues[29] found approximately a 50 percent reproducibility in clinically normal subjects after a 3-year interval—not too surprising. However, Sheps and associates[18] repeated the exercise test after 45 minutes and found the second test resulted in a significant decrease in irritability. Jelinek and Lown[30] reported a reproducibility of 30 percent for PVCs and 50 percent for V-tach. Thus, when using a stress test to evaluate the efficacy of an antiarrhythmic agent, the degree of unreliability must be kept in mind. An even lower rate of reproducibility in Holter monitoring (10 percent) was reported by Jelinek and Lown.[30] Ryan and associates[31] and Glasser and coworkers[32] have reported, however, that for the detection of ventricular dysrhythmias the Holter, on the average, outperformed the exercise test.

CONDUCTION DISTURBANCES

Exercise initiates a complex set of events that impinge on the conduction system. There is an increase in sympathetic drive and a withdrawal of vagal tone. Sympathetic enhancement of conduction is mediated somewhat by the increased sinus firing rate causing an increased number of impulses arriving at the atrioventricular node. The fatigue of the conduction tissue as a result of the increased traffic, and a relatively greater segment of the conduction time being occupied by the refractory period, may mitigate the effect of the excess sympathetic influence. In coronary artery disease patients, ischemia may also alter the conduction process depending on its severity and location. In normals at maximum exercise, the P-Q interval shortens to about 110 msecs. Barrow and Ouer[33] reported that immediately after exercise, the P-R interval is either decreased to a greater extent than would be predicted from the heart rate or is independent of the heart rate. Atrial pacing at increased heart rates almost always prolongs the P-Q interval, probably because vagal tone is still intact and there is very little increase in sympathetic drive.

FIRST DEGREE ATRIOVENTRICULAR BLOCK

First degree AV block at rest commonly disappears with exercise owing to the vagal withdrawal. The same effect can be induced with Atropine.[34] The development of a prolonged P-Q segment after exercise has been reported in a patient with triple-vessel disease, by Glasser and Clark[35] who state that they have seen three patients with AV block after exercise in 2000 treadmill examinations. Sandberg[34] describes this phenomenon in two patients who have had myocarditis. This rare finding probably has little clinical significance.

SECOND DEGREE ATRIOVENTRICULAR BLOCK

Lepeschkin and colleagues[36] report a case of Type II, second degree block after norepinephrine effusion. The absence of this type of abnormality in exercise testing is probably due to the fact that we rarely exercise a patient with a known infectious disease or active rheumatic fever. Bakst's group[37] reports a 74-year-old woman with coronary artery disease and a first and second degree AV block at rest. Both exercise and atropine produced a second degree Type II block. No change in P-R interval occurred with either of these maneuvers when the sinus rate exceeded 68 BPM. Cases have also been reported by Moulopoulos and Anthopoulos[38] and Goodfriend and Barold.[39] The latter did HIS bundle studies and reported the lesions to be above the HIS spike and below the AV node. Gilchrist[40] in 1958 pointed out that Type I block improves with exercise while Type II deteriorates. This effect has also been emphasized by Rozanski's group[41] who state "an exercise-induced increase in sympathetic drive will enhance conduction through the AV node, but will have no effect on tissue below this level." As previously mentioned, first degree AV block may be prolonged with atrial pacing at high heart rates until it becomes a second degree block.

FASCICULAR BLOCK

Left Anterior Division Block

To my knowledge, there are no data on the likelihood of the occurrence of left-anterior division hemiblock with exercise. Oliveros and associates[42] have reported two cases where exercise-induced left-anterior hemiblock was associated with a high-grade paroxysmal left anterior descending lesion. Both patients also had typical S-T segment depression when normal conduction returned during recovery. During the period when hemiblock was evident, however, the S-T changes tended to be masked in the frontal plane and to some degree in the precordial leads. Although Oliveros and associates failed

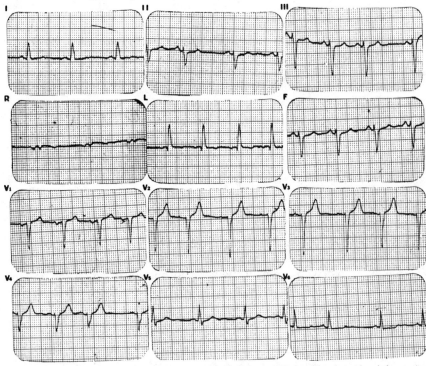

FIGURE 13-3. A resting 12-lead tracing of a 66-year-old asymptomatic man with a left-anterior division hemiblock (see Fig. 13-4).

STRESS TESTING: PRINCIPLES AND PRACTICE

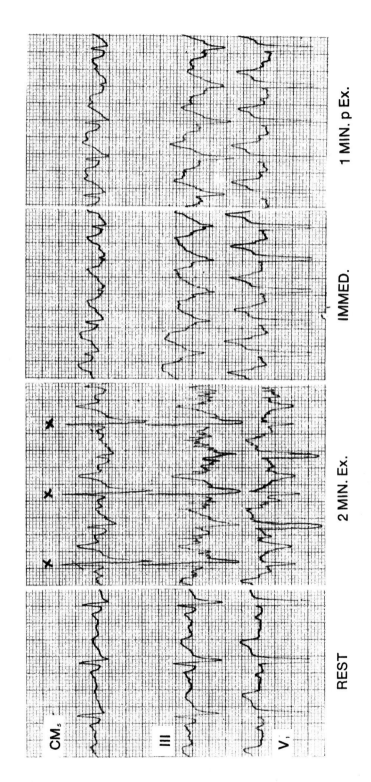

FIGURE 13-4. The exercise tracing of the man illustrated in Figure 13-3. He developed intermittent alterations in axis deviation and S-T segment elevation in V_1 with exercise.

to comment on this in their paper, Gergueira-Gomes and colleagues[43] in a general discussion of hemiblock emphasized this point. They believe the changes were due to transient ischemia of the septum as one case, following successful bypass surgery, reverted to normal. In spite of the tendency of the axis shift to mask ischemia, the incidence of a positive test tends to increase when the presence of left anterior hemiblock is established. Miller and co-workers[44] described abnormal exercise test results in 14 out of 20 subjects with left axis deviation, who were thought otherwise to be normal. Nine of these subjects had left anterior hemiblock using the criteria of more than 35 degree axis. A matched control group who had normal axis had an incidence of 40 percent positive tests for ischemia. This high incidence is rather surprising and makes me suspect that their control patients were a very selected group. Mean age of the control group was 50.1 and from the experience in our laboratory, we would expect an abnormal response in this age group to be somewhere between 15 and 20 percent.

Figure 13-3 depicts the tracing of a 66-year-old man who had never experienced any symptoms of cardiac disease. The resting electrocardiogram clearly demonstrated left-anterior division block. As exercise progressed, temporary alterations in the axis resulted presumably due to a change in the degree of block from beat to beat. In addition, the R-wave in CM_5 diminished and returned toward that recorded at rest during recovery. The patient experienced no symptoms during the test except for the usual fatigue and dyspnea. The S-T segment elevation in V_1 at rest, which was accentuated by exercise, might have been due to a dyskinetic area or an ischemic area in the septum (Fig. 13-4).

Left Posterior Hemiblock and Right Bundle Branch Block

The interpretation of this pattern poses a difficult problem in evaluation of S-T segments because of the unusual electrocardiographic axis. The usual CM_5 lead in this condition presents a small R-wave and because of this, one might suspect that the S-T segment forces would also be very minimal. Figure 13-5 displays the resting 12-lead tracing of a 56-year-old man, four months after he experienced a myocardial infarction that resulted in the development of a left posterior hemiblock and RBBB. During the exercise period, the patient developed S-T segment elevations in the CM_5 and vertical leads and S-T segment depression in the V_1 lead suggesting that the S-T segment depression is still opposite to the major QRS forces even when they are shifted anteriorly and inferiorly.

Left Posterior Hemiblock

Bobba and associates[45] from Italy, reported four cases in which they proposed that the left posterior hemiblock was initiated by exercise. In their patients, the

STRESS TESTING: PRINCIPLES AND PRACTICE

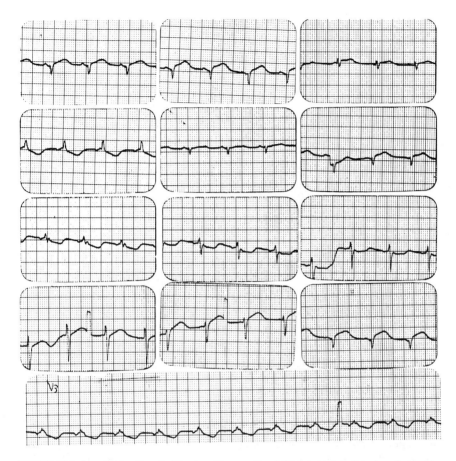

FIGURE 13-5. A resting tracing of a 56-year-old man with a left posterior hemiblock and a RBBB taken one week following an acute myocardial infarction.

axis shifted inferiorly and to the right from 0 to approximately 110 degrees. S-T segment depression developed in the classical V_4 and V_5 positions so that the recognition of ischemic changes was similar to that of the patient with a normal axis. They described four such cases in 100 subjects indicating that it may not be too unusual. Most of the time, this shift would be missed because of failure to record the three standard leads, thus, being unable to identify the axis change they reported.

RATE-RELATED BUNDLE BRANCH BLOCK

Sandberg[34] studied nine cases of bundle branch block initiated by exercise, two of which were right bundle branch block (RBBB). In the subjects who were quite young (ages 30 to 40), the onset of the block appeared only at high workloads and in the absence of S-T segment depression. It was his feeling that this was not associated with coronary disease and produced little change in function. He also found that it could be caused by means other than exercise, such as the administration of amyl nitrite or atropine. There did not appear to be an exact heart rate or R-R interval at which the patient would shift to a block pattern, but there was definitely a range after which this would invariably occur. The terms rate-related BBB often implied the absence of significant coronary or myocardial pathology. Like so many findings in medicine, it cannot be judged without taking the total clinical picture into consideration. Evidence now suggests that in patients in the coronary age group this process can often be due to ischemia.[46] It was Sandberg's belief that in older subjects with coronary disease, the block would occur at slower heart rates. Wayne and colleagues,[46] however, found that 14 of 16 patients with "rate-related bundle branch blocks" had strong evidence in favor of coronary artery disease. Their patients' average age was 59 $\pm$ 9. Eleven had left bundle branch block and 5 had right.

Whenever a block pattern spontaneously occurs during exercise or with hyperventilation, one should consider the possibility of WPW syndrome. It is very important to recognize this entity because the S-T segment depression in this condition does not mean ischemic heart disease and the short PQ and delta wave are easy to overlook. Kattus[47] described a patient with variable right bundle branch block who had ischemia in the normally conducted complexes, but not in those with the block pattern.

RIGHT BUNDLE BRANCH BLOCK

The reliability of exercise-induced S-T segment depression as a predictor of ischemia in patients with right bundle branch block has been debated.[47] Most investigators argue that while the wide S-wave makes the identification of the J-point somewhat more difficult, changes in the lateral precordial leads should be reliable.[49,50] It may be that the sensitivity is less satisfactory with this abnormality. Tanaka and coworkers[49] make the point that the S-T depression must be manifested in the lateral precordial or similar leads to have significance. Several of their patients with normal coronary arteries had S-T depression in V_1 to V_3. Kattus[47] also has made this point. In our laboratory, we have seen many patients with right bundle branch block develop S-T segment depression with exercise. The electrocardiogram of the 51-year-old man depicted in Figure 13-6, who exhibits this finding, had suffered two previous myocardial infarctions and exhibited S-T segment depression and experienced anginal pain immediately after exercise and during cardiac catheterization. The elevation of left-ventricular end-diastolic pressure can be seen to correlate with the S-T segment depression. Although the QRS is wide in right bundle branch block, the total Q-T interval is not significantly prolonged. Therefore, the duration of the S-T segment depression is relatively shorter in right bundle because the wide S-wave in the CM_5 lead or in the lateral precordial lead encroaches on the S-T segment. Even so, *right bundle branch block in contraindication to left bundle*

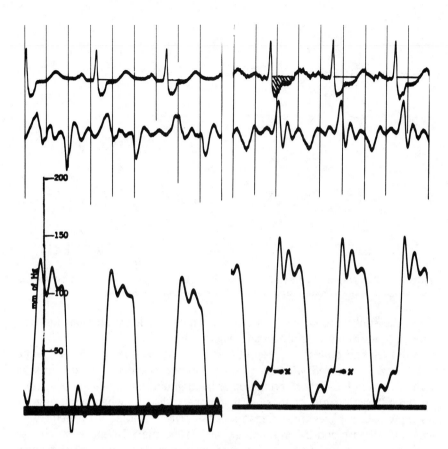

FIGURE 13-6. Resting and exercise left-ventricular pressures in a 51-year-old man with advanced three-vessel disease by angiography. Note the increase in the LVEDP associated with S-T segment depression in a subject with RBBB. The wide S-wave encroaches on the S-T segment.

branch block may but does not usually mask ischemic changes, at least in the CM_5 lead (Fig. 13-7).

LEFT BUNDLE BRANCH BLOCK

In general, LBBB tends to be associated with decreased left-ventricular function and with a poor prognosis. In patients who have LBBB alternating with normal conduction, the function of the ventricle, during the beats associated with the block, has been demonstrated to be less effective in subjects with reduced left-ventricular function. This may be due to degenerative changes in the conduction system and not associated with coronary disease per se. It can also be due to myocarditis, severe left-ventricular hypertrophy or myocardiopathy. Under such circumstances, the electrocardiographic changes associated with stress are difficult to evaluate with certainty. In symptomatic sub-

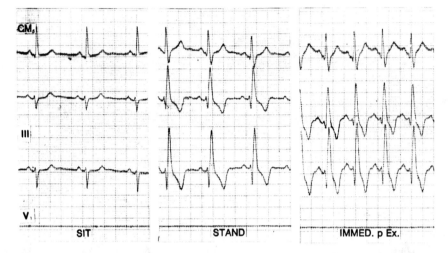

| SIT | STAND | IMMED. p Ex. |

FIGURE 13-7. A 48-year-old man who developed RBBB on standing. Subsequent catheterization revealed normal coronary arteries and normal left-ventricular function.

jects, the stroke output and other measurements of left-ventricular function may at times be very near normal[50] (Fig. 13-8).

Cooksey and colleagues[51] report that if S-T depression of 1.5 mm, more than at rest, occurred with exercise one should suspect coronary disease. Whinnery and Froelicher[50] on the other hand, found no significant difference in the S-T depression of those with coronary disease when analyzing 31 asymptomatic air crewmen. Orzan and associates[52] studied 30 patients with coronary disease and 27 without, and also found the S-T depression change with exercise to be of little value in identification. In their discussion, they commented that anginal pain was rarely associated with significant S-T change and suggested that in LBBB the S-T depression is probably not a manifestation of ischemia. Discussions of the possible electrophysiologic reasons for these findings can be found in the work of Walston and colleagues[53] and Abildskov.[54]

In the CM$_5$ lead, a fair number of patients with LBBB have a positive rather than a negative T-wave. In these patients, the S-T segments become more and more depressed during progressive exercise. I believe this may be a reflection of decreased left-ventricular function with a higher filling pressure in some patients, similar to the mechanisms producing S-T segment depression in a patient with normal conduction. It does not necessarily follow, however, that there is coronary disease present. This phenomenon often occurs in patients with hypertensive or idiopathic cardiomyopathies and may even occur when the disease is localized in the bundle itself. For this reason, I agree with those who believe that LBBB and the S-T segment depression seen with it is not indicative of coronary disease (Fig. 13-9).

A number of patients with normal ventricular conduction at rest develop LBBB during stress testing. They may or may not have coronary disease. Figure

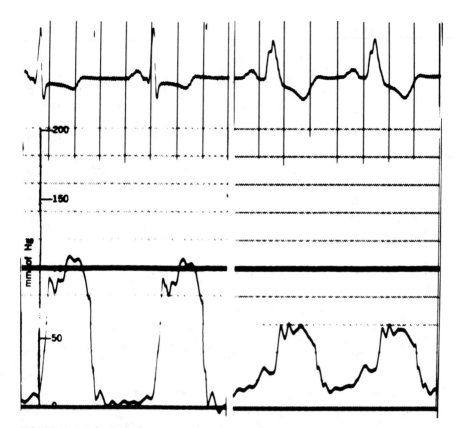

FIGURE 13-8. Left-ventricular tracings taken during catheterization in a 56-year-old man. LBBB suddenly developed after the catheter was placed in the left ventricle. The decrease in left-ventricular systolic pressure and the increase in the LVEDP in the tracing on the right indicated a severe decrease in function.

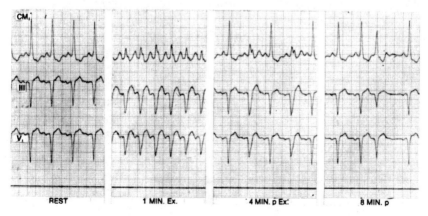

FIGURE 13-9. A 53-year-old woman with severe three-vessel disease and very poor left-ventricular function developed LBBB almost immediately with the onset of exercise. Note return to a resting configuration during the recovery period.

RHYTHM AND CONDUCTION DISTURBANCES IN STRESS TESTING   293

13-10 illustrates the ECG of a patient who not only had LBBB with a stress test, but also after administration of atropine. The coronary angiograms in this case were perfectly normal although there was mild evidence of left-ventricular dysfunction as indicated by LVEDP elevations after angiography. The report of Wayne and colleagues[46] previously mentioned, supports the growing trend to suspect ischemia in these patients. Bellet and associates[55] reported a patient with LBBB at rest who maintained a normal pattern during exercise and reverted to LBBB during recovery. They claim the patient had clearcut hypertensive arteriosclerotic heart disease (ASHD) with congestive failure. I have seen one patient with left bundle branch block consistently convert to a normal pattern with exercise, who was shown to have normal coronaries and good left-ventricular function. The recent report by Lee and colleagues[55] suggests that R-wave changes may be useful in identifying coronary disease in patients with LBBB.

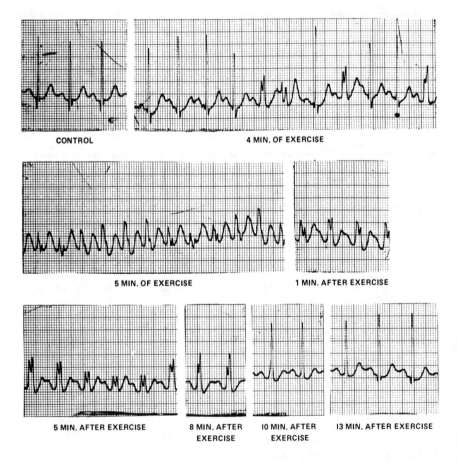

CONTROL   4 MIN. OF EXERCISE

5 MIN. OF EXERCISE   1 MIN. AFTER EXERCISE

5 MIN. AFTER EXERCISE   8 MIN. AFTER EXERCISE   I0 MIN. AFTER EXERCISE   I3 MIN. AFTER EXERCISE

FIGURE 13-10. Exercise tracing of a 44-year-old woman who developed LBBB with exercise. Subsequent coronary angiography revealed normal vessels and normal left-ventricular function.

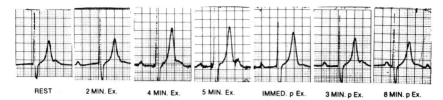

| REST | 2 MIN. Ex. | 4 MIN. Ex. | 5 MIN. Ex. | IMMED. p Ex. | 3 MIN. p Ex. | 8 MIN. p Ex. |

FIGURE 13-11. Tracings from a 23-year-old man with congenital heart block. The T-wave amplitude increases and exercise progresses.

THIRD DEGREE ATRIOVENTRICULAR BLOCK

In older patients with known or suspected coronary disease, third degree heart block at rest should be a relative contraindication to stress testing. HIS bundle electrograms demonstrate that the block may be proximal to, within, or distal to the HIS spike. Congenital block is usually proximal to the HIS bundle and it may be that even in acquired block this location may have a lesser risk to the patient during exercise. No data to support this contention are available in acquired disease, however. It is well-known that when patients with coronary disease develop complete block, the prognosis is very poor. Whether or not this would be the case in pre-HIS bundle blocks is not known. On the other hand, if it is a congenital block or is present in vigorous younger patients with no other evidence of heart disease, testing may be done (Fig. 13-11).

ACCELERATED CONDUCTION (WPW SYNDROME)

It is now well established that patients with WPW have S-T segment depression when the accelerated conduction pathway intervenes. When accelerated conduction occurs intermittently, the changes in the S-T segment depression can be seen associated with each delta wave. A few isolated reports of coronary angiographic data on such patients have demonstrated normal coronaries.[57] Sandberg[34] reported 35 instances of patients with pre-excitation syndrome who underwent exercise tests. He found that exercise may bring on the delta wave and pre-excitation, or it may cause disappearance of the syndrome with a return during recovery, or it may not affect the presence or the absence of the syndrome at all. In two of his patients, both in their 50s, this phenomenon was initiated by exercise. He suggested that these patients had acquired WPW due to coronary disease or some other myocardial dysfunction. In our laboratory, we have seen WPW initiated by exercise several times. On one such occasion, one patient who underwent coronary angiography had a normal coronary tree. Gazes[58] reported that 20 out of 23 patients with WPW had S-T segment depression of 1.0 mm or more after exercise. During our studies, we have also seen it initiated by hyperventilation. The tracings in Figure 13-12 depict the stress test of a 46-year-old man with resting accelerated conduction who had S-T segment depression during exercise even though the abnormal

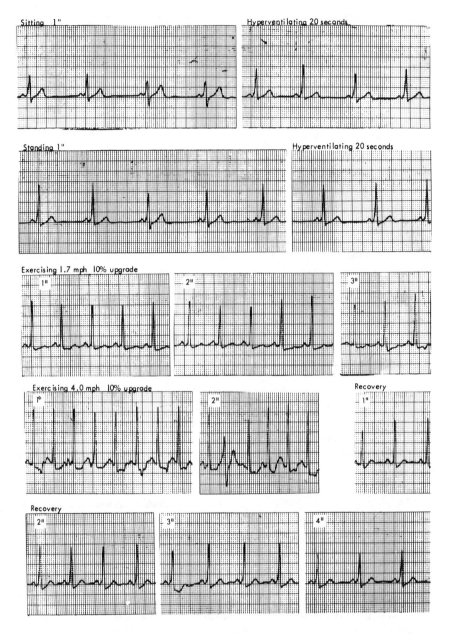

FIGURE 13-12. Exercise tracings of a 46-year-old man with normal coronary arteries manifesting S-T segment depression with exercise and accelerated conduction at rest.

conduction pathways could not be recognized when the heart rate became rapid. In eight of Sandberg's[34] cases, the pre-excitation pattern disappeared with exercise and returned later. These patients were mostly between the ages of 23 and 50, which suggests that the process was not associated with underly-

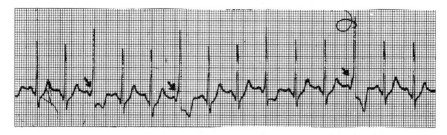

FIGURE 13-13. Tracing of a 52-year-old man illustrating transient WPW and S-T segment depression associated with each complex that exhibits a delta wave.

ing coronary disease. For the remaining patients, ages 18 to 56, no definite conclusions could be drawn as to why exercise did not alter the pre-excitation pattern. It is interesting to note that in the five cases that were over 50 years of age in Sandberg's series, coronary disease was present in every one by history and examination, although no coronary angiograms had been done. The pre-excitation syndrome may be initiated in young patients whenever they exercise sufficiently and is almost invariably associated with S-T segment depression. The exercise performance and aerobic capacity for Sandberg's patients were perfectly normal, suggesting that there were probably only minimal coronary abnormalities within the group. We have never seen a patient with WPW develop supraventricular tachycardia on the treadmill even though those with the disease have a history of attacks at unexpected times. Fourteen cases of accelerated conduction initiated by exercise have been recognized in our laboratory (Fig. 13-13).

SUMMARY

Exercise-induced arrhythmias and conduction disturbances are abnormal in most cases. As with other findings during stress testing, however, they must be viewed in light of other clinical findings in each patient. In most cases who come to stress testing, they are potential cases for concern, but in special cases such as endurance athletes, especially young ones, certain of the arrhythmias have no clinical significance (see Sports Medicine, Chapter 19).

REFERENCES

1. BIGGER, JT, JR, ET AL: *Ventricular arrhythmias in ischemic heart disease: Mechanism, prevalence, significance, and management.* Prog Cardiovasc Dis 19:255, 1977.
2. FARIS, JV, ET AL: *Prevalence and reproducibility of exercise-induced ventricular arrhythmias during maximal exercise testing in normal men.* Am J Cardiol 37:617, 1976.
3. ELLESTAD, MH AND WAN, MKC: *Predictive implications of stress testing: Follow-up of 2700 subjects after maximum treadmill stress testing.* Circulation 51:363, 1975.

4. CHIN, CF, ET AL: *Chronotropic incompetence in exercise testing.* Clinical Cardiol 2:12–18, 1979.
5. ABBOTT, JA, ET AL: *Graded exercise testing in patients with sinus node dysfunction.* Am J Med 62:330, 1977.
6. LEWIS, T: *Fibrillation of the auricles: Its effects upon the circulation.* J Exp Med 16:395, 1912.
7. KAPLAN, MA, GRAY, RE, AND ISERI, LT: *Metabolic and hemodynamic responses to exercise during atrial fibrillation and sinus rhythm.* Am J Cardiol 22:543, 1968.
8. KILLIP, T AND BAER, RA: *Hemodynamic effects after reversion from atrial fibrillation to sinus rhythm by precordial shock.* J Clin Invest 45:658, 1966.
9. GRABOYS, TB AND WRIGHT, RF: *Provocation of supraventricular tachycardia during exercise stress testing.* Cardiovasc Review & Reports 1(1):57–58, 1980.
10. GOOCH, AS: *Exercise testing for detecting changes in cardiac rhythm and coinduction.* Am J Cardiol 30:741–746, 1972.
11. FISHER, FD AND TYROLER, HA: *Relationship between ventricular premature contractions in routine electrocardiograms and subsequent death from coronary heart disease.* Circulation 47:712, 1963.
12. GOLDSCHLAGER, N, SELZER, A, AND COHN, K: *Treadmill stress tests as indicators of presence and severity of coronary artery disease.* Ann Intern Med 85:277, 1976.
13. RODSTEIN, M, WOLLOCH, L, AND GUBNER, RS: *A mortality study of the significance of extrasystoles in an insured population.* Trans Assoc Life Ins Med Dir Am 54:91, 1971.
14. LOWN, B AND WOLF, M: *Approaches to sudden death from coronary heart disease.* Circulation 44:130, 1971.
15. ALEXANDER, S, DESAI, DC, AND HERSHBERG, IH: *Resting PVC's and their influence on mortality.* Am Cardiol Conf, February 1973.
16. BUCKINGHAM, TA, LABOVITZ, AJ, AND KENNEDY, HL: *The clinical significance of ventricular arrhythmias in apparently healthy subjects.* Practical Cardiology 9(8):37–46, 1983.
17. UDALL, JA AND ELLESTAD, MH: *Predictive implications of ventricular premature contractions associated with treadmill stress testing: A follow-up of 6,500 patients after maximum treadmill stress testing.* Circulation 56:985–989, 1977.
18. SHEPS, DC, ET AL: *Decreased frequency of exercise induced ventricular ectopic activity in the second of two consecutive treadmill tests.* Circulation 55:892, 1977.
19. MCHENRY, PL, MORRIS, SN, AND KAVALIER, M: *Exercise-induced arrhythmias-recognition, classification, and clinical significance.* Cardiovasc Clin 6:245, 1974.
20. FROELICHER, VF, ET AL: *Epidemiologic study of asymptomatic men screened by maximal treadmill testing for latent coronary artery disease.* Am J Cardiol 34:770, 1974.
21. CALIFF, RM, ET AL: *Prognostic value of ventricular arrhythmias associated with treadmill exercise testing in patients studied with cardiac catheterization for suspected ischemic heart disease.* J Am Coll Cardiol 2(6):1060–1067, 1983.
22. MCHENRY, PL, ET AL: *Comparative studies of exercise-induced ventricular arrhythmias in normal subjects and in patients with documented coronary artery disease.* Am J Cardiol 37:609, 1976.
23. GOOCH, AS AND MCCONNELL, D: *Analysis of transient arrhythmias and conduction disturbances occurring during submaximal treadmill exercise testing.* Prog Cardiovasc Dis XIII(3):293–307, 1970.
24. BOURNE, G: *An attempt at the clinical classification of premature ventricular beats.* QJ Med 20:219, 1977.
25. HELFANT, RH, ET AL: *Exercise related ventricular premature complexes in coronary heart disease.* Ann Intern Med 80:589, 1974.
26. DIMSDALE, J: *Etiology of post exercise sudden death.* Discover 514:10, April 1984.
27. SANDBERG, L: *Studies in electrocardiogram changes during exercise tests.* Acta Med Scand (Suppl)169:365, 1969.
28. CASTLE, LW, ET AL: *Ventricular fibrillation and coronary atherosclerosis with normal maximal exercise test: Report of a case.* Cleve Clin Qtr 39:163, 1973.

29. FARIS, JV, ET AL: *Prevalence and reproducibility of exercise-induced ventricular arrhythmias during maximal exercise testing in normal men.* Am J Cardiol 37:617, 1976.

30. JELINEK, MV AND LOWN, B: *Exercise stress testing for exposure of cardiac arrhythmia.* Prog Cardiovasc Dis 16:497, 1974.

31. RYAN, M, LOWN, B, AND HORN, H: *Comparison of ventricular ectopic activity during 24 hour monitoring and exercise testing in patients with coronary heart disease* (abstr). N Engl J Med 292:224, 1975.

32. GLASSER, SP, CLARK, PI, AND APPLEBAUM, H: *The occurrence of frequent complex arrhythmias detected by ambulatory monitoring in a healthy elderly population.* Chest 75:565, 1979.

33. BARROW, WH AND OUER, RA: *Electrocardiographic changes with exercise: Their relation to age and other factors.* Arch Intern Med 71:547, 1943.

34. SANDBERG, L: *Studies in electrocardiogram changes during exercise tests.* Acta Med Scand (Suppl)365:169, 1969.

35. GLASSER, SP AND CLARK, PI: *The clinical approach to exercise testing.* Harper & Row, New York, 1980, p 158.

36. LEPESCHKIN, E, ET AL: *Effect of nifedipine and norepinephrine on the electrocardiograms of 100 normal subjects.* Am J Cardiol 5:594, 1960.

37. BAKST, A, GOLDBERG, B, AND SHAMROTH, L: *Significance of exercise-induced second degree atrioventricular block.* Br Heart J 37:984, 1975.

38. MOULOPOULOS, SD AND ANTHOPOULOS, LP: *Reversible atrio-ventricular conduction changes during exercise.* Acta Cardiol (Brux) 23:352, 1968.

39. GOODFRIEND, MA AND BAROLD, SS: *Tachycardia-dependent and bradycardia-dependent Mobitz Type II atrioventricular block within the bundle of HIS.* Am J Cardiol 33:908, 1974.

40. GILCHRIST, AR: *Clinical aspects of high-grade heart block.* Scottish Med J 3:53, 1958.

41. ROZANSKI, JJ, ET AL: *Paroxysmal second degree atrioventricular block induced by exercise.* Heart & Lung 9(5):887–890, 1980.

42. OLIVEROS, RS, ET AL: *Intermittent left anterior hemiblock during treadmill exercise test.* Chest 72:492, 1977.

43. GERGUEIRA-GOMES, M, ET AL: *Repolarization changes in left anterior hemiblock.* Adv Cardiol 14:148, 1975.

44. MILLER, AB, NAUGHTON, J, AND GORMAN, PA: *Left axis deviation: Diagnostic contribution of exercise stress testing.* Chest 63:159, 1973.

45. BOBBA, P, SALERNO, JA, AND CASARI, A: *Transient left posterior hemiblock: Report of four cases induced by exercise test.* Circulation 44:931, 1972.

46. WAYNE, VS, ET AL: *Exercise-induced bundle branch block.* Am J Cardiol 52:283–286, 1983.

47. KATTUS, AA: *Exercise electrocardiography: Recognition of the ischemic response: False positive and negative patterns.* Am J Cardiol 33:726, 1974.

48. JOHNSON, S, ET AL: *The diagnostic accuracy of exercise ECG testing in the presence of complete RBBB* (abstr). Circulation 51,52(11):48, 1975.

49. TANAKA, T, ET AL: *Diagnostic value of exercise-induced ST segment depression in patients with RBBB.* Am J Cardiol 41:670, 1978.

50. WHINNERY, JE AND FROELICHER, V: *Acquired BBB and its response to exercise testing in asymptomatic air crewmen: A review with case reports.* Aviation, Space and Environmental Medicine; November, 43: 1217, 1976.

51. COOKSEY, JD, PARKER, BM, AND BAHL, OP: *The diagnostic contribution of exercise testing in left bundle branch block.* Am Heart J 88:482, 1974.

52. ORZAN F, ET AL: *Is the treadmill exercise test useful for evaluating coronary artery disease in patients with complete LBBB?* Am J Cardiol 42:36, 1978.

53. WALSTON, AL, BOINEAU, JP, AND SPOCH, MS: *Relationship between ventricular depolarization and the QRS in right and left BBB.* J Electrocardiol 1:155, 1968.

54. ABILDSKOV, JA: *Effects of activation sequence on the local recovery of ventricular excit-*

ability in the dog. Circ Res 38:240, 1976.
55. BELLET, S, ET AL: *Radioelectrocardiographic changes during strenuous exercise in normal subjects.* Circulation 25:686, 1962.
56. LEE, G, ET AL: *Accuracy of left precordial R wave analysis during exercise testing in reliably detecting coronary disease in LBBB patients.* Am J Cardiol (in press).
57. GOOCH, AS AND EVANS, JM: *Extended applications of exercise electrocardiography.* Med An DC 38:80, 1969.
58. GAZES, PC: *False-positive exercise test in the presence of Wolff-Parkinson-White syndrome.* Am Heart J 78:13, 1969.

14

PREDICTIVE IMPLICATIONS

EFFECT OF AGE
EFFECT OF PREVIOUS MYOCARDIAL INFARCTION
MULTIVARIATE ANALYSIS
CONCLUSIONS

The prediction of disease is one of the primary functions of stress testing. We would like to be able to predict in each patient:
1. The anatomic condition of the coronary arteries.
2. The functional status of the heart.
3. The ultimate outcome of the patient as influenced by the above two parameters.

It is commonly, but erroneously assumed, that the last two items are easy to determine if we know the first. So many factors impact the ultimate outcome of any given patient with clinically significant coronary disease, that knowing the anatomic condition of the coronary arteries may give us very little information about items two and three. We should not be too surprised when a patient with a normal maximum exercise test suddenly has an infarction or sudden ventricular fibrillation a few weeks later. Although this is an infrequent occurrence, the dynamic nature of coronary atheroma certainly can result in sudden reductions in perfusion with all the attendant dramatic sequelae. In this chapter, I present some of the concepts necessary to understand how information derived from stress testing can be applied to the individual.

One of the difficulties in interpreting a diagnostic report stems from the fact that many of us are not used to being precise in our statements. We all know that very few tests are 100 percent reliable, but rarely do we stop to consider just how reliable our tests are. Unfortunately, there are limited data to allow us to derive the degree of certainty of stress testing in its present form. Most of us combine so many different variables in arriving at the final conclusion that it should be called a consultation rather than a test. However, if we limit our discussion for now, to S-T segment depression, about which there is a great deal of information, we can illustrate some important principles.

BAYES' THEOREM

Bayes' Theorem is a mathematic rule relating the interpretation of present observation in light of past experience[1] (Fig. 14-1).

BAYES' THEORUM

PAST EXPERIENCE + PRESENT OBSERVATIONS = FUTURE INTERPRETATION

FIGURE 14-1. Bayes' Theorem.

It relates the probability of disease (pre-test probability) in the patient before the test is performed to the probability of disease after the test (post-test probability). This is best understood by considering Figure 14-2. If the *pre-test probability* of disease in question is 10 percent and the information content (power of the test to increase information) is known, for example, 50 percent, then we can calculate the post-test uncertainty or conversely the probability.

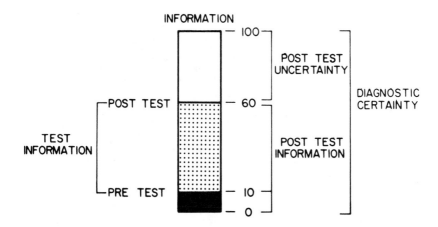

FIGURE 14-2. The total information about the patient's diagnosis depicted by the bar is divided into pre-test (black), which is the probability of disease as estimated from clinical data. The test information (stippled) represents the increase in information supplied by the diagnostic test. The uncertainty after the test is finished is the diagnostic difference between the post-test probability or post-test information content and 100 percent. (From Diamond, et al.,[2] with permission.)

In the case of Figure 14-2, the information content is 50 percent, leaving us with a *post-test probability* of 60 percent or a remaining uncertainty of 40 percent. The *information content* varies with the nature of the test and the prevalence of disease in the population under study, which also determines the *pre-test* probability. Therefore, the information content of a test varies to some degree with each individual being tested. This concept may be difficult for some clinicians because we think in terms of individual patients and consider the value of the test to be intrinsic to the test. If we use Bayes' Theorem, we must consider the test in the context of the population to which the patient belongs. By collating data from large population studies, Diamond and Forrester[3] have estimated the information gained by the discovery that 1 mm of S-T segment depression varies according to the type of chest pain, because of the difference in the pre-test probability. Thus, the information gained or diagnostic use is five times more in a subject with atypical angina than in a subject without symptoms, and two and one-half times that of someone with typical angina (Fig. 14-3).

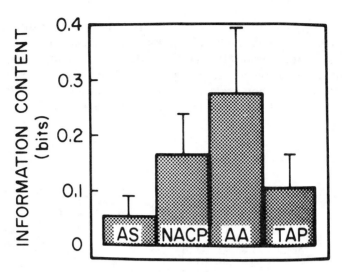

FIGURE 14-3. The pre-test information content (equivalent to the black part of the bar in Fig. 14-2) according to the patient's symptoms. AS = asymptomatic, NACP = non-anginal chest pain, AA = atypical angina, TAP = typical anginal pain. It is well known that typical angina is a very reliable symptom and thus starts with the largest pre-test probability. (From Diamond, et al.,[2] with permission.)

The diagnostic use of the test is highest when applied to a population in which the diagnosis is most uncertain. S-T depression in patients with typical angina adds little because this group already has a high likelihood of coronary disease.

For the purpose of this discussion, we will assume that prevalence of disease is accurate in each of Diamond's pain categories. We know, of course, that the prevalence of disease in each of these categories would also be influenced by sex, age, cholesterol, family history, smoking habits, and other determinants.[4]

SENSITIVITY AND SPECIFICITY

We have fallen into the acceptance that the coronary angiogram is the "gold standard" when deciding whether coronary disease is present or not. Most of the literature assumes that a coronary artery obstruction of 70 percent or greater is significant and one that is less than this, is not. Although this is highly arbitrary and is probably untrue, we will accept it for now in order to explain the principle. A group of patients studied by angiography and exercise testing can be categorized with the contingency table (Table 14-1).

Sensitivity

The measure of reliability in identifying the presence of disease, or the percent-

TABLE 14-1. 2 × 2 Contingency Table

TEST RESULT	DISEASE	
	PRESENT	ABSENT
Positive	True-positives (TP)	False-positives (FP)
Negative	False-negatives (FN)	True-negatives (TN)

age of patients with an abnormal stress test out of all those studied with coronary disease.

$$\text{Sensitivity} = \frac{\text{Patients with abnormal stress tests and abnormal angiograms}}{\text{All patients with abnormal angiograms}} \times 100$$

True-positives: Patients with both abnormal stress tests and abnormal angiograms.

False-positives: Patients with abnormal stress tests and normal angiograms.

Sensitivity is not only a function of the prevalence of disease in the population under study. It can be enhanced by increasing the stress applied, by using more leads, and by liberalizing the criteria for an abnormal test. If this is done, for example, accepting 0.5 mm of S-T depression instead of 1.0 mm, we will identify more of those with disease, but there will also be more false-positives identified. False-negative tests will be increased by reducing the stress applied, increasing the amount of S-T depression required for a positive test, the balancing of S-T vectors, inadequate critical mass of ischemic muscle, and so forth.

Specificity

The measure of reliability in identifying by stress test, the absence of disease or the percentage of those with a normal stress test out of all studied with normal angiograms.

$$\text{Specificity} = \frac{\text{Patients with normal stress tests and normal angiograms}}{\text{All patients with normal angiograms}} \times 100$$

True-negatives: Patients with normal stress tests who have normal angiograms.

False-negatives: Patients with normal stress tests who have abnormal angiograms.

Note: Abnormal angiograms are used in this example for illustration purposes. Coronary artery abnormalities are only one cause of abnormal stress tests.

As specificity increases, the false-positives decrease. The false-positive, or subject who has S-T depression and normal coronary arteries, creates the biggest problem for clinicians at present. The term *specificity* in this sense has a slightly different meaning than is commonly understood. In common parlance, specificity refers to the reliability or the predictive power of a test. We term this—the correct classification rate.

PREDICTIVE VALUE AND RELATIVE RISK

The data to be presented in this chapter describing sensitivity and specificity of stress testing are of necessity, usually based on patients being admitted for coronary angiography. This results in a cohort of patients with a high prevalence of disease. Let us examine how this affects the results.

$$\text{PREDICTIVE VALUE} = \frac{\text{TRUE-POSITIVES}}{\text{TRUE-POSITIVES and FALSE-POSITIVES}}$$

The predictive value of a positive or an abnormal test is defined as the true-positives over true-positives plus false-positives. The predictive value is the percentage of those identified correctly. It can be for a positive or for a negative test. The predictive value of a positive test does not tell us how many abnormal patients have been diagnosed as normal, however. Bayes' Theorem states that the predictive value of a test is directly related to the prevalence of disease in the population being studied[1] (Table 14-2).

TABLE 14-2. Relation of prevalence of a disease and predictive value of a test*†

Actual disease prevalence (%)	Predictive value of a positive test (%)	Predictive value of a negative test (%)
1	16.1	99.9
2	27.9	99.9
5	50.0	99.7
10	67.9	99.4
20	82.6	98.7
50	95.0	95.0
75	98.3	83.7
100	100.0	—

*From Vecchio,[54] with permission.
†Sensitivity and specificity rates each equal 95 percent.

If we now examine a population with a 1 percent prevalence of disease, with a test that has a 60 percent sensitivity and a 90 percent specificity (values not far removed from those reported for S-T segment depression), the result will be as shown in Table 14-3. It we select another population to study with the prevalence of disease at 10 percent, the predictive value will increase to 40 percent (Tables 14-3 and 14-4).

TABLE 14-3. Performance of a test with a 60 percent sensitivity and a 90 percent specificity in a population with a 1 percent prevalence of disease

Subjects	No. with abnormal test		No. with normal test	
100 diseased	60	(TP)	40	(FN)
		(Sensitivity)		
9900 nondiseased	990	(FP)	8910	(TN)
		(Specificity)		
Total	1050		8950	

$$\text{Predictive value of an abnormal test} = \frac{TP}{TP + FP} = \frac{60}{1050} = 5.7\%$$

False-positive rate $= 100 - 5.7 = 94.3\%$

TABLE 14-4. Performance of a test with a 60 percent sensitivity and a 90 percent specificity in a population with a 10 percent prevalence of disease

Subjects	No. with abnormal test		No. with normal test	
1000 diseased	600	(TP)	400	(FN)
		(Sensitivity)		
9000 nondiseased	900	(FP)	8100	(TN)
		(Specificity)		
Total	1500		8500	

$$\text{Predictive value of an abnormal test} = \frac{TP}{TP + FP} = \frac{600}{1500} = 40\%$$

False-positive rate $= 100 - 40 = 60\%$

It can be seen from the above numbers that the inherent accuracy of the test as previously stated, is defined by the sensitivity and specificity and that the results when applied to the individual, are dependent on the prevalence of disease in the population to which the individual belongs.

It becomes obvious that two of the most important factors in analysis of our patients undergoing stress testing are: (1) pre-test prevalence of disease and, (2) sensitivity and specificity of the test.

DISEASE PREVALENCE

There are a number of ways to estimate prevalence and there is considerable disagreement in this area. Diamond and Forrester[3] believe that the patients should be categorized according to their pain pattern (Fig. 14-4).

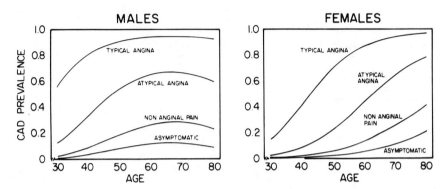

FIGURE 14-4. Prevalence of coronary artery disease according to age, sex, and symptom classification. (From Diamond and Forrester[3] with permission.)

This is then modified by age, sex, and so forth. They have published tables that provide information gleaned from a review of the literature. One can use these tables or purchase their computer program (Cadenza)[3] to evaluate the likelihood of disease. It will calculate both pre-test and post-test likelihood after a stress test or a series of noninvasive tests including CKG, coronary calcification by fluoroscopy, and thallium scintography.

Hossack and colleagues[5] believe one can do as well with the conventional risk factors combined with "exercise risk factors" obtained during treadmill stress testing. The Framingham Risk Factor Tables are well known and have been used by the Seattle Group in their "Heart Watch" study for a number of years. The use of symptoms for disease prevalence presumes the patient will tell you about pain. Many subjects withhold or modify information for various reasons, commercial airline pilots are a typical example.

EFFECT OF PREVALENCE ON EXERCISE-INDUCED S-T DEPRESSION

In order to proceed with the application of Bayes' Theorem, the likelihood of significant coronary disease is presented from Diamond's calculations based on the pre-test likelihood. Figure 14-5 illustrates the degree of diagnostic uncertainty according to the magnitude of S-T segment depression and the pre-test likelihood.

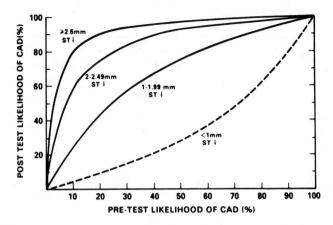

FIGURE 14-5. Family of S-T segment depression curves and the likelihood of coronary artery disease. (From Epstein,[6] with permission.)

The data suggest that even if the pre-test probability was only 20 percent, exercise-induced S-T depression of greater than 2.5 mm gives a probability of disease in the range of 90 percent, while slightly less than 2 mm of S-T depression results in a probability of about 50 percent. This information can be used after the exercise test and in other tests such as a thallium scintigram. If the post-test probability is, for example, 70 percent after a stress test and the information content of a thallium test is 25 percent, an abnormal thallium will then give a probability of 95 percent; however, a normal thallium following the abnormal stress test will reduce the probability to 55 percent.

CRITIQUE OF THE BAYESIAN THEOREM

The numbers presented here provide a highly simplified approach to a complex problem. Although the concept is valid, when we apply it to our patients, we must remember that important elements in the calculations used are not actually known with certainty.

The sensitivity and specificity of stress testing, as used in the day-to-day management of our particular patients, is uncertain. Most of the data available to us comes from cardiac centers where the referral pattern may influence the prevalence of disease in the study.[7] It is known that sensitivity and specificity from such centers vary quite a bit. How then do we relate these data to our own individual patients? In clinical practice, most of us instinctively use a number of variables to determine the presence of disease. In our laboratory, we use a computer generated probability based on a multivariate analysis of 10 variables. Recent analysis of this method resulted in a correct classification of between 88 and 94 percent. However, we have no information to tell us how well this approach would work in an outpatient-oriented clinic, a private practice of cardiology, or an internal medical office.

POPULATION GROUPS

In a cardiology practice in an area where coronary prevalence is very high (especially if the physician is a recognized expert in this field), there would be a larger percentage of patients with coronary disease than in the office of a general internist, an industrial clinic, or a military installation. An example of this concept is illustrated in Table 14-5, in which two groups of subjects were studied with relationship to the prevalence of exercise-induced S-T depression (positive stress tests).

TABLE 14-5. Percent of positive stress tests according to age and sex in two studies

Age	MHIB* Female	LBHA† Female	MHLB Male	LBHA Male
21-30	0	0	2.5	1.2
31-40	10.1	2.1	11.7	4.3
41-50	19.9	2.0	29.5	11.4
51-60	29.1	7.4	48.0	26.9
Over 60	43.3	12.1	58.2	29.3
Mean	23.3	4.6	34.3	13.5

*Memorial Hospital Cardiology Laboratory
†Long Beach Heart Association
(From Ellestad, Allen, and Stuart, with permission.[42])

Those referred for evaluation in the Memorial Hospital Cardiology Laboratory, as expected, resulted in from two to four times as many positive tests as those studied in an asymptomatic group solicited by the Long Beach Heart Association.[8] Actually, most physicians do stress tests on subjects who, by their age and sex, are in a population with a higher prevalence of coronary disease.

Using Table 14-5, it would be fair to estimate a disease prevalence of approximately 19 percent ($\frac{26.9 + 11.4 = 19}{2}$) in men between ages 40 and 60. In this population, there would be a significant number of false-positives and false-negatives. If we were to agree that about 20 percent were false-positives, we might calculate the predictive value if we analyzed 500 men as follows:

	# with abnormal test	# with normal test
100 diseased	70 (TP)	30 FN
	(Sensitivity = 70%)	
400 non-diseased	80 (FP)	320 TN
	(Specificity = 80%)	
	Total 150	350

$$\text{Predicted value of abnormal test} = \frac{TP}{TP + FP} = \frac{70}{150} = 46\%$$

Thus, almost one half of this group of men would be correctly identified by S-T segments and age alone. It would be prudent to evaluate the abnormal responders by considering risk factors and other exercise variables (see Chapter 18).

The final caveat has to do with the recently recognized difficulties with angiographic estimates of coronary narrowing and their effect on coronary flow during metabolically-induced hyperemia.[9] When we consider that all our data, using angiographically estimated percentages of narrowing, are subject to considerable question (Chapter 4), it may take a few years before the reliability of any test in estimating coronary ischemia can be based on more certain criteria. For a more detailed critique of this subject, I suggest that the serious reader review Feinstein's[10] essay "The Haze of Bayes, Aerial Palaces of Decision Analysis, and the Computerized Ouija Board."

CORRELATION OF S-T DEPRESSION WITH CORONARY ANGIOGRAPHY

Published reports correlating the association of exercise-induced S-T depression with coronary angiography shed some insight into the reliability of this method in a population being referred to a cardiac center.[11,12] A few are illustrated in Table 14-6.

TABLE 14-6. Sensitivity and specificity of stress testing reported by various investigators

			Sensitivity			
Study	N	Specificity	1 Vessel	2 Vessels	3 Vessels	Total
Kassebaum, et al.,[13]	68	97%	25%	38%	85%	53%
Martin, et al.,[14]	100	89%	35%	67%	86%	62%
McHenry, et al.,[12]	166	95%	61%	91%	100%	81%
Helfant, et al.,[15]	63	83%	60%	83%	91%	79%
Bartel, et al.,[19]	609	94%	39%	62%	73%	63%
Goldschlager, et al.,[37]	410	93%	40%	63%	79%	64%

The above investigators (see Table 14-6) considered 1 mm of horizontal or downsloping S-T depression to denote a positive test, and used from 50 to 75 percent cross sectional narrowing as a significant coronary lesion. In spite of the fact that coronary stenosis is often misjudged on angiography and other factors often cause ischemia, such as embolism and coronary spasm, the results are quite similar. It becomes evident that the similar results are due in part to similar prevalence of coronary disease in the groups studied. Other factors would be the lead systems employed, criteria for doing and terminating the test, and the mix of single- versus three-vessel disease in the population.

Some time ago Weiner and associates[16] attracted a good deal of attention in the press because they reported that stress testing had very little diagnostic value. They found that a "positive stress test," that is, one resulting in horizontal or downsloping S-T segments, increased the post-test risk of coronary disease by only 6 to 20 percent, and a negative test decreased the post-test risk by only 2 to 28 percent. They really presented nothing new, but emphasized that in the subjects with typical angina, depressed S-T segments added little to the diagnosis. What they failed to say was that it added a great deal to the prognosis. The reasons for their findings are understandable from our discussion of prevalence and the Baysian Theorem.

Claims are being made that computer evaluation of S-T segments can give a better discrimination between diseased and normal patients in this type of population. Simoons and Hugenholtz[17] report that by using measurements of the S-T segments at 20 and 80 milliseconds after the QRS in the X-lead they found a sensitivity of 85 percent and a specificity of 91 percent. The specificity is similar to other investigators but their sensitivity is somewhat better. The major improvement reported is in the sensitivity or the ability to correctly identify diseased patients. Simoons[18] also found that correcting for heart rate enhanced the results.

Bartel and colleagues[19] report a specificity of from 88 to 97 percent, but a sensitivity from 53 to 73 percent. One can see the false-negatives remain a prominent shortcoming when using S-T segments alone.

We found between 70 to 80 percent of those with high-grade and two- and three-vessel disease will have an abnormal S-T segment response to exercise (Fig. 14-6). On the other hand, the reliability of the S-T segment decreases in single-vessel disease in our study[20] and studies by others. Most reports suggest one can detect single-vessel disease in about 50 to 60 percent of men if an obstruction of 70 percent or more is present. We must then accept at least a 40 percent false-negative response using the S-T segment alone as an identifier. It has been demonstrated by Bruschke and associates[21] and later by McNeer and colleagues[22] that this is a group of patients with a relatively good long-term outlook, however. Chaitman and coworkers[23] who originally suggested the subgrouping according to symptoms, discussed under Baysian analysis, used a 14-lead system and reported the predictive value of a positive test was 100 percent in men with typical angina, 85 percent in men with probable angina, and only 45 percent in men with atypical chest pain. The predictive value of a negative test was 83 percent in men with nonspecific chest pain, 70 percent in men with probable angina, and 55 percent in men with typical angina. When men with probable or typical angina and a limited work time of less than 360 seconds on the Bruce Protocol had a positive test, the predictive value of multivessel disease was 92 percent. It is important to mention, however, that a good exercise tolerance does not rule out severe disease. They found 47 percent of their patients reaching Bruce Stage IV had significant disease.

From the data available at this time, the following statements regarding average correlations between catheterization data and maximal stress testing seem in order if S-T segments are taken as the only marker for coronary ischemia, in a cohort referred for angiography, most of whom are sent in for chest pain.

% POSITIVE STRESS TESTS

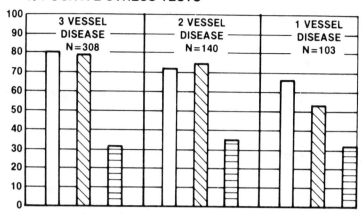

% NEGATIVE STRESS TESTS

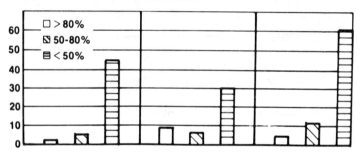

FIGURE 14-6. The bar graph illustrates the percentage of those having a positive test according to the number and severity of coronary artery narrowing. It can be seen that patients with lesions of less than 50 percent only have a positive test about 30 percent of the time, even if there are low-grade plaques in all three vessels. The percentages in the bar graphs do not add up to 100 percent because those with equivocal tests were not included. It can be seen that this constitutes a sizeable number of subjects in each group.

1. Men with single-vessel disease and significant coronary narrowing of 70 percent of luminal diameter have about 50 to 60 percent chance of an abnormal test result.
2. Men with two-vessel disease have a 65 percent change of an abnormal test result.
3. Men with three-vessel disease have a 78 percent chance of an abnormal test result.
4. Men with left-main disease have an 85 percent chance of an abnormal test result.
5. Men admitted for evaluation of chest pain who are over age 45 with 1.0 mm of S-T segment depression have a 90 percent chance of having coronary disease or evidence of significant left-ventricular dysfunction.

6. Men in the above category with 1.5 mm of S-T depression have a 94 to 95 percent chance of having coronary disease or evidence of significant left-ventricular dysfunction.
7. Men over age 45 with 2.0 mm or more S-T segment depression have a 98 percent chance of having coronary disease or evidence of significant left-ventricular dysfunction.
8. When evaluating subjects with lesser degrees of coronary narrowing, the number of false-negative tests will increase.

FALSE-POSITIVE TESTS

Because S-T depression has been equated with coronary disease, patients with this finding who have less than a critical coronary narrowing have been called false-positives. Upon careful scrutiny of these patients, however, it turns out that most of them have some process or condition that could explain the repolarization abnormality[24] (Table 14-7). In a study of 95 patients with S-T segment depression and normal coronaries, we found only 13 percent without some possible explanation. Erikssen and Myhre[25] followed 36 men for 7 years with normal coronaries and S-T depression. The prevalence of cardiac events after 7 years was the same in this group as those who were found to have significant coronary disease. Moreover, none were believed upon entry to have any of

TABLE 14-7. Summary of Cardiac Catheterization Data

	Stress Test (%)	
	True Positive	False Positive
Contraction patterns in ventriculogram		
Normal	46	73
Akinesia	33	9
Hypokinesia	5	18
Dyskinesia	16	1
LVEDP > 12 mm Hg		
At rest	41	35
After exercise	64	57
Other findings		
Mild mitral insufficiency	6	3
Papillary muscle dysfunction	3	0
Mild aortic insufficiency	4	6
Mild cardiomyopathy	1	22
Infarction	31	9
Left ventricular hypertrophy	6	8
Bundle branch block	3	5
IHSS	0	2
Hypertension	9	20
Hyperdynamic heart	1	14

the conditions listed in the above table. They believe many of these patients represent early myocardiopathies and the S-T changes were due to abnormalities in the vasodilator reserve or other, as yet poorly understood mechanisms that would eventually lead to clinically evident disease. Thus, the term "false-positive" S-T depression should be abandoned and replaced with "abnormal S-T depression of unknown cause."

FALSE-NEGATIVE TESTS

When patients are found to have significant coronary narrowing and fail to have exercise-induced S-T depression, they have been labeled "false-negative." We can understand this when the obstructed artery subtends an area of scar, suggesting that there is no ischemic muscle to produce the characteristic electrocardiographic changes. Indeed, the prevalence of an ischemic S-T response is reduced in subjects with a previous infarction, especially if it is a large anterior wall scar.[26] Harder to understand is the patient with no known previous infarction, but who has classical angina on exercising, yet has no detectable S-T change. This has been observed even in patients with left-main disease.[27] In one series it occurred in 22 percent of those with left-main stenosis. It might be postulated that if we had enough leads this would never occur, but even with precordial maps false-negatives occur in about 10 percent. Weiner and colleagues[28] analyzed the false-negative tests from the CASS Study and reported they were as common in patients with multi-vessel disease as in those with single-vessel disease. They found that even in patients with three-vessel disease, the absence of S-T depression (horizontal or downsloping) predicted a very low probability of a coronary event in four years. They also claim that the achieved heart rate response had no effect on the likelihood of a false-negative, although this would be at odds with reports from other workers.[14,17,20] The results must be viewed with the knowledge that they excluded upsloping S-T depression and, therefore, increased the number of false-negative patients considerably.

In some patients, it seems likely that the magnitude of ischemia is inadequate to produce a significant current of injury; in others, the ischemia may be in a part of the myocardium that is electrically silent. Because S-T depression is due to subendocardial ischemia with the attendant potassium shift (see Chapter 4), factors that would alter this process may come into play. Probably the most common, in patients with severe three-vessel disease, is patchy scarring of the subendocradium, often undetected in the resting electrocardiogram.

Hakki and colleagues[29] report that when evidence of infarction on the electrocardiogram is taken into consideration, false-negatives should constitute only about 10 percent of a population referred in for angiography (less than half that found by Weiner and associates[28]) and 75 percent of these would be identified by thallium scintigraphy. A few more can be identified with kymocardiograms and by analysis of multiple variables such as heart rate response,

Q peaked T, septal Q-wave changes, intraventricular conduction abnormalities, and the presence of anginal pain.

It would appear that by combining a number of noninvasive parameters, most significant but not all coronary narrowing will be detectable by stress testing.

LONG-TERM FOLLOW-UP STUDIES

A knowledge of the capacity of stress test findings to predict subsequent coronary events becomes important when making clinical judgments in managing individual patients. Events are influenced by myocardial function and many other factors besides the coronary anatomy.

Master's Test

The first large actuarial study of survival following a stress test was that of Robb and coworkers[30] in 1957, later enlarged in 1967. They reported that the mortality was 56.8 per 1000 patient-years of observation when an abnormal test was present in patients with CAD and that this was more than five times higher than in those with a normal test with a mortality of 11.5 per 1000. When evaluating sudden death, the mortality of those with abnormal tests increased to six times that of the normal. When they reviewed the data on 2224 patients in 1967, the maximal period of observation was 15 years and the average was 5 years. This time they reported a mortality of 25 per 1000 patient-years of observation in the subjects with abnormal tests. The mortality ratio was 1.2 for normal responders, 0.9 for those with J-point depression, and 4.3 for those with an abnormal test. In 1972, Robb[31] again reviewed the data and those subjects with more than 2.0 mm S-T depression had an average mortality of approximately 8 percent per year for eight years. Those subjects whose tests were read as abnormal, including all those with 0.5 mm S-T segment depression or more, had an average mortality of about 3 percent per year with the standard insurance risk being about 2 percent. His data would suggest that some of Robb's abnormal responders (those with 0.5 mm S-T depression) probably had normal hearts, but had abnormal appearing S-T segments due to abnormalities not associated with coronary disease. However, our six-year study of 658 abnormal responders to a treadmill test showed a mortality of 20 percent or 3.3 percent per year.[20]

In 1962, Mattingly[32] reviewed data compiled over a 10-year period on 1920 military personnel. He reported 56 coronary episodes in 145 abnormal responders (with 0.5 mm or more S-T segment depression), which is about 3.8 percent per year. The subjects with abnormal tests had approximately 10 times the prevalence of coronary events as did those with normal tests.

The significant differences reported between the abnormal and normal responders to the Master's test indicated that stress testing was of definite value

TABLE 14-8. Risk ratio, sensitivity, specificity, and predictive value of stress testing calculated from follow-up data of various investigators

Study	Risk Ratio	Sensitivity	Specificity	Predictive Value
Bruce	13.6x	60%	91%	13.6%
Aranow	13.6x	67%	92%	46%
Froelicher	14.3x	61%	92%	20%
Cumming	10x	58%	90%	25%
Ellestad	6.3	75%	86%	75%

When using follow-up data, it must be emphasized that if coronary disease is present but still not symptomatic it will result in false-negatives and will reduce the sensitivity.

in predicting death as a result of coronary heart disease. The data to follow extend this concept to the maximum treadmill stress test.

The predictive capacity reported in several follow-up studies is summarized in Table 14-8. The sensitivity and specificity in these studies are surprisingly similar to those reported in the angiographic studies.

When S-T segment depression occurs in subjects who have yet to have a clinical manifestation of coronary narrowing, even though they may have high-grade stenosis, they would be termed false-positive.

Memorial Medical Center Follow-Up Study—1975

We obtained follow-up data[20] on about 6000 patients previously referred for maximal treadmill tests. Most subjects were referred for evaluation of pain syndromes with 17 percent being referred for a routine screening test. The events recorded as significant in follow-up were: (1) progression of angina, (2) myocardial infarction, and (3) death due to heart disease.

Subjects were diagnosed as abnormal if they had S-T segment depression of 1.5 mm of more 0.08 second from the J-point. Flat, upsloping, or downsloping S-T segments were included. Subjects diagnosed as equivocal included those with S-T segment depression of 0.5 to 1.4 mm, multifocal or frequent PVCs with exercise, and poor chronotropic response falling more than one standard deviation below the mean heart rate response for age and sex.

The prevalence of any coronary event by year is depicted in Figure 14-7 for normal, equivocal, and abnormal responders. The prevalence of coronary events in the abnormal responders is almost 10 percent per year. Those with equivocal results fall so far below those with a normal pattern that there must be a large number of subjects with coronary disease in this group. The prevalence of coronary events over a four-year period in those diagnosed as positive is 46 percent as opposed to the normal responders of 7 percent, almost a sevenfold difference. The 25 percent prevalence of coronary events in subjects with equivocal results resulted in our revision of the criterion for an abnormal

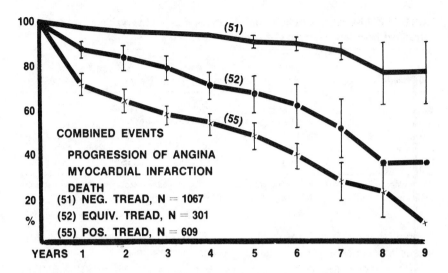

100

80

(51)

60

COMBINED EVENTS

40   PROGRESSION OF ANGINA
     MYOCARDIAL INFARCTION
     DEATH
20   (51) NEG. TREAD, N = 1067
%   (52) EQUIV. TREAD, N = 301
     (55) POS. TREAD, N = 609

YEARS 1   2   3   4   5   6   7   8   9

FIGURE 14-7. Incidence of all coronary events in the negative responders (51). Incidence of events in equivocal responders (those with S-T segment depression from 0.5 to 1.4 mm) (52). Classically positive responders (S-T segment depression of 1.5 or more mm) (55).

stress test to 1.0 mm S-T segment depression at 0.08 second from the J-point.

After 8 years, 76 percent of the abnormal responders had some coronary event; this amounts to 9.5 percent per year. Figure 14-8 depicts the data for myocardial infarction in the same group. The prevalence of myocardial infarction over a 4-year period is 15 percent in positive as opposed to 1 percent in negative responders. The prevalence of 5 percent in those with equivocal results (5 times that of normals) also suggests that some of these tests should have been read as abnormal. The data compiled for an 8-year period are quite similar, showing a 27 percent prevalence of infarctions in those with abnormal tests, resulting in an average of about 3.5 percent per year. It is interesting how closely this fits Mattingly's data[32] from the double Master's test in which the prevalence of death is similar to that for infarction, averaging about 3.3 percent per year.

We subsequently analyzed a similar group for death and myocardial infarction together, omitting angina as being an end-point more difficult to character-ize. Figure 14-9 illustrates that the abnormal S-T segment still identifies a popu-lation subject to more coronary events. We then analyzed 804 subjects who were sent for screening tests that had no symptoms and no history of heart disease (Fig. 14-10). The prevalence of coronary events in the abnormal re-sponders is well below the first cohort made up mostly of symptomatic pa-tients, but still significantly above the normals. When we exclude angina as an event, and only consider the "harder" data of myocardial infarction and death in this asymptomatic group (Fig. 14-11), it becomes apparent that only 1 per-cent of the normal responders have an MI or death, while about the same number of those with abnormal S-T responses have events as in the previous group.

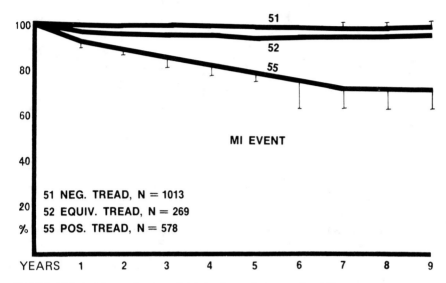

FIGURE 14-8. Incidence of myocardial infarction only in negative (51), equivocal (52), and positive (55) responders.

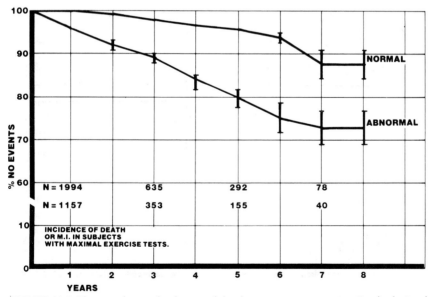

FIGURE 14-9. The prevalence of only two of the three coronary events previously depicted (death and/or myocardial infarction). It will be noted that with angina removed as an event, slightly less than 30 percent of those with abnormal tests have events as compared with the previous study on a smaller cohort where all three events were tabulated.

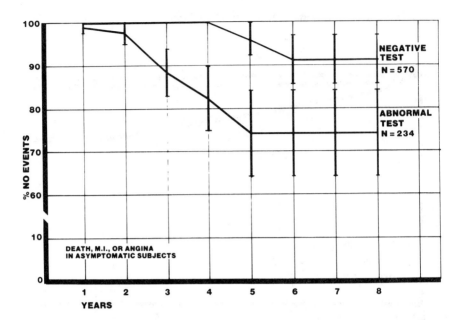

FIGURE 14-10. When only those who denied any symptoms were evaluated, all coronary events occurred well below those reported in the study in which 83 percent were symptomatic (see Fig. 14-7).

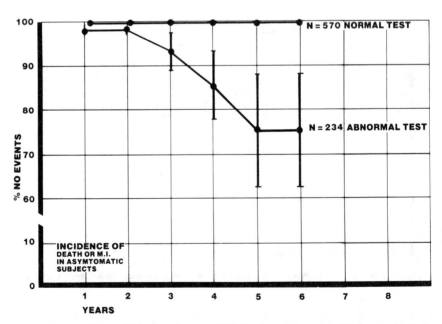

FIGURE 14-11. When only death and myocardial infarction were predicted in the asymptomatic cohort, the specificity of a negative test increases dramatically, while those with a positive test have almost the same prevalence of events as in Figure 14-10.

STRESS TESTING: PRINCIPLES AND PRACTICE

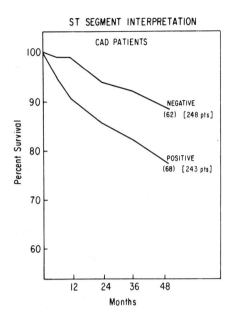

ST SEGMENT INTERPRETATION

CAD PATIENTS

NEGATIVE
(62) [248 pts]

POSITIVE
(68) [243 pts]

FIGURE 14-12. In patients with angiographically demonstrated coronary disease, the mortality is greater in those with ischemic S-T segments. (From McNeer et al.,[33] with permission.)

Duke Study—1978

The excellent registry at Duke has made it possible to publish follow-up data in subjects who have had not only exercise tests, but angiograms[33] (Fig. 14-12). The mortality in their patients with S-T depression is about 6 percent per year, about double our findings, undoubtedly due to patient selection. Also, the 3 percent annual mortality compared with our normals, reflects the same bias. I would suspect their subjects with a normal S-T response may have a high prevalence of single-vessel disease.

Heart Watch—1980

Although the early reports from this excellent multicenter study by Bruce and colleagues[34] began to appear in the late 1970s, we will report their data on patients with atypical chest pain here[35] (656 men). Their earlier work is re-ported in Chapter 18.[5] Because it had been recognized how important multi-ple variables can be, they categorized the subjects in three groups. High risk were those with S-T depression and a short exercise time (FIA = less than 30 percent). Moderate risk included subjects with one or more risk factors but no exercise findings. The low-risk group consisted of no risk factors and normal exercise tolerance without S-T changes. Figure 14-13 illustrates the impor-

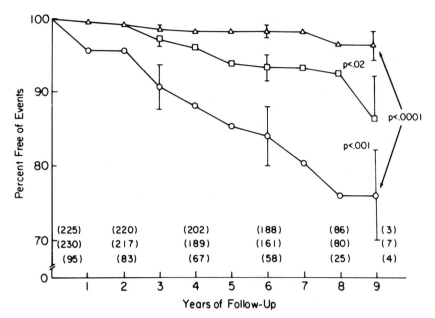

FIGURE 14-13. A life table depicting the effect of S-T depression in coronary events in men with atypical chest pain.

△ Low risk = no risk factors, no S-T depression, and excellent exercise tolerance.

□ Medium risk = one or more risk factors but no abnormal exercise findings.

0 High risk = either exercise-induced S-T depression or exercise capacity greater than 30 percent below predicted for age and sex. (From Hossack, et al.,[35] with permission.)

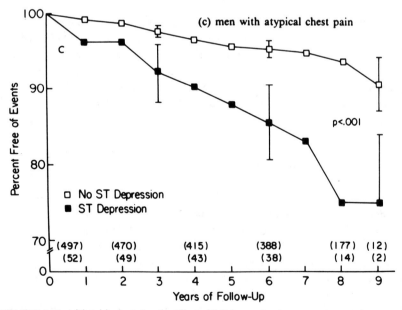

FIGURE 14-14. A life table depicting the effect of S-T depression in coronary events in men with atypical chest pain. (From Hossack, et al.,[35] with permission.)

STRESS TESTING: PRINCIPLES AND PRACTICE

tance of S-T depression, especially when coupled with a short exercise time, the coronary event rate being about seven times more likely than those without these findings. Figure 14-14 illustrates the significant difference is still present when S-T depression alone is used as a discriminator.

CASS Study—1982

This multicenter study[36] based on 4083 patients deals with a different population but provides us with similar evidence that exercise S-T segment depression is a good discriminator of events. Patients in this study were stratified according to various risk factors and in essence confirmed the previously cited studies. They found a short exercise time and S-T depression of greater than 2 mm identified a cohort with a high risk of developing coronary events; by combining and quantifying exercise duration and S-T depression, they could identify subjects with an annual mortality of less than 1 percent. By contrast, those who had 1 mm of S-T depression and could not exceed Bruce Stage I, had an annual mortality of over 5 percent. The predictive importance of short exercise duration reported by our group in 1975,[20] has now been confirmed by subsequent studies.[22,34,35]

TIME OF ONSET OF S-T SEGMENT DEPRESSION

It would be a logical conclusion to believe that ischemia reflected by S-T segment depression resulting from very mild exercise is more severe than that occurring at a workload near peak capacity. We analyzed the follow-up events in those who had S-T depression of 2.0 mm or more manifested at the various work levels of our protocol, that is, three, five, and seven minutes.

Figure 14-15 clearly supports the concept that the workload at which the ischemic changes are determined is of prime importance in the evaluation of the severity of the disease. The incidence of coronary events in a subject with a 2.0 mm S-T segment depression at three minutes of our protocol (walking at 1.7 miles per hour on a 10 degree incline) is four times that of a subject requiring 4 miles per hour to initiate S-T segment changes (seventh minute of our protocol). It is interesting to note that the prevalence of anginal pain associated with ischemia at high levels of exercise is also decreased.

When the onset of 1 mm of S-T depression is used as an indicator, the difference at various workloads is also significant, although not so marked. Goldschlager and colleagues,[37] McNeer and associates[22] and Weiner and co-workers[36] have confirmed our life table studies by demonstrating a higher proportion of multivessel disease in those with onset of ischemia at low workloads. Schneider and colleagues[38] report that the onset of S-T depression in Bruce Stage I or II predicts a 30 percent incidence of left-main coronary stenosis.

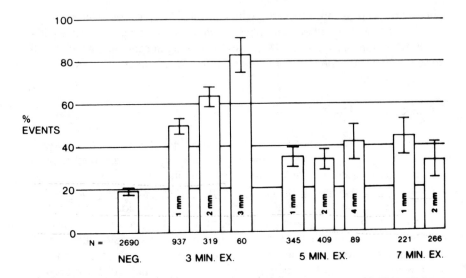

FIGURE 14-15. The incidence of subsequent coronary events (progression of angina, myocardial infarction, and death) increases with the magnitude of the S-T segment depression only when analyzed at a light workload (3 min of exercise = 4 METS; time span = 6 years).

MAGNITUDE OF S-T SEGMENT DEPRESSION

The original work of Robb and associates[30] indicated that the deeper the S-T segment depression, the more serious the disease. This seems valid when considering the progression of S-T segment depression during exercise. We reported in 1975[20] that there appeared to be no predictive value in the magnitude of S-T depression measured immediately after exercise. In a subsequent study,[8] however, it became evident that when analyzed at low workloads, those subjects with deep S-T depression definitely have a more serious prognosis (see Fig. 14-15).

The debate over the importance of the magnitude of S-T depression has continued into the more recent literature. Podrid and colleagues[39] reported "profound S-T segment depression" or a "strongly positive test" did not have a serious prognosis in 212 men followed from 20 to 59 months. When examining their report carefully, it turns out that their patients who had early onset S-T depression with a short exercise tolerance of six minutes or less, however, contained four patients or 26 percent requiring bypass surgery and four others who were treated medically died. The event rate of 17 percent annualized at approximately 4 percent per year. Deganis and coworkers[40] from Quebec Heart institute reported similar data confirming that when the onset of S-T depression is early, it is a serious prognosis, but when combined with a good exercise tolerance, deep S-T depression must be suspect as being noncoronary or at least associated with less severe disease.

TIME OF RECOVERY FROM S-T SEGMENT DEPRESSION

It had been our opinion that the longer it took a patient to recover from S-T segment depression, the more serious the degree of ischemia and, therefore, the more serious the prognosis. However, we were unable to demonstrate this with follow-up data. This was surprising to us and may be due to the fact that in those with more severe disease, exercise is terminated sooner; therefore, their recovery was more rapid than those who had less severe disease and exercised longer before they were forced to terminate exertion.

Goldschlager and associates,[37] however, reported that the severity of coronary narrowing correlates with the duration of the ischemic response after exercise is terminated. It is of interest that their protocol calls for the termination of exercise after clearcut S-T segment depression is established. Thus, on the average, their ischemic patients were exposed to less exercise after onset of significant abnormalities. On the evidence available, the time necessary for resolution of S-T segment depression should correlate with the severity of ischemia and, in most cases, the severity of coronary narrowing, but is dependent on the indications for termination of exercise.

POOR CHRONOTROPIC RESPONSE

When the heart rate response to exercise falls considerably below average for age and sex, the incidence of a future myocardial infarction and all coronary events is slightly greater than in those with ischemic S-T segment depression and a normal heart rate response. Figure 14-16 demonstrates the prevalence of any coronary event in subjects with normal S-T segments and a slow rate as compared with all subjects whose tests were diagnosed as normal. It can be seen that a poor heart rate response appears to have the same long-term significance, even in the absence of ischemic S-T segments, as an early classical ischemic response. Approximately 15 percent per year of those with slow pulse had some coronary event. Figure 14-17 compares those with S-T segment depression and bradycardia with all abnormal responders.

Our study group was characterized by a consistently low heart rate response to each workload, but even those who have an appropriate response to a given workload but failed to achieve their predicted maximum heart rate have an increased incidence of events. Figure 14-18 illustrates that there is almost a twofold increase in events when achieved heart rate is significantly reduced. The data of McNeer and colleagues[22] confirm this, even when limiting the population to those with significant coronary disease. More recently Hammond and associates[41] studied this in patients with radionuclide imaging and found a high prevalence of angina or myocardial scarring (Fig. 14-19).

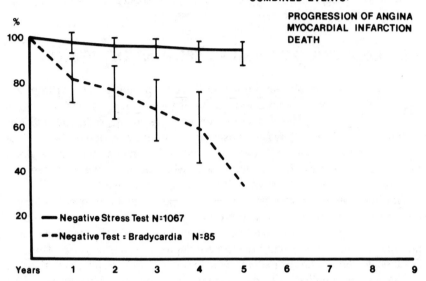

FIGURE 14-16. Those with bradycardia (pulse below the 95 percent confidence limits for age and sex) and normal S-T segments have a high incidence of combined events (similar to those with S-T segment depression).

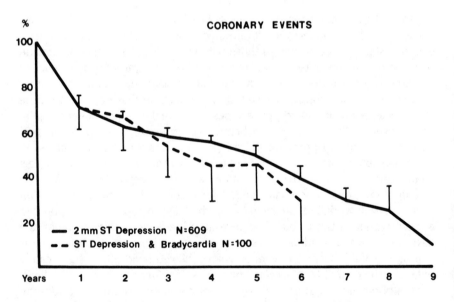

FIGURE 14-17. Those with S-T segment depression and bradycardia have a high incidence of coronary events (50 percent in five years).

STRESS TESTING: PRINCIPLES AND PRACTICE

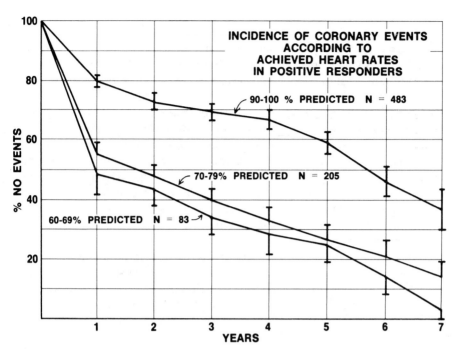

FIGURE 14-18. When all patients with abnormal S-T segments are stratified according to achieved heart rate, it becomes evident that those stopping at lower heart rates have a higher prevalence of events and presumably more severe coronary disease.

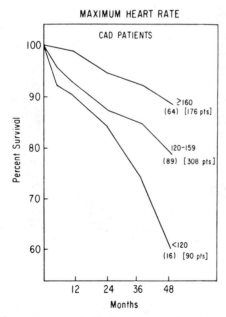

FIGURE 14-19. When patients are stratified according to the achieved heart rate, the survival is reduced in those with the lowest rate. (From McNeer, et al.,[22] with permission.)

ANGINAL PAIN

Although, in our experience, anginal pain occurs in less than half of those manifesting S-T segment depression,[42] it has been shown by Cole[43] working in our laboratory that this symptom gives added significance to the presence of the ischemic S-T segment. Subjects with pain associated with ischemic S-T segments have double the incidence of subsequent coronary events as those with S-T changes and no pain. This difference was also present when analyzing for any of the events (myocardial infarction, increased angina, and coronary death) individually (Fig. 14-20). The difference was even more striking when the analysis was restricted to men between ages 41 and 50. In this relatively young group, pain was associated with a threefold increase in events. It was also demonstrated that pain manifested early in the test, at low workloads, also was a marker for a higher incidence of future events (Fig. 14-21).

Weiner and colleagues[44] from Boston City Hospital have reviewed the importance of chest pain during testing and report that classical angina during testing, even in the absence of S-T depression, has a 90 percent predictive accuracy. Other authors[45] have found a similar reliability.

There is a high correlation between those unable to attain high heart rates

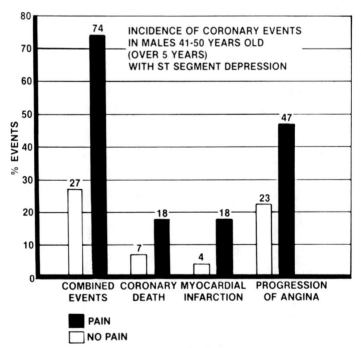

FIGURE 14-20. The five-year incidence of coronary events is significantly greater in subjects with anginal pain manifested during the stress test as compared with those without pain. (From Ellestad, et al.,[42] with permission.)

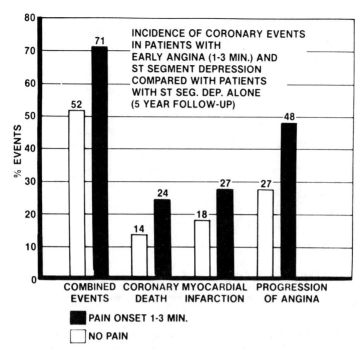

FIGURE 14-21. When pain manifested early in the test is analyzed, it identified a group with a higher incidence of events. (From Ellestad, et al.,[42] with permission.)

and those with early onset of ischemia and pain. Thus, these various indicators are probably all telling us the same thing, although not always appearing together. They indicate that there is a larger area of ischemic heart muscle during exercise and that ventricular function is seriously compromised.

Hayet and Kellerman[46] from Tel Aviv have used the heart rate, anginal threshold as a predictor of a subsequent coronary event. In a five-year follow-up study, their group found an increased prevalence of bypass surgery, infarction, and cardiac death as compared with those who developed pain at a heart rate greater than 120 beats per minute.

EFFECT OF AGE

There has been some divergence in our studies when considering the influence of age on those with an abnormal S-T response. In our earlier life table analysis, it appeared that age had no effect on subsequent coronary events. In another study[8] on a much larger sample (2667 subjects), we found that age seemed to have a definite influence on coronary events when 1 mm of S-T depression was used as an indicator (Fig. 14-22). When 2 mm of S-T depression at a prescribed time of onset (5 min) was used, less difference in the age groups was found (Fig. 14-23).

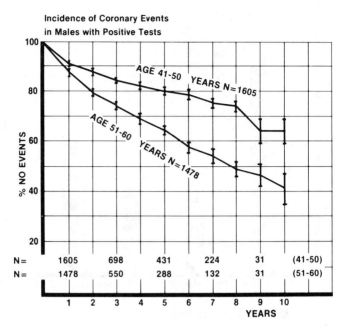

FIGURE 14-22. When the coronary events are stratified according to age and 1 mm of S-T depression, it appears that the older subjects are at higher risk.

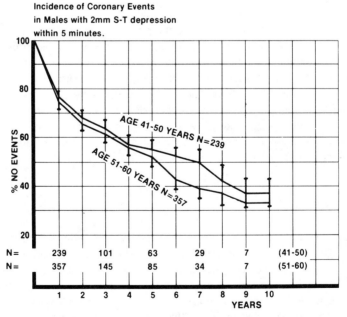

FIGURE 14-23. When an abnormal test is characterized by 2 mm of S-T depression, age then loses some of its impact on the ultimate outcome. It would appear in those with more severe degrees of ischemia, age has less effect on the long-term outcome.

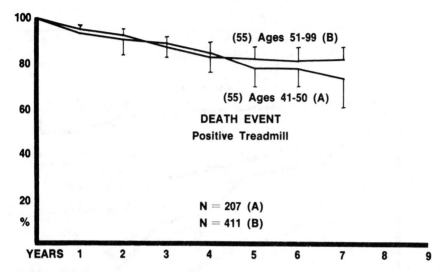

FIGURE 14-24. The incidence of death in the two age groups is similar, as well as the incidence of the events depicted in Figure 14-25.

The prevalence of abnormal test results in any large study will increase with age. If one analyzes the abnormal tests for death only and compared age group 41 to 50 with age group over 50, there is no difference (Fig. 14-24).

The slight trend for the younger groups to manifest a greater mortality at seven years is not statistically significant. If the negative responders are divided into age groups and analyzed for death alone, there is a tendency for the older subjects to have an increased prevalence, as would be expected. The same trend for myocardial infarction was also found.

EFFECT OF PREVIOUS MYOCARDIAL INFARCTION

Early stress testing after an MI was reviewed in Chapter 10. The data here deal with the effect of a stable scar on the predictive value of exercise testing. Bruce[47] has shown that when using S-T depression as a marker for coronary disease the prevalence of abnormal stress tests is decreased if there is evidence of a previous myocardial infarction. Even though a previous infarction decreases the sensitivity of the test, patients who had suffered this complication have a more serious prognosis than those who had not, averaging 7.5 percent per year.

Figure 14-25 shows that even a negative stress test in a subject with a previous infarction is no protection against the appearance of a coronary event. Those who have S-T depression after sustaining an infarction, however, have an 81 percent likelihood of having some coronary event within five years; whereas, those who have not had an infarction have a 34 percent chance—the

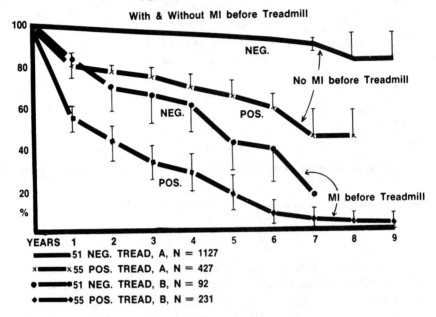

COMBINED EVENTS:

PROGRESSION OF ANGINA
MYOCARDIAL INFARCTION
DEATH

With & Without MI before Treadmill

NEG.

No MI before Treadmill

NEG.   POS.

POS.

MI before Treadmill

YEARS 1   2   3   4   5   6   7   8   9

▬▬▬51 NEG. TREAD, A, N = 1127
✕▬▬✕55 POS. TREAD, A, N = 427
●▬▬●51 NEG. TREAD, B, N = 92
◆▬▬◆55 POS. TREAD, B, N = 231

FIGURE 14-25. Those with previous infarction (B) have a much higher risk of a coronary event than those without (A) even if they have a negative stress test.

difference is more than twice as great. It can be seen from the standard deviations that the difference is highly significant between these groups.

In order to fully evaluate postinfarction testing, however, localization of the scar must be considered. Castellanet and colleagues[26] have studied the effect of various infarction patterns on the reliability of the S-T segment to identify ischemia in noninfarcted areas of the heart. They have shown that in those with inferior infarction, the sensitivity of the stress test is 84 percent. When a large anterior wall scar is present, it may mask ischemia in other areas, and reduce the sensitivity to 33 percent. Reliability of the test in patients with anterior infarction is inversely related to the magnitude of the scar. Their work has been confirmed by Pain and associates[48] and Weiner and coworkers.[49] Thus, one is on fairly safe ground when coming to a clinical decision based on the stress test when the infarction is inferior, but when the test appears normal following a large anterior infarction, other areas of muscle may be ischemic without influencing the S-T segment.

MULTIVARIATE ANALYSIS

It must now be quite obvious that the patient's S-T segments must be consid-

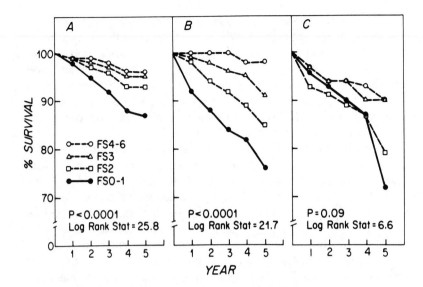

FIGURE 14-26. Life tables from the study by Weiner and colleagues[51] depicting survival according to S-T depression and final stage of exercise (Bruce). A = Those with less than 1 mm S-T depression. B = Those with S-T depression from 1 to 2 mm. C = Those with S-T depression greater than 2 mm.
The 5-year survival is a function of both S-T response and exercise time, with those with a long exercise time having the best survival unless the S-T depression is greater than 2 mm.

ered in light of a whole host of clinical observations in order to obtain the maximum amount of information. Obviously, a 19-year-old girl with a midsystolic click, a late systolic murmur, and S-T segment depression on exercise does not have coronary artery disease.

By using a number of findings, it is possible to calculate a probability score, combining and weighing the clinical variables in such a way as to characterize all of the test findings as well as the patient's clinical characteristics.

We developed a program in 1976[24] that gave increased discrimination, when compared with S-T depression alone. A number of centers[11,50,51] have since applied this method and found it to be very useful. Weiner and colleagues[51] used exercise time and magnitude of S-T depression among other variables to predict survival. Figure 14-26 illustrates the value of this approach. Recent work in our laboratory[8] suggests predictive accuracy of at least 90 percent is possible with this method in a population referred to a Cardiac Center. The details of the methodology are presented in Chapter 23.

CONCLUSIONS

The predictive power of the normal as well as the abnormal maximum stress test can now provide us with a very useful tool in the clinical management of coronary patients. The early studies of the Master's test suggested this, but validation with the maximum test was needed to confirm it.

The fact that all abnormal responders to stress tests are not the same, needed re-emphasis. Marked differences exist between those with the early onset of ischemia and those with changes near peak cardiac output. Among those with early onset are patients who have lesions in the left-main coronary and proximal branches of the circumflex and left-anterior descending arteries. When the blood pressure and heart rate responses, S-T configuration, R-wave changes, and other variables are compared by computer, we can eliminate many of the previous weaknesses of the method.

It has long been believed that coronary angiography would be the ultimate test allowing us to predict the future of subjects with coronary heart disease. As new information identifies the limits of angiography in defining flow it would appear that some type of dynamic evaluation is probably superior.[52] If our preliminary data are confirmed, it may be that stress testing will be as reliable. When comparing the life table figures of Bruschke and associates[53] with our subjects having early onset of ischemia, the curves are statistically equivalent (Fig. 14-27). The usefulness of the maximal stress test in predicting future events seems well established. It would appear that subsequent experiences can only result in further refinements in enhancing the usefulness of a test that has gained wide acceptance.

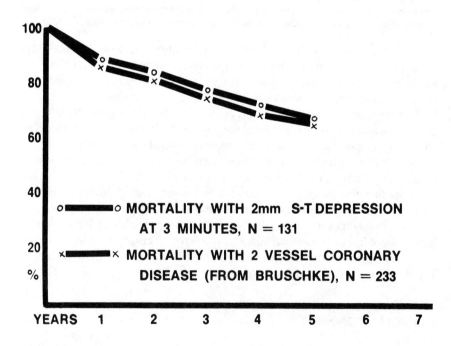

FIGURE 14-27. The mortality predicted by two-vessel coronary disease and by 2.0 mm S-T segment depression on the third minute of our protocol is the same. (Coronary angiogram mortality data from Bruschke, et al.,[53] with permission.)

REFERENCES

1. DIAMOND, GA: *Bayes' Theorem: A practical aid to clinical judgment for diagnosis of coronary artery disease.* Prac Cardiol 10(6):47–77, 1984.
2. DIAMOND, GA, ET AL: *Application of information theory to clinical diagnostic testing.* Circulation 63(4):915–921, 1981.
3. DIAMOND, GA, AND FORRESTER, JS: *Analysis of probability as an aid in the clinical diagnosis of coronary artery disease.* N Engl J Med 1350–1358, 1979.
4. *Coronary Risk Handbook.* New York Heart Association, 1973.
5. HOSSACK, KF, ET AL: *Prognostic value of risk factors and exercise testing in men with atypical chest pain.* Int'l J Cardiol 3:37–50, 1983.
6. EPSTEIN, SE: *Implications of probability analysis on the strategy used for noninvasive detection of coronary artery disease.* Am J Cardiol 46:491–499, 1980.
7. ELLESTAD, MH: *MVA: Improved diagnostic discrimination in exercise testing.* In Press.
8. ELLESTAD, MH AND HALLIDAY, WK: *Stress testing in the prognosis and management of ischemic heart disease.* Angiology 28:149, 1977.
9. MARCUS, ML: *The coronary circulation in health and disease.* McGraw-Hill, New York, 1983.
10. FEINSTEIN, AR: *The haze of Bayes, the aerial palaces of decision analysis, and the computerized Ouija board.* Clin Pharmacol Ther 21:482–495, 1979.
11. CHAITMAN, BR, ET AL: *Improved efficiency of treadmill exercise testing using a multile lead ECG system and basic hemodynamic response.* Circulation 57:71, 1978.
12. MCHENRY, PL, PHILLIPS, JF, AND KNOBEBEL, SB: *Correlation of computer quantitated treadmill exercise ECG with arteriographic location of coronary artery disease.* Am J Cardiol 30:747, 1972.
13. KASSEBAUM, DG, SUTHERLAND, KI, AND JUDKINS, MP: *A comparison of hypoxemia and exercise electrocardiography in coronary disease.* Am Heart J 7:371, 1932.
14. MARTIN, CM AND MCCONAHAY, DR: *Maximal treadmill exercise electrocardiography: Correlations with coronary arteriography and cardiac hemodynamics.* Circulation 46:956, 1972.
15. HELFANT, RH, ET AL: *Exercise related ventricular premature complexes in coronary heart disease.* Ann Intern Med 80:589, 1974.
16. WEINER, DA, ET AL: *Correlations among history of angina, ST segment response and prevalence of coronary artery disease in the Coronary Artery Surgery Study.* N Engl J Med 301:230, 1979.
17. SIMOONS, ML AND HUGENHOLTZ, PG: *Estimation of probability of exercise-induced ischemia by quantitative ECG analysis.* Am J Cardiol 56:552, 1977.
18. SIMOONS, ML: *Optimal measurements for detection of coronary artery disease by exercise ECG.* Comput Biomed Res 10:483, 1977.
19. BARTEL, AG, ET AL: *Graded exercise stress tests in angiographically documented coronary artery disease.* Circulation 49:348, 1974.
20. ELLESTAD, MH AND WAN, MKC: *Predictive implications of stress testing: Follow-up of 1700 subjects after maximum treadmill stress testing.* Circulation 51:363, 1975.
21. BRUSCHKE, AVG, PROUDFOOT, WL, AND SONES, FM, JR: *Progress study of 590 consecutive nonsurgical cases of coronary disease followed 5-9 years: Arteriographic correlations.* Circulation 42:1154, 1973.
22. MCNEER, JF, ET AL: *The role of the exercise test in the evaluation of patients for ischemic heart disease.* Circulation 57:64, 1978.
23. CHAITMAN, BR, ET AL: *The importance of clinical subsets in interpreting maximal treadmill exercise test results: The role of multiple lead ECG systems.* Circulation 59:560, 1979.
24. ELLESTAD, MH, ET AL: *The false positive stress test multivariate analysis of 215 subjects with hemodynamic, angiographic and clinical data.* Am J Cardiol 40:681–685, 1977.
25. ERIKSSEN, J AND MYHRE, E: *False positive exercise ECG: A misnomer?* Int'l J Cardiol 6:263–268, 1984.

26. CASTELLANET, M, GREENBERG, PS, AND ELLESTAD, MH: *Comparison of ST segment changes on exercise testing of angiographic findings in patients with prior myocardial infarction.* Am J Cardiol 42:24–35, 1978.

27. STONE, PH, LAFOLLETTE, LE, AND COHN, K: *Patterns of exercise treadmill test performance in patients with left main coronary artery disease: Detection dependent on left coronary dominance or coexistent dominant right coronary disease.* Am Heart J 104(1):13–19, 1982.

28. WEINER, DA, ET AL: *Assessment of the negative exercise test in 4,373 patients from the coronary artery surgery study (CASS).* J Cardiac Rehab 2(7):562–568, 1982.

29. HAKKI, AH, ET AL: *Implications of normal exercise electrocardiographic results in patients with angiographically documented coronary artery disease: Correlation with left ventricular function and myocardial perfusion.* Am J Med 75:439–444, 1983.

30. ROBB, GP, MARKS, HH, AND MATTINGLY, TW: *The value of the double standard 2 step exercise test in detecting coronary disease in a follow-up study of 1,000 military personnel.* Research Report AMSGS-21-54, Army Medical Service Graduate School, Walter Reed Army Medical Center, Washington, DC, September 1957.

31. ROBB, GP: Metropolitan Life Statistical Bulletin, 53, 1972.

32. MATTINGLY, TW: *The postexercise electrocardiogram: Its value in the diagnosis and prognosis of coronary arterial disease.* Am J Cardiol 9:395, 1962.

33. MCNEER, JF, ET AL: *The role of the exercise test in the evaluation of patients for ischemic heart disease.* Circulation 57:64, 1978.

34. BRUCE, RA, DEROUEN, TA, AND HOSSACK, KF: *Value of maximal exercise tests in risk assessment of primary coronary heart disease events in healthy men: Five years' experience of the Seattle Heart Watch Study.* Am J Cardiol 46:371–378, 1980.

35. HOSSACK, KF, ET AL: *Prognostic value of risk factors and exercise testing in men with atypical chest pain.* Int'l J Cardiol 3:37–50, 1983.

36. WEINER, DA, ET AL: *Prognostic importance of a clinical profile and exercise test in medically treated patients with coronary artery disease.* JACC 3(3):772–779, 1984.

37. GOLDSCHLAGER, H, SELZER, Z, AND COHN, K: *Treadmill stress tests as indicators of presence and severity of coronary artery disease.* Ann Intern Med 85:277, 1976.

38. SCHNEIDER, RM, BAKER, JT, AND SEAWORTH, JF: *Early positive exercise test: Implications for prognosis.* Primary Cardiol, December:49–55, 1983.

39. PODRID, PJ, GRAYBOYS, TB, AND LOWN, B: *Prognosis of medically treated patients with coronary artery disease with profound ST segment depression during exercise testing.* N Engl J Med 305(19):1111–1116, 1981.

40. DEGANIS, GR, ET AL: *Survival of patients with strongly post exercise ECG.* Circulation 65:452, 1982.

41. HAMMOND, HK, KELLY, TL, AND FROELICHER, V: *Radionuclide imaging correlatives of heart rate impairment during maximal exercise testing.* JACC 2(5):826–833, 1983.

42. ELLESTAD, MH, ALLEN, WH, AND STUART, RJ: *Diagnostic and prognostic information derived from stress testing.* In WENGER, NK (ED): *Exercise and the Heart.* FA Davis, Philadelphia, 1978.

43. COLE, J AND ELLESTAD, MH: *Significance of chest pain during treadmill exercise.* Am J Cardiol 41:227, 1978.

44. WEINER, DA, ET AL: *The predictive value of anginal chest pain as an indicator of coronary disease during exercise testing.* Am Heart J 96(4):458–462, 1978.

45. JELINEK, VM, ET AL: *The significance of chest pain occurring with the Master Two Step test.* Aust NZ J Med 6:22, 1976.

46. HAYET, M AND KELLERMAN, JJ: *The angina pectoris, heart rate threshold as a prognostic sign.* Cardiology (Suppl 2)68:78, 1981.

47. BRUCE, RA: *Exercise testing of patients with coronary heart disease.* Ann Clin Res 3:323, 1971.

48.   PAIN, RD, ET AL: *Relationship of graded exercise test findings following myocardial infarction to the extent of coronary artery disease and left ventricular dysfunction.* Am J Cardiol (in press.)

49.   WEINER, DA, ET AL: *Exercise induced ST changes, post-infarction: Predictive value for multivessel disease* (abstr). Circulation (Suppl)55&56 111:111, 1977.

50.   BERMAN, JL, WYNNE, J, AND COHN, PF: *Value of a multivariate approach for interpreting treadmill exercise tests in coronary heart disease* (abstr). Am J Cardiol 41:375, 1978.

51.   WEINER, DA, ET AL: *Prognostic importance of a clinical profile and exercise test in medically treated patients with coronary artery disease.* JACC 3(3):772–779, 1984.

52.   MARCUS, ML, ET AL: *Measurements of coronary velocity and reactive hyperemia in humans.* Circ Res 49:877, 1981.

53.   BRUSCHKE, AVG, PROUDFOOT, WL, AND SONES, FM, JR: *Progress study of 590 consecutive nonsurgical cases of coronary disease followed 5-9 years: Arteriographic correlations.* Circulation 42:1154, 1973.

54.   VECCHIO, TH: *Predictive value of a single diagnostic test in unselected populations.* N Engl J Med 274:1171, 1966.

15

STRESS TESTING IN WOMEN

PREVALENCE OF CORONARY ARTERY DISEASE IN WOMEN VERSUS MEN
DIFFERENCES IN SENSITIVITY AND SPECIFICITY
FINDINGS ACCORDING TO SYMPTOMS
Typical angina
Probable angina
MECHANISMS
STRATEGY TO SEPARATE TRUE- FROM FALSE-POSITIVE PATIENTS
CONCLUSIONS

Since the early days of exercise stress testing, S-T segment depression has been the focus of interest as a marker for ischemia. Because coronary disease has been so much more common in men than in women, the reduced reliability of this finding in women has been of lesser importance. If the trends in coronary artery disease parallel those of lung cancer, another disease often induced by smoking, we will soon be treating a larger number of women with this problem than ever before. Is there a way to deal with this discrepancy? What is the cause? Is S-T depression in women with normal coronary arteries truly a false-positive? Is it due to ischemia?

This chapter reviews information available bearing on these perplexing problems, suggests answers, and offers guidelines that we have found useful.

PREVALENCE OF CORONARY ARTERY DISEASE IN WOMEN VERSUS MEN

Exact information on prevalence in women is difficult to acquire because we are dependent on symptoms to lead us to the diagnosis, especially in younger subjects. Data on mortality, however, suggest that women lag behind men by about 10 years and the age adjusted mortality in men is about 2.5 times that of women[1] (Fig. 15-1). At younger ages, however, prevalence of coronary disease in men exceeds women by 5 to 1. It has been said that in premenopausal nondiabetic women with coronary disease, smoking and the use of birth control pills are almost always present.[2] On the other hand, Engel and colleagues[2] found family history to be the most important risk factor in these patients. It is paradoxical that exercise-induced S-T depression in normal women under age 45 has been found to be much more common than in men (almost 4 times), by both Wu's group[3] in Milan and Profant and associates[4] in Seattle. Because it is known that coronary artery disease prevalence is lower than in men, these changes must be presumed to be due to some process independent of coronary atherosclerosis. As the women in Wu's study[3] aged, however, the preva-

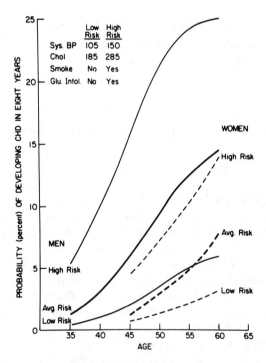

FIGURE 15-1. Probability of women developing CAD in eight years according to age, sex and risk. (From the Framingham Heart Study, with permission.)
Men ————————————
Women ————————————

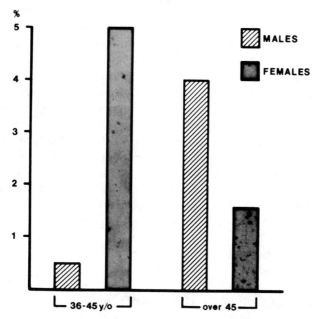

PREVALENCE OF ST SEGMENT DEPRESSION
WITH EXERCISE

MALES

FEMALES

FIGURE 15-2. Prevalence of exercise-induced S-T depression in normal subjects according to age. The young women with a low prevalence of CAD and a high estrogen level exceed that in men. This ratio reverses over age 45. (Drawn from data in Wu.[3])

lence of S-T depression fell. In women over age 45, during the years we know them to be more susceptible to coronary artery disease, the prevalence of S-T depression was exceeded by the men in their study (Fig. 15-2). Our experience with a group of normal volunteers did not reflect this trend, however (see Table 14-5).

DIFFERENCES IN SENSITIVITY AND SPECIFICITY

As in all studies, we must remind ourselves that the population under scrutiny will determine the findings. Most reported series analyzing S-T depression in women are from cardiac centers where women with chest pain syndromes are sent for angiography. Thus, the symptoms and the signs determine the sampling. When women with chest discomfort, for whatever cause, finally come to angiography, they are quite likely to have been screened with an exercise test. If the test was normal, few will be sent for angiography—thus, the sampling favors those with S-T depression. This is also partly true for men as well. Of the various studies comparing men and women, Sketch and associates[5] in Nebraska found 8 percent of men had false-positive S-T changes and 67 percent of women. Linhart and coworkers,[6] on the other hand, found only 22 percent of their female subjects had S-T depression and only 5 percent when they excluded abnormal resting electrocardiograms and those on drugs. It seems unlikely that women in Omaha were that much different from those in Philadelphia. Koppes and colleagues[7] report false-positive rates of between 24 to 35 percent in 4 studies they reviewed, and Amsterdam and associates[8] reviewed 96 men and 65 women with normal coronary angiograms and reported the false-positive rate of 15 percent in women versus 11 percent in men. Weiner and coworkers[9] reported on 3153 patients in the CASS study and reported a false-positive rate of 3 percent in men and 14 percent in women. The false-negative rate was 38 percent and 22 percent respectively. They then matched men and women for age, previous infarction, and coronary anatomy and found the false-positive and false-negative rates to be almost identical. When Guiteraz and associates[10] and Chaitman and colleagues[11] at the Montreal Heart Institute evaluated 112 women according to symptoms, as well as by different lead systems, the overall sensitivity was 79 percent and specificity 66 percent using 14 leads. Similar results were obtained using only CC_5 or CM_5. They had previously reported a specificity of 82 percent in men using this lead system, when they stratified them by symptoms.

FINDINGS ACCORDING TO SYMPTOMS

Typical Angina

In women with typical angina, the pre-test risk was 0.75 and post-exercise test risk with abnormal S-T depression was 0.83. These data were similar to that in men with typical angina.

Probable Angina

In women with probable angina, the pre-test risk was 0.36 and after S-T depression with exercise 0.5.[10] This group turns out to have a high false-positive rate and a low specificity. In those with nonspecific chest pain, the post-test likelihood was zero. They found that typical angina during testing and exercise S-T elevation to be 100 percent reliable in detecting coronary disease, however. On the other hand, S-T depression found only during exercise and not immediately afterward, has a low specificity (89 percent false-positive).

Sketch and Aronow[12] categorized their data according to symptoms and constructed Figure 15-3. Their sensitivity varied more between sexes than does the specificity, thus their false-positive rate remained quite low in all groups. Some of the above data[5] suggest the false-positive tracings are due to prevalence alone. This would pre-suppose that many known causes such as mitral prolapse, vasoregulatory asthenia, and drug effects are excluded. It seems certain that some of these problems are more common in women than men.

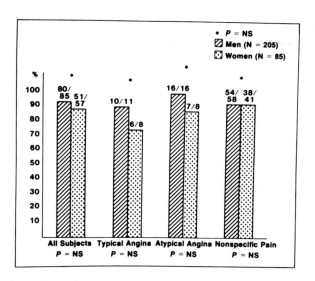

FIGURE 15-3. The specificity of an abnormal exercise test for all men and women and according to chest pain syndrome. (From Sketch and Aronow[13] with permission.)
These data differ from other workers in that there is a lower prevalence of false-positive responders among the women. This would be expected if most of the women were older.

MECHANISMS

Estrogens have been implicated as a cause for S-T depression. Oral estrogens have been shown to increase the prevalence of S-T depression and androgens to decrease the effect.[13] Estrogens have a similar chemical structure to digitalis, which is known to cause S-T depression and may function as a coronary vasoconstrictor. This mechanism is believed to be a likely explanation for some of the changes seen.

Subclinical disturbances in muscle function that are associated with reduced left-ventricular compliance may be more common in women. These changes may be due to a nonspecific cardiomyopathy or the hypertrophy associated with hypertension.[14] Kassumi and coworkers[15] studied left ventricular dynamics in women with S-T depression as compared with normals and described higher vascular resistance and an increased oxygen demand, especially at the subendocardial level. They postulate this is an important cause for false-positive changes.

Syndrome X patients, mostly women with angina, relieved by nitroglycerin who have normal coronary arteries may well have reduced coronary vasodilator reserve.[16] Abnormal lactate excretion has been shown in these patients with atrial pacing. Whether this phenomenon is hormonal, autonomic, or mechanical has yet to be elucidated.

I expect that in time, some of the mechanisms will become better understood. Various maneuvers are now under study to help in their identification.

STRATEGY TO SEPARATE TRUE-FROM FALSE-POSITIVE PATIENTS

Careful attention to the history of pain, medications, physical signs, and other laboratory signs of disease will go a long way in helping to discriminate the true disease process.

Analysis of the exercise electrographic tracing at rest, during hyperventilation and after exercise, is important. The presence of ST-T wave changes after hyperventilation are strong negative predictors.[17] Rapid upsloping S-T, increasing septal Q amplitude, and very rapid resolution of the S-T change after exercise can also alert us to the probability of a "false-positive."

Repeating the test in a fasting state, if the abnormal one was done soon after a meal may help.[18]

The use of beta blockers has been shown to correct abnormal S-T changes in the absence of coronary artery disease.[19] (See Chapter 18.)

The simultaneous use of a CKG during testing.[20] This "poor man's" wall motive device gives some of the wall motion information found on the more expensive nuclear blood pool studies.

Multivariate analysis. We have found the use of multiple variables in a simple computer program (Chapter 23) to be very helpful in reducing the uncertainty, based on S-T findings alone.

If indicated, thallium stress testing[21] done in high quality laboratories may add data to confirm or negate the results suggested by S-T segment depression, after the standard exercise test has been completed.

There are times in appropriate clinical situations when angiography is indicated—even when normal coronary arteries are suspected. Clearing up uncertainty is important, especially as the risk of angiography is virtually zero in top-flight laboratories. We should be reminded, however, that normal epicardial coronary arteries, on angiography, do not rule-out myocardial ischemia. Labeling a patient with Syndrome X as a neurotic is a disservice to the patient as well as to the physician.

CONCLUSIONS

It would appear at this time that by using careful clinical analysis, and all the information available to us during stress testing, the reliability of the stress test in women is not far below that of men. In most cases, when the S-T depression is suspected to be due to non-coronary causes, it can be confirmed with a high degree of accuracy, short of an angiogram.

It is important to remember that the prevalence of "false-positive" S-T depression is high in younger women who are unlikely to have CAD on the basis of age alone. As they age, the number of "false-positive" changes decreases and S-T depression becomes a more reliable marker for coronary disease.

When dealing with women with pain and normal coronaries; reassurance, understanding, and careful follow-up are essential in providing a proper program to minimize disability.

REFERENCES

1. LEVY, RI AND FEINLEIB, M: *Risk factors for coronary artery disease and their management.* In BRAUNWALD, E (ED): *Heart Disease.* WB Saunders, Philadelphia, 1984, p 1206.
2. ENGEL, HJ, PAGE, HL, JR, AND CAMPBELL, WB: *Coronary artery disease in young women.* JAMA 230(11):1531–1534, 1974.
3. WU, SC, ET AL: *Sex differences in the prevalence of ischemic heart disease and in the response to a stress test in a working population.* Eur Heart J 2:461–465, 1981.
4. PROFANT, GR, ET AL: *Responses to maximum exercise in healthy middle-aged women.* J Appl Physiol 33:595, 1972.
5. SKETCH, MH, ET AL: *Significant sex differences in the correlation of electrocardiographic exercise testing and coronary arteriograms.* Am J Cardiol 36:169–173, 1975.
6. LINHART, JW, LAWS, JG, AND SATINSKY, JD: *Maximum treadmill exercise electrocardiography in female patients.* Circulation 50:1173–1178, 1974.
7. KOPPES, G, ET AL: *Treadmill exercise testing.* Curr Prob Cardiol 8:1, 1977.
8. AMSTERDAM, EA, ET AL: *Exercise stress testing in patients with angiographyically normal coronary arteries: Similar frequency of false positive ischemic responses in males and females.* Am J Cardiol 41:378, 1978.
9. WEINER, DA, ET AL: *Correlations among history of angina, ST segment response and prevalence of coronary artery disease in the coronary artery surgery study (CASS).* N Engl J Med 301:230, 1979.
10. GUITERAS, P, ET AL: *Diagnostic accuracy of exercise ECG lead systems in clinical subsets of women.* Circulation 65(7):1465–1474, 1982.
11. CHAITMAN, BR, ET AL: *Improved efficiency of treadmill exercise testing using a multiple-lead ECG system and basic hemodynamic exercise response.* Circulation 57:71, 1978.
12. SKETCH, MH AND ARONOW, WS: *Continuing education: Diagnostic and prognostic value of exercise testing.* J Cardiac Rehab 3:495–508, 1983.
13. JAFFE, MD: *Effect of testerone cypionate on post exercise ST segment depression.* Br Heart J 39:1217, 1977.
14. ELLESTAD, MH, ET AL: *The false positive stress test multivariate analysis of 215 subjects with hemodynamic, angiographic and clinical data.* Am J Cardiol 40:681–685, 1977.
15. KUSUMI, F, ET AL: *Elevated arterial pressure and post-exertional ST segment depression in middle-aged women.* Am Heart J 92(5):576–583, 1976.
16. MARCUS, ML: *The coronary circulation in health and disease.* McGraw-Hill, New York, 1983.
17. KEMP, GL AND ELLESTAD, MH: *Treadmill stress testing as a means of objectively evaluating coronary revascularization.* Vascular Dis J 5:96–103, 1968.
18. MCHENRY, PL AND MORRIS, SN: *Exercise electrocardiography-current state of the art.* In SCHLANT, RC AND HURST, JW (EDS): *Advances in Electrocardiography.* Grune & Stratton, New York, 1976, p 265–304.
19. MARCOMICHELAKIS, J, ET AL: *Exercise testing after beta-blockade: Improved specificity and predictive value in detecting coronary heart disease.* Br Heart J 43:252–261, 1980.
20. WEINER, DA, ET AL: *Cardiokymography during stress testing.* Am J Cardiol 51:1307, 1983.
21. GREENBERG, PS, BIBLE, M, AND ELLESTAD, MH: *Prospective application of the multivariate approach to enhance the accuracy of the treadmill stress test.* J Electrocardiol 15(2):143–148, 1982.
22. FRIEDMAN, TD, ET AL: *Exercise thallium-201 myocardial scintigraphy in women: Correlation with coronary arteriography.* Am J Cardiol 49:1632–1637, 1982.

16

CHEST PAIN AND NORMAL CORONARY ARTERIES

A relieved 42-year-old woman upon being told she had just sustained a myocardial infarction exclaimed "Thank God, now everyone will know the pain wasn't all in my mind." Somewhere between 10 and 30 percent of patients subjected to coronary angiograms have epicardial coronary arteries thought to be normal or to have disease inadequate to explain their chest pain.[1] In an age when many people are obtaining relief of symptoms with coronary bypass surgery or angioplasty, the failure to demonstrate anatomic stenosis is frustrating to both the physician and the patient. The finding is even more perplexing when exercise-induced S-T depression or relief of pain by nitroglycerin is also present. This chapter reviews present concepts pertinent to the understanding of this syndrome and the place of exercise testing in diagnosis and management.

PREVALENCE

The occurrence of this syndrome in any center or hospital depends on a good deal on the referral patterns. In areas where only those with late, severe, typical angina are referred for study, it would be quite low. Centers where the sensitivity and specificity of stress testing is reported to be very high must not be seeing many of these types of patients because a significant number (approximately 20 percent) have S-T segment depression with exercise.[2] After ergonovine testing became popular, many patients in this category were subjected to provocative testing, but those who failed to have classical epicardial coronary spasm and S-T segment elevation (the majority) were still left without a clear-cut diagnosis. The majority of cardiac centers[3,4,5,6] report that about 10 to 12 percent of their patients referred for angiography would fall into this class, if those with well-understood mechanisms for their pain are excluded. These known conditions responsible for false-positive S-T depression include aortic stenosis, severe hypertensive left-ventricular hypertrophy, classic obstructive cardiomyopathy, and mitral prolapse.

CLINICAL SYNDROMES

Myocardial Infarction

Although these patients rarely have classic angina, they are included here because this sub-set may be important in understanding this syndrome as a whole. Classically they are younger, often under age 35. The sex ratio seems to be similar, although our experience favors women. The most common risk factors are smoking and oral birth control pills.[7] The three mechanisms involved are coronary spasm, thrombosis, or coronary embolus. All the evidence to implicate spasm is somewhat scant; Maseri and colleagues[8] reported a patient with spasm at the onset of an infarction who died 6 hours later. A fresh thrombus was found at necropsy in the area seen on angiography to be in severe spasm. Engle and associates[9] have attributed infarcts during angiography to a spasm and infarction has been reported following the withdrawal of nitrates.[10]

In women on birth control pills, abnormalities in clotting have been demonstrated and blamed for the infarction.[11] Post-infarction angios lend some credence to the concept that thrombosis, which later is lysed out, may be the villain. The rare case of coronary embolus, barring those from bacterial colonies on the aortic valve, remain hard to explain. The natural history of this syndrome is yet to be fully described.

Prinzmetal's Angina

The syndrome of vasospastic angina should be suspected when patients with known coronary heart disease have rest pain, or when the early morning spontaneous anginal attacks, described by Prinzmetal and coworkers[12] so long ago, recur repeatedly. These are usually relieved by nitroglycerin and may be initiated by ergonovine, hyperventilation, or the cold pressure test. When S-T elevation accompanies pain and rhythm disturbances are seen, one can predict the provocative use of ergonovine is likely to be positive during the coronary angiogram. Because this syndrome has been so well described, I will only mention that these subjects may have either S-T elevation or depression during stress testing. Those with S-T depression are more likely to have coexisting coronary atheroma. The majority with pure spasm and normal coronary anatomy will have a normal exercise test.

Cardiomyopathy

In patients without overt cardiac enlargement caused by congestive or obstructive cardiomyopathy, it is common to find abnormalities in contraction or increased left-ventricular end-diastolic pressure, especially after contrast injection.[13] Goodin and colleagues[2] found 46 percent had an increased left-ventricular end-diastolic pressure after contrast was injected. Erikssen and associates[14] from Oslo did coronary angiograms on 105 asymptomatic men who had S-T depression on a treadmill and identified 36 with normal coronary arteries. After a 7-year follow-up, three were dead of heart failure, four had clear-cut cardiomyopathies, one had aortic incompetence and left-ventricular dilatation, and one had developed severe angina thought to be caused by coronary disease by an abnormal Muga scan. Thus, 22 percent had developed significant myocardial disease and about one-half had an abnormal ejection fraction with exercise Muga scan on follow-up. In asymptomatic men S-T depression and normal coronary arteries may identify a cohort who has poor function and a poor long-term prognosis. Pasternac and associates[15] have shown that in hypertrophic and congestive cardiomyopathy, subendocardial ischemia occurs at rest and during exercise and most patients develop chest pain and lactate excretion with atrial pacing. They implicate a reduced diastolic pressure time interval to systolic pressure time interval ratio and the compressive forces associated with the myocardial hypertrophy. We analyzed 100 "false-positive" stress test patients and found 57 percent had an increased left-ventricular end-diastolic pressure,[16] and Goodin and colleagues[2] found 18 percent of their 60 patients with chest pain and normal coronary arteries had the same finding. Thus, a significant percentage of this population may have some type of poorly understood cardiomyopathy (see Chapter 4).

Syndrome X

This term was first applied by Likoff and coworkers[17] in Philadelphia, recognizing that the mechanisms explaining the pain were unknown. It was their belief, however, that most of these patients had myocardial ischemia, because their classic pain was often relieved by nitroglycerin, even though coronary atheroma could not be demonstrated. It is only recently, that we are beginning to understand more about the underlying mechanisms responsible for this process. Following Marcus's[18] demonstration in the operating room that some patients with normal coronaries are unable to increase flow appropriately during reactive hyperemia, Cannon and colleagues[1] at the National Heart, Lung, and Blood Institute have used coronary sinus flow measurements to demonstrate a reduced increase in coronary perfusion following atrial pacing. They also found a reduction in coronary sinus flow after ergonovine and the cold pressure tests—even though no epicardial narrowing was present. They labeled this condition "reduced vasodilator reserve" and believed the obstruction is in the arterioles and explains many of the findings heretofore hard to understand. When this type of study is done, those with S-T depression are likely to have an increase in lactate excretion, confirming that the S-T depression is not a "false-positive," but reflects ischemia, even in those who have normal epicardial coronary arteries. S-T depression with exercise on atrial pacing was demonstrated in 72 percent of a series of cases reported by Bemiller and associates[19] but were found in only 36 percent of another series by Waxler and colleagues.[20] When Berland and coworkers[21] divided their patients into those who had abnormal lactate excretion and those who did not, typical anginal pain and S-T depression on exercise were more common in the former.

ESOPHAGEAL DYSFUNCTION

Esophageal dysfunction is so common and so difficult to separate from angina by symptoms alone that it warrants a few words. Tibbling[22] from Sweden studied 217 patients diagnosed as having esophageal dysfunction by acid perfusion or by esophageal mammetry and found between 60 and 70 percent had effort-related pain. Tibbling and Wranne[23] found that 50 percent of one group referred for exercise tests had esophageal dysfunction (ED). In their data, however, more than half their patients described their symptoms as "heart burn," a term that should not be ignored by the physician. Kramer and Hollander[24] inflated esophageal balloons in patients with ischemic heart disease and 7 of 19 complained of pain identical to their angina, which was relieved immediately when the balloon was inflated. Most of the reports suggest ischemic S-T depression in patients with esophageal dysfunction is rare (2 to 5 percent), although nonspecific T-wave changes are common.

The reason for exercise-induced chest pain in esophageal dysfunction may be explained by the recent work of Harrison and colleagues[25] who found gastroesophageal reflex (GER) in exercising patients who had eaten or who had previous acid loading. The GER was measured with a pH electrode in the esophagus above the gastroesophageal junction. Only 1 of 33 fasting patients had GER, however. It is of interest that smoking aggrevates this response. Thus, when our patients with anginal pain have a negative coronary angiogram, esophageal disease must be suspected, but if they are tested in a fasting state confusion is less likely to occur.

OTHER MECHANISMS

We don't know at this time how many patients with Syndrome X are due to the above mechanism. Myocardial bridging, musculoskeletal syndrome, esophageal spasm, and psychosomatic disorders have all been proposed.

Bass and colleagues[26] report that these patients have a high prevalence of psychologic syndromes such as sighing and gasping during rest, breathlessness after trivial exertion, during conversation, and with emotional tension. They believe the angina is often a somatic expression of anxiety. They also report that chronic hyperventilation in some of these subjects may cause peripheral and coronary vasoconstriction due to hypocapnea. Case[27] has adequately demonstrated marked myocardial hypoxia secondary to hypocapnea and alkalosis. Waxler and associates[20] also found 40 percent had some type of anxiety neurosis. The presence of an abnormal hemoglobin dissociation curve reported by Eliot and Bratt[28] has not been confirmed by others.

TREADMILL FINDINGS

Are there any tips that can help separate these subjects from those with anatomically significant coronary disease? We selected a group of false-positive patients and compared them with true-positive to try to answer this question.[16] We found that in men, they were more likely to be younger, be able to exercise longer, have atypical chest pain, and have hyperventilation-induced S-T changes. This can be suspected when S-T depression is associated with significant septal Q-waves. In women, exercise time was not helpful, but the patients were younger, had more atypical pain, were more likely to have significant changes on hyperventilation, and some had abnormal electrocardiograms at rest.

If their angina is due to myocardial ischemia, however, and induced by exercise, it would be likely that a number of our patients would be clinically indistinguishable from those with epicardial coronary narrowing. These patients, as long as they are with us, promised to keep stress testing from being 100 percent reliable in predicting anatomic coronary disease.

THERAPY

If our present perceptions are accurate, and a significant number of these patients have significant myocardial ischemia, then the use of nitrates, calcium blockers, and beta blockers would seem appropriate. A significant proportion of our patients failed to be relieved by these agents, however, suggesting that there may be mechanisms yet to be elucidated. When the symptoms are atypical, a careful search for noncardiac causes for the pain may be rewarding. Chest wall pain and esophageal pain can usually be recognized once one suspects the heart may not be the culprit.

PROGNOSIS

Most of the studies[19,29] indicate patients with this syndrome have a good prognosis. Goodin and coworkers[2] report after a 2-year follow-up, 49 percent of 80 patients are improved or have no symptoms. Myocardial infarction and death was absent in this short follow-up. Bemiller and colleagues[19] report that after 4 years, 80 percent of their patients claim their angina was decreased and the other 19 percent reported it had remained stable. They also reported one patient with sudden death, however, who was found to have normal coronary arteries at autopsy. The patients of Goodin and colleagues report—50 percent had marked improvement or a complete loss of pain in 2 years.

CONCLUSIONS

It seems clear that patients with this syndrome are not all they seem. At one end of the spectrum there may be a few who have significant coronary disease that was missed on the angiogram and at the other end are patients with a neurosis or a noncardiac pain of some type. In the middle, probably representing 40 to 50 percent are a group who have definite myocardial ischemia. Many of these will have ischemic S-T depression on exercise and lactate excretion when challenged by atrial pacing. There are some who have lactate excretion and who have negative exercise tests and vice versa, however. Many of those with true ischemia probably have a reduced vasodilator reserve.

This syndrome can be enormously disabling. Goodin and coworkers[2] reported that 78 percent of their patients had one or more hospitalizations for chest pain in the year prior to study. To complete a cardiac study will often relieve anxiety, allow for a more sensible approach to therapy, and minimize subsequent hospitalizations. No longer should these patients be embarrassed by their pain syndromes and live in fear of imminent infarction and death.

A few conclusions can be listed:
1. Typical angina and the exercise S-T depression is more likely associated with myocardial ischemia.
2. Atypical angina and negative exercise tests are more likely to be found in those in whom ischemia cannot be demonstrated.

REFERENCES

1. CANNON, RO, III, ET AL: *Angina caused by reduced vasodilator reserve of the small coronary arteries.* J Am Coll Cardiol 1(6):1359–1373, 1983.
2. GOODIN, RR, ET AL: *Exercise stress testing in patients with chest pain and normal coronary arteriography: With review of the literature.* Cathet Cardiovasc Diagn 1:251–259, 1975.
3. OCKENE, IS, ET AL: *Unexplained chest pain in patients with normal coronary arteriograms.* N Engl J Med 303:1249–1252, 1980.
4. LIKOFF, W, SEGAL, BL, AND KASPARIAN, H: *Paradox of normal coronary arteriograms in patients considered to have unmistakable coronary heart disease.* N Engl J Med 276:1063–1066, 1966.
5. PROUDFOOT, WL, SHIREY, EK, AND SONES, FM: *Selective cine coronary arteriography: Correlation with clinical findings in 1,000 patients.* Circulation 33:901–910, 1966.
6. KEMP, HG, ET AL: *The anginal syndrome associated with normal coronary arteriograms: Report of a six year experience.* Am J Med 54:735–742, 1973.
7. KHANDHERIA, B AND SEGAL, BL: *Myocardial infarction in patients with normal coronary arteries.* Practical Cardiol 10(3):68–73, 1984.
8. MASERI, A, ET AL: *Coronary vasospasms as a possible cause of myocardial infarction.* N Engl J Med 299:1271–1277, 1978.
9. ENGLE, HJ, ET AL: *Coronary artery spasm as the cause of myocardial infarction during coronary arteriography.* Am Heart J 91(4):500–506, 1976.
10. LANGE, RI, ET AL: *Nonatheromatous ischemia heart disease following withdrawal from chronic industrial nitroglycerin exposure.* Circulation 46:666, 1972.
11. SCHUSTER, EH, ET AL: *Multiple coronary thromboses in previously normal coronary arteries: A rare cause of acute MI.* Am Heart J 99(4):506–509, 1980.
12. PRINZMETAL, M, ET AL: *Correlation between intracellular and surface electrograms in acute myocardial ischemia.* J Electrocardiol 1:161–166, 1968.
13. OHLMEIER, H AND GLEICHMANN, U: *Abnormal left ventricular complicance as a cause of exercise-induced angina in patients without coronary-artery disease.* Practical Cardiol 10(4):97–104, 1984.
14. ERIKSSEN, J, ET AL: *False suspicion of coronary heart disease: A 7 year follow-up study of 36 apparently healthy middle-aged men.* Circulation 68(3):490–497, 1983.
15. PASTERNAC, A, ET AL: *Pathophysiology of chest pain in patients with cardiomyopathies and normal coronary arteries.* Circulation 65(4):778–789, 1982.
16. ELLESTAD, MH, ET AL: *The false-positive stress test multivariate analysis of 215 subjects with hemodynamic, angiographic and clinical data.* Am J Cardiol 40:681–685, 1977.
17. LIKOFF, W, SEGAL, BL, AND KASPARIAN, H: *Paradox of normal coronary arteriograms in patients considered to have unmistakable coronary heart disease.* N Engl J Med 276:1063–1066, 1966.
18. MARCUS, ML: *The Coronary Circulation in Health and Disease.* McGraw-Hill, New York, 1983.
19. BEMILLER, CR, PEPINE, CJ, AND ROGERS, AK: *Long-term observations in patients with angina and normal coronary arteriograms.* Circulation XLVII:36, 1973.
20. WAXLER, EB, KIMBIRIS, D AND DREIFUS, LS: *The fate of women with normal coronary arteriograms and chest pain resembling angina pectoris.* Am J Cardiol 28:25–31, 1971.

21. BERLAND, J, ET AL: *Angina pectoris with angiographically normal coronary arteries: A clinical, hemodynamic, and metabolic study.* Clin Cardiol 7:485–492, 1984.

22. TIBBLING, L: *Angina-like chest pain in patients with oesophageal dysfunction.* Acta Med Scand (Suppl)644:56–59, 1981.

23. TIBBLING, L AND WRANNE, B: *Oesophageal dysfunction in male patients with angina-like pain.* Acta Med Scand 200:391, 1976.

24. KRAMER, P AND HOLLANDER, W: *Comparison of experimental esophageal pain with clinical pain of angina pectoris and esophageal disease.* Gastroenterology 29:719, 1955.

25. HARRISON, MR, LEHMAN, GA, AND FARIS, JV: *Gastroesophageal reflux occurring during treadmill exercise testing* (in press).

26. BASS, C, WADE, C, AND GARDNER, WN: *Angina-like chest pain: Is it the somatic expression of anxiety?* Modern Medicine, September: 161, 1983.

27. CASE, RB: *The response of canine coronary vascular resistance to local alterations in coronary arterial pCO_2.* Circ Res 39:558, 1976.

28. ELIOT, RS AND BRATT, G: *The paradox of myocardial ischemia and necrosis in young women with normal coronary arteriogram.* Am J Cardiol 23:633, 1969.

29. SELZER, A: *Cardiac ischemic pain in patients with normal coronary arteriograms.* Am J Med 63(5):661–665, 1977.

17

BLOOD PRESSURE MEASUREMENT DURING EXERCISE

The recording of blood pressure has plagued those of us doing exercise testing for a number of years, and we are still beset with problems. The importance of recording accurate blood pressure cannot be overestimated, in view of the influence of the aortic pressure on the oxygen requirements of the heart. It has long been known that the so-called double product, or systolic blood pressure multipled by the heart rate, is an excellent index of myocardial oxygen consumption. A simple, noninvasive method of measuring the central aortic pressure has yet to be found. Although we use the brachial artery pressure recorded in the standard way, its accuracy diminishes rapidly as the speed of the treadmill increases. There are patients who, because of their well-coordinated gait, walk very smoothly or even jog with a minimum of jiggle, and, therefore, it is easy to take their blood pressure at even 5 or 6 miles an hour. Other patients vibrate so much that even at 3 or 4 miles per hour their blood pressure is extremely difficult or impossible to record by the usual method. Simultaneous pressures taken by two examiners on the same patient on opposite arms are fairly widespread (Fig. 17-1). Measurement of blood pressure by catheter in the brachial artery and the aorta often reveals a significant increase as one proceeds distally, even at rest. This difference during exercise may well be accentuated, especially in patients with inadequate cardiac outputs, because of their well-known tendency to develop peripheral vasoconstriction. The measurement of blood pressure by automated means has been studied by a number of equipment companies. By filtering the Kortakoff sounds and blocking the sound pickup except at the appropriate time by triggering the sound circuit from the ECG, the accuracy of the mechanical device, according to vendors, exceeds that obtained by the conventional method. If this accuracy is confirmed by careful experimental work, it will be a major advance.

In spite of the inherent inadequacies, blood pressure should be recorded frequently before, during, and after the stress test. We do this at minute inter-

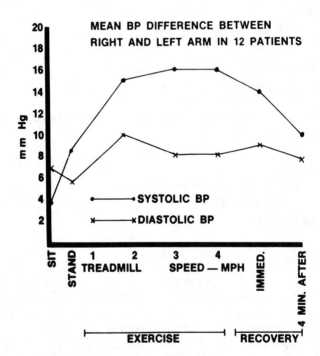

FIGURE 17-1. The difference between two simultaneously recorded blood pressures using aeronoid manometers on the right and left arms is plotted. The difference between the two measurements tends to increase during exercise and to decrease again as soon as exercise is terminated.

STRESS TESTING: PRINCIPLES AND PRACTICE

vals as long as is possible as the rate of exercise increases and continues during eight minutes of recovery.

PHYSIOLOGY

Many complex factors are involved in the control of blood pressure response with exercise, and an understanding of these various factors and how they interact with each other is necessary in order to draw conclusions concerning blood pressure response and the patient's condition based on blood pressure changes with exercise and the degree of underlying myocardial impairment.

NORMAL BLOOD PRESSURE RESPONSE

The interaction between the peripheral vasculature and the heart during exercise is modulated through the central nervous system via the sympathetic nervous system as well as locally by factors that are responsible for autoregulation on an arteriolar level. With the onset of exercise, the resistance to blood flow through contracting muscles decreases significantly and results in a fall in peripheral vascular resistance. Other perfusion beds in nonworking areas, primarily the splanchnic, undergo significant vasoconstriction, thereby directing blood to working areas and away from nonworking areas. Constriction of the capacitance vessels on the venous side of the circulation aids in returning blood to the heart; thereby, facilitating increased cardiac output by maintaining preload. Venous constriction is of prime importance in enabling cardiac output to rise normally in the face of a net reduction in total peripheral vascular resistance.[1] A rise in resistance to flow in the splanchnic circulation, skin, and non-exercising muscles also occurs. When the patient begins to exercise, the normal blood pressure response is a gradual elevation of systolic pressure with increasing workloads and essentially no significant change in diastolic pressure. Near peak workload, the systolic blood pressure levels off and often declines, only to rise again within a minute or two after exercise is terminated. As the patient recovers, the pressure gradually returns to control levels. Factors that alter blood pressure response are reviewed below and their clinical significance discussed.

HYPERTENSIVE RESPONSE

Hypertension at rest has long been known to be a risk factor for the development of coronary artery disease.[2] Significant elevation of blood pressure during exercise above the expected normal response has, until recently, been of questionable clinical significance. Recent reports[3-6] indicate that when subjects with normal resting pressure develop an abnormally high systolic pressure with exercise, they increase their probability of developing clinically significant hypertension in the future. Miller-Craig and colleagues[7] suggest that exercise-induced hypertension is a better predictor of eventual clinical hypertension than elevated blood pressure at rest, although Kannel and associates[8] report that labile hypertension in young adults also has definite predictive value.

BLOOD PRESSURE RESPONSE WITH AGE

As patients get older, although the cardiac output with exercise increases in about the same ratio as in younger subjects, the peripheral resistance is greater so that the systolic pressure is higher. As exercise increases, however, resistance drops, as in younger subjects, but not enough to lower the pressure to the range seen in youth. The normal maximal systolic pressure in older subjects is higher as age progresses proving cardiac function is good and cardiac output can increase[9] (Fig. 17-2).

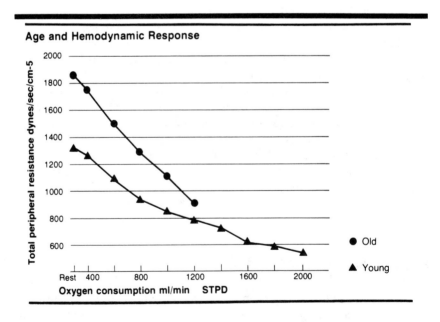

FIGURE 17-2. The drop in peripheral resistance with increased work in older subjects is similar to the younger ones, although it always remains somewhat higher. (From Julius,[9] with permission.)

STRESS TESTING: PRINCIPLES AND PRACTICE

BLOOD PRESSURE RESPONSE IN PATIENTS WITH RESTING HYPERTENSION

Exercise blood pressure in most hypertensive patients increases at about the same rate as it does in normals, but starting from a higher baseline the maximum systolic blood pressure will usually be greater. There are some, however, who as exercise progresses, have less of a rise and their peak pressure may be similar to that of a normal age-matched subject. This would indicate that the peripheral resistance drops in a more normal manner and responds more like a nonhypertensive subject. This might suggest that exercise would be a good therapeutic measure. Others not only have a steep rise during exercise, but the pressure continues to climb for several minutes after exercise and stays high during the recovery. This subject probably responds with an increase in peripheral resistance and would be a greater risk. Such a patient might be expected to receive little benefit from an exercise program; it could even be detrimental.

HYPERTENSIVE RESPONSE IN CORONARY ARTERY PATIENTS

An exercise rise in systolic blood pressure (well over 200 mm of mercury) has been used as a reason to terminate exercise in some centers or hospitals. We have never done this because we have failed to see any complications related to a rising blood pressure. There is a general tendency for the pressure to rise more in older subjects, and in those who are deconditioned. We followed a large group of patients who had a maximum systolic blood pressure response of over 200 for up to eight years.[10] These patients were selected because they had S-T segment depression as well as an abnormal increase in blood pressure response. When they were compared with patients with S-T segment depression and a normal blood pressure response, the prevalence of subsequent coronary events (death, myocardial infarction, and new angina) was reduced. This suggested to us that the increased blood pressure response identified a cohort who had good left-ventricular function and could thus generate higher pressures. The possibility that the increased pressure also provided better coronary perfusion during exercise has to be considered. Irving and colleagues[11] found similar data in the Seattle Heart Watch subjects. They found a decrease in sudden cardiac death per year as maximum systolic blood pressure increased. Morris and associates[12] correlated peak systolic blood pressure with the number of coronary vessels obstructed and also with the ejection fraction. They found the higher the pressure, the less disease and thus provided us with an anatomic explanation of our findings (Fig. 17-3).

Sheps and coworkers[13] found that when the diastolic pressure increased with exercise, it identified a sub-set of patients with a higher probability of coronary artery disease. This has not been confirmed by other authors, possibly due to the difficulty in recording diastolic pressure during exercise accurately.

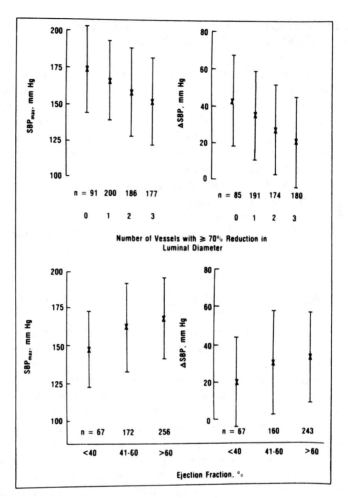

FIGURE 17-3. The peak systolic blood pressure (SBP_max), and change in systolic blood pressure with exercise (Δ SBP) is correlated with the number of significantly narrowed vessels on angiography (upper graph), and ejection fraction (lower graph). The higher the peak systolic blood pressure, and change in systolic blood pressure, the less severe the myocardial impairment. Conversely, patients with lower systolic blood pressure with exercise tended to have more severe vessel involvement and lower ejection fractions. (From Morris, et al.,[12] with permission.)

HYPOTENSIVE RESPONSE

Systolic hypotension during exercise occurs under a number of circumstances that must be clearly identified in order to assess its significance.

Late in Exercise

Many normals as well as those with cardiac pathology extend exercise beyond their aerobic threshold. At this point, which is usually around 60 percent or more of their maximum capacity, they have a more rapid increase in heart rate and ventilation and the systolic blood pressure levels off and then begins to fall because of increasing acidosis. This is probably due to the accummulation of lactic acid, which causes a drop in peripheral resistance as well as a decrease in myocardial contractility. When exercise is stopped, this decrease will rapidly abate and the systolic pressure will rebound to a point considerably greater than that recorded at the end of exercise. This response has no predictive value in our experience except to indicate that the patient has exercised past anaerobic threshold and probably has done about as well as the patient is capable of (Fig. 17-4).

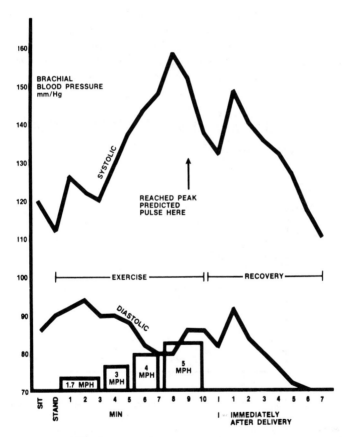

FIGURE 17-4. A typical blood pressure change as seen during our exercise protocol recorded with an aeronoid manometer on the arm. Systolic pressure rises as the workload increases until it gets near the peak capacity of the subject. At this point, it tends to drop sharply, probably due to a decrease in peripheral resistance or a drop in cardiac output, or both. The rebound phenomenon then occurs shortly after exercise is terminated.

Early in Exercise

Anxious patients occasionally will have a sudden rise in blood pressure for a minute or two and then a drop to 10 or 20 mm even as the exercise progresses followed by a gradual increase again. This is probably due to an excess of norepinephrine, the effect of which is quickly dissipated by the increased metabolic demands. This can be differentiated from a more serious decrease in cardiac output, by the vigor of the patient, the respiratory rate, and the absence of signs of ischmia. The blood pressure does not go below control in this situation.

Blood Pressure Response With Ischemia

As early as 1959, Bruce and colleagues[14] reported that failure to increase the systolic blood pressure over 130 was a risk factor for subsequent coronary events and Thompson and Kelemen[15] in 1975 and Irving and Bruce[16] in 1977, emphasized the correlation of severe ischemia with a drop in pressure early in the exercise protocol. Hammermeister and associates[17] believe that in true

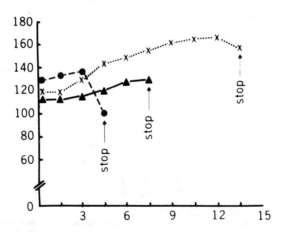

NORMAL & ABNORMAL SYSTOLIC BLOOD PRESSURE RESPONSES TO EXERCISE TESTS

FIGURE 17-5. Normal and abnormal systolic blood pressure responses to exercise tests.
X   = Normal response—subject able to exercise 13½ minutes, drops blood pressure at peak of normal exercise capacity.
● = Abnormal—subject increases systolic pressure initially, but pressure drops early in exercise before normal exercise capacity is reached.
▲ = Abnormal—subject fails to raise systolic pressure to 130 mmHg or higher, even though exercise duration may be nearly normal.
(From Sheffield and Roitman,[21] with permission.)

ischemic hypotension, the pressure must drop during exercise below the resting level. This is often associated with deep S-T segment depression and identifies a group of patients likely to have left-main disease or severe three-vessel disease. San Marco and associates[18] found that exertional hypotension was as reliable as "marked S-T segment depression" in predicting severe three-vessel disease or left-main coronary disease.

Weiner and colleagues[19] studied over 400 consecutive patients with exercise testing and cardiac catheterization. Forty-seven patients manifested a fall in blood pressure with exercise. Of this group, approximately one half were randonized to medical therapy, and one half to surgical therapy. Cardiac catheterization revealed three-vessel or left-main coronary artery disease in 55 percent of the patients. Repeat exercise testing verified the reproducibility of this blood pressure response in the medical group. Repeat exercise testing in the surgical group revealed normal blood pressure response in all patients after successful coronary bypass surgery. In the last few years, many reports[17,20] have confirmed that a drop in pressure during exercise reflects severe ischemic left-ventricular impairment. The pressure changes are often correlated with other findings, such as an appearance of reduced vitality, skin palor, and other signs of inadequate perfusion (Fig. 17-5).

RECOVERY BLOOD PRESSURE

The rate of the systolic blood pressure drop during recovery is usually fairly rapid after maximum exercise, although a rebound with a temporary rise about one minute after exercise termination is common. As previously mentioned, this is believed to be due to the recovery from the anaerobic metabolism, that has occurred near peak workload. Recently, the group from San Antonio[22] has reported that systolic blood pressure in patients with significant coronary artery disease fails to drop as fast as normals and has suggested that this response may help discriminate those with ischemia. Because the recovery blood pressure is so dependent on the magnitude of exercise, and because the systolic blood pressure at high workloads is so difficult to record accurately, I am skeptical of the validity of this concept. We were unable to verify their work by retrospective analysis of our own data (Fig. 17-6). A review of the systolic blood pressure data in Appendix 1 will suggest to the reader that normals often exhibit a delayed decrease in pressure.

CARDIOMYOPATHIES

Any process that reduces left-ventricular function may cause exertional hypotension with exercise testing. The common denominator of this clinical event appears to be that the upper limit of cardiac output cannot continue to meet the increased peripheral demands of the working tissues when the peak car-

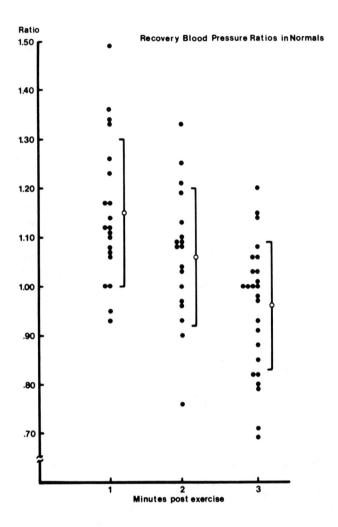

FIGURE 17-6. Systolic blood pressure as a percent of blood pressure at end of exercise. The systolic blood pressure during recovery was plotted in a group of normal subjects studied in our laboratory during the first three minutes. The majority were above a ratio of 0.9 and would have been classified as abnormal using the criteria of Amon and coworkers.

diac output is reached. The increasing demand of the peripheral tissues results in a rise in lactic acid and a generalized drop in pH, which causes a progressive decrease in peripheral vascular resistance and in blood pressure. Cardiomyopathic processes, both hypertrophic as well as congestive will produce this effect.[23] Decreases in pressure with obstructive cardiomyopathies are likely to be more abrupt than in other conditions and may be associated with syncope and serious arrhythmias. Because these patients are often suspected

STRESS TESTING: PRINCIPLES AND PRACTICE

of having coronary artery disease due to anginal pain, special care should be exercised when angina is found in a patient with a murmur of undetermined etiology.

DRUGS

Various types of medications have been shown to produce a fall in blood pressure with exercise testing, the most common are antihypertensives.[24,25] Various classes of these agents such as the sympatholytic drugs, beta blockers, or peripheral vasodilators have all been implicated in abnormal blood pressure response to exercise. These responses may be mediated either through a central mechanism inhibiting sympathetic outflow such as beta blockers or sympatholytics or by decreasing the ability of peripheral vasculature to respond to sympathetic activity. The peripheral vasodilators are notoriously likely to produce sudden drops in pressure. Diuretics will not produce much exertional hypotension, their major effect seems to be on the resting pressure. The psychoactive drugs either major or minor tranquilizers have been shown to cause moderate blood pressure changes through both central and peripheral mechanisms. The effects of various drugs and metabolic processes on stress testing is covered in more detail in Chapter 22.

CONCLUSIONS

Careful observation of blood pressure during exercise can yield important information not only about the peripheral resistance, but also about the contractile state of the left ventricle. A heart that can function well when ejecting against a very high resistance (BP over 200 mmHg) is usually fairly well perfused, as well as free from very much fibrosis.

When we observe a fall in pressure, despite continuing exercise early in the test, poor perfusion or inadequate function for other reasons is almost certainly the case.

It now seems well established that a blood pressure response to exercise that is greater than normal in a young healthy person is likely to predict clinically significant hypertension in the future.

Thus, careful monitoring of blood pressure at each increment of workload and during recovery is an essential part of stress testing.

REFERENCES

1. GUYTON, A: *The relation of cardiac output and arterial pressure control.* Circulation 64:1079–1089, 1981.
2. BRAUNWALD, E: *Heart Disease: A Textbook of Cardiovascular Medicine,* ed 2. WB Saunders, Philadelphia, 1980, p 1246.

3. DLIN, RA, ET AL: *Follow-up of normotensive men with exaggerated blood pressure response to exercise.* Am Heart J 106(2):316–320, 1983.
4. WILSON, NV AND MEYER, BM: *Early prediction of hypertension using exercise blood pressure.* Prev Med 10:62–68, 1981.
5. JACKSON, AS, ET AL: *Prediction of future resting hypertension from exercise blood pressure.* J Cardiac Rehab 3:263–268, 1983.
6. WILHEMSEN, L, ET AL: *13-year followup of a maximal exercise test in a population sample of 803 men aged 50 at entry* (abstr). European Cardiology Symposium on Prognostic Values of Exercise Testing, Vienna, April 2-5, 1981.
7. MILLER-CRAIG, M, ET AL: *Use of graded exercise testing in assessing the hypertensive patient.* Clin Cardiol 3:236–240, 1980.
8. KANNEL, WB, SORLIE, P, AND GORDON, T: *Labile hypertension: A faulty concept?* Circulation 61:1183, 1980.
9. JULIUS, S: *Exercise and the hypertensive patient mediguide to hypertension.* Geigy Publications 1:1, 1984.
10. SCHRAGER, BR AND ELLESTAD, MH: *The importance of blood pressure measurement during exercise testing.* Cardiovasc Rev & Rpt 4(3):381–394, 1983.
11. IRVING, J, BRUCE, RA, AND DEROUEN, T: *Variations in and significance of systolic pressure during maximal exercise (treadmill) testing.* Am J Cardiol 40:841–848, 1977.
12. MORRIS, S, ET AL: *Incidence and significance of decreases in systolic blood pressure during graded treadmill exercise testing.* Am J Cardiol 41:221–226, 1978.
13. SHEPS, DS, ET AL: *Exercise-induced increase in diastolic pressure: Indicator of severe coronary artery disease.* Am J Cardiol 43:708, 1979.
14. BRUCE, RA, ET AL: *Exertional hypotension in cardiac patients.* Circulation 19:543–551, 1959.
15. THOMPSON, P AND KELEMEN, M: *Hypotension accompanying the onset of exertional angina.* Circulation 52:28–32, 1975.
16. IRVING, JB AND BRUCE, RA: *Exertional hypotension and post exertional ventricular fibrillation in stress testing.* Am J Cardiol 39:849–851, 1977.
17. HAMMERMEISTER, KE, ET AL: *Prognostic and predictive value of exertional hypotension in suspected coronary heart disease.* Am J Cardiol 51:1261–1266, 1983.
18. SAN MARCO, M, PONTIUS, S, AND SELVESTER, R: *Abnormal blood pressure response and marked ischemic ST segment depression as predictors of severe coronary artery disease.* Circulation 61:572–578, 1980.
19. WEINER, D, ET AL: *Decrease in systolic blood pressure during exercise testing: Reproducibility, response to coronary bypass surgery and prognostic significance.* Am J Cardiol 49:1627–1632, 1982.
20. ERIKSSEN, J, JEWELL, J, AND FOGLANG, K: *Blood pressure response to bicycle exercise testing in apparently healthy middle aged men.* Cardiology 66:56–63, 1980.
21. SHEFFIELD, LT AND ROITMAN, D: *Stress testing methodology.* Prog Cardiovasc Dis XIX(1):33–49, 1976.
22. AMON, KW, ET AL: *Value of post exercise systolic blood pressure in diagnosing coronary disease* (abstr). Circ II 6B:36, 1983.
23. WEINDER, DA: *Clinical significance of abnormal blood pressure response during exercise stress testing.* Practical Cardiology 10:37–45, 1984.
24. PICKERING, TG: *Immediate and delayed hypotensive effects of propanolol at rest and during exercise.* Trans Assoc Am Physicians 92:271–285, 1979.
25. FRANCIOSA, J, JOHNSON, S, AND TOBIAN, L: *Exercise performance in mildly hypertensive patients: Impairment by propranolol but not oxprenolol.* Chest 78:291–299, 1980.

18

ISCHEMIA
IN ASYMPTOMATIC SUBJECTS

Although the absence of chest pain and other symptoms of coronary heart disease were once believed to provide assurance that its presence was unlikely, this concept must now be laid aside.[1,2] Gordon and Kannel[3] report that the first symptom of coronary disease was myocardial infarction or death in 55 percent of the Framingham men. Most of us will agree that these two end-points are unacceptable. There are two groups of asymptomatic patients commonly considered for stress testing. This chapter deals primarily with those who have never had symptoms recognized as being of cardiac origin. Another group, those who have had recognized myocardial infarction but have been asymptomatic following this event, are commonly believed to be free of ischemia but limited somewhat by scar tissue replacing functional myocardium. In actuality, more than half of this group have other vessels significantly narrowed. The use of exercise testing in these patients is covered in Chapters 10 and 14.

PREVALENCE

There are a number of ways to estimate how many people have silent myocardial ischemia.

Autopsy Data

Allison and colleagues[4] found only 19 percent of subjects dying of sudden death had a history of angina, although 66 percent had pathologic evidence of infarction. Spickerman and associates[5] in a similar study found 32 percent had angina. If one reviews autopsy findings on subjects dying of noncardiac causes[6] on the other hand, it appears that a 6 percent mean prevalence rate in men (ages 30–69) and a 2.6 percent mean rate for women characterizes the amount of coronary disease in people who are truly asymptomatic.

Epidemiologic and Screening Studies

Diamond and Forrester[6] reviewed reports of patients undergoing catheterization for reasons other than chest pain (for example, valvular heart disease, abnormal ECGs) and found 4.5 percent prevalence of coronary narrowing. Erikssen and coworkers[7] catheterized subjects with abnormal S-T segment response to stress testing and found 3.4 percent of the total had significant narrowing; however, their methodology suggests at least 50 percent would be missed because of a false-negative test. Again, using S-T depression with exercise as a case finding method, Buckendorf and colleagues[8] found coronary artery disease in 6 percent of their asymptomatic military aviation personnel (mean age 36). The five-year follow-up heart study by Bruce and associates[9] of 2365 asymptomatic subjects, identified 2 percent who had a coronary event. If one assumes a 5 percent per year event rate in a coronary disease population, then 75 percent of those manifested would yet to be discovered during the five-year period resulting in a prevalence of 8 percent. Allen and coworkers,[10] however, reported that 5.4 percent of 888 subjects followed for 5 years developed coronary artery disease, which by the above reasoning could suggest a prevalence in their material of at least 20 percent. Moreover, when the initial abnormal exercise tests were stratified by age and sex (see Table 14-5), the prevalence of a hospital-based study would be higher with 25 percent of men over age 41 demonstrating S-T depression. In this age range, estimating a 50 percent specificity, the prevalence would be approximately 12 percent. If the prevalence of coronary artery disease in asymptomatic men in a population over 40 is only 10 percent, there are at least four million people in the United States at risk with this syndrome.

S-T DEPRESSION AND NORMAL CORONARY ARTERIES

We all are also faced with the problem of dealing with those who appear to have ischemia on the ECG, but have normal coronaries. The followup of Erikssen and colleagues[11] reports on this group and found them also at risk of a cardiac disability and death. This is discussed in Chapter 16.

MECHANISMS AND PATHOPHYSIOLOGY

When patients are referred for exercise testing because of a history of chest pain, a high percent fail to have angina during the test, even though they have S-T segment depression. Are they having ischemia? Deanfield and Shea[12] have studied ischemia with rubidium, an isotope with a short half-life using positron emission tomography, and report that S-T depression has been associated with reduced myocardial perfusion in every case studied. The evidence is quite conclusive that in patients with coronary artery disease, and suggestive even in its absence, that S-T depression usually represents myocardial ischemia.[11] Data from Maseri, at Hammersmith in London,[13] as well as several papers using Holter techniques[14,15] indicate about 75 percent of the ischemic episodes in patients with typical angina are silent. They suggest that lesser degrees of ischemia and shorter time periods are more likely to be "silent." On the other hand, Kunkes and associates[16] using Holter monitoring, found that silent ischemia was more common in patients with multivessel disease. Shell and Penny[15] believe an average period of ischemia of five to seven minutes is necessary before angina appears. My own angioplasty experience, however, indicates that in many cases severe ischemia is followed by pain in as little as 10 to 15 seconds.

PAIN PERCEPTION

The failure of the patient to perceive ischemic pain may be related to a number of factors. It has been stated that the transmission of pain is interrupted in some diabetic patients due to a neuropathy.[17] Diabetic individuals are reported to have a higher prevalence of silent MI.[17] Droste and Roskamm[18] have reported that asymptomatic subjects have a higher pain threshold when their cutaneous perception of pain is measured.

Because endorphins are reported to mitigate pain under certain circumstances, we tested 10 patients with angiographically proven coronary disease during stress testing.[19] Each patient had 2 mm or more of S-T depression, but intravenous naloxone (an endorphin antagonist) failed to bring on pain or influence the exercise test in any significant way. Thus, it appears that high endorphin levels are not involved in painless ischemia.

We have repeatedly observed that conditioning will reduce or abolish exercise-induced angina. Sim and Neill[20] reported on eight patients with this phenomenon and found that when the angina was produced by atrial pacing, it was not influenced by training. They found the double product at anginal threshold was also increased, suggesting an increase in myocardial oxygen supply. However, when atrial pacing was used to increase cardiac work, the double product at the anginal threshold and lactate secretion was the same before and after conditioning. The reasons for this are as yet to be explained.

DETECTION

The failure to detect subjects with exercise testing in an asymptomatic population who will eventually have a coronary event is not surprising, considering the known false-negative rate (20 to 40 percent) and the propensity for atherosclerotic lesions to progress sometimes quite rapidly. Cumming and associates[21] and Bruce and colleagues[9] emphasize that more than half their patients who developed coronary events failed to manifest S-T segment depression on the initial exercise test. On the other hand, an abnormal exercise ECG, especially when combined with other risk factors, has been shown to identify a cohort of high-risk subjects for a subsequent coronary event, in spite of the application of Baysian Theory. It will be recalled from Chapter 14 that the post-test probability in an asymptomatic subject with S-T depression is low because of the low prevalence of disease. If one uses known risk factors, in conjunction with stress testing, however, the predictive power becomes more acceptable. Giagnoni and coworkers[22] from Milan compared 135 asymptomatic subjects with S-T depression with a group without S-T depression controlled for age and other risk factors. They found that after six years, the risk for coronary events of those with S-T depression was 5 times the controlled subjects.

We found similar results when analyzing subjects who were referred to our laboratory for screening tests rather than for chest pain syndromes (Fig. 18-1).

Hopkirk and coworkers[23] studied 225 asymptomatic men from the Air Force who had undergone stress testing for various reasons. They found that 0.3 millivolts (3 mv) of S-T depression, persistence of S-T depression for six minutes into recovery, and total duration of exercise of less than 10 minutes

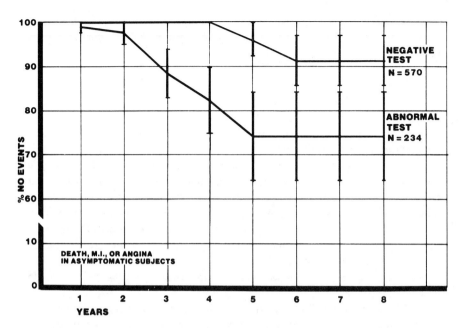

FIGURE 18-1. When only those who denied any symptoms were evaluated, all coronary events occurred well below those reported in the study in which 83 percent were symptomatic (Fig. 14-7).

(equivalent to seven minutes on the Bruce Protocol) resulted in a high likelihood of disease. They found any two of the exercise variables were highly predictive (89 percent), but relatively insensitive (37 percent). When studying the false-positives they found that normalization of the S-T segment depression in the first 20 seconds of recovery was present in 18 percent.

When Allen and colleagues[10] analyzed their data on 888 asymptomatic subjects, they also needed a combination of findings for best results. S-T segment depression, R-wave increase, and a short exercise duration had reasonable sensitivity in five years and a very high specificity. Other tests found useful in this population have been exercise thallium, kymocardiograms, and coronary calcium, detected on fluoroscopy. When any of these is abnormal in conjunction with an exercise test, the likelihood of coronary disease is above 95 percent.[24]

PROGNOSIS

Although many subjects with silent coronary disease have a sudden coronary event, it seems likely that the risk of an event is less than if ischemia is associated with typical anginal pain. Data from our files[25] indicate the risk of an event with asymptomatic ischemia is about half that when classical angina accompanies the electrocardiographic findings during stress testing. Cohn[26] also found an improved survival in a small group of asymptomatic patients followed for seven years with coronary artery disease as compared with those with anginal pain.

IMPLICATIONS

In spite of the apparent lower risk in this group of patients, the implications need some discussion. There appears to be three subsets of patients.

(1) Those who never have pain. Cohn has characterized this group as having a "defective anginal warning system." Raper and associates[27] report patients with repeated massive infarction without chest pain and comment that these people are at risk because of the lack of pain. Our patients tested with naloxone[19] were also in this category. There seems no doubt that angina in many is protective, and in this group its absence is a hazard and should be recognized as such. When we find patients before they are stricken by catastrophe, they should be carefully evaluated for severity of disease prior to deciding on therapy.

(2) Those who have pain with ischemia on some occasions, but not on others. This comprises a majority of patients who are recognized with coronary heart disease. Factors that influence the variability are occasionally detectable, such as changes in myocardial work, magnitude of ischemic myocardium, coronary spasm, durations of ischemia, and so forth. Many, however, have angina or chest pain at different times and under different conditions that seem to defy categorization. As we learn more about the pathophysiology of coronary artery disease, some of these will be easier to understand.

(3) Those who have chest pain with ischemia on most occurrences are a minority to be sure, yet a few years ago we believed most of our coronary patients fell into this group. Although we have learned a great deal about this process, there are many questions still unanswered.

CLINICAL STRATEGY

Epstein and coworkers,[28] Selzer and Cohn,[29] and others[30] have criticized the use of exercise testing in asymptomatic individuals. There are probably also those who would be against the detection of asymptomatic prostatic cancer.[1] On the whole, however, exercise testing is justified in asymptomatic subjects suspected of having an increased prevalence of disease. The presence of the classic risk factors in conjunction with the findings on an exercise test will go a long way to determine the presence or absence of significant coronary narrowing. If clinically indicated, a patient should proceed to other noninvasive diagnostic measures after the exercise test is evaluated. Findings usually associated with true-positive stress tests are:

1. Short exercise time.

ASYMPTOMATIC ST DEPRESSION

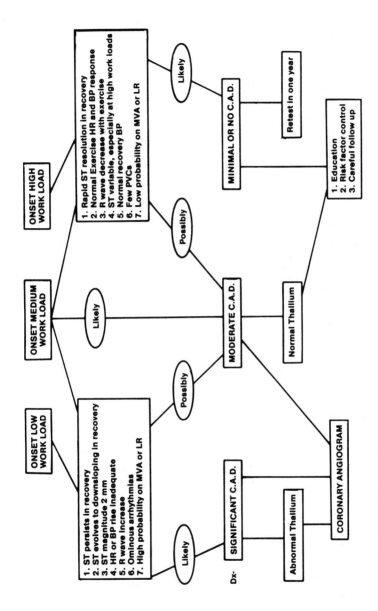

FIGURE 18-2. Diagnostic Flow Chart. Those patients with findings in the right hand box may not need angiography if one can follow them on a regular basis.

2. Less than normal increase in heart rate or blood pressure during the test.
3. Early onset of S-T segment depression with progression during exercise.
4. Evolution to downsloping S-T pattern during recovery.
5. Persistence of systolic hypertension during the first two or three minutes of recovery.
6. Marked increase in R-wave amplitude.
7. Reduction in amplitude of the septal Q, if present.
8. Prolongation in Q peak T interval with exercise.
9. Widening of the QRS with exercise.
10. High post-test probability on MVA or likelihood ratio.
11. Abnormal CKG (part of our routine exercise test).
12. Confirmation with radionuclide stress testing.

The above flow chart (Fig. 18-2) might serve as a guide when encountering an asymptomatic man with exercise-induced S-T depression. Clinical findings not shown will shade the decision to follow a more aggressive or conservative pathway. These might include the family history, hypertension, smoking, cholesterol, the cooperativeness of the patient, degree of denial, and many others.

TESTING WITH BETA BLOCKADE

A significant number of patients with S-T segment depression on exercise may be suspect of having some other cause, rather than coronary disease. Mitral prolapse, hypertensive heart disease, hyperdynamic heart disease due to excess catechol stimulation, and cardiomyopathy are some of the well-known examples. The latter two, when completely subclinical, are difficult to detect.

Kattus and colleagues,[31] as early as 1970, demonstrated that the S-T changes could be altered by beta blockade. Marcomichelakis and colleagues[32] in London compared ischemia in 50 patients with coronary artery disease and in 50 normals with S-T segment depression. They report that beta blockade failed to eliminate S-T depression in the coronary patients and normalized the S-T segments in all the false-positives. We have used this approach with success, but have not found it to be 100 percent reliable, as did the British group.

NITROGLYCERIN TEST

Zohman and Carroll from New York[33] have tested patients by giving nitroglycerin during graded exercise testing. They report that subjects who have true ischemia (true-positives) have normalization of their S-T segment depression with nitroglycerin administration, while those with ischemic changes not related to coronary disease (false-positives) demonstrated no change in their S-T segment depression.

Because S-T segment depression may, in some cases, be due to ischemia not associated with epicardial coronary narrowing, one would expect that patients with this mechanism would reduce their S-T depression when coronary disease is absent. This has turned out to be the case when we used Dr. Zoman's method.[33] Thus, patients with limited perfusion of their subendocardium for various reasons will correct their S-T depression with nitroglycerin and be indistinguishable from coronary artery diseased patients.

COMMENT

We often explain to the patient that the abnormal stress test findings are another risk factor, which along with other findings influence the clinical course to follow. In this situation, I believe education of the patient and family is one of the most important aspects of good patient care. If the patient understands the problem, we will have made a major step in the direction of initiating a sensible course of management.

ANGINAL EQUIVALENT

Even though the patient may come in with a story of no chest pain, a careful review of any type of chest discomfort, upper abdominal gas or bloating, inordinate dyspnea with exercise, or just increasing fatigue, may be an angina equivalent. Quite commonly, when the possible implications of the test are explained, the patient may then report symptoms withheld prior to the test. The need for denial of possible illness is a powerful force in many men, yet when they find a friend who understands their problem, they may let down and fill in some of the blanks heretofore withheld.

S-T DEPRESSION WITH PRIOR NEGATIVE TEST

These patients usually manifest S-T segment depression at high workloads and can be managed as if it were the first test. However, now the patient is identified as having an increased risk. If the S-T changes should be manifested at low workloads, the implications become more serious. Men who convert from a normal to an abnormal S-T segment response almost invariably have coronary narrowing and are rarely false-positive.

SURGICAL THERAPY

Although therapy is not strictly within the scope of this book, a few words about management of patients with silent ischemia may be in order. When we look for hard scientific data to direct us, there is little to go on. A number of studies[34,35] including CASS[36] would suggest that surgery on an asymptomatic patient, unless the patient has left-main disease, will not increase longevity.

On the other hand, Cohn,[26] Kent,[36] and others[37] who have had an active interest in this subset of patients for some time, would favor an invasive approach in certain circumstances. Severe three-vessel disease, low exercise tolerance, early onset of S-T segment depression, and other signs of major ischemia are reliable predictors[38] of a more serious prognosis in asymptomatic, or mildly symptomatic patients. One might, therefore, expect they would have a similar impact on the outcome of the asymptomatic patient. Indeed, S-T depression in the asymptomatic post-infarct patient is the most reliable predictor of subsequent coronary events.[39] If we had evidence that these subjects would eventually have angina prior to infarction, thus warning us to intervene, it would make sense to wait for the onset of symptoms. The fact is, however, that most patients with infarctions do not have angina as a warning.[1] Therefore, we can either be content to wait for the "axe to fall" or try to develop criteria for intervention. Thurer and associates[40] and others have documented that bypass surgical mortality in this group is almost zero in the best surgical centers.

Few would argue that open coronaries are more preferable than stenotic ones. The real issue is, what price should we pay, or what risks should we take to open them up for a time at least? If angioplasty continues to improve, and the high percentage of re-stenosis can be eliminated, it will make the decision to intervene somewhat easier.

MEDICAL THERAPY

A possibility, yet to be well documented, is that repeated episodes of ischemia may cause myocardial cell death and ultimately permanent reduction in left-ventricular function. We know this happens in aortic stenosis and hypertensive heart disease. Evidence is accummulating that it may also occur in coronary artery disease.[41,42]

Some reports[43] suggest that medical therapy will to some degree reduce the percentage of ischemic episodes and lessen their severity. The beta blocker trials indicate that in post-infarction patients, mortality will also decrease.[44] It has also been shown that beta blockers result in favorable re-distribution of blood flow in the ischemic myocardium.[45] The Oslo randomized trial[46] in healthy men clearly demonstrates diet and risk factor control also reduces mortality and morbidity. Is this enough? No one can be sure. When dealing with individual patients, physicians will probably act on their own experiences, it is hoped, combined with a sound knowledge of pathophysiology and familiarity with the recent literature.

At this time, I tend to be more aggressive in those with multi-vessel high-grade stenosis or very proximal left-anterior descending disease when they demonstrate severe ischemia and/or other signs of limited left-ventricular performance. On the other hand, if some new chemical can be shown to consistently cause regression of atheromata, the situation will change rapidly and intensive attacks on the coronary tree will dwindle.

CONCLUSION

In spite of those who oppose stress testing in asymptomatic patients, I firmly believe we will continue to search for ways to identify asymptomatic coronary disease. The use of exercise or other types of stress is by far the most practical approach we have today. When all the data available are combined to calculate the probability of disease, we have an excellent tool that warrants continued application. With the information obtained, we can act to prevent infarction and death in an ever increasing number of our patients.

REFERENCES

1.   GORDON, T AND KANNEL, WB: *Premature mortality from coronary heart disease.* JAMA 215(10):1617–1625, 1971.

2.   KEMP, GL AND ELLESTAD, MH: *The incidence of "Silent" coronary heart disease.* California Medicine 109:363–367, 1968.

3.   GORDON, T AND KANNEL, WB: *Multiple risk functions for predicting coronary heart disease: The concept, accuracy, and application.* Am Heart J 103(6):1031–1039, 1982.

4.   ALLISON, RB, ET AL: *Clinicopathologic correlations in coronary atherosclerosis.* Circulation 27:170, 1963.

5.   SPICKERMAN, RC, ET AL: *The spectrum of coronary heart disease in a community of 30,000.* Circulation 25:57, 1962.

6.   DIAMOND, GA AND FORRESTER, JS: *Analysis of probability as an aid in the diagnosis of CAD.* N Engl J Med 300:350, 1979.

7.   ERIKKSEN, J, ET AL: *False-positive diagnostic tests and coronary angiographic findings in 105 presumably healthy males.* Circulation 54:371–376, 1976.

8.   BUCKENDORF, W, WARREN, SE, AND VIEWEG, WVR: *Suspected coronary artery disease among military aviation personnel.* Aviation, Space, & Environ Med, October:1153–1158, 1980.

9.   BRUCE, RA, DEROUEN, TA, AND HOSSACK, KF: *Value of maximal exercise tests in risk assessment of primary coronary heart disease events in healthy men.* Am J Cardiol 46:371–378, 1980.

10.   ALLEN, WH, ET AL: *Five year follow-up of maximal treadmill stress test in asymptomatic men and women.* Circulation 62:522–527, 1980.

11.   ERIKSSEN, J, ET AL: *False suspicion of coronary heart disease: A 7 year follow-up study of 36 apparently healthy middle-aged men.* Circulation 68(3):490–497, 1983.

12.   DEANFIELD, J AND SHEA, M: *ST segment change as a marker of ischemia.* Circulation (Suppl III)68:22, 1983.

13.   MASERI, A: *Pathogenic mechanisms of angina pectoris expanding views.* Br Heart J 43:648, 1980.

14.   ARMSTRON, WF AND MORRIS, SN: *The ST segment during continuous ambulatory electrocardiographic monitoring* (editorial). Ann Int Med 98:249, 1983.

15.   SHELL, WE AND PENNY, WF, JR: *Mechanisms and therapy of spontaneous angina: The implications of silent myocardial ischemia.* Vascular Medicine. Apr/June 85–96, 1984.

16.   KUNKES, SH, ET AL: *Silent ST segment deviations and extent of coronary artery disease.* Am Heart J 100:813, 1980.

17. FAERMAN, I, ET AL: *Autonomic neuropathy and painless MI in diabetics.* Diabetes 26:1147, 1977.

18. DROSTE, C AND ROSKAMM, H: *Experimental pain measurement in patients with asymptomatic myocardial ischemia.* J Am Coll Cardiol 1(3):940–945, 1983.

19. ELLESTAD, MH AND KUAN, P: *Naloxone and asymptomatic ischemia: Failure to induce angina during exercise testing.* Am J Cardiol 54:982–984, 1984.

20. SIM, DN AND NEILL, WA: *Investigation of the physiological basis for increased exercise threshold for angina pectoris after physical conditioning.* J Clin Invest 54(3):763–770, 1974.

21. CUMMING, GR, ET AL: *Electrocardiographic changes during exercise in asymptomatic men: 3-year follow-up.* CMA J 112:578–581, 1975.

22. GIAGNONI, E, ET AL: *Prognostic value of exercise EKG testing in asymptomatic normotensive subjects.* N Engl J Med 309(18):1085–1089, 1983.

23. HOPKIRK, JAC, ET AL: *Discriminant value of clinical and exercise variables in detecting significant coronary artery disease in asymptomatic men.* JACC 3(4):887–894, 1984.

24. LASLETT, LJ, AMSTERDAM, EA, AND MASON, DT: *Evaluating the positive exercise stress test in the asymptomatic individual.* Chest 81(3):364–367, 1982.

25. COLE, JP AND ELLESTAD, MH: *Significance of chest pain during treadmill exercise: Correlation with coronary events.* Am J Cardiol 41:277, 1978.

26. COHN, PF: *Asymptomatic coronary artery disease.* Modern Concepts of Cardiovascu Dis 50(10):55–60, 1981.

27. RAPER, AJ, HASTILLO, A, AND PAULSEN, WJ: *The syndrome of sudden severe painless myocardial ischemia.* Am Heart J 107(4):813–815, 1984.

28. EPSTEIN, SE, ET AL: *Strategy for evaluation and surgical treatment of the asymptomatic or mildly symptomatic patient with coronary artery disease.* Am J Cardiol 43:1015–1025, 1979.

29. SELZER, A AND COHN, K: *Asymptomatic coronary artery disease and coronary bypass surgery.* Am J Cardiol 39:614–616, 1977.

30. REDWOOD, DR, EPSTEIN, SE, AND BOVER, FS: *Whither the ST segment during exercise.* Circulation 54:703–706, 1976.

31. KATTUS, AA, MACALPIN, RN, AND ALVARO, A: *Reversibility of nonischemic postural and exercise-induced ECG abnormalities of the T wave and ST segments by beta adrenergic blockade.* In KATTUS, A, ROSS, G, AND HALL, V (EDS): *Cardiovascular Beta Adrenergic Responses.* UCLA Forum in Medical Sciences Vol. 13, University of California Press, Los Angeles, 1970.

32. MARCOMICHELAKIS, J, ET AL: *Exercise testing after beta-blockade: Improved specificity and predictive value in detecting coronary heart disease.* Br Heart J 43:252–261, 1980.

33. ZOHMAN, LR AND CARROLL, LR: *The nitroglycerine exercise test.* Cardiology (Suppl 2)68:169, 1981.

34. NORRIS, RM, ET AL: *Coronary surgery after recurrent myocardial infarction: Progress of a trial comparing surgical with nonsurgical management for asymptomatic patients with advanced coronary disease.* Circulation 63(4):875–792, 1981.

35. MURPHY, ML, ET AL: *Treatment of chronic stable angina: A preliminary report of survival data of the randomized VA Cooperative Study.* N Engl J Med 297:621–627, 1977.

36. KENT, K: *Silent ischemia, pathophysiology still a mystery.* Heart Lines 4:4, 1983.

37. MYERBURG, RJ AND SHEPS, DS: *Evaluation of management of the asymptomatic patient with ECG evidence of myocardial ischemia.* Practical Cardiol, September:113–123, 1978.

38. MCNEER, JF, ET AL: *The role of the exercise test in the evaluation of patients for ischemic heart disease.* Circulation 57:64, 1978.

39. THEROUX, P, ET AL: *Prognostic value of exercise testing soon after myocardial infarction.* N Engl J Med 301:341, 1979.

40. THURER, RL, ET AL: *Asymptomatic coronary artery disease managed by myocardial revascularization.* Circulation (Cardiovascular Surgery) August:39 1979.

41. Braunwald, E and Kloner, RA: *The stunned myocardium: Prolonged, postischemic ventricular dysfunction*. Circulation 66(6):1146–1149, 1982.
42. Geft, IL, et al: *Intermittent brief periods of ischemia have a cumulative effect and may cause myocardial necrosis*. Circulation 66(6):1150–1153, 1982.
43. Schang, SJ and Pepine, CJ: *Transient asymptomatic ST segment depression during daily activity*. Am J Cardiol 39:396, 1977.
44. Wilhelmsson, C, et al: *Reduction of sudden deaths after myocardial infarction by treatment with alprenolol: Preliminary results.* Lancet 2:1157, 1974.
45. Kalischer, AL, et al: *Effects of propranolol and timolol on left ventricular volumes during exercise in patients with coronary artery disease*. JACC 3(1):210–218, 1984.
46. Hjermann, I, et al: *Effect of diet and smoking intervention on the incidence of coronary heart disease*. Lancet 44:1301–1310, 1981.

19

SPORTS MEDICINE
AND REHABILITATION

USE OF EXERCISE TESTING IN SPORTS
  Alerting the Patient and Physician to Occult Dysfunction
  Following Progress in Known Disease
  Evaluating Drug Regimens
COMMENT
EXERCISE TESTING IN CARDIAC REHABILITATION
DISCHARGE EXERCISE TEST
EXERCISE TESTING PRIOR TO FORMAL OUT-PATIENT REHABILITATION
EXERCISE PRESCRIPTION
CONFIRMATION OF IMPROVEMENT OR DETECTION OF
PROGRESSION

Although the performance of the fit athlete and the cardiac patient needing rehabilitation are at opposite ends of the spectrum, many of the concepts in exercise physiology apply to both. Each is involved in an attempt to improve function using the same basic mechanisms. Coronary patients under the supervision of Kavanaugh and colleagues[1] in Toronto dramatically demonstrate that sports and coronary artery disease are no longer incompatible. The use of exercise testing in each case provides us with a way to detect dysfunction if present, as well as providing a measure of conditioning and a tool for prescribing a subsequent exercise program in evaluating progress. This chapter presents some of the special problems arising when dealing with each group and suggests guidelines we have found useful.

PERFORMANCE OF ATHLETES VERSUS NONATHLETES

Henry Blackburn[2] claims "the modern affluent human is a species of animal that, shortly after maturation is confined in special cages. One is a mobile steel and plastic cage with exposure to complex decisions, frustration, and danger. The atmosphere is high in carbon monoxide while being transported to other stationary cages. There the subject is required to sit motionless most of the day while conditioned to self-adminster 20 potent doses of the poison nicotine and at least 5 doses of "caffeine alkaloids."

  This commentary on our modern lifestyle dramatizes how far we have come from the environment our evolution has prepared us for. In these artificial, unhealthy surroundings, disease can be far advanced and be undetected and unsuspected. On the other hand, in subjects who regularly stress their cardiovascular systems to near maximum capacity, dysfunction is more likely to be detected earlier. Thus, besides the benefits mentioned in Chapters 2 and 3, earlier awareness of declining function is another benefit of an active lifestyle. Although changes in cardiovascular function are of chief interest to us, improvement in bones, muscles, tendons, lungs, and other organs can be achieved with regular activity. Because we have, through custom, considered the sedentary human to be normal, which may not be the case, it is important to recognize the common cardiovascular changes seen in athletes. These include reduced heart rate, increased sinus arrhythmia, second-degree heart block, larger cardiac volume, some degree of ventricular hypertrophy, and the electrocardiographic patterns that are listed later.[3] Static exercise produces fewer cardiovascular alterations, but may be associated with significant hypertension; therefore, left-ventricular hypertrophy may be greater than with dynamic exercise.

RISKS OF CORONARY EVENTS IN SPORTS

Rhythm Disturbances

Rhythm disturbances are more common if warm-up is inadequate, isometric exercise is sustained, isotonic exercise is near maximal capacity, and are also found during the early recovery period. Scherer and Kaltenbach,[4] however, reported no mortality in 353,000 exercise tests done in sports centers for evaluation of fitness. The risks usually come with older subjects and in patients with occult disease.

Sudden Death

As many as 25 percent of primary infarctions occur during exercise.[5] Contributory factors include excitement, excessive pressure to continue when exhausted and sustained isometric activity. The immediate risk of sudden death is threefold to fourfold during exercise.[6] It is believed by some that the increased risk during exercise is balanced by a decreased risk between bouts. Sudden death during marathon running is fairly common.[7] The recent death of Jim Fixx, a well-known writer and lecturer, has dramatized the risk and placed another nail in the concept that marathon running provides a dispensation from coronary heart disease (the Bassler hypothesis).[8] A recent authoritative treatise by Noakes and colleagues[9] reviews this subject in detail. Sudden death during or immediately after exercise is especially common in cardiomyopathies—usually hypertrophic cardiomyopathies in young asymptomatic athletes.[10] This is probably due to ventricular tachycardia and ventricular fibrillation.

Infarction

Infarction, arrhythmias, and sudden death often coexist and can be initiated by exercise. In younger runners infarction occasionally occurs even with normal coronary arteries.[11,12] The cause for this is poorly understood, but some theories are presented in Chapter 16.

HEALTH AS RELATED TO PREVIOUS ATHLETIC EFFORTS

There seems to be little evidence that athletic performance as a youth has much effect on cardiovascular health in later years. On the other hand, life expectancy may be increased slightly in those who persist in strenuous sports for many years. Karvonen and associates[13] reported a maximum gain in longevity of three years in 396 Finnish championship skiers. Of interest is that 37 percent of these men continued to ski regularly on into their 60s. Soviet athletes have been reported to have a shorter life expectancy unless they reach age 64, after which they also manage to live longer. We know so little of the lifestyle in Russia that these data are hard to evaluate. Certain types of sports seem to be associated with different risks. Middle-aged British rugby players seem to have the highest risk and marathon runners the lowest.[14]

ENVIRONMENTAL FACTORS

It has long been recognized that cold may initiate angina and myocardial infarction in subjects with coronary disease. It is presumed that peripheral resistance increases and, thus, myocardial work is greater with moderate activity. As the time and intensity of work increases, however, this increased peripheral resistance disappears in normal subjects. Every distance runner knows that exercise during times of increased heat and humidity presents problems. If occult disease is present, these factors constitute serious hazards, as low cardiac function is associated with a reduced capacity to eliminate heat and to overcome increased peripheral resistance. Thus, the risk of serious cardiac events increases when subjects push themselves in climatic extremes.

QUANTITY AND QUALITY OF EXERCISE TO MAINTAIN FITNESS

Because a training effect is so dependent on the level of fitness at the onset of the program, it is difficult to give rigid guidelines. In a subject who is very sedentary, or in one who has been at bed rest, minimal exercise will increase fitness. The more fit one is, the more one has to do to improve or to maintain this level. This was established by the classic study of Saltin and associates[15] in Dallas where normal subjects on bed rest had a rapid increase in VO_2max in a short time after they resumed training; but as they progressed, the benefits and percentage change per unit of work steadily declined. Their function finally reached a plateau after about six weeks of training. It seems clear that on the average, the higher the intensity and the longer exercise intervals, the faster the training effect will progress, as long as excessive fatigue does not limit the program, which may constitute a sign of overtraining.

HOW MUCH IS ENOUGH?

The answer to this is dependent upon the goals of the individual. If the subject believes that exercise is good for general health and will decrease the likelihood of developing coronary heart disease, the subject should probably exercise for from thirty to forty-five minutes at least three days per week. This was recommended by Pollock[16] after evaluating a number of training schedules for their ability to increase VO_2max as well as the likelihood of causing an injury. The data of Paffenbarger and coworkers[17] suggest that about 2000 Kcal per week give maximum protection from coronary heart disease. Exceeding this failed to increase protection. It is important that the exercise program is carried out at an intensity of at least 60 to 80 percent of maximum capacity. These guidelines are for sedentary subjects planning to engage in sports and for coronary patients who would improve their function. If the sport envisioned requires a high level of fitness, increased intensity and training time will be required.

TYPE OF EXERCISE TEST IN SPORTS

The design of the exercise test may need to be specific for evaluation of certain activities; on the other hand, if only the aerobic capacity or maximal oxygen uptake is to be evaluated, a progressive exercise test, either on a treadmill or bicycle will be appropriate. We often use the same protocol for analyzing athletes as we do for patients. It is necessary to markedly extend the speed and grade for those who are highly conditioned, however. If research work requires knowledge of VO_2, direct measurement of the oxygen consumption must be done. There are many approaches to this depending on the experience of the examiner and the facilities available. We use the Beckman metabolic cart in our laboratory. If less accuracy is deemed satisfactory, there are a number of formulas and nomograms that allow fairly reproducible estimates of oxygen capacity from the speed and grade or the time on the treadmill protocol, or the watts achieved on the bicycle (see Chapter 7).

FINDINGS IN ATHLETES

Duration and Intensity

As would be expected, indurance-trained athletes can perform at high levels for longer periods. Those who train isometrically, however, such as weight lifters, may have little increase in their aerobic capacity.

Heart Rate and Blood Pressure

The lower resting heart and the average lower heart rate at any given workload is a recognized result of conditioning and has led to a method of predicting

VO$_2$max from submaximal performance.[18] Maximum heart rate is also occasionally moderately reduced as compared with the value predicted for age.

The expected increase in blood pressure is often lower in highly trained athletes, but this effect is frequently absent in the older age groups.

Electrocardiographic Changes at Rest

As early as 1954,[19] it was recognized that the electrocardiogram of athletes was often different from other subjects and findings correlated with pathology in nonathletes may be the result of a normal response to vigorous training. These include left- and right-ventricular hypertrophy, abnormalities in repolarization, (T and S-T segment changes), sinus bradycardia, and atrioventricular conduction disturbances[3] (Fig. 19-1).

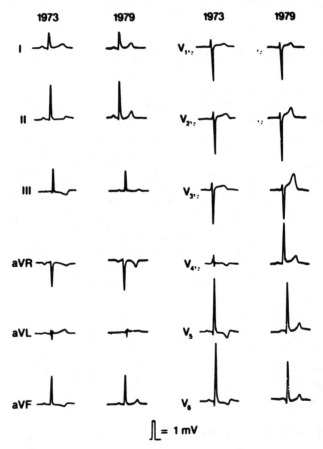

FIGURE 19-1. Electrocardiogram of an olympic walker prior to and six years after stopping training. Note loss of voltage and normalization of the T-waves in V$_5$ and V$_6$. (From Oakley, with permission.[20])

STRESS TESTING: PRINCIPLES AND PRACTICE

TABLE 19-1. Incidence of Left and Right
Ventricular Hypertrophy by ECG and VCG
in 42 Professional Basketball Players

	LVH		RVH	
	No.	%	No.	%
ECG	11	26	29	69
VCG	12	29	18	43
Both	9	21	16	38
Neither	28	67	11	26

LVH = left-ventricular hypertrophy; RVH = right-
ventricular hypertrophy.

VENTRICULAR HYPERTROPHY

Both right- and left-ventricular hypertrophy are common as estimated by
R-wave criteria. ST-T wave changes are seen, but are less common. The incidence of these abnormalities in 42 professional basketball players reported by
Roeske and colleagues[21] is illustrated in Table 19-1. It appears that right axis
deviation is common, and right-ventricular hypertrophy is frequently seen as
well as left-ventricular. S-T elevation in the lateral precordial leads termed
early repolarization is also frequently seen. It has been demonstrated by echocardiography, that the electrocardiographic changes are associated with left-
ventricular dilation and sometimes myocardial hypertrophy. It seems well established that this type of hypertrophy is simple work-related and has no
untoward implications.

RHYTHM AND CONDUCTION DISTURBANCES

Sinus bradycardia is common and is correlated to some degree with the level
of fitness. Resting heart rates in the 40s are frequent and occasionally less than
40 may be seen. AV junctional rhythm and first- and second-degree heart
block occur in from 1 to 5 percent of subjects.[3] These seem to be invariably
normalized by exercise and are believed to be due to increased vagal tone.
Occasional examples of WPW and other varieties of preexcitation syndrome
have also been described.[3]

Exercise-Induced Abnormalities

The majority of endurance athletes have normal electrocardiographic complexes during exercise. In fact, it is common for even senior runners to have
patterns quite similar to those seen in very young subjects. Rogers and col-

leagues[22] studied 43 boys, ages 12 to 15, none of whom had exercise-induced S-T depression.

S-T SEGMENT DEPRESSION

On the other hand, a significant number of young, symptom-free athletes have S-T depression with exercise, although this may be no more common than in nonathletes.[20] When it does occur—is there a way to differentiate those who have coronary artery disease from those who don't?

If the resting electrocardiogram shows hypertrophy, benign S-T depression is more likely, although those with coronary artery disease, of course, may have this finding also. High aerobic capacity—those athletes with coronary artery disease may have a very high aerobic capacity, but will usually report a decrement from previous performances.

DURATION OF S-T SEGMENT DEPRESSION

During exercise, S-T depression may occur at a moderate workload and then evolve to a lesser magnitude at higher levels of work. Or it may appear only at maximum workload and then disappear within a few seconds into the recovery. When significant S-T depression occurs during exercise and remains for several minutes during recovery and evolves to a downsloping pattern, it is more likely to be due to ischemia.

SEPTAL Q-WAVES

Because of hypertrophy of the heart wall with training, the septal Q in the lateral precordial leads is often prominent at rest. If this increases with exercise and is associated with S-T depression,[23] ischemia is rarely present.

T-WAVES

Inverted T-waves are seen in the resting electrocardiogram and this will usually become upright with exercise. This has no clinical significance. Very tall T-waves in the immediate recovery are common and probably represent an increased stroke volume (see Chapter 12).

S-T ELEVATION

Resting S-T elevation (early repolarization) in the precordial leads invariably disappears with exercise. This process is poorly understood, but has no special significance. S-T elevation induced by exercise is rare in the absence of ischemia.

USE OF EXERCISE TESTING IN SPORTS

Alerting the Patient and Physician to Occult Dysfunction

In today's fitness-conscious society, there are many individuals who have a number of coronary risk factors who decide to mend their ways. Engaging in a regular fitness program may aggravate ischemia or predispose them to serious arrhythmias. Part of a complete examination in this group should include an exercise test. Jim Fixx[24] would probably be alive today if he had been tested. In age groups over 40, a high percentage of sedentary subjects have hypertension. The blood pressure response to exercise is important to determine. It may provide information as to the likelihood of blood pressure progression in the future[25] as well as determine the need for present treatment. In those who are serious about improving performance, the exercise capacity, maximum VO_2 and blood pressure response to exercise, and anaerobic threshold may be of interest. Guidelines as to the mode of training may be made more intelligently with this information in mind.

Following Progress in Known Disease

In patients with recognized cardiac disability, the exercise prescription has traditionally been based on the treadmill or bicycle performance. The safety of exercise is predicted by adjusting its intensity after observation of the response to known workloads and extrapolating this to the daily regimen. Details of this approach have been provided in a number of monograms and texts.[12,26,27]

Not infrequently, we have determined, after retesting patients who have been on exercise programs, that they should stop exercising and consider some invasive procedure to improve coronary flow. This decision is usually based on the onset of S-T segment depression or anginal pain at an earlier workload than previously. The occurrence of ominous ventricular arrhythmias or a marked decrease in exercise heart rate or blood pressure would also be of concern.

Evaluating Drug Regimens

A large number of drugs are now available to treat ischemia, hypertension, and cardiac arrhythmias. Only by exercise testing can we determine how our patients are responding to whatever regimen has been prescribed. All too often, estimates of effects are based on resting performance only to find out later that during exercise, the program is ineffective and may not be providing the desired result.

COMMENT

Exercise testing was first used almost exclusively as a method for evaluating athletes. As more and more of our population engages in various types of sports, it is becoming routine. It will continue to be an essential tool in our management of sportsmen, especially in those with known or suspected disease, as well as in research on the effects of exercise on our health and well-being.

EXERCISE TESTING IN CARDIAC REHABILITATION

Although there is widespread disagreement as to the use of exercise testing in apparently healthy people prior to the institution of an exercise program, it is generally agreed that it plays an important role in the patient with known cardiac disease.

DISCHARGE EXERCISE TEST

This is discussed extensively in Chapter 10, but its value should be emphasized here, in that it provides guidelines as to the likelihood of problems induced by exercise. When a low level test is completed on discharge without abnormalities, it is usually safe to allow rapid return to moderate activity. Within four to six weeks, a near-maximum test should be done to plan the activity for the next few months.

EXERCISE TESTING PRIOR TO FORMAL OUT-PATIENT REHABILITATION

This test provides:
1. Patient reassurance.
2. Risk prediction.
3. Triage to various types of therapy.
4. Formulation of an exercise prescription.

EXERCISE PRESCRIPTION

Most dynamic exercise programs are based on the concept that a heart rate of 60 percent of maximum or more is necessary for the training effect to occur. Because there is so much individual variation in heart rate and exercise capacity, the exercise test is an ideal way to arrive at the proper workload geared to each individual. If the patient can reach maximal predicted heart rate without symptoms or signs of ischemia or arrhythmias, the optimal heart rate for training can then be selected. If, on the other hand, the patient should develop S-T displacement, anginal pain, or arrhythmias during the test, a heart rate of approximately 10 beats less than that necessary to initiate the aberration is usually a safe level to maintain during a daily workout. At times, monitoring the patient during the workout is desirable to confirm the original level selected. As the patient gains experience the patient can often perceive the level of exertion necessary to judge the amount of work prescribed.

After a time (usually four weeks or so) the patient will be able to increase the work level without increasing the heart rate, a sign of improved aerobic capacity or conditioning.

CONFIRMATION OF IMPROVEMENT OR DETECTION OF PROGRESSION

At some time interval, after the onset of the rehabilitation program (three to six months), a repeat exercise test will either document the improvement, providing a new safe level of performance or occasionally indicate disease progression. The latter is extremely important to alert the physician and the patient that some change in therapeutic plans may be in order. By this time, the subject will have a better understanding of the mechanisms of the disease process and the validity of the determinations made during exercise as well as the signs of cardiac dysfunction. Objective evidence is very important as we have seen many patients who have no angina, but have more ischemia as determined by the onset of S-T depression at a workload lower than during the previous test. This is particularly valid if it occurs after a good training effect has been obtained.

In summary, the exercise test in rehabilitation is a yardstick useful in measuring exercise capacity, the severity of disability and in demonstrating to the patient the signs of progress. We find it indispensable.

REFERENCES

1. KAVANAUGH, T, ET AL: Marathon running after myocardial infarction. JAMA 229:1602, 1974.
2. BLACKBURN, H: Disadvantages of intensive exercise therapy after myocardial infarction. In INGELFINGER, FJ, ET AL (EDS): Controversy in Internal Medicine, II. WB Saunders, Philadelphia, 1974, pp 169–170.
3. HANNE-PAPARO, N, ET AL: Common ECG changes in athletes. Cardiology 61:267–278, 1976.
4. SCHERER, D AND KALTENBACH, M: Frequency of life-threatening complications associated with stress testing. Dtsch med Wschr 104:1161, 1979.
5. MCHENRY, PL, PHILLIPS, JF, AND KNOEBEL, SB: Correlation of computer-quantitated treadmill exercise electrocardiogram with arteriographic location of coronary artery disease. Am J Cardiol 30:747, 1972.

6. SHEPHARD, RJ: *The cardiac athlete: When does exercise training become overexertion?* Practical Cardiology 6(2):39, 1980.

7. MILVY, P: *Statistics, marathoning and CHD.* Am Heart J 95(4):538–539, 1978.

8. BASSLER, TJ: *Athletic activity and longevity.* Lancet 2:712, 1972.

9. NOAKES, TD, OPIE, LH, AND ROSE, AG: *Marathon running and immunity to CHD.* Clinics in Sports Med 3:527, 1984.

10. MARON, BJ, EPSTEIN, SE, AND ROBERTS, WC: *Hypertrophic cardiomyopathy: A common cause of sudden death in the young competitive athlete.* Eur Heart J (Suppl)4:135–144, 1983.

11. GREEN, LH, COHEN, SI, AND KURLAND, G: *Fatal myocardial infarction in marathon racing.* Ann Intern Med 84(6):704–706, 1976.

12. FRANKLIN, BVA: *Clinical Exercise Testing.* Clinics in Sports Med 3:295, 1984.

13. KARVONEN, MJ, ET AL: *Longevity of endurance skiers.* Med Sci Sports 6:49, 1974.

14. CRAWFORD, MH AND O'ROURKE, RA: *The Athlete's Heart: Year Book of Sports Medicine.* Year Book Medical Publishers, Chicago, 1979, p 311.

15. SALTIN, B, ET AL: *Response to exercise after bed rest and after training.* Circulation 37(7):VII–1, 1979.

16. POLLOCK, ML: *How much exercise is enough?* The Physician and Sportsmedicine 6(6), 1978.

17. PAFFENBERGER, RS, ET AL: *Epidemiology of exercise and coronary heart disease.* Clinics in Sports Med 3:297, 1984.

18. NAUGHTON, JP AND HELLERSTEIN, HK: *Exercise testing and exercise training in CHD.* Academic Press, New York, 1973.

19. BECKNER, G AND WINSOR, T: *Cardiovascular adaptations to prolonged physical effort.* Circulation 9:835–846, 1954.

20. OAKLEY, CM: *Treatment of primary pulmonary hypertension.* In SOBEL, B, JULIAN, DG, AND HUGENHOLTZ, PG (EDS): *Perspectives in Cardiology.* Current Med Lit Ltd., 1984.

21. ROESKE, WR, ET AL: *Non-invasive evaluation of ventricular hypertrophy in professional athletes.* Circulation 53:286, 1976.

22. ROGERS, JH, JR, HELLERSTEIN, HK, AND STRONG, WB: *The exercise electrocardiogram in trained and untrained adolescent males.* Med & Sci in Sports 9(3):164–167, 1977.

23. FAMULARO, M, ET AL: *Identification of septal ischemia during exercise by Q wave analysis: Correlation with coronary angiography.* Am J Cardiol 51(3):440–443, 1983.

24. *Jim Fixx Ran a Risky Race.* Medical World News, August 27, 1984, p 27.

25. SCHRAGER, B AND ELLESTAD, MH: *The importance of blood pressure measurement during exercise testing.* Cardiovascular Reviews and Reports 4(3):381–394, 1983.

26. LONG, C: *Prevention and Rehabilitation in Ischemic Heart Disease.* Williams & Wilkins, Baltimore, 1983.

27. FLETCHER, GF: *Exercise in the Practice of Medicine.* Futura Publishing Co., Mt. Kisco, NY, 1982.

20

PEDIATRIC STRESS TESTING

In recent years, there has been an increasing interest in stress testing as a means of evaluation of children with cardiac abnormalities. Although ischemic disease caused by coronary insufficiency is rare, the presence and degree of abnormal cardiovascular function can be determined and quantitated effectively with this method. Congenital lesions with valvular abnormalities as well as other cardiac abnormalities in which arrhythmias can be a major problem are most likely to yield findings useful in their management and evaluation. Interest in hypertension in children and teenagers and the abnormal pressor response to exercise in the young may be a forerunner of a clinically important syndrome.[1] Also, the presence of ventricular dysfunction in children with mitral prolapse and various other cardiomyopathies is probably much higher than previously believed. Finally, many disorders in respiratory function can best be demonstrated with exercise, especially exercise-induced asthma.

Although stress testing in children has not been as widely used as in adults, the available data will be presented.

EXERCISE IN NORMAL CHILDREN

Considerable information on the exercise response in normal children has been published. An extensive review of the physiologic responses in normal children has been released by Godfrey[2] and should be reviewed by the serious student.

Responses of the normal child will be presented as a basis for understanding those with diseased states. It is also important to be aware of the differ-

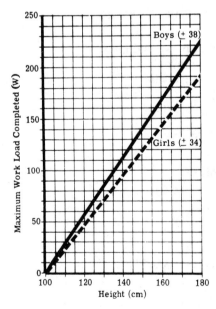

FIGURE 20-1. Maximum power output achieved in simple progressive exercise related to height in boys and girls. The numbers in parentheses in this and subsequent illustrations indicate the approximate 95 percent confidence limits. (From Godfrey,[2] with permission.)

ences and similarities when comparing children with adults. We will see that besides their size and age, the circulatory physiology of children varies in some important ways.

The maximum capacity to exercise increases with height as does the heart rate (Fig. 20-1). The level of peak heart rate rises to about 210 beats per minute at age 10, and then steadily declines, falling to about 200 beats per minute at about age 20. Because stroke volume reaches its maximum value considerably earlier than heart rate, the major contribution to cardiac output at peak level is, as in adults, dependent upon heart rate. The VO_2max in children as well as adults, remains the classic measure of physical fitness. It increases from 1 liter per minute in 6-year-old boys to about 3 liters per minute in 15-year-old boys.[3] The consistently lower level in girls was difficult to explain until it was shown to correlate with leg muscle volume. Therefore, the larger and heavier leg muscles in boys explain this discrepancy at least in children.

The majority of earlier work in this field comes from England and the Scandinavian countries.[4,5] There is increasing evidence that at least in the Nordic countries the degree of fitness exceeds that in American youth, so that some differences in VO_2 values are to be expected.

ANAEROBIC AND AEROBIC POWER

The increase in anaerobic power has been measured by running up a steep flight of stairs as fast as possible, as well as on a bicycle or treadmill. The changes in this parameter are related to age and are listed in Figure 20-2. The power is calculated from the time of exercise, body weight, step size, and velocity of motion. It is possible to calculate the maximum anaerobic power, which is about 2.5 times the aerobic power at all ages tested. These values also correlate well with maximum VO_2. Endurance as measured by the time on the Bruce Protocol[6] increases with age until about 17 or 18 years and then declines (Fig. 20-3).

James[7] reported on the maximal working capacity measured on the bicycle ergometer in 103 normal children. His data are depicted in Figure 20-4.

RESPIRATION

The respiratory capacity of children increases with body size, so that the minute ventilation manifested when a child reaches VO_2max depends on the sum of the level of aerobic metabolism and the resultant acidosis due to the excess carbon dioxide produced, as well as the level of anaerobic metabolism.

These relationships are shown in Figure 20-5 based on the work of Astrand and associates.[8] The maximum exercise ventilation is higher than in other studies subsequently done, probably owing to the exceptional fitness of the children in their study. The reduced frequency with age has been correlated with a

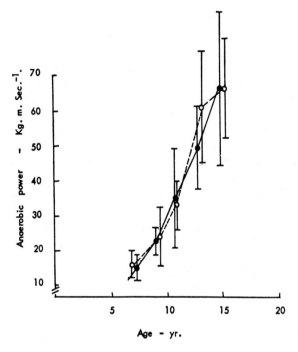

FIGURE 20-2. Anaerobic maximum power output in relation to age in boys (•) and girls (o). (From Godfrey,[2] with permission.)

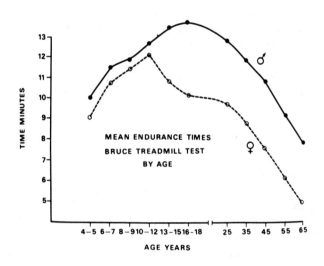

MEAN ENDURANCE TIMES
BRUCE TREADMILL TEST
BY AGE

FIGURE 20-3. Endurance times according to age. (From Cummings, et al.,[6] with permission.)

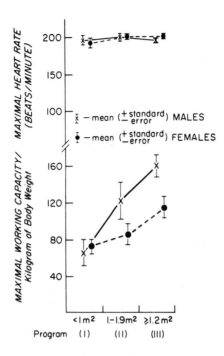

FIGURE 20-4. Maximum working capacities and heart rate in 103 normal children. Maximum working capacity increases with growth without changing the heart rate. (From James,[7] with permission.)

fall in airway resistance and a rise in lung compliance. The tidal volume with maximum exercise tends to be about 60 percent of the vital capacity at all ages.

The limiting factor for maximum exercise in children then appears to be the limitations of the heart as a pump, rather than the ability to move the respiratory gases or factors related to diffusion. As in adults, the ability of tissues to metabolize oxygen and other substrates is related to the number and concentration of mitochondria in the cells. This is clearly altered by the level of fitness. It has been shown that children tolerate a larger AV-Q2 difference, which makes up for the slightly smaller stroke volume, and might suggest that the efficiency of oxygen use at all levels is somewhat better than adults. Finally, the ability to tolerate lactic acid is reduced in children and increases with age as shown in Figure 20-6. How much this can be increased by training is unknown in children, although it has been demonstrated to be a factor in adults.

Eriksson[9] reported on the results of a four- to six-month training program in 11- to 13-year-old boys in Sweden. He found that their response to training was similar to that in adults except in two areas: they seemed to increase their stroke volume more than adults with an equivalent exercise program, but were unable to develop the same capacity to withstand anaerobic exercise. These findings reinforce those of other workers.[10]

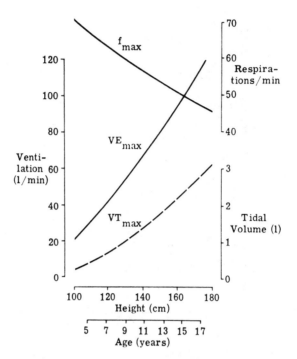

FIGURE 20-5. Relationship among maximal exercise values for respiratory frequency (f_{max}), ventilation (VE_{max}), tidal volume (VT_{max}) and height. The approximate age corresponding to the height is shown in the lower scale. (From Godfrey,[2] with permission.)

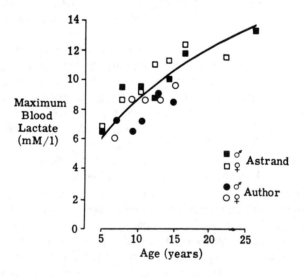

FIGURE 20-6. Relationship between maximum blood lactate resulting from maximal exercise and age. (From Godfrey,[2] with permission.)

ELECTROCARDIOGRAPHIC CHANGES

Bengtsson[3] in 1956, published an extensive study on the ECG responses of 84 children and compared them with a group of adults. He outlined a number of differences that he considered significant. Sinus arrhythmia with variable atrial contractions was much more common than in adults, and sudden sinus slowing after exercise was also often seen. He also reported that almost no ventricular ectopic beats were present in normal children. Although most of the children were not taken to their peak predicted heart rate, he constructed tables characterizing the P-Q interval, the QRS duration, and the amplitude of R- and T-waves. He found that severe (over 1.5 mm) S-T segment depression was extremely rare, but that it was fairly common to have a very moderate amount (up to 0.7 mm in several leads). Fifty-six children tested had orthostatic changes when standing characterized by minor S-T changes and T-wave flattening. The incidence was much more common than in his normal adult series. In general, his conclusions were that children reacted to exercise quite similarly to adults with the exceptions listed above.

Goldberg[11] in 1966 studied a group of normal children and listed some of the ways in which they differed from adults as follows: (1) a lower incidence of T-wave abnormalities, (2) increased incidence of J-point depression with rapid upsloping of the S-T segment, (3) higher achieved heart rates, and (4) lower average blood pressure responses. James[12] has studied children and has compared normals with a number of disease states. The heart rate and blood pressure response in a heterogeneous group of subjects from age 9 to 25 exercised on a bicycle ergometer is shown in Figure 20-7. The bicycle protocol used by James[7] is illustrated in Table 20-1.

James'[7] protocol exercises patients on a bicycle using the maximal voluntary capacity as an end-point, attempting to have the patients reach 180 beats per minute and a respiratory rate of at least 40 breaths per minute. His indications for termination of exercise are depicted in Table 20-2.

The following sections present some of the diseases in which stress testing has been found to be of value.

TABLE 20-1. A continuous, progressive bicycle exercise protocol*

Program	I(BSA < 1 m^2) kg-m/min	II(BSA 1-1.19 m^2) kg-m/min	III(BSA ≥ 1.2 m^2) kg-m/min
Level 1	200	200	200
Level 2	300	400	500
Level 3	500	600	800
Increments	100	100	200
	Pedal speed: 60–70 rpm	Duration of levels: 3 min	

*The three exercise programs are used for three ranges of body surface area. The duration at each exercise level is three minutes.

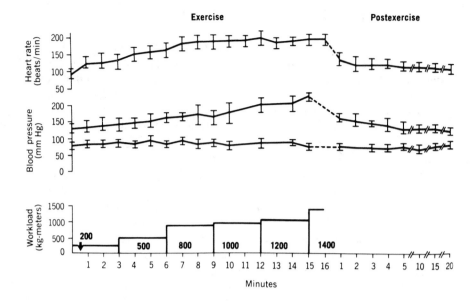

FIGURE 20-7. Mean changes in heart rate and blood pressure during and after exercise in 25 normal subjects age 9 to 25 (body surface area ≥ 1.2 sq m). (From James,[12] with permission.)

Cardiomyopathies

The incidence of primary muscle disorders in children and adolescents is unknown; however, if one includes those with mitral prolapse it must be much higher than previously believed.

Mitral Prolapse (Barlow's Syndrome)

This disorder is believed to be present in some form in 6 percent of presumedly healthy young women.[13] Markiewicz and associates[14] found more than 10 percent in a random study of college students who were asymptomatic when analyzed by echocardiography. Although there are no data on how many of these will eventually become clinically significant, it now seems well established that the abnormality in valve function is often associated with some type of muscle disorder. It has been reported to be related to a congenitally small circumflex coronary artery;[15,16] however, Classman and Kronzon[17] have challenged the importance of abnormalities in the coronary tree.

The presence of arrhythmias, sometimes life threatening, has been established by Schwartz and coworkers,[18] who tested 30 patients ages 8 to 12, diagnosed by echocardiography. They found three with frequent PVCs initi-

TABLE 20-2. Indicators for terminating exercise tests prior to reaching maximal voluntary capacity level

1. The onset of serious cardiac arrhythmias (e.g., ventricular tachycardia, supraventricular tachycardia)
2. Any appearance of potential hazard to the patient
   a. Failure of electrocardiographic monitoring system
   b. Symptoms such as pain, headache, dizziness, or syncope precipitated by exercise.
   c. Segmental S-T depression or elevation $\geq$ 3 mm during exercise
   d. Arrhythmia (over 25 percent of beats) precipitated or aggravated by exercise
   e. Recognized types of intracardiac block precipitated by exercise
   f. Inappropriate rise in blood pressure with systolic pressures exceeding 230 mmHg and diastolic pressures exceeding 120 mmHg
   g. Inappropriate fall in blood pressure
   h. Marked signs of cutaneous vascular insufficiency (e.g., pallor)

ated by exercise, and six with PVCs during the recovery. They also found three with ischemic S-T segment depression, which was believed to be due to the now well-known muscle dysfunction seen in this disorder.[19] S-T segment depression associated with prolapsed valves and initiated by exercise is often seen in adults as well as children and now has been recognized as one of the causes for a positive exercise test in a young adult. The careful search for a midsystolic click and a late systolic murmur can often explain the findings that were previously confusing. While chest pain is occasionally found in these patients, it fails to correlate well with ischemic changes in the stress test. Therefore, in children and adolescents with this syndrome, stress testing is used to determine if their pain is related to exercise and increasing cardiac output, and can also help establish the incidence of exercise-induced arrhythmias, which may be a major threat. I believe that a young adult with unexplained chest pain and abnormal S-T changes on the treadmill should have an echocardiogram as the next diagnostic procedure. Because sudden death has been estimated to occur in about 1.2 percent of these patients, O'Rourke and Crawford[16] have recommended that all subjects with this syndrome have some type of arrhythmia monitoring, either Holter or stress testing.

Hypertrophic Cardiomyopathy

When evaluating chest pain associated with exercise in children and adults, hypertrophic cardiomyopathy must always be a prime suspect. The incidence of pain in this condition is unknown, but is often associated with an abnormal resting electrocardiogram and also S-T segment depression initiated by exercise. The presence of an apical systolic murmur, a loud fourth sound, and a prominent sustained double apical impulse should alert the examiner when a positive stress test in a child or young adult occurs. The exercise test in this condition is especially helpful in evaluating the presence or severity of arrhythmias, as it is in the click murmur syndrome. A sudden burst of ventricular ectopy is often seen within two or three minutes of the end of the exercise test. This may indicate the danger present in allowing those children to engage in strenuous sports, as malignant rhythms often occur at this time.

Unclassified Cardiomyopathies

A wide variety of primary muscle disorders as well as those due to the known metabolic disturbances, such as Tay-Sachs, glycogen storage disease, muscular dystrophy and others, will present the pediatrician with problems in management. The hemodynamic implications of these disorders are important to evaluate. Using the stress test gives useful longitudinal information when comparisons of aerobic power at appropriate intervals are made. When using the stress test in this way, a standard protocol makes it much easier to compare the same patient at different times. Again, in these disorders, arrhythmias may play a very important role and the control by pharmacologic means can best be evaluated with an exercise test. If the process has progressed to the point of heart failure, the time has passed when stress testing should be used.

AORTIC STENOSIS

Although catheterization has long been considered the best method to determine the status of this condition, some doubt often remains after the gradient and valve area have been calculated. The response of the myocardium to the outflow obstruction, as observed during stress testing, may be a definite adjunct. In adults, aortic stenosis has long been considered a relative contraindication to exercise testing; however, in children and adolescents it is being used with increasing frequency.[5] The calculation of the diastolic pressure time interval over systolic pressure time interval (DPTI/SPTI) at various levels of stress may give insight into the risk of myocardial fibrosis due to intermittent severe subendocardial ischemia. It now seems clear that as diastole shortens and the left-ventricular pressure rises with increasing work, the time necessary to perfuse the inner layers of the myocardium becomes inadequate (see Chapter 4). James and Kaplan[5] have pioneered in the application of exercise in the evaluation of patients with congenital aortic stenosis, and believe the decisions regarding surgery can be made with more precision when stress testing is used. The risk of stress testing in this syndrome is believed by them to be much less than that in adults. When studying 52 children with aortic stenosis, S-T depression occurred in 46 percent with left-ventricular resting gradient of less than 30. It occurred in 58 percent of those with a gradient of between 30 and 59 mm, and 87 percent in those with gradients of 70 mm or more.

Chandramoule and colleagues[20] reported on 44 children, ranging in age from 5 to 19, and found S-T depression in 12, or 27 percent. They found that a resting gradient of 55 mmHg or more was present in all those with S-T depression, and suggest that it appears to be the most reliable noninvasive way to evaluate the severity of the hemodynamic burden. This finding was also confirmed by Halloran[21] in a study of 31 children. She suggested that this might help to identify those at risk for syncope and sudden death. Exercise studies by Cueto and Moller[22] during catheterization indicate that those with higher gradients have a significant rise in left-ventricular end-diastolic pressure, which could presumably correlate with the observed S-T segment depression. Because prolonged subendocardial ischemia may result in permanent fibrotic replacement of muscle, Lewis and coworkers[23] suggest that those who have T-wave inversion and S-T depression with exercise should be seriously considered for surgery. It is recognized that children are not only very active in an aerobic sense, but often engage in isometric type exercises; thus, it might also be desirable to evaluate their response to this type of stress. Rosenthal and associates[24] have demonstrated that isometric handgrip increases the left-ventricular work in children and, in those with aortic stenosis, may unbalance the supply/demand ratio to dangerous levels.

POSTOPERATIVE EVALUATION

It is well known that aortic valvulotomy and valve replacement in children often fails to produce ideal results, and it is suggested that balloon valvuloplasty will be similar. Residual systolic gradients as well as various degrees of aortic insufficiency are fairly common. By stress testing postoperatively, decisions regarding functional impairment can be documented and followed on a longitudinal basis. Tuboku-Metzger and associates[25] found that postoperative S-T segment depression is not as reliable in predicting the gradient as before surgery. They do believe, however, that these abnormalities in the postoperative patient may help to identify those with residual muscle dysfunction. As in adults, decreased exercise tolerance, a decrease in maximal systolic blood pressure and a reduction in heart rate are also useful in identifying those with decreased function.[7]

AORTIC INSUFFICIENCY

Patients with aortic insufficiency tolerate their defect for a longer period than do those with aortic stenosis. The reasons for this are easy to understand when considering that pressure work requires more oxygen than does a volume load. On the other hand, there are a few clearcut hemodynamic measurements to use as markers for intervention. Recent information suggests that these patients also may sustain myocardial injury while we wait for signs that the valve should be replaced. The "Venturi" effect at the coronary ostium, incident to the diastolic regurgitant flow, may well minimize the coronary flow even more than estimated from the low aortic diastolic pressure. As the muscle undergoes degenerative changes, the rate tends to slow, causing an increased regurgitant volume with a resultant increase in ventricular diameter. This then increases the myocardial metabolic requirements. Stress testing is a useful way to follow such patients, using both the appearance of S-T segment depression and a reduction in heart rate response to each workload as a marker for decreasing function. The DPTI/SPTI calculated at rest and at peak heart rates can also help estimate the stress being placed on the muscle in relationship to the factors responsible for perfusion. As technology in prosthetic valves improves, it may be advisable to intervene prior to the appearance of hemodynamic abnormalities rather than wait for their appearance.

COARCTATION

Although the surgical correction of coarctation was an early triumph of cardiac surgery, it is now known that the results are not as clearcut as once believed. Growth in small children has resulted in continued stenosis at the site of the anastomosis, and hypertension in the upper part of the body may remain a problem.[26] Even in those with apparent ample relief of obstruction, total body hypertension is often a postoperative finding.

Because the pressure is a function of cardiac output as well as resistance, it is useful to evaluate the blood pressure response to exercise as well as attempt to determine the degree of stress placed on the heart during the child's activity.[27] Exercise-induced systolic blood pressure elevation of 300 mmHg has been reported by Taylor and Donald.[26] It has been proposed that extreme pressures such as this constitute an indication for surgery. They also have recorded increases in end-diastolic pressure in these patients during exercise, documenting that they very likely also have subendocardial ischemia. James and Kaplan[27] have shown that the blood pressure response to exercise after surgery for coarctation may be quite variable, and a knowledge of this may help to determine how much activity should be recommended for the child.

James[7] reports significant S-T depression postoperatively in 28 percent of boys and 67 percent of girls found in a series of 47 patients. He also believes that if the patients are hypertensive at rest postoperatively or if the systolic pressure with exercise reaches 200, antihypertensive medication should be recommended. He recommends response to the drugs should be determined with an exercise test.

A widening of pulse pressure during exercise in the postoperative patient has been documented, and is believed to indicate permanent stiffening of the large arteries. Valodaver and Neufeld[28] have studied the coronary arteries in 15 patients and found that the caliber is increased due to the increased metabolic demand. They found a high incidence of coronary intimal proliferation and atherosclerosis even in young people. They state that these changes must be suspected in young adults and children who have had coarctation and the accompanying hypertension for a number of years. Stress testing can give us clues to these changes and is being used more and more in this disorder.

The exercise-induced S-T depression occasionally seen postoperatively may indicate subendocardial ischemia and can be due to either coronary disease or the presence of a residual obstruction at the operative site. Therefore, the use of stress testing can help us evaluate ventricular function and plan how much exercise to permit in children after the surgeon is no longer involved.

TETRALOGY OF FALLOT

Since the so-called "primary total repair" of Fallot's tetralogy has become popular, the question then arises: How near normal is cardiac function after surgery? This is especially important as the children become older and may desire to engage in strenuous sports or occupations. It is well known that a systolic pressure gradient often remains across the pulmonic valve or infundibulum. Pulmonary or tricuspid insufficiency may also be present and, if shunting operation predated the total repair, pulmonary hypertension may be an important factor. The associated tendency for pulmonary shunting with this lesion must be actively sought. Arrhythmias have proved to be a problem and exercise testing may document the level of exercise necessary to elicit the irritability so that it might be avoided.

Strieder and colleagues[29] studied 12 patients with complete correlations for tetralogy and found only seven to have normal exercise tolerance. Ten of the 12, however, had been treated with either a Potts or a Blalock shunt for a number of years prior to surgery. They found the oxygen uptake at peak workload to be inversely correlated to age at the time of repair. Pulmonary dysfunction, including reduced diffusing capacity, high physiologic deadspace and airway obstruction, and an abnormal alveolar arterial PO_2 difference were also identified. There is an inverse relationship between age at time of repair and pulmonary function.

The use of postoperative stress testing in this disorder is a practical aid in the determination of exercise capacity and the tendency for the development of arrhythmia.[12] James[7] reports that 10 of 43 postoperative patients have multifocal PVCs or ventricular tachycardia requiring antiarrhythmic therapy.

It is known that postoperative gradients, pulmonary insufficiency, and right-ventricular dysfunction are also seen in isolated pulmonary stenosis. Although there seems to be limited experience with stress testing in this lesion, it would be expected that useful information could also be required in these patients by observing their response to exercise.[29]

CONGENITAL HEART BLOCK

Nowhere is the adaptive capacity of the human cardiovascular system demonstrated more beautifully than in congenital heart block. Many examples of

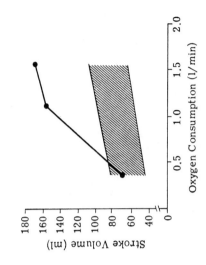

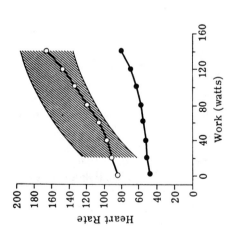

FIGURE 20-8. *Left,* Atrial rate (o) and ventricular rate (•) during simple progressive exercise test in a young adult with congenital heart block. *Right,* Stroke volume at rest and during steady-state exercise in a patient with congenital heart block. (From Taylor and Donald,[26] with permission.)

outstanding, if not world class, athletic achievements have been reported in these children and young adults. A stress test is an ideal way to determine how well they perform. Because many with otherwise normal hearts have a systolic murmur, the documentation of their aerobic capacity is essential in separating those with other cardiac defects from those who have adapted by an increase in stroke output. Godfrey[2] has reported studies on these children and has demonstrated the enormous increase in stroke volume and the difference in the atrial and ventrical response to exercise (Fig. 20-8).

Because heart block is often seen in conjunction with congenital and acquired heart disease in children, and as the size is reduced and sophistication of pacemakers is improved, there is need to evaluate the exercise capacity as part of the decision to pace or not to pace. It is also necessary to determine if the atrial rate increases appropriately with exercise as pacemakers are now available that will link the ventricular response to the atrial contraction. I have seen a number of children and young adults in heart failure because a fixed-rate ventricular pacer was used when an atrial-triggered pacemaker would have provided a more physiologic solution to the problem.

SICKLE-CELL ANEMIA

An excellent article by Lindsay and colleagues[30] describing the cardiovascular manifestations of sickle-cell disease should be reviewed by the serious student. Changes are nearly always present in the cardiovascular response of patients with sickle-cell anemia because an increased output is necessary to adjust for the reduced oxygen content of arterial blood. This is complicated by the propensity of the sickled erythrocyte to occlude small blood vessels, especially those in the pulmonary vascular bed.[13,31] The evidence is inconclusive, but it seems likely that the capillary bed of the myocardium may also be partly obliterated by this process.[32,33] Regardless of the underlying pathology, cardiac enlargement and reduced cardiac function are often present, and stress testing provides a method to document the degree of disability and a way to follow the progress of the patients.[34] Right-ventricular hypertrophy is often present and, as exercise increases, the increased pulmonary resistance would be expected to result in right-ventricular ischemic changes, characterized by S-T depression in V_1 to V_3 as seen in pulmonary stenosis. Evidence is now available to demonstrate that while cardiovascular dysfunction is often present in homozygous sickle-cell disease, the same is not usually true for the heterozygous subject with a sickle-cell trait. There has been a tendency to recommend that these children be restricted. A stress test is an ideal way to demonstrate their capacity to exercise. By judiciously applying this modality it may be possible to allow many children to live a normal life when exercise has been demonstrated to be well tolerated.

ARRHYTHMIAS

Although the literature abounds with data on exercise-induced arrhythmias in adults,[35,36] the interest in evaluating children is increasing. Ventricular arrhythmias are fairly common in children, and may be of concern to their physicians and parents. In some cases, they constitute a serious risk, but in most they are abolished by exercise and can be largely ignored. Kupersmith and colleagues[37] have carefully studied ventricular arrhythmias in children and have come to the following conclusions:

1. Ventricular arrhythmias during exercise are predictably reproducible in children.
2. Exercise may reveal serious arrhythmias not apparent in other forms of testing.
3. It allows precise exercise and antiarrhythmia prescriptions so as to insure the safety of the patients.

We still are unable to predict whether certain types of ventricular tachycardia are serious in children or require therapy by their response to exercise testing. If they fail to cause symptoms, even during strenuous exercise, it would appear that they are more benign. On the other hand, in obstructive cardiomyopathies and postoperative surgical patients, they constitute a more serious threat.

James[12] has reported the value of the exercise test in the evaluation of arrhythmias, especially in postoperative patients. He believes it is especially valuable in the evaluation of the response to antiarrhythmia drugs, and has found it useful as an aid in prescribing medication for the control of idiopathic ventricular tachycardia in children.

HYPERTENSION

An abnormal increase in blood pressure response to exercise in children and young adults has been observed in a number of clinics.[17] The evidence suggests that this response is a significant risk for future clinical hypertension[1] (see Chapter 17). Because there appears to be a genetic tendency to develop this disease, it would be sensible to test the children of parents with severe hypertension, and if they have an abnormal response, alterations in lifestyle and diet may be in order.

EXERCISE-INDUCED ASTHMA

There is now a significant volume of data on the mechanics of respiration during exercise and its alterations in asthmatic children. Although exercise-induced asthma is often considered an isolated entity, Godfrey[2] believes it only occurs in the already asthmatic child. For a detailed review of this subject,

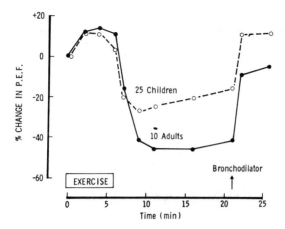

FIGURE 20-9. Typical patterns of exercise-induced asthma in children and adults assessed by measurements of peak expiratory flow rate (PEF). Each point is the mean for the number of subjects indicated. The magnitude of the postexercise fall is often very similar in adults and children. (From Godfrey,[2] with permission.)

the publications by Godfrey and colleagues,[38] Anderson and Godfrey,[39] and Silverman and Henderson[40] should be reviewed. When the asthmatic subject runs at a reasonably fast pace, the peak flow rate is reduced from 30 to 50 percent (Fig. 20-9). There is a marked variation in obstructive changes depending on the severity of the allergy and clinical manifestations of disease (Fig. 20-10). Manifestations of this entity are also present in wheezy children and even in their asymptomatic families[13] suggesting a common genetic basis for this disorder. The spirogram of such a patient as compared with normal is depicted in Figure 20-11. It has been shown that the bronchospasm is most marked with running, less with cycling, and least with a horizontal exercise such as swimming. The exact reasons for this are not evident at this time. In order to detect and evaluate these changes, some type of measurement of airway obstruction is necessary during and after exercise. Godfrey[2] has demonstrated that measurements with a Wright peak flow meter closely reflects parameters measured with more costly and complex equipment. Because this syndrome responds to bronchodilators, an exercise test in combination with a treatment regimen is the most satisfactory method of evaluating therapy.

CYSTIC FIBROSIS

Other chronic lung disorders also lend themselves to evaluation by exercise tests. Cystic fibrosis is one. The response to exercise is a most useful way to fully determine the degree of disability and the usefulness of a therapeutic modality. We all too often forget that most of our patients, even those with chronic lung disease, are not at rest most of the day. The knowledge of their

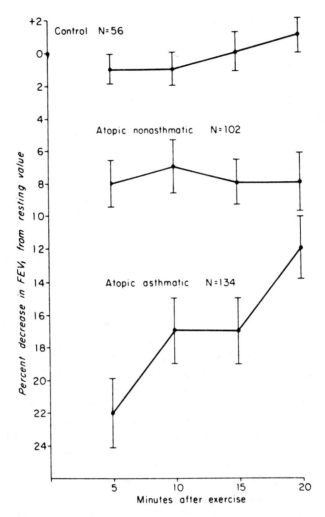

FIGURE 20-10. Comparison of the average percent change ($\pm$ SEM) from pre-exercise values at 5, 10, 15, and 20 minutes following the end of exercise of the control, atopic nonasthmatic, and atopic asthmatic groups. (From Bierman, et al.,[4] with permission.)

function during exercise is as important to a thorough evaluation as that measured while at rest.

SUMMARY

Stress testing in children and young adults is becoming a more acceptable method for evaluating circulatory dynamics. A few investigators such as Godfrey[2] and James and Koplan[5] have been especially influential in this regard. Because my own experience in pediatric stress testing has been limited primar-

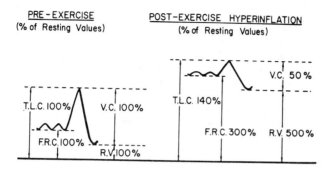

FIGURE 20-11. Schematic representation of changes in lung volumes in children with exercise-induced asthma. The magnitude of changes shown corresponds to those observed in our patients with severe exercise-induced airway obstruction and hyperinflation. (From Bierman, et al.,[4] with permission.)

ily to the evaluation of arrhythmias and a few children with congenital heart block and valvular disease, I have drawn heavily on the literature and my conversations with some of the experts, especially Dr. Fred James of Cincinnati. I suspect our use of exercise testing in the pediatric age range will expand rapidly in the next few years.

REFERENCES

1. JACKSON, ES, ET AL: *Prediction of future resting hypertension from exercise blood pressure.* J Cardiac Rehab 3:213–268, 1983.
2. GODFREY, S: *Exercise testing in children.* WB Saunders, Philadelphia, 1974.
3. BENGTSSON, E: *The exercise electrocardiogram in healthy children and in comparison with adults.* Acta Med Scand 154:3, 1956.
4. BIERMAN, CW, KAWABORI, I, AND PIERSON, WE: *Incidence of exercise-induced asthma in children.* Pediatrics (Suppl)56:847, 1975.
5. JAMES, FW AND KOPLAN, S: *Exercise testing in children.* Primary Cardiol 3:34, 1977.
6. CUMMINGS, GR, EVERATT, D, AND HASTMAN, L: *Bruce treadmill test in children, normal values in a clinic population.* Am J Cardiol 41:69, 1978.
7. JAMES, FW: *Exercise testing in children and young adults: An overview.* In WENGER, NK (ED): *Exercise and the Heart.* Cardiovascular Clinics 15(2). FA Davis, Philadelphia, 1978.
8. ASTRAND, PO, ET AL: *Cardiac output during maximal and submaximal work in girl swimmers.* Acta Paediatr (Suppl) 147, 1963.
9. ERIKSSON, BO: *Physical training, oxygen supply and muscle metabolism in 11 to 13 year old boys.* Acta Phys Scand (Suppl) 384, 1972.
10. EKBLOM, B: *Effect of physical training in adolescent boys.* J Appl Physiol 27:350, 1969.
11. GOLDBERG, J: *Comparison of work requirements by normal children and those with congenital heart disease.* J Pediatr 69:56, 1966.
12. JAMES, FW: *Effects of physical stress in adolescents.* Postgrad Med 56:52, 1974.
13. PROCOCCI, PM, ET AL: *Prevalence of clinical mitral valve prolapse in 1169 young women.* N Engl J Med 294:1086, 1976.
14. MARKIEWICZ, W, ET AL: *Mitral valve prolapse in one hundred presumably healthy females.* Circulation (Suppl II)52:77, 1975.

15. MOSER, KM AND SHEA, JG: *The relationship between pulmonary infarction, corpulmonale and the sickle states.* Am J Med 22:561, 1957.

16. O'ROURKE, RA AND CRAWFORD, MH: *The Systolic Click-murmur Syndrome,* Vol 1. Year Book Medical Publishers, Chicago, 1976.

17. CLASSMUN, E AND KRONZON, I: *Coronary artery distribution in patients with prolapse of the mitral valve.* Am J Cardiol 35:139, 1975.

18. SCHWARTZ, DC, JAMES, FW, AND KOPLAN, S: *Exercise induced ST segment depression in children with mitral valve prolapse* (abstr). Circulation 52:258, 1975.

19. JERESATY, RM: *Etiology of mitral valve prolapse syndrome.* Am J Cardiol 36:110, 1975.

20. CHANDRAMOULE, B, EHMKE, DA, AND LAUER, RM: *Exercise induced electrocardiographic changes in children with congenital aortic stenosis.* J Pediatr 87:725, 1975.

21. HALLORAN, KH: *The telemetered exercise electrocardiogram in congenital aortic stenosis.* Pediatrics 47:31, 1971.

22. CUETO, L AND MOLLER, J: *Hemodynamics of exercise in children with isolated aortic valvular disease.* Br Heart J 35:93, 1973.

23. LEWIS, AB, ET AL: *Evaluation of subendocardial ischemia in valvular aortic stenosis in children.* Circulation 59:978, 1974.

24. ROSENTHAL, A FREED, MD, AND KEANE, JF: *Isometric exercise in adolescents with congenital aortic stenosis* (abstr). Circulation (Suppl 2)54:183, 1976.

25. TUBOKU-METZGER, A, ET AL: *Hemodynamic correlates of exercise testing in children with aortic stenosis.* Circulation (Suppl 2)54:183, 1976.

26. TAYLOR, SH AND DONALD, KW: *Circulatory studies at rest and during exercise in coarctation of the aorta before and after operation.* Br Heart J 22:117, 1960.

27. JAMES, FW AND KAPLAN, S: *Systolic hypertension during submaximal exercise after correction of coarctation of the aorta.* Circulation (Suppl 49,50)51:11, 1974.

28. VALODAVER, Z AND NEUFELD, HN: *The coronary arteries in coarctation of the aorta.* Circulation 37:449, 1968.

29. STRIEDER, DJ, ET AL: *Exercise tolerance after repair of tetralogy of Fallot.* Am Thorac Surg 19:397, 1975.

30. LINDSAY, J, MISHEL, JC, AND PATTERSON, RH: *The cardiovascular manifestations of sickle-cell disease.* Arch Intern Med 133:643, 1974.

31. YATER, WN AND HANSMANN, GH: *Sickle cell anemia: A new cause of cor pulmonale.* Am J Med Sci 191:474, 1936.

32. OLIVIERA, E AND GOMEZ-PATINIO, N: *Falcemic cardiopathy.* Am J Cardiol 11:686, 1963.

33. WINSOR, R AND BURCH, GE: *The electrocardiogram and active cardiac state in active sickle cell anemia.* Am Heart J 29:685, 1945.

34. MILLER, GJ, ET AL: *Cardiopulmonary responses and gas exchange during exercise in adults with homozygous sickle cell disease.* Clin Sci 44:113, 1973.

35. FARIS, JV, ET AL: *Prevalence and reproducibility of ventricular arrhythmias during maximal exercise testing in normal men.* Am J Cardiol 39:617, 1976.

36. UDALL, JA AND ELLESTAD, MH: *Predictive implications of ventricular premature contractions associated with treadmill stress testing.* Circulation 56:985, 1977.

37. KUPERSMITH, J, ET AL: *Maximal treadmill exercise in the evaluation of arrhythmias in children.* Circulation (Suppl 11)54:146, 1976.

38. GODFREY, S, DAVIS, CTM, AND WOZNIAK, E: *Cardiorespiratory response to exercise in normal children.* Clin Sci 40:419, 1971.

39. ANDERSON, SD AND GODFREY, S: *Cardiorespiratory response to treadmill exercise in normal children.* Clin Sci 40:433, 1971.

40. SILVERMAN, M AND HENDERSON, SD: *Standardization of exercise tests in asthmatic children.* Arch Dis Child 47:882, 1972.

21

NUCLEAR STRESS TESTING

MYOCARDIAL PERFUSION IMAGING

History of Myocardial Perfusion Imaging

Since the pioneering work by Zaret and colleagues[1] and Strauss and associates,[2] stress perfusion scanning has rapidly evolved into a widely used and useful adjunct to the more established approach to stress testing. The first application of radioactive tracers to the investigation of physiology occurred in

1927 when Blumgart and Weiss[3] used radon gas administered intravenously in a cloud chamber as a radiation detector to measure the circulation time in intact man. In 1947, Prinzmetal and his colleagues[4] used sodium 22 and a Geiger counter placed over the heart to record the transit time through the heart. They called their curves a radiocardiogram. They were able to calculate cardiac output and derive some evidence of shunting from their data. In 1962, Carr and associates[5] used cesium as a radio tracer. It was not until the development of the Anger/scintillation camera where high resolution of the heart and great vessels could be made that real progress occurred.[6] In 1969, Mason and coworkers[7] recorded the "nuclear angiocardiogram" in the detection of congenital abnormalities, aortic aneurysm, and valvular regurgitation. They also suggested the use of gaiting the scintillation camera so that portions of the cardiac cycle could be visualized. Finally, in 1971 Zaret and colleagues[8] reported their pioneering work using potassium 43 to image stress-induced myocardial ischemia. Perfusion scanning is a measure of cardiovascular physiologic function as are the electrophysiologic alterations seen in S-T segment analysis. Although there has been an attempt to correlate both these findings with anatomic changes in the coronary arteries, they are of necessity only partly related. This method has become, however, a major adjunct to our evaluation of patients with ischemic heart disease.

Characteristics of Tracer Elements

All tracers used for evaluation of regional perfusion follow the Sapirstein principle.[9] They are substances that are rapidly cleared from the blood and are concentrated in the organs under investigation. This allows for the distribution of the tracer to indirectly measure the blood flow to that area. The most important tracers used in cardiac stress testing are the monovalent cations of potassium, rubidium, cesium, and thallium. A terminally labeled 16-iodohexadecanoic acid has also been shown to distribute in the myocardium in relation to the regional perfusion.[10] This fatty acid, however, is quite difficult to image and it is expected that it will be some time before it can become useful. None of the above agents bind exclusively to the heart. Significant concentrations of tracer in the liver, kidney, thyroid, and intestine as well as skeletal muscles are seen. It is believed that the distribution of the tracer represents the product of the regional distribution of blood flow and the activity of sodium, potassium ATPase in each organ. The blood brain barrier effectively excludes thallium. These cations do not all behave identically, however, and studies performed reveal that thallium concentrates in the myocardium to a greater extent than potassium, rubidium, or cesium. Over a time, the myocardial concentration diminishes with potassium and rubidium turning over most rapidly, thallium next, and cesium the slowest. Potassium half life in the human myocardium is approximately 90 minutes in normal patients, whereas thallium half life is about five to seven hours. Control experiments, in normal animals and those with partial occlusion of coronary arteries checked against radioactive microspheres, reveal a linear relationship between the regional distribution of potassium-43 and microspheres; similar experiments seem to suggest that thallium and rubidium react in the same way.[11,12]

Static Myocardial Perfusion Imaging

When intravenous thallium-201 is given in a resting state, the left-ventricular myocardium is well visualized because it has a mass approximately three times greater than the right and a greater blood flow.[13] Although the right ventricle concentrates thallium, it is usually not seen clearly because of the underlying activity of the lung and because of the minimal blood flow. In right-ventricular hypertrophy, however, it becomes well defined and in such a situation one should suspect pulmonary hypertension. Patients with transmural myocardial infarctions have resting perfusion deficits in about 80 percent of those tested,[14] and these must be separated from those seen with stress injections. Data have suggested that nontransmural infarctions are more difficult to define and can be seen in about 50 percent of subjects in a clinical setting.

Dynamic Myocardial Perfusion Imaging

METHOD

Because perfusion of the left ventricle at rest in a patient without previous infarction is usually normal even in the face of severe coronary narrowing, a scan at rest and after isotope injection at peak exercise is necessary. It appears that with exercise, the ratios of blood flow to the normally perfused myocardium and the ischemic myocardium change dramatically. Therefore, a larger dose may be delivered to the working myocardium with normal flow, and the ischemic muscle picks up a relatively much smaller amount of isotope, resulting in a difference in tracer concentration. Recent data, however, suggest that the uptake in exercising heart muscle may not be increased so much as the ischemic muscle decreased.[15] It is important to inject the intravenous isotope at peak exercise and then maintain a period of exercise for at least a minute following the injection so that the tracer can be picked up by the muscle according to the distribution of blood flow. Data suggest that the tracer redistributes within about an hour so that imaging should be completed within 45 minutes, if at all possible. Within four hours, the redistribution of the tracer will be almost identical to a resting scan. This makes it possible to do a second scan without a second injection of isotope[16] (Figs. 21-1 and 21-2).

During the stress test, the patient's ECG, blood pressure, and clinical findings must be monitored exactly the same as with regular stress testing. It is of interest that when the tracer is injected at peak stress, the background activity

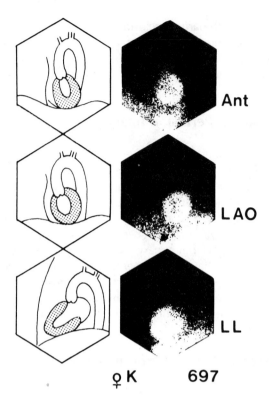

FIGURE 21-1. The three views commonly used for analysis of thallium or stress imaging in a normal patient. (From Wackers, FJTh, et al: Atlas of [201]Tl Myocardial Scintigraphy. Clin Nucl Med 2:64, 1977, with permission.)

in the pulmonary bed all but disappears. The ischemic myocardium tends to be correlated with the area of perfusion by the diseased coronary artery, particularly if there is a single vessel involved. When there are multiple vessels involved, it is difficult to anticipate which vessels will play a major roll by observing the perfusion defect. The knowledge of the ischemic area, however, can at times be very useful in determining which area of narrowing seen on the angiogram is of most importance. Figure 21-3 illustrates the idealized changes seen on the perfusion images in typical clinical situations.[17]

RELIABILITY

Because the intensity of gamma emitters falls off rapidly with distance from the camera and because of overlapping areas of perfusion, the lateral wall and, to some degree, the inferior wall, is more difficult to image and thus, the detection is reduced. Selwyn and colleagues[18] compared S-T depression with thallium and krypton-81M in dogs made ischemic by a ligature around the left-anterior descending. They found that when flow was approximately 49 percent decreased, krypton-81M demonstrated abnormal metabolism, but the

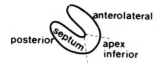

Ant

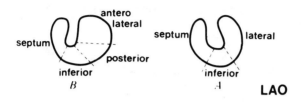

B   *A*   **LAO**

L L

FIGURE 21-2. The anatomic areas visualized in the various views can be correlated with the appropriate coronary artery perfusing each area. (From Wackers, FJTh, et al: Atlas of ^{201}Tl Myocardial Scintigraphy. Clin Nucl Med 2:64, 1977, with permission.)

thallium and the epicardial electrocardiogram failed to identify the change. When the flow was further decreased and electrocardiographic S-T depression occurred, then thallium scintigrams also became abnormal. They predicted that in patients, the electrocardiogram and thallium should have about the same sensitivity in identifying reduced myocardial perfusion. Other workers report that it only takes a decrease in blood flow to the ischemic myocardium of between 30 and 40 percent, as compared with the area normally perfused to facilitate detection.[19]

The original reports[20,21] suggested that sensitivity and specificity were very high, probably owing to their study series being based on patients with a high prevalence of disease. When patients with intermediate prevalence and difficult or atypical presentations are studied, however, the picture changes somewhat. Bungo and Leland[22] report that in a population with a disease prevalence of 67 percent, the sensitivity and specificity were both 70 percent, while the exercise electrocardiogram was 69 percent and 74 percent, respectively—not significantly different. These same authors report a sensitivity for the right coronary artery of 71 percent, circumflex 62 percent, and LAD 78 percent. Lesions in obtuse marginal and diagonal were also less likely to be detected.

Sens, tint / spec = ~ 70%

EXERCISE   REST

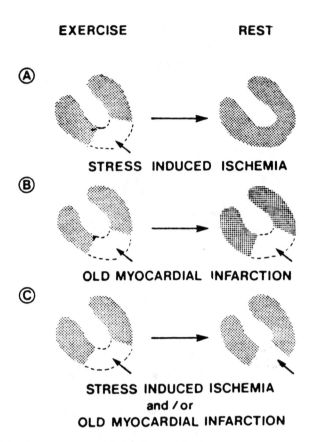

Ⓐ

STRESS INDUCED ISCHEMIA

Ⓑ

OLD MYOCARDIAL INFARCTION

Ⓒ

STRESS INDUCED ISCHEMIA
and / or
OLD MYOCARDIAL INFARCTION

FIGURE 21-3. Patterns seen with ischemia and infarction.
A. The "cold spot" observed after exercise, fills in on redistribution (rest), indicating reversible ischemia.
B. The "cold spot" fails to fill in on redistribution, indicating an area of scar tissue.
C. When the "cold spot" gets smaller on redistribution but remains, there may be a zone of reversible ischemia adjacent to the area of infarction.

Many cases where typical S-T segment depression is seen on the electrocardiogram and the thallium scan is negative, have been explained by the presence of well-developed collaterals.[23] It appears that the subendocardial ischemia is usually revealed by S-T segment depression, but unless a larger amount of muscle mass is ischemic, a "cold area" may not be discernible on the scan. When we find a clearly identifiable exercise-induced area of reversible ischemia on the thallium scan, we feel more certain about coronary disease. On the other hand, the absence of disease is less certain when the scan is negative.

The problems come, according to Bungo and Leland,[22] and the findings in the thallium images and the electrocardiogram disagree. In their data, they only agreed in 47 percent of the cases and when the tests are discordant, the probability of disease drops. Table 21-1 illustrates this problem with the pre-

TABLE 21-1. Usefulness of Noninvasive Predictors of CAD

	Sensitivity %	Specificity %	Predictive Value of Pos Result, %	Predictive Value of Neg Result, %
Resting or exercise ECG	69	74	84	54
Exercise thallium scan	70	70	83	54
ECG/ETT or thallium	94	52	80	82
ECG/ETT and thallium	. . .	. . .	92	82

dictive value of a negative result being approximately 50 percent unless the results are concordant. Figure 21-4 from Gitler[24] illustrates the concept using Bayes Theorem where the electrocardiogram is abnormal with S-T depression of 1.0 mms. The likelihood of disease is 75 percent. However, if the thallium test is normal, which often occurs (thallium false-negative tests occur from 30 to 40 percent), the likelihood drops to 41 percent. However, if the thallium test was abnormal, the likelihood would increase to 90 percent.

One can find numerous reports in the literature describing wide variations in the results with this test.[25,26] One problem is the interobservation differences when viewing the scintigrams. In our own laboratory, this is often the case

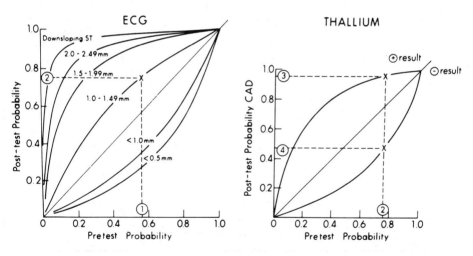

FIGURE 21-4. Illustration of data obtained from both ECG and thallium (Bayes Theorem). *Left,* The subject, a 55-year-old man with atypical angina, starts with a 59 percent pretest probability of CAD (point 1). Because he has 1 mm of S-T depression, he has a 75 percent probability of disease (point 2). *Right,* Starting from this probability (point 2), an abnormal thallium will result in a 90 percent probability of CAD (point 3) but if the thallium test is normal, the likelihood of CAD would be decreased to .41 (point 4). Thus, discordant results, which are common in clinical situations, force us to use our clinical acumen. It may be necessary to do a coronary angiogram for a definite diagnosis. (From Gitler, et al.,[24] with permission.)

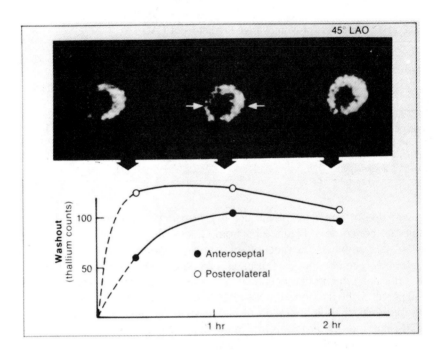

FIGURE 21-5. Normal and abnormal exercise thallium scintigrams of patients having chest pain. *Far left panel,* Serial postexercise [201]thallium scintigrams in 45 degree LAO projection for a patient who had chest pain and angiographically normal coronary arteries. Initial image *(left)* shows uniform thallium uptake in anteroseptal and posterolateral segments. Myocardial computer-derived quantitative time activity curves show normal washout of thallium in mid-anteroseptal and posterolateral walls (designated by arrows in *middle image). Near left panel,* Serial postexercise [201]thallium scintigrams in 45 degree LAO projection from a patient who had left-anterior descending coronary artery stenosis. Initial image *(left)* shows perfusion defect in anteroseptal wall. Delayed images *(center and right)* show "redistribution" into this region (arrows indicate anteroseptal and posterolateral walls). Quantitative time activity curves confirm this abnormal study. (LAO = left anterior oblique.) (From Tubau, et al.,[23] with permission.)

with considerable disagreements occurring between the nuclear specialists and the cardiologists. Beller and colleagues[27] and others[28] have proposed that the sensitivity can be improved by a computerized time activity curve (Fig. 21-5). When rather diffuse ischemia occurs, as is often seen with three-vessel disease, differentiation between normal and reduced areas of perfusion becomes more difficult.

Mehrotra and coworkers[29] have reported abnormal perfusion scans in six patients with chronic obstructive pulmonary disease who were demonstrated to have normal coronary arteries. Three also had S-T segment depression. Even though the epicardial coronaries were normal, the probability remains that these subjects had ischemia, possibly due to a limited vasodilator reserve (see Chapter 4).

Thallium Scintigraphy With Dipyridamole

A relatively new application has been the use of thallium scintigraphy after intravenous dipyridamole, in lieu of exercise. Areas of ischemia can be identified because the agent vasodilates the normal coronary arteries and augments the difference between underperfused areas and the hyperemia induced by the drug. Schmoliner and associates[30] reported the sensitivity with disease in the left-anterior descending to be 75 percent, right coronary 73 percent, and circumflex 37 percent. They claim that this method tends to identify the most severe areas of ischemia and miss the lesser areas, however.

Indications for Perfusion Imaging

The test is particularly useful in a number of special situations.

1. The patient with a previous myocardial infarction suspected of having coronary disease in other areas that have not yet infarcted. The appearance of a new area of underperfusion during exercise tends to implicate arteries not already responsible for an area of infarction.
2. Patients with chest pain but who have ECGs that are difficult to interpret, such as those with LBBB, left-ventricular hypertrophy, or patients on digitalis. McGowan and colleagues,[20] using potassium-43 and rubidium-81, have found that resting scans in patients with LBBB may show areas of decreased radionuclide uptake in the septum suggesting an area of regional ischemia. However, most of these patients who have normal coronary arteries have a clearing of this finding after exercise. In their patients who had coronary disease and LBBB, the ischemic area became more pronounced or new areas of ischemia developed when injections were made at peak exercise.
3. False-positive responders on the stress test who are in population groups that suggest that they may not have coronary disease. Such as angina with normal coronary arteries in women, young athletes, and in people who have no symptoms but positive stress tests where their occupation or lifestyle makes it extremely important to gather more evidence about their coronary circulation.
4. Patients with an intermediate degree of coronary stenosis on the angiogram and it is not known if it is functionally significant.
5. When the ventriculogram shows hypokinesis or akinesis and the coronary is highly obstructed, thallium may indicate viable muscle that would benefit from an intervention to provide reperfusion.
6. Recent reports suggest that an abnormal thallium scan identifies a subset of patients with a higher probability of coronary events in the future.[28] This is particularly true if multiple defects and abnormal lung uptake occur.

RADIONUCLIDE ANGIOGRAPHY

This technique is a measure of ventricular performance rather than myocardial perfusion. Although performance is often related to perfusion, other factors such as afterload and preload, as well as catecholamines play significant roles.

First Pass Studies

Radionuclide angiography or blood pool imaging can be accomplished by the first pass method or by equilibrium blood pool imaging. In the first pass method, an intravenous bolus of radioactivity is recorded by a gamma scintillation camera. Time activity curves are derived for the various chambers and stroke volume and systolic and diastolic volumes are calculated by computer analysis. In the equilibrium method, the blood is labeled by a radioactive substance and the gamma camera images the chambers by electrocardiographic gaiting. The resultant computer generated facsimile of the heart chambers provides data on wall motion, systolic and diastolic volumes, and ejection fraction. These volumes have been shown to correlate well with cineangiographic measurements as well as with casts of animal heart chambers.[31,32] Both the first pass and gaited pool studies are accomplished with technetium-99M. The first pass method has not been popular because a second injection will be necessary if exercise measurements are to be compared to the resting. Also the camera position must be predetermined prior to injection and if improperly placed, discrimination between chambers may be less than ideal. Also, the low count rates may reduce the reliability. Small "nuclear stethoscopes" have been designed for this method, however, and have been reported to be quite reliable while dramatically reducing the equipment cost.[33]

Equilibrium Blood Pool Imaging

In this technique, the isotope must stay tightly bound to the blood for a considerable time while data are being acquired. Thus, technetium-99M, labeled autologous red cells, are usually used because of minimal leakage from the vascular compartment. Imaging can be started after about 10 minutes has elapsed so that the tracer has equilibrated with the blood. The computer divides the cardiac cycle into 12 to 50 frames. Data are collected for each segment and stored until high enough count densities (usually several hundred cardiac cycles) will allow synthesis of satisfactory images. These have been called "Muga" scans, which stands for multiple gaited acquisition blood pool imaging—now a trade name. The camera is positioned so as to separate the right and left ventricle (45 percent LAO with a 15 degree caudal tilt) to prevent counts from one chamber contaminating those from another.

Areas of interest are identified either by the computer or by the operator, both are usually but not invariably quite accurate. Regional wall motion, total ejection fraction,* and regional fractions may be analyzed at rest and after exercise or after some other intervention.

Numerous papers now have reported on the ability of this method to identify changes in the ejection fraction and wall motion at rest and after exercise in coronary patients and in normals.[17,34,35] The ejection fraction usually increases about 10 percent with exercise and patients who show less than this increment are designated as abnormal. Reduction in contraction of isolated wall segments are also frequently diagnostic of coronary ischemia.[36]

When the patient is exercised on a bicycle with data acquired at each increase in workload using the above criteria, sensitivity and specificity as high as 95 percent[17,37] has been reported. Results with this degree of accuracy must come from a highly selected population, however. Studies on women[38] with cardiomyopathies (even mild) and those with valve disease decrease reliability a great deal.[39] Using the ejection fraction, the blood pool method is usually more sensitive but less specific than thallium in our experience. Beller and colleagues[27] report wall motion abnormalities to have a sensitivity of 76 percent and a specificity of 95 percent. When patients are on beta blockers,[26] when they fail to exercise adequately,[40,41] or when they have an atypical pain pattern, the sensitivity and specificity fall significantly. Seaworth and associ-

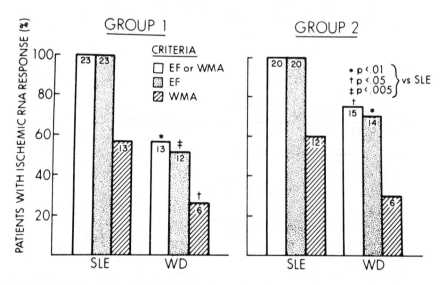

FIGURE 21-6. Effect of workload reduction on test sensitivity. In group I, 23 patients had ejection fraction (EF) reductions of over 5 units with maximal symptom-limited exercise, and 13 had wall motion abnormalities with a 50 percent work reduction. Only 13 had an EF decrease, and only 6 had abnormal wall motion.

In group 2, only a small reduction in workload was tried and approximately 75 percent had an abnormal EF indicating maximum exercise is necessary for optimal diagnostic power.

---

*Ejection fraction is the percent of left-ventricular diastolic volume ejected during systole. Normal is between 60 and 70 percent.

ates[40] have evaluated reductions in workload on indexes of ischemia and has found a 40 percent reduction in sensitivity when this happens (Fig. 21-6). Christopher and coworkers[42] believe that abnormal exercise-induced changes in ventricular function are better predictors of future cardiac events than they are of the anatomy. This may also be true of exercise-induced S-T segment depression. When we consider the recent data[19] on the inaccuracies in predicting ischemia from the coronary angiogram, this is not too surprising.

Which Procedure Should Be Used When?

When we have decided after conventional stress testing that we need another relatively noninvasive test, which one should be used? Should the radiation dosage be considered? With these studies the amount is small, with the red marrow receiving about 510 millirads with myocardial perfusion imaging and 1000 millirads with equilibrium blood pool imaging. This compares with a dosage of 24 to 64 rads per minute, with conventional cinecoronary angiography at 60 frames a second.[17]

As previously mentioned, left-ventricular function studies have been reported to be more sensitive in the detection of coronary disease than conventional thallium-201 (90 percent versus 75 percent). But the latter is more specific (95 percent versus 80 percent).[17] In our experience, all these numbers can be reduced by at least 5 to 10 percent. Be that as it may, the interobserver disagreement with thallium makes it somewhat less reliable; however, newer methods of collumation for tomographic enhancement are improving the sensitivity somewhat. The ability to apply numbers to the ventriculographic measurements gives it a certain appeal, even though we know computer generated numbers may not add as much accuracy as they seem. Ventricular function studies are particularly helpful in evaluating changing patterns of function after interventions such as coronary bypass surgery, angioplasty, or valve replacement. If the patient has had a previous myocardial infarction we might be asking—is further myocardium in jeopardy? Blood pool imaging appears superior, although we must realize that conditions of preload, afterload, and medication such as beta blockers and nitrates, all affect the ejection fraction during exercise. Gibbons and colleagues from Duke[43] reported ejection fraction response to exercise in patients with angina and normal coronary arteries varied from an increase of 24 percent to a decrease of 23 percent and counsels against its use in the diagnosis of coronary artery disease because of its low specificity. Because of these factors, wall motion abnormalities may be more reliable markers for ischemia than ejection fraction trends.[44]

SUMMARY

In recent years, enormous strides in exercise nuclear techniques have given us an exciting and useful tool in evaluation of our coronary patients. It will serve us well if we understand the weaknesses and strength of these tests. Unfortunately, the costs are still quite high owing to the expensive equipment and isotopes. Because modern therapeutic techniques often require an accurate knowledge of the coronary anatomy, many patients will proceed from standard exercise stress testing or from the consultation room directly to the catheterization laboratory without the use of the type of information acquired from these techniques, however.

REFERENCES

1, ZARET, BL, ET AL: Noninvasive regional myocardial perfusion with radioactive potassium: Study of patients at rest, with exercise and during angina pectoris. N Engl J Med 288:809–812, 1973.

2. STRAUSS, HW, ET AL: Noninvasive evaluation of regional myocardial perfusion with potassium 43: Technique in patients with exercise-induced transient myocardial ischemia. Radiology 108:85–90, 1973.

3. BLUMGART, HC AND WEISS, SL: Studies on the velocity of blood flow, VII: The pulmonary circulation time in normal resting individuals. J Clin Invest 4:399–425, 1927.

4. PRINZMETAL, M, ET AL: Radiocardiography: A new method for studying the blood flow through the heart in human beings. Science 108:340–341, 1948.

5. CARR, EA, ET AL: The detection of experimental myocardial infarcts by photoscanning. Am Heart J 64:650–660, 1962.

6. COOPER, M: Myocardial imaging: An overview. In STRAUSS, HW, PITT, B, AND JAMES, AE, JR (EDS): Cardiovascular Nuclear Medicine. CV Mosby, St. Louis, 1974, Chapter 9.

7. MASON, DT, ET AL: Rapid sequential visualization of the heart and great vessels in man using the wide field Anger scintillation camera. Circulation 39:19–28, 1969.

8. ZARET, BL, ET AL: A noninvasive scintiphotographic method for detecting regional ventricular dysfunction in man. N Engl J Med 284:1165–1170, 1971.

9. SAPIRSTEIN, LA: Regional blood flow by fractional distribution of indicators. Am J Physiol 193:161–168, 1958.

10. POE, ND, ROBINSON, GD, AND MACDONALD, NS: Myocardial extraction of variously labeled fatty acids and carboxylates (abst). J Nucl Med 14:440, 1973.

11. BECKER, L, FERREIRA, R, AND THOMAS, M: Comparison of ^{86}Rb and microsphere estimates pf of left ventricular blood flow distribution. J Nucl Med 15:969–973, 1974.

12. SCHELBERT, HR, ET AL: Comparative myocardial uptake of intravenously administered radionuclides. J Nucl Med 15:1092–1100, 1974.

13. COOK, DJ, ET AL: Thallium 201 for myocardial imaging: Appearance of the normal heart. J Nucl Med 121:257–268, 1976.

14. STRAUSS, HW: Cardiovascular Nuclear Medicine: New look at an old problem: Noninvasive approaches to the evaluation of coronary heart disease: New Horizons for Radiologists lecture. Radiology 121:257–268, 1976.

15. BAILEY, IK, ET AL: Thallium 201 myocardial perfusion imaging at rest and during exercise: Comparative sensitivity to electrocardiography in coronary artery disease. Circulation 55:79–87, 1977.

16. POHOST, GM, ET AL: Thallium 201 redistribution following transient myocardial ischemia (abstr). J Nucl Med 17:535, 1976.

17. WISENBERG, G AND SCHELBERT, HR: Radionuclide techniques in the diagnosis of cardiovascular disease. Current Problems in Cardiology 4(7):1–58, 1979.

18. SELWYN, AP, ET AL: The interpretation of thallium 201 cardiac scintigrams. Circ Res 43(2):287–293, 1978.

19. MARCUS, ML: *The Coronary Circulation in Health and Disease.* McGraw-Hill, New York, 1983.

20. McGOWAN, RL, ET AL: *Noninvasive myocardial imaging with potassium-43 and ribidium-81 in patients with left bundle branch block.* Am J Cardiol 38:422, 1976.

21. ROSENBLATT, A, ET AL: *Post-exercise thallium 201 myocardial scanning: A clinical appraisal.* Am Heart J 94(4):463–470, 1977.

22. BUNGO, MW AND LELAND, OS, JR: *Discordance of exercise thallium testing with coronary arteriography in patients with atypical presentations.* Chest 1:112–116, 1983.

23. TUBAU, JF, ET AL: *Importance of coronary collateral circulation in interpreting exercise test results.* Am J Cardiol 47:27–32, 1981.

24. GITLER, B, FISHBACH, M, AND STEINGART, RM: *Use of electrocardiographic-thallium exercise testing in clinical practice.* JACC 3(2):262–271, 1984.

25. CARRILLO, AP, ET AL: *Correlation of exercise [201]thallium myocardial scan with coronary arteriograms and the maximal exercise test.* Chest 73(3):321–326, 1978.

26. STEELE, P, ET AL: *Thallium 201 myocardial imaging during maximal and submaximal exercise: Comparison of submaximal exercise with propranolol.* Am Heart J 106(6):1353–1357, 1983.

27. BELLER, GA, GIBSON, RS, AND WATSON, DD: *Radionuclide tests for coronary artery disease: How do you choose?* J Cardiovasc Med, August:892–910, 1983.

28. BONOW, RO, GREEN, MV, AND BACHARACH, SL: *Radionuclide angiography during exercise in patients with coronary artery disease: Diagnostic, prognostic and therapeutic implications.* Int J Cardiol 5:229–233, 1984.

29. MEHROTRA, PP, WEAVER, YJ, AND HIGGINBOTHAM, EA: *Myocardial perfusion defect on thallium 201 imaging in patients with chronic obstructive pulmonary disease.* JACC 2(2):233–239, 1983.

30. SCHMOLINER, R, ET AL: *Thallium 201 imaging after dipyridamole in patients with coronary multivessel disease.* Cardiology 70:145–151, 1983.

31. ALAZRAKI, NP, ET AL: *Utilization of radionuclide cardiac angiogram for determination of cardiac output and ejection fraction.* J Nucl Med Biol 19:112, 1971.

32. MADDAHI, J, ET AL: *Validation of two minute technique for multiple gated scintigraphic assessment of left ventricular ejection fraction and regional wall motion* (abstr). J Nucl Med 19:669, 1978.

33. WAGNER, HN, JR: *Cardiovascular nuclear medicine: A progress report.* Hospital Practice, July:76–83, 1976.

34. JONES, RH, GOODRICH, JK, AND SABISTON, PM: *Quantitative radionuclide angiocardiography in evaluation of cardiac function.* Surg Forum 22:128, 1971.

35. PULIDO, JI, ET AL: *Submaximal exercise testing after acute myocardial infarction: Myocardial scintigraphic and electrocardiographic observations.* Am J Cardiol 42:19, 1978.

36. BODENHEIMER, M, ET AL: *Comparative sensitivity and specificity of radionuclide angiographic assessment of wall motions and ejection fraction at rest and during exercise in the diagnosis of coronary heart disease.* Proc Soc Nucl Med 18:73, 1978.

37. SLUTSKY, R, ET AL: *Response of left ventricular volume to exercise in man.* Circulation 60:565, 1979.

38. GREENBERG, P, ET AL: *The value and limitation of radionuclide angiography with stress in women.* Clin Cardiol 6:312–317, 1983.

39. OSBAKKEN, MD, ET AL: *Comparison of exercise perfusion and ventricular function imaging: An analysis of factors affecting the diagnostic accuracy of each technique.* JACC 3(2):272–283, 1984.

40. SEAWORTH, JR, ET AL: *Effect of partial decreases in exercise work load on radionuclide indexes of ischemia.* JACC 2(3):522–529, 1983.

41. BROWN, EJ, ET AL: *Effect of timolol on exercise-induced reduction in regional ejection fraction in patients with coronary artery disease.* Chest 84(3):258–263, 1983.

42. CHRISTOPHER, TD, KONSTANTINOW, G, AND JONES, RH: *Bayesian analysis of data from radionuclide angiocardiograms for diagnosis of coronary artery disease.* Circulation 69(1):65–72, 1984.

43. GIBBONS, RJ, ET AL: *Ejection fraction response to exercise in patients with chest pain and normal coronary arteriograms.* Circulation 64(5):952–957, 1981.

44. CAMPOS, CT, ET AL: *Comparison of rest and exercise radionuclide angiocardiography and exercise treadmill testing for diagnosis of anatomically extensive coronary artery disease.* Circulation 67(6):1204–1210, 1983.

22

METABOLIC ABNORMALITIES AND DRUGS

AMPHETAMINES

ISOPROTERENOL

PSYCHOTROPIC DRUGS

Tricyclic Antidepressants
Lithium
Phenothiazines
Diazepam (Valium)

ANTIHYPERTENSIVE AGENTS

DIURETICS

METHYLDOPA (ALDOMET)

CLONIDINE

GUANETHIDINE

VASODILATORS

ANGIOTENSIN-CONVERTING ENZYME INHIBITORS

ALCOHOL

Information on changes in cellular physiology, cardiopulmonary function, and exercise tolerance, associated with metabolic abnormalities and various drug regimens, is proliferating so fast that what we know today may be out-of-date tomorrow. Many of the drugs we now use can profoundly alter ischemia, afterload and preload, and the chronotropic and ionotropic response. It is essential to consider these changes when undertaking exercise testing. The information to follow should help the physician deal with most of the more common conditions and drugs in use. Careful study of new agents being introduced to determine their effects on patients during exercise testing will be mandatory.

METABOLIC ACIDOSIS

Acidosis produces a depressive effect on cardiac contractility, especially during exercise. The accumulation of lactic acid and the ability to tolerate this buildup is one of the most important determinants of endurance in performance in sports.[1] As the pH level drops with acidosis, the strength of myocardial contraction decreases, and the cardiac output also decreases. There appears to be a variation in individual susceptibility to this, and conditioning and age seem to be factors in this discrepancy.[2] The same drop in pH level seems to have somewhat of a protective effect against ventricular irritability. The only significant findings on the ECG may be some lowering of the T-waves and slight prolongation of the Q-T interval. These changes are, however, nonspecific. If exercise is carried to maximum capacity, all subjects become acidotic, but this is quickly corrected during the recovery period.

ALKALOSIS

It has long been recognized that carbon dioxide (CO_2) has important vasoactive properties. The vasoconstrictive properties of a low PCO_2 and the dilatation seen with a high PCO_2 on the vasculature of the brain are the most notable.[2] More recently, the capacity of a low PCO_2 to cause intense coronary vasoconstriction with the resultant decrease in myocardial perfusion has been demonstrated by Case and coworkers.[3] An increase in coronary vascular resistance occurs with alkalosis even when the arterial PO_2 is maintained in the normal range. Thus, it may be that S-T depression following hyperventilation may actually represent myocardial ischemia.

Chronic hyperventilation is one of the most common types of alkalosis seen in ambulatory patients. This condition is common in emotionally labile women who are often subject to vague chest symptoms and may be suspected of having coronary heart disease. Chronic alkalosis involves intracellular potassium depletion with a subsequent increase in urinary potassium loss. A lower than normal level of total body potassium may account for fatigue, loss of strength, and characteristic changes reflected in the ECG. The ECG of such a patient is illustrated in Fig. 22-1. A 28-year-old woman was referred to our Pulmonary Rehabilitation Clinic because of suspected asthma or emphysema.

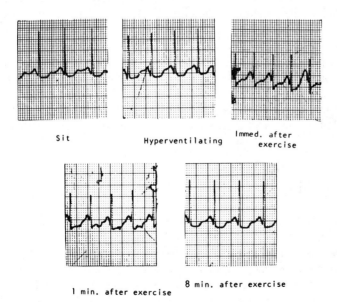

Sit   Hyperventilating   Immed. after
                                        exercise

1 min. after exercise   8 min. after exercise

FIGURE 22-1. The CM_5 leads recorded from a 28-year-old woman with chronic hyperventilation, a low PCO_2, and a high pH. The tendency for the depressed S-T segments to evolve toward normal immediately after exercise and then to assume a more pathologic appearance during recovery is common in people with metabolic abnormalities.

Her spirometric measurements were normal, but the blood gas studies revealed a pH of 7.51 and a PCO_2 of 32; serum potassium was 3.2. The stress test disclosed S-T segment depression at rest, which was accentuated by hyperventilation. The results were considered by some observers to be suggestive of coronary disease. After potassium-level correction, prolonged psychotherapy and an exercise program, the patient became relatively free of her symptoms, and her resting ECG returned to normal. This patient is an extreme example of the electrocardiographic changes seen in those who are chronically anxious and neurotic. One of the reasons for using a period of hyperventilation prior to the stress test is to help identify such individuals and separate the S-T segment changes caused by the metabolic defect from those resulting from ischemia secondary to coronary narrowing. As discussed in Chapter 12, excessive diuretic use is another cause of alkalosis. The low potassium and ECG changes associated with this condition are illustrated in Figure 12-19.

THYROID ABNORMALITIES

Hyperthyroidism

High levels of thyroid hormone (T_3 and T_4) profoundly influence cardiac function as well as the metabolism of all body tissues. The increase in heart rate, systolic blood pressure, ejection rate, and coronary blood flow is associated with a decrease in systemic resistance. Iskandrian and colleagues[4] studied 10 thyrotoxic patients with exercise radionuclide angiograms. They found the exercise capacity, heart rate, and blood pressure to be quite similar to normals. But at maximum capacity the ejection fraction was reduced, thus supporting the previous data[5,6] indicating that hyperthyroidism is associated with cardiac dysfunction. S-T segment changes are not usually seen in this condition, however.

Hypothyroidism

A decrease in thyroid hormone is known to reduce cardiac output, produce decreased myocardial contractility and heart rate. These changes are of sufficient magnitude that ^{131}I was once proposed as a treatment for severe angina, in spite of the known fact that it was associated with acceleration of the atherosclerotic process. Hypothyroidism is often associated with T-wave flattening and S-T segment depression. Exercise has been reported to produce S-T depression in about 50 percent of patients with severe myxedema. Thus, thyroid function should be taken into consideration when S-T depression occurs, especially in a lethargic woman with a slow heart rate. Hylander and associates[7] have studied the cardiovascular response to thyroid replacement and have found that it takes twelve weeks or more for the exercise-induced S-T segments to return to normal, at about the same time it takes for TSH to normalize. On the other hand, it takes about thirty-five weeks for the exercise capacity to return to normal. They proposed that the heart returns to normal function before the peripheral response can recover.

DIABETES

Stress testing in diabetic patients requires some knowledge of the disturbances in metabolism and physiology brought on by this protean disease. Besides hypertension and hyperlipidemia, diabetes is known to be associated with alterations in the microvasculature and with deposits of mucopolysaccharides in the myocardium.[8,9] These latter changes may explain the report[10] from the Framingham Study that twice as many diabetic patients develop congestive failure as compared with aged-matched controls. The inadequate insulin supply has been shown to inhibit the transportation of glucose across the myocardial cell membrane,[11] and glucose phosphorylation by ATP is altered so that an excess of ammonium is liberated.[12] Not only does the ammonium decrease myocardial contractility secondary to the acidosis, but the increased use in free fatty acids results in a decrease in glucose use and an excess deposit of glycogen in the heart muscle as well. These changes decrease myocardial compliance as well as the contractile force and can best be identified by measuring the isovolumetric relaxation time, which is abnormally prolonged, especially after exercise.

Rubler[9] and Rubler and Arvan[13] have described a reduction in exercise capacity, higher systolic and diastolic pressures, and a lower maximum heart rate in asymptomatic diabetics. This latter finding may be an expression of the dysautonomia under study in diabetes.[14] This is believed to be due to a generalized neuropathy.[15] Rubler,[9] however, failed to document a higher incidence of S-T depression in diabetics when compared with patients of the same age in other studies.

Persson,[16] on the other hand, studied 84 diabetic men with exercise and followed them for nine years. He found an increased prevalence of S-T depression in diabetic patients as compared with controls, as well as a correlation with duration of the diabetes. A similar increase in S-T depression during exercise was also reported by Bellet and Roman[17] and Karlefors.[18]

When testing diabetic subjects, it might seem prudent to do so in a fasting state if they are on insulin, as it has been reported by Riley and colleagues[19] that intravenous glucose accentuates the incidence of S-T segment depression. It still remains to be determined if a glucose meal would have the same effect, however. When subjects on insulin are studied in our laboratory, we proceed to do stress testing approximately two hours after either breakfast or lunch without altering either their diet or their insulin schedule. I am aware of no case in which this practice has resulted in a false-positive test or any complications related to blood sugar levels.

ESTROGENS

It has been recognized for some time that exercise-induced S-T depression is often seen in women with normal coronary arteries.[20,21] Although it is still uncertain as to whether estrogen is a cause, there now seems to be adequate evidence that the hormone clearly functions as a vasoconstrictor.[22] Engel's group[23] in Hanover has presented evidence of decreased myocardial perfusion in women on estrogens. Various estrogens have been found to have an adverse effect on the incidence of myocardial infarction in subjects in the Coronary Drug Project,[24] and in men treated for carcinoma of the prostate.[25]

Jaffe[26] found that when treating patients with established coronary disease, 90 percent had more S-T segment depression after two weeks of treatment with 10 mg of conjugated estrogens or 5 mg of stilbestrol. When treating 10 patients (five men and five women) without coronary disease or S-T depression, however, he failed to produce S-T changes. Because he only used the Master's Test, we do not know for certain if S-T depression would be manifested at higher workloads. At this juncture, when patients on estrogens have an abnormal S-T response to exercise, one must always consider the possibility of a drug-induced response (Table 22-1), especially if seen in a woman in the age group in which the prevalence of coronary disease is known to be very low. Because estrogens have some pharmacologic similarity to digitalis, more careful studies need to be carried out to determine their role in myocardial metabolism.

ANDROGENS

Very little data are available on the possible influence of androgens on the heart. It only seemed logical that Jaffe,[26] after having studied the effect of estrogens, would extend this to the evaluation of androgens. Because women have a lower incidence of infarction than men, it was long believed that estrogens protected against coronary disease, and that androgens must have an adverse effect. The findings released by the Coronary Drug Project[24] implicating estrogen as a possible added risk factor were a surprise to most of us. The added evidence that estrogens aggravated exercise-induced ischemia, however, tended to confirm the concept that the physiologic effect of this steroid has an

TABLE 22-1. Agents reported to alter exercise-induced S-T segment changes

False positive	False negative
digitalis	nitrites
estrogens	beta blockers
diuretics	quinidine
catecholamines ?	androgens ?
lithium ?	diazepam ?

adverse effect on cardiac function. Jaffe[27] has now reported that ethylestrenol, an anabolic steroid, and testosterone cypionate both reduce S-T segment depression in patients with coronary heart disease. When testosterone 200 mg intramuscularly was compared with a placebo for from four to eight weeks, the treated subjects had a decrease in the sum of the S-T depression in leads II, V_4, V_5, and V_6 immediately after a two step test by 32 percent after four weeks of treatment and by 51 percent after eight weeks of treatment. The reason for this improvement was not established; however, the exercise heart rate was significantly lower in those who showed improvement. The blood pressure was not altered. Testosterone is known to improve muscle strength[28] and to increase the sense of vigor. This could have resulted in those treated actually needing less caloric expenditure because of the increased muscle strength. Androgens also increase the 2,3 diphosphoglycerate in red cells, thus enabling them to carry more oxygen[11] as well as increasing the concentration of hemoglobin.[29] The men in Jaffe's study, however, failed to have a measurable increase in hemoglobin. Finally, a decrease in smooth muscle tone has been reported,[30] which might decrease coronary resistance. Holma[31] has studied the hemodynamic changes in athletes following a 2-month oral dose of metandierone, an anabolic steroid. He found an increase in stroke volume, a reduction in heart rate, and improved peak forearm blood flow, which would also support the concept that smooth muscle relaxation is an important component.

At this juncture, the final mechanism for the improvement is unknown; however, angina was also decreased so that it would appear that there may actually be less ischemia after the administration of male hormones.

DIGITALIS

The alterations in S-T segments produced by digitalis are well documented, and there is little doubt that ischemic S-T segment changes can be accentuated when a patient who has taken the drug exercises. It is also clear that digitalis will produce exercise-induced S-T segment depression in people with normal coronary arteries.

It seems odd that although digitalis is the drug enjoying the longest usage in cardiac disorders, there is still some doubt about some of its pharmacology. It seems definite, however, that some of its actions are fairly well understood.

1. In the normal sized heart, the ionotropic effect is associated with an increased oxygen uptake.
2. In the failing heart, the size of the ventricle can be reduced, and thus the oxygen consumption is actually decreased.[32] Vogel and colleagues[33] have demonstrated with thallium-201 uptake that myocardial perfusion actually increases in the failing heart when a patient is digitalized. These subjects have been shown to have better left-ventricular function during exercise as well.[34]

3. A definite vasoconstrictor effect has been demonstrated, both in the heart and in peripheral tissue.[35,36] This seems to be due to a direct effect on the smooth muscles of both arteries and veins. In the heart, a reduction of flow to the subendocardium has been demonstrated by both rubidium-86 and radioactive microspheres.[37] When this happens, there is usually an increase in left-ventricular systolic pressure associated with the drug. There is evidence also that, at times, the epicardium may be relatively overperfused and act as a physiologic shunt.[38]
4. Even though the above decrease in subendocardial flow is present, the S-T depression may not be due to significant ischemia[39] because though oxygen inhalation tends to correct the S-T depression, nitroglycerin fails to have the same effect.
5. It has been demonstrated that digitalis causes an increase in intracellular calcium,[40] a change also present in ischemia.

Studies to elucidate the incidence and mechanism of digitalis-induced S-T depression during exercise are numerous,[33,34,41] but still leave us with some uncertainties. Kawai and Hultgren[39] report that approximately 50 percent of their normal subjects placed on a maintenance dose of digoxin and tested on a Master's protocol had significant S-T depression, but that the changes could be minimized by oxygen inhalation or potassium infusion. Goldbarg[42] reported about the same incidence of S-T depression in normal subjects taking digitalis. Tonkon and colleagues[43] reported that S-T changes occurred in all subjects with digoxin levels about 0.5 mg per milliliter. They also found that when these patients reached a workload of over 75 percent of their maximal predicted heart rate, the S-T depression disappeared, thereby enabling them to separate those subjects with ischemia from those with drug changes alone. They also found that most of their subjects had a J-point or upsloping pattern and that there was a rough correlation when comparing the depth of the S-T depression and the serum digoxin level (R = 0.57).

Sketch and colleagues,[21] on the other hand, found that their normal patients given digoxin continued their S-T depression to maximum workload and in a few, the changes persisted up to six minutes into recovery. They also reported that the incidence of S-T depression increased with age. One hundred percent of those over 60 had S-T depression while only 25 percent of the total cohort exhibited this finding. After five years, they retested most of their subjects and found that those who had digitalis-induced S-T depression originally were likely to have S-T changes without the drug on follow-up. They postulate that digitalis unmasks ischemia and that some of those with S-T depression after digoxin were really false-negative responders. This hypothesis, I believe, requires further verification. Degre and associates[44] from Belgium report that an increase in R-wave amplitude will add discrimination to those on digitalis. The specificity of the S-T depression was 30 percent and 70 percent for the increase in R-wave amplitude. Sensitivity was 100 percent and 50 percent, respectively. It has also been reported that S-T depression due to ischemia will be improved by nitroglycerin, but no change will be seen if digitalis is the cause.

It has been our experience that when S-T depression of 4 to 5 mm occurs, it almost always signals ischemia, even in patients who are taking digitalis. The maximum magnitude in Sketch's normal patients was 1.9 mm. If a patient on digitalis is tested and has no S-T depression, it provides us with strong evidence against the presence of myocardial ischemia.

It is of interest that Kawai and Hultgren[39] reported a normal Q-T interval in subjects with digitalis-induced S-T changes, while those with ischemia had prolonged Q-T intervals. This important finding has not been confirmed.

Davidson and Hagan[45] have proposed the use of stress testing in digitalized patients with atrial fibrillation to assess the adequacy of the dose. When an adequate drug level is on board, the ventricular response to exercise will be similar to those patients in sinus rhythm and when this has been accomplished, exercise tolerance will improve.

QUINIDINE

Although it has been stated that quinidine will result in a false-positive stress test, I have been unable to find a documented example of this and we have never observed such a response in our laboratory. Although this agent, in toxic doses, may prolong conduction at any level in the conduction system, it is very useful when blood levels are in the therapeutic range as an antiarrhythmic agent during exercise. Gey and colleagues[46] gave quinidine gluconate orally in doses of 10 and 15 mg per kg of body weight to 29 subjects prior to a standard Bruce test. Some subjects were normal, while others had documented coronary disease. They observed an excellent antiarrhythmic effect, but were unable to identify a change in either heart rate or blood pressure and no evidence of S-T segment depression was observed. They reported that pronestyl, however, has been shown to produce significant S-T depression during exercise.[47] Fluster and coworkers[48] report that quinidine increases resting as well as exercise heart rate. This issue seems to be up in the air at this time.

Surawicz and coworkers[49,50] have stated that the prolongation of Phase 2 of the ventricular action potential by quinidine will decrease the repolarization gradient during inscription of the S-T segment and thereby diminish the manifestation of S-T depression even during ischemia. Freedberg and associates[51] have also reported that quinidine will produce a false-negative stress test.

MECHANISMS OF ACTION FOR ANTIANGINAL DRUGS

Simoons and Balakumaran[52] have claimed that antianginal drugs act through two primary mechanisms. Drugs that slow heart rate such as the beta blockers and a new agent alidine,[53] a derivative of clonidine, characterize the first. The reduction in heart rate decreases myocardial oxygen demand and velocity of contraction and allows for a longer diastolic period, which favors an increased myocardial perfusion through compromised coronary arteries.[52] The second mechanism, illustrated by nitroglycerin, increases venous capacitance and decreases arterial resistance, thereby reducing inflow into the heart. This results in a decrease in left-ventricular volume and reduced wall stress and afterload. Calcium blockers may do both of the above. They may also have a direct effect on the myocardial cell membrane, but this is believed to be of lesser importance.

NITRITES

Although the reduction in arterial resistance is an important mechanism, there are a number of others that play a significant role. The simplistic concept that the nitrites function as coronary dilators does not help much in understanding this complex process. It must be obvious that an agent that increases flow to a normal segment of myocardium might well shunt blood away from an ischemic area. Thus, the precapillary sphincters, believed to be under local metabolic control, are probably not significantly altered by these agents. It now seems well established that the nitrites serve to "redistribute" blood to the ischemic areas.[54] The possible mechanism of this redistribution is still a matter of considerable speculation. The demonstrated capacity of the nitrites to reduce venous tone and thus allow the blood to sequestrate in the capacitance vessels, with the resultant decrease in cardiac filling,[55] must be an important part of the reduction in cardiac work. The drop in left-ventricular end-diastolic pressure immediately after nitroglycerin administration is familiar to every catheterizing cardiologist. One explanation for the favorable redistribution of blood may be related to the anatomic location of many collateral vessels. Fulton[56] has shown that in occlusive coronary disease the major communications between normal and ischemic zones of myocardium are in the subendocardial plexus, and are thus subject to cavity pressure. This effect in subjects with a high diastolic pressure, which is common during an ischemic episode, would be important. If the venous filling were to drop suddenly, the reduction of 10 to 20 mm of diastolic filling pressure might well favor a redistribution of blood to the ischemic areas through these pathways that are so vulnerable to the forces of compression present in the left-ventricular cavity. This mechanism has been attractively presented by McGregor[57] and supported by Vineberg and associates,[58] and others.[59] When Ganz and Marcus[60] injected nitroglycerin directly into the coronary arteries, they could not document an increased flow in the coronary sinus. On the other hand, others seem to have documented an increase in flow in both dog[61] and man[62] after nitroglycerin. It seems, then, that even though these agents have a demonstrated ability to provide smooth muscle relaxation,[63] which in many cases affects the larger branches of the coronary tree, other mechanisms considered may be more important than the increase in flow.

LONG-ACTING NITRITES

When the long-acting preparations, such as the sterioisomers of pentitol (Pentanitrate), d-isosorbide dinitrate (Isordil), and erythrol tetranitrate, are taken sublingually, they act much like glyceryl trinitrate but with longer activity.[64] Goldstein and colleagues[65] found that only a small percentage of their subjects had a favorable effect one hour after sublingual d-isosorbide dinitrate, and in most cases, it was indistinguishable from those changes related to nitroglycerin.

When taken by mouth, there was some question as to their effectiveness; however, Russek and Funk[66] found 20 to 60 mg of pentaerythritol tetranitrate (Peritrate) to be effective in reducing the S-T changes on a Master's test for up to five hours. Others have had difficulty confirming these findings, however.[67]

The data on these agents can be summarized by concluding that when given prior to an exercise test, they may reduce the S-T depression associated with exercise, and should be withheld for an appropriate interval. In most subjects the S-T changes will not be eliminated, but may appear at a higher workload than without the drug.

DIPYRIDAMOLE (PERSANTINE)

Because of the widespread belief that the nitrites owe their effectiveness to an increase in coronary flow, other agents with this capacity have been tried clinically.[68] Dipyridamole is one of these and falls far short of the nitrites in its ability to mitigate ischemic changes associated with exercise, even though it will increase coronary flow by 300 to 400 percent.[69] When this agent is given, the coronary sinus oxygen concentration increases significantly, suggesting that perfusion of the myocardium may increase excessively without improving delivery to areas of ischemia. Reports of its ability to produce collateral growth after long-term administration as well as the alteration in platelet adhesiveness may augur its clinical usefulness.

Because of its propensity to redistribute blood away from areas of ischemia, intravenous administration has been used to initiate ischemia. Usually 0.75 mgs per kg is administered intravenously in a ten minute period during electrocardiographic monitoring. S-T depression or anginal pain is a marker for ischemia as it is in exercise testing. Tavazzi and coworkers[70] in Italy found a 74 percent sensitivity in patients with angina on effort, but there were no positive responders in those with angina at rest. Dipyridamole produced a positive test in 74 percent of those with an abnormal exercise test. None of their normal subjects had a positive test. Thus, it provides a low sensitivity and possibly higher specificity in exercise testing. Apparently, when given orally, it fails to alter the S-T segments or the response to exercise significantly.

BETA BLOCKERS

Although there were some who denied the obvious benefits of beta blockers on the angina syndrome,[71] many clinicians began to use them to treat their patients with coronary disease soon after the drug became available.

MECHANISMS OF BETA BLOCKADE

It is now well established that propranolol and beta blockers act by the following mechanisms:

1. Decrease in contractility. This is apparently due to its ability to isolate the beta receptors from the intrinsic catecholamines present in the circulation by reducing the metabolic demands associated with this stimulating hormone.
2. Decrease in heart rate. When the number of contractions per minute decreases, the total energy per minute necessary to sustain contraction is not only less, but the longer diastole results in a better perfusion because of the known attenuating effect on coronary flow during systole. The ratio of the systolic pressure time interval (SPTI) to the diastolic pressure time interval (DPTI) is a very important parameter in the determination of the magnitude of coronary flow. The longer diastole is sustained, the better redistribution takes place through the subendocardial collateral channels between the normal and ischemic areas, as mentioned in the previous section on nitrites.[72]
3. Depression of arterial pressure. This is due primarily to a reduction in cardiac output, which is a function of both heart rate and ionotropism.
4. Change in myocardial intermediary metabolism. Evidence now suggests that oxidative catabolism is reduced and more glucose is used—a more efficient system.[73]
5. A shift in AV-O_2 dissociation curve. There are now reports that propranolol shifts the hemoglobin dissociation curve to the right, thus facilitating a better release of oxygen as it perfuses the coronary bed. This is due to a redistribution of 2,3-diphosphoglycerate in the red cell.[74]

It is now well established that these agents are very useful in the treatment of ischemia and a significant part of those presenting for exercise testing will be on a maintenance dose. Although it may limit the diagnostic value of the test somewhat, the practical approach is to test the patient while on the drug. The maximum heart rate will be decreased, but it has been reported it will not obscure ischemic S-T depression in patients with epicardial coronary narrowing.

Not all the effects of propranolol are beneficial, however. It increases the systolic ejection period, probably due to the reduction in velocity of ejection, increases the left-ventricular end-diastolic pressure, and causes some cardiac dilatation. Beta blockers also result in a higher plasma epinephrine in exercising subjects as compared with those who are not blocked.[75] This is thought to be stimulated by the lower cardiac output and heart rate in exercising subjects, and may be the cause for the higher peripheral resistance, probably due to the effect of the epinephrine on the alpha receptors. While all these factors increase myocardial oxygen uptake, they fail in most patients to outweigh the benefits, so that on balance, patients with coronary disease do better during exercise with propranolol. Thus, a higher workload can be achieved with an equivalent heart rate or double product after propranolol has been administered.[75,76]

Many subjects not only exercise longer on the treadmill after having taken propranolol, but also have less S-T segment depression and less angina. It is our feeling that one can predict this event fairly well by knowing something about the patient's general cardiac function. Those with a large fibrotic left ventricle and a slow resting pulse are not usually benefited. On the other hand, if they smoke, have a high resting pulse, and have never had an infarction, they are likely to be improved by this agent.

CALCIUM BLOCKERS

The mechanism of the antianginal effect of calcium blockers has been widely documented. The ability of these agents to reduce peripheral resistance, and in many cases heart rate provides us with obvious examples and the reasons for the salutory effects. The inhibition of the transmembrane calcium transport may not only have a peripheral effect, but may also have a primary effect on the heart itself. This is due in part to its ability to dilate the epicardial coronary arteries, especially in the areas adjacent to stenotic segments, but also to the overall increase in flow to the capillary bed. This is probably due to its effect on the precapillary sphincters. The inhibition of calcium overloading in ischemic myocardial muscle cells is possibly also important. When performing exercise tests in patients who are on calcium blockers, as would be expected, ischemia may come on at higher workloads and systolic blood pressure and heart rate may be decreased for a given level of exercise. If exercise is terminated by angina, work tolerance may also be increased by these drugs.

The commonly used drugs now available in the United States provide a range of action. Verapamil has the most profound direct cardiac effect with a lesser degree of action in the peripheral vasculature, while nifedipine has the least cardiac effect and the most profound in the peripheral circulation. Diltiazem has some of both and is intermediate between the two. These drugs have been demonstrated to delay the time of onset of S-T depression; however, if the blood pressure drop is excessive, as may occur in some patients with nifedipine,[77] the reduced diastolic pressure may decrease myocardial perfusion and reduce exercise tolerance.[78]

AMIODARONE

This agent, a benzfuran derivative was introduced as an antianginal agent in 1967, because of its depressant effect on sinus node function. It has emerged as a potent antiarrhythmic agent, especially for malignant ventricular tachycardia. A study by Rod and Shenasa[79] in Milwaukee found that it suppresses resting heart rate an average of 15 beats per minute and maximal exercise heart rate an average of 20 beats per minute. The systolic blood pressure at each heart rate prior to administration of the drug was the same as during the drug therapy, as was the functional capacity expressed in METS.

The mechanism of heart rate suppression has been studied by Touboul and colleagues[80] and others.[81] They believe an increase in action potential duration, a prolongation in sinus node recovery time along with a normal sinus mode conduction time explains the findings. This drug, then, differs from beta blockers in that resting and exercise blood pressures are not reduced.

ATROPINE

Atropine, which increases the heart rate in most patients, would be expected to make S-T segment changes more likely during exercise because of the increased metabolic demands associated with more contractions per minute. In fact, this rarely occurs. Apparently, this is because the patient's catecholamines normally play an important role in the increase in heart rate and the enhancement of ventricular contractility during exercise. These catecholamine changes override those due to the atropine. The loss of the patient's ability to sweat after administration of atropine has a definite effect on heat elimination, however, and if exercise lasts very long, a definite decrease in exercise capacity will occur.

PROPRANOLOL AND ATROPINE

Jose and Taylor,[82] in their studies on intrinsic heart rate, proposed the administration of propranolol and atropine to obtain a medically denervated heart. The resultant resting heart rate seemed to correlate well with the contractility of the left ventricle. They termed this the "intrinsic heart rate." Figure 22-2 illustrates the pulse response on our treadmill protocol before and after a

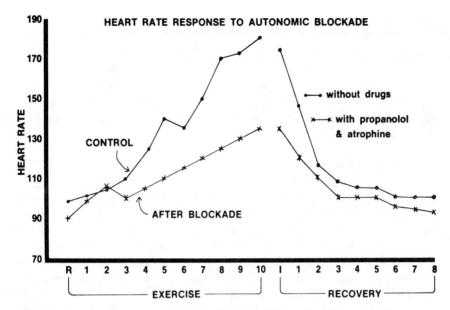

FIGURE 22-2. The heart rate response to a stress test before and after autonomic blockade by propranolol and atropine illustrates the magnitude of the catecholamine effect on heart rate during exercise.

blocking dose of these two agents was given intravenously. It can be seen that the exercise heart rate is considerably lower at the upper end of the scale when the patient's intrinsic catecholamines are major factor in acceleration. As would be expected, these pharmacologic agents decrease the exercise capacity somewhat, as well as the heart rate.

CATECHOLAMINES

The effect of the catecholamines on the heart has been studied extensively.[83-85] Their well-known stimulatory effect on contractility, heart rate, and myocardial oxygen uptake would suggest that they should be avoided by most subjects with suspected coronary disease, and thus rarely present a problem in stress testing. In fact, one of the most common habits of coronary patients is smoking, which stimulates an increase in catechols,[86] as well as decreasing the oxygen-carrying capacity to a variable degree depending on the concentration of carbon monoxide fixed in the red cells. Cryer and colleagues[86] have shown a marked increase in both norepinephrine and epinephrine and the expected secondary hemodynamic changes associated with smoking two nonfiltered cigarettes. Aronow[87] has reported that S-T segment depression occurs at a low workload after smoking. We have urged patients to abstain from smoking for several hours prior to an exercise test; abstinence will also help minimize arrhythmias associated with exercise.

AMPHETAMINES

Another family of agents in common usage, which may produce all the familiar changes associated with catecholamine ingestion, are the amphetamines. Not only will they cause the expected acute manifestations of these agents, but also they will produce a chronic cardiomyopathy,[88] which might well be predicted in view of the well-known experimental cardiomyopathies associated with isoproterenol.[89]

ISOPROTERENOL

Because he wanted to produce a higher incidence of positive stress tests, Gubner[90] administered sublingual Isuprel prior to the Master's test. Surawicz and Sata[85] have studied the effects of catecholamines extensively and have reported that in subjects with inverted T-waves, intravenous administration of isoproterenol will correct the inversion in a high percentage of subjects with normal hearts and also in some heart disease. We have found that exercise often results in the normalization of inverted T-waves because of the catecholamine effect that normally comes with strenuous exercise. We have not used catecholamines to add an additional stimulus to stress testing because of our standard practice of using a maximal test. In Gubner's[90] case, he was using a Master's test, which is often far from maximum, and there is no evidence at this point to determine whether or not the use of an extra catecholamine stimulus might correct some of the so-called false negatives.

PSYCHOTROPIC DRUGS

Tricyclic Antidepressants

Thirty million prescriptions are written in the United States each year for tricyclic antidepressants.[91] The Aberdeen General Hospital Group[92] studied the cardiovascular effects in 119 cardiac patients and found that 2.2 percent of the patients on the wards were on one or more of these antidepressant compounds, and that the mortality in forty months was 19 percent in treated patients as opposed to 12 percent in matched controls for age, sex, and cardiac diagnosis. The heart rate is higher and the T-waves are lower with these drugs, and S-T depression is common. The P-R interval is prolonged as is the H-V interval when His-bundle recordings are performed. The QTC and QRS are increased as well in 15 percent of the patients, and a Mobitz Type 2 atrioventricular (AV) block is not uncommon. Vohra and colleagues[93] report an excellent correlation between the degree of prolongation of the QRS and the plasma concentration of the tricyclic antidepressants (TCA). There is good evidence that in subjects with bundle branch block a lower dose will bring about a complete AV block as compared with those with normal conduction.[94,95] Kantor and associates[94] and Bigger and colleagues[96] have reported that arrhythmias are very rare, and there is a growing body of evidence that these agents have some antiarrhythmic properties. In fact, the pharmacologic properties are strikingly similar to those of quinidine. Muller and Burckhard[97] evaluated left-ventricular function with systolic time intervals and found a prolongation of the pre-ejection period and a decrease in the PEP/VET ratio as well as a decrease in velocity of fiber shortening by echocardiography. The same finding has also been reported in rats by Thorstrand and coworkers.[98] These data and the reported cases of hypotension clearly point to a depression of left-ventricular function.

Although there have been no reports of exercise-induced S-T depression due to these drugs, they are in such common usage that it becomes important to be aware of their suppressive effect on the left-ventricular function and their tendency to produce both hypotension and increasing degrees of heart block. Caution would be the watchword if called upon to do stress testing in a patient on this type of medication.[99]

Lithium

Like the tricyclics, lithium has become a very popular agent especially for the treatment of depression. Its metabolic and cardiovascular implications are well documented. By interfering with the hormones mediated through cyclic AMP it can cause:[100]
1. Diabetes insipidus.
2. Hypothyroidism and goiters.
3. Hypoglycemia-like symptoms.
4. Replacement of intracellular potassium from the myocardium.
5. Inhibition of the chronotropic effects of epinephrine.
6. T-wave inversion.
7. Conduction defects, that is, sinus mode dysfunction with prolonged sinus recovery time.[101]
8. Ventricular arrhythmias.[102]

In spite of all these changes, when Tilkian and colleagues[102] reported on 10 patients who underwent stress testing before and after a full therapeutic dose of lithium, they found no decrease in exercise tolerance and no S-T segment depression associated with this drug. Some years ago, we tested a patient on lithium who developed S-T depression and had a normal response after the drug was withdrawn. Although T-wave inversion or flattening is common, it would seem at this juncture that S-T changes caused by this agent are relatively rare, although a systematic evaluation, using blood levels to measure the dosage, is yet to be done.

Phenothiazines

The pharmacologic responses are complex owing to both a direct effect on the heart and blood vessels and an indirect effect due to secondary central nervous system changes with the resultant autonomic alterations. The following responses have been reported:
1. A direct depressant effect on cardiac muscle.[103]
2. A reduction in the rate of rise of Phase zero of the transmembrane action potential.
3. Decrease in the duration of Phases two and three of the actual potential.
4. Antiarrhythmic properties similar to quinidine.[92]
5. The above results in prolongation of the R-R and Q-T intervals, decreased amplitude, and prolongation of the QRS, and it may at times cause S-T depression.[104] On the other hand, Linhart and Turnoff[105] have reported that a false-negative test was found in 5 of 13 subjects on these drugs and claimed this was due to the quinidine-like action.
6. Hypotension caused by both the alpha blockade and the direct effect on the smooth muscle of the vasculature,[106] as well as a reduction in cardiac output.

Although in small doses these agents have antiarrhythmic properties, the toxic doses have been reported to cause ventricular ectopic beats, ventricular tachycardia, and ventricular fibrillation,[107] atrial fibrillation, complete heart block, and sudden death.[108]

Diazepam (Valium)

There are few psychotropic drugs that enjoy the popularity of diazepam. It has been claimed that 2.5 billion 5 mg tablets were sold in the United States in 1977.[109] It is also very popular in hospitals as a quick sedative when given intravenously. The cardiovascular effects are as follows:
1. Coronary vasodilation lasts at least thirty minutes.
2. Increase in left-ventricular contractility secondary to the above effect on coronary flow. When coronary flow is held constant in dogs, contractility is unchanged.
3. When injected directly into the coronary circulation, vasodilatation results, but when the systemic and coronary circulation are isolated in an experiment so that systemic blood cannot enter the cardiac circulation, diazepam does not alter coronary flow.
4. The coronary flow in patients with diseased coronary arteries is augmented two or three times as much as those with normal coronary anatomy.[110]
5. Aortic blood pressure is reduced slightly.
6. Heart rate and cardiac output are usually unchanged.[111]

7. Left-ventricular end-diastolic pressure is decreased suggesting dilatation of the capacitance vessels.[111]

Although the increase in coronary flow does not in itself establish it as useful in angina, the fact that it may often improve angina, result in a reduced left-ventricular end-diastolic pressure, and increase coronary flow more in patients with diseased coronary circulation, suggests that redistribution to the ischemic area, as with nitrites, is very likely. This information then tells us that diazepam should be withheld prior to stress testing if the true picture of cardiovascular dynamics is to be documented. Although we know of no specific tests demonstrating an alteration in ischemic changes, it seems likely that it has the capacity to do so.

ANTIHYPERTENSIVE AGENTS

Because hypertension is commonly seen in coronary patients and because these subjects are often under treatment when they come in for testing, a knowledge of the alterations to be expected with the various agents is important. Although physicians soon become familiar with the patterns of blood pressure alterations at rest in the supine and upright postures, they rarely consider the changes with exercise, which are probably equally as important.

DIURETICS

Lund-Johansen[112] studied polythiazide, hydrochlorothiazide, and chlorthalidone at rest and during exercise when the patients were on a usual maintenance dose. The heart rate was not altered during exercise by these agents as compared with controls. The thiazides caused a reduction in exercise blood pressure and peripheral resistance and a 7 percent reduction in plasma volume. The cardiac output, however, was not altered. The peripheral resistance was reduced 12 percent at rest, but only 7 percent at peak exercise. This was also reflected in a less dramatic decrease in blood pressure during exercise.

The chlorthalidone patients, however, failed to show a drop in peripheral resistance, their decrease in blood pressure resulted from a decrease in cardiac output. The reason for the difference in mechanisms could not be determined. Ogilvie[113] found that exercise hypotension increased with dosage up to 100 mg per day with chlorthalidone, after this the hypotensive effect began to be lost, and at 200 mg per day there was a paradoxic increase in diastolic blood pressure and heart rate. Thus, in this drug at least, there seems to be an optimum dose after which the exercise effects are lost.

These agents all may induce S-T segment depression of a moderate degree if hypokalemia becomes significant.

METHYLDOPA (ALDOMET)

This agent, along with guanethidine, reserpine, and clonidine, causes a reduction in heart rate during exercise but, unlike the others, there is no change observed at rest. The primary hypotensive effect is due to a decrease in peripheral resistance with no change in cardiac output. The decrease in resistance and in heart rate actually is associated with an increase in the stroke volume during exercise, as compared with the control patients. In some subjects studied by Sannerstedt and coworkers,[114] the resting blood pressure did not change even though a significant drop was seen at peak exercise. Methyldopa, along with clonidine and the beta blockers, suppresses renin release, which may increase the amount of exercise-induced hyperkalemia usually seen; thus, these drugs should be used carefully when exercise is contemplated in patients with a precarious potassium balance.[115]

CLONIDINE

This agent, which is generically related to pentolamine and tolazoline, has been used successfully in hypertension and seems to be gaining in popularity. There is a moderate decrease in both systemic resistance and cardiac output, thus resulting in a drop in pressure at all workloads as well as at rest.[116] Circulatory function seems to be well maintained, probably because the decrease in venous tone in the legs at rest seems to be compensated by an increase in resistance in the upper extremities during exercise. It seems that the circulatory dynamics are somewhat better during exercise with this agent than either methyldopa or guanethidine.

When stress testing is planned, the above effects of antihypertensive agents must be kept in mind. At this time, the cumulative effects of a number of drugs are not yet reported. It seems almost certain that the response will vary according to whether the pressure is fixed or labile, and will be especially dependent on the degree of ischemia or myocardial dysfunction if present.

GUANETHIDINE

This agent can be considered to be classic for the sympathetic blockers that are used to treat hypertension. It is usually only used in severe cases in conjunction with diuretics and/or beta blockers. Studies to evaluate the degree of peripheral vasoconstriction show a sharp drop in vasomotor tone when this drug is administered. There is not only a decrease in vasoconstriction in terms of the arterial circulation, but also an increase in volume in the legs owing to venous relaxation. Khatri and Cohn[117] believe that all patients on this agent should be exercised for better determination of the degree of potential hypotensive response because of the marked tendency for postural changes to be masked until exercise is used to demonstrate their presence. As might be expected with this agent, the cardiac output drops considerably in the upright position owing to distal dependent pooling; however, with exercise, the decrease in peripheral resistance allows the cardiac output to rise more rapidly than would occur with a higher afterload. Because this agent produces a rather marked decrease in heart rate, the stroke output increases during exercise and the decrease in cardiac filling results in an increased contractile velocity and greater DP/DT. No S-T changes have been reported with methyldopa, clonidine, or guanethidine.

VASODILATORS

These agents are playing an increasing role in antihypertensive therapy. Hydralazine, the earlier agent, is now joined by prazosin and minoxidil.

Exercise can be augmented by the decrease in peripheral resistance, which causes some increase in heart rate with hydrolazine, however. There is less of an increase in heart rate with prazosin and minoxidil.[118] This may explain the likelihood of excessive blood pressure drops with starting doses of these agents. All three may improve exercise tolerance, especially if left-ventricular function is very limited.[119]

ANGIOTENSIN-CONVERTING ENZYME INHIBITORS

Captopril is the most commonly used agent in this category. Although Pickering and coworkers[120] reported no change in exercise blood pressure, more recent studies all seem to find a drop in both systolic and diastolic pressures with exercise in this agent as well as with sarolosin.[121,122] Little change in heart rate occurs, however.

ALCOHOL

Alcohol will reduce cardiac output when taken in excessive amounts by normal persons, but after only 3 to 4 ounces in patients with significant coronary heart disease. If a subject has a normal heart, the acute effect of alcohol on coordination will be more evident than electrocardiographic changes associated with exercise. On the other hand, if there is underlying heart disease due to hypertension or coronary narrowing, alcohol will reduce the cardiac output and, therefore, the exercise capacity of the patient. Subjects with alcoholic cardiomyopathy may have S-T segment depression or may develop left bundle branch block with exercise as their ventricular filling pressure increases. Experimental studies on the isolated rat atrium have shown an almost linear decrease in contractility as the concentration of alcohol rises at levels commonly seen in human alcoholics.[123] The exact influence on the heart may be due to alcohol's effect on membrane permeability.[1] Thus, one should expect to see repolarization abnormalities if alcoholic myocardiopathy is present or if the subject has recently ingested large amounts of alcohol, even if no underlying heart disease is recognized.

REFERENCES

1. SIMONSON, E: *Physiology of Work Capacity and Fatigue.* Charles C Thomas, Springfield, Illinois, 1971.
2. GANONG, WF: *Review of Medical Physiology.* Lang Medical Publications, Los Altos, California, 1973.
3. CASE, RB, ET AL: *Relative effect of CO_2 on canine coronary vascular resistance.* Circ Res 42:410, 1978.
4. ISKANDRIAN, AS, ET AL: *Cardiac performance in thyrotoxicosis: Analysis of 10 untreated patients.* Am J Cardiol 51:349–352, 1983.
5. SHAFER. RB AND BIANCO, JA: *Assessment of cardiac reserve in patients with hypertension.* Chest 78:269–273, 1980.
6. FORFAR, PG, ET AL: *Abnormal left ventricular function in hyperthyroidism.* N Engl J Med 307:1165, 1982.
7. HYLANDER, B, EKELUND, LG, AND ROSENQVIST, U: *The cardiovascular response at rest and during exercise in hypothyroid subjects to thyroxine substitution.* Clin Cardiol 6:116–124, 1983.
8. JAMES, TN: *Pathology of small coronary arteries.* Am J Cardiol 20:679, 1967.
9. RUBLER, S: *Cardiac manifestations of diabetes mellitus.* Cardiovasc Med 2:823, 1977.
10. KANNEL, WB, HJORTLAND, M, AND CASTELLI, WP: *Role of diabetes in congestive heart failure.* Am J Cardiol 31:29, 1974.
11. PARKER, JP, ET AL: *Androgen-induced increase in red cell 2,3 diphosphoglycerate.* N Engl J Med 287:381, 1972.
12. NEELY, TF AND MORGAN, HE: *The relationship between carbohydrate and lipid metabolism and the energy balance of heart muscle.* Ann Rev Physiol 36:413, 1974.
13. RUBLER, S AND ARVAN, SB: *Exercise testing in young asymptomatic diabetes.* Angiology 27:539, 1976.
14. EWING, DJ, ET AL: *Vascular reflexes in diabetic autonomic neuropathy.* Lancet 2:1354, 1973.
15. BISHU, SK AND BERENZ, MR: *Circulatory reflex response in diabetic patients with and without neuropathy.* J Am Geriat Soc 19:159, 1971.
16. PERSSON G: *Exercise tests in male diabetics.* Acta Med Scand (Suppl) 605:7–23, 1977.
17. BELLET, S AND ROMAN, L: *The exercise test in diabetic patients as studied by radioelectrocardiography.* Circulation 36:245–254, 1967.
18. KARLEFORS, T: *Exercise tests in male diabetics.* Acta Med Scand (Suppl) 449:19–43, 1966.
19. RILEY, GP, OBERMAN, A, AND SCHEFFIELD, LT: *ECG effects of glucose ingestion.* Arch Intern Med 130:703, 1972.
20. ELLESTAD, MH AND HALLEDAY, WK: *Stress testing in the prognosis and management of ischemic heart disease.* Angiology 28:149, 1977.
21. SKETCH, MH, ET AL: *Significant sex differences in the correlation of electrocardiographic exercise testing and coronary arteriograms.* Am J Cardiol 36:196, 1976.
22. PINTO, RM, ET AL: *Action of estradiol upon uterine contractility.* Am J Obstet Gynecol 90:99, 1964.
23. ENGEL, HJ, HUNDESHAGEN, H, AND LICHTLEN, P: *Transmural myocardial infarction in young women taking oral contraceptives.* Br Heart J 39:477–484, 1977.

24. Coronary Drug Project Research Group. JAMA 214:1030, 1970.
25. BLACKARD, CE, ET AL: *Incidence of cardiovascular disease and death in patients receiving diethylstilbestrol for carcinoma of the prostrate.* Cancer 26:249, 1970.
26. JAFFE, MD: *Effect of oestrogens on post-exercise electrocardiogram.* Br Heart J 38:1299, 1977.
27. JAFFE, MD: *Effect of testosterone cypionate on post exercise ST segment depression.* Br Heart J 39:1217, 1977.
28. MURAD, F AND GILMAN, AG: *Androgens and anabolic steroids.* In GOODMAN, LS AND GILMAN, AG (EDS): *The Pharmacological Basis of Therapeutics,* ed 5. MacMillan, New York, 1970, p 1451.
29. SHAHIDI, NT: *Androgens and erythropoiesis.* N Engl J Med 289:72, 1973.
30. GREENBERG, S, HEITZ, DA, AND LONG, JP: *Testosterone-induced depression of adrenergic activity in the perfused canine hindlimb.* Proc Soc Exp Biol Med 142:883, 1973.
31. HOLMA, P: *Effect of an anabolic steroid (metandienone) on central and peripheral blood flow in well-trained athletes.* Ann Clin Res 9:215, 1977.
32. GROSS, GJ, ET AL: *The effect of ouabain on nutritional circulation and regional myocardial blood flow.* Am Heart J 93:487, 1977.
33. VOGEL, R, ET AL: *Effects of digitalis on resting and isometric exercise myocardial perfusion in patients with coronary artery disease and left ventricular dysfunction.* Circulation 56:355, 1977.
34. GLANCY, DL ET AL: *Effects of ouabain on the left ventricular response to exercise in patients with angina pectoris.* Circulation 43:45, 1971.
35. MASON, DT, AND BRAUNWALD, E: *Studies on digitalis. X. Effect of ouabain on forearm vascular resistance and venous tone in normal subjects and patients in heart failure.* J Clin Invest 43:532, 1964.
36. ROSS, J, JR, WALDHAUSEN, JA, AND BRANWALD, E: *Studies on digitalis. 1. Direct effects on peripheral vascular resistance.* J Clin Invest 39:930, 1960.
37. RUDOLPH, AM AND HEYMAN, MA: *The circulation of the fetus in utero, methods for studying distribution of blood flow, cardiac output, and organ blood flow.* Circ Res 21:163, 1967.
38. GAMBLE, WJ, ET AL: *Regional coronary venous oxygen saturation and myocardial oxygen tension following abrupt changes in ventricular pressure in the isolated dog heart.* Circ Res 34:672, 1974.
39. KAWAI, C AND HULTGREN, HN: *The effect of digitalis upon the exercise electrocardiogram.* Am Heart J 80:409, 1964.
40. KATZ, AM: *Physiology of the Heart.* Raven Press, New York, 1977, p 189.
41. LEWINTER, MM, ET AL: *The effects of oral propranolol, digoxin, and combination therapy on the resting and exercise electrocardiogram.* Am Heart J 93:202, 1977.
42. GOLDBARG, AN: *The effects of pharmacological agents on human performance.* In NAUGHTON, J, HELLERSTEIN, HK, AND MOHLER, IC (EDS): *Exercise Testing and Exercise Training in Coronary Heart Disease.* Academic Press, New York, 1973.
43. TONKON, MJ, ET AL: *Effects of digitalis on the exercise electrocardiogram in normal adult subjects.* Chest 72:714, 1977.
44. DEGRE, S, ET AL: *Analysis of exercise induced R wave amplitude changes in detection of coronary artery disease in patients on digitalis.* Cardiology (Suppl 2) 68:178–185, 1981.
45. DAVIDSON, DM AND HAGAN, AD: *Role of exercise stress testing in assessing digoxin dosage in chronic atrial fibrillation.* Cardiovascu Med, June: 671–678, 1979.
46. GEY, GO, ET AL: *Quinidine plasma concentration and exertional arrhythmia.* Am Heart J 90:19, 1975.
47. GEY, GO, ET AL: *Plasma concentration of procainamide and prevalence of exertional arrhythmias.* Ann Intern Med 80:718, 1974.
48. FLUSTER, PE, ET AL: *Effect of quinidine in the heart rate and blood pressure response to exercise.* Am Heart J 104:1244–1247, 1982.

49. SURAWICZ, B AND LASSETER, KC: *Effects of drugs on the electrocardiogram.* Prog Cardiovasc Dis 13:26, 1970.
50. SURAWICZ, B AND SAITO, S: *Exercise testing for detection of myocardial ischemia in patients with abnormal electrocardiograms at rest.* Am J Cardiol 41:943, 1978.
51. FREEDBERG, AS, RISEMAN, JEF, AND SPIEGEL, ED: *Objective evidence of the efficiency of medical therapy in angina pectoris.* Am Heart J 22:494, 1941.
52. SIMOONS, ML AND BALAKUMARAN, K: *The effects of drugs on the exercise electrocardiogram.* Cardiol (Suppl 2) 68:124–132, 1981.
53. KOBINGER, W, LILLIE, C, AND PICHLER, L: *N-allyl-derivative of Clonidine, a substance with specific bradycardiac action at a cardiac site.* Arch Pharmacol 306:255–262, 1979.
54. FAM, WM AND MCGREGOR, M: *The effect of coronary vasodilator drugs on retrograde flow in areas of chronic myocardial ischemia.* Circ Res 15:355, 1964.
55. MASON, DR AND BRAUNWALD, E: *The effects of nitroglycerin and amylnitrite on arteriolar and venous tone in the human forearm.* Circulation 32:755, 1965.
56. FULTON, WF: *The coronary arteries.* Charles C Thomas, Springfield, Illinois, 1965.
57. MCGREGOR, M: *Drugs for the treatment of angina pectoris.* In LASAGNA, L (ED): *International Encyclopedia of Pharmacology and Therapeutics,* Sec. 6, Vol. 11. Clinical Pharmacology. Pergamon Press, Oxford, 1966, p 377.
58. VINEBERG, AM, ET AL: *The effect of Persantin on intercoronary collateral circulation and survival during gradual experimental coronary occlusion: A preliminary report.* Can Med Assoc J 87:336, 1962.
59. MAUTZ, FR AND GREGG, DE: *The dynamics of collateral circulation following chronic occlusion of coronary arteries.* Proc Soc Exp Biol 36:797, 1937.
60. GANZ, WM AND MARCUS, HS: *Failure of intracoronary nitroglycerin to alleviate pacing-induced angina.* Circulation 46:880, 1972.
61. ESSEX, HE, ET AL: *The effect of certain drugs on the coronary blood flow of the trained dog.* Am Heart J 19:554, 1940.
62. ROSS, RS, ET AL: *The effect of nitroglycerin on the coronary circulation studied by cineangiography and xenon[133] myocardial blood flow measurements.* Trans Am Clin Climatol Assoc 76:70, 1964.
63. NICKERSON, M: *Vasodilator drugs.* In GOODMAN, LS AND GILMAN, A (EDS): *The Pharmacology Basis of Therapeutics,* ed 5. MacMillan, New York, 1970, p 736.
64. RISEMAN, JEF, KORETSKY, S, AND ALTMAN, GE: *Stereo-isometric nitrates in the treatment of angina pectoris.* Am J Cardiol 15:220, 1965.
65. GOLDSTEIN, RE, ET AL: *Clinical and circulatory effects of isosorbide dinitrate, comparison with nitroglycerin.* Circulation 43:629, 1971.
66. RUSSEK, HI AND FUNK, EH, JR: *Comparative responses to various nitrates in the treatment of angina pectoris.* Postgrad Med 31:150, 1962.
67. COLE, SL, KAYE, H, AND GRIFFITH, GC: *Assay of anti-anginal agents: I.A. curve analysis with multiple control periods.* Circulation 15:405, 1957.
68. CHARLIER, R: *Coronary Vasodilators.* Pergamon Press, New York, 1961.
69. GREGG, DE: *Physiology of the coronary circulation.* Circulation 27:1128, 1963.
70. TOVAZZI, L, ET AL: *Prognostic value of exercise hemodynamics after myocardial infarctions.* Cardiology (Suppl 2) 68:53–66, 1981.
71. ARONOW, WS AND KAPLAN, MA: *Propranolol combined with isosorbide dinitrate versus placebo in angina pectoris.* N Engl J Med 280:847, 1969.
72. MOIR, TW *Subendocardial distribution of coronary blood flow and the effect of anti-anginal drugs.* Circ Res 30:621, 1972.
73. EPSTEIN, SE AND BRAUNWALD, E: *Beta andrenergic receptor blocking drugs: Mechanisms of action and clinical application.* N Engl J Med 275:1106, 1966.
74. OSKI, FA, ET AL: *Oxygen affinity in red cells: Changes induced in vivo by propranolol.* Science 175:1372, 1972.
75. IRVING, MH, ET AL: *Effect of beta adrenergic blockade on plasma catecholamines in exercise.* Nature 248:531, 1974.

76. JORGENSEN, CT, ET AL: *Effect of propranolol on myocardial oxygen consumption and its hemodynamic correlates during upright exercise.* Circulation 68:1173, 1973.

77. DEPONTI, C, ET AL: *Effects of nifedipine, acebutolol, and their association on exercise tolerance in patients with effort angina.* Cardiology (Suppl 2) 68:195–199, 1981.

78. FOX, KM, ET AL: *The dose-response effects of nifedipine of ST segment changes in exercise testing: Preliminary studies.* Cardiology (Suppl 2) 68:209–212, 1981.

79. ROD, JL AND SHENASA, M: *Functional significance of chronotropic response during chronic amiodarone therapy.* Cardiology 71:40–47, 1984.

80. TOUBOUL, P, ET AL: *Effects of amiodarone on sinus node in man.* Br Heart J 42:573–578, 1979.

81. MELMED, S, ET AL: *Hyperthyroxinemia with bradycardia and normal thyrotropin secretion after chronic amiodarone administration.* J Clin Endocrinol Metab 53:997–1001, 1981.

82. JOSE, AD AND TAYLOR, RR: *Autonomic blockade by propranolol and atropine to study intrinsic myocardial function in man.* J Clin Invest 48:2109, 1969.

83. DAOUD, FS, SURAWICZ, B, AND GETTES, LS: *Effect of isoproterenol on the abnormal T wave.* Am J Cardiol 30:810, 1972.

84. SANO, T, SUZUKI, F, AND SATO, S: *Mechanism of inotropic action of catecholamines and ouabain in cardiac muscle in relation to changes in action potential.* Jpn Heart J 11:269, 1970.

85. SURAWICZ, B AND SATO, S: *Exercise testing for detection of myocardial ischemia in patients with abnormal electrocardiograms at rest.* Am J Cardiol 41:943, 1978.

86. CRYER, PE, ET AL: *Smoking, catecholamines and coronary heart disease.* Cardiol Med 23:471, 1977.

87. ARONOW, ES: *The effect of smoking cigarettes on the apexcardiograms in coronary heart disease.* Chest 59:365, 1971.

88. SMITH, RR, ET AL: *Cardiomyopathy associated with amphetamine administration.* Am Heart J 91:792, 1976.

89. KOHN, DE, RONA, G, AND CHAPPEL, CT: *Isoproterenol-induced cardiac necrosis.* Ann NY Acad Sci 156:286, 1969.

90. GUBNER, RS: *Newer developments in exercise electrocardiography and evaluation of chest pain.* Trans Assoc Life Ins Med Dir Am 52:125, 1969.

91. BISHNU, SK AND BERENZ, MR: *Circulatory reflex response in diabetic patients with and without neuropahy.* J Am Geriat Soc 19:159, 1971.

92. BASSETT, AL AND HOFFMAN, BF: *Antiarrhythmic drugs, electrophysiological actions.* Ann Rev Pharmacol 11:143, 1971.

93. VOHRA, J, BURROWS, GD AND SLOMAN, F: *Assessment of CV side effects of therapeutic doses of tri-cyclic antidepressant drugs.* Austr NZ J Med 5:7, 1975.

94. KANTOR, SJ, ET AL: *Imipramine-induced heart block, a longitudinal case study.* JAMA 231:1364, 1975.

95. SMITH, RR AND RUSBATCH, BJ: *Amitriptyline and the heart.* Br Heart J 3:311, 1967.

96. BIGGER, JT, JR, ET AL: *Cardiac antiarrhythmic effect of imipramine hydrochloride.* N Engl J Med 287:206, 1977.

97. MULLER, V AND BURCKHARD, D: *Die wirkung tri-und tetrazyklischer antidepressiva auf Herz und Kreislauf.* Schweiz Med Wschr 104:1911, 1974.

98. THORSTRAND, J, BERGSTROM, R AND CASTENFORS, J: *Cardiac effects of amitriptyline in rats.* Scand J Clin Lab Invest 36:7, 1976.

99. SURAWICZ, B AND SATO, S: *Exercise testing for detection of myocardial ischemia in patients with abnormal electrocardiogram at rest.* Am J Cardiol 41:943, 1978.

100. SINGER, L AND ROTENBERG, D: *Mechanisms of lithium action.* N Engl J Med 289:254, 1973.

101. WELLENS, HJ, CATS, VM AND DUREN, DR: *Symptomatic sinus node abnormalities following lithium carbonate therapy.* Am J Med 59:285, 1975.

102. TILKIAN, AG, ET AL: *Effect of lithium on cardiovascular performance: Report on extended ambulatory monitoring and exercise testing before and during lithium therapy.* Am J Cardiol 38:701, 1976.

METABOLIC ABNORMALITIES AND DRUGS

103. JARVIK, ME: *Drugs in the treatment of psychiatric disorders.* In GOODMAN, LS AND GILMAN, A (EDS): *The Pharmacological Basis of Therapeutics,* ed 5. MacMillan, New York, 1970.

104. CRANE, GE: *Cardiac toxicity and psychotropic drugs.* Dis Nerve Syst 31:534, 1970.

105. LINHART, JW AND TURNOFF, HB: *Maximum treadmill exercise tests in patients with abnormal central electrocardiograms.* Circulation 49:667, 1974.

106. FOWLER, NO, ET AL: *Electrocardiographic changes and cardiac arrhythmias in patients receiving psychotropic drugs.* Am J Cardiol 37:223, 1976.

107. GILES, TD AND MODLIN, RK: *Death associated with ventricular arrhythmias and thioridazine hydrochloride.* JAMA 205:180, 1968.

108. HOLLISTER, LE AND KOSEK, JC: *Sudden death during treatment with phenothiazine derivatives.* JAMA 192:1035, 1965.

109. ROCHE SALES REPRESENTATIVE: Personal communication, 1978.

110. IKRAM, H, RUBIN, AP AND JEWKES, RJ: *Effect of diazepam on myocardial blood flow of patients with and without coronary artery disease.* Br Heart J 35:626, 1973.

111. COTE, P, CAMPEAU, L AND BOURASSA, MG: *Therapeutic implications of diazepam in patients with elevated left ventricular filling pressure.* Am Heart J 91:747, 1976.

112. LUND-JOHANSEN, P: *Hemodynamic changes in long term diuretic therapy of essential hypertension: A comparative study of chlorthalidone, polythiazide and hydrochlorothiazide.* Acta Med Scand 187:509, 1970.

113. OGILVIE, RI: *Cardiovascular response to exercise under increasing doses of chlorthalidone.* Eur J Clin Pharmacol 9:339, 1976.

114. SANNERSTEDT, E, VARNAUSKAS, E AND WERKO, L: *Hemodynamic effects of methyldopa (Aldomet) at rest and during exercise in patients with arterial hypertension.* Acta Med Scand 171:75, 1962.

115. LOWENTHAL, DT, ET AL: *Biochemical and pharmacodynamic responses to anti-renin, antihypertensives during exercise.* Ann Sports Med 1 (2):59–65, 1983.

116. MOIR, TW: *Subendocardial distribution of coronary blood flow and the effect of anti-anginal drugs.* Circ Res 30:621, 1972.

117. KHATRI, AM AND COHN, JN: *Mechanism of exercise hypotension after sympathetic blockade.* Am J Cardiol 27:329, 1970.

118. LUND-JOHANSEN, P: *Hemodynamic changes at rest and during exercise in long-term prazosin therapy for essential hypertension.* Proceedings of Postgraduate Medicine Symposium on Prazosin, New York, November 1975, p 45.

119. NELSON, GIC, DONNELLY, GL AND HUNYOR, SN: *Haemodynamic effects of sustained treatment with prazosin and metoprolol, alone and in combination, in borderline hypertensive heart failure.* J Cardiovasc Pharm 4:240–245, 1982.

120. PICKERING, TG, ET AL: *Comparison of antihypertensive and hormonal effects of captopril and propranolol at rest and during exercise.* Am J Cardiol 49:1566–1568, 1982.

121. MANHEM, P, ET AL: *The effect of captopril on catecholamines, renin activity, angiotensin II and aldosterone in plasma during physical exercise in hypertensive patients.* Eur J Clin Invest 11:389–395, 1981.

122. FAGARD, R, ET AL: *Effects of angiotensin antagonism on hemodynamics, renin and catecholamines during exercise.* J Appl Physiol 43:440–444, 1977.

123. GIMENO, AL, GIMENO, MF AND WEBB, JL: *Effects of ethanol on cellular membrane potentials and contractility of isolated rat atrium.* Am J Physiol 203:194, 1962.

23

COMPUTERS

At this time, there are numerous programs for analysis of the resting electrocardiogram that have become accepted as having a high degree of accuracy. The proliferation of devices offering this option for stress testing requires a general discussion of the method and a few comments about the hardware as well. As far as I know, the first effort to computerize the exercise electrocardiogram was an "off line" system developed by Gunner Blomqvist in 1965.[1] This was followed by investigative programs by other investigators.[2-6] These systems are now being followed by commercial devices because of the increased power and availability of microcomputers.

ADVANTAGES OF COMPUTER ANALYSIS

The resting electrocardiogram is an instantaneous cross section of the electrical behavior of the heart and can be acquired with a minimum of muscular artifact. Only a few complexes in a series of leads are necessary for study. The nature of the analysis necessary is ideal for computer processing and very accurate time and voltage measurements are easily acquired. Wave patterns can be stored or described mathematically and diagnostic probabilities calculated. The exercise electrocardiogram, however, requires that the time course of electrical behavior be analyzed and may require up to 2000 cardiac cycles to be recorded and analyzed.[7] Even with good electrodes and technique, considerable artifact at near maximal exercise is almost always present, which interferes with optimal wave form analysis. Thus, the computer must record the signals, determine the magnitude of myogenic and other high frequency artifacts and process this signal so as to minimize its effect. The noise level may be very high in relation to that found on a resting tracing, but also multiple samples must be acquired, stored, analyzed, and compared with the previous samples. Processing should be done in only a few seconds as decisions pertinent to the conduction of the test depend on the output.

The measurements during and after exercise, however, are relatively simple, being primarily concerned with the low frequency changes occurring during repolarization. Also useful are elapsed time, heart rate, and treadmill work capacity. The final comparison between the resting and exercise data requires a fairly powerful computer, because of the multiple acquisitions and need to compare one with the other.

Why should we use computers? As mentioned in Chapter 4, visual analysis of electrocardiographic changes vary widely from one physician to another, and are also different when the same person re-interprets the test on separate days. The repeatability of the computer measurements can be consistent within very narrow margins. The reduction of the exercise-induced artifact is probably one of the major benefits of this approach. One finds fairly frequently that a standard exercise electrocardiogram is almost uninterpretable by visual inspection. In spite of careful skin preparation and electrode application, this happens all too often. Computer averaging techniques can minimize an enormous amount of myogenic artifact and 60 cycle interference.

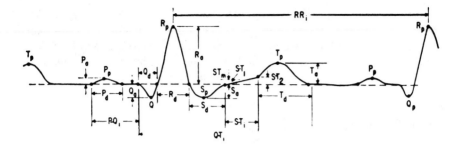

FIGURE 23-1. An electrocardiographic signal is analyzed by computer. The points illustrated here are identified as to the magnitude of the voltage change and as to their temporal occurrence by the diagnostic program. These measurements are then compared with those known to be related to normal and abnormal patients and an appropriate diagnostic impression is printed out. (From Caceres, CA, and Rikli, AE,[8] with permission.)

The high degree of accuracy inherent in the newer analog digital (A/D) converters makes it possible to make measurements impossible with the older methods. The A/D converter is actually a digital vote meter and may operate at 1000 times a second or greater in some cases, and can resolve voltage changes of 5 microvolts accurately and thus record 0.2 mms (equivalent to 20 microvolts) of S-T change with consistency (Fig. 23-1).

METHODS USED IN SIGNAL PROCESSING

Analog to Digital Conversion

As previously mentioned, this involves the repeated measurement of voltages in very rapid sequence with storage of these numbers in such a way that the linear array of voltages actually describes the electrocardiographic wave form. The frequency of the observations determines the details of the wave form acquired. The more frequently sampled, the more accurate the data. Some exercise programs sample at only 200 cycles per second, which is probably only accurate for very low frequency measurements, such as are found during the S-T segment and T-wave, but will miss details in areas where high frequency data may be found such as the Q-wave, peak of the R-wave, and occasionally the J-junction. A sampling rate of from 300 to 500 is preferred.

Signal Averaging

Consecutive beats are stored in memory and averaged, which reduces noise and derives a representative complex. The larger the sample size, the more smoothing occurs—however, if too many beats are included, important variations will be "averaged out." Some programs select a fixed number of beats; for example, 20. Others record for a fixed time frame; for example, 20 seconds. Thus, when the rate is fast and more subject to artifact, more beats will be included and thus better smoothing will occur.

Beat Recognition

In order that ectopic beats will not be included in the above averaging, the program must store normal complexes and when an atypical one occurs, for example, a PVC, it must be rejected so as not to distort the average normal complex. Most programs also count the number of abnormal beats and print this out for the record.

Wave Form Recognition

Various algorithms have been written to identify the important points on the electrocardiographic wave form. The most commonly measured voltage is the S-T segment. This may be arbitrarily sampled at a set time after the R-wave peak (80 milsec), which is fairly adequate unless a block pattern is present, which will distort the fiduciary point (the R peak), and result in a measurement in the wrong section of the S-T segment. If the rate is very fast, the delay time may be too great and miss the horizontal part of the S-T segment. A more satisfactory way is to identify the J-point using a more complex algorithm and measure the S-T segment at 60 or 80 milsec from this point. Sometimes the end of the QRS or J is calculated from changes in special velocity; usually a fairly reliable method.

ANALYSIS OF THE NORMAL EXERCISE ELECTROCARDIOGRAM

Computer analysis of the normal electrocardiogram has demonstrated that some of our assumptions about the S-T segment response during exercise may be in error. Bruce and associates,[2] as early as 1966, demonstrated that some degree of S-T depression with increasing workloads is a normal response. This was confirmed and augmented by Blomqvist and Mitchell[9] in the orthogonal leads, demonstrating the variations seen in each plane as exercise increased (Fig. 23-2). They have shown that the deviations from the isoelectric line are greater in the vertical (Y) and anteroposterior (Z) leads, and differ according to sex. Their data demonstrate that as exercise and heart rate increase, there is a progressive displacement of the S-T segment to the right, upward, and posteriorly. Fortunately, for those using a lead similar to V_5 or CM_5, deviations in the

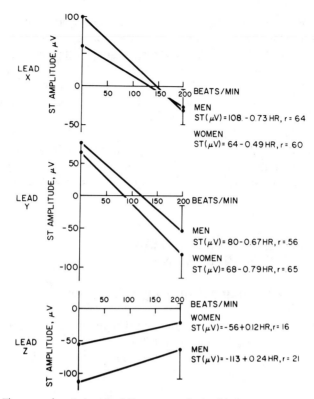

FIGURE 23-2. The normal variations in S-T segments obtained by computer analysis in the orthogonalleads. (From Blomqvist, CG and Mitchell, JH,[9] with permission.)

X or frontal lead are of lesser magnitude. Simoons[10] has confirmed Blomqvist's work and has proposed a heart rate correction when measuring the exercise-induced S-T depression. By applying this correction and analyzing S-T depression down to 0.01 millivolts by computer, he has been able to increase the sensitivity and specificity of the S-T determination significantly. He has also analyzed the use of converting the S-T segment to 6 Chebysliev polynomials and has not found this approach to be helpful. The computer was also used to analyze the polargraphic spatial coordinates of Dower,[11] without additional benefit. The approach used by these investigators is to capture the analog data on tape, digitize them, and use this material to correlate any number of variables with the angiographic data.

McHenry and colleagues[12] used a digital computer to plot the S-T segment from average signals as well as the magnitude of S-T segment depression. They believe that accurate identification of abnormal tracings is possible in this way. Dwortezky and coworkers[13] have applied Fourier analysis to the harmonic characteristics of the exercise ECG in an attempt to more clearly define changes related to exercise. They feel this method is useful, but have had too limited an experience to be convincing.

Wolf and associates[14] have employed a computer program that selects clusters of complexes and then finally a single representative complex, which is then analyzed. Noise is evaluated by the filtered spatial velocity and limits are set beyond which no diagnostic applications will be made. Klingeman's and Pipberger's[15] diagnostic program based on a modified multivariate analysis is then applied. A visual check of 10,473 ECGs, 6,275 resting, and 4,198 during exercise, disclosed a 2.6 percent error in estimation of S-T segment depression, usually because of excessive noise. However, the end of the T-wave was missed in only 0.7 percent and P-wave detection in 1.8 percent. These both constitute traditionally difficult elements in computer analysis. Although their program did not deal well with PVCs, they found it very satisfactory for S-T segment analysis.

MEASUREMENTS OTHER THAN CLASSIC S-T DISPLACEMENT

Division of Repolarization Into Subsegments

Blomqvist[16] divided the ST-T segment into eight equal subsegments. He found that measurement of the mid-point (ST-4 in Fig. 23-3a) was the most productive. Simoons and colleagues[18] divided the J, peak T similarly, again using a number of subdivisions.

S-T Index

McHenry and associates[3] introduced the S-T index, defined as the algebraic sum of the S-T amplitude in mms and the S-T slope in millivolt seconds, measured between 70 and 110 milliseconds after the R-wave peak (see Fig. 23-3b). The index is abnormal if it is less than zero (negative index) and normal if positive. They found the overall sensitivity of the index was 92 percent. In those with false-negatives, the disease was usually confined to the left circumflex or right coronary artery. Ninety-two percent of those with left-anterior descending disease had a negative index.

S-T Slope

The slope (see Fig. 23-3b) has also been used independently of the index and was believed originally to have a major impact, as those with a positive slope were believed to be normal.[19] At present, this concept has been discarded, but because slope is easy to measure is included in a number of the commercial computer programs.

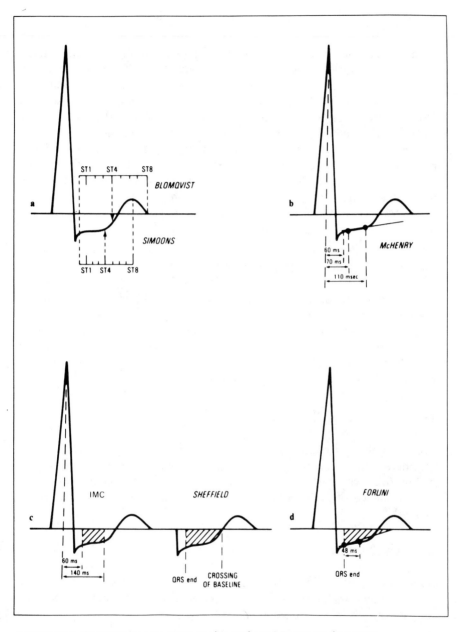

FIGURE 23-3. Computer measurements used to evaluate S-T segment depression.

    a) Blomqvist and Simoons divided parts of the S-T segment in equal units and measured depression at ST-4.

    b) McHenry calculated the S-T index by multiplying slope in mvs by magnitude of S-T depression.

    c) The IMC described by Sketch and Sheffield method of calculating the integral.

    d) Integral as calculated by Forlini. (From Savvides and Froelicher,[17] with permission.)

S-T Integral

Sheffield and coworkers[4] have measured the area from the QRS to the point where S-T segment crosses the baseline (see Fig. 23-3c). They found that normals had a maximal integral of minus 4.3 microvolt seconds (at 25 mms per second paper speed with a 1 cm calibration to 1 millivolt, a 1 mm squared block equals 4 microvolt seconds). They selected minus 7.5 microvolt seconds as the normal cut-off and found a sensitivity of 81 percent and a specificity of 95 percent. Sketch and colleagues,[20] using an integral between 60 and 140 miliseconds after the R peak and a normal cut-off of minus 6 microvolt seconds, reported a sensitivity of 71 percent during exercise, but only 54 percent immediately after exercise. The specificities were 73 and 96 percent respectively. More work still needs to be done in large populations to confirm the increased value of integral measurements.

Sum of S-T Amplitudes and Slope

Hollenberg and associates[21] have devised a score based on adding the sum of the S-T depression and slope from the beginning of exercise to the end of recovery in two leads and dividing the value by the duration of exercise in minutes. They found that patients with three-vessel or left-main disease could be distinguished from lesser disease as well as the fact that they could identify normals. The sensitivity was 85 percent and specificity was 91 percent.

Lead Strength Ratio

Correcting the magnitude of S-T depression for R-wave amplitude has been recommended.[22] Evidence has been proposed that the diagnostic accuracy can be improved with this calculation.[23] Also when R-wave amplitude is very low, the prevalence of false-negative exercise tests has been reported to be increased.[27]

R-Wave Amplitude

Although the value of this measurement is yet to be agreed upon, the computer simplifies the acquisition of data, especially if the R-wave changes in a number of leads are to be summed.

NONELECTROCARDIOGRAPHIC CALCULATIONS AND PRESENTATIONS

Estimate of VO₂max

A number of formulae are available that can derive a reasonable estimate of this value, especially if the patient exercises without hanging on to the handrail (see Chapters 7 and 9).

Estimate of Aerobic Capacity

This value popularized by Bruce and colleagues[25] which compares the exercise capacity of the subject to others of the same age and sex, can be easily calculated from the data collected by the computer.

Efficiency Index

This index, which is derived by dividing the estimated VO_2max by the double product, was introduced by the Aptecars and associates in Buenos Aires.[26] It provides an excellent way to record the ratio of the myocardial oxygen consumption to the body as a whole during exercise.

Treadmill Score

This number, in our laboratory, is derived by adding the magnitude of S-T

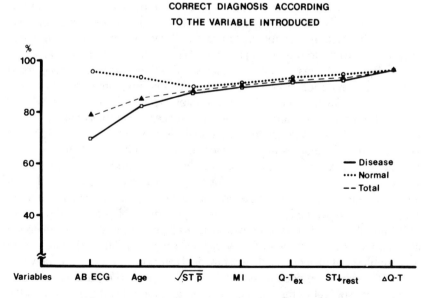

FIGURE 23-4. As the computer selects each variable for its discriminating power, it lists the percent correct diagnosis for subjects with disease, with no disease, and the total correct classification. The accuracy increases rapidly with the first three variables and then the improvement is less significant as additional variables are added.

depressions at each minute of exercise and recovery after multiplying by a factor adjusted for the workload and the persistence of S-T depression during the recovery period. The score has helped us discriminate between patients with mild and severe ischemia (see Fig. 9-7).

The score ranges from 0 to 180 and is calculated as illustrated in Figure 23-4. Patients with no disease or single-vessel disease usually score from 0 to 15, those with two-vessel disease in the range of 50, and above this usually characterizes severe ischemia. We have found this correlates with a new coronary score that quantitates myocardial ischemia much better than with the familiar one-, two-, or three-vessel designation.

Multivariate Analysis

Multivariate analysis is done by selecting a group of patients for analysis with known coronary artery anatomy, evaluated by angiography, and who have had treadmill testing.[27] Data are entered by selecting variables that we believe might have value in discriminating between those with and without disease. The computer performs a discriminate analysis by selecting the variables that best identify the groups under study. First, a univariate analysis is done (Table 23-1). The variables are then subjected to a multivariate discriminate analysis (Table 23-2) using a CYBE 730-750 computer. Discriminate analysis is a statistical technique designed to maximize separation of predefined groups; in this case, the normal versus diseased patients. The analysis proceeds in a step-wise fashion taking first, the variable that makes the largest contribution to the separation of the groups (diseased and normals). This variable is the one that generates the largest F value in a one-way analysis of variance and, after it is entered in the discriminate function, the variable with the next largest F value is selected, and so forth. Ultimately, all variables are ranked according to their relative discriminatory importance. Because successive entries of variables are based on the F values generated in an analysis of variance after conditional consideration of variables already entered, final ranking of all the variables may be quite different from that based on the original (independent) F values. All F values, however, may be tested for significance in the conventional manner. It is of interest that most of our analysis of large groups of patients demonstrate that the first variable has the greatest single discriminatory power and, as each variable is added, discrimination is gradually improved and levels off after, sometimes only three or four variables are added. Thus, although up to 20 variables have been used, for practical purposes somewhere between 6 and 10 seem to be equally as good (see Fig. 23-4). The program will also display each subject in the analysis according to their distribution around the centroid of those with and without disease (Fig. 23-5).

The multiple discriminate function, thus, ultimately generates a series of coefficients that weigh each variable according to its relative discriminatory

TABLE 23-1. Men: Univariate Analysis

Variables	F Value	Mean		Standard Deviation	
		Normal	Diseased	Normal	Diseased
1. Test Duration (minutes)	31.80**	7.98	6.02	1.52	2.18
2. M.I. By ECG (0=no) (1=yes)	22.50**	0.06	0.41	0.24	0.50
3. % Maximal HR Achieved	16.74**	93.56	85.68	8.43	12.10
4. Maximal HR Achieved (beats/min)	16.02**	163.60	149.18	15.83	22.62
5. M.I. By History (0=no) (1=yes)	14.88**	0.06	0.34	0.24	0.48
6. R Wave Change (mm)	12.34**	−1.80	0.71	4.05	4.09
7. Maximal Systolic BP (mm mercury)	8.49**	175.60	160.88	31.71	27.04
8. ST Depression-Immediate Period (mm)	7.61**	0.58	1.36	1.36	1.69
9. Anginal Pain During TST (0=no) (1=yes)	7.28**	0.14	0.35	0.35	0.48
10. Age (years)	6.91**	49.98	53.60	8.33	7.55
11. History of Elevated Cholesterol (0=no) (1=yes)	1.96	0.14	0.24	0.35	0.43
12. Downsloping ST-Recovery Period (0=no) (1=yes)	1.92	0.02	0.08	0.14	0.27
13. Drugs (Non-Cardiac) (0=no) (1=yes)	0.93	0.32	0.40	0.47	0.49
14. Type of ST Depression	0.64	10.80	9.54	8.98	8.87
15. Resting Systolic BP (mm mercury)	0.35	126.38	124.75	15.05	16.01
16. History of Diabetes (0=no) (1=yes)	0.33	0.06	0.09	0.24	0.28
17. Hyperventilation ST Changes (0=no) (1=yes)	0.22	0.13	0.09	0.41	0.48
18. Smoking History (0=no) (1=yes)	0.14	0.50	0.47	0.51	0.50
19. Family History of Heart Disease (0=no) (1=yes)	0.04	0.44	0.46	0.50	0.50
20. ST Changes-Control Period (0=no) (1=yes)	0.03	0.15	0.14	0.47	0.46
21. Abnormal ECG at Rest (0=no) (1=yes)	0.01	0.18	0.17	0.39	0.38

Shown are the means and standard deviations of all 21 variables for normal and diseased male patients. The variables are ranked in decreasing order of significance as given by the F values from univariate analysis of variance.
** = P <0.01.

TABLE 23-2. Calculations Used in Multivariate Analysis*

	A	B	C	D	E
		Coefficient 1	Coefficient 2	Score 1	Score 2
Variable	Value	(Nondiseased)	(Diseased)	(Nondiseased)	(Diseased)
1 Age	60	0.53659	0.75965	(A1*B1)	(As*C1)
2 S-T Rest	0	-8.13821	-11.33283	(A2*B2)	(As*C2)
3 S-T Exercise	2	4.88535	5.78042	(A3*B3)	(A3*C3)
4 AB ECG	1	5.47845	13.62379	(A4*B4)	(A4*C4)
			Constant	-236.60221	-229.9304
			Total	Σ(D1 thru D5)	Σ(E1 thru E2)
			Post Prob	Exp D6	Exp 86
				Exp D6+Exp E6	Exp D6+Exp E6
1 Age	60	0.53659	0.75965	32.19540	45.57900
2 S-T Rest	0	-8.13821	-11.33283	0.000	0.000
3 S-T Exercise	2	4.88535	4.78042	9.7707	11.56084
4 AB ECG	1	5.47845	13.62379	5.47845	13.62379
			Constant	-236.60221	-287.07024
			Total	-189.1577	-159.1668
			Post Prob Exp	7.007^{-83}	7.4944^{-70}

$$7.077^{-83} + 7.4944^{-70} = 9.4432^{-14}$$

$$7.4944^{-70} + 7.077^{-83} = 1.000$$

*Illustration of calculations used in multivariate analysis of one patient. The value for each variable (A) is multiplied by the coefficient for no disease (B) and for disease (C). These scores (D and E) are added to arrive at the exponent used in the final calculation of posterior probability.

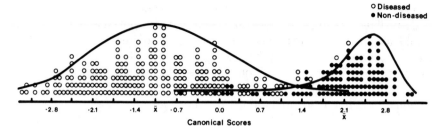

FIGURE 23-5. The computer program distributes each patient according to the canonical score that groups those with disease (0) around the mean, and those without disease (•) around their own mean. The overlap between these groups illustrates misclassifications.

power. These coefficients are then used to complete the discriminate score. The scores are then summed to compute the probability of disease and no disease. The probability of *no disease* equals:

$$\frac{\text{Exp Score 1 (no disease)}}{\text{Exp Score 1 + Exp Score 2 (no disease)}}$$

and the probability *of disease* equals:

$$\frac{\text{Exp Score 2 (diseased)}}{\text{Exp Score 1 + Exp Score 2}}$$

The final step of this analysis has been written for small computers and can be done on any of the personal computers now on the market or even on a fairly complicated hand-held calculator. Although our earlier results with MVA were better than with S-T depression alone, it is only recently that we have been able to select variables and assign appropriate function values that have allowed us to obtain an accuracy in discriminations of 90 percent or above. Although we are not certain this will hold up in other populations, the results are encouraging at this time.

Likelihood Ratio

This concept, explained in Chapter 14, allows the input of symptoms and risk factors and computes a pre-test probability. When the results of the exercise tests are entered, a post-test probability is calculated.[28] Thus, using Baysean statistics, a probability and the confidence limits of the estimate are printed out.

CORRELATING DATA IN FINAL PRINT-OUT

The efficiency of a computer in assemblying, calculating, and printing out the above data cannot be underestimated. If demographic information, blood pressure, and a few symptoms and risk factors are entered before or after the test, a final report can be generated efficiently and can contain information that would take many hours to produce manually. This requires that a good quality printer be part of the stress testing equipment as well as the now familiar oscilloscope and some type of multichannel electrocardiographic recorder. Although an ideal package, in my opinion, is yet to be released commercially, it should be forthcoming in the not too distant future.

COMMENT

The concepts presented in this chapter are intended to help the reader conceptualize the capabilities of the computer. The hardware, in the form of microprocessors, various types of disk storage, printers of all types, and oscilloscopes are now off-the-shelf items. It remains now for innovative people to write the programs and package the system. I predict the use of computers in our stress labs will proliferate rapidly and in a few years we will wonder how we were able to work without them.

REFERENCES

1. BLOMQVIST, G: *The Frank lead exercise electrocardiogram: A quantitative study based on averaging technic and digital computer analysis.* Acta Med Scand (Suppl 440) 178:5–98, 1965.
2. BRUCE, RA, ET AL: *Quantification of QRS and ST segment response to exercise.* Am Heart J 71:455, 1966.
3. MCHENRY, PL, PHILLIPS, JF, AND KNOEBEL, SB: *Correlation of computer quantitated treadmill exercise electrocardiogram with arteriographic location of coronary artery disease.* Am J Cardiol 30:747–752, 1972.
4. SHEFFIELD, LT, ET AL: *On-line analysis of the exercise electrocardiogram.* Circulation 40:935, 1969.
5. SIMOONS, ML: *Optimal measurements for detection of coronary artery disease by exercise electrocardiography.* Comput Biomed Res 10:483–499, 1977.
6. ASCOOP, CA: *ST Forces During Exercise.* Thesis, Groningen, The Netherlands, 1973.
7. SHEFFIELD, LT: *The use of the computer in exercise electrocardiography.* Practical Cardiology, January 101–118, 1978.
8. CACERES, CA AND RIKLI, AE: *Diagnostic Computers.* Charles C Thomas, Springfield, Illinois, 1969.
9. BLOMQVIST, CG AND MITCHELL, JH: *Heart disease and dynamic exercise testing.* In WILLERSON, JT AND SANDERS, RA (EDS): *Clinical Cardiology.* Grune & Stratton, New York, 1977.
10. SIMOONS, ML: *Optimal measurements for detection of coronary artery disease by exercise ECG.* Comput Biomed Res 10:483, 1977.
11. DOWER, GA: *Polarcardiography.* Charles C Thomas, Springfield, Ill, 1971.
12. MCHENRY, PL, PHILLIPS, JF, AND KNOEBEL, SB: *Correlation of computer quantified treadmill exercise ECG with arteriographic location of coronary artery disease.* Am J Cardiol 30:747, 1972.
13. DWORTEZKY, LH, ET AL: *Fourier analysis of exercise electrocardiograms.* In BLACKBURN, H (ED): *Measurement in Exercise Electrocardiography.* Charles C Thomas, Springfield, Illinois, 1967.

14. WOLF, HK, ET AL: *Computer analysis of rest and exercise electrocardiograms.* Comput Biomed Res 5:329, 1972.

15. KLINGEMAN, J AND PIPBERGER, HV: *Computer classifications of electrocardiograms.* Comput Biomed Res 1:1, 1963.

16. BLOMQVIST, G: *The Frank lead exercise electrocardiogram.* Acta Med Scand (Suppl) 178:1–98, 1968.

17. SAVVIDES, M AND FROELICHER, V: *Non-invasive non-nuclkear exercise testing.* Cardiology 71:100–117, 1984.

18. SIMMONS, ML, BOOM, HBK, AND SWALLENBURG, E: *On-line processing of orthogonal exercise ECG's.* Comput Biomed Res 8:105, 1975.

19. ASCOOP, CA, DISTELBRINK, CA, AND DELAND, PA: *Clinical value of quantitative analysis of ST slope during exercise.* Br Heart J 39:212, 1977.

20. SKETCH, MH, ET AL: *Automated and nomographic analysis of exercise test.* J Am Med Assn 243:1052–1055, 1980.

21. HOLLENBERG, M, ET AL: *Treadmill score quantifies electrocardiographic response to exercise and improves test accuracy and reproducibility.* Circulation 61:276–285, 1980.

22. HOLLENBERG, M, ET AL: *The magnitude of exercise-induced ST depression is influenced by QRS amplitude* (abstr). J Am Coll Cardiol 1(2):736, 1983.

23. BLACKBURN, H, ET AL: *The electrocardiogram during exercise: Findings in bipolar chest leads of 1,449 middle-aged men, at moderate work levels.* Circulation 34:1034, 1966.

24. HAKKI, AH, ET AL: *R wave amplitude: A new determinant of failure of patients with coronary heart disease to manifest ST segment depression during exercise.* JACC 3(5):1155–1160, 1984.

25. BRUCE, RA, KUSUMI, MS AND HOSMER, D: *Maximal oxygen intake and nomographic assessment of functional aerobic impairment in cardiovascular disease.* Am Heart J 85:546, 1973.

26. APTECARS, M, ET AL: *The assessment of myocardial efficiency by an exercise testing index.* J Cardiac Rehabil 2:271–279, 1982.

27. GREENBERG, PS, ELLESTAD, MH, AND CLOVER, RC: *Comparison of the multivariate analysis and CADENZA systems for determination of the probability of coronary artery disease.* Am J Cardiol 53:493–496, 1984.

28. DIAMOND, GA AND FORRESTER, JS: *Analysis of probability as an aid to the clinical diagnosis of coronary artery disease.* N Engl J Med 360:1350, 1979.

APPENDICES

1. BLOOD PRESSURE GRAPHS

These graphs were prepared from subjects tested on our protocol depicted in Chapter 10. The data were taken from those with normal stress tests. The dark line is the mean for the group and the shaded area represents two standard deviations of the mean. It will be noted that in the group with small numbers the standard deviations are much larger.

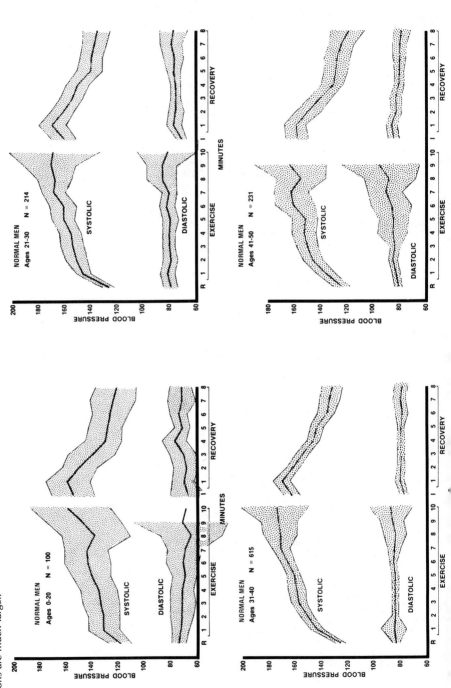

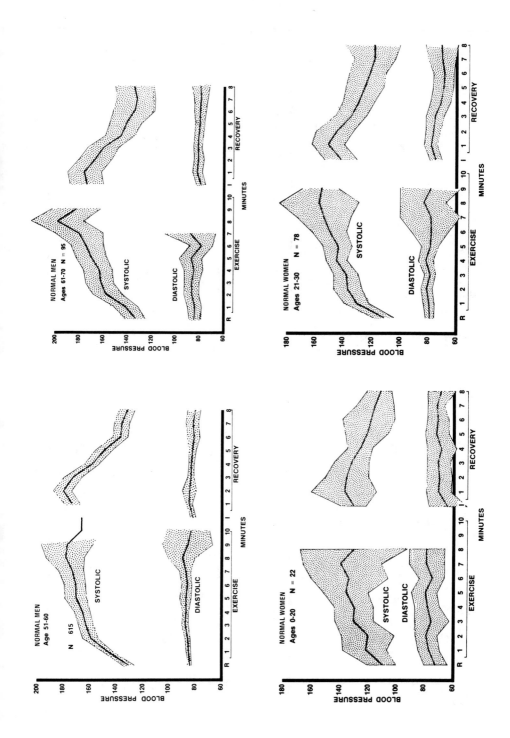

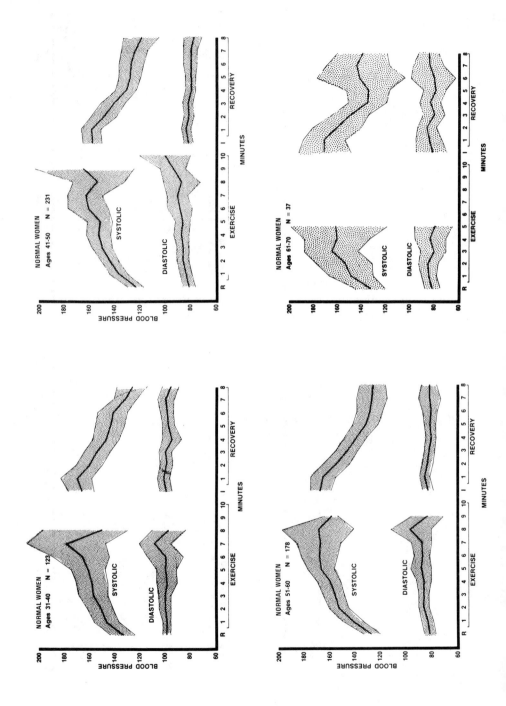

STRESS TESTING: PRINCIPLES AND PRACTICE

2. CONSENT FORM

MEMORIAL HOSPITAL MEDICAL CENTER

In order to evaluate the ability of my heart to respond to exercise I voluntarily agree to undergo an exercise stress test in the Division of Clinical Physiology, Memorial Hospital Medical Center of Long Beach.

I understand that this test, like all medical procedures in a hospital, may involve an extremely remote possibility of death and also that this test may in very rare cases cause symptoms such as abnormal heart rhythms, fainting or heart attacks.

However, this test will be conducted by trained experts in a careful manner and will be discontinued if any abnormality is observed.

I have read the above and give my consent to proceed with the test and will not hold the hospital or personnel involved responsible if untoward events or injury results.

Signed: _____

Time: _____

Date: _____

Witness: _____

CONSENT FOR TREADMILL STRESS TESTING

---

3. CORONARY ANGIOGRAPHIC CORRELATION

Table 1. Maximal S-T segment depression in 179 patients with 3 vessel disease*

S-T segment depression	% of group
0 mm	22
1 mm	6
2 mm	27
3 mm	22
4 mm	12
5 mm or more	4.5

*3 vessels with obstruction of 51 per cent or more.
Of those with 3 vessel disease 88 per cent have 1 mm or more S-T segment depression.

Table 2. Maximal S-T segment depression in 44 patients with left main disease

S-T segment depression	% of group
0 mm	20
1 mm or more	80
2 mm or more	67

Although 20 per cent of those with 51 per cent obstruction or more had no S-T segment depression the remainder had significant ischemic changes.

Table 3. Time to onset of 2.0 mm S-T segment depression

Minutes of exercise	1	2	3	4	5	N
3 vessel disease	20%	20%	16%	17%	28%	115
2 vessel disease	14%	16%	8%	13%	46%	82
No disease	23%	11%	11%	14%	40%	64

It might be expected that those with the more severe disease would develop S-T segment depression earlier at lower work loads; however, the data shows little evidence of this. Most of those with no coronary disease had some type of myocardial dysfunction manifested by reduced diastolic compliance.

Table 4. Findings on 683 patients with coronary angiograms and stress tests

Stress test results		No disease (%)	Mild disease* (%)	Severe disease* (%)	N
Normal	51	41	25	34	112
Equivocal	52	35	22	43	117
Positive	55	17	10	73	279
Probably positive	56	20	28	52	115
No myocardial infarction + normal test		46	22	32	96
No myocardial infarction + positive test		20	19	61	194
Myocardial infarction + positive test		7	10	83	85

*Mild disease = 1 vessel 51 per cent obstructed or more and/or several vessels with less than 50 per cent obstruction. Severe disease = 2 or 3 vessels 51 per cent or more obstructed.

APPENDICES

Table 5. Incidence of coronary disease on angiography by ECG pattern

Pattern	No disease %	2 or 3 vessel disease	Number
F	13.6	60.0	116
G	33.3	46.6	45
H	43.7	31.2	16
I	5.0	65.0	20
J	27.2	40.0	55
K	0	81.2	16
L	0	77.7	9
M	38.2	29.4	34
N	65.0	31.0	86
O	20.9	67.7	62
P	17.0	57.0	70
Q	20.5	58.9	39
S	36.4	45.5	11
U	27.3	54.5	11
V	42.9	21.4	14
X	18.2	72.7	11

Illustrations of the various patterns are listed in the Appendix.

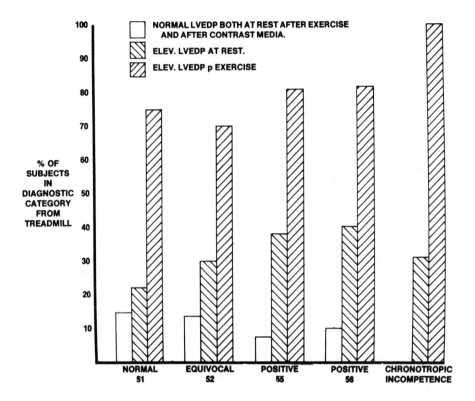

Table 6. Left Ventricular Filling Pressure by Treadmill Diagnosis. In Order to correlate left ventricular function with the treadmill diagnosis, the filling pressure during heart catheterization was recorded at rest and after exercise and the injection of contrast media. Only a small percentage had completely normal pressures, even in those with normal coronaries and a normal stress test.

The percentage of those with elevated LVEDP after exercise is almost the same in the patients with a normal stress test as in those who have a positive response. It is interesting that subjects with chronotropic incompetence are the only group who fail to have any incidence of normal left ventricular function.

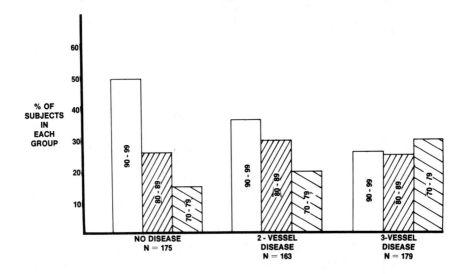

Table 7. The ability of subjects who were catheterized to reach their peak heart rate was somewhat limited. Only 50 percent of those with normal coronary arteries could attain 90 to 99 percent of their predicted heart rate; 92 percent of the normal subjects, however, were able to exceed 70 percent of their predicted rate.

Although a much smaller percentage (27%) of those with three-vessel disease could attain 90 to 99 percent of their predicted rate, 82 percent could reach 70 percent of this value.

4. ELECTRODE POSITIONS

1. The bipolar CH lead - forehead to chest.
2. The bipolar CR lead - right arm to chest.
3. The bipolar CC lead - $C_5 R$ to C_5.
4. The bipolar CB lead - right back to apex.
5. The bipolar CM_5 lead - manubrium to C_5.
6. The bipolar CS lead - right subclavicle to C_5.
7. The bipolar O lead - right subclavicle at sternal border to approximately C_8.
8. The X lead is the right to left derivation of the orthogonal system of Frank.
9. The bipolar A lead - manubrium to sacrum.
10. The bipolar B lead - $C_6 R$ to C_6 but at lower rib cage margin.
11. The bipolar CN lead - second thoracic vertebra to C_5.
12. The V lead is the conventional Wilson central terminal to chest positions.
13. The RV system - reference electrodes at each clavicle and the left ilium below the crest.
14. The R system is similar to the CC bipolar transthoracic system except that a central terminal network is used and three reference electrodes placed on the right chest.
15. The L system, or the E-E-P system - a central terminal network with reference electrodes on the right ear, at the ensiform, and at C_7 and exploring electrodes at C_4, C_5, C_6.

(From Blackburn, H.: *Measurement for Exercise Electrocardiography.* C. C Thomas, Springfield, Ill., 1969, with permission.)

5. ELECTROCARDIOGRAPHIC PATTERNS CODES

In each pair of complexes the one on the left represents the resting tracing and on the right that recorded immediately after exercise is discontinued.

A

Ta-WAVE

B

LEFT BUNDLE BRANCH BLOCK AFTER EXERCISE

C

LEFT BUNDLE BRANCH BLOCK

D

RIGHT BUNDLE BRANCH BLOCK
WITH S-T DEPRESSION

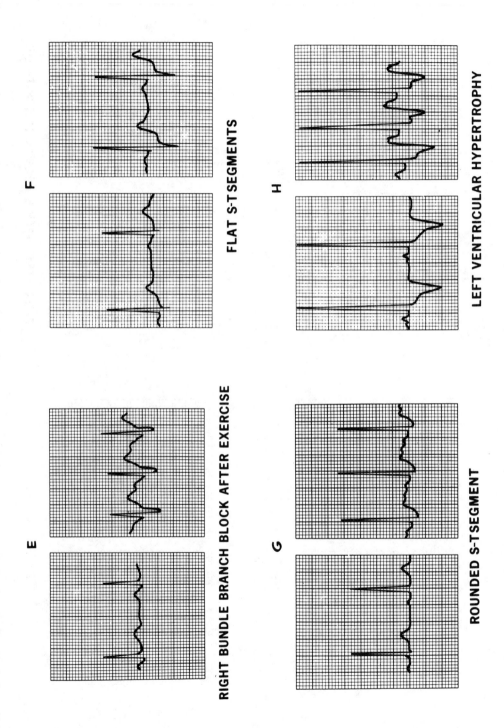

E

RIGHT BUNDLE BRANCH BLOCK AFTER EXERCISE

F

FLAT S-T SEGMENTS

G

ROUNDED S-T SEGMENT

H

LEFT VENTRICULAR HYPERTROPHY

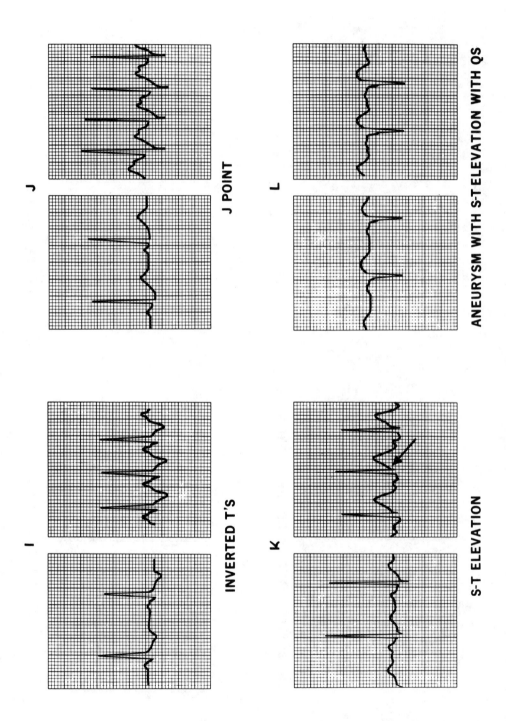

I

INVERTED T'S

J

J POINT

K

S-T ELEVATION

L

ANEURYSM WITH S-T ELEVATION WITH QS

STRESS TESTING: PRINCIPLES AND PRACTICE

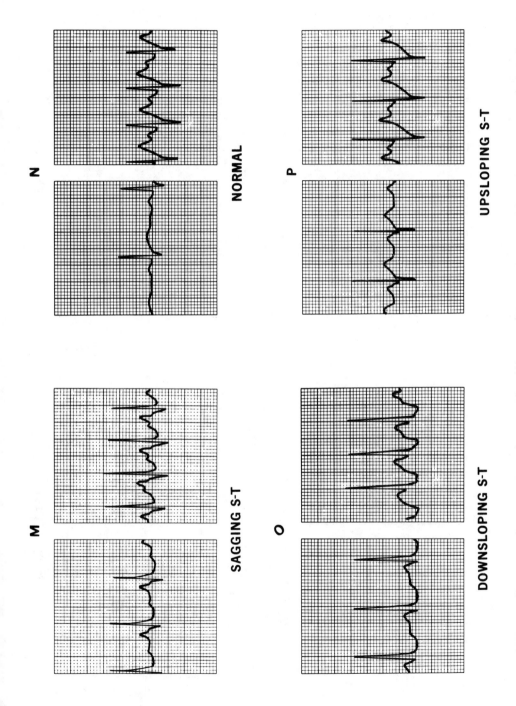

N

NORMAL

M

SAGGING S-T

P

UPSLOPING S-T

O

DOWNSLOPING S-T

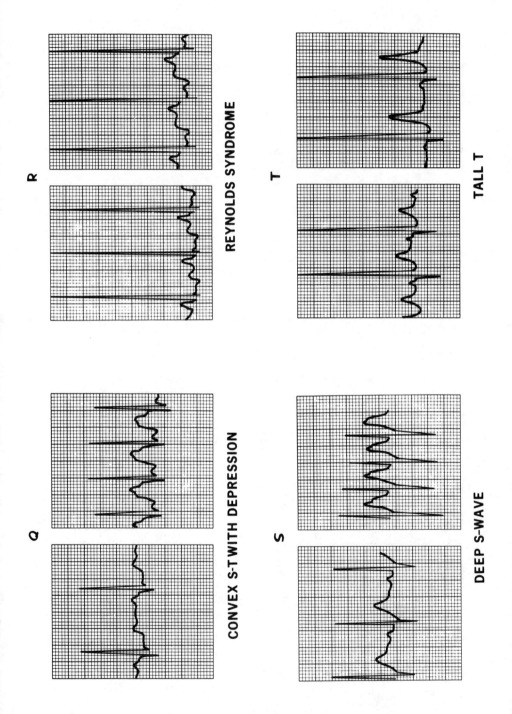

Q

CONVEX S-T WITH DEPRESSION

R

REYNOLDS SYNDROME

S

DEEP S-WAVE

T

TALL T

STRESS TESTING: PRINCIPLES AND PRACTICE

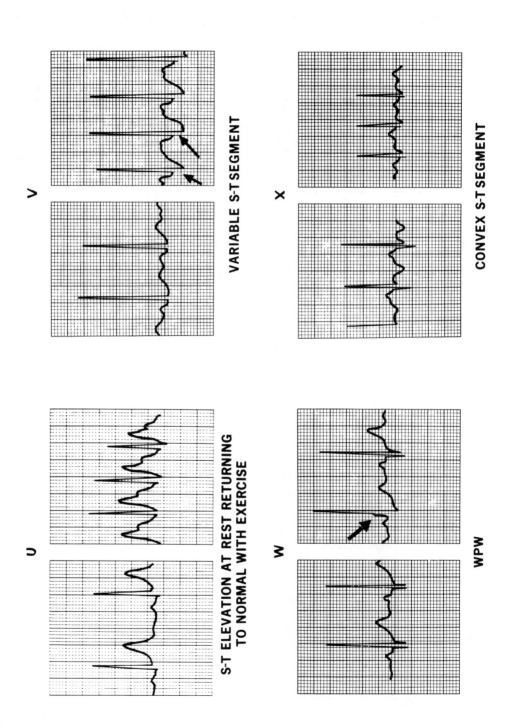

V — VARIABLE S-T SEGMENT

X — CONVEX S-T SEGMENT

U — S-T ELEVATION AT REST RETURNING TO NORMAL WITH EXERCISE

W — WPW

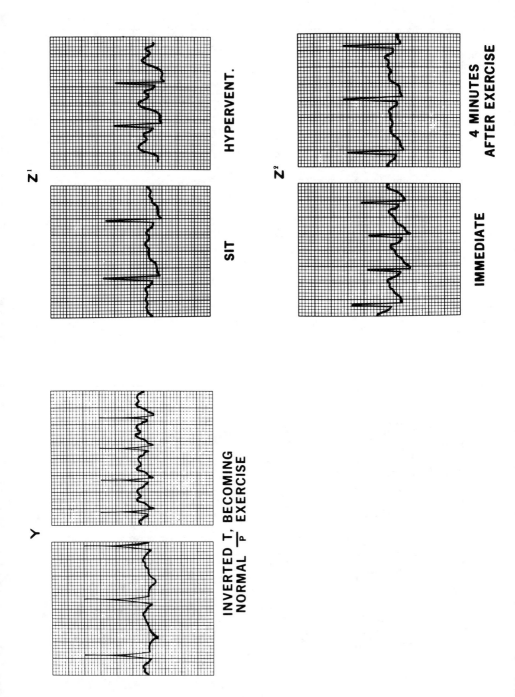

STRESS TESTING: PRINCIPLES AND PRACTICE

6. HEART RATE GRAPHS

The heart rate response to our protocol described in Chapter 10 is segregated into age groups and sex. Data were taken from those with negative tests.

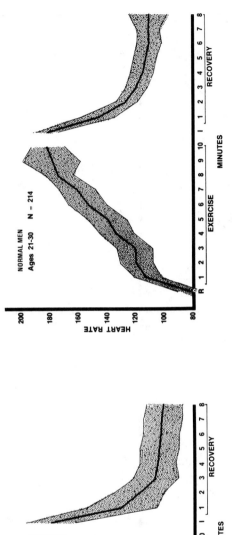
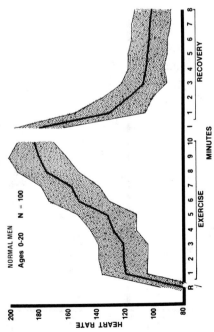

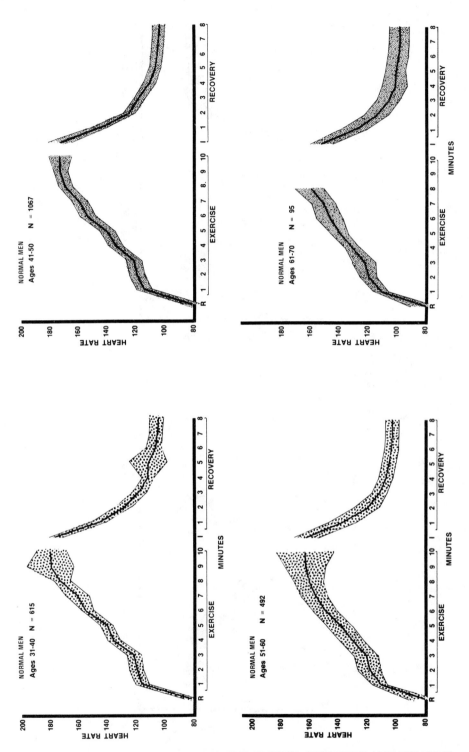

STRESS TESTING: PRINCIPLES AND PRACTICE

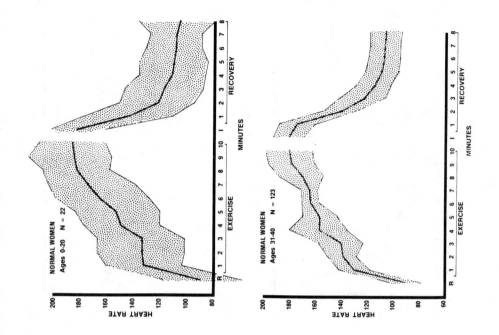

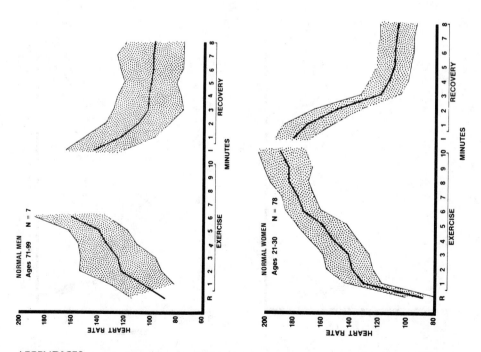

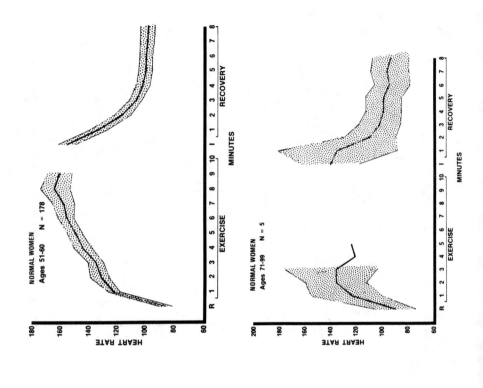

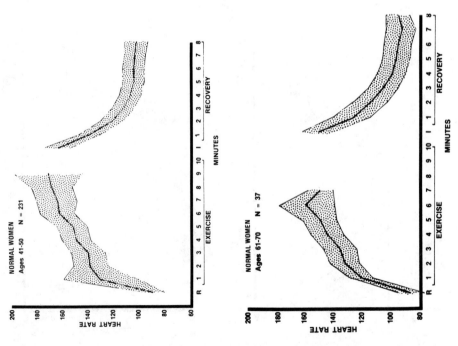

STRESS TESTING: PRINCIPLES AND PRACTICE

7. STANDARD EXERCISE FOR THE MASTER'S TEST
Standard Number of Ascents for Men

Weight (lb)	5 - 9	10 - 14	15 - 19	20 - 24	25 - 29	30 - 34	35 - 39	40 - 44	45 - 49	50 - 54	55 - 59	60 - 64	65 - 69
40 – 49	34	36											
50 – 59	33	35											
60 – 69	31	33	32										
70 – 79	28	32	31										
80 – 89	26	30	30	29	29	28	27	27	26	25	25	24	23
90 – 99	24	29	29	28	28	27	27	26	25	25	24	23	22
100 – 109	22	27	28	28	28	27	26	25	25	24	23	22	22
110 – 119	20	26	27	27	27	26	25	25	24	23	23	22	21
120 – 129	18	24	26	26	27	26	25	24	23	23	22	21	20
130 – 139	16	23	25	25	26	25	24	23	23	22	21	20	20
140 – 149		21	24	24	25	24	24	23	22	21	20	20	19
150 – 159		20	23	24	25	24	23	22	21	20	20	19	18
160 – 169		18	22	23	24	23	22	22	21	20	19	18	18
170 – 179			21	22	23	23	22	21	20	19	18	18	17
180 – 189			20	21	23	22	21	20	19	19	18	17	16
190 – 199			19	20	22	21	21	20	19	18	17	16	15
200 – 209			18	19	21	21	20	19	18	17	16	16	15
210 – 219				18	21	20	19	18	17	17	16	15	14
220 – 229				17	20	20	19	18	17	16	15	14	13

Age in years

STANDARD EXERCISE FOR THE MASTER'S TEST (Cont.)
Standard Number of Ascents for Women

Weight (lb)	5 - 9	10 - 14	15 - 19	20 - 24	25 - 29	30 - 34	35 - 39	40 - 44	45 - 49	50 - 54	55 - 59	60 - 64	65 - 69
							Age in years						
40 – 49	35	35	33										
50 – 59	33	33	32										
60 – 69	31	32	30										
70 – 79	28	30	29										
80 – 89	26	28	28	28	28	27	26	24	23	22	21	21	20
90 – 99	24	27	26	27	26	25	24	23	22	22	21	20	19
100 – 109	22	25	25	26	26	25	24	23	22	21	20	19	18
110 – 119	20	23	23	25	25	24	23	22	21	20	19	18	18
120 – 129	18	22	22	24	24	23	22	21	20	19	19	18	17
130 – 139	16	20	20	23	23	22	21	20	19	19	18	17	16
140 – 149		18	19	22	22	21	20	19	19	18	17	16	16
150 – 159		17	17	21	20	20	19	19	18	17	16	16	15
160 – 169		15	16	20	19	19	18	18	17	16	16	15	14
170 – 179		13	14	19	18	18	17	17	16	16	15	14	13
180 – 189			13	18	17	17	17	16	16	15	14	14	13
190 – 199			12	17	16	16	16	15	15	14	13	13	12
200 – 209				16	15	15	15	14	14	13	13	12	11
210 – 219				15	14	14	14	13	13	13	12	11	11
220 – 229				14	13	13	13	13	12	12	11	11	10

The prescribed number of ascents should be completed in 1½ minutes for a single and 3 minutes for a double Master's Test.

8. QUESTIONNAIRE

TREADMILL QUESTIONNAIRE

Division of Clinical Physiology
Name _____ Physician _____ Date _____
Age _____ Ht. _____ Wt. _____ Sex _____ Case# _____ Comp# _____

Please circle the number
that indicates your answer.

Previous treadmill test here?
1. Yes
2. No

Hospitalization for myocardial infarction (Heart Attack)?
3. Never
4. Once
5. More than once   Date(s) _____

Heart Surgery?
6. None
7. Vineberg Implant
8. Bypass Graft (aorta to coronary)
9. Combined Vinebert & Bypass Graft
10. Cardiac Valve
11. Other   Date(s) _____

Chest Pain?
12. None (go on to #26)
13. Slight
14. Moderate
15. Severe
16. Occurs infrequently
17. More than once a month
18. More than once a week
19. More than once a day
20. Lasts less than 5 minutes
21. Lasts longer than 5 minutes
22. Relieved by Nitroglycerin
23. Unrelated to activity
24. Occurs with exertion
25. Occurs at rest

Physical activity at work?
26. None
27. Light
28. Moderate
29. Heavy

Exercise Pattern
30. None (go on to #39)
31. Light (walking, golf)

32. Moderate (jogging, bicycling)
33. Heavy (running, competitive sports)
34. Regular
35. Irregular
36. Less than 2 times a week
37. 2 times a week
38. More than 2 times a week

Have you ever smoked Cigarettes?
Indicate average usage
39. Never
40. Less than 5 years
41. 5 years or longer
42. Less than ½ pack per day
43. ½ to 1 pack per day
44. More than one pack per day

Have you ever used alcoholic beverages?
45. None (go on to #55)
46. Beer
47. Wine
48. Whiskey

Indicate frequency of use
49. Rarely (holidays, special occasions)
50. Occasionally
51. Weekly
52. Daily

Indicate duration of use
53. Less than 5 years
54. 5 years or longer

Have you ever been treated for high blood pressure?
55. Never
56. In a physician's office
57. In the hospital

Have you ever been treated for "sugar diabetes"?
58. Never
59. With pills
60. With insulin injections

Did either of your parents ever have a "heart attack"?
61. Do not know
62. Neither
63. One
64. Both

Does your present occupation subject you to emotional stress?
65. None
66. Moderate degree
67. High degree

Have you ever had an elevated blood cholesterol level?
68.   Do not know
69.   No
70.   Yes

Are you taking any of the following drugs?
71.   Nitroglycerin
72.   Digitalis
73.   Diuretics (water pills)
74.   Propranolol (Inderal)

FEMALES ONLY

Are you still Menstruating?
75.   Yes
76.   No
If not, fill in the blanks: **Age at Menopause** _____
                                              OR
                        Age at time of hysterectomy _____

Are you taking estrogen medication?
77.   Yes
78.   No

9. WORKLOAD NOMOGRAM

Grade units of elevation per hundred horizontal expressed as percent
10 percent grade constant

Estimated watts within ≈ ± watts

Weight		Speed – 1.7 mph (45.6 met/min)			Speed – 3 mph (80.5 met/min)			Speed – 4 mph (107.3 met/min)			Speed – 5 mph (134.1 met/min)		
lbs	kg	VO_2	watts	work/min kg/met	VO_2	watts	work/min kg/met	VO_2	watts	work/min kg/met	VO_2	watts	work/min kg/met
50	22.7	322	9	179	569	25	316	569	37.5	421	949	50	527
55	25	355	10	197	626	25	348	835	50	464	1044	62.5	580
60	27.3	387	12.5	215	684	37.5	380	913	50	507	1139	75	633
65	29.5	419	12.5	233	740	37.5	411	986	62.5	548	1231	75	684
70	31.8	452	12.5	251	797	37.5	443	1062	62.5	590	1328	87.5	738
75	34.1	484	12.5	269	855	50	475	1139	75	633	1424	100	791
80	36.4	517	12.5	287	913	50	507	1217	75	676	1519	100	844
85	38.6	547	25	304	968	50	538	1291	87.5	717	1611	112.5	895
90	40.9	581	25	323	1026	62.5	570	1366	87.5	759	1708	112.5	949
95	43.2	614	25	341	1084	62.5	602	1444	100	802	1804	125	1002
100	45.5	646	25	359	1141	75	634	1521	100	845	1901	137.5	1056
105	47.7	677	37.5	376	1195	75	664	1593	112.5	885	1993	137.5	1107
110	50	709	37.5	394	1253	75	696	1670	112.5	928	2088	150	1160
115	52.2	742	37.5	412	1309	87.5	727	1744	125	969	2180	150	1211
120	54.5	774	37.5	430	1366	87.5	759	1822	125	1012	2275	162.5	1264
125	56.8	806	37.5	448	1424	87.5	791	1897	137.5	1054	2372	175	1318
130	59.1	839	50	466	1481	100	823	1975	137.5	1097	2468	175	1371
135	61.4	871	50	484	1539	100	855	2052	150	1140	2563	187.5	1424

140	63.6	904	50	502	1595	112.5	886	2126	150	1181	2657	187.5	1476
145	65.9	936	50	520	1652	112.5	918	2201	162.5	1223	2752	200	1529
150	68.2	968	50	538	1710	112.5	950	2279	162.5	1266	2848	200	1582
155	70.5	1001	62.5	556	1768	125	982	2356	175	1309	2945	212.5	1636
160	72.7	1031	62.5	573	1822	125	1012	2430	175	1350	3037	212.5	1687
165	75	1066	62.5	592	1883	137.5	1046	2506	175	1392	3132	225	1740
170	77.3	1098	62.5	610	1939	137.5	1077	2583	187.5	1435	3227	225	1793
175	79.5	1129	75	627	1993	137.5	1107	2657	187.5	1476	3319	237.5	1844
180	81.8	1163	75	646	2050	150	1139	2732	187.5	1518	3416	250	1898
185	84.1	1193	75	663	2108	150	1171	2810	200	1561	3512	250	1951
190	86.4	1228	75	682	2165	150	1203	2887	212.5	1604	3607	262.5	2004
195	88.6	1258	75	699	2221	162.5	1234	2961	212.5	1645	3699	262.5	2055
200	90.9	1291	87.5	717	2279	162.5	1266	3037	212.5	1687	3796	275	2109
205	93.2	1323	87.5	735	2336	162.5	1298	3114	225	1730	3892	275	2162
210	95.5	1355	87.5	753	2394	175	1330	3191	225	1773	3989	287.5	2216
215	97.7	1388	87.5	771	2450	175	1361	3265	237.5	1814	4081	287.5	2267
220	100	1420	87.5	789	2507	175	1393	3341	237.5	1856	4176	300	2320
225	102.3	1453	100	807	2565	187.5	1425	3418	250	1899	4271	300	2373
230	104.6	1485	100	825	2623	187.5	1457	3496	250	1942	4369	312.5	2427
235	106.8	1517	100	843	2677	187.5	1487	3569	250	1983	4460	312.5	2478
240	109.1	1549	100	861	2734	200	1519	3645	262.5	2025	4556	325	2531
245	111.4	1582	112.5	879	2792	200	1551	3722	262.5	2068	4651	325	2584

WORKLOAD NOMOGRAM (continued)

Grade units of elevation per hundred horizontal expressed as percent 10 percent grade constant

Estimated watts within ≲ ± watts

Weight		Speed – 1.7 mph (45.6 met/min)			Speed – 3 mph (80.5 met/min)			Speed – 4 mph (107.3 met/min)			Speed – 5 mph (134.1 met/min)		
lbs	kg	VO₂	watts	work/min kg/met	VO₂	watts	work/min kg/met	VO₂	watts	work/min kg/met	VO₂	watts	work/min kg/met
250	113.6	1613	112.5	896	2848	200	1582	3796	275	2109	4743	337.5	2635
255	115.9	1646	112.5	914	2905	212.5	1614	3872	275	2151	4840	337.5	2689
260	118.2	1678	112.5	932	2963	212.5	1646	3949	287.5	2194	4936	350	2742
265	120.5	1711	112.5	951	3020	212.5	1678	4027	287.5	2237	5033	350	2796
270	122.7	1742	125	968	3076	225	1709	4100	287.5	2278	5125	362.5	2847
275	125.0	1775	125	986	3134	225	1741	4176	300	2320	5220	362.5	2900
280	127.3	1808	125	1004	3191	225	1773	4253	300	2363	5315	375	2953
285	129.5	1839	125	1022	3245	237.5	1803	4327	312.5	2404	5407	375	3004
290	131.8	1871	125	1040	3305	237.5	1836	4405	312.5	2447	5504	387.5	3058
295	134.1	1904	137.5	1058	3362	237.5	1868	4480	312.5	2489	5600	387.5	3111
300	136.4	1937	137.5	1076	3420	250	1900	4558	325	2532	5695	387.5	3164
305	138.6	1967	137.5	1093	3474	250	1930	4631	325	2573	5787	400	3215
310	140.9	2002	137.5	1112	3532	250	1962	4709	337.5	2616	5884	400	3269
315	143.2	2034	150	1130	3589	262.5	1994	4784	337.5	2658	5980	412.5	3322
320	145.5	2066	150	1148	3647	262.5	2026	4862	337.5	2701	6075	412.5	3375
325	147.7	2097	150	1165	3703	262.5	2057	4936	350	2742	6169	425	3427
330	150	2129	150	1183	3760	275	2089	5011	350	2784	6264	425	3480
350	159	2258	150	1254	3986	275	2214	5315	350	2953	6640	425	3689

The predicted O₂ work per minute in kg-ms is presented for each work level of our protocol according to body weight. The data were calculated from the formulae by Balke and Ware by Mrs. Frances Weiss, our chief technician, and by Joseph Nargy, M.D.

INDEX

A "t" following a page number indicates a table; an italic page number indicates a figure.

Block
  atrioventricular
    first degree, 285
    second degree, 285–286
    third degree, 295, *295*
  fascicular
    left anterior division block, 286–288,
      286, 287
    left posterior hemiblock, 288–289
    left posterior hemiblock and right bundle
      branch block, 288, *289*
  heart, congenital
    pediatric stress testing and, 405–407, *406*
  left anterior division, 286–288, *286, 287*
  left bundle branch, 291–294, *293, 294*
  rate-related bundle branch, 289–290
  right bundle branch, 290–291, *291, 292*
  left posterior hemiblock and, 288, *289*
Blockade, beta
  mechanisms of
    metabolic abnormalities and, 440–441
Blockers
  beta, metabolic abnormalities and, 440
  calcium, metabolic abnormalities and,
    441–442
Blood
  clotting of, exercise and, 41–42
  exercise and, 40–41
Blood flow
  coronary
    exercise and, 19–20, *19*
  redistribution of
    exercise and, 45–46, *45*
  regulation
    studies in, 20–21
  skin
    exercise and, 31
Blood pool imaging
  equilibrium
    radionuclide angiography in
      nuclear stress testing and, 422–424,
        423
  nuclear
    recent studies in
      stroke volume and, 12
Blood pressure
  graphs, 472–474
  measurement of
    age and response of, 358, *358*
    cardiomyopathies in, 363–365
    conclusions in, 365
    coronary artery patients and hypertensive
      response of, 359–360, *360*
    drugs in, 365

hypertensive response of, 357–358
  coronary artery patients and, 359–360,
    360
hypotensive response of
  early in exercise, 362
  ischemia and, 362–363, *362*
  late in exercise, 360–361, *361*
  importance of, 355–357, *356*
  normal response of, 357
  physiology of, 357
measuring of, 136
recovery, 363, *364*
resting hypertension and response of, 359
sports medicine and, 385–386
systemic
  ischemia and, 86
  peripheral resistance and
    exercise and, 60–61
Blood volume
  exercise and, 60
Body position
  stroke volume and, 11
Body temperature
  measuring of, 146, *147*
Bruce protocol, 164, *165*

CALCIUM blockers, metabolic abnormalities
  and, 441–442
Calculations and presentations
  nonelectrocardiogram
    computers and
      efficiency index, 463
      estimate of aerobic capacity, 463
      estimate of VO_2max, 462–463
      likelihood ratio, 467
      multivariate analysis, *463*, 464–467,
        465t, 466t, *467*
      treadmill score, 463–464, *463*
CA lead, 129
Capacity
  estimate of aerobic
    computers and, 463
  functional
    evaluation of, 109–110, *110*
Carbohydrates
  exercise and, 28–29
  muscles and
    exercising, 48–50, *49, 50*
Carbon dioxide
  coronary resistance and
    exercise and, 26–28, 26t, *27, 28*
Cardiokymogram, 148–149, *149*
Cardiomyopathy(ies)
  blood pressure measurement and, 363–365

Drugs—*Continued*
    malities and, 448
  nitrites
    metabolic abnormalities and, 438–439
  nitrites, long-acting
    metabolic abnormalities and, 439
  Persantine, metabolic abnormalities and,
    439–440
  phenothiazines, metabolic abnormalities
    and, 446
  propranolol, metabolic abnormalities and,
    442–443, *443*
  psychotropic
    diazepam (Valium)
      metabolic abnormalities and, 446–447
    lithium, metabolic abnormalities and,
      445
    phenothiazines, metabolic abnormalities
      and, 446
    tricyclic antidepressants, metabolic ab-
      normalities and, 444–445
  psychotropic
    tricyclic antidepressants
      metabolic abnormalities and, 444–445
    Valium, metabolic abnormalities and,
      446–447
  quinidine, metabolic abnormalities and,
    437
  regimen
    evaluation of
      sports medicine and, 389
  safety and, 119
  tricyclic antidepressants, metabolic abnor-
    malities and, 444–445
  Valium, metabolic abnormalities and,
    446–447
  vasodilators, metabolic abnormalities and,
    449
Duke Study—1978, 321, *321*
Duration
  exercise and, 18
  Memorial Hospital protocols for, 193
Dysfunction
  esophageal
    normal coronary arteries and, 350–351
  occult
    alerting patient and physician to
      sports medicine and, 389
  valvular
    congenital heart disease and, 110–111

ECG patterns
  alternating S-T segment depression,
    252–253, *252*

  convex S-T segment depression, 254–255,
    254
  distribution of S-T segment depression, 241
  flattened or inverted T-waves, 265–267
  horizontal and downsloping S-T segments,
    236–240, 236t, *237, 238, 239*
  hyperventilation and orthostatic changes,
    270, *271*
  hypokalemia, 242–244, *243*
  increased sympathetic tone (Reynolds syn-
    drome) (vasoregulatory asthemia),
    244, *244*
  intermittent S-T segment depression associ-
    ated with respiration, 246–250,
    247, 248, 249
  intraobserver agreement and, 240–241
  normal exercise electrocardiogram,
    224–227, *225, 226*
  normalization of T-waves with exercise,
    267–268, *268*
  Q peak T (QPT) wave intervals, 261
  QRS changes, 227
  Q-T intervals, 259–261, *259, 260,* 261t
  QX/QT ratio, 261–262, *261*
  rounded S-T segment depression, 255, *255*
  R-wave amplitude, 227–231, *228, 229,*
    230, 231, 232
  septal Q-waves, 262–263, *262*
  severe hypertrophy patterns, 263, *264*
  S-T integral and slope, 241–242, *242*
  S-T segment and J-point depressions,
    231–233, *233*
  S-T segment depression associated with
    long diastolic filling, 250, *250*
  S-T segment depression at rest evolving to-
    ward normal with exercise,
    244–245, *245, 246*
  S-T segment depression late in the recovery
    period, 253–254, *253*
  S-T segment depression with nodal prema-
    ture contractions, 250–252, *251*
  S-T segment elevation at rest normalized by
    exercise (early repolarization),
    256–259, *258*
  S-T segment elevation with exercise, 256,
    257
  summary of, 270–272
  tall T-waves, 263–265, *265, 266*
  upsloping S-T segments, 233–235, *234,*
    235, 235t
  U-wave, 268, *269*
Electrocardiogram
  normal exercise
    computer analysis of, 458–460, *459*

significance of, 224–227, *225, 226*
patterns of. *See* ECG patterns.
Electrocardiographic patterns. *See* ECG patterns.
    codes, 482–488
Electrocardiography, ischemia and, 1
Electrode(s)
    disposable, 189, *189*
    position and attachments
        Memorial Hospital protocols for, 189, *190*
    positioning of, 481
    skin preparation for
        Memorial Hospital protocols for, 188–189, *189*
Elements, tracer
    characteristics of
        myocardial perfusion imaging and nuclear stress testing and, 414–415
Elevation, S-T segment. *See also* S-T segment elevation.
    exercise and, 256, *257*
    ischemia and, 99
    sports medicine and, 388
    stress testing after myocardial infarction and, 205
    termination of testing and, 118
Endorphins, pain and
    ischemia and, 92–93
Equation(s), myocardial supply/demand, *24, 25*
Equipment, safety and, 118
Ergonovine testing, 179
Estrogens, metabolic abnormalities and, 434, 434t
Evaluation
    arrhythmic, 109
    functional capacity, 109–110, *110*
    patient
        computers and, 196, *196*
        chest pain and, 107
        congestive heart failure and, 109
    postoperative
        pediatric stress testing and, 403
    prognosis and severity of disease and, 107
    therapy and, 107–108
Examination, explanation and
    Memorial Hospital protocols for, 189–190
Exercise
    abolition of ventricular arrhythmias and, 283
    arm
        equipment for, 174–175

maximal work in, 174
complications of, 65–66
coronary disease and
    danger in, 1–2
    S-T segment depression in, 1
duration of
    Memorial Hospital protocols and, 193
energy cost of, 47, 47t
extra-cardiac effects of
    immediate
        autonomic responses, 40
        blood and plasma, 40–41
        blood clotting, 41–42
        gastrointestinal function, 46
        lipids, 41
        metabolic cost of contraction, 46–47
        muscles, 46
        redistribution of blood flow, 45–46, *45*
        renal function, 46
        substrate use in exercising muscles
            carbohydrates, 48–50, *49, 50*
            energy cost of exercise, 47, 47t
            fats, 51–52, *51, 52, 53*
            glucoregulatory hormones, 53–56, *54, 56*
            hormonal influences, 52
            proteins, 50–51
            steady state and oxygen debt, 48, *48*
        temperature, 42–45, *43, 44*
    long-term
        AV-O_2 difference, 59–60
        bed rest, 56–57
        blood volume, 60
        complications of exercise, 65–66
        effects of conditioning, 58
        fibrinolysis, 42
        heat dissipation, 61
        heart rate, 61–62
        influence on aging, 66
        lipid metabolism, 62, *63*
        maximum oxygen uptake, 58–59, *59*
        peripheral resistance and systemic blood pressure, 60–61
        personality, 62–64
        resistance to sequelae of coronary atherosclerosis, 64–65
        weightlessness, 57
    summary of, 66–67
heart rate response to
    measuring of, 138–140, *139, 140*
how much is enough, sports medicine and, 385
hyperpnea, 33
intensity of, 169–171, 170t, *171*

Exercise—*Continued*
Memorial Hospital protocols for, 191, *191*
peak heart rate and
  knowledge of, 15
performance, postoperative
  coronary artery bypass surgery and,
    218–219, *219*
prescription for
  sports medicine and, 390–391
respiration and
  rate versus depth of, 34
responses to
  cardiovascular and pulmonary
    aerobic metabolism, 30
    anaerobic metabolism, 30
    carbon dioxide, ph, and bicarbonate,
      26–28, *27, 28*
    contractility, 13–14, *14*
    coronary blood flow, 19–20, *19*
    coronary resistance, 20–21
    heart rate, 14–15, *16*
    heart rate with training, 17, *17*
    hypoxia and ischemia, 30–31
    intramyocardial tension, 23–25, *24*
    mechanisms leading to, 10
    myocardial oxygen demand, 21–22, *22*
    oxygen uptake and metabolism
      maximum oxygen uptake, 25–26, 26t
    preload and stroke volume, 10–12, *11,*
      12
    respiration
      diffusion, 34–35
      exercise hyperpnea, 33
      rate versus depth, 34
    substrate use in the heart
      carbohydrates, 28–29
      noncarbohydrates, 29
      role of nucleotides and phosphory-
        lase, 29–30
    stroke volume and training, 12–13, *13*
    summary of, 35
    systolic and diastolic time intervals, 25
    temperature, *32*
      cold, 32–33
      heat, 31–32
    tension time index, 22–23, *23*
    training methods
      duration, 18
      frequency, 18
      intensity, 18
      mode, 19
  risk factors
    treadmill stress testing and, 308
  skin blood flow and, 31

S-T segment depression at rest and,
  244–245, *245, 246*
S-T segment elevation and, 256, *257*
S-T segment elevation at rest normalized by,
  256–259, *258*
Exercise testing
  serial postoperative, coronary artery bypass
    surgery and, 220
Exhaustion, stage of, 54
Explanation, examination and
  Memorial Hospital protocols for, 189–190

FACTORS, environmental
  sports medicine and, 384
Fallot, tetralogy of
  pediatric stress testing and, 405
False-negative tests
  predictive implications and, 315–316
  specificity and, 305–306
False-positive tests
  predictive implications and, 314–315, 314t
  sensitivity and, 305, 305t
Fascicular block
  left anterior division, 286–288, *286, 287*
  left posterior hemiblock, 288–289
Fats, muscles and
  exercising, 51–52, *51, 52, 53*
FFA. *See* Free fatty acids.
Fibrillation, atrial
  flutter and, 279
Fibrinolysis, exercise and, 42
Fibrosis, cystic
  pediatric stress testing and, 409–410
Filling pressures
  ischemia and, 84–86, *84, 85*
First pass studies
  radionuclide angiography in
    nuclear stress testing and, 422
Fitness, maintenance of
  quantity and quality of exercise for
    sports medicine and, 384
Flow
  blood
    redistribution of
      exercise and, 45–46, *45*
  transmural
    distribution of
      myocardial perfusion and
        ischemia and, 78–79, *78*
Flutter, atrial fibrillation and, 279
Follow-up, extended
  stress testing after myocardial infarction
    and, 209–210
Formation

STRESS TESTING: PRINCIPLES AND PRACTICE

collateral
exercise stimulus to
ischemia and, 75
coronary collateral
stimulus to
ischemia and, 74
Form, consent, 188, 475
Frank system, 133
Free fatty acids
ischemia and, 94–95
Frequency, exercise and, 18
Function
gastrointestinal
exercise and, 46
left ventricular wall
testing of, 180
renal
exercise and, 46

GASTROINTESTINAL function
exercise and, 46
General Adaptation syndrome, 53–55
Glucoregulatory hormones
muscles and
exercising, 53–56, 54, 56
Graphs
blood pressure, 472–474
heart rate, 489–492
Groups, population
predictive implications and, 310–311, 310t
Growth hormones, response of, 55
Guanethidine, metabolic abnormalities and,
448–449

HANDRAIL support
Memorial Hospital protocols for, 191
Harvard Step Test, 3, 159
protocol for, 159
Health, previous athletic efforts related to,
384
Heat
dissipation
exercise and, 61
exercise and, 31–32
Heart
substrate use in
exercise and, 28–30
Heart block
congenital
pediatric stress testing and, 405–407, 406
Heart disease
congenital
valvular dysfunction and, 110–111
Heart failure

congestive, 116
evaluation of patients with, 109
Heart rate
autonomic nervous system and, 14–15
exercise and, 14–15, 16, 61–62
graphs, 489–492
increase in, 15
maximum
age and, 15, 16
peak
knowledge of
exercise and, 15
response of
exercise and, 17, 17
response to exercise, measuring of,
138–140, 139, 140
sports medicine and, 385–386
target
submaximal, 117
training and
exercise and, 17, 17
training methods of
duration, 18
frequency, 18
intensity, 18
mode, 19
Heart rate targeted testing, 160
Heart sounds
aortic murmur, measuring, 150
first and second, measuring, 150
fourth, measuring, 150
mitral murmur, measuring, 150–152, 151
third, measuring, 150
Heart Watch—1980, 321–323, 322
Hemiblock
left posterior, 288–289
right branch bundle and, 288, 289
Hemodynamic responses
stress testing after myocardial responses
and, 204–205
Histamine testing, 179–180
History(ies)
case
death in, 119–124, 121, 122, 123
patient
safety and, 114
Hormonal influences, muscles and
exercising, 52
Hormones, glucoregulatory
muscles and
exercising, 53–56, 54, 56
Hyperpnea exercise, 33
Hypertension
pediatric stress testing and, 408

Vasodilator reserve
  intramyocardial perfusion and
    ischemia and, 79–80, 79
Vasomotion, ischemia and, 72–74, 73
Vasoregulatory asthemia, significance of, 244,
    244
Vector, S-T
  direction of
    ischemia and, 95–99, 97, 98
Vectrocardiographic analysis, 133
Ventriculography, radionuclide
  stress testing after myocardial infarction
    and, 208–209
Viscous resistance, 20
Volume
  blood, exercise and, 60
  stroke, left ventricular
    ischemia and, 89–90, 89
VO₂ max. See also Maximum oxygen uptake.
  estimate of
    computers and, 462–463

WALK through phenomenon, measuring, 149
Walk versus run
  exercise and, 47, 47t
Wall motion
  contractility and
    ischemia and, 86–88, 87
  measuring, 148–149, 149
Wave(s)
  atrial repolarization. See Ta-wave
  Q
    septal
      significance of, 262–263, 262
      sports medicine and, 388
    Q peak T, intervals
      significance of, 261
  R
    amplitude of
      significance of, 227–231, 228, 229,
        230, 231, 232
    measuring of, 135
  S-T
    changes, ischemia and, 1

T
  amplitude of
    coronary disease and, 241
    vasoregulatory asthenia and, 241
  changes, ischemia and, 1
  flattened, hypokalemia and, 242–243
  flattened or inverted, significance of,
    265–267
  normalization of, exercise and, 267–268,
    268
  sports medicine and, 388
  tall, significance of, 263–265, 265, 266
  Ta, ischemia and, 254–255
  U
    significance of, 268–269
    superimposition of
      ischemia and, 225, 254–255
Weightlessness, exercise and, 57
Women
  stress testing in
    conclusions drawn in, 344
    differences in sensitivity and specificity
      between men and, 341–342
    findings according to symptoms
      probable angina, 342, 343
      typical angina, 342
    mechanisms of, 343
    prevalence of coronary artery disease in
      women versus men, 340–341, 340,
        341
    strategy to separate true- from false-
      positive patients, 344
Work
  maximal, arm exercise testing and, 174
Work
  stroke, ischemia and, 90
Workload
  coronary size as related to
    ischemia and, 75–76
  nomogram for, 498–500

XYZ orthogonal lead systems
  measuring of, 131–133

STRESS TESTING: PRINCIPLES AND PRACTICE